FIRST
FARMERS

For Claudia, Tane, Hannah, and Charlie

FIRST FARMERS

The Origins of Agricultural Societies

Peter Bellwood

Blackwell
Publishing

@ 2005 by Peter Bellwood

BLACKWELL PUBLISHING
350 Main Street, Malden, MA 02148-5020, USA
9600 Garsington Road, Oxford OX4 2DQ, UK
550 Swanston Street, Carlton, Victoria 3053, Australia

First published 2005 by Blackwell Publishing Ltd

3   2006

Library of Congress Cataloging-in-Publication Data

Bellwood, Peter S.
  The first farmers: origins of agricultural societies / Peter Bellwood.
    p. cm.
  Includes bibliographical references and index.
  ISBN 0-631-20565-9 (hardcover: alk. paper) – ISBN 0-631-20566-7 (alk. paper)
1. Agriculture – Origin.   2. Agriculture, Prehistoric.   3. Plants, Cultivated – Origin.
I. Title.

  GN799.A4B45 2004
  630'.9'01 – dc22

                                                                    2004003944

ISBN-13: 978-0-631-20565-4 (hardcover: alk. paper) – ISBN-13: 978-0-631-20566-1 (alk. paper)

A catalogue record for this title is available from the British Library.

Set in 10.5/13pt Dante
by Graphicraft Ltd, Hong Kong
Printed and bound in Singapore
by C.O.S. Printers Pte Ltd

The publisher's policy is to use permanent paper from mills that operate a sustainable
forestry policy, and which has been manufactured from pulp processed using acid-free and
elementary chlorine-free practices. Furthermore, the publisher ensures that the text paper
and cover board used have met acceptable environmental accreditation standards.

For further information on
Blackwell Publishing, visit our website:
www.blackwellpublishing.com

Summary Contents

Detailed Contents

Figures

Tables

Preface

To present a reconstruction of human prehistory that has worldwide significance is no easy task. There are probably none alive who are fully trained practitioners in all the disciplines that contribute to the subject matter of this book, which is essentially focused on the origins and dispersals of ancient agricultural populations. I can claim professional training only in archaeology. But archaeology is a central discipline in the reconstruction of the human past, with a tentacle-like interest in the results of many other scientific fields.

The task set for this book is therefore a daunting one. The multidisciplinary correlations that point to major foundation layers of farming dispersal in human prehistory, on almost a worldwide scale within temperate and tropical latitudes, cannot be subjected to formal proof. But they can be presented as part of a very powerful hypothesis to be presented in more detail in the introductory chapter. At this point, as a backdrop, I would like to describe how I came to reach my current level of obsession with the history of human cultural, linguistic, and biological variation on such a broad scale.

As a student in Cambridge in the mid-1960s, I focused on the archaeology of the north-western provinces of the Roman Empire, and on the post-Roman (Germanic migrations) period. At that time, most of the glamor associated with the Cambridge department under the headship of Grahame Clark was attached to the Paleolithic/Mesolithic and Neolithic/Bronze Ages, so perhaps I had chosen a dark horse (not to mention a Dark Age!). But my reasons for choosing to study the later portion of the northwest European archaeological record related essentially to my desire to work in periods where the lives of *real* people ancestral to modern living populations could be reconstructed from written documents, combined with a dense and detailed record from archaeology.

In my final year at Cambridge I began to realize that, while Romans and Anglo-Saxons provided some extremely rewarding topics of investigation, nothing learned in those arenas would or could ever revolutionize understanding of the human condition on a world scale. My late teachers, Joan Liversidge and Brian Hope-Taylor, would probably have agreed. The great beyond was beginning to beckon. Having taken part in an undergraduate expedition with Norman Hammond to trace a Roman road in Tunisia and Libya in 1964, followed by archaeological expeditions to Turkey and Iran with Seton Lloyd and Clare Goff in 1966, I decided to look for more stimulus in remote and exciting places.

The excitement came quickly, following my appointment to a lectureship at Auckland University in New Zealand in 1967. This gave me six valuable years to undertake research in Polynesia, specifically in the Marquesas and Society Islands with Yosihiko Sinoto, then with my own projects in New Zealand and the Cook Islands. It was during this research period that I discovered the value of historical linguistics, and also a population of transparently shared and very recent origin, namely the Polynesians. I began to wonder how such a vastly spread grouping of humanity had been created in the first place, and how its members had subsequently differentiated after the islands were settled. Of course, even back in 1967 I was not the only person intrigued by the origins of the Polynesians. Following a tradition of enquiry that began with the explorers Cook and Forster in the 1770s, I found myself working at Auckland in the good company of Roger Green and Andrew Pawley, both strong advocates of an archaeolinguistic approach to prehistory (e.g., Pawley and Green 1975).

In 1973 I moved to the Australian National University, where research fever about the peopling of the Pacific Islands and Australia was at a peak during the 1970s. With John Mulvaney's encouragement I began research in Indonesia, and witnessed at first hand what I had long realized while in New Zealand. The Polynesians, while widespread, were really only a side chapter to the whole quite staggering phenomenon of Austronesian dispersal. At the same time, as a result of my undergraduate teaching, periodic fieldwork, and sabbatical travels, I had acquired a good working knowledge of several regions of world archaeology, especially at the Neolithic/Formative level, in Asia, Europe, and the Americas.

It was during the early 1980s that I began to think seriously about the significance of agriculturalist dispersal in human prehistory, at a time when most archaeologists, reacting against Childe's concept of the "Neolithic Revolution," were regarding early agriculture as a very slow and laborious development for most populations. The idea that all the world's peoples had been relatively immobile since their origins, and had evolved their cultural characteristics essentially by independent and *in situ* processes, ruled the archaeological roost with little dissent. Western scholarship, in its most intensive phase of post-imperial guilt, was leveling the playing field of cultural evolution to mirror-smoothness. My knowledge of the Roman Empire, and Barbarian and Polynesian migrations, led me to be suspicious.

During the late 1980s and 1990s, I began to wonder just how smooth the reality had been, particularly with respect to two very important questions. Firstly, why was the real world of the last few centuries, in terms of its tempo of change and the patterns of human behavior on a group or "ethnic" level, so many light years away from the prehistoric world of slow change, cozy interaction, and long-term stasis favored by many archaeologists in their reconstructions? Secondly, why has so much of the world been inhabited, since written history began, by speakers belonging to a small number of very widespread language families? To many, the latter question might seem odd, especially coming from an archaeologist. But as I will attempt to demonstrate later, a widespread language family must have a zone of origin relatively restricted in extent, and a history of dispersal involving at least some movement of native speakers. "Widespread" in this context means far greater in extent than any polity, empire, or trade system known to us from ethnography or pre-Columbian world history.

In fact, language history was almost shouting out important facts of which the majority of nonlinguistic scholars seem to have been quite unaware. I began to realize that some aspects of the human past must have been completely different from the rather gradualist reconstructions being presented by archaeologists, based as were the latter on comparative observations of human behavior as preserved in the ethnographic record. Ethnography was, in my mind, beginning to look more and more like a biased database.

I have no idea when I first locked all the pieces of the jigsaw into place, but the 1980s was clearly a formative decade (Bellwood 1983, 1988, 1989). Colin Renfrew (1987) was then developing his ideas on Indo-European dispersal, and others were examining the Bantu spread in Africa (Ehret and Posnansky 1982). Getting up steam took a while for me owing to the vast amount of data to be brought under control, in so many disciplines. My resolve also dissipated frequently as I realized that seemingly attractive hypotheses emanating from other disciplines nearly always attracted as much internal dissent as any major hypotheses emanating from archaeology. All historically oriented disciplines face problems in establishing the authenticity of data and the relative strengths of inferences drawn from those data. How could an archaeologist expect to offer any useful observations on the historical reconstructions of linguists and geneticists? Today, the answer is clearer to me. Archaeologists do have an important role to play because their data, like those of skeletal anthropologists, are direct witnesses from the past. The majority of linguists and geneticists deal with data from the present, except in the specific cases of languages with ancient scripts and bones which preserve ancient DNA (both rather rare in the contexts discussed in this book).

Direct witnesses surviving from the past are important, just as they are in the academic discipline which modern universities refer to as "history" (i.e., based on written records). But it is no more possible to reconstruct the past entirely from data recovered from the ground, or from ancient texts, than it is to reconstruct it entirely from living linguistic and biological data that can be reduced to phylogenetic trees. Both kinds of data matter. Both need the independent perspective that the other provides, just as do the three disciplines of archaeology, comparative linguistics, and biological anthropology around which this book is based.

It remains to add some acknowledgments. My greatest debt is to Jenny Sheehan of the Cartography Unit in the Research School of Pacific and Asian Studies at ANU. She has prepared most of the maps, a massive job indeed. Others have been drawn by Clive Hilliker of the Geography Department, and by Lyn Schmidt and Dominique O'Dea in Archaeology and Natural History, all at ANU. Without these maps, this book would be far less of an achievement.

Numerous colleagues have read parts of the manuscript. Here they are, more by order of chapter than alphabet: Nic Peterson, Ofer Bar-Yosef, Lloyd Evans, Sunil Gupta, Dilip Chakrabarti, Vasant Shinde, Virendra Misra, David Phillipson, Norman Hammond, Colin Renfrew, Roger Blench, Jane Hill, Andrew Pawley, Robert Attenborough. To all I am most indebted, and any errors are mine.

Finally, I need to thank my university and the two departments to which I am attached (Archaeology and Anthropology, Archaeology and Natural History) for allowing me the facilities in time, study leave, libraries, and sharp-witted colleagues to undertake this research. The Australian-American Educational Foundation (Fulbright Commission) and the British Academy gave me visiting awards at Berkeley (1992) and Cambridge (2001) respectively, both immensely useful for broadening my horizons. Students innumerable, both graduate and undergraduate, have asked hundreds of curly questions over the years, as have my many colleagues who don't agree with me. But most of all I wish to thank my family for putting up with all this obscure burrowing into the past – Claudia, Tane, Hannah, and Charlie. I hope they all enjoy reading the results.

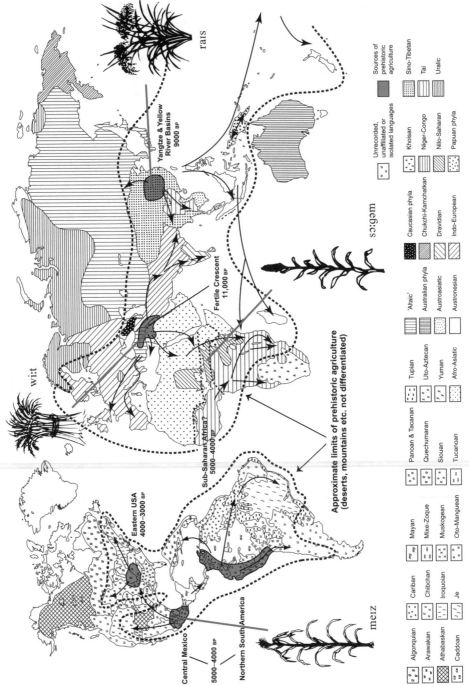

Figure 0.1 Map of some major geographical trends in the spreads of agricultural systems and language families during the past 11,000 years. From Bellwood and Renfrew 2003. Map prepared by Dora Kemp and Clive Hilliker.

Chapter 1
The Early Farming Dispersal Hypothesis in Perspective

Most of us subsist today, and always have done in historical memory, on foods derived mainly from the products of domesticated plants and animals. Even "wild" foods such as fish, lobsters, and mushrooms are frequently farmed. The human status as top mammal depends without question on food production. Hunting and collecting entirely from the wild could not possibly support even a tiny fraction of the world's current population.

The development of the agricultural systems that provide virtually all of the world's food has occurred over many millennia, and still proceeds apace. The nature of farming today is under continuous pressure as environments react to the load of billions of hungry humans and to the curse of climatic unpredictability. Genetic modification of crops and animals promises (for some) a brave new world. We are living through a crucial period in human history, perhaps a turning point with respect to the future, a period of colossal technological, economic, and demographic change. We have good right to think that the current rapid rate of change in all aspects of life has never been matched in history or prehistory.

But was the world of "real" prehistory, for instance in 5000 or 3000 BC, just a quiet forgotten fuzz of peaceful background noise, enlivened only by the occasional glimmer of action in places such as Egypt and Mesopotamia? In actuality, there are indications that the world then was just as busy in its own way as it is now, albeit without such huge populations or global networks of communication. This book suggests that major episodes of human movement occurred from time to time, in various parts of the world, as different populations developed or adopted agriculture and then spread farming, languages, and genes, in some cases across vast distances. To unravel the histories of these upheavals, which impacted eventually upon all the world's populations, even those living far from agricultural latitudes, is a complex matter. This is partly because the tales told by archaeologists, linguists, and geneticists often do not correlate very conveniently.

In order to approach what often appears to be a debate in which specialists all talk past each other, concerned only with data from their own discipline, this book is framed around a fairly simple *multidisciplinary* hypothesis. The *early farming dispersal hypothesis* postulates that the spreads of early farming lifestyles were often correlated with prehistoric episodes of human population and language dispersal from agricultural homelands. The present-day distributions of language families and racially varied populations across the globe, allowing for the known reassortments that have ensued in historical times, still reflect to a high degree those early dispersals.

Of course, there are some provisos. The early farming dispersal hypothesis is not claimed to have any absolute explanatory power. It is only by understanding why it works for some situations, and not for others, that we can improve understanding of the last 12,000 years of the human past in a meaningful way. Furthermore, the hypothesis suggests that major episodes of population expansion occurred as dependence upon farming grew, and such expansions tend to imply fairly strong correlations between populations, languages, and cultures, just as they have in the recent colonial past. However, it is an easy matter to point to situations where cultural complexes, language families, and complexes of related genes do *not* correlate in their distributions at all well, particularly in the record of ethnography and amongst living peoples. For instance, people of quite different biological appearance often speak related languages, even the same language. But such situations need not imply that the hypothesis is automatically wrong, or that language, culture, and biology never correlate at the population level. Indeed, many of these seemingly disjunctive situations reflect normal and expectable processes of population admixture occurring sometimes during, and sometimes long after, the episodes of dispersal described in the following chapters.

It is also important to emphasize right from the start that the early farming dispersal hypothesis is not claiming that *only* farmers ever dispersed into new lands or established language families in prehistory. Hunter-gatherers feature widely in this book since their lifestyle, in terms of long-term stability and reliability, has been the most successful in human history. It fueled the initial human colonization of the whole world, apart from a number of oceanic islands. It is not my intention to put farming on a pedestal, but merely to examine its impact on the world of our post-Paleolithic ancestors.

The farming story also gives all of the world's ancient farming populations a kind of equality, in the sense that so many peoples and cultures contributed, not just an elite few. We have clear signs of relatively independent agricultural origins in western Asia, central China, the New Guinea highlands, Mesoamerica, the central Andes, the Mississippi basin, and possibly western Africa and southern India. These developments occurred at many different times between about 12,000 and 4,000 years ago. The agricultural systems concerned spread at remarkably different rates – some quickly, some slowly, some hardly at all.

In order to understand these cultural and biological expansions in historical perspective, we need to examine data drawn from several different fields of study. Firstly, we have archaeology, the study of ancient human societies from their material traces left in or on the ground. Archaeology occupies most of this book and is a discipline that has the advantage of dealing directly with evidence created at the time in question, evidence which often can be precisely dated by radiocarbon dating or other absolute methods. But it has the obvious disadvantage that such evidence is always fragmentary and sometimes very ambiguous, often reflecting trivial aspects of human existence. Interpretation of the archaeological record in terms of the patterns and relationships of ancient societies, especially in prehistory, is not an easy matter.

Secondly, we have *comparative* linguistics, with the emphasis on *comparative* reflecting the fact that our periods of concern are so long ago that they always predate the invention of writing and thus directly documented history. Admittedly, some anciently written languages such as Egyptian and Hittite can add valuable data, but, for the most part, comparative linguists present their reconstructions of the histories of language families from a comparison of many languages either still spoken or recorded very recently. There is an advantage here over archaeology in that the database, in the case of a living language, is normally complete (a whole society cannot operate using only half a language), but linguists have no *direct* window through time on ancient preliterate people actually conversing. Neither do they have precise chronological methods in the absence of historical or archaeological dates. A proto-language or family tree is a reconstruction; an ancient village or cemetery is real.

Thirdly and fourthly, we have the two disciplines contained within the overarching field of biological anthropology, these being skeletal anthropology and archaeogenetics. The former, like archaeology, is the study of material drawn directly from the past, in this case human skeletons (or parts thereof), items which are of course quite common in archaeological contexts. Ancient bone can also contain traces of DNA and methods are now available to extract and study this, although in practice this kind of research is still in its infancy and so far few results have been published which reflect directly on the large-scale historical issues under discussion here.

Archaeogenetics (Renfrew 2000) is the other side of the biological coin, and this discipline is currently undergoing a major growth spurt. Archaeogeneticists study genetic material drawn from living populations and create their historical interpretations in several ways, mainly by reconstructing the molecular ages and dispersal geographies of lineages within non-recombining mitochondrial DNA (mtDNA) and the non-recombining portion of the Y chromosome, or by comparing populations in terms of multiple genetic systems within their recombinant nuclear DNA. Like comparative linguists, therefore, archaeogeneticists draw their data from the present, but their samples are rarely complete in the way that a living language can be complete, because of sampling constraints at both the population and genomic levels.

In support of these major disciplines we have many others which provide very important data. Within the natural sciences we have paleoclimatology and geomorphology, both studying changes in the earth's environments over time, and those fields within zoology and botany which study the origins and histories of domestic animals and plants. We also have anthropology with its ethnographic corpus of observations about real human behavior in traditional societies. Then we have physical dating methods based on radioactivity, and chemical methods of tracing artifacts to sources. A multitude of sciences contain somewhere within their vast fields of endeavor some techniques or observations which can help us to understand the deep past.

But the ultimate discipline that transcends all others is *history*, not just history as written down in books, but the history of humanity as it has unfolded worldwide over at least the past 12,000 years. Historical interpretation from a comparative perspective is our goal, and in this quest the disciplines of archaeology, comparative linguistics, and archaeogenetics are just handmaidens.

Broad Perspectives

This book owes its origin to a consideration of two primary observations:

1. Prior to the era of European colonization there existed (and still exist) a number of very widespread families of languages, the term "family" in this sense meaning that the languages concerned share common ancestry, having diverged from a common forebear (Figures 1.1 and 1.2). These language families exist because they have spread in some way from homeland regions, not because they have converged in place out of hundreds of formerly unrelated languages.

2. Within the early agricultural past of mankind there have existed many widespread archaeological complexes of closely linked artifactual style, shared economic basis, and relatively short-lived temporal placement. In the archaeological literature these complexes are generally referred to as (Early) Neolithic in the Old World, and (Early) Formative in the New. Again, these spreads have occurred from homeland regions, and most such complexes tend to become younger as one moves away from regions of agricultural origin (Figure 1.3). Most importantly, many agricultural homelands overlap geographically with major language family homelands, in highly significant ways.

Let us look at these two observations in a little more detail. Firstly, the language families. Why, for instance, does the Austronesian family of languages have more than 1,000 member languages, spread more than halfway around the world? By what mechanisms did the languages ancestral to this family spread over such a vast area? Similarly, why did the Indo-European family have almost an equal extent of spread prior to AD 1500, from Bangladesh to northwestern Europe, but in this case across continents rather than oceans? Both of these language families had virtually attained their AD 1500 distributions long before the existence of any written records or conquest empires. The ethnographic record gives us no comparative examples of spread on

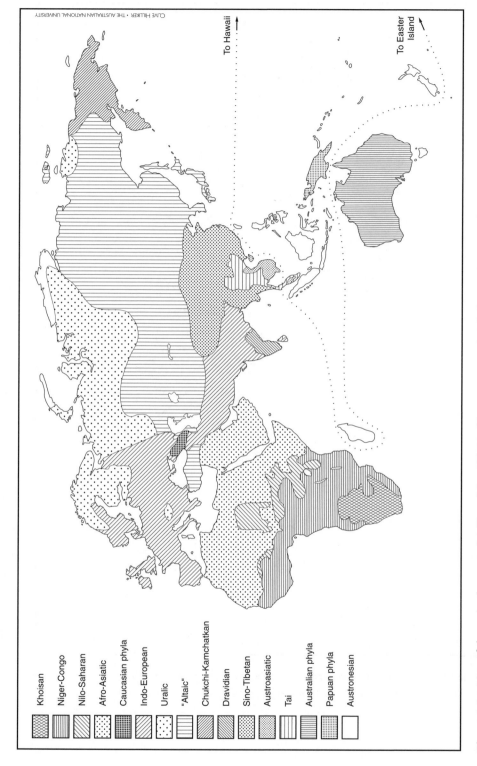

Legend:

- Khoisan
- Niger-Congo
- Nilo-Saharan
- Afro-Asiatic
- Caucasian phyla
- Indo-European
- Uralic
- "Altaic"
- Chukchi-Kamchatkan
- Dravidian
- Sino-Tibetan
- Austroasiatic
- Tai
- Australian phyla
- Papuan phyla
- Austronesian

To Hawaii

To Easter Island

CLIVE HILLIKER • THE AUSTRALIAN NATIONAL UNIVERSITY

Figure 1.1 Map of the major language families of the Old World. Locations with "phyla" contain more than one language family. After Ruhlen 1987.

Figure 1.2 Map of the major language families of the New World. Modified from *Encyclopaedia Britannica*, 15th edn (1982), Macropaedia vol. 11, p. 957; vol. 13, p. 210; vol. 17, p. 110.

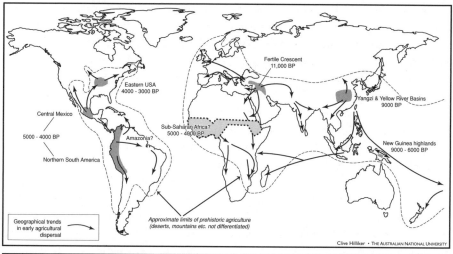

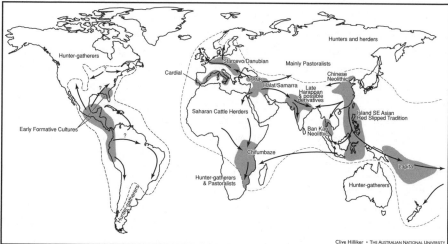

Figure 1.3 The origins and approximate directions of expansion of agricultural systems and early farming cultural complexes. The upper map shows the major regions of agricultural origin attested in the archaeological record (see also Diamond and Bellwood 2003, figure 1). The lower shows some very widespread cultural complexes of the early agricultural world (see also Bellwood 2001b, figure 1).

such scales. The recent historical record most certainly does, especially for recently spread languages (not language families!) such as English, Spanish, Malay, Arabic, Mandarin, and Cantonese. But when, why, and how did the prehistoric spreads occur? Are the recent situations of large-scale language spread relevant for comparative purposes?

Secondly, why do we find, from time to time, immense spreads in the archaeological record of stylistically related material culture over huge distances, far greater in homogeneity and total extent than in previous or following cultural periods? In prehistory, examples include the Pre-pottery Neolithic cultures of the early farmers of Southwest Asia; the Balkan, "Danubian," and Mediterranean coastal cultures of early Neolithic Europe; the early Iron Age cultures of eastern and southern Africa; the Early and Middle Formative cultures of the Americas; the Lapita culture of the western Pacific and its antecedents in the islands of Southeast Asia; and the earliest prehistoric assemblages of the islands of Eastern Polynesia and New Zealand (Figure 1.3). All are far greater in extent than any conceivable single political unit, at least as far as the ethnographic record of small-scale farming societies is concerned.

It will be noted that these archaeological spreads tend to correlate fairly closely with relatively early phases in the agricultural prehistories of the regions concerned, or with initial human settlement in the (eastern) Lapita and Polynesian cases. Again, the ethnographic record as it pertains to material culture does not appear to reflect linked spreads of such vast extent. For example, the ethnographic artifact assemblages (stone adzes, fishhooks, personal ornaments, and the like) of the various Eastern Polynesian archipelagos in AD 1770, at the time of Cook's voyages, reveal to us many more differences between island groups than those visible in the archaeological record of these islands 1,000 years ago, soon after initial settlement occurred. The same is even truer of the Melanesian islands, if the very varied ethnographic assemblages are compared with those of the more uniform Lapita cultural horizon of 3,000 years ago. We discuss these complexes in more detail later, but both illustrate a situation of increasing cultural divergence through time following the establishment of a widespread and relatively homogenous foundation culture across a very broad region.

Some of these spreads in the linguistic and archaeological records may be hard to explain, but common sense dictates that dispersals of related populations with common lifestyles and languages must have occurred in human prehistory, and deserve careful consideration as causes of ancient homogeneity of patterning. The archaeological record is sufficient to suggest this, since with early agriculture there commenced in many agricultural homeland regions an unprecedented growth in the size and density of the human population. This was especially true for Southwest Asia, China, Mesoamerica, and the northern Andes. The potentials here for cultural, language, and population spread are not hard to visualize.

The expansions of early farming populations that form the subject matter of this book reflect two consecutive processes:

1. the periodic genesis of new cultural (archaeological) or linguistic configurations in homeland circumstances;
2. the dispersal of such configurations into surrounding regions and their subsequent transformations, in situations either of pristine colonization (no prior humans), or in the presence of other populations.

The transformations within such configurations, both during and after dispersal, can occur via adaptive or chance modifications to the inherited pattern (thus giving relationships of descent, or *phylogeny*), or via interactions with other contemporary human populations, including culturally and linguistically related as well as unrelated groups (thus giving rise to a process termed *reticulation*). Throughout history, the relative significances of these two kinds of modification have not been unchanging. Human societies within, or just emerging from, a dispersal or colonization mode, especially if the dispersal has been relatively rapid and extensive, will reflect descent-based relationships very clearly. It is within societies of this kind that we can expect to see clear correlations between cultural/linguistic and biological variation. Societies long embedded in an interactive mode under conditions of geographical stability will not reveal such correlations.[1]

One of the suggestions that will dominate the chapters in this book is that short bursts, or "punctuations," of dispersal by closely related populations over very large areas have occurred from time to time in human prehistory, especially following the regional beginnings of agriculture or the acquisitions of some other material, demographic, or ideological advantages. Punctuations also occurred when humans first entered regions previously uninhabited, such as Australia, the Americas, and the Pacific Islands. These bursts have actually occupied very little of the total time span of human history. Often their effects are confusingly hidden beneath the reticulate interactive networks that have linked varied populations through the long millennia of subsequent history. But their underlying impacts on the course of human history and on the generation of subsequent patterns of human diversity have been immense.

Some Key Guiding Principles

At this point it is necessary to present a number of key guiding principles held with respect to certain essential aspects of human behavior and history. These inform much of the reconstruction of early farming dispersal presented in this book.

1.   *The range of individual human behavior patterns can be treated as relatively uniform during the time span of agriculture.*
Given the modern biological unity of mankind, individual human behavior patterns of 10,000 years ago were probably essentially similar in their range to those of today. Thus, desires for economic and reproductive success, peer-recognition, freedom from fear and disease, plus capacities for calculated altruism and morality, have presumably always characterized anatomically modern humans like ourselves. So too have abilities to be acquisitive and destructive. There is no evidence to suggest otherwise, although this opinion is impossible to justify with complete certainty. It is maintained as a working hypothesis underpinned by uniformitarian principles.

2.   *Specific events in the prehistoric past cannot necessarily be reconstructed through direct analogy with the ethnographic record.*
Despite the uniformitarian perspective on individual human behavior just offered, the overall historical trajectory of the human prehistoric past at the group/population level cannot be interpreted in uniformitarian fashion, and certainly not from the comparative perspective of events observed in the ethnographic record. Ethnography is not a complete and reliable guide to the structure of pre-ethnographic history.

Concatenations of events (particular historical situations with contingent and unique causative trajectories) occurred in prehistory for which the ethnographic record need have absolutely no parallels. One class of such situations involves ethnolinguistic dispersal on the scale of the major language families. Another involves the colonization of new continents and archipelagos by hunter-gatherers and Neolithic farmers – Australia, the Americas, and Oceania.

The world of ethnography is not one which reflects an expansive mode – it contains no records of trans-continental population dispersal of the kinds we see, for instance, in recent Western colonial history, and it is mostly a record of societies under pressure from Western civilization (with some marked exceptions, of course, but insufficient to disprove the majority rule). This does not mean that the ethnographic record is worthless in terms of the issues discussed here. It is extremely valuable, and aspects of it will be discussed at length from a comparative perspective below. But this record will not be privileged as a mechanism for supporting or refuting hypotheses of major historical significance derived from archaeology or linguistics.

3. *Specific events in the prehistoric past cannot necessarily be reconstructed through direct analogy with the written historical record, although the written record may be more relevant than the ethnographic for situations involving population expansion.*

The written historical record is less affected by the strictures that afflict ethnography and covers a full record of human activity replete with ethnolinguistic expansion and retraction, from the first documentary records bequeathed to us by the Sumerians, Akkadians, and Egyptians of the third millennium BC to the historically recent dispersals of Arabs, Chinese, and western Europeans. This record may be, *in general*, more valuable for comparative evaluation of the broad-scale ethnolinguistic hypotheses raised in this book than that from recent tribal ethnography. The historical record is particularly useful for a comparative perspective on how languages have spread over vast territories in recent history, territories far greater in extent than any single polity, yet of similar extent to those we must visualize for the dispersal of the foundation levels of many of the world's most extensive language families.

4. *Scale is a significant factor in culture-historical explanation.*

Reality at the single-society level is a cross-cutting mosaic, a result of generations of cultural diffusion, intermarriage, and bilingualism – in general, of the activities of socialized and advantage-seeking human beings. If one takes a comparative worldwide view, however, the perspective can change. On this level, it is possible to progress beyond the cross-cutting mosaics of localized human diversity to a different and much greater scale, where both history and geography extend far beyond the boundaries of particular ethnographic or archaeological communities. In such continental-scale situations, the irregularities of small-scale reality become "ironed out." Prehistory at this scale is more than just the sum of an infinitude of archaeological and ethnographic situations; it involves a different vista on humanity, one totally unimaginable from the activities recorded in the shrinking and circumscribed world of ethnography. The expansion, for instance, of the Austronesian language family cannot be explained simply by invoking the interactive processes involving bilingualism and even language shift that we witness between the members of adjacent ethnographic villages. *Scale* matters in interpreting prehistory. Archaeological and historical linguistic interpretations on continental scales are far more than just ethnographic observation written large.

Population dispersal has undoubtedly been a very important process in human affairs at all times. It has occurred throughout prehistory and in the light of written history, both into empty spaces and into previously occupied continents. It has been a fundamental driving force in the development of many cultures since humanity began, going back into the primeval days of the first hominid exodus from Africa. It might also have led, especially with landowning agricultural societies, to an intensification of some of those concepts of social ranking and property around which many historical societies have been built (Bellwood 1996d).

Admittedly, population dispersal has always been a symptom of prior causes in the long-term evolution of humanity, rather than an external cause or prime mover in its own right. But that does not lessen its significance. Without it, humans would still be living in some African Eden, or indeed might not exist at all.

Chapter 2

The Origins and Dispersals of Agriculture: Some Operational Considerations

The origins of agriculture involve both human intentionality and a set of underlying ecological and evolutionary principles. (Kent Flannery, 1986:4)

The main theme of this book revolves around the large-scale Neolithic/Formative dispersals of agricultural systems and communities that can be detected in the linguistic and archaeological records. Such dispersals, it is held, would have occurred most positively and coherently if the agricultural communities involved in the process already *depended* on agriculture (including animal husbandry) for the greater part of their subsistence needs, and if they had the technology and skills to establish such agricultural systems in new environments. Many hunters and gatherers of the ethnographic record have resource management skills that can mimic agriculture, and some have even adopted minor forms of casual cultivation. But such low-energy economies cannot account for the episodes of massive cultural and linguistic punctuation with which we are concerned. So we must first examine several important questions:

1. What is agriculture and what levels of productivity and population density can it support?
2. How did agriculture originate?
3. How does it relate in terms of productivity and scheduling to hunting and gathering?
4. How might hunter-gatherers have reacted when they first came into contact with agriculturalists?
5. How can a hunter-gatherer economic system be transformed into a fully agricultural one through contact and borrowing?

To examine such questions, it is necessary to start with a few definitions.

Resource management, a generalized set of activities that can be carried out by farmers, hunters, and gatherers alike, can be defined as any technique that propagates, tends, or protects a species, reduces competition, prolongs or increases the harvest, insures the appearance of a species at a particular time in a particular place, extends the range of or otherwise modifies the nature, distribution, and density of a species (after Winter and Hogan 1986:120; the authors actually use this definition for what they call *plant husbandry*). Resource management is not synonymous with agriculture or cultivation and it has obviously been practiced to some degree by all plant and animal exploiters since long before agriculture began.

Cultivation, an essential component of any agricultural system, defines a sequence of human activity whereby crops are planted (as a seed or vegetative part), protected, harvested, then deliberately sown again, usually in a prepared plot of ground, in the following growing season. Cultivation is a conscious activity, and the seasonal cycle of planting played a crucial role in the evolution of the first domesticated plants. Wild plants as well as domesticated ones can be cultivated, although in cases where seed crops are harvested fairly ripe and later replanted one would expect the cultivation activity to select for domesticated features in plant phenotypes fairly quickly. This process is discussed more fully in the following chapter.

Domesticated plants in the archaeological record are those that show recognizable indications of morphological change away from the wild phenotype, attributable to human interference in the genotype through cultivation, via the conscious or unconscious selection of traits. Certain domesticated plants have become dependent on humans for their propagation – the seed heads of many cereals, for instance, have lost their ability to disintegrate when ripe and to disperse their seeds, a characteristic most visible in the modern maize cob. Here, however, the concept of domestication is simply used for any recognizable degree of phenotypic change that can be attributed to human management, and no assumption is made that the plant in question could not have propagated itself under natural conditions.

For animals, the concept of domestication is invoked when there are relatively undisputed signs of human control and breeding of a species. Such signs can normally be claimed in situations where animals were transported out of their homeland regions – for instance, goats and sheep from Southwest Asia into Europe and Africa, pigs and chickens from China and Southeast Asia into the Pacific. In putative homeland areas for such animals, especially where there was exploitation of wild ancestral species in pre-agricultural times, it can often be difficult to distinguish animal husbandry from hunting in early agricultural contexts. Also, the criteria for identifying domestication in many animal species are rather diffuse and based on long-term trends rather than sudden changes in bone metrics and age/sex ratios. Animal domestication led in certain regions to great increases in productive capacity and hence played a major role, particularly in the Old World, in the kinds of agricultural population growth and geographical dispersal to be described below. Indeed, animal domestication may well be one of the major determinants of the differences in expansionary success between the Old and New World early agricultural situations.

It should be added that the term *agriculture* will be used to apply in a general sense to all activities involving cultivation and domestication of plants. There has been a tendency in some archaeological literature to distinguish agriculture, as a monocropping field-based activity, from *horticulture*, as a multicropping garden-based activity, but since the two cannot often be differentiated in the archaeological record the term horticulture is only used here in documented ethnographic instances. The same applies to the term *arboriculture*, often used to refer to production systems dependent on tree products.

The Significance of Agriculture: Productivity and Population Numbers

The significance of agriculture in history is that it has served as the ultimate economic foundation for the past 10,000 years of population growth amongst the human population, indeed for the phenomenon of civilization as we know it, although there is no intention here to push the chain of causality into the domains of urbanization, statehood, and literacy. We are still reaping the harvest of the several agricultural revolutions in world history in our overcrowded and highly stressed world today.

The demographic potential of agriculture vis-à-vis hunting and gathering is a crucial factor that perhaps needs little emphasis. In general, whereas a family of hunters and gatherers might need several square kilometers of territory for subsistence, an average family of shifting cultivators will be able to get by with a few hectares of crop-producing land. A family of irrigation agriculturalists will normally be able to manage with less than one hectare. Thus, along the scale of increasing intensification of production, less land is needed to feed a standard unit such as a family or individual. Fekri Hassan's ethnographic tabulations indicate that hunters and gatherers generally live at densities below one person per square kilometer, with a maximum approaching ten in the case of the Haida of British Columbia, although there is uncertainty as to how far back in prehistoric time such high Northwest Coast densities can be projected (Hassan 1981; Butler 2000). Non-urbanized shifting cultivators range from three persons per square kilometer to almost one hundred. Irrigation agriculturalists can reach far higher densities. There is thus some overlap between the most affluent foragers, especially those on the American Northwest Coast, and the least intensive cultivators, but only to a very small extent.

Since this book is about the earliest expansions of agriculturalists, in the days when the world was otherwise peopled by hunters and gatherers, any data on the potential maximum rates of agricultural population increase and territorial expansion are obviously of interest. The early centuries of agricultural development were probably fairly healthy, in the sense that the major epidemic diseases of history, many known to have derived from domesticated animals, had probably not yet developed. Neither, perhaps, had many major crop diseases (Dark and Gent 2001). Of course, once they did develop, in crowded and unsanitary living conditions, the impacts of disease on both farmers and hunter-gatherers alike were doubtless often devastating. But we are here concerned with "first-farmer" situations in which relatively healthy farmers moved into territories either previously uninhabited, or inhabited by low density hunter-gatherers.

In comparative situations recorded in recent history, rates of human population growth and territorial expansion have sometimes been quite remarkable. Recent colonial history in Australia, South Africa, and the Americas, together with the Chinese colonization of Taiwan and the progenitive exploits of the descendants of the Bounty mutineers on Pitcairn Island (Figure 2.1), provide very important comparative data.[1] These examples all suggest that internally fueled population growth among agriculturalist settlers could be quite phenomenal in frontier situations, especially where

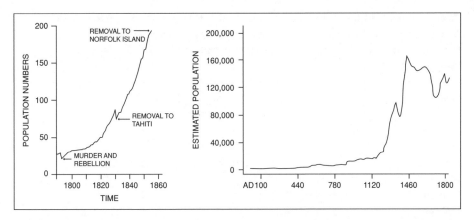

Figure 2.1 Two examples of internally fueled population growth in frontier situations, without significant immigration. Left: The population of Pitcairn Island between 1790 and 1860. During this time the population increased, without immigration, from 27 to 193 people – a seven-fold increase in 66 years. After Terrell 1986. Right: Plot of increasing population size over time estimated for Hawaiian prehistory, based on the distribution of archaeological radiocarbon dates for habitation activities as a proxy indicator for past intensities of human activity. See page 18 for explanation. After Dye and Komori 1992.

preexisting populations either did not exist or could offer only limited resistance. Such high growth rates soon came to an end as landscapes filled or as socioeconomic expectations changed, but it is instructive to observe that Australian-born white women bore children during the mid-19th century at more than three times the average rate for the early 20th century (Table 2.1). This was a situation, especially when compared to that in the British homeland, of culturally sanctioned population growth in a situation of rapid colonization, ample resources, and low infant mortality. The archaeological record suggests that similar instances could have occurred following the beginnings of systematic agriculture in many parts of the world when populations were, for a few centuries at least, given the opportunity to increase their numbers at a compound rate of interest. The human capacity for massive fecundity is not in question (Shennan 2002; LeBlanc 2003a), at least not when circumstances are right.

Some archaeological observations also offer food for thought. Fekri Hassan (1981: 125) has suggested that the population increase consequent upon early agriculture was very rapid, with a possible increase in world population from 10 million to 50 million across the total of world transitions to agriculture. Philip Smith (1972:9) has suggested that the population of Southwest Asia, the scene of one of the major transitions to agriculture in world prehistory, could have increased from 100,000 to 5 million people between 8000 and 4000 BC. Brian Hayden (1995) estimates a 1,600 percent increase in human population from the Natufian to the PPNB in the Levant (ca. 10,000 to 7500 BC). Mark Hudson (2003:312), commenting on research by Shuzo Koyama, notes a possible population increase in Japan from 75,000 in the Final Jomon (300 BC) to 5.4 million in the 7th century AD.

Table 2.1 Rapid frontier population growth: Birth rates for children born to married Australian women of European origin (but Australian birth) between 1841 and 1897. Note the continuous falling of the rate, to less than half its original value. Data from Vamplew 1987:55.

Women's birth years	Average number of live births per married woman
1841–46	6.8
1846–51	6.5
1851–56	6.3
1856–61	5.7
1861–66	5.1
1866–71	4.6
1871–76	4.0–4.2
1877–82	3.8
1882–87	3.6
1887–92	3.3
1887–97	3.0–3.1

Unfortunately, archaeologists can never know exactly how many people occupied an area in prehistoric times, but they can get good relative estimates from changing site locations, site numbers, and surface areas through time. As an example, the two major islands of New Zealand illustrate the demographic importance of agriculture within a single ethnolinguistic population spread across a varied landscape (Figure 2.2). Maori ancestors with a full knowledge of tuber agriculture colonized previously uninhabited New Zealand from tropical Polynesia about 800 years ago. Unfortunately for them, the New Zealand temperate climate straddled the growing-season limit of the only available tuber that was agriculturally viable beyond the northern fringes of their new home – the South American sweet potato. Over much of the country, despite their full knowledge of agriculture, early Maoris were persuaded by the agricultural marginality of their situation (especially in central and southerly regions) to make an initial "reverse" adaptation to a predominantly hunting and collecting economy focused on plentiful marine resources and flightless land birds (*moa*). For a century or so, until decimated, these resources undoubtedly provided a good living, especially in the South Island. Thus, colonizing agriculturalists became hunters and gatherers with either subsidiary agriculture (in the north) or no agriculture at all (in the south), a salutary observation of potential relevance for considering Mesolithic–Neolithic transitions elsewhere.

Both islands of New Zealand appear to have been settled at similar coastal-focused hunting and gathering population densities for the first few centuries of their prehistory, perhaps with denser populations in the eastern South Island, in terms of site numbers. Subsidiary agriculture was maintained in the northern and central coastal

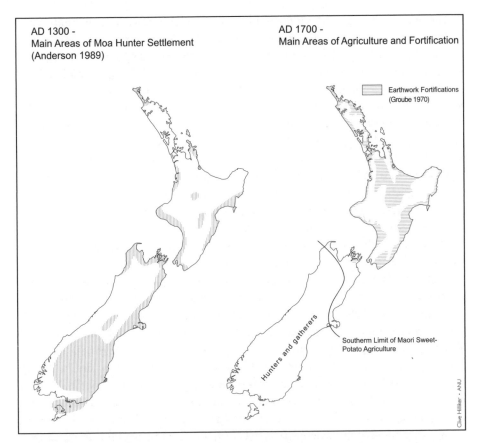

Figure 2.2 The significance of agriculture in New Zealand Maori prehistory. Left: The distribution of Archaic (moa hunting) sites around the whole country, ca. AD 1300, soon after initial settlement. Right: The distributions of hill forts and sweet potato agriculture in the north, and of the hunter-gatherer southern culture, ca. AD 1700.

regions of the North Island. However, by the time of Cook's visit in 1769, when the moas were extinct and marine mammal resources highly depleted, dependence on agriculture had become absolutely essential wherever it was climatically possible. By this time, perhaps 80–90 percent of the Maori population (100,000 people?) was living in the most suitable agricultural areas, both coastal and inland, in the northern half of the North Island. The high North Island population densities of this time are revealed by literally thousands of earthwork fortifications (*pa*), mostly constructed in the post moa-hunting phase after AD 1500. The remainder of the country, including the North Island interior and virtually all of the South Island, climatically marginal or impossible for sweet potato and even fern root propagation, was very thinly populated in comparison, with less than 10 percent of the population occupying perhaps 75 percent of the land area of New Zealand. The environmental availability of agriculture, even if it was a rather marginal kind of agriculture in this instance, was clearly the main contributor to this highly skewed situation of difference between north and south.

The reason why agriculturalists can live at much higher densities than hunters and collectors is because food is produced, on average, more intensively per unit of exploited area. Food-collecting mothers also tend to space births more widely than sedentary cultivators for reasons believed to relate in part to factors of mobility and diet,[2] leading in combination to biologically reduced frequencies of conception. This form of birth control maximizes the number of hunter-gatherer children able to survive to adulthood, but keeps the overall population small. Sedentary cultivator mothers are able to wean earlier, partly because cereals allow the cooking of gruel/porridge-type foods that can be used for infant foods (as long as one has utensils such as pottery to cook such foods). Thus, they conceive more frequently and have high fertility levels. Sedentism, whether linked with intensive food collecting or true agriculture, can also promote population increase in many situations. To the general significance of sedentism as a precursor for agriculture we will return.

The health of the earliest agriculturalists was also probably quite good compared to that of their more numerous and crowded descendants. Infant mortality and the incidence of osteological stress markers amongst the earliest cultivators in many regions were not high by later standards,[3] unless people moved into environments with latent health hazards. An example of this comes from the pioneer agricultural site of Khok Phanom Di in coastal Thailand, where Neolithic people settled at about 2000 BC in a swampy and malarial coastal situation. The infant death rate here was alarmingly high due to the combined effects of both anemia and malaria, although the general health of the population was otherwise good.[4] But, in general, the early agricultural world was far less crowded and presumably far less subjected to highly contagious epidemic diseases (especially outside the tropics) than in the recent past. Early agriculturalists in epidemic-free circumstances could have both *increased* their birth rates and perhaps also *decreased* their infant death rates, a package of profound significance for population growth.

The big question, of course, is *how rapidly* could human populations have increased their numbers and territorial extents in early agricultural situations, at times when competition from other populations and threats from disease and mortality rates were probably at fairly minimal levels compared to what was to come in later millennia? Pitcairn and 19th-century Australia give us clues, but we also have good prehistoric data from Pacific islands first settled in quite recent centuries. An excellent example comes from the Hawaiian Islands, settled about 1,000 years ago by Polynesians. Figure 2.1 shows an estimate of changing population size through time for this archipelago, with data at the recent end tied into 19th-century census data, thus allowing very rough estimates of real population sizes. The long tail of rare dates older than AD 1000 is believed to represent dates mainly from wood that was already old when burned, rather than contemporary human activity. The fall-off in dates close to European contact may reflect the introduction of diseases by Europeans. This diagram therefore suggests that the Hawaiian population size reached its ethnographic level (150,000 people?) within 300–400 years of initial settlement. Early Polynesian agriculturalist populations in pristine and disease-free conditions were able to increase population numbers with remarkable speed.

What, finally, of the "affluent forager" viewpoint (Sahlins 1968) that has enlivened much recent ethnographic discussion, which tends to regard hunters and gatherers as happier, healthier, and less overworked than their unfortunate agricultural cousins? It would obviously be quite misguided to suggest that hunter-gatherers who developed agriculture were always embarking on a downhill trajectory into hard labor and disease. Such a view pays no attention to specifics, whether ethnographic or archaeological, it ignores chronology, and it ignores some very basic facts of recent colonial history. Some hunters may indeed have been quite affluent before agriculturalists destroyed their livelihood, but the *earliest* agriculturalists in healthy food-rich environments probably had even more enviable lives from the viewpoint of many inhabitants, including many hunter-gatherers, of our crowded and starvation-inflicted modern world. True, the rats, diseases, overcrowding, malnutrition, and environmental devastation caught up with the descendants of the first agriculturalists, in some cases very quickly indeed. But the generally low incidence of crowd diseases in hunter-gatherer societies and presumably also in loosely packed earliest agricultural situations, like those on the colonial period temperate-latitude European frontiers in Australasia and the Americas, should make us think instead about "affluent earliest cultivators" rather than their hunter-gatherer counterparts.

Why Did Agriculture Develop in the First Place?

This is one of the most enduring questions posed by archaeologists and one that probably generates more debates than any other major archaeological question. We still do not really know the full answers for all regions. Most of the theorizing about agricultural origins has obviously been driven by the situation in Southwest Asia, with Mesoamerica and China following, but it is essential to remember that what may work for one region may not necessarily work well for another. Environments, chronologies, and cultural trajectories differed. Yet it may still be asked if there are any cross-regional regularities across the worldwide set of primary transitions. At the outset, there would appear to be two.

Firstly, the primary development of agriculture could not have occurred anywhere in the world without deliberate *planting* and a regular annual cycle of *cultivation*. Such would have been necessary for the selection to operate that ultimately produced the domesticated plants, and both of these activities would obviously have begun, in the first instance, with plants that were morphologically wild. Planting away from the areas where the wild forms grew would also have helped immensely in fixing and stabilizing any trends toward domestication, especially in the cases of those plants that were cross- rather than self-fertilizing, and thus subject to constant back-crossing with wild individuals.

Secondly, agriculture seemingly could not have occurred without the postglacial amelioration and ultimate Holocene *stabilization* of warm and rainy climates in those tropical and temperate zones where food production was ultimately developed. This is a most significant finding of recent paleoclimatic research. Basically, the argument

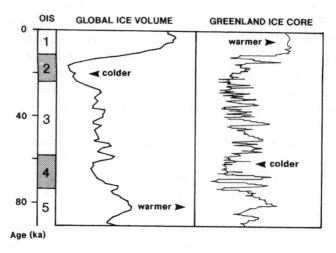

OIS   GLOBAL ICE VOLUME   GREENLAND ICE CORE

Age (ka)

Figure 2.3   Synthetic diagram to show the rapid changes in world climate after the peak of the last glaciation. The Holocene with its relatively stable warm conditions is at the top of both diagrams (OIS = oxygen isotope stage, ka = millennia ago). From van Andel 2000.

runs that postglacial climates of the period between 20,000 and 11,500 years ago were not only mostly cold and dry, but also extremely variable, such that major swings of temperature and moisture supply could have taken place literally on decadal scales. This is now well established from ice cores, deep sea cores, and continental pollen profiles. Under such conditions, according to an increasing number of authors (van Andel 2000; Chappell 2001; Richerson et al. 2001), any incipient attempts to cultivate and domesticate plants would have been doomed to early failure. Indeed, as we will see in the next chapter, at least one short-lived attempt to domesticate rye does seem to have occurred at Abu Hureyra in northern Syria at about 13,000 years ago.

With the Holocene amelioration of climate to conditions like those of the present, a rapid change that occurred about 11,500 years ago, the world's climates became warmer, wetter, and a good deal more *reliable* on a short-term basis (Figure 2.3). It was this reliability that gave the early edge to farming, by means of a chain of circumstances leading on from an increasing density of wild food supplies, through increasing settlement sedentism and population size, and so to the "competitive ratchet" between regional populations intent on maximizing their economic and demographic well-being vis-à-vis other groups (Richerson et al. 2001). Once agricultural trends began they *almost* never turned back (although, as we will see later in this chapter, some farmers did return to being hunters and gatherers).

At first sight, this explanation might seem so obvious as to render all previous attempts to explain early agriculture superfluous. But it does not explain everything, since the whole world population did not suddenly switch to farming, wherever it was climatically possible, in 9500 BC. Holocene climate was clearly the *ultimate enabler* of early farming, but it was not the *proximate cause* behind individual transitions. To understand proximate causes we need to review the history of early agricultural causation theory within archaeology.

Those who ask why agriculture developed, as a form of human behavior different from hunting and gathering, adopt many differing theoretical perspectives. Some explanations focus on a background of affluence, others on stress, especially environmental or population stress. Some favor conscious choice, others prefer unconscious Darwinian selection. Some like revolution, others prefer gradualism.

Many early theories were focused on affluence, combined with shots of good luck. William Perry (1937:46), for instance, believed that "year after year the gentle Nile would, by means of its perfect irrigation cycle, be growing millet and barley for the Egyptians. All that would be necessary, therefore, would be for some genius to think of making channels to enable the water to flow over a wider area, and thus to cultivate more food." Carl Sauer (1952) preferred situations of hunter-gatherer affluence and leisure time in riverine and coastal situations in Southeast Asia. Robert Braidwood (1960:134) favored cultural readiness in western Asia: "In my opinion there is no need to complicate the story with extraneous 'causes'. The food producing revolution seems to have occurred as the culmination of the ever increasing cultural differentiation and specialization of human communities." Stress received little recognition in these particular theories and none offered coherent chains of causality for the beginnings of cultivation. Indeed, we now know that agriculture did not begin at all in a primary sense in either Egypt or Southeast Asia.

Perhaps the most famous of the early stress-based theories was that of Gordon Childe, who believed that desiccation forced humans and animals together in oasis situations in Southwest Asia at the end of the last glaciation, eventually leading to domestication – hence the famous "propinquity hypothesis" (Childe 1928, 1936). We now know that domestication really took off in earnest in the wetter climatic conditions of the early Holocene. But, as will be indicated in chapter 3, there is a twist to the situation that means that Childe could have been partly right. Periodic spells of drought stress, especially during the Younger Dryas (11,000–9500 BC), are known to have affected Southwest Asia and probably China as the overall postglacial climatic amelioration occurred. Such stresses could have stimulated early, maybe short-lived, attempts at cultivation to maintain food supplies, especially in the millennia before 9500 BC. Childe was perhaps not too far off the mark.

Most modern explanations for the origins of agriculture bring in at least one "twist" of this type, in the sense of a factor of stress imposed either periodically or continuously over a situation of generalized affluence. But there are deep debates as to exactly what were the fundamental stress factors that led people to cultivate plants. Were they social, demographic, or environmental in nature, or a combination of all three? Were they continuous or periodic? Were they mild or severe?

One school of thought favors a primacy of social stress (perhaps better termed "social encouragement" in this context), fueled by competition between individuals and groups. Developments toward agriculture in resource-rich environments could have been stimulated by conscious striving for opportunities and rewards, including the reward of increased community population size and strength vis-à-vis other communities (Cowgill 1975). In similar vein, many have suggested that competitive social demands for increased food supplies could have led to food production.[5] We would expect such developments to occur in societies that valued competitive feasting or an accumulation of exotic valuables, via exchanges involving food, to validate status. Brian Hayden (1990) stresses that such developments would have occurred in relatively rich environments, in which groups would have been allowed to circumvent the strong ethic of inter-family food sharing that characterizes many ethnographic hunter-gatherers. In food-rich environments, families could have stored food for their own use under conditions of relatively high sedentism, thus leading to the individual or family accumulation of wealth that a system of competitive feasting demands. In poor and continually stressful environments such accumulation would have been replaced by more survival-oriented modes of sharing, and these form structural impediments to any shift to food production and consequent private accumulation of surplus.

Other authorities have stressed the significance of demographic stress, rather than social encouragement or competition. The clearest statement of this is by Mark Cohen (1977a), foreshadowed in part by Philip Smith (1972) and Ester Boserup (1965). Cohen's model focuses on continuous population growth during improving environmental conditions in the later Pleistocene, leading to dietary shifts into more productive but less palatable resources (for instance, from large game meat toward marine resources, cereals, and small game). Eventually, people were obliged to shift into plant cultivation, essentially to feed growing populations. Population packing led via necessity to increased sedentism, thus further promoting a higher birth rate and a gradual snowballing of ever-increasing population density. The adoption of agriculture by Cohen's model was a gradual process, but one occurring in varying environments around the world whenever and wherever food production became demographically necessary. Animal domestication followed later as wild meat resources declined.

Related population growth or "packing" models were favored even earlier for Southwest Asia and Mesoamerica. Lewis Binford (1968) and Kent Flannery (1969) both proposed that increasing post-Pleistocene population densities in favorable coastal zones, occupied by relatively sedentary fisher-foragers, led to an outflow of people into marginal zones, resulting in cereal cultivation in order to increase food supplies. This hypothesis also emphasized that initial plant cultivation would be most likely to have taken place on the *edges* of the wild ranges of the plants concerned, because stresses in supply here would obviously be higher than in core areas of plentiful and reliable supply (Flannery 1969). The evidence that hunter-gatherer populations were indeed growing in various places in the Old World after the last glacial maximum and prior to the beginnings of agriculture is quite strong for some regions, and the significance of such population growth will be highlighted for Southwest Asia later. There is no doubt that this could have been a significant factor.

Another very important factor amongst the last hunter-gatherers involved in transitions to agriculture, and one undoubtedly related to increasing population density, is widely believed to have been settlement sedentism (Harris 1977a; LeBlanc 2003b). Many scholars now believe that agriculture, especially in the Levant, could only have arisen among sedentary rather than seasonally mobile societies.

Unfortunately, however, the demonstration of sedentism in prehistory is one of the most difficult tasks that an archaeologist can face. Biological indicators (for instance, presence of bones of migratory bird species, age profiles of mammal species with seasonal reproduction cycles) can sometimes give ambiguous results – the presence of people during a certain season can often be identified, but not the absence. Archaeologists are often forced to fall back on generalized assumptions about the existence of sedentism made in terms of the presence in sites of commensal animal species (mice, rats, sparrows etc. in the Levant) and in terms of the seeming permanence of houses and other structural remains. The whole issue can be extremely uncertain for there are many ethnographic situations, amongst hunter-gatherers and agriculturalists alike, where settlements can have a degree of permanence but the populations that inhabit them can fluctuate from season to season.[6] The same probably applies to many of the seemingly sedentary settlements of "affluent" hunter-gatherers in prehistory. Perhaps in awareness of this, Susan Kent (1989) has defined sedentism as requiring residence for more than six months of a year in one location. Ofer Bar-Yosef (2002:44) suggests nine months for the pre-Neolithic Levant.

Given that sedentism to some degree was apparently so important in agricultural origins, it becomes necessary to ask where sedentary societies were located in the pre-agricultural world of the terminal Pleistocene and early Holocene. So far, the archaeological record gives few indications of absolute sedentism, and even a high degree of sedentism was perhaps not present in many places apart from the Levant and southeastern Turkey, Jomon Japan (where sedentary hunter-gatherers seemingly resisted the adoption of agriculture), Sudan, perhaps central Mexico, and perhaps the northern Andes.[7] No doubt, archaeological specialists in various parts of the world will have data to claim that sedentism existed in other areas, but in the context of terminal Pleistocene and early Holocene hunter-gatherers it is my impression that it was rather rare, especially if one demands all-year-round permanence of a total population in a village-like situation.

Despite these conceptual problems, any major increase in the degree of sedentism would have become a stress factor in itself because it would have encouraged a growing population, via shorter birth intervals, and would also have placed a greater strain on food supplies and other resources in the immediate vicinity of a campsite or village.[8] Fellner (1995) has suggested that the development of plant cultivation in Southwest Asia was a deliberate act to allow small and already sedentary hunter-gatherer villages to amalgamate into much larger, and better-fed, agriculturalist ones – more food, more political and social power (Cowgill 1975).

These social and demographic stress hypotheses are convincing as a group, but they by no means explain everything. For instance, why did agriculture not develop in all "affluent" hunter-gatherer regions in prehistory, and especially amongst many of the more affluent groups of the ethnographic record who inhabited agriculturally possible regions, such as those in some parts of coastal or riverine Australia, California, or British Columbia? The American groups, in particular, had relatively high degrees of settlement sedentism. Despite such apparent situations of non-fit, however, some form of reduction of continuous sharing behavior must have been an essential ingredient in the early agricultural equation, and affluence and feasting combined with a shift toward a sedentary residence pattern with concomitant storage are good ways to reduce this. The affluence models are not to be dismissed lightly and they certainly reflect substantial common sense.

Nevertheless, somewhere in all of this there has to be another factor. What if the full story was not just affluence tilted by the sedentizing and productive demands of social or demographic pressures, but also affluence overshadowed by the threat of episodes of environmental stress? Severe environmental or food stress alone is probably not the answer – the starving or devastated populations who tragically inhabit our TV screens are the least likely, without massive outside help, to revolutionize their economies. But there are gradations of environmental stress, and stress can vary in intensity and in periodicity. Perhaps the sharp retraction of resources at about 11,000 BC associated with the onset of the Younger Dryas could have led to some early experiments in agriculture in the Levant. Most actual establishments of farming economies apparently followed later, and in this regard it needs to be stressed that early Holocene climates were not *absolutely* stable, never changing at all from year to year. Climatic variability in the Pleistocene may have been too great to allow agriculture to develop permanently at all, but the opposite – unchanging conditions – could presumably have been just as unrewarding. The old saying, "necessity is the mother of invention," was surely not founded in total vacuity. A combined explanation of affluence alternating with mild environmental stress, especially in "risky" but highly productive early Holocene environments with periodic fluctuations in food supplies, is becoming widely favored by many archaeologists today as one explanation for the shift to early agriculture. Indeed, in an analysis of ethnographic "protoagricultural" activities by hunter-gatherers, Lawrence Keeley (1995) points out that most such activity has been recorded for groups in high risk environments in low to middle latitudes. Risk, and smart circumvention thereof, has been a clue to many successes in life and history.

There is one other general theory to be discussed here, one rather different from the theories related above and one that requires neither affluence nor stress of any kind, nor even conscious awareness or choice on the part of the human populations involved. The view of Eric Higgs and Michael Jarman (1972), that animal domestication had been developing since far back in Pleistocene times as humans gradually refined their hunting and husbandry practices, is an early precursor of this, but it has been most powerfully presented for plants by David Rindos (1980, 1984, 1989). Rindos took a very gradualist and Darwinist view of co-evolutionary selection and change, in which plants were thought to have co-evolved with humans for as long as they have been predated by humans, adapting to the different seed dispersal mechanisms and selective processes set in train by human intervention. From this viewpoint, plants have always been undergoing some degree of phenotypic change as a result of human activity and resource management. However, Rindos did recognize that the actual transition to conscious cultivation ("agricultural domestication") was probably driven by population increase, and that it was the cause of much subsequent human population instability and expansion.

The essence of Rindos' theory was really unconscious Darwinian selection as opposed to conscious choice, and it was not tailored to fit any specific region. In my view, a long process of pre-agricultural co-evolution might fit with what we know of the New Guinea and Amazon situations with their focus on tuber and fruit crops, perhaps better than, for instance, Southwest Asia, China, or Mesoamerica, where cereals seem to have undergone rather explosive episodes of domestication. But it does not tell us anything about the historical reasons why particular groups of prehistoric foragers crossed the Rubicon into systematic agriculture, any more than Darwin himself was able to state how animal species could acquire completely new genetic features through mutation.

It is necessary, therefore, to emphasize that the regional beginnings of agriculture must have involved such a complex range of variables that we would be blind to ignore any of the above factors – prior sedentism, affluence and choice, human–plant co-evolution, environmental change and periodic stress, population pressure, and certainly the availability of suitable candidates for domestication. And this is not all. Charles Heiser (1990) suggested that planting began in order to appease the gods after harvests of wild plants – a hypothesis incapable of being tested, but interesting nevertheless. Jacques Cauvin (2000; Cauvin et al. 2001) suggested that a "revolution of symbols" formed an immediate precedent to the emergence of plant domestication in the Levant, the symbolism in this case involving human female figurines and representations of bulls. Again, this is an intriguing but rather untestable hypothesis, and a little imprecise on causal mechanism.

Indeed, most suggested "causes" overlap so greatly that it is often hard to separate them. Environmental change and increasing stability into the Holocene may be the most significant underlying facilitator, but even this will produce little in the absence of the "right" social and faunal/floral background combinations. Thus, there can be no one-line explanation for the origins of agriculture. Neither can we ignore the possibility of human choice and conscious inventiveness. Any overall explanation for a trend as complex as a transition to agriculture must be "layered in time," meaning that different causative factors will have occurred in sequential and reinforcing ways.

The Significance of Agriculture vis-à-vis Hunting and Gathering

There is a point of view, quite commonly held by anthropologists and archaeologists, that hunting-gathering and agriculture are merely extremes of a continuum, along which ancient societies were able to move with relative ease (Schrire 1984; Layton et al. 1991; Armit and Finlayson 1992). Such a point of view obviously minimizes the significance of agricultural origins and in extreme form would render the concept valueless. It is true that hunter-gatherers often engage in resource management activities. But chameleon-like societies that switch from hunter-gatherer *dependence* to agricultural or pastoral *dependence* and then back again are remarkably hard to document, whether in the archaeological or ethnographic records. One really wonders if they have ever existed, outside those well-known cases in which former agricul-turalists made short-term adaptations to the presence of naïve faunas in previously uninhabited islands, especially in Oceania (the example of New Zealand was discussed above).

Certainly, many recent hunter-gatherers have been observed to modify their environments to some degree to encourage food yields, whether by burning, replant-ing, water diversion, or keeping of decoy animals or domesticated dogs; that is, by resource management techniques which might mimic proto-agriculture in the archaeological record. Most agriculturalists also hunt if the opportunity is presented and always have done so throughout the archaeological record. Indeed, in the Ameri-cas, hunted meat was a major source of supply for all agriculturalists because of the absence of any major domesticated meat animals. This is probably one essential reason why the American record of agricultural and language family expansion was quite low key compared to that in the Old World.

All of this means that there is good evidence in recent societies for some degree of overlap between food collection and food production. But the whole issue here revolves around just what level of "food production" is implied. Any competent food gatherer can also be a resource manager, maybe plant an occasional garden or even keep a few tame animals. Yet any idea that mobile hunters and gatherers can just shift in and out of an agricultural (or pastoral) *dependent* lifestyle at will seems unrealistic in terms of the major scheduling shifts required by the annual calendars of resource availability, movement, and activity associated with the two basic modes of production. There are very few hints of such circumstances ever occurring in the ethnographic record, and certainly none that are unchallengeable in historical vera-city. Mobile foragers must give an increasing commitment to sedentism if agriculture is to become a successful mainstay of their economy – fields of growing crops can of course be abandoned for several months while people go hunting, but under such circumstances yields will be expectably low. If the foragers were sedentary prior to adopting agriculture then the transition may be less traumatic, but the difficulties that archaeologists face in tracing sedentism in pre-agricultural contexts have already been alluded to.

There is another way to approach this question of the "hardness" of the transition between hunting-gathering and agriculture. If casual shifts between agriculture and foraging had been occurring with high frequency in recent centuries, we might expect to find lots of societies still passing between the two states when they were first captured in the ethnographic record. We might also expect to see a gradual progression in the relative importance of produced versus gathered food from one extreme of dependence to the other. Is this the case?

The answer to this question is not particularly obvious since so many traditional economies were transformed by contact with the Western world before the ethno-graphic record began to be compiled. But we have hints in the entries in the *Ethnographic Atlas* (Murdock 1967; Hunn and Williams 1982) for the proportional contributions of five subsistence modes (gathering, hunting, fishing, animal husbandry, and cultivation) in the diets of a total of 870 societies distributed throughout the world. In Figure 2.4

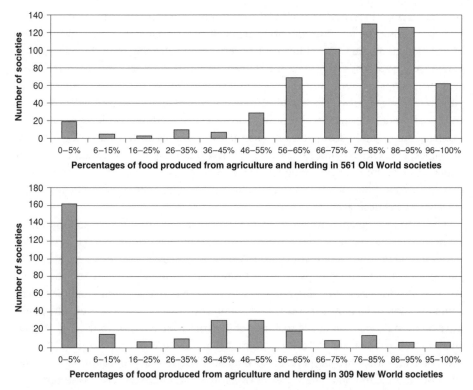

Figure 2.4 Top: The percentages of produced food in the diets of a sample of 561 Old World societies. Bottom: The percentages of produced food in the diets of a sample of 309 New World societies. Data from Murdock 1967.

the percentages for agriculture and animal husbandry (i.e., "produced" food) are summed as one combined percentage of the total food supply for all the societies listed in the *Atlas*. We see some very interesting patterns.

In the Old World (Figure 2.4 top), virtually all societies which practice agriculture and/or stockbreeding derive more than 50 percent of their food supply from these two sources. Very few combine them with any major reliance on hunting and gathering. Most exceptions to this generalization, where agricultural dependence drops in a few cases to below 50 percent, occur in Pacific Island communities where the high importance of fishing and absence of major herd animals clearly push the figures for food production downwards. In general for the Old World, we see that hunters and gatherers may practice a small amount of agriculture, and agriculturalists may practice a small amount of hunting and gathering, but the two modes of production most decisively *do not merge* or reveal a gentle cline. Almost no societies occupy "transitional" situations, deriving for instance 30 percent of their food from agriculture and 70 percent from hunting and gathering. In terms of Old World cultural history, such a combination has clearly not been stable since ethnographic records began to be compiled.[9]

This suggests, in terms of the Old World cultural trajectory, that hunting-gathering and agricultural modes of production cannot be indiscriminately mixed. Being good at one alone is a better option for most societies than balancing both. Mobile hunters cannot stay near crops to protect them from predators, farmers cannot always abandon their crops to hunt, and often do not need to do so if there are hunters and gatherers living nearby. Trade-and-exchange forms of mutualism between the two modes of production tend to keep them apart in many ethnographic situations, and hunters often benefit from the presence of wild animals attracted by agricultural activities. This Old World observation, of a sharp ethnographic separation between dependence on hunting-gathering and farming, is contrary to the views of those who believe that hunting-gathering and agriculture are simply alternative strategies which societies can choose at will.

The graph for the 309 American societies listed in the *Atlas* (Figure 2.4 bottom) is by no means as striking as that for the Old World in terms of the degree of dependence on food production. Of course, the Americas (especially North America) had, at European contact, an immensely greater number of hunter-gatherer societies than the Old World (excluding Australia). But it is clear that the graph is still a much-muted version of its bimodal Old World counterpart, with a lesser degree of dependence on food production in the majority of American societies. As in the Old World, there is an obvious nadir at 16–25 percent, but in the New World we also find very few societies more than 60 percent dependent on agriculture and herding. This reflects some fundamental differences between the Old and New Worlds in terms of environments and history.

The New World, from the perspective of early agriculturalists, had a much greater extent of landscapes marginal or prohibitive to agriculture than the Old. It also had virtually no major stockbreeding economies and its agricultural trajectory has occupied much less time than in much of the Old World. Without stockbreeding, food production was necessarily reduced in proportional importance because most societies needed to obtain meat from wild sources, whether by fishing or hunting, and both these modes tended to be more important in combination than gathering amongst those American societies listed as having agriculture. In the New World, agriculture was in general not the basis of such powerful subsistence economies as in the Old World. Even so, and despite these differences, the fact remains that both Old and New World populations evidently found it problematic to shift in and out of agricultural dependence on a regular basis.

Under What Circumstances Might Hunters and Gatherers Have Adopted Agriculture in Prehistory?

The agricultural dispersals described in this book involved populations who appear, according to archaeological evidence and linguistic reconstructions, to have depended quite highly on agriculture for their subsistence. If ancient hunter-gatherers did adopt agriculture through cultural diffusion, then we must consider under what circumstances they would have shifted into fully agricultural economies. This is not a trivial question, at least not for those who wish to understand the spread of agriculture in more depth than that offered by the botanical and archaeological databases alone.

We can attack this issue comparatively, to some extent, from the ethnographic and historical records pertaining to hunter-gatherer behavior in agricultural latitudes in the recent past. But the issue becomes complex when the precise nature of those hunter-gatherer groups who survived to enter the ethnographic record is taken into consideration. Ethnographic hunters survive because they have never adopted agriculture, but most are also oppressed by current political and social conditions that discourage them from doing so. They can, for the most part, only offer negative information, about why people did *not* adopt or invent agriculture. We simply have no detailed historical records of hunter-gatherers actually adopting agriculture in a successful and long-term manner, even though many practice minimal cultivation on a casual basis.

There are historical provisos, however. On the one hand, the ethnographic record is essentially a creation of Western colonial societies and belongs to a period of history when conditions for successful agricultural adoption have been extremely discouraging. One could perhaps reject it as irrelevant to issues of agricultural adoption in the Neolithic. On the other hand, we have records from northern Australia and California of people who were technically in a position to adopt agriculture from neighboring cultivators for several centuries prior to major European domination of their lives, but who never did so. We also have circumstantial evidence for many groups of former hunter-gatherers who probably did adopt agriculture or pastoralism in relatively recent times, although these adoptions predate direct ethnographic records and so are rather uncertain in historical trajectory. From these behavioral perspectives ethnography is surely relevant as a comparative database, even if the comparisons cannot be extended to the interpretation of trajectories of long-term human history.

In order to approach the ethnographic record systematically and to extract useful comparative information, it is essential *not* to treat all recorded ethnographic hunter-gatherer societies as being one simple category, or as having had the same basic historical trajectories stretching back far into the Pleistocene past (Kent 1996). None of these societies are fossils. Hunter-gatherers have had histories just as tumultuous in many cases as have agriculturalists (Lee and Daly 1999). This chapter favors a separation of the world's surviving hunter-gatherers into three groups based on historical understanding, albeit often rather faint, of their origins and relationships with cultivators in the past. Not all hunter-gatherer groups can be placed unequivocally in one of the three groups, but there are sufficient that can to allow a number of fairly convincing observations.

Of the three groups, the first two can be distinguished as "original" hunter-gatherers in the sense that they are presumed, at least by most authorities, to have unbroken ancestries within the hunter-gatherer economy extending back into the Pleistocene. Group 1 hunter-gatherers are enclosed within farming and pastoralist landscapes, whereas those of group 2 are (or were) free of such constraints. Group 3

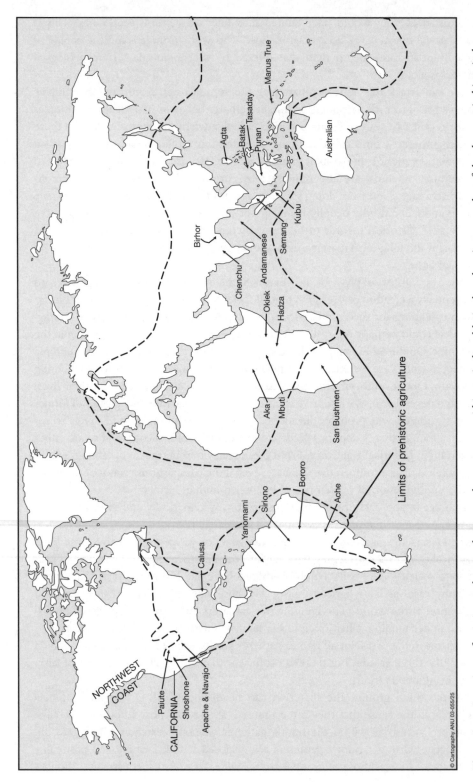

Figure 2.5 Locations of existing and recent hunter-gatherer groups within agricultural latitudes, showing examples of the three main historical types, and also the limits of prehistoric farming societies.

hunter-gatherers have a range of apparently derived hunter-gatherer economies, created by specialization out of former lifestyles that in many cases included agriculture.

Hunter-gatherers who live completely (or mostly) beyond the range of agriculture in the cold latitudes are excluded for obvious reasons from the following discussion. Such groups include the Ainu (who did have a marginal foray into agriculture in recent centuries), plus of course the many cold temperate, Arctic, and southern South American hunter-gatherer populations. The members of the three groups to be discussed below all live in, or just beyond, those tropical and temperate latitudes within which agriculture was or is generally possible (Figure 2.5).

Group 1: The "niche" hunter-gatherers of Africa and Asia

These populations are classified together because all have survived to the present in agriculturally poor environments in the interstices between much larger agriculturalist and pastoralist populations. All have fairly non-ranked "band" forms of social organization and all have apparently been essentially hunter-gatherer in economic orientation throughout their known or reconstructable histories. Classic populations of this type include the San (Bushmen) of the Kalahari and Namib regions, the Hadza of northern Tanzania, the Aka and Mbuti (Pygmies) of the African rain forest, and the Semang and Agta (Negritos) of Peninsular Malaysia and the Philippines. It is possible that some Amazonian interfluvial hunter-gatherers, located between the major riverine farming populations, also belong in this group, but this is a contested issue. Most examples in this section will be drawn from the Kalahari and Southeast Asian rain-forest populations.

Group 1 hunter-gatherer societies live in areas decidedly marginal for cultivation, particularly semi-deserts and equatorial rain forests, and today are surrounded by or live adjacent to more fertile agricultural or pastoralist landscapes. In James Woodburn's (1982, 1991) terms they are "encapsulated" by their more powerful neighbors. Some groups, such as the Malaysian Semang and Philippine Agta, have entered states of severe encapsulation very recently with the march of logging, cash cropping, and other activities completely antithetical to hunter-gatherer survival (Dentan et al. 1997; Headland and Reid 1989; Headland 1997). With all these populations, however, varying degrees of less threatening long-term contact, intermarriage, and sometimes hostility with agriculturalist populations, often over millennia, mean that many have surely undergone substantial change away from any "Paleolithic" behavioral norms that might have existed before agriculture appeared.

The impact of encapsulation is highlighted by Woodburn's categorization of them as having *immediate return* systems characterized by sharing, together with an absence of storage and accumulation of food and property. Such groups often occupy low-status economic positions in partial dependence on nearby agriculturalist or pastoral populations, rapidly losing ethnic identity in the process. The stresses that result from such subordination, described in some detail for the Philippine Batak by James Eder (1987), ensure that such groups lack any form of social hierarchy. In social terms, they can be described as living in mobile multi-family bands, usually bilateral in kinship terms and egalitarian in terms of authority. Such groups, in Woodburn's view, are most unlikely ever to become agriculturalists. None have ever seemed very determined in this regard as far as the ethnographic record is concerned, and their general lack of concern with accumulation and/or inheritance of wealth is so far from the mind-set of many farmers and herders that any successful shift would require some very fundamental reorganization of their societies and ideologies.[10]

Indeed, detailed studies of the Philippine Agta and Batak reveal that they find it extremely difficult to adopt agriculture successfully, even when all their hunting land has been taken by agriculturalists (Headland 1986; Eder 1987). According to Rai (1990), immigrant tobacco farmers in northeastern Luzon nowadays drive out native agriculturalists, who in turn impinge on Agta hunter-gatherers and take their hunting land. Not only do the Agta and Batak lack the necessary skills for a firm commitment to agriculture, but even when they wish to learn them the surrounding cultivators and cash-croppers normally do not allow the hunters to farm successfully. It suits the farmers better to keep them in a semi-dependent relationship, hunting and collecting for trade and laboring in fields from time to time. Eder (1987:93) states with respect to the Batak of Palawan: "The proximate causes of the desultory state of Batak agriculture are found in an array of poor management practices, scheduling conflicts, social pressures, and cultural values."

Andrew Smith (1990:65, 1998) makes the same point for San populations living adjacent to Bantu herders in southern Africa: "even if a hunter would aspire to be a herder, the social conditions are against it." He also notes that the current low status of hunter-gatherers who live in association with African pastoralists probably goes back deeply into the prehistoric record. Vierich points out that "rather than undergoing a contemporary 'Neolithic Revolution' . . . the hunter-gatherers of the southeastern Kalahari are becoming increasingly dependent on the encroaching Bantu economy." She also states that amongst Basarwa (Botswana Bushman) populations, "the more dependent a [Basarwa] family is on livestock and agricultural products, the less likely they are to actually own livestock or plant their own fields" (Vierich 1982:217, 219). This reinforces the fairly obvious conclusion that as encapsulation increases in intensity, so the opportunities for successful and stable long-term adoption of food production rapidly fade.

Sedentism also has its problems for these populations. Kent (1996) notes in the African context how adoption of a sedentary lifestyle can lead to a profound increase in social disorder and homicide amongst egalitarian societies without authoritarian leadership. Hitchcock (1982) states, again in an African (Basarwa) context: "Considering all the problems incurred by sedentism, it comes as no surprise that hunter-gatherer groups would attempt to keep moving if at all possible."

The recent histories of all these circumscribed populations suggest that remaining a hunter-gatherer was actually an attractive prospect in the past, when pressure from farmers or herders was not so high as recently. In such circumstances, people had sufficient hunting land and could establish exchange partnerships with farmers in order to acquire cereals and other domesticated foods. In return, the hunter-gatherers exchanged meat and other wild products, especially important for farmers who lacked large herds (Spielman and Eder 1994). Many examples exist of such exchange systems in all hunter-gatherer situations in the Old World, particularly in West Africa, Malaysia, and the Philippines.[11] Geoffrey Benjamin's (1985) linguistic and anthropological observations suggest that the Semang hunter-gatherers and the Senoi farmers of the Malay Peninsula have differentiated their lifestyles in situations of continuing inter-action over about 4,000 years, toward hunting-gathering and farming specializations respectively. The Semang have adopted aspects of social organization, such as local group exogamy and bilateral descent, that encourage wide-ranging movement and social ties, free of any of the links between lineages and specific territories that characterize many sedentary agriculturalists. Thomas Headland (1986) observes similar features amongst the Casiguran Agta.

Such interactive networks between farmers and hunter-gatherers, in situations of non-severe circumscription, are presumably stable until the farmers increase their numbers (hardly a rare circumstance in many modern developing countries) and thus require more land. Then, the hunter-gatherers either join the farmers as an underclass of field workers, or, if they are lucky, they can adopt agriculture. The catch-22 situation here is that by the time the farmer pressure is sufficient to make agricultural adoption worthwhile, it can be already too late, as some of the Philippine Negrito populations have discovered so tragically, and as have some marginalized San with respect to pastoralism. The process in the 21st century would appear to be similar to trying to jump aboard a fast-moving train.

For those who miss the train through choice or circumstance, the future can be grim indeed. Colonial period attempts to persuade the Malaysian Semang to settle and farm have not been very successful owing to problems with seasonal food scarcity and reduced dietary diversity (Kuchikura 1988; Polunin 1953). The same has been the case for the Philippine groups, although here the enormous population density in the Philippines compared to Malaysia renders the future of Agta foragers as independent groups even more tenuous. Headland (1986, 1997; Early and Head-land 1998) gives average life expectancy for the Casiguran Agta as 22 years, with 50 percent of children dying before puberty, one woman in seven dying in childbirth, and one man in five dying as a result of homicide. Malnutrition is severe, and Agta gardening is on such a small scale that it adds little to the diet. Headland suggests that nutritional deficiencies in the past may be a major reason for the short stature of the Agta, indeed for all the Southeast Asian Negrito populations. Eder paints a similar picture for the Batak of Palawan.

However, when some of these groups are looked at from a historical perspective, it is clear that their world has not always been as pressured as now. Some of the Agta in the Philippines adopted agriculture and even changed their languages to those of the Austronesian agriculturalists deep in prehistoric time (Fox 1953; Reid 1994a, 1994b), although today the Ayta of Zambales, now full-time agriculturalists, rather paradoxic-ally derive 90 percent of their diet from introduced American rather than native Southeast Asian crops (maize, manioc, sweet potato, *Xanthosoma* taro) (Brosius 1990). This is surely a reflection of the fact that these people are obliged to live in a relatively marginal agricultural location where only these non-irrigated and hardy crops will grow.

The San, in particular, have been the center of a broad and rather vituperative debate in anthropology and archaeology as to how "genuine or spurious" they are as hunters.[12] The San live mostly now in an area beyond the range of agriculture, but not of pastoralism, and their relations with Bantu mixed farmers and Khoikhoi herders have been very intense at times in the past, particularly for those groups who live around the edge of the Kalahari. The Khoikhoi are one group of Khoisan peoples who actually adopted sheep pastoralism on a permanent basis about 1,500–2,000 years ago (pages 109–10). Some San have also adopted agriculture from Bantu farmers, planting tobacco and sorghum on a casual basis, but rarely tending the crop according to Richard Lee (1979:409–411). Others, however, such as the Dobe San of the dry Kalahari interior, remained relatively uninfluenced hunter-gatherers until early in the 20th century. As Solway and Lee (1990:119) state: "Thus . . . the complete incorporation, as dependants, of the San into the agro-pastoralist system was delayed as long as the bush held the possibility of an alternative livelihood."

Despite the existence of occasional cases of agricultural adoption amongst societies within group 1, it is apparent that all such cases of adoption for which we have records, or which can be surmised from proxy data, have been small in scale and certainly not of the strength likely to set off a process of agricultural dispersal. Indeed, they probably represent lucky escapes from situations of developing encapsulation. It is very hard to see in the records of these "niche" hunter-gatherer societies anywhere in Africa or Asia any potential for agricultural adoption on a large scale, similar for instance to the major spreads of agriculture we witness in the world's Neolithic and Formative periods.

Group 2: The "unenclosed" hunter-gatherers of Australia, the Andamans, and the Americas

This group comprises those hunter-gatherers who inhabited agricultural latitudes in Australia, the Andaman Islands, and many regions of North America, especially the West Coast and Florida, but who (unlike the members of group 1) lived lives generally apart from farmers prior to European colonization. Many of these societies in North America lived in coastal regions with prolific maritime resources and were thus able to attain chiefdom modes of social organization, often with ranked lineages. Some were also in periodic but non-threatening contact with farmers in adjacent regions in prehistory and thus had opportunities, never taken, to adopt agriculture (e.g., the northern Australians, the Andamanese, and the southern Californians). The Calusa of Florida could also be included in this group, but Keegan (1987) suggests that they ate domesticated maize on bone isotope evidence, so perhaps care is needed in interpretation. Others had limited or no contact with farmers at all, partly through remoteness and by virtue of being "protected" from agricultural contact by extensive intervening hunter-gatherer landscapes. The tribes of British Columbia and the southern half of Australia belonged in this category.

In James Woodburn's terminology, some of these hunter-gatherer populations, especially the maritime chiefdoms of western North America and Florida, had delayed-return systems for reciprocal repayment of obligation and debt. They were as a result less egalitarian than the encapsulated African and Asian hunter-gatherers. Such groups often recognized formal rights over territories and resources at many levels ranging from the individual to the community (Richardson 1982; Widmer 1988). They had lineage rather than bilateral social organization for marriage and ritual purposes, they stored food (a necessary development for delayed-return systems – Testart 1988), were often less mobile, more sedentary than the immediate return groups, and in general had the kind of social characteristics which *in theory* could render a shift to the accumulating and storing lifestyle of the successful farmer a little easier. Socially, therefore, such groups overlapped greatly with agriculturalists, indicating that social complexity of the chiefdom type can relate in terms of origin more to the intensity and reliability of resources and population density than to any simple presence of food production as opposed to hunting and gathering. This is not a new observation, but it is one worth reiterating nevertheless.

Complex hunter-gatherer chiefdoms of the North American type seem not to have existed in Australia at European contact, although Harry Lourandos (1991, 1997) and Colin Pardoe (1988) provide archaeological and burial evidence to suggest that complex societies in Woodburn's "delayed-return" mold could have existed in the prehistoric past, especially in some of the more fertile southern parts of the continent. Ethnographically, Australia is too complex for easy categorization, with some societies now being strongly "immediate-return" and focused on sharing. Nevertheless, intensely maritime-oriented societies with complex technology and lineage ranking did not occur in Australia and neither was food storage highly developed, except in drier regions (Peterson 1993; Cane 1989:104).

What do we know about opportunities for agricultural adoption amongst these group 2 hunters and gatherers, before the incorporation of most into modern nations? Australia, uniquely, formed a vast continent of hunter-gatherers who survived into ethnographic times with no traces of pre-contact agricultural adoption, yet who lived sometimes in regions of high potential agricultural productivity. Cape York Aborigines were in contact with Torres Strait and southern New Guinea gardeners, all living within a zone of similar ecology, climate, and floral resources (Harris 1977b). Indeed, the crops that supported New Guinea cultivators – yams, aroids (particularly taro), arrowroot, palms, pandanus, and occasional coconuts – grew wild in the Cape York landscape without evincing any agricultural interest.

Arnhem Land and Kimberley Aborigines also had contact with male Indonesian maritime collectors and traders ("Macassans"), but here we perhaps must accept that seamen and farming knowledge do not easily travel together. Macassan visits to northern Australia for *bêche-de-mer* collection since perhaps the 16th century (Macknight 1976) seem to have been frequent enough for Macassan–Aboriginal trade pidgins to form (Urry and Walsh 1981), and some Aborigines were even taken by ship to Macassar (Ujung Pandang). But in this case, the Indonesians did not settle permanently or farm in Australia. Similar contacts occurred with the Andamanese, who were visited by trading ships sailing between India and Southeast Asia from at least 2,000 years ago, such that they were able to acquire pigs and to adopt pottery-making (Cooper 1996). But they also did not become farmers.

According to some authorities, Australian Aboriginal societies also enshrined behavioral characteristics that would have made adoption of settled agriculture a difficult process. Nicolas Peterson refers to the lack of materialism, need for portability, and ethic of generosity in Aboriginal society, regarding these as removing any motivation for the development of labor-intensive subsistence patterns such as agriculture. He gives the example of an Arnhem Land group who made a garden in 1971 for the specific purpose of convincing officials that their land was in use, thus not available for expropriation. When the group moved camp it uprooted the plants and replanted them beside the new camp, thus giving a new meaning to the concept of shifting cultivation. Not surprisingly, the plants died. A. K. Chase also suggests, with respect to northern Aboriginal societies, that agriculture "implies a radically different perception of the environment and its legitimate human occupants, and it authorizes a radically different manipulation of plants and their habits".[13]

Some of the drier inland riverine regions of Australia supported populations who harvested wild grasses in prehistory, and still do today (Allen 1974; Cane 1989). But, unlike the situation in the Levant or China, we witness no trajectory here toward domestication. The reasons for this are probably that the hand-stripping harvesting method recorded ethnographically never selected for grains with a non-shattering habit. Even if such selection were to occur, no planting was practiced for the next season. In addition, processing of these small grass seeds was so laborious (six hours' work to feed one person for one day according to Cane) that the bread-like "dampers" produced from the husked and ground grain never provided more than a supplement to the diet. Whether agriculture would eventually have developed here if the harvesters had been left alone by the outside world for another few millennia we will never know, but with existing processing methods it would certainly be unlikely. The regions concerned are also marginal for agriculture, with recurrent problems of drought.

But what of agricultural adoption by ethnographic group 2 hunter-gatherer societies in other parts of the world? The Yanomama of Venezuela possibly adopted banana cultivation into a basically hunter-gatherer economy in post-Columbian times, after this plant was introduced from Southeast Asia into the Americas (Rival 1999:81). Another example of agricultural adoption has occurred in recent centuries in the Southwest USA. The ancestors of the Athabaskan-speaking Apache and Navajo migrated from Canada into northern Arizona and northwestern New Mexico, apparently after the collapse around AD 1400 of many of the former Anasazi and Mogollon (pueblo-building) agricultural societies made famous by such evocative ruins as Cliff Palace in Mesa Verde and Pueblo Bonito in Chaco Canyon (Matson 2003). The Athabaskans migrated, probably down the western Plains, as bison hunters, but some Navajo in close contact with surviving Pueblo societies had adopted sheep-herding and some casual cultivation of maize by 1705. Ethnographically, the Apache and Navajo habitats were relatively arid and the degree of agricultural investment prior to the 19th century was apparently only slight; attempts to force the Navajo to adopt agriculture more intensively prior to 1863 failed. Some Apache living at high altitudes (e.g., the Mescalero) planted maize in spring but harvested it while still green (unripe) to avoid frost. They then needed to roast and sun-dry the grains in order to make them edible, which meant that they lacked any viable planting stock for the next season. This, they probably had to trade for. So agricultural adoption here was evidently both encouraged and yet at the same time limited in intensity by environmental marginality (Hester 1962; Snow 1991).

So far, it seems that the ethnographic record with respect to both group 1 and group 2 hunter-gatherer societies offers few hints of eager and successful agricultural adoption. This seems to be the case regardless of whether societies were immediate or delayed return, encapsulated or unenclosed, ranked or egalitarian, sedentary or mobile, "collectors" or "foragers".[14] The ranked and populous hunter-gatherer societies of northern California were no more interested in adopting agriculture than were the Cape York Aborigines or the Semang, and perhaps even the majority of hunter-gatherers in prehistory. It does not follow that hunter-gatherers who have "complex" social institutions will necessarily become farmers whenever they are introduced to the farming concept. Indeed, the Apache and Navajo were probably small and mobile egalitarian bands at the time of their adoption of agriculture and herding.

Thus, whatever the social and environmental conditions conducive to agricultural adoption, the "bottom line" observation still holds. Nowhere in the ethnographic record do we observe any adoption of agriculture that has imparted expansionary success to the adopting population. However, it is not my intention here to claim that this could *never* have happened in the prehistoric past, and of course we will return to this issue on many occasions in later chapters.

Group 3: Hunter-gatherers who descend from former agriculturalists

This group has deliberately been left until last because of the uniqueness of its historical trajectory. Some hunter-gatherers appear to have descended from original farming or pastoralist societies, via specializations into environments where agriculture was not possible or decidedly marginal. Some also exist in direct contact with agriculturalist groups closely related in terms of cultural and biological ancestry. The so-called "Manus True" fishing communities of the southern coast of Manus Island in the Admiralty Islands of Melanesia are a good example here,[15] existing as they do side by side with a land-based agricultural population from whom they are not sharply separated in an ethnic sense. In terms of history, such trajectories obviously necessitate that these societies be considered separately from the "original/pristine" hunter-gatherers of groups 1 and 2.

But this is a difficult group to deal with in terms of authentication. Often the suggestions of a partial agricultural ancestry are based on linguistic and biological relationships rather than concrete eye-witness evidence. Examples of this group are claimed (and sometimes counterclaimed) to occur in East Africa, southern India, interior Borneo, southern New Zealand, the Sepik Basin of New Guinea, the Great Basin and western Great Plains of the USA, and in relatively infertile interfluvial regions of the Amazon Basin. Indeed, it is a very large group, amongst whom the southern Maoris and some of the northern Uto-Aztecan peoples were the only ones actually *obliged* by environmental factors to abandon true agriculture. The existence of this group renders "hunting and gathering" rather an uncertain concept from a historical point of view, but our concern in this section is more with behavior than with history *per se*. As far as behavior is concerned these people are, of course, genuine hunter-gatherers.

Some of the rain-forest hunters and gatherers of Island Southeast Asia, particularly the Punan of Borneo, the Kubu of Sumatra, and the much-debated Tasaday of Mindanao (fake or genuine!), descend from original agricultural populations, if the linguistic and biological data are any guide.[16] In this view, the ancestral Punan and Kubu became hunter-gatherers, especially wild sago collectors in the case of the Punan, via conscious decisions to move into interfluvial rain-forest hunting and gathering in regions that riverine agriculturalists found hard to penetrate.

Other hunter-gatherers descended from cultivators include some Bantu speakers in southern Africa, possibly the honey-collecting Dorobo or Okiek of the Kenyan Highlands of East Africa, probably some marginal sago-collecting groups (most of whom practice minor horticulture) in the Sepik Basin of New Guinea, and some Indian groups such as the Chenchu and Birhor.[17] In South America there are other such potential group 3 hunter-gatherer populations in the poorer interfluvial regions of the Amazon Basin, such as the Ache of Paraguay and the Siriono and Bororo of Brazil.[18] Perhaps the most interesting are the Numic-speaking Uto-Aztecan peoples of the Great Basin and adjacent areas, who appear to have abandoned a former agricultural lifestyle around 1,000 years ago. These people, linguistic descendants of original maize-cultivators in Mexico and the Southwest, eventually found themselves in a dry region where maize agriculture had become marginal or no longer possible (see chapter 8). Some groups still have give-away characteristics of their remote agricultural ancestry, such as pottery-making, irrigation of stands of wild plants, and farmer-like attitudes to resource ownership (Kirchhoff 1954; Madsen and Rhode 1994; Hill 2001, 2003).

Group 3 hunter-gatherer societies are of especial interest because it is far easier for a relatively marginal food-producing community to turn to hunting and gathering than it is for hunters and gatherers to move in the opposite direction. Thus, it is a fair expectation that members of this third group of hunter-gatherers will always have been quite numerous, particularly around the ecological margins of expanding agricultural societies. As to the value of these groups with respect to debates concerning hunter-gatherer adoptions of agriculture, one might protest that having given up agriculture they are quite likely to adopt it again. This is perhaps true, particularly if some technological or economic habits survive from the former agricultural phase. Yet those who lived ethnographically in regions of agricultural possibility (i.e., excluding southern New Zealand and the Great Basin) still behaved essentially as other living hunter-gatherer groups with respect to general lack of interest in agricultural adoption. For instance, Bernard Sellato (1994) notes how resistant the Punan of parts of Borneo are to taking up farming, although Punan women often marry men from Kayan farming communities.

Indeed, the marriage of hunter-gatherer women to food-producer men is so commonly recorded in ethnography that it is clearly a major avenue of cultural and genetic interchange. Hunter-gatherer men can rarely afford to acquire farmer wives, especially if bride-price payments are involved. Despite the intermarriage, however, Kayan communities still like to keep the Punan in a subservient collector relationship, just as Philippine farming communities do the Agta and as some Bantu farmers do their Pygmy and San neighbors.

Thus, the group 3 hunter-gatherers overlap with those of groups 1 and 2 in terms of behavior and social situation, and only appear to differ in terms of origin. The factor of origin in this respect, however, is very significant, for the group 3 societies offer one trajectory of cultural evolution that can terminate for ever the idea that evolution from foraging to farming is a one-way street.

Why Do Ethnographic Hunter-Gatherers Have Problems with Agricultural Adoption? A Comparative View

They live in a Tranquillity which is not disturb'd by the Inequality of Condition: The Earth and sea of their own accord furnishes them with all things necessary for life, they covet not Magnificent Houses, Household-stuff &c^a, . . . In short they seem'd to set no value upon any thing we gave them, nor would they ever part with any thing of their own for any one article we could offer them; this in my opinion argues that they think themselves provided with all the necessarys of Life and that they have no superfluities. (Captain James Cook, describing the Natives of New-Holland [New South Wales, Australia] in 1770; Beaglehole 1968:399)

The absence of farming in areas susceptible of it, like California, is thus not due to natural limitations but to cultural limitations of a historical character – the feebleness of agricultural stimuli. (Kirchhoff 1954:533)

The above descriptions of the three groups of ethnographic hunter-gatherer societies indicate that some have shifted into fairly marginal economies of agricultural production in recent centuries. But very few, it seems, have actually been observed in ethnographic times adopting a full-time farming livelihood supported by only minimal hunting and gathering. Why not? Is it because there are special factors that have made such adoptions almost impossible in the face of a torrential outpouring of European colonization and conquest during the past 500 years? Did hunter-gatherers adopt agriculture much more frequently before this? Perhaps, but the fact still remains that there are obviously many aspects of mobile hunter-gatherer society that are antithetical to adoption of the sedentary lifestyle of the cultivator. On top of this, we have the attitudes of the farming and pastoralist societies themselves, often ranked and status-conscious, with whom some of the ethnographic hunter-gatherers have come into contact and by whom many have eventually been encapsulated. We have, therefore, two pincer-like reasons why hunter-gatherers face a catch-22 situation and find it hard to adopt agriculture – unsuitable social relations on the inside, combined with adverse relationships with other populations on the outside.

What about those societies for whom encapsulation has not been an issue? Here, we still have to explain why Cape York Aborigines did not adopt yam and taro gardening across Torres Strait, given all the other material borrowings, including outrigger canoes, that are known to have crossed the same route. We also have to ask why southern Californians did not adopt maize cultivation from the peoples of the lower Colorado valley long before Spanish arrival. In a detailed review of this question for California, Bean and Lawton (1976:47) seem to hit the nail right on the head when they state: "The abundance of California's food resources and highly developed techniques of energy extraction, however, made it unnecessary to adapt an agricultural mode, except in some of the marginally productive desert areas."

This suggests, so far, that we have two basic sets of reasons for agricultural non-adoption – the social reasons, and the economic lack-of-necessity reasons. There is a third reason, presented by the Californians and northern Australians. Although relatively affluent in food supplies, the people of both southern California and Cape York were also *separated* from their nearest agricultural neighbors by small but significant geographical transitions. In the case of northern Australia it was a sea gap and increasing dry-season length toward the south, moving away from agriculturalist New Guinea. In the case of California it was desert and the shift from a semi-arid Arizona environment to a Mediterranean-type climate with very marked winter rainfall seasonality. Bean and Lawton tend to dismiss the latter problem on the grounds that maize was grown widely by Indians in California in the colonial conditions of the 18th and 19th centuries, but this development merely demonstrates that "where there is a will there is a way." Prior to the mid-18th century it seems there was no will.

In addition to this, the low-density Yuman and Uto-Aztecan agricultural populations in Arizona probably saw no reason to attempt to expand their ranges across the Mojave Desert into California, except for hunting and gathering purposes. These populations had low levels of production tied to localized irrigation systems and it is unlikely they would have seen any necessity to cross forbidding desert terrain to enter a quite different climatic zone. Elsewhere in the world where bio-geographical transitions needed to be crossed, as from Pakistan into India and from temperate China into tropical Southeast Asia, agriculture also spread very slowly. Into Australia and California agriculture never spread at all and the indigenous hunter-gatherers simply continued, prior to the European period, in the lifestyle they knew best.

Having reviewed the varied reasons why hunters and gatherers should not adopt agriculture, it is now necessary to ask what kind of hunter-gatherers could have dodged the overall catch-22 situation with success and aplomb, avoiding encapsulation in the process, back in the Neolithic or Formative? Under what circumstances would hunters and gatherers have positively and successfully adopted agriculture, *such that they were able to "take over" the economy, technology, and maybe even language of a neighboring farming group and convert their takeover into a powerful force for expansion?* This, after all, is what any claim for local hunter-gatherer adoption of agriculture as a major driving force for both language and material culture expansion in prehistory must imply. Mere adoption of low-energy sporadic cultivation by a hunter-gatherer population, or incorporation of a hunter-gatherer group and its genes into a dominant agriculturalist society, is not a relevant issue in this regard.

The answer to the above question is not an easy one, for it is of course possible that hunter-gatherer societies existed 10,000 years ago quite unlike any of the recent past with respect to their attitudes toward adopting an agricultural lifestyle. But again, one must express some doubt on this. There is nothing in the archaeological record to indicate that ancient hunter-gatherers were structured beyond the range, from band to chiefdom, that we witness in hunter-gatherer ethnography. If we wish to ask what would have happened when agriculturalists and hunter-gatherers came face to face in regions of very high agricultural potential, such as the fertile alluvial plains of temperate Europe, central China, or northern India, then comparative ethnography and history suggest the following possibilities:

a) Hunter-gatherers would have been unlikely to adopt agriculture if they were not in direct and continuous contact with agriculturalists. They would also not have adopted agriculture by remote action across bio-geographical transition zones or uninhabited terrain.

b) When the contacts were direct, that is, when the agriculturalists were actually living within the territories used by hunter-gatherers, then the initial trends would have been for mutualism and exchange.[19]

c) The hunter-gatherers would have begun to adopt agriculture as the agriculturalist pressures on land increased. But here we have that catch-22 situation again – as the pressures increased, so would the encapsulation and domination, thus reducing the social likelihood of successful agricultural adoption. There would always have been a window of opportunity for hunters and gatherers to adopt agriculture. But if it was an ephemeral one, as it would have been in situations of rapid farmer demographic increase, then most hunter-gatherers would have been less likely to pass through it.

So far, therefore, there appear to be no compelling reasons why any ancient hunters and gatherers would have commonly adopted agriculture on a permanent basis, or would have tried to do so unless pushed, or even why the many Neolithic farmer populations would simply have sat by quietly and watched hunter-gatherers adopting the livelihood from which they derived their social and symbolic power. But, of course, there is a very important loophole here for those disposed to vote for hunter-gatherer adoption of agriculture as the main means of agricultural spread in Neolithic times. This concerns environmental specifics and issues of farmer-hunter comparative demography. In regions that were marginal for agriculture, or in coastal regions where maritime food-collecting populations were quite dense, it is obvious that the chances of the native hunter-gatherer populations "taking over" a tentatively introduced agricultural system could have been higher, at least according to pure logic. Much would depend on how rigidly the farmers wished to protect their ethnic identity, on how much they would have been willing to recruit new members through intermarriage with hunter-gatherers, and on how much their economy was coming under stress with the move into less favorable environmental conditions. These are complex issues that cannot be dispatched with one-line answers, and many examples of such situations are discussed later. But let us not forget again that high productivity in a rich coastal hunter-gatherer economic system, even with sedentism and storage, does not necessarily make agricultural adoption any more likely.

Despite these fairly negative views on the possibility of agricultural adoption by hunter-gatherers, it is certainly not being suggested here that ancient hunter-gatherers could *never* have adopted agriculture from outside sources. But they would only have been likely to do so in situations where they had some demographic or environmental advantage over any farmers in the vicinity, and where there would have been significant reasons why the normal hunter-gatherer disinterest in agricultural adoption should be overturned. We cannot assume that hunter-gatherers would automatically adopt agriculture just because it was sitting under their noses. We also need to remember that many populations of hunters and gatherers survived alongside agriculturalists in many parts of the world for *millennia*, without adopting agriculture, just as we witness in the ethnographic record.

The following chapters will demonstrate that the spread of agriculture in the past could not simply have occurred only because hunter-gatherers everywhere adopted it. Agriculture spread in Neolithic/Formative circumstances mainly because the cultural and linguistic descendants of the early cultivators increased their demographic profiles and pushed their cultural and linguistic boundaries outwards. Occasionally, existing hunter-gatherers were offered short-lived windows to do the same. But such windows were probably rare, at least in terms of unilateral adoption of farming by hunter-gatherers without a substantial presence of farmers in the vicinity.

To the Archaeological Record

According to the archaeological record, agriculture emerged as the predominant form of food production directly from a hunter-gatherer background, without any major significance attributable to external diffusion,[20] in at least five major regions of the world (Figure 1.3):

1. the Fertile Crescent of Southwest Asia (wheat, barley, pea, lentil, sheep, goat, pig, cattle);
2. the middle and lower courses of the Yangzi and Yellow river basins of China (rice, foxtail millet, many tubers and fruits, pig, poultry);
3. New Guinea, probably in the interior highlands (taro, sugar cane, pandanus, banana, no domestic animals);
4. the tropical regions of the Americas, perhaps with one or more foci in central Mexico and northern South America (maize, beans, squashes, manioc, many fruits and tubers, minor domestic animals);
5. the Eastern Woodlands of the USA (squashes and various seed-bearing plants, no domestic animals).

It is possible that central (Sub-Saharan) Africa also witnessed early agricultural developments, particularly in the Sahel zone for millets and north of the rain forest in West Africa for yams and African rice. There are also claims of a similar nature for southern India.

In understanding the origins of agriculture in these regions we need to consider for each of them, wherever data exist, a number of botanical/zoological, environmental, and archaeological questions:

a) Where did the progenitors of the major domesticated plants and animals live when domestication first occurred (bearing in mind that modern environments and species distributions can be very different from those of several millennia ago)?

b) How did climatic conditions and environments change during the time spans in which agriculture emerged in the various regions? What were the results of these changes on faunas, floras, and human economies?

c) What kinds of hunting and gathering cultures made the transition to agriculture in the various regions? How important were preexisting patterns of sedentism, food storage, and opportunities for asymmetrical accumulations of wealth as opposed to egalitarian sharing?

d) How rapidly did particular transitions occur, and over what extents of territory initially?

e) What patterning in archaeological/cultural terms is associated with the transition?

These questions will be addressed in more detail as we proceed through the evidence from each region. Coverage for different areas is very uneven and our understanding, in terms of sheer quantity of archaeological data, is dominated very much by the transition in the Levant. But we have enough information to know that the Levant model is unlikely to be valid for any other regions, apart perhaps from China, and even here only with modification. The routes to agricultural dependence were multiple.

Chapter 3
The Beginnings of Agriculture in Southwest Asia

Southwest Asia is by far the best-known region in world prehistory for the transition to agriculture, especially its western portion, generally known as the Levant. The Southwest Asian trajectory does not necessarily provide the model for all the other areas of transition, but it had, in terms of world significance, the greatest impact on subsequent human affairs, followed closely by that in China.

The setting for the transition to agriculture in Southwest Asia was a zone of open woodlands and grasslands, with stands of wild cereals and legumes, that forms part of what has become famous in archaeology as the "Fertile Crescent" (Figure 3.1). This runs from the Jordan Valley northwards through inland Syria, into southeastern Turkey (Anatolia), then eastwards through northern Iraq, and finally southeastward along the Zagros foothills of western Iran. Today, the Fertile Crescent receives annually more than 200 millimeters of relatively reliable winter-focused rainfall, being flanked to its south by desert and to its north and east by high mountains. It is essentially a zone of gentle gradients with ample areas of alluvial soil, where climatic conditions allowed rain-fed agriculture to develop without elaborate irrigation requirements.

Some very significant points may first be noted about the transition to agriculture and plant/animal domestication in the Fertile Crescent:

1. It was closely related in timing with the first *stable* and *continuing* amelioration of post-glacial climate, focused on the period between 9500 and 7500 BC (calibrated radiocarbon dates).
2. It occurred in a region of winter rainfall with very marked rainfall seasonality.
3. It involved a combination of cereal, legume, and animal domestication, a combination of unrivalled productive significance in world prehistory (Diamond 2002).
4. It was aceramic and Neolithic in technological orientation (i.e., no pottery in the early stages, and no smelted as opposed to hammered metal).

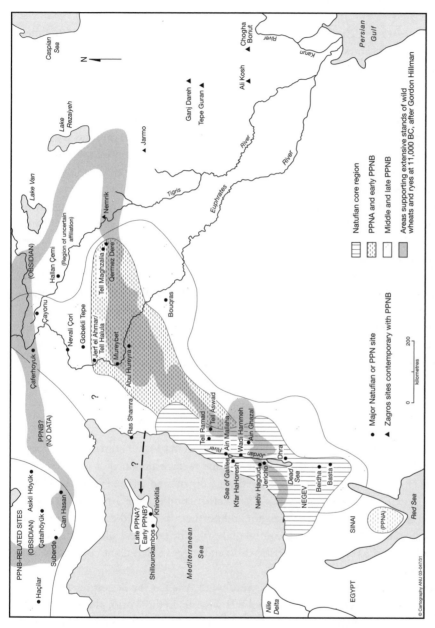

Figure 3.1 Natufian/Epipaleolithic, PPNA, and PPNB site distributions, from many sources, especially Hours et al. 1994. Also shown is the extent of wild cereal stands as reconstructed by Gordon Hillman for about 11,000 BC, close to the onset of the Younger Dryas cold and dry phase.

5. It evolved from a baseline of complex hunting and gathering, with presumed sedentary or near-sedentary settlements.
6. It was revolutionary, both in tempo and in impact on the western/central Eurasian and northern African cultural canvases.[1]

The Quaternary pollen record from Southwest Asia, in combination with other paleoclimatic indicators, outlines the transformations of climate and vegetation that have occurred since 20,000 years ago.[2] In the Fertile Crescent, the last glacial maximum was a period of cold dry conditions, with widespread relatively treeless steppes. Average temperatures were 4° or more below present and wild cereals apparently existed only in protected refuge areas. Between 15,000 and 12,000 BC there were rises in temperature, rainfall, and atmospheric carbon dioxide almost to present-day levels, but they were episodic (see Figure 2.3). About 11,000 BC, an unusually rapid and severe swing took the region back into cold and dry glacial conditions, a situation that lasted until about 9500 BC. This cold phase is termed the Younger Dryas.

The Younger Dryas was followed after 9500 BC by a very rapid re-warming, by as much as 7°C in average annual temperature, to Early Holocene conditions; warm and wet, with increased winter rainfall, and increased summer monsoon rainfall in some southerly regions. These conditions were excellent for a widespread radiation of wild cereals and legumes. Just as important, they were associated with the establishment of a high level of climatic stability. Between about 9000 and 7300 BC, domesticated cereals, legumes, and herd animals rapidly acquired dominant roles in human subsistence throughout Southwest Asia. If this association with the onset of a relatively stable and encouraging Holocene climate was pure coincidence, then it was one of the most remarkable coincidences ever to occur in human prehistory.

The Domestication of Plants in the Fertile Crescent

Using available palynological data (van Zeist and Bottema 1991; Hillman 1996; Moore et al. 2000), it is possible to offer a fairly specific reconstruction of where the wild cereal species ultimately to be domesticated were distributed on the eve of domestication and agriculture. If Gordon Hillman's reconstruction (Figure 3.1) is correct, they would have grown mainly in the western and northern parts of the Fertile Crescent, rather than in the colder and more continental east. The botanical and archaeological evidence is in accord with this reconstruction and suggests that plant cultivation also began in this area.[3]

As stressed by Jared Diamond (1997), Southwest Asia has the largest area of Mediterranean climate (hot dry summers, cool wet winters) in the world, plus the greatest range of altitudinal variation within this climatic category. It also has the largest number of large-seeded annual wild cereal and pod-bearing legume species (legumes include broad beans, peas, chick peas, and lentils) of any region of Mediterranean climate, all genetically programmed to germinate and grow through the short day-lengths of the wet winter and to remain dormant in seed form in the ground during the hot dry summer. Annual cereals tend to have larger grains than perennial ones because of the function of the grains as food stores during dormancy. Fortunately for humans, those cereals and legumes chosen for ultimate domestication also happened to be self- rather than cross-pollinating. In other words, useful characters developed as a result of human management would not be easily swamped out of successive generations by back-crossing with wild plants, especially if such modified varieties were planted beyond the normal ranges of the wild forms. Stable lines of domesticates could be developed from the beginning. These botanical advantages possessed by Southwest Asian cereals were of fundamental importance.

Moving now to the cereals themselves, the wheat species termed emmer (a hulled tetraploid[4]) and einkorn (a hulled diploid) were the first to be widely cultivated in the Fertile Crescent, together with barley and rye. Actual domesticated (morphological) features in these cereals are present in a few sites by about 8500 BC, although domesticated rye is currently claimed much earlier than this at Abu Hureyra in Syria. By 8000 BC, naked-grained (free-threshing) tetraploid and hexaploid wheats had also made an appearance. Bread wheat, a naked-grained hexaploid, was brought into domestication following an introgression between emmer and a wild species of goat grass. Barley was cultivated initially in its natural 2-row form, with the higher-yielding 6-row barley developing rapidly through cultivator selection in well-watered environments. Wild 2-row barley has a widespread distribution across Southwest Asia extending to western Anatolia, North Africa, and Afghanistan, but occurrences in archaeological contexts[5] suggest initial cultivation in the Fertile Crescent. Emmer is of Levant origin, and einkorn is currently believed to have originated in southeastern Anatolia.

The legumes pea, lentil, and chickpea were all of Levant origin, possibly from an area encompassing northern Syria and southeastern Anatolia, but none of these occur in domesticated form until after 8000 BC, later than emmer and barley on present evidence (Ladizinsky 1999; Lev-Yadun et al. 2000; Garrard 1999). Another important domesticate of the Fertile Crescent was flax, the fiber source for linen, attested in Neolithic textile remains from dry caves in Israel.

From the viewpoint of those populations making the transition to agriculture, wild cereals and legumes have characteristics that we might consider not very user-friendly. Their ears and pods disintegrate or burst open when they are ripe so that the grains can disperse – for cereals this is referred to as shattering, or dehiscence in the case of the legumes. The grains are also encased in tough protective glumes (Figure 3.2B) so they can survive predation during dispersal and dormancy. Individual grains, ears or pods on a single plant will not ripen synchronously, causing difficulties for efficient harvesting. The wild Southwest Asian cereals and legumes will only germinate and mature during a relatively fixed period each year (autumn to spring), owing to their sensitivity to temperature, moisture, and day-length variations and their requirements for vernalization. Early wild cereal and legume exploiters would probably have wanted to harvest the ears or pods slightly unripe, before the seed dispersal phase triggered by full ripeness. They would then have needed to dry the grains in the sun or roast them, before grinding.[6]

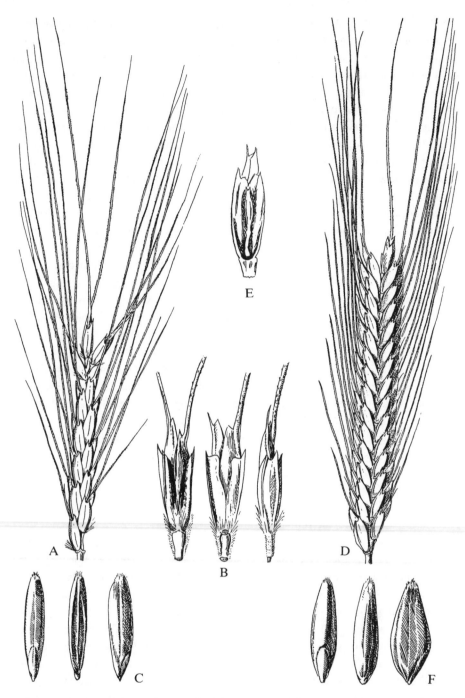

Figure 3.2 Ear, spikelet, and grain of wild (A, B, C) and domesticated (D, E, F) einkorn wheat, *Triticum monococcum*. From Zohary and Hopf 2000.

The overall impact of the domesticatory process by humans has been to alter, especially for the Southwest Asian cereals (but also for all other major world cereal crops), all the wild states listed above toward a non-shattering habit when ripe, grains held loosely within weak glumes (naked grains), synchronous ripening in individual plants and across stands, lessened dormancy of the grains (meaning they can be planted year-round as long as water is available), larger grains, and larger and more compact ears (Figure 3.2D). Obviously, cereals with such features will not be well equipped to survive by themselves in the wild – but then they will not need to with human cultivators at their service. From a perspective of population numbers, domesticated plants and animals can be stated to benefit just as much as humans from a mutualistic domesticatory relationship.

A major question that arises with all these crops is that of how many independent domestications occurred for each of them. This is an important issue, since if most crops were only domesticated once, as believed by Daniel Zohary (1996, 1999) and Mark Blumler (1998), then it could imply that hunter-gatherers all over late Pleistocene Southwest Asia did not simply start, independently, cultivating the wild cereals that just happened to be growing near their camps. It implies that, once domesticated, the major cereals and legumes spread "pre-emptively" throughout the burgeoning agricultural world, rendering it non-economic for anyone to attempt to domesticate separate local wild varieties. At present the genetics behind this issue are a little clouded; whereas einkorn is claimed to have been domesticated in just one locality in the Karacadag Mountains of southeastern Anatolia (Heun et al. 1997), the evidence for the other crops is not so clear and more than one domestication event is likely, especially for barley (Jones and Brown 2000; Willcox 2002).

Despite the uncertainty, it has recently been claimed that all the main founder crops of the Near East were domesticated within a single small area of northern Syria and southeastern Anatolia, an idea driven partly by the limited distribution of the chick pea in wild form. This suggests almost a single point of origin for the Near Eastern Neolithic, a possibility that cannot easily be negated and one that would be of great importance were it to be independently verified (Lev-Yadun et al. 2000; Gopher et al. 2001).

The Hunter-Gatherer Background in the Levant, 19,000 to 9500 BC (Figure 3.3)

The archaeological course toward domestication in the Levant can be traced from around 19,000 BC, at the peak of the last glaciation. At that time, people camped at a locality called Ohalo II, on the shoreline of the Sea of Galilee, were exploiting local wild stands of emmer, barley, pistachio, grape, and olive (Nadel and Herschkovitz 1991; Herschkovitz et al. 1995; Nadel and Werker 1999). The Sea of Galilee formed the northern part of the much larger Pleistocene Lake Lisan, which filled the Jordan Valley for a continuous 220 kilometers. The Ohalo II camp covered 1,500 square meters, a surprisingly large area for a site of this period. The inhabitants constructed

Figure 3.3 The basic archaeological chronology of the Middle East, showing sites and cultural complexes dating between 15,000 and 5000 BC, together with the generalized pattern of climate change. Adapted, with modifications, mainly from Cauvin 2000. The unbroken lines show the spread of the PPNB, according to Cauvin, from a source region in the Middle Levant/Middle Euphrates.

Cal. BC	Climatic Phases	Cultural phases in Levant	Western Anatolia	Central Anatolia	Medit. Coast, Cyprus	Southern Levant	Jordan Valley, Damascus Basin	Middle Euphrates	Southeastern Turkey	North Syria	Northern Iraq	Zagros
6000	Drying	Pottery	Ilipinar, Hoça Cesme	Haçilar	Byblos	*YARMUKIAN*	(Pastoralists)	Sabi Abyad		(Pastoralists)	*HASSUNA* Dabaghiyah	Jarmo
7000	Drying	*PPNC*		Çatalhöyük / Aceramic Haçilar	*KHIROKITIA* Ras Shamra	Ain Ghazal *PPNC*	*Late PPNB*	Abu Hureyra 2C	Cafer Höyük	Bouqras	*Late PPNB* Maghzalia	Ali Kosh Ganj Dareh
8000	Holocene optimum: Stable	*PPNB*		Aşıklı Höyük	Cyprus *PPNB*	Ain Ghazal *PPNB*	Beidha / Jericho PPNB	*Middle PPNB* Abu Hureyra 2 / *Early PPNB* Jerf el Ahmar	Nevali Cori / Göbekli / Çayönü grills		Nemrik	
9000		*PPNA*				*KHIAMIAN*	*SULTANIAN* Jericho *PPNA* *KHIAMIAN*	Mureybet III / Mureybet IIA	Çayönü basal / Hallan Çemi		Qermez Dere	
10,000	Younger Dryas: Cold, dry	*NATUFIAN*			*NATUFIAN*	*NEGEV LATE NATUFIAN*	*NATUFIAN* Eynan / Hayonim	Mureybet IA		*NATUFIAN*		Zawi Chemi Shanidar
11,000	Alleröd: Warm but unstable							*NATUFIAN* Abu Hureyra I				
12,000		*GEOMETRIC KEBARAN*			*GEOM. KEBARAN*		*GEOM. KEBARAN*	*GEOM. KEBARAN*		*GEOM. KEBARAN*		
13,000	Unstable, warming	*GEOMETRIC KEBARAN*										
14,000												
15,000												*ZARZIAN*

at least three oval pole and thatch huts, stored their food supplies in pits, buried their dead in flexed postures in shallow pits covered by large stones (like the Natufians much later), and utilized a toolkit of Upper Paleolithic blade type, together with basalt bowls and pestles. At this time, available data suggest a very low population density for Southwest Asia, with most regions having a cold climate with perennial shrubby vegetation. Ohalo was an environmental "refuge" zone, possibly a fairly ephemeral one, and cereals would not have flourished outside warm sheltered areas such as this.

After 15,000 BC, an archaeological complex known as the Geometric Kebaran developed in the southern Levant ("geometric" here refers to the shapes of the characteristic microlithic stone tools). These people lived in caves or small campsites mostly under 300 square meters in area, reaching about 1,000 square meters maximum. They are assumed to have been seasonally mobile and possibly to have moved between winter lowland camps in valleys and summer camps at higher altitudes. They also used stone mortars and pestles, and at Ein Gev III near the Sea of Galilee they built small circular huts with stone foundations. One presumes they harvested wild cereals like their Ohalo predecessors, but, unlike their Natufian successors, they apparently still did not use stone sickles. The *Atlas des Sites du Proche Orient* (Hours et al. 1994) lists 51 archaeologically investigated locations occupied during the Geometric Kebaran period in the Levant, and only three contemporary locations for all other regions of Southwest Asia. But this may, of course, be telling us more about current foci of archaeological research rather than any absolute patterning.

By 12,500 BC, the Geometric Kebaran microlithic industry was evolving into its Natufian descendant.[7] In an overall sense, sites increased markedly in number and area during the Natufian; the *Atlas des Sites du Proche Orient* shows 74 locations of this period for the Levant, and 26 contemporary non-Natufian locations in Anatolia and the Zagros. But numbers are not all, for site areas through the whole Natufian region are estimated to have ranged up to five times larger on average than those of the Geometric Kebaran. This suggests that the human population was increasing rapidly, especially during the early Natufian, before the commencement of the Younger Dryas cold phase (11,000 to 9500 BC). Belfer-Cohen and Hovers (1992) give a total of 417 excavated Natufian burials as opposed to only three from the preceding Upper Paleolithic – also an apparent indication of increasing human numbers at this time.

Unfortunately, soil conditions in most Natufian sites mean that few plant remains survive, but there are some hints that wild cereals, especially barley, were being exploited, in the drier regions at least. As in the Geometric Kebaran, many sites have basalt mortars and pestles. The early Natufian site of Wadi Hammeh 27 (11,500 BC) has remains of wild barley, together with bone sickle handles with microlithic stone blade inserts (Edwards 1991). The stone-bladed sickle, indeed, seems to have come into common use in the central Levant during the Natufian, although as Patricia Anderson (1994) points out, such tools could have been used for cutting reeds as well as cereals. The Natufian-related site of Mureybet IA in northern Syria also has remains of wild barley, einkorn, and lentils at about 10,500 BC (van Zeist 1988).

Newly published observations from the site of Abu Hureyra, near Mureybit on the Middle Euphrates, bring the Natufian (or a close cousin – here perhaps better termed

Epipaleolithic) right into the forefront of the debate about early domestication. According to Gordon Hillman and his colleagues (Hillman 1989; Hillman et al. 2001; Moore et al. 2000), the inhabitants of this site were impacted upon quite heavily by the Younger Dryas cold dry phase, after 11,000 BC. This caused a disappearance of woodland and encouraged the inhabitants to harvest wild wheat and rye. The rye, quite surprisingly, shows domesticated characteristics as early 10,700 BC, three grains being dated by AMS radiocarbon. At the same time in the site record there is an appearance of the seeds of weed species known to favor arable land. However, it is likely that the extreme levels of climatic variability made the experiment a relatively short-lived one at Abu Hureyra, because the site was almost abandoned for a millennium immediately after the Younger Dryas. Yet the situation indicates that cereal domestication was perhaps imminent in many terminal Pleistocene contexts in Southwestern Asia.

Full and continuing domestication as a basis of village life was not to occur at Abu Hureyra for another two thousand years or so, when the site was reoccupied at about 8500 BC, after an apparent abandonment. The arrival of domesticated cereals can clearly be seen in the paleobotanical record from the site, as well as from the population estimates offered by the excavators. In the Epipaleolithic Phase (Abu Hureyra 1) the population was perhaps 100 to 200 people, living in an apparently sedentary small village mainly by hunting and gathering, plus a minor amount of rye cultivation. In the Neolithic phase (Abu Hureyra 2) at about 8000 BC, by which time domesticated crops were absolutely dominant in the economy, the population had risen dramatically to between 4,000 and 6,000 people (see Figure 3.4).

The Natufian also reveals some intriguing cultural developments in the direction of increasing "social complexity." Some sites have large cemeteries – about 60 burials, for instance, in the cave of Mugharet-el-Wad and 50 in Nahal Oren, both in Israel. Some settlements were quite large; the early Natufian site of Ain Mallaha, on the ancient shoreline of Lake Huleh in northern Israel, covered about 2000 square meters and is estimated to have contained up to 12 circular huts with sunken stone-lined floors at any one time. Ain Mallaha and Abu Hureyra both produced small amounts of imported Anatolian obsidian. All such indications, not to mention the bone-carving art, the edge-ground axes, and the sickle blades, make the Natufian and its Middle Euphrates cousins look something akin to an "affluent forager" expression, complete with a significant degree of settlement sedentism, some degree of social differentiation, and a high population density. What better background for a trajectory toward planting and cultivation, given the instability of such a forager adaptation in the risky and changeable environment imposed on the Levant by the Younger Dryas? The choice for village-dwelling plant collectors, faced by shrinking supplies in circumstances of increasing cold and dryness, would have been either to fall back on increasing nomadism and population shrinkage, or to move toward deliberate planting and cultivation of food supplies and further population growth. The post-Natufian archaeological record leaves no doubt as to which option was the more successful.

There is a strong attraction in this viewpoint of cultural change driven by a Younger Dryas engine of stress, a viewpoint favored by many current authorities,[8] albeit

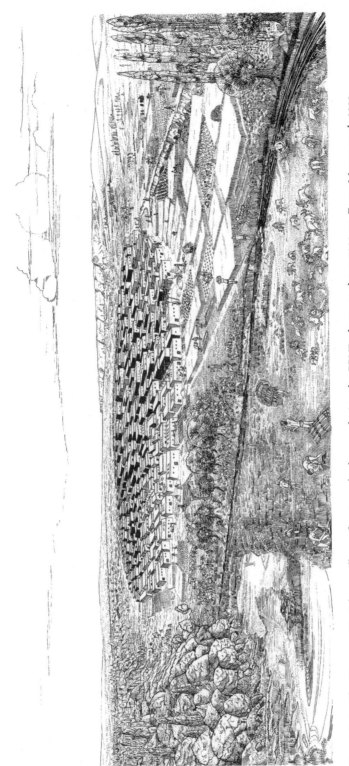

Figure 3.4   Abu Hureyra 2B: A large village of rectangular houses during the PPNB phase, at about 7200 BC. From Moore et al. 2000.

recently challenged by Tchernov (1997) and Cauvin (2000). However, it should be pointed out that the *actual* archaeological evidence for Natufian sedentism (based on settlement complexity, presence of commensal animals, etc.) is by no means perfect, and neither is that for social differentiation.[9] Neither, as we will see later, is there any precise correlation, outside the single example of the few grains of morphologically domesticated rye at Abu Hureyra, between the Younger Dryas and the widespread appearance of domesticated plants in the archaeological record. The latter, on present indications, only appeared in quantity perhaps 500–1,000 years after the Younger Dryas and the Natufian had both ended. So if the Younger Dryas was a trigger, the gun took quite a while to go off.

The Pre-Pottery Neolithic and the Increasing Dominance of Domesticated Crops

The initial millennium after the Natufian in the Levant was termed by Kathleen Kenyon the Pre-Pottery Neolithic A (PPNA, ca. 9500 to 8500 BC), in her reports on the 1950s excavations in Jericho. Not surprisingly, the PPNA was followed in Kenyon's terminology by the PPNB (ca. 8500–7000 BC) (Figure 3.3). Then followed a period of agricultural and environmental decline in the central Levant, currently termed the PPNC, although Kenyon herself did not use this term since it reflects the results of more recent research. Apart from the rather ephemeral rye at Abu Hureyra, domesticated cereals and legumes first appeared in the later part of the PPNA or early PPNB, after 9000 BC (Garrard 1999; Colledge 2001).

There are a number of cultural aspects which either first appeared or became more emphasized in the Pre-Pottery Neolithic as a whole, emphasizing that society was changing from a hunter-gatherer to an agriculturalist mode. Such aspects include:

1. Very major increases in maximum settlement sizes, with some PPNA settlements reaching 3 hectares and some late PPNB ones reaching an almost-urban 16 hectares (Figure 3.4), sizes which leave no doubt that the settlements were permanently occupied by essentially food-producing populations by the end of the PPNA (Bar-Yosef and Belfer-Cohen 1991; Kuijt 1994, 2000a).
2. Architectural innovations, expressed in the common use of sun-dried mud bricks, use of lime plaster on walls and floors, and a gradual shift from the prevailing Natufian and PPNA circular house forms into the PPNB subdivided rectilinear forms which have dominated Old World domestic architecture ever since (Flannery 1972).
3. The appearance of "monuments" and communal structures in many of the larger sites, for instance the PPNA round tower and walls at Jericho, and many other examples of shrine-like buildings excavated recently in sites from southern Jordan to southeastern Anatolia. Associated with some of these are monumental stone carvings, the most celebrated being the T-shaped pillars carved with relief animals and humans from the sites of Göbekli Tepe and Nevali Çori in southeastern Anatolia.

4. Widespread modeled clay figurines of human females (the famed and much-discussed "Mother Goddesses"), often emphasizing aspects of sexuality and fertility, together with the architectural display of cattle skulls, as in Jerf el Ahmar and Mureybet in Syria, ca. 9000–8500 BC, and later in the shrines of Çatalhöyük in Anatolia. Jacques Cauvin has recently identified this "revolution of symbols" as one of the major underlying driving forces behind the evolution of the Southwest Asian Neolithic.
5. The removal of the skulls from human burials and apparent veneration of them as ancestors by placing them inside houses, even in the PPNB modeling their faces in clay with painted features and shell eyes (Kuijt 1996; Garfinkel 1994). Associated with this interesting phenomenon there appear, in the PPNB especially, large communal burial facilities, with bones placed either in pits or in constructed charnel houses. Flexed headless burials were commonly placed under house floors.
6. An early decline in the frequency of microliths, and their replacement by fully polished axes and some widespread and very uniform categories of sickles and "projectile points" or awls made on large blades (Figure 3.5).
7. A trend, according to examination of use-wear and gloss on sickle-blade edges, toward increased harvesting of *ripe* grain during the course of the Pre-Pottery Neolithic (Unger-Hamilton 1989, 1991; Quintero et al. 1997). Successful harvesting of large quantities of ripe grain, using flint sickles, could only occur if the grain had already developed a non-shattering habit through domestication.

Most importantly, the economic record of the Pre-Pottery Neolithic period as a whole indicates increasing reliance on domesticated crops, matched by an appearance of the first domesticated animals, especially sheep and goats. By soon after 7000 BC we witness a common and widespread use of pottery, an item of great significance in allowing the preparation of soft cereal-based foods such as gruels and porridges – foods which seem rather minor to us today but which, for a population consuming mainly gritty bread beforehand, could have opened a door toward early weaning, more rapid population growth, and much less toothache (Molleson 1994; de Moulins 1997).[10] Pottery-making also required an appreciation of pyrotechnics, and this undoubtedly led eventually to the discovery of metallurgy. PPN sites do not have smelted metal, but they often contain small items of hammered copper such as beads and awls, a sure sign that technological innovation was well on its way.

Of course, not all these changes appeared *de novo* in the Pre-Pottery Neolithic. Female figurines played a profound role in Upper Paleolithic art in Eurasia, and skull removal is also known from the Natufian. But head- (or skull-) veneration certainly indicates an increasing interest in "ancestors," as does communal burial. The ethnographic record leaves no doubt that ancestors often correlate with the existence of lineages. In turn, lineages often correlate with concepts of ownership of defined pieces of food-producing land – the "corporate land-holding descent group" has long been a major attraction for anthropological research. Many hunters and gatherers, and cultivators who live at low population densities where land is a free good, have

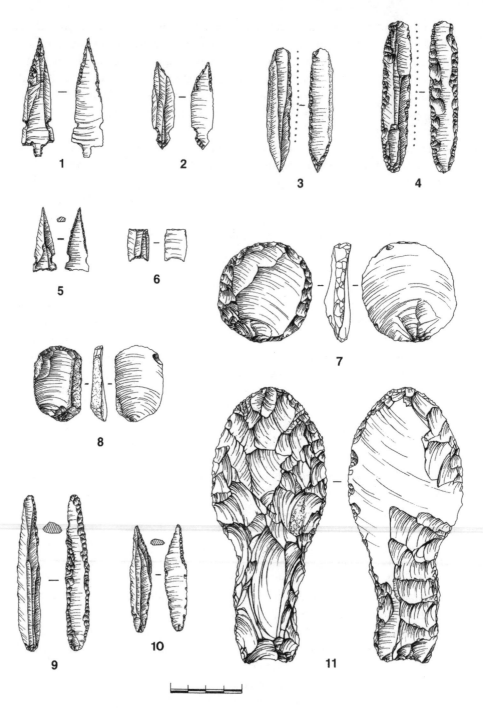

Figure 3.5 Stone tools of the PPNA and PPNB phases from Jerf el Ahmar and Tell Halula, Middle Euphrates. 1) Helwan point; 2) Jerf el-Ahmar point; 3 and 4) lustred sickle blades; 5) El-Khiam point; 6) Hagdud truncation; 7) semi-circular scraper; 8) endscraper; 9) awl; 10) piercer; 11) flaked adze of Euphrates Valley type (*Erminette de Mureybet*). Drawn by Mandy Mottram.

bilateral social structures without clearly defined lineages. But when populations become more packed, when access to land becomes worthy of some formal recognition, when "ownership" has to be demonstrated by something tangible, then we see the existence of rights of access to land expressed through genealogy or descent. And a genealogy requires an ancestor, from whom descent needs to be traceable to the satisfaction of one's peers (perhaps by having the skull of such a person on display!).

Indeed, the archaeological record reveals that early agriculture in Southwest Asia first appeared in areas where small parcels of fertile and doubtless valuable (and inherited?) land were located close to good water resources. This was the main attraction of those late PPNA sites in the Levant which have the oldest potentially domesticated cereal remains; all were located near springs, lakes, or riverine water sources. Such sites include Jericho, Netiv Hagdud, Gilgal, Tell Aswad, Abu Hureyra, and Mureybet. Early agricultural sites elsewhere, such as Ali Kosh in Khusistan, had similar advantages. Some of these sites were also located outside the regions where wild cereals would have grown naturally, thus requiring purposeful importation and planting by the human populations resident there.

It may be little more than common sense to observe that early cultivation required water, and given rainfall unreliability in the Fertile Crescent the obvious place to grow plants would be close to a reliable water source from which simple "irrigation" techniques (filling an animal skin with water, for instance) could be applied when necessary. For instance, carbon isotope discrimination research suggests that some form of irrigation was practiced at PPNB Tell Halula in Syria (Araus et al. 1999). But the main point, of course, is that such land was relatively scarce and valuable. This in itself could have stimulated a growth in the size of individual settlements such as Jericho with its remarkable perennial spring, for reasons of its access to well-watered farmland. Such growth doubtless stimulated in time a parallel growth in the ranking of the population into those with more and those with less – the roots of institutionalized inequality. But that is another story.

How Did Cereal Domestication Begin in Southwest Asia?

Experiments by Gordon Hillman and Stuart Davies have revealed that non-shattering genomes in wheat and barley could be selected for very quickly if people consistently sickle-harvested their grain fairly ripe, and replanted it. They suggest (1990:189) that "domestication could be achieved within 20–30 years if the crop is harvested near-ripe by sickle-reaping or uprooting, and if it is sown on virgin land every year [with seed] taken from last year's new plots." George Willcox (1999), however, notes that wild and domesticated cereals occurred together for over a millennium before the latter became fully dominant, so it is likely that the domestication process in reality was not quite so single-minded, despite its ultimate ascent to glory.

One key to domestication seems to have been presented to those ancient harvesters who used stone sickles to cut non-domesticated and ripe cereal ears (ripeness is an important feature here). They would have shaken each plant during the cutting process, with the result that grain from those ripe ears with a genetic predisposition to non-shattering would have been collected more successfully than normal free-shattering grain. The latter would have been lost into the ground in fairly large quantities. Uprooting of the plant would have had a similar effect, but beating or shaking of grain into a basket or bag would have been selective in the opposite direction. If the non-shattering grains selected by sickle harvesting or uprooting were later planted, especially in a new plot away from existing wild stands, it is easy to understand how an extremely powerful selective process toward non-shattering forms could have commenced, leading rapidly to the appearance of visibly domesticated plants (Wilke et al. 1972; Heiser 1988).

Yet, the first *widespread* occurrence of morphologically domesticated cereal remains, as determined from rachis segments and glume structures, only appears in the archaeological record at the end of the PPNA or in the Early PPNB, at about 8500 BC, and several centuries after the end of both the Younger Dryas and the Natufian.[11] The Natufians, it seems, did not domesticate their cereals on a permanent basis. It is of great interest in this regard that studies of the glossed edges of Natufian sickle blades suggest that people were frequently harvesting moist *unripe* grain, a practice that would have avoided the shattering problem in order to maximize yields from wild cereals (Unger-Hamilton 1989, 1991; Anderson 1994). Unripe stalks are also easier to cut than fully ripe ones, although unripe wild grain can be more time-consuming than ripe grain to dehusk if it needs to be dried or roasted beforehand (Wright 1994). However, any Natufian combination of an unripe harvest plus consumption of all the grains harvested, rather than storing some for replanting next season, could never have led to domestication. Something else had to occur to encourage the process.

We may never know exactly how the process finally occurred in such an irreversible way, but three activities would certainly have helped it along. One was surely the adoption of sickle harvesting and thus selection for non-shattering, as noted above. Another would have been the planting of sickle-harvested grain in new areas away from wild stands. A third would have been delaying the harvest until the plants were partly or fully ripe, increasing the representation of grains from non-shattering ears.

Thus, Gordon Hillman (2000) has recently suggested that the Epipaleolithic inhabitants of Abu Hureyra at about 11,500 BC, prior to the Younger Dryas and in conditions of relatively high warmth and humidity, chose to harvest by beating wild cereals into baskets. Such would have led to no selection toward domestication. Then, during the Younger Dryas, the shrinkage of wild stands of cereals prompted the inhabitants to plant their wild rye. At the same time, some form of sickling or uprooting method of harvesting must have been adopted, at least by some families. Did they also at some point, perhaps deliberately, begin to cut off ripe ears for storage and replanting and leave any remaining unripe ears for later processing as food? We do not know. But somehow, the result at Abu Hureyra was a development of plump-grained domesticated rye by soon after 11,000 BC, strangely ephemeral at this time and seemingly unconnected directly with the much more massive appearance of domesticated cereals after 8500 BC. Many mysteries remain.

The Archaeological Record in Southwest Asia in Broader Perspective

Where did systematic agriculture and associated villages originate? From a small area such as the central or northern Levant followed by expansion, or in several different early-cultivator environments linked by cultural contacts right through the Fertile Crescent, all at much the same time? What were the ultimate consequences of "full-on" Neolithic agriculture, particularly when linked to animal domestication, with truly massive settlement agglomerations eventually attaining up to 16 hectares in extent? We have, in the PPNB in particular, a manifestly unstable combination of powerfully developing human economies in fragile environments. There were consequences at that remote time, just as there are consequences (unpleasant ones) for the similar situation humanity finds itself in today.

To approach the questions asked above we need to examine the distributions of contemporary cultural variation within the Natufian and Pre-Pottery Neolithic cultural complexes in the Levant. We need also to expand the debate into nearby areas, such as Anatolia and western Iran, where related developments occurred.

Firstly, for the Natufian and its contemporaries, the archaeological record reveals a dense cluster of "Classic" Natufian sites in the southern and central Levant, concentrated in the Jordan Valley and the Mediterranean coastal hinterland (Figure 3.1). Related sites such as Mureybit and Abu Hureyra were located on the Middle Euphrates. These sites share sufficient material culture for us to suggest that their inhabitants shared a similar lifestyle, and similar stylistic traditions in their art, burial methods, architecture, and so forth. There are regional differences in the proportions of different classes of stone tools, but these are no more than one would expect given that the Natufian was spread over a range of both wooded and open environments, even into the desert fringes in the south and east. In archaeological terms, the Classic Natufian in Israel and Jordan rates as a fairly genuine "culture" (Bar-Yosef 1998b). Ofer Bar-Yosef and Anna Belfer-Cohen (1992:39) regard "the emergence of the Natufian from a background of Epi-Paleolithic hunter-gatherers as a revolutionary event which took place in a geographical, well-delineated Levantine 'homeland'."

Contemporary sites of this period in Anatolia and Iran are not classifiable as Natufian in terms of microlithic technology, indeed those in Iran are separately classified as Zarzian in lithic terms. Few of these Anatolian or Iranian sites have yielded evidence for cereal or legume exploitation, and at present there is little evidence that their inhabitants were involved directly in the origins of agriculture.

The Pre-Pottery Neolithic A (ca. 9500 to 8500 BC)

In the PPNA we find a wider spread of cultural relationships than occurred in the Natufian. Expansion occurred into northern Iraq and Anatolia, but it is very difficult to determine if this expansion originated in one region or if it developed contemporaneously over a much larger area.[12] The available C14 dates, with their inherent error ranges, overlap greatly in the 10,000 to 9000 BC time period, and there is also a radiocarbon calibration "plateau" in this time span which makes chronological precision currently impossible. But, however the PPNA evolved, it did so quickly.

The extent of the PPNA, as defined by the varying presences of certain marker stone tools (Figure 3.5) such as "projectile points" (El Khiam, Salibiya, Helwan, and Jordan valley variants), the small "Hagdud truncations," ground stone axes, and unretouched sickle blades, is considerably greater than that of the Natufian. It incorporates sites such as Mureybet, Abu Hureyra, and Jerf el Ahmar in northern Syria, and, with less certainty, Qermez Dere in northern Iraq.[13] Jerf el Ahmar (9600 to 8500 BC) has yielded some of the most interesting architecture recovered from the PPNA, comprising a sunken-floored circular community house surrounded by both circular and rectangular buildings. Circular houses, lime plastered floors, headless burials, female figurines, flint sickles, querns and hand stones, central Turkish obsidian, ground stone axes, notched projectile points, and a Natufian-derived flint industry all combine within the PPNA to produce a fairly tight unity, albeit with minor differences in expression if one compares sites as far apart as Jericho and Mureybet.

But where do the sites and complexes of Anatolia and the Zagros fit when compared to the PPNA pattern? The northern Iraqi site of Nemrik 9 (Kozlowski 1992, 1994) has many Levantine PPNA features (circular houses of cigar-shaped bricks, El Khiam points, for instance), but on the other hand it has aspects of lithic and ground stone technology claimed to relate to the Zarzian of the Zagros and to Hallan Çemi in eastern Anatolia. Interestingly, the presence of embedded projectile points in some Nemrik 9 burials suggests that ethnic coexistence in this region left something to be desired – perhaps this site lay in or close to a border zone between Levantine and Zagros spheres of influence. Sites located in the Zagros foothills in northeastern Iraq and western Iran at this time, such as M'lefaat, Karim Shahir, Zawi Chemi, Asiab, and Ganj Dareh level E, still remain poorly understood, but there seems to be unanimous agreement that they cannot be incorporated within the Levantine PPNA. Neither do any of these sites have unequivocal evidence for domesticated plants or animals during the PPNA or early PPNB time span. Current indications are that agriculture was introduced into these Zagros regions from the Levant (Hole 1998; Dollfus 1989; Kozlowski 1999).

It is uncertain if the same conclusion applies to southeastern Anatolia since einkorn might have been domesticated in this region, as discussed above. But during PPNA times, positive Levantine cultural links are few. Presumed-sedentary circular house settlements are reported from Hallan Çemi (ca. 10,000 BC) and the basal level of Çayönü (both in the Upper Tigris basin), in neither instance with positive evidence for agriculture (the former site has no cereal remains at all). Recent reports suggest that Hallan Çemi might have witnessed management of pigs during the Younger Dryas, contemporary with the later Natufian and the experiments in rye domestication at Abu Hureyra. If this conclusion is substantiated it could alter our perspectives on the course of animal domestication, at least in regions around the peripheries of the Levant.[14]

My inclination from present evidence is to regard the PPNA, with Susan Colledge et al. (2004), as a marker of the origins of agricultural communities within the Levant. There is no strong evidence to extend it beyond the boundaries shown in Figure 3.1.

This implies that the contemporary sites in Iran and Anatolia were mainly "complex forager" settlements, possibly with some animal management,[15] continuing alongside the PPNA with a lifestyle similar to that of the Natufian. The inhabitants of some of these sites might well have been harvesting wild cereals, but with the possible exception of einkorn there is no good evidence that they domesticated these cereals independently. As suggested by Jacques Cauvin, the full incorporation of the Turkish and Iranian wild cereal regions into the agricultural lifestyle seems to have occurred as a result of later PPNB expansion, again from a heartland located somewhere in the Levant.

The Pre-Pottery Neolithic B (ca. 8500 to 7000 BC)

We need first to bear in mind an important observation. The Southwest Asian environment is a fragile one, particularly when assaulted by human populations intent on population growth, woodland clearance, soil tillage, animal pasturing, and many other activities which can, in combination, lead toward land degradation, veg-etation loss, salinization, soil erosion, and general resource decline.[16] Southwest Asian PPN sites were rarely occupied continuously into historical times; even the largest such as Jericho and Abu Hureyra were abandoned. A major phase of environmental decline is attested for the later phases of the PPN in the Levant, fueled by both human activity and by a climatic trend toward aridity, and to this we return in due course. Common sense and history dictate that such episodes would always have given an impetus for a human population to seek new land. The alternative is inten-sification, or "agricultural involution" in the terminology of Clifford Geertz (1963), a course of action obviously taken many times in world history by civilizations and small-scale cultivators alike. But not all societies will automatically seek to intensify production locally to feed a growing population or avoid a resources shortfall, par-ticularly if new land, previously undamaged by heavy-handed cultivators, is available within reach. This observation brings us to the PPNB and its expansive history.

Brian Hayden (1995) estimates that the PPNB population in the Levant was 16 times that of the Natufian, yet the actual number of reported sites is much fewer than during the Natufian. This is because many PPNB sites are now virtually towns – some site areas cover up to 16 hectares (Figure 3.4), or about four times the size of the largest PPNA sites. Ian Kuijt (2000a) notes a 50-times increase in the sizes of the largest sites from late Natufian to late PPNB, over a period of about 2,500 years. Two-storey houses are attested from a number of PPNB sites in Jordan (Ain Ghazal, Basta, Ba'ja), with stone walls in Ba'ja surviving to a remarkable height of over 4 meters (Gebel and Hermanson 1999). Some of the smaller sites were also fortified, at least in part, like late PPNB Tell Magzaliyah in northern Iraq (Bader 1993). Large town-like settlements, of course, mean that the inhabitants can afford to be settlement-endogamous if they wish – mates are not hard to find when a population of several thousand people live cheek by jowl. People can also be forced into defensive postures by high population densities and environmental instability, and this can lead to an efflorescence of tribalism and ethnicity. Thus we have two opposing trends in the PPNB, as in all successful Neolithic cultures – one toward expansion, the other toward regional differentiation. It is essential to remember this, otherwise we are forced toward choosing between two ridiculous polar hypotheses, one seeing the PPNB as totally monolithic, the other seeing it as a coincidental appearance of independently generated traits in many different areas. It was neither.

Like the PPNA, the PPNB of "classical" form existed only in the Levant. But the signs of an extension of some of its basic elements across larger parts of Southwest Asia are very compelling, especially in the typical late PPNB agglutinative rectangular house architecture and the powerful mixed farming economy, improved by the addition of hexaploid bread wheat. Certainly by the end of the PPNB, and probably well before, the full complement of major domestic animals – goat, sheep, cattle, and pig – had been added to the domesticated repertoire as wild species declined in numbers owing to intensive hunting (Legge and Rowley-Conwy 1987, 2000).

In terms of extent, the classic PPNB of the middle and late phases covers a larger area than the PPNA, probably much larger if one allows for future discoveries in the unsurveyed regions in Syria and Anatolia between the main distributions shown in Figure 3.1. It spread throughout the Levant, described as "one cultural sphere" for the PPNB by Bar-Yosef and Belfer-Cohen (1989b, 1991:192), onward into northern Iraq, and with more local cultural input into southeastern and central Anatolia. The core origin region of the PPNB, if indeed there was a circumscribed origin, remains uncertain, although some scholars favor the northern Levant.[17] Bar-Yosef and Belfer-Cohen point out that many cultural traits typical of the PPNB seem to have a north-to-south momentum in their chronological and geographical distributions. These include obsidian (all from Turkish sources), einkorn wheat and chickpeas (both of northern Levant/Anatolian origin), domestic animals (especially sheep and goat, perhaps of northern Levant or Zagros origin), rectilinear architecture (marginally dated oldest by C14 in the northern Levant, in sites such as Mureybet and Jerf el Ahmar), and the gypsum-plaster antecedents of pottery termed "white wares." On the other hand, many outstanding aspects of PPNB culture are best known from the southern Levant, including the remarkable plastered and painted portrait skulls from Jericho and the slaked lime plaster "ancestor" figures built around frames of reeds and sticks found at Ain Ghazal in Jordan.

In terms of PPNB regionality, the picture differs slightly in terms of the artifact class being considered. For instance, PPNB sites in the Levant and southeastern Anatolia have fairly homogenous lithic technologies, focused on the production of large percussion blades from naviform cores to serve as blanks for tanged projectile points. Of these, the basally tanged "Byblos Point" seems to have been the most widespread and typical. Beyond the Levant, pressure-flaked blade cores are dominant, particularly in the Zagros and across northern Iran into Pakistan (Inizan and Lechevallier 1994; Quintero and Wilke 1995). The distributional boundary between the naviform and pressure-flaked cores seems to correlate with the division between the earlier Levantine PPNA cultures and those of the Zagros region, suggesting that the regionality observed for the PPNA time span was still continuing into the PPNB. Apart from the naviform cores and Byblos Points, the Turkish and middle

Euphrates sites (Çaferhöyük, Çayönü, Aşiklihöyük, Mureybit, and Jerf el Ahmar) also have similar types of incised stone pebbles or "plaques," suggesting an overall pattern of close cultural relationship. Plastered skulls and skull veneration derived from the PPNA tradition also occur from the southern Levant to as far away as Hacilar in central Anatolia, and various kinds of artificial cranial deformation seem to be present all over Southwest Asia (including Cyprus and the Zagros) in the PPN and Early Ceramic periods (Meiklejohn et al. 1992).

In terms of house plans there is much regional variation, with single-roomed houses at Ramad and Byblos, porched "megaron"-style houses in Jericho and Ain Ghazal, and, during the later PPNB, complex structures of small seemingly doorless cubicles in many sites around the edges of the distribution (e.g., Beidha and Basta in Jordan, Bouqras in Syria, at Çayönü and Nevali Çori in Anatolia, and in early ceramic sites such as Umm Dabaghiyah and Yarim Tepe I in northern Iraq). It is this "doorless cubicle" architectural style that characterizes some of the earliest agricultural communities in regions far beyond the Levant, for instance in Ganj Dareh level D in Iran, Mehrgarh in Pakistan, and Çatalhöyük in central Anatolia.[18] Related "grill-plan" layouts of close-set parallel foundation walls, possibly to support floors within reed and post houses, are also reported from Çayönü, Nevali Çori, and Basta, at opposite ends of the PPNB distribution (Özdoğan 1999). I believe these later PPNB architectural similarities to be important in indicating widespread cultural linkages. It is interesting also that Nissen et al. (1987) note that the gracile skulls of flexed burials excavated from Basta resemble skulls from Çayönü. These two sites are close to the furthest north–south extremities of the PPNB distribution, 1,000 kilometers apart.

Potential community structures seem to illustrate aspects of local identity and style even more than ordinary houses since they would, of course, have been more popular vehicles for "heraldic" statements about group identity, affiliation, and ritual (Verhoeven 2002). Large numbers of such structures have been excavated in recent years, and all have their idiosyncrasies. As examples we have the large circular sunken "community houses" at Jerf el Ahmar and Mureybit (some of PPNA date); the mud brick rectangular "shrine" with an end niche at Jericho; circular and apsidal "shrines" at Ain Ghazal; the stone-walled rectangular "cult building" at Nevali Çori in Anatolia; and the large mud brick platform 10 by 7 meters in size and 60 centimeters high at PPNB Sabi Abyad II in northern Syria.

Most remarkably, a 9-hectare mountain sanctuary at Göbekli Tepe in eastern Anatolia (ca. 8300–7200 BC) has a possible total of 20 (4 have been excavated) stone-walled circular enclosures 10 to 30 meters in diameter, with sunken floors, and inner wall surfaces set with radial arrangements of 10 massive T-shaped pillars up to 3 meters high. Some of these pillars are decorated with relief carvings of animals. Each enclosure also had two high central T-shaped pillars, and one unfinished pillar found on the site would have stood over 6 meters high. These enclosures contain no primary habitation debris and were presumably used for community ceremonial activities of some kind – the whole complex was eventually deliberately buried under a transported layer of occupation soil 3 to 5 meters thick. Similar T-shaped pillars, in this case with carvings of humans, occur at Nevali Çori.

Communal burial in charnel houses was also a marked feature of the PPNB: we have the remarkable "skull building" or charnel house at Çayönü, containing the jumbled remains of about 400 deceased members of the community placed in slab-covered stone cists across one end of the building; also a painted and plastered chamber with secondary burials at Ba'ja in Jordan; a charnel room and other examples of collective burial at Abu Hureyra; and a remarkable series of human and wild cattle burials in pits sealed with lime plaster layers up to 3 tonnes in weight at Kfar HaHoresh near the Sea of Galilee. In the case of one pit at this last site, 50 human long bones appear to have been arranged in the shape of an aurochs or wild boar.[19]

Intercommunity contact within the PPNB is highlighted by the developing obsidian trade, with obsidian from sources in both central and eastern Anatolia now very widespread. During the PPNA, only central Turkish obsidian appears to have reached the central and southern Levant, but eastern Turkish sources were added in the PPNB. Obsidian appears to have been generally absent in the Levant during the Natufian, or at least extremely rare.

As noted already for the PPNA, if we take present evidence at face value there is really no good evidence to suggest a spread of agricultural communities into the Zagros region of Iran much before 8000 BC, during the period of the PPNB in the Levant (Kozlowski 1999; Hole 2000; Dollfus 1989). By this time, sites such as Ganj Dareh, Tepe Guran, and Ali Kosh all have PPNB-like architecture and economies, although Ganj Dareh apparently lacked emmer wheat. All three sites have evidence for goat herding, and Ali Kosh has claimed evidence for sheep domestication. Ali Kosh is also located in the dry Deh Luran Plain of Khusistan where none of the major wild cereals would originally have grown. Agriculture clearly had to be introduced to this region, just as it had to be introduced to other regions beyond the agricultural homeland, such as Europe and Egypt.

Without going into more detail, we can see from the above that the PPNB has a general appearance of overall homogeneity in the Levant and adjacent regions of Anatolia and northern Iraq, but it also has many clear expressions of regionalism in style, especially in its later phases (the period, after all, lasted for over 1,500 years). The Zagros sites presumably belonged to other cultural configurations, despite the obvious existence of contact. Many authorities regard the PPNB as an "interaction sphere," without committing themselves too strongly on whether the interaction did or did not involve spreading populations.[20] Mehmet Özdoğan (1998:35), for instance, suggests: "What is most striking in the Near Eastern Neolithic is that it is a period of experimentation, carried out in the most orderly and organized way, as if experimenting in a lab; any change or innovation was, almost instantly, shared through all of the Near Eastern Neolithic region." We might argue for ever about how many ethnic groups constituted the PPNB, but one thing is clear – they communicated efficiently. Likewise, Jacques Cauvin regarded the PPNB as a unified spreading phenomenon with a northern Levant origin and a powerful religion based on the veneration of human and animal fertility. As it spread, so it replaced or incorporated the regional late hunter-gatherer and PPNA cultures into a relatively homogeneous whole, albeit with continuing foci of regional diversity.

We move now to some of the consequences of PPNB population growth, consequences that might give some insight into how the processes of farming spread beyond the Levant might have occurred.

The Real Turning Point in the Neolithic Revolution

For most people, the concept of the Neolithic Revolution refers to the actual origin of agriculture with domesticated plants, this occurring in Southwest Asia in the late PPNA or early PPNB at around 9000–8500 BC. True, there was an economic revolution here, without which later civilizations could never have existed. But there is also another aspect to this revolution, and that concerns the spread of the agricultural lifestyle far beyond its homeland. After 8000 BC, a concatenation of events came together, literally to "lift the lid" off the PPN pressure cooker. Two of these event categories are of absolutely fundamental importance, these being regional episodes of resource shortfall caused by land degradation, and the increasing importance of animal domestication combined with an increasing dependence on legumes to serve as fodder (Miller 1992:51). Both trends reflected the results of inexorable human and animal population growth. This period witnessed the origins of specialized sheep and goat pastoralism, and it witnessed the laying down of the immediate proto-urban groundwork for the impressive Mesopotamian cultural sequence still to come; successive cultures such as Ubaid, Uruk, Susa, and the ultimate magnificence of third millennium BC Sumerian, Akkadian, and Elamite civilization. The Mesopotamian lowlands where these later civilizations developed were colonized by Early Ubaid irrigation farmers at about 6000 BC, with an economic and cultural tradition that owed a great deal to the PPNB.

All this growth in the size of the PPNB human population and in the complexity of the economy required to support such growth had, of course, a downside. This becomes apparent in considering developments between about 7000 and 6500 BC in the Levant. It is worth noting here that very few large PPNB sites in the Levant show continuous long-term occupation into the succeeding pottery-using Neolithic phase. Many were abandoned or shrank (sometimes only temporarily) at about the time that pottery was putting in a widespread appearance, during the seventh millennium BC. We see this clearly in the cases of Bouqras, Jericho, Beidha, and Abu Hureyra. The circumstances behind this seeming downturn of fortune have been researched in detail at the site of Ain Ghazal in the Jordan Valley (Kohler-Rollefson 1988; Rollefson and Kohler-Rollefson 1993). Here, there is evidence at about 6500 BC of cultural degradation of a fragile ecosystem, a trend perhaps exacerbated by a drying climate (Bar-Yosef 1996; Hassan 2000).[21] Ain Ghazal grew from 5 to 10 hectares during the PPNB to reach a massive 13 hectares during the "PPNC" at around 6750 BC. This development of peak size occurred as other sites in the region were also being abandoned (Ain Ghazal itself continued to be occupied into the Yarmukian Pottery Neolithic phase), suggesting that the site was briefly "booming," as many cities do today when the surrounding countryside loses some of its ability to support a large population. Large numbers of shaped clay tokens were in use in Ain Ghazal at this time – these are believed to be early precursors of accounting systems and even writing, so the complexities of managing the affairs of a large population may be evident, more than 3,000 years before writing was actually invented in Sumer.

However, during this phase of phenomenal growth at Ain Ghazal, the houses became further apart, room sizes became smaller, post-hole diameters decreased, and sickle blades and mortars decreased in numbers. Trees were cut for housing, cooking, and the firing of limestone to make plaster for covering floors and walls – the PPNB site of Yiftahel has a house measuring 7.5 by 4 meters, with a lime plastered floor estimated to weigh 7 tonnes (Garfinkel 1987). At Ain Ghazal, increases occurred in infant mortality, and in the importance of domesticated goats and the legume species which they probably liked as fodder. Many authorities see this trajectory as recording the local collapse of a cereal-based agricultural economy due to environmental degradation and extensive deforestation, with a consequent shift toward an increasingly pastoral economy and consequent human population decline or dispersal. Zarins (1990) has suggested that a major phase of dispersal by pastoralists occurred from the PPN Levant in the seventh millennium bc, extending into desert/oasis regions such as the Palmyra Basin and northern Arabia.

Similar hints of stress are reported from other sites. Beidha in southern Jordan was occupied into the PPNC and then abandoned, possibly to be replaced by the one-hectare and very densely inhabited terraced pueblo-like settlement of Ba'ja, a site which gives the impression of being a short-lived last-ditch attempt to keep settled life going in a region where its future was limited (Gebel and Bienert 1997; Gebel and Hermansen 1999). Abu Hureyra rose to an impressive 16 hectares in the Middle PPNB, then shrank back again to about half this size, with much less dense housing, by 7300 bc. Peter Akkermans records widespread site abandonment in the Balikh Valley in northern Syria during the seventh millennium bc, in the early pottery Neolithic, especially in drier regions. Even though Akkermans, like Ofer Bar-Yosef and Alan Simmons, favors a climate-change rather than a human-impact explanation in this regard, the results for human societies in general would have been similar (Akkermans 1993; Bar-Yosef 1996; Simmons 1997). On the other hand, abandonment was never universal and seems at present to be less marked in the northern Levant than elsewhere. The site of Tell Halula, for instance, seems not to have been abandoned at all between the PPNB and the subsequent Pottery Neolithic, despite some temporary shrinkage (Mandy Mottram, pers. comm.).

A combination of site abandonment in some regions, and a development of pastoral mobility around the edges of the continuing settled areas, would probably have encouraged two developments. These can be succinctly described as regional interaction and population dispersal, the two seemingly opposed factors which together led to the second, and major, stage of the Agricultural Revolution. After about 2,000 years of gestation amongst the early farming communities of south-western Asia, the process of agricultural dispersal into northeastern Africa, Europe, central Asia, and the Indus region was about to take off, in earnest.

Chapter 4
Tracking the Spreads of Farming beyond the Fertile Crescent: Europe and Asia

We move in this chapter to our first examination of the "full steam ahead" mode of agricultural dispersal. Focused within the two and a half millennia from 6500 to 4000 BC, the farming system that developed in Southwest Asia spread over vast areas of the Old World – to Britain and Iberia in one direction; to Turkmenistan, the Altai Mountains, and Pakistan in the other; as well as to Egypt and North Africa. At the other end of Asia, East Asian agricultural systems were also on the move by this time, reaching toward Southeast Asia and eastern India.

For most regions of farming spread in both the Old and New Worlds, there has been much contentious debate about whether or not the archaeological record reveals some kind of cultural continuity from pre-farming into farming (Mesolithic to Neolithic in the Old World, Archaic to Formative in the Americas). Europe plays a very central role in these debates. In actuality, there are very few archaeological sites anywhere in the world, including Europe, that show unarguable, on-the-spot, continuity from a hunter-gatherer subsistence into farming, with no outside influence being present in material form. The main exceptions to this generalization, as we might expect, occur in regions believed to be independent homelands of agriculture (Figure 1.3). In most other areas, agricultural systems were variously acquired or imposed, sometimes by a combination of both processes.

Nevertheless, however the people of an area came to be agriculturalists, there would always have remained hunting-gathering populations who would have continued to exist, if allowed, for centuries or perhaps even millennia after agriculture began. The histories of European colonization in the Americas and Australia make this crystal clear, even through in these cases the hunters and gatherers were decimated by lethal diseases and territorial dispossession at rates many times greater than any which could conceivably have occurred during the early Neolithic. Agriculturalist dispersal does not automatically mean instant hunter-gatherer demise, and any hints of *in situ* cultural continuity in archaeological site records during transitions to agriculture need not automatically mean that indigenous adoption was the only, or even the major, process behind the change on a regional basis. Hunting/gathering and agriculture can exist side by side very successfully for as long as stable relations exist between the foragers and the farmers, separately but in interaction.

Chapter 3 plotted the spread of early agricultural economies from the northern Levant into adjacent regions of Anatolia and Iran. It described the growth of the agricultural economy, the addition of domesticated animals, and the resulting, seemingly rather unhappy, human impact on some regions with fragile resources. It examined periods, especially the PPNB, during which archaeological cultures seem to have had a coherence beyond the merely parochial and to have been associated with high levels of geographical expansion. But the PPNB was only the beginning of a continent-wide process of farming dispersal in four major directions – to Europe, central Asia, the Indian subcontinent, and North Africa.

The Spread of the Neolithic Economy through Europe

Because of its broad latitudinal extent and because it extended well beyond the northern limits of Neolithic agriculture, Europe (Figure 4.1) has become one of the major regions of debate in world prehistory with respect to the question of how agriculture spread. Was it mainly by hunter-gatherer adoption? Or, following the terminology used by Albert Ammerman and Luca Cavalli-Sforza (1984), was it mainly by a "wave of advance" of farmers? Evidence suggests that it probably spread by a mixture of both processes, with rapid farmer dispersals in some regions such as Greece, the Mediterranean coastline, the Danube Valley, and onward into Germany and the Low Countries, but much slower spreads with substantial Mesolithic population involvement or resistance in western Europe and around the rugged and/or colder Atlantic and Baltic coastlines.

A recent analysis of European earliest Neolithic radiocarbon dates by Gkiasta et al. (2003) shows quite clearly how Mesolithic cultures existed side by side with Neolithic cultures for several centuries in some parts of western Europe, especially southern and central France, Portugal, the British Isles and Ireland (see also Zilhão 2000; Perrin 2003) (Figure 4.3). This is no more than one would expect given understanding of climatic factors and Mesolithic hunter-gatherer population densities at the time, the latter being most concentrated in maritime regions, but the details are nevertheless important to tease out since tempo of spread is an essential element in any overall and balanced interpretation of the whole situation.

Before moving into the details, six points require preliminary emphasis:

1. The Neolithic spread into Europe occurred, in the main, from western Anatolia. Connections across the Mediterranean with northwestern Africa and through the steppes north of the Black Sea were only of minor significance, the latter reflecting mainly expansion out of Europe rather than in during this time period (Telegin 1987; Yanushevich 1989).

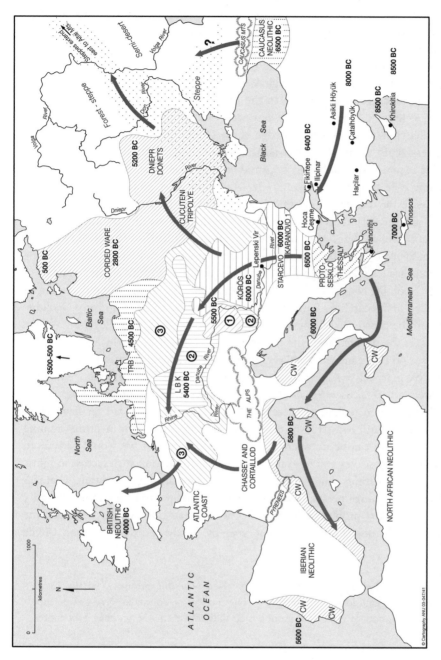

Figure 4.1 The earliest Neolithic cultures of Europe. 1) LBK origin region; 2) Early LBK expansion; 3) Later LBK expansion (after Zvelebil 2000); CW, Cardial Ware. Other shading is simply to delineate cultural regions. Dates refer to the first attested evidence for agriculture and/or Neolithic assemblages.

2. With the marked exception of the Preceramic Neolithic of Cyprus, geographically closer to Asia than to Europe, and apart from a faint aceramic echo in Crete and mainland Greece, the Neolithic period in Europe was entirely ceramic, with a full complement of Southwest Asian cereals, legumes, and domestic animals. Genetic data indicate that European cattle descend from Western Asian rather than European wild stock (Troy et al. 2001), and the wild ancestors of sheep and goats were not native to Europe.

3. The spread of agriculture through Mediterranean and temperate Europe south of the Baltic, from the Aegean to the British Isles, spanned about 2,500 years, from 6500 to 4000 BC. Along the east–west axis there was a standstill of perhaps a millennium near the western edge of the Great Hungarian Plain (Sumegi and Kertesz 2001). Along the south–north axis, initial agricultural settlements in the Baltic region and Scandinavia occurred only after 3500 BC, and in colder Boreal regions only as recently as AD 500 (Zvelebil 1996a, 1998; Taavitsainen et al. 1998).

4. Evidence for the spread of agriculture around the coastlines of the Mediterranean and the Atlantic is bedeviled by the fact that the sea surface only reached its present level at about 4000 BC, having risen from a level of minus 35 meters at about 8000 BC. Although postglacial isostatic uplift of the North Sea and Baltic regions has lessened the problem in the north, further south a large quantity of early Neolithic coastal archaeology is presumably drowned, to the detriment of detailed understanding. Barnett (1995), for instance, refers to an early Neolithic site off the coastline of Languedoc, now 5–6 meters below sea level.

5. Some of the debate about the transition from Mesolithic to Neolithic has been focused on caves and rock shelters, especially in the Mediterranean zone. A comparative perspective suggests that caves were far more likely to harbor surviving hunter-gatherers, users no doubt of gifted, borrowed, or looted farmer goods, than they were to harbor successful farmers. Many caves are far from good agricultural land by virtue of their karst geology, but often in prime hunting terrain. There can be no overall generalization here, but we would be wise to take care with caves and to examine their records bearing such factors in mind.

6. Virtually all authors who have written about the European Neolithic, whatever their interpretative persuasions, seem to agree that patterns of cultural diversity start off in low profile, in situations of widespread homogeneity, but become sharper and more localized as time goes by. In the words of Gordon Childe (1956:86):

> If one studies in detail several closely allied Neolithic groups – on the Central European löss, for example – one notices a continual divergence, the multiplication of individual groups each differing from one another ever more pronouncedly . . .

Cultural diversity across much of Europe in the Early Neolithic was considerably less than it was in either the later part of the preceding Mesolithic, or in the subsequent Late Neolithic.

Cyprus, Turkey, and Greece

Agricultural dispersal into Cyprus occurred during the PPNB, perhaps even in the late PPNA, at about 8500 BC. The settlers presumably crossed the Mediterranean from the Syrian coast, although likely source regions in the northern Levant are now beneath the sea – existing sites such as Ras Shamra and Byblos in the modern coastal region are too young to represent direct sources. As Edgar Peltenberg et al. (2001:60) comment: "The Mediterranean [i.e., Cyprus] evidence, therefore, provides firmer evidence than was previously available from the mainland alone that migration played a significant role in the earliest spread of farming" (see also Colledge et al. 2004).

One of the first tasks of the new settlers in Cyprus seems to have been the hunting to extinction of a native and doubtless naïve fauna of pygmy hippos.[1] They established several villages with a full Levantine PPNB material culture, including Byblos Points, naviform cores, glossed sickle blades, and Anatolian obsidian (Peltenberg et al. 2000, 2001; Knapp and Meskell 1997; Simmons 1998). They brought with them their crops – domesticated einkorn, emmer, and barley. Cattle, sheep, goat, pigs, and fallow deer (the latter presumably wild) also made the sea crossing, and animals were kept in a palisaded enclosure at the site of Shillourokambos. The most famous of the Neolithic villages of Cyprus is Khirokitia (Le Brun 1989) in the southern part of the island, where a village of dozens of stone-walled honeycomb-like circular houses, reminiscent of the Levantine PPNA, was founded about 7000 BC in a steep valley close to the sea. The Khirokitia houses are divided by a wall which probably reflected some kind of social/lineage division in the community.

Current opinion on the western Anatolian sequence also favors population incursion, in this case from central and southeastern Turkey, and somewhat later in time than Cyprus. Western Turkey, on current evidence, appears to have witnessed a cultural trajectory into the Neolithic during the early ceramic period. The site of Ilipinar on the Bosporus (6200–5500 BC) has an initial phase of single-roomed houses built of mud slabs, followed by a phase with mud brick multi-roomed two-storied houses of central Anatolian type. The inhabitants had a fully agropastoral economy with pigs, cattle, and caprovines (goats and sheep), and made female figurines and a variety of chaff-tempered pottery. The excavator of Ilipinar, Jacob Roodenberg, derives this population from the Hacilar region of central Turkey, and specifically notes the close relationship between Ilipinar and the early Neolithic of the Balkans (Roodenberg 1999; Özdoğan 1997a, 1997b).

Further to the west, in Thrace, an exotic ceramic Neolithic tradition appeared in the site of Hoça Cesme at about 6400 BC, in association with stone-walled circular houses, a defensive wall, painted and monochrome pottery, and a large-blade tradition which does not descend from the local Epipaleolithic. Mehmet Özdoğan also traces the Hoça Cesme tradition to central Turkey, and notes that its pottery is related to that of some early Neolithic sites in the eastern Balkans, such as Karanovo I in Bulgaria.

The perspective from Greece matches that from western Anatolia quite smoothly, with the introduction of a Neolithic cultural tradition with both Anatolian and deeper "Near Eastern" features, as postulated by Özdoğan. Aceramic Neolithic occupation is attested in Stratum X at Knossos on Crete at about 7000 BC, with a full agropastoral complement of bread wheat, cattle, pigs, sheep, and goats. According to Cyprian Broodbank, this represents a fairly large-scale episode of maritime colonization, from an uncertain origin point, of an island that, like Cyprus, apparently had no prior inhabitants (Broodbank and Strasser 1991; Broodbank 1999). Together with the evidence from Cyprus, Knossos Stratum X suggests that the oldest dispersals westward from the Levant might have been by sea, rather than by the land route through western Turkey. Likewise, the Greek mainland itself has only a shadowy and very late Preceramic Neolithic, represented at Argissa in Thessaly and a few other sites. Otherwise, most mainland Greek Neolithic sites appear to postdate 6500 BC, and contain pottery (Perlès 2001).

Greece, in environmental terms, represents a direct westward extension of the Anatolian landmass. Like much of Turkey, it has limited agricultural land and a fairly scarce record of Mesolithic occupation, circumstances which would allow any incoming Neolithic population to move freely between the best pockets of fertile alluvial soil. This is exactly what we see in the record, if we pool the observations of several authorities.[2] Tjeerd van Andel and Curtis Runnels (1995) discuss the distribution of Neolithic sites in Thessaly, mostly on terrace fans next to active flood plains and close to cultivable raised levees. Like Andrew Sherratt (1980), they favor a saltatory movement of pioneer Neolithic societies, moving rapidly from one circumscribed environment to another (Figure 4.2). Thessaly is quite rich in such alluvial environments and during the Early Neolithic supported a remarkable density of sites averaging 2.5 hectares in size, located about 2.7 kilometers apart on average and heavily dependent on agricultural production (Perlès 1999).

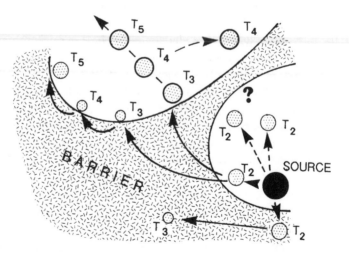

Figure 4.2 The saltatory Neolithic colonization in Greece, moving from fertile across infertile regions to new farmlands. From van Andel and Runnels 1995.

Jean-Paul Demoule (1993) and Catherine Perlès (2001) both see the Greek Neolithic economy as heavily agropastoral from the start, with very little hunting and no lithic continuity from the Mesolithic. Greek Early Neolithic painted pottery is homogeneous (Vitelli 1995), and closely paralleled in the early Hoça Cesme pottery of Thrace, as well as in the Proto-Sesklo, Starcevo, and Karanovo assemblages of the southern Balkans (ca. 6100 BC) (Figure 4.1). Over time it developed greater regional expressions, particularly after 5300 BC. As far as specific parallels with the Anatolian Neolithic are concerned, we can point to a number of items which appear in the earliest Greek Neolithic sites: female figurines, marble bracelets, painted pottery with no very clear "primitive" phase, earplugs of stone or clay, clay stamp seals, flexed burials under house floors, wattle and daub associated with mud brick and timber-framed house construction techniques, and the build-up of tells (Perlès 2001:52–56). Greek and Balkan Neolithic houses tend to be single-roomed and separate, as we see in some contemporary Neolithic sites in the northern Levant (Tell Ramad and Byblos, for instance).

An important perspective on the introduction of the agricultural economy into Greece is provided by Franchthi Cave in the Argolid. Here, Mesolithic populations utilized wild forms of oats, lentils, pistacchio, almond, and barley. Then, domesticated emmer, barley and lentils, with domesticated sheep, goats, and pigs, appeared fairly suddenly in the sequence at about 6900 BC, after a period of virtual abandonment of the site. Julie Hansen (1991, 1992) sees this appearance as a result of introduction from Anatolia. What role the local Mesolithic people played in all of this is unclear, but a cave situation such as Franchthi is one place where we might expect some degree of continuity. However, in her recent survey of the Greek early Neolithic, Catherine Perlès (2001, with Colledge et al. 2004) favors colonization by many groups crossing the Aegean from Anatolia, rather than continuity from a faint preceding Mesolithic phase. She notes (2001:44) that Greece has only 12 recorded Mesolithic sites, as opposed to between 250 and 300 Neolithic sites.

As in the Levant, so too in Greece there was perhaps an ultimate price to pay for the early Neolithic episode of colonization and population growth. Soil erosion became evident about 500–1,000 years after the beginnings of the Greek Neolithic in parts of Thessaly and the Peloponnese (van Andel et al. 1990). Neolithic agriculture impacted heavily on the slopes around the Argive Plain, site of the future Bronze Age citadel of Mycenae:

> This expansion of human activity triggered an environmental catastrophe that altered the landscape forever . . . It appears that in a very short period massive erosion stripped the soil from the hills above Berbati and Limnes, leaving behind bare rock where the Neolithic farmers [had] grazed their flocks and had their fields. The soil and debris flowed out into the Argive Plain to the south, depositing as much as 20 feet of alluvium over a large area. (Wells et al. 1993:56)

True, the later civilization of Mycenae might have waxed rich on the agricultural produce of all these anthropogenic alluvial lowlands, as did many island cultures in the Pacific whose ancestors also caused similar soil erosion (Spriggs 1997b). But the fact remains that the immediate impact might have been a little unsettling, at least for a while. According to van Andel and Runnels (1995:497), the settlement history of eastern Thessaly underwent a decline in the late Neolithic, with few new settlements founded and many abandoned. One might legitimately wonder about the consequences of such developments as a trigger for ensuing population dispersal.

The Balkans

The answer to this question was probably two-pronged. In the first direction, moving northward, early Balkan Neolithic cultures closely related to those of Anatolia and northern Greece are represented by the Proto-Sesklo culture of Macedonia, the Starcevo culture of parts of the former Yugoslavia, the Karanovo I of Bulgaria and Thrace, and the Körös of Hungary. Perlès (2001:304) believes that the earliest Balkan Neolithic populations arrived from Anatolia via Thrace, rather than from Greece itself. Whatever the exact origins, the full agropastoral economy with domesticated cattle traveled too, with the addition of broomcorn millet, a cereal not native to Southwest Asia which must, presumably, have been introduced from the steppes of the Ukraine or central Asia (Dennell 1992; Zohary and Hopf 2000). The Balkan Neolithic cultures continued the same general PPNB/Anatolian-related elements as those in Greece, including, in the southern Balkans, tell-like settlements of wattle and daub houses, a form of wall construction better suited to wetter climates than mud brick.

The local Mesolithic populations were not entirely unaffected by all of this (see the range of views in Kertesz and Makkay 2001), and chronological overlap with them appears to be documented (albeit with controversy) at the site of Lepenski Vir in the Iron Gates region of the middle Danube, where acculturated descendants of a Mesolithic population are claimed to have continued in occupation until possibly 4400 BC. A rather piecemeal impact of the Neolithic in the Balkans is suggested by palynological evidence, indicating that forest clearance only registered on a large scale at about 4000 BC (Willis and Bennett 1994).

The northwestward spread of the Balkan style of Neolithic, in form of the Körös culture of Hungary, evidently ran out of steam for about a millennium toward the western limits of the Great Hungarian Plain, owing perhaps to variations in soil conditions, climate, and topography (Sumegi and Kertesz 2001). But by about 5400 BC, after a likely episode of cultural and perhaps biological reformulation, there emerged the temperate climate phenomenon of remarkable colonizing power known to archaeologists as the Linear Pottery Culture, or Danubian, to which we return below.

The Mediterranean

In the second direction of expansion into Europe, agricultural populations had also begun to move along the northern Mediterranean coastline by at least 6000 BC; the earliest pottery in Albania and Italy is related to that of the Starcevo culture in the southern Balkans. On the Tavoliere Plain in southeastern Italy, commencing about 6200 BC, there is a remarkable concentration in an area of 70 by 50 kilometers of about 500 ditched settlement enclosures up to 30 hectares in size, some with multiple outer ditches and internal compounds (Malone 2003). Ruth Whitehouse (1987) notes that there is no evidence for Mesolithic continuity here, but neither are there obvious signs of direct origin in the tell settlements of Greece or the Levant. What we appear to have is an adaptation to continuously unfolding new landscapes as the agricultural complex and its associated material culture spread westward. Tells were replaced by more ephemeral villages as people moved to regions of more widespread agricultural potential than obtained in the Levant, Anatolia, or Greece,[3] allowing timber to replace mud bricks for construction and a more frequent foundation of new settlements, instead of continuous occupation of single localities.

Beyond Italy we see the continuing spread of Neolithic cultures, characterized by so-called Cardial (shell-impressed) pottery, along the northern coastline of the Mediterranean to reach southern France, Iberia, Malta, and the nearby coast of North Africa between 5800 and 5400 BC (Rowley-Conwy 1995; Zilhão 1993, 2001). According to João Zilhão, the complex traveled via maritime colonization focusing on regions not densely settled by Mesolithic hunters, forming a sharp break with the preceding Mesolithic in most regions, despite some hints of overlap in certain marginally located limestone caves. But of course, Mesolithic populations were not all absent-mindedly looking the other way while farming blossomed behind their backs. In Portugal, the end of the line for this particular episode of Neolithic dispersal and also a good location for maritime hunter-gatherers, Mesolithic populations appear to have overlapped for at least 1,000 years with Neolithic farmers (Figure 4.3). In such a circumstance it is not surprising that some fairly strong debate has emerged recently on the question of Mesolithic continuity into the Neolithic in Iberia, with skeletal evidence from Portugal taking centre stage.[4]

Temperate and Northern Europe

After 5400 BC, at roughly the same time that farming was spreading westward along the Mediterranean coastline, pioneer farming populations spread quite rapidly, following a 600-year standstill on the western edge of the Hungarian Plain, up the Danube Valley, and through Europe north of the Alps to as far as the Rhineland and the Paris Basin. The approaches to the northern European coastline brought another marked slowing of the rate of spread, and a marked increase in the potential evidence for Mesolithic population incorporation into the farming communities. Agriculture probably did not spread into Latvia and much of Scandinavia until after 3500 BC, or into Finland until well into the Bronze Age.

An interesting economic perspective on the two-pronged spread of Neolithic societies through Europe is given by archaeobotanist Ursula Maier (1996). The economy which spread initially through the Balkans, up the Danube and into temperate Europe north of the Alps, was dominated by hulled emmer and einkorn wheats. However, the wheats which spread along the northern Mediterranean were all of the naked variety, probably tetraploids. The technicalities here suggest that the agricultural

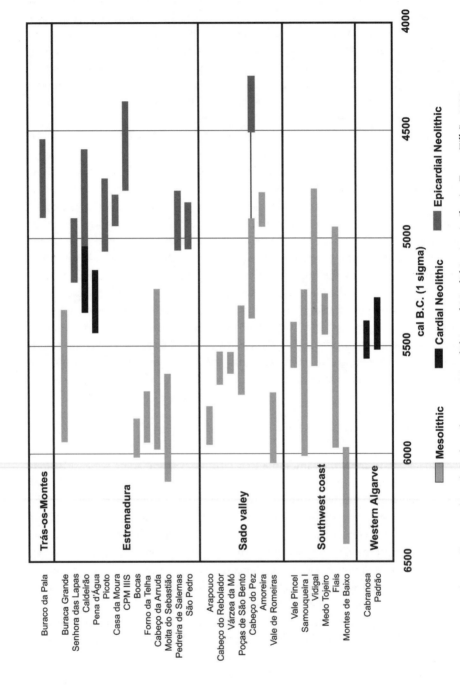

Figure 4.3 The overlap in radiocarbon dates between Mesolithic and Neolithic sites in Iberia. From Zilhão 2000.

colonization of Europe involved not only two axes of movement, but also two different cereal complexes, both eventually meeting west and north of the Alps.[5]

The Danubians and the northern Mesolithic

The northerly and westerly expansion of pioneer farmer communities from the Hungarian Plain through the former Czechoslovakia, Austria, Poland, Germany, and the Low Countries, but stopping short of extension on to the alluvial coastal plain of northern Europe, belongs to one of the most dramatic episodes of cultural replacement in European prehistory. After 5400 BC, Linear Pottery Culture (otherwise termed Danubian, Linear Bandkeramik, or simply LBK) populations with their characteristic timber longhouse settlements and incised pottery spread through the fertile loesslands, favoring floodplain-edge situations for their permanent villages, with an economy focused on small clearings in the forest where they raised hulled emmer and einkorn wheat, broomcorn millet, cattle, sheep, goats, and pigs.[6] LBK origins can be located at the southeastern end of the distribution (Figure 4.1), and the spread was very rapid – perhaps 200 years from Slovenia and Poland to the Paris Basin. There is very little evidence for interaction with Mesolithic communities, except in the peripheral westerly and northerly parts of the region. Large-blade tools, including sickles, replaced the bladelets and burins of the local Mesolithic, although Gronenborn (1999) suggests that there was some lithic continuity in blade manufacture.

The LBK reflects remarkable homogeneity in pottery decoration and longhouse construction, a homogeneity soon to break up with the settling-down process and the inevitable decay of long-distance colonizer networks. LBK settlements reveal high densities in some areas, with villages (Figure 4.4) located as little as one kilometer apart, but with few sites in other areas, suggesting as in Greece and Iberia that early farmers were quite selective in their choice of territory and prepared to move long distances if necessary. The longhouses, as in parts of ethnographic Borneo, might have reflected non-lineage societies in which early landownership patterns were fluid – a pattern within which people could move frequently from one village or longhouse to another, as with the remarkably expansive Iban of western Borneo in the 19th century. Such a society can be characterized as oriented toward the acquisition of labor rather than land, at least in the initial phase of territorial expansion into previously unfarmed terrain. Longhouses thus correlate from this perspective with a society in pioneer mode, where individual families need mobility. Such mobility has recently been demonstrated from a study of strontium isotopes in the teeth and bones of Rhineland LBK people, indicating that many people spent their childhoods in places with different environmental chemistries from those where their bones were finally laid to rest (Price et al. 2001).

North of the LBK distribution, however, the pattern of agricultural spread differed markedly. Entrenched Mesolithic populations located on the North European alluvial plain and around the Baltic and North Sea coastlines, together with the less favorable soil and climatic conditions, held up the spread of agriculture in a major way. The details are complex and differ from place to place; this lack of homogeneity of course

Figure 4.4 An undefended Bandkeramik settlement on a Meuse River terrace, from Kooijmans 1993. Kooijmans notes that house sizes, in reality, were perhaps not as regular as shown here.

being a sure sign in itself that Neolithic settlers did not just spread in a vacuum. But before we look at some aspects of this complexity, let us consider a quotation about this interesting situation of hunter-farmer "confrontation":

> it seems to me important, first to realize that we have here a situation that has no good modern analogy. We are studying the confrontation of stone-technology hoe cultivators, and colonist-settlers, with broad spectrum hunter-gatherers with presumably restricted mobility, all this in an unspoiled temperate environment with full opportunities for all communities involved to select optimal site locations in their perception. Both popula-tions, the colonists and the natives, had widely different cultural roots. Those of the Bandkeramik are to be traced to southeastern Europe and ultimately to the Near East . . . The "natives", in contrast, had their roots far back in the Late Palaeolithic of northern Europe . . . My point is that differences in mentality can explain the lack of adoption of Neolithic elements [by the Mesolithic populations] in the early centuries of contact. Fundamentally different attitudes had to be bridged. This implies that both culture complexes gradually had to transform in the other's direction. (Kooijmans 1993:137)

It is possible to make further observations on the nature of this Mesolithic–Neolithic interface in northern Europe. The edges of the LBK distribution in the Low Coun-tries were marked by the construction of numerous longhouse settlements fortified by deep ditches and timber palisades, possibly reflecting defense against Mesolithic communities, although other kinds of within-LBK instability due to population growth (Shennan 2002:247–251) clearly cannot be ruled out. Lawrence Keeley refers to a no-man's-land along the frontier between Mesolithic and LBK sites in Belgium (Fig-ure 4.5) and to a massacre of 34 members of an LBK population at Talheim in Germany. He also suggests that many of the LBK stone axes found in Mesolithic sites were used as weapons of war and points out (Keeley 1997:309) that "whatever interactions there were between these two groups, they were at best chilly and at worst violent."

Relevant here for the rather long and drawn-out episodes of hunter–farmer inter-action on the northern fringes of Europe is the idea that domesticated crops and animals will be adopted by hunter-gatherers by means of passing through three successive phases, termed by Marek Zvelebil and Peter Rowley-Conwy (1986; Zvelebil 1998) the *availability*, *substitution*, and *consolidation* phases. The availability phase could have been quite long. For instance, the Ertebølle hunter-fishers of the coastlines of Denmark and northern Germany maintained a frontier with farmers to the south between about 4800 and 4000 BC, after which agriculture finally spread rapidly into the region in the form of the TRB (Funnel Beaker) culture.[7] Ertebølle sites have no clear signs of any agricultural products, apart from occasional goat bones, indicating that they probably did not trade regularly for produce from farmers (unlike many recent "niche" hunter-gatherers – see chapter 2). They did adopt pottery-making at about 4500 BC, and imported some LBK antler and stone adzes. So in this case we witness long-term contact without agricultural adoption, prior to the ultimate entry of Ertebølle descendants into the agricultural TRB lifestyle.

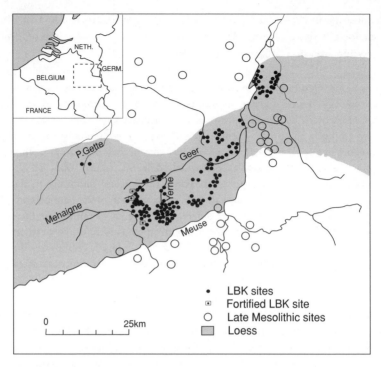

Figure 4.5 The non-overlapping distributions of Mesolithic and LBK sites in a section of the Meuse Valley in Belgium, in the vicinity of Liège and Maastricht. After Keeley and Cahen 1989. The LBK sites are restricted to loess soils and are ringed by Mesolithic sites. Note the separation to the north between the nearest Mesolithic and Neolithic settlements; such settlements are only in proximity where the Meuse River intervenes.

The TRB and the Baltic

The TRB, a derivation from the earlier LBK, spread across the northern coastal plain of Europe starting about 4500 BC and replaced or incorporated the Mesolithic Ertebølle culture. It reflects both a high level of early homogeneity and a fairly clear derivation from the Lengyel variant of the later LBK. As with the LBK, this early homogeneity hints strongly at dispersal from a source region, rather than piecemeal origin amongst native Mesolithic groups. Of course, there are sometimes traces of Mesolithic continuity within the TRB trajectory, emphasized by many authors.[8] Bergljot Solberg (1989), however, favors a sharp replacement of the Ertebølle by the TRB in Denmark, with only a faint degree of continuity (see also Skak-Nielson 2003; Raemakers 2003). Peter Rowley-Conwy (1999) also comments on the sharpness of the change in dietary terms, despite middle Neolithic switches in some regions to hunting and gathering (such switches are common in agricultural boundary zones – see chapter 2). It is clear that the process of becoming Neolithic in northern Europe was essentially driven by an LBK–TRB cultural phylogeny rather than by a native Mesolithic one, regardless of how many "native" hunter-gatherers there might have been around who were willing or allowed to join the farmer villages.

Another interesting region of long-term agricultural availability, here more clearly associated with actual *substitution* (i.e., eventual agricultural adoption by Mesolithic communities), was located around the eastern shoreline of the Baltic (Zvelebil 1998). Rimuté Rimantiené (1992) proposes a long "Early Neolithic" phase between 5500 and 3400 BC, associated with the use of pottery but no agriculture,[9] followed by a Middle Neolithic between 3400 and 2800 BC, when agriculture, with foxtail and broomcorn millet, emmer, and domesticated animals, was finally adopted. The resulting Mesolithic-derived economic amalgam was, in turn, overtaken by incoming Corded Ware farmers during the late Neolithic (2800 to 2000 BC).

Both the Ertebølle and the Baltic examples raise an interesting question. We see, on the agricultural fringes, with some examples carrying more conviction than others, situations whereby native Mesolithic populations adopted aspects of a Neolithic life-style, with or without agriculture, and eventually blended, or simply disappeared, into the "full Neolithic" and Bronze Age cultural records which ensued. So, we may ask if the full Neolithic cultures of northern Europe beyond the LBK heartland existed *entirely* because Mesolithic populations adopted agriculture, or did the real impetus behind the process lie with expanding and land-hungry farmers moving mainly from the south and east? This is one of those everlasting questions that seem to torment archaeologists all over Europe. Just observing that some Mesolithic populations probably became incorporated into a Neolithic cultural landscape tells us nothing very useful at all. What we want to know is what really *drove* the Neolithic expansion, a question for which the activities of those Mesolithic hunters who happened to be somewhere in the vicinity of the action may not have been terribly relevant.

The British Isles

A similar debate exists for the British Isles. Lowland Britain ("England") is a fertile region with a warm maritime climate which would have been attractive to agriculturalists from the start, just as were the lowlands of Europe, apart from the sandy and rather infertile North European Plain. Mesolithic adoption of agriculture is more likely in the fastnesses of Scotland, Wales, and Ireland, where Iron Age inhabitants 4,000 years later were much more successful in resisting the Roman and the later Anglo-Saxon onslaughts than their lowland eastern contemporaries. Nevertheless, most archaeologists today favor a purely Mesolithic adoption of a continental agricultural economy into the British Isles. Douglas Price (1987:282) has suggested that "the 'Neolithic revolution' in Britain was an inside job," thus relegating any arrival of a farmer population from the continent as of minimal significance.

However, the transition from Mesolithic to Neolithic in Britain and Ireland was quite sharp and decisive, just as on the continent. No British Mesolithic sites have ever been reported to have evolved Neolithic economies or material cultures entirely from internal resources. New data on large LBK-like timber houses, field systems, and some fairly impressive cereal inventories in British Neolithic sites indicate that many of the inhabitants were serious farmers with continental cultural traditions.[10] Indeed, given the negative perspective on adopting agriculture at a distance given in chapter 2, even if the English Channel is only 33 kilometers wide, a totally Mesolithic engine of adoption seems most unlikely.

The debate over Mesolithic adoption of farming often extends to considerations of the earthen burial mounds and megalithic monuments characteristic of many western European Early Neolithic cultures from about 4600 BC onward. These are seen by many as reflectors in part of a Mesolithic ideological input into a Neolithic landscape, even though there seems no unequivocal evidence to trace them precisely to a Mesolithic source. Chris Scarre (1992) and Andrew Sherratt (1997a) adopt a middle course, regarding the early long burial mounds with timber chambers as reflecting a central European Neolithic, perhaps LBK, ultimate origin, with the very frequent expressions of megalithicism and circularity in monument design (especially passage graves) as being of native Mesolithic origin (Figure 4.6). As Sherratt (1997a:336–367) has recently expressed the situation, clearly wishing to maintain the best of both worlds: "The Neolithic cultures of western and northern Europe . . . created a unique synthesis of an ultimately Near Eastern form of social organization . . . and an indigenous population with its own forms of culture and subsistence base."

Hunters and farmers in prehistoric Europe

Thinking in a general way, we may ask what range of situations might have given rise to some perceived degree of continuity from Mesolithic to Neolithic in regions not suspected to have witnessed independent origins of agriculture. Mesolithic adoption of agriculture in isolation is highly unlikely, at least from the perspective taken in this book, unless the agriculture can be shown to have been generated locally, as in Southwest Asia. But there are many intermediate possibilities. One is suggested for formerly Mesolithic populations by Ian Armit and Bill Finlayson (1992): "Whether actual economic practices themselves or whether only material symbols originally associated with agricultural economies were initially adopted, archaeologically these people would become Neolithic." In other words, hunters can adopt outsider artifacts, as have many in the recent ethnographic record, without actually adopting agriculture itself. They can thus appear to be Neolithic without being so in economic reality.

R. E. Donahue and colleagues (1992) give a good example of this from Tuscany, in which a Mesolithic cave-dwelling population acquired Neolithic pottery. Milutin Garasanin and Ivana Radovanovic (2001) give another example, this time of a Neolithic pot in a "Mesolithic" house in Lepenski Vir (Danube Basin). As noted above, the late hunter-gatherers of the North Sea and Baltic coastlines also acquired farmer goods such as polished axes. Some late Mesolithic sites in the Netherlands contain cereal remains, presumed traded in rather than locally cultivated. The archaeological record of the late Mesolithic in Europe must contain many more examples of this type, often difficult to recognize if the transition to agriculture occurred rapidly. Such situations carry no necessary implications for a unilateral Mesolithic adoption of agriculture.

At the opposite end of the spectrum, farmers who inhabit game-rich agricultural frontiers can switch temporarily to hunting and almost lose their agricultural heritage, becoming virtual hunters and gatherers again, as did many early Polynesian

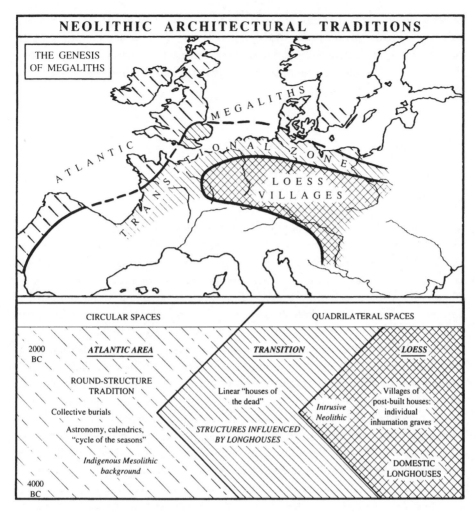

Figure 4.6 The genesis of megalithic monuments from interaction between the LBK farming tradition and the Mesolithic "round-structure tradition" in northwestern Europe, mid-sixth to third millennia BC, according to Andrew Sherratt 1997a.

populations in the Pacific Islands.[11] Admittedly, the Pacific islands east of the Solomons had no Mesolithic hunters – the first farmers found them pristine and well stocked with wild avifaunas. But clearly it is possible for frontier Neolithic populations to masquerade as Mesolithic hunters, a circumstance noted for the earliest Neolithic in central Europe by John Alexander (1978). Marek Zvelebil (1989) has also noted that many Neolithic sites in Europe do not appear to have actual evidence for agriculture, perhaps reflecting temporary shifts into foraging (although this could as well reflect poor preservation of organic remains).

There can also be side-by-side interdigitated coexistence of hunters and farmers for long periods, a situation not to be confused with the long-term and rather hostile hunter–farmer frontier suggested by Keeley for Belgium during the LBK (above). As in many ethnographic situations, hunters and farmers can exchange and coexist in a mosaic of neighboring territories. Susan Gregg (1988) favors such a scenario for LBK farmers and their presumed Mesolithic contemporaries in southern Germany. As long as there are niches, hunters can of course survive for millennia amongst farmers, but only if the conditions are right.

Agricultural Dispersals from Southwest Asia to the East

Central Asia

The agricultural movement that gave rise to the Zagrosian agricultural Neolithic by about 7500 BC continued on to reach Pakistan, the Caucasus, and Turkmenistan in central Asia during the seventh millennium BC. The spread to Pakistan probably occurred through northern Iran, rather than through the desert core of the Iranian Plateau, but current lack of information from northern Iran and Afghanistan makes further speculation rather difficult. However, the remarkable site of Mehrgarh in Baluchistan, on the Kachi alluvial plain about 150 kilometers southeast of Quetta, has a Preceramic Neolithic sequence through about 10 meters of archaeological deposit. Baluchistan lies toward the eastern limit of the winter rainfall zone and Mehrgarh itself provides a remarkable beacon-like outpost, close to the eastern limits of Fertile Crescent Neolithic expansion.

The foundation of Mehrgarh probably occurred a little before 7000 BC. The site has mud brick constructions of small rectangular doorless rooms arranged in rows, like those of some PPNB settlements. The stone tools are dominated by microlithic forms such as trapezes and lunates, similar to Epipaleolithic industries such as the Natufian and Zarzian, the latter perhaps indicating the most likely source of the tradition. Bitumen-hafted glossed sickle blades indicate cereal harvesting, and grain impressions in mud bricks indicate that a naked (i.e., domesticated) form of 6-row barley was the dominant crop. Hulled emmer and einkorn, 2-row barley, possibly durum or bread wheat, and dates were also present. In the lower levels there were no domesticated animals, but sheep and goats were domesticated toward the end of the Preceramic phase, together with the native Indian humped bovid (*Bos indicus*) that rapidly came to dominate the animal economy. Water buffalo bones occur as well, but it is unclear if this animal, so fundamental to the rice-farming economy of later South and Southeast Asia, was also domesticated in Preceramic Mehrgarh. Female figurines are of generalized Middle Eastern type.[12]

Although there have been suggestions that Mehrgarh represents a local independent generation of a Neolithic economy, this is really stretching the evidence rather far. *Zebu* cattle (*Bos indicus*) were presumably domesticated locally, and possibly even goats (MacHugh and Bradley 2001), but everything about the site suggests a cultural origin further to the west. Local domestication of a plant or animal need not mean a totally independent generation of an agricultural economy. Perhaps we have here, as so often, a combination of a cultural spread assimilating to some degree a "native" tradition.

The appearance of the first agricultural communities in Turkmenistan, east of the Caspian Sea, occurred somewhat later than at Mehrgarh. The Neolithic of Turkmenistan had pottery from the beginning, with the key site of Jeitun being founded around 6000 BC. Jeitun lies in a region which would have required irrigation to make agriculture successful, hence perhaps its relative lateness and seeming marginality on the northeastern edge of the Middle Eastern early agricultural sphere. The village covered about 0.4 hectares, with one-roomed square houses built of clay bricks with plastered floors and grain bins. Domestic sheep and goats were present from the start, together with einkorn and barley and a possible irrigation ditch. The Jeitun painted pottery seems related to that of the site of Jarmo in Iraqi Kurdistan, and it is probably to this region or northern Iran that the Jeitun culture will ultimately be traced. Here, as at Mehrgarh, the Middle Eastern economy was required to come to grips with its ecological boundaries, in this case on the fringes of the central Asian arid zone (Harris et al. 1996; Harris 1998b).

Farming probably reached the Caucasus by about 6500 BC, and large numbers of Neolithic sites are reported from the eastern hinterlands of the Black Sea, on the Kura and Araxes riverine plains and close to some of the other small rivers that flow into the Caspian. According to Karine Kushnareva (1997), the oldest Neolithic sites have pottery and a full complement of domestic animals and plants, but she also notes continuity of Mesolithic technology in some of the remoter regions. As we will see, this is in accord with the linguistic situation in the Caucasus; an incoming farming economy was spread by farmers moving in from the south, but it was also clearly adopted to some degree by native populations whose languages survive in descendant form to the present.

To the north of about latitude 36°, a belt of rather forbidding desert extends east of the Caspian, through the Tian Shan ranges, and into the Taklimakan and Gobi desert regions of China and Mongolia. Early farmers did not penetrate these desert regions as far as we know, at least not until horse riding and the use of bronze allowed Andronovo pastoralists to spread through vast regions during the second millennium BC, as far to the east as the Altai and Tian Shan (Dergachev 1989). However, the grassland steppes to the north of these deserts, together with the belt of forest-steppe further north again, did witness a spread of mainly caprovine pastoralists with some cereal production after 5000 BC. The western steppes run from the mouth of the Danube, around the northern sides of the Black and Caspian Seas (Figure 4.1), and then fade eastward at the feet of the Altai and Sayan Mountains, virtually in the exact center of Asia. They then commence again in Mongolia. As far as the western steppes are concerned, the Kelteminar, Mariupol, Samara, and Botai complexes were all cultures of westerly derivation in the period down to 3500 BC, with Botai being the most easterly and reaching a little beyond the Urals. The succeeding Afanasievo culture reached the Altai by 2500 BC.

The more westerly of these groups in the vicinity of the Black Sea grew cereals such as emmer, einkorn, barley, common millet (*Panicum miliaceum*), and foxtail millet (*Setaria italica*), as well as herding sheep, goats, and occasional cattle (the latter perhaps used for traction in later prehistoric periods). To the east of the Urals, it is unlikely that cereal production would ever have been a very viable activity, at least not prior to the Bronze Age, and the early emphasis seems to have been mainly pastoralist. Horses were hunted initially, and the invention of horse riding during the second millennium BC (Levine et al. 1999) allowed for much greater mobility and population expansion.

The Neolithic steppe cultures seem all to have moved in from the west or south; from the Cucuteni and Tripolye cultures north of the Black Sea, perhaps from the Caucasus, and perhaps even from Turkmenistan in the case of the Kelteminar culture of the Aral Sea region. At this time, no serious relationships appear to have existed with Neolithic cultures in China. But during the Iron Age of the first millennium BC, we know that cultures of oasis regions in the Tarim Basin of Xinjiang, and a little to the north in the alluvial outwashes from the Tian Shan in Kazakhstan, were based on the production of crops such as wheat, common millet (*Panicum*), and rice, together with sheep, goats, and cattle (Chang and Tourtelotte 1998; Rosen 2001). Given that the Tarim Basin once contained Indo-European languages of one of the earliest-differentiated subgroups in the family (Tocharian), and given the occurrence of common millet cultivation in Neolithic China, Iran, and the western steppes by 5000 BC, one begins to wonder if there were earlier Neolithic movements through these desert regions. Common millet perhaps originated somewhere between the Caspian Sea and Xinjiang (Zohary and Hopf 2000). Did Neolithic settlers ever penetrate the Tarim Basin from Afghanistan, the Russian steppes, or even western China? Only future research will tell.

The Indian Subcontinent

The Indian subcontinent – Pakistan, India, Bangladesh, Nepal, and Bhutan – is separated from Central Asia by the Himalayas and their westerly extension, the Hindu Kush. We can divide the environments of South Asia, at least as far as the history of early agriculture is concerned, into five zones of climate, rainfall seasonality, and agricultural colonization history (see Figure 6.2 for rainfall seasonality):

1. *The Indus Valley and Baluchistan.* Baluchistan witnessed the oldest agriculture in South Asia, documented by the introduction of a Southwest Asian economy at Mehrgarh by the seventh millennium BC. This economy continued in Baluchistan with no significant outside introductions until the appearance of one of the world's greatest early urban civilizations – the Harappan (or Indus Valley, or Sarasvati) civilization of Pakistan and northwestern India. By the end of the Mature Harappan Phase (2600 to 1900 BC), a number of important new food crops had appeared, especially rice from China or eastern India, and millet species from tropical Africa (Fuller 2002, 2003; Fuller and Madella 2002). These introductions would have allowed, by perhaps 2000 BC, a regime of both summer and winter cropping

(Fentress 1985), the latter depending on irrigation because the Indus river system receives most of its floodwater during the spring and summer.

2. *The Ganges Valley.* This region, much wetter generally than the Indus and with increasing summer monsoon rainfall reliability, had a mixed economy of both Southwest Asian winter crops *and* rice (a monsoon crop) established at the start of the Neolithic, ca. 3000 BC, although the possibility of earlier rice cultivation should not be overlooked. The Southwest Asian crops were initially of more importance in the west, but rice increased its dominance as time went by, to attain the enormous significance it holds in the Ganges Basin today. The Ganges farming story thus began, on current evidence, perhaps 4,000 years after Mehrgarh, presumably by partial derivation from a westerly Pre-Harappan source combined with a more shadowy hint of influence, in the form of domesticated rice (*Oryza sativa*), from China or Southeast Asia.

3. *Inland peninsular India.* South of the Indus and Ganges basins, the interior Deccan Plateau regions of India have a dry monsoonal climate and were first settled in the north and west by Pre-Harappan farmers around 3500 BC, in this case with an economy based on the Southwest Asian cereals together with native grams (legumes) and millets. New research is suggesting the possibility of an indigenous domestication of at least two species each of grams and millets in Karnataka by 2800 BC (Mehra 1999; Fuller 2002, 2003). African pearl millet and sorghum were introduced via Harappan sea contacts, by about 2000 BC. In some drier regions of Rajasthan, Gujarat, Maharashtra, and Karnataka there were also developments of cattle pastoralism, together with long-term survival of hunter-gatherers in exchange contact with the farmers (Misra 1973; Possehl and Kennedy 1979).

4. *The humid coastal regions* of southwestern, eastern, and northeastern India are generally *terra incognita* as far as evidence of early agriculture is concerned, as is Sri Lanka.[13] Eastern and northeastern India must have played roles in either an independent development of rice cultivation or its successful introduction into the subcontinent from the east, perhaps around 3000 BC, but we have no clear archaeological evidence for this as yet from countries such as Bangladesh or Burma.

5. Likewise, *the Himalayan region* has no detailed archaeological record of early agriculture, except for the presence of sites with a mixture of Southwest and East (or Central) Asian Neolithic affinities in Kashmir.

What we have in South Asia is therefore quite a complex situation. Unlike Southwest Asia, a firm and fairly unitary homeland and expansion history for agriculture cannot be established. The reality was clearly a mix of external introduction from several sources, combined with some currently rather faint hints of independent internal development, especially in the south.

The domesticated crops of the Indian subcontinent

The crops involved in the South Asian story fall into four groups in terms of ultimate origin: Southwest Asian, African, East Asian, and native South Asian (Willcox 1989).

The major Southwest Asian cereals and legumes were introduced into the region in domesticated form, with the possible exception of barley, which could have been domesticated locally. It is also possible that a species of hexaploid wheat (*Triticum sphaerococcum*), grown widely in Harappan sites, was domesticated from a wild forebear in the northwestern subcontinent.

The African millets and legumes appear to have been introduced initially into the Indus region during the period of trading activity with Mesopotamia and the Persian Gulf, focused on the Akkadian, Third Dynasty of Ur, and Isin-Larsa periods (2350 to 1800 BC). The two main millet species are sorghum (*Sorghum bicolor*) and pearl millet (*Pennisetum* sp.), both of which appeared in the late Harappan and Deccan Chalcolithic around 2000 BC. These are both highly productive summer crops, well attuned to the drought conditions that frequently occur in monsoonal areas. Finger millet, *Eleusine coracana*, is believed to be of Ethiopian origin, although its actual presence in South Asian sites is still under debate. The African legume species *Vigna unguiculata* (cowpea) and *Lablab purpureus* (hyacinth bean) had also arrived in South Asia by Late Harappan times.[14]

The third group of crops is of East Asian origin. The most important is Asian rice, *Oryza sativa*, domesticated first in the Yangzi Basin by about 7000 BC, although since many eastern and northeastern parts of India are also significant homelands of wild rice it is likely that some local long-grained (*indica*) varieties were brought into cultivation here as the rice economy developed. However, there is no clear-cut evidence so far for any early and *independent* Indian domestication of rice, which occurs widely in northern India by at least 2500 BC (Singh 1990; Kajale 1991). Two of the millets widespread from the late Harappan onward are also possibly of external origin, these being foxtail millet (*Setaria italica*), probably domesticated first in the Yellow Basin of China, and broomcorn millet (*Panicum miliaceum*), probably domesticated in central Asia (Weber 1998; Zohary and Hopf 2000).

The domesticated food plants native to the subcontinent are all summer crops, such as the legumes black and green gram (*Vigna* sp.) and horse gram (*Dolichos* sp.), a number of grain-bearing plants in the *Paspalum* and *Chenopodium* genera, and two minor species of millet (*Brachiaria ramosa* and *Setaria verticillata*). Dorian Fuller (2003) has suggested that a number of these plants were domesticated independently in the Karnataka region of south India. All are of relatively minor significance today.

The upshot of the above is that the pre-Iron Age South Asian Neolithic and Chalcolithic cultures, between 3000 and 1000 BC, flourished on the basis of combinations of crops introduced from Southwest Asia via the Indus Valley, from central Africa via the Harappan trading system, from other regions of central and eastern Asia, as well as crops of local origin. Given that the agricultural colonization of South Asia required a crop register to be compiled from such disparate sources, it is not surprising that the earliest Neolithic and Chalcolithic cultures in India proper should date to around 3000 BC, perhaps four millennia after the establishment of indigenous or unblended economies such as those of Mehrgarh in Pakistan and Pengtoushan in the Yangzi Basin. Agricultural spread into the Indian subcontinent clearly required considerable gestation and adjustment.

Regional Trajectories from Hunter-Gathering to Farming in South Asia

The consequences of Mehrgarh

In the Indus Basin, the Southwest Asian agropastoral economy introduced to Mehrgarh by 7000 BC developed to become the economic foundation for Mature Harappan civilization, via a number of successive Pre-Harappan cultures (Possehl 2002) dating variously to between 5000 and 2600 BC in sites such as Mehrgarh, Kot Diji, Amri, and Harappa (Figure 4.7). By 3500 BC, aspects of these cultural traditions had extended

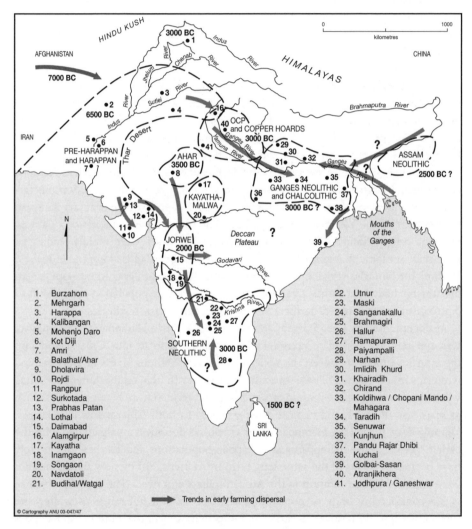

Figure 4.7 The early farming cultures of South Asia. Modified from Misra 2001; Chakrabarti 1999.

southeast of the Indus, to occur in the basal deposits of sites such as Dholavira and Prabhas Patan in Gujarat, and Kalibangan and Balathal in Rajasthan. As well as villages and towns, camps of hunters and pastoralists also appeared east of the Indus system. Agriculture had certainly entered northwestern Peninsular India, by movement around the southern side of the Thar Desert, many centuries before the opening of the Mature Harappan around 2600 BC.[15]

Another spread at a similar date seems also to have occurred around the northern peripheries of the Indus basin, to carry the Southwest Asian economy to Neolithic sites such as Burzahom and Gufkral in Kashmir (ca. 3000–2500 BC),[16] and possibly also by this time into the upper Ganges and Yamuna Valleys. The basal layer in Gufkral reveals a rather recent (ca. 3000 BC) and puzzling aceramic Neolithic, a situation made more complex by the fact that some cultural items from these two Kashmir sites, especially the cord-marked pottery and ground stone harvesting knives, have apparent Chinese Neolithic affinities. At this stage, however, we have no coherent traces in these sites of rice, or of the African millets.

During the later third millennium BC, continuing contact between the Indus region and Gujarat led to the appearance in the latter region of a number of Mature Harappan settlements, some fortified. Examples include Surkotada, Dholavira (already settled in pre-Harappan times), Rojdi, and Lothal (Figure 4.7). Mature Harappan sites were also founded in the Yamuna Valley, for instance at Alamgirpur near Delhi, and Harappan-influenced settlements were established at Balathal in Rajasthan and Daimabad in Maharashtra. By 1900 BC, the decline of core-region sites such as Harappa and Mohenjo-Daro in the Indus Valley system was already under way. Various factors, including movement of the Indus course in Sind, capture of the tributary Sarasvati river system by the Yamuna/Ganga, and possible human over-exploitation of a fragile environment (salinization? too many kiln-fired bricks?), were rapidly leading to large-scale settlement abandonment in the Harappan heartlands along the Indus and its Punjab tributaries (Possehl 1997; Flam 1999). Harappan agricultural populations presumably had to face three overlapping choices – reduce population *in situ*, shift to pastoralism, or continue as farmers and move out into new territories.

As documented by Greg Possehl, the Late or Post-Urban Harappan (1900–1400 BC) was apparently a period of considerable population spread into Gujarat and into the interfluve (*doab*) between the upper Ganges and Yamuna rivers in Haryana and western Uttar Pradesh. These spreads occurred with the establishment of small villages rather than urban settlements and lacked typical Mature Harappan traits such as seals, use of script, and cubical stone weights. In both Gujarat and the Ganges-Yamuna *doab*, these Late Harappan eastward pulses doubtless amalgamated with the earlier spreads of Pre-Harappan and Harappan populations, indeed they may merely have been later stages of the same long-term movement. But by now the economies were enriched by the addition of the African millets and rice.[17] The result by 1800 BC was a considerably body of population with access to a full range of winter and summer crops, domesticated cattle and caprovines, painted pottery and copper metallurgy, expanding to north and south around an ever-desiccating Thar Desert, toward the Ganges Basin and Peninsular India.

The big question at this point is whether the earliest farming cultures which eventually spread into western India and the Ganges Basin were derived *exclusively* from the Pre-Harappan and Harappan complexes, or whether they incorporated other, perhaps local, ancestries. This question cannot be answered easily, but the latter situation seems likely, as we will see.

Western India: Balathal to Jorwe

In western India, extending from Balathal and Ahar in southeastern Rajasthan southward to Songaon on the upper Krishna River in Maharashtra, the archaeological record reveals a number of closely related Chalcolithic cultures dating from 3500 BC in the north, continuing to an ultimate phase of decline and abandonment late in the second millennium BC.[18] These cultures have copper tools of Harappan derivation, hence there is strictly speaking no Neolithic in this region, although there is a Neolithic to the south, as there is in northeastern India. The west coast of India, as indeed also the east coast, is currently a region almost devoid of archaeological information pertinent for early agricultural questions.

Into this monsoonal region focused on the rather dry Deccan Plateau spread the farming economy characteristic of the Harappan in Gujarat, complete with the Southwest Asian cereals and legumes, the African and native millets, and rare occurrences of rice, the latter for instance at the site of Dangawada in Madhya Pradesh, directly dated by C14 to almost 2000 BC (IAR 1982–83:144). With it came an animal economy dominated, as in the Indus Valley itself, by cattle, with sheep and goats usually in minor proportions. Black cotton soils were favored for settlement, usually near rivers so that agriculture could proceed with irrigation when necessary. Traces of an irrigation canal have been discovered at Inamgaon in Maharashtra. Presumably, as in the Late Harappan, a double-cropping economy was practiced, together with a good deal of cattle-based pastoralism in drier regions.

The cultures concerned are normally differentiated through minor variations in pottery typology, but most Indian archaeologists regard them all as very closely related to one another. Vasant Shinde (2000, 2002) divides the Chalcolithic sequence of western India into a number of phases running successively from 3500 BC onward, being represented first by the Pre-Harappan basal layer at Balathal in Rajasthan, then the successive Kayatha, Ahar, Malwa, and Jorwe ceramic complexes, culminating in the final decline of Jorwe settlements around 1000 BC, just before the dramatic cultural changes of the Iron Age. For our purposes the details of these successive ceramic phases are not essential, except to note that many artifact types do show fairly obvious relationships with the Pre-Harappan and Harappan cultures of the Indus region. These include black-on-red painted and wheel-made pottery, pottery kilns and clay ovens, pressure-flaked lithic blade industries, simple copper tools made mostly in open molds, clay models of bulls and humans, urn burials of children, mud or stone-walled rectangular houses, lime plastered floors, and even Harappan-like defended enclaves ("citadels") located in third millennium BC layers at Balathal and Daimabad.

The Balathal "citadel" was quite a remarkable construction, enclosing an approximate square of 600 square meters, with stone-faced mud walls 7 meters wide at the base and 4 meters high, the whole filled from top to bottom with cow dung cakes after its abandonment. As V. N. Misra (2002) notes, this construction is rather an enigma, but its cow-dung fill is reminiscent of the ashmound sites in Karnataka that are about to be described below. These Chalcolithic settlements were up to 20 hectares in size (Daimabad), often with houses arranged in rectilinear blocks separated by lanes, as at Inamgaon, a 5-hectare site that appears to have been fortified with a mud wall with rubble bastions and a ditch (Dhavalikar et al. 1988).

The essential question with this western Indian Chalcolithic complex is to determine how it relates to the Pre-Harappan and Harappan sequences on the one hand, and to the southern Neolithic cultures that lay beyond it on the other. Most observers clearly favor either direct derivation from the Pre-Harappan and Harappan cultural traditions, or very strong influence from them (e.g., Dhavalikar 1988, 1994, 1997; V. N. Misra 1997, 2002; Shinde 2000, 2002). Yet there seems to be more to the western Chalcolithic than just an Indus Valley overflow. For instance, non-Harappan types of circular houses with wattle and daub walls are present in Navdatoli in Madhya Pradesh, and in the basal layer at Balathal in Rajasthan (ca. 3200 BC). They later became entirely dominant in the Late Jorwe phase in Maharashtra during the late second millennium BC (Dhavalikar 1988). At face value this might mean little, but there is at least a hint here of a "native" element not immediately derivable from the sidewalks of Mohenjo-Daro. V. H. Sonawane (2000:143) notes that circular huts also appear in several sites of the Post-urban Harappan Phase in Gujarat, again suggesting that these Chalcolithic cultures contained an ethnic tradition not simply derivable from the Harappan.

Southern India

In Karnataka, Andhra Pradesh, and Tamil Nadu, the picture is slightly different from that just described for western India. We have no good Neolithic data from Kerala, and Sri Lanka seems only to have been settled by farmers during the Iron Age, after 1000 BC. Virtually the whole archaeological record in the south comes from the dry monsoonal regions in the southern inland part of the Deccan Plateau. In northern Karnataka, the earliest Neolithic sites appear to have been based on cattle pastoralism, and date back to about 2800 BC. A classic site in this series is the Utnur ashmound, which had a sub-rectangular stockaded enclosure about 60 meters long fenced with palm trunks, sufficient in area for perhaps 500 cattle. Inside the stockade was a thick layer of burned cow dung, with several hoof impressions. Dwelling huts (presumably circular) were constructed between the enclosure and a separate outer stockade (Allchin 1963; Allchin and Allchin 1982:123).

Another ashmound site at Budihal, dated to 2300 BC, had possibly four cattle pens, of which the major excavated example (Budihal Locality 1) contained a 3-meter-high mound of burned dung, an adjacent animal pen fenced by a rubble embankment, and a flanking habitation area of about 1.3 hectares with the stone foundations of rectangular and oval houses. The dung is believed to have been derived from nocturnal cattle-corralling, perhaps burned periodically to reduce flies. Such periodic burning suggests that the dung was not in demand as fertilizer, thus that field agriculture might have been absent. However, the plant remains from Budihal do contain some barley, horse gram, bean, and millet-type seeds, so we cannot assume that these people were purely pastoralists (Paddayya 1993, 1998; Kajale 1996b).

The ashmound sites contain querns, stone axes, a blade industry, and pottery comprising plain gray, incised, and painted wares, handmade and not kiln-fired in the earliest layers. Antecedents are obscure, but the recently excavated non-ashmound site of Watgal, near Budihal, has a number of features reminiscent of Chalcolithic sites further north in the Deccan – a child urn burial and clay-lined basins paralleled at Inamgaon, and painted pottery, including some in Jorwe style (Deavaraj et al. 1995; DuFresne et al. 1998). Budihal has also yielded urn burials of children. Watgal, which has occupation dating from as early as 2700 BC, also has remains of a rather interesting plant found widely in Southeast Asia and the western Pacific – the betel nut.

Elsewhere in southern India, Neolithic occupation sites such as Hallur, Tekkalakota, Paiyampalli, Brahmagiri, and Sanganakallu (Figure 4.7) have varying combinations of painted pottery, child urn burials, blade industries, circular houses with bamboo walls (Tekkalakota and Sanganakallu), and cattle figurines. Most of these sites appear to have commenced occupation in the early second millennium BC, with copper appearing fairly soon after this date in sites such as Ramapuram, Hallur, and Maski. In general, the focus on domesticated cattle, painted pottery, and circular houses links this region loosely with the northern Deccan Chalcolithic sites, and indeed in some sites there is a fairly late spread of Jorwe-type ceramics, particularly into northern Karnataka. Plant remains from these southern sites include the native grams and millets (with apparently no African millets present until 1500 BC), with less frequent occurrences of wheat, barley, and rice (Kajale 1996b; Venkatasubbaiah and Kajale 1991; Korisettar et al. 2002; Fuller 2003).

As far as origins of the southern Neolithic and Chalcolithic are concerned, the radiocarbon series indicates a slight time-cline from north to south, from Rajasthan to Karnataka, between about 3000 and 2500 BC. This suggests that the whole series may belong to a single episode of agricultural dispersal. There is considerable local variation, but over such a vast area this is to be expected. However, the possibility that southern India also witnessed an independent domestication of a number of local and relatively minor millets and grams has recently been suggested. If Fuller's (2003) suggestions of a native and independent South Indian course toward plant domestication, dating from about 2800 BC in the ashmound phase, prove to be correct, then our understanding of the South Asian Neolithic will be greatly enriched.

The Ganges Basin and northeastern India

The Ganges Basin, with major tributaries such as the Yamuna, witnessed a cultural trajectory from Neolithic onward which is superficially similar to that of Chalcolithic western India, but rather different in style and detail. There is another complication with the Ganges, especially in its middle and lower portions from Allahabad eastward, this being that the spread of agriculture might have been two-layered, with a period of rice cultivation in the east older than, or at least contemporary with, the arrival of the Southwest Asian crops. But the evidence is currently most unclear on this. The Southeast Asian evidence offers little help, for while we know that rice cultivation was present in Thailand by 2500 BC, we have no good data on this question from Burma, Bangladesh, or northeastern India.

As far as Assam and the other provinces of far northeastern India are concerned, it is clear that some form of Southeast Asian Neolithic with cord-marked pottery (sometimes with tripods), spindle whorls, and occasional shouldered stone adzes was making a presence by soon after 3000 BC, succeeding a rather poorly known series of late hunter-gatherer lithic industries (Rao 1977; Singh 1997). Presumably, these Neolithic people grew rice, but we cannot be certain of this. In the central and eastern Ganges basin there is much stronger evidence in many sites for rice cultivation associated with the use of a style of cord-marked pottery that could have Southeast Asian antecedents. But one problem here is that cord-marked pottery also occurs in some Harappan-derived assemblages to the west.[19] In addition, there are still many problems of chronology, especially in the identification of any real precedence of Southeast Asian markers beneath those elements of the Ganges Neolithic (for instance, Black and Red Ware pottery, barley, copper technology, sheep, and goat) derived from westerly sources.

Three of the key sites here are Koldihwa, Mahagara, and Chopani-Mando in the Belan valley, which drains north into the Ganges near Allahabad. They have stirred a debate within South Asian archaeology focused on claimed radiocarbon dates for rice and cord-marked pottery, especially from Koldihwa, extending back to 6500 BC (Sharma et al. 1980; IAR 1975–76:85). But Mahagara, which has pottery like that from Koldihwa, is dated by C14 to the second millennium BC. Another related site called Kunjhun II dates to about 2000 BC (IAR 1977–78:89; Clark and Khanna 1989). The upshot of all this is that few people now believe that the early Koldihwa dates relate to the Neolithic material from the site at all (e.g., Dhavalikar 1997:230; Glover and Higham 1996; but they are accepted by Chakrabarti 1999:328).

The current situation in most Ganges sites is that rice and cord-marked pottery occur *together* with non-impressed pottery styles (Black and Red Ware in particular), and elements of the Southwest Asian agropastoral complex. This appears to be the actual situation at Koldihwa (Misra 1977:108), and in a group of culturally related sites at Senuwar, Imlidih Khurd I, Chirand, and Narhan, together covering an occupation sequence from about 2500 to 1000 BC. These sites have between them an economy based on rice, barley, bread wheat, lentils, grams, sorghum, and pearl millet (the last two reported at Imlidih Khurd).[20] Sites downstream in West Bengal, such as Pandu Rajar Dhibi, appear to have focused more on rice cultivation, as befitting their higher rainfall. Domesticated animals include cattle, water buffalo, pig, sheep, and goat, with horse claimed at Imlidih Khurd in the late second millennium BC. Houses have wattle and daub walls and are generally of circular plan. Some sites (especially Chirand, but not Narhan) have microblade and bone industries like those in Koldihwa and Chopani-Mando.[21]

In order to gain a better perspective on the Ganges basin as a whole we need to retreat westward to Punjab and the Ganges-Yamuna *doab*, since it is in these regions that the non-corded (Black and Red) pottery styles appear to have originated before spreading downstream toward Bengal. This area has both Pre-Harappan and Mature Harappan occupation extending east to the vicinity of Delhi on the Yamuna River. Between the Yamuna and Ganges rivers, downstream as far as Allahabad, the oldest pottery is termed "Ochre Colored Pottery" (OCP) – normally wheel-made, red-slipped, and frequently painted with black patterns. Much of this pottery is water rolled and often in poor condition when found, and there is considerable disagreement about its immediate antecedents. Some OCP sites in Rajasthan could be pre-Harappan, but others clearly indicate a degree of Harappan influence and contact (Lal 1984:33). For instance, many artifacts found in OCP sites, such as pottery toy cart wheels, bull figurines, and carnelian beads, have definite Harappan affinities. Many OCP sites also have a basically Harappan economy with very few summer crops apart from rice. On the other hand, the copper tool industry (including the famous "copper hoards") associated with the OCP cannot clearly so be derived from the Harappan. The copper itself was local to northeastern Rajasthan (Khetri-Ganeshwar region), and was supplied from here to Harappan cities as well as to the Ganges sites.

For the OCP, a general origin at about 3000–2500 BC in Punjab or Rajasthan would seem to be indicated (Agrawala and Kumar 1993; Chakrabarti 1999; Sahi 2001). Clearly, it evolved side by side with the Harappan and was strongly influenced by it, but its main significance is that it remains the first attested episode of agricultural dispersal into the Ganges Basin from the west. In some OCP sites, such as Atranjikhera and Jodhpura (Gaur 1983; Agrawala and Kumar 1993), the OCP developed into the Black and Red Ware (BRW) with slipped and burnished red exteriors of the type found widely in the middle and lower Ganges Basin. Dates for BRW in Bihar appear to follow 2500 BC, perhaps 2000 BC in Bengal. The BRW was then succeeded during the Iron Age, after 1000 BC, by a different style of Painted Gray Ware (PGW). Many archaeologists clearly regard the sequence of OCP through BRW to PGW in the Ganges Basin as continuous,[22] and the issue of continuity (versus cultural disruption) in the Ganges sequence, from OCP through to early historical times, lies at the crux of the debate about early Indo-European settlement in the subcontinent. We return to this issue later.

In my opinion, the best explanation for the spread of agriculture through the Ganges Basin is that a cultural assemblage with cord-marked pottery and rice cultivation was moving upstream from the east at about the same time as a separate complex with Southwest Asian crops and OCP pottery was moving downstream from the west, that is at about 3000 BC. The resulting fusion appears to have been rapid and without undue social upheaval.

Europe and South Asia in a Nutshell

The several dispersals of agriculture into and through South Asia were even more multiplex than those in Europe. We have three external sources of crops – Southwest

Asia, northern Sub-Saharan Africa, and East Asia – together with a degree of local domestication. In Europe, farming took 3,000 years to spread from Anatolia to the British Isles. In South Asia, it seems to have taken even longer to spread from northern Pakistan to Sri Lanka, without considering the relatively unknown chronology for early rice cultivation in the northeast. These early spreads of farming were clearly inexorable, even unstoppable in the long term, but they were not instantaneous. Along a given latitude, yes, there could be relative swiftness, as in the case of the northern coastline of the Mediterranean from Greece to Portugal. But across latitude, or across climatic divides, such as that from winter to summer rainfall that separates Iran and Afghanistan from the Ganges Basin, the rate was reduced to a heavy plod. However the farming spread, it was neither by quick-smart adoption by clever hunter-gatherers, nor was it by express trains carrying hungry farmers ever toward the horizon, leaving astonished and landless hunters in their wake.

Chapter 5
Africa: An Independent Focus of Agricultural Development?

The African continent, with the exception of Egypt, does not yet have the density of archaeological coverage which would allow a discussion as detailed as that presented in chapters 3 and 4 for Southwest Asia, Europe, or South Asia. It is also orders of magnitude vaster than western Eurasia and was never dominated by just one region, similar in size to the Fertile Crescent, where evolution of agriculture from an indigenous hunter-gatherer background can so easily be demonstrated. We search for needles of information in a huge range of environments – deserts, savannas, mountains, and rain forests.

Until recently, the belt of grassland (the Sahel zone) and parkland (the Savanna zone) that today stretches across the continent between the Sahara and the rain forest, between about 5° and 15° north, was believed to be the homeland for a number of important native crops (Figure 5.1). New discoveries concerning Holocene climatic zonation in the Sahara, detailed below, now render this zone much more extensive toward the north. The most significant crops are summer-rainfall cereals, particularly African rice (*Oryza glaberrima*), pearl millet (*Pennisetum glaucum*), and sorghum (*Sorghum bicolor*). Guinea yam (*Dioscorea rotundata*) was domesticated in the rain-forest fringes to the south, and finger millet (*Eleusine coracana*) further east, in Ethiopia or southern Sudan. Sub-Saharan agricultural populations subsisted on these and other African crops throughout their prehistory, whereas Egyptian and North African Neolithic populations depended on cereals and legumes of Southwest Asian origin, as did many populations of the Ethiopian Highlands (Barnett 1999; D'Andrea et al. 1999). No major crops or animals were ever domesticated in Africa south of the Equator.

In addition, Indonesian visitors contributed Southeast Asian crops such as bananas, taro, and greater yams to tropical Africa, through movements perhaps connected with the Austronesian settlement of Madagascar at about 1,500 years ago. However,

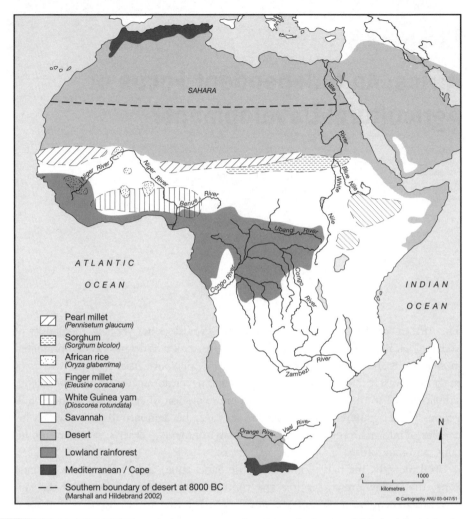

Figure 5.1 The major present-day vegetational regions of Africa, with Harlan's homelands for some of the major crops domesticated there. Also shown is the southern boundary of desert at about 8000 BC, when the Sahara was experiencing moister conditions than now. It should be noted that Harlan's homelands reflect present-day plant distributions; during the wetter phases of the Holocene these distributions would have moved significantly northward, especially for sorghum and pearl millet. Data from Harlan 1992; Marshall 1998; Marshall and Hildebrand 2002.

the recent finding of banana phytoliths in Cameroon dated to 500 BC (Watson and Woodhouse 2001; Mindzie et al. 2001) raises intriguing possibilities of Indian Ocean travel in much earlier times, a topic already discussed in connection with the transfer of African crops to India and Pakistan.

A major question for Africa is whether or not the Sahel and Savanna zones, and also the Ethiopian Highlands, contained one or more regions of *primary* agricultural origin. Currently, this is a most difficult question to answer, since sub-Saharan Africa has no archaeological evidence for domesticated crops until after 2000 BC. It does appear, however, that the Saharan region was much wetter than now in the early Holocene, owing to a northward shift of the monsoon and the belts of grassland and savanna, with a consequent shrinkage of the desert. The wild cereal "homelands" shown in Figure 5.1 would also have moved northward, as we know from the presence of wild sorghum in archaeological sites dating to the end of the Pleistocene in Egypt's Western Desert. This situation doubtless encouraged an increasing emphasis on wild annual cereal collection and possibly also native cattle management by about 8500 BC, and some groups also began to use incised, stamped, and impressed pottery in several Saharan and Nilotic regions by this time.

Since these developments seem to have occurred before the first evidence for Asian sheep and goats in northeastern Africa (ca. 5500 BC), they presumably owed nothing to the Southwest Asian agricultural economy or cultural sequence. However, no *certain* remains of domesticated animals or plants have ever been found in these early Saharan sites and there is as yet insufficient evidence to claim a food-producing subsistence pattern with full confidence. Before examining these issues further it is necessary to outline one aspect of African early agricultural prehistory that does have relatively clear definition.

The Spread of the Southwest Asian Agricultural Complex into Egypt

By virtue of its origins in the African monsoon rainfall zone, the Nile Valley in Egypt has a flood regime almost perfect for the cereals and legumes that originated in Southwest Asia. This is why, of course, many scholars in the past regarded Egypt, erroneously, as a locus of agricultural origin. The Nile floods reach southern Egypt from mid-August and the delta four to six weeks later. The water is relatively free of salt and floods dampen the soil for about two months in autumn and winter, allowing crops to be grown with little further irrigation and without the hazards of salinization and low winter river levels which so afflicted contemporary Sumerians in Mesopotamia.

The main problem for the idea that Egypt was an origin locus for agriculture is that none of the relevant crops existed there in the wild. Paleolithic Egyptians, such as those who used the Wadi Kubanniya campsites (Figure 5.2) about 20,000 years ago, exploited fish, migrant birds, wild cattle, gazelle, and hartebeest, and used grindstones to prepare a toxic tuber (*Cyperus rotundus*) for leaching prior to consumption (Wendorf et al. 1980; Hillman 1989; Jensen et al. 1991; Close 1996). Although grains of barley and einkorn were found in Wadi Kubanniya early in the investigations, more accurate dating has shown that they are intrusive into the sediments, and of recent date. It now seems that the late glacial Nile Valley in Egypt, at that time hyper-arid, supported no major cereals at all. The glossed stone blades once regarded as cereal harvesters are now assumed to have been used for harvesting wetland tubers and possibly palm fruits.

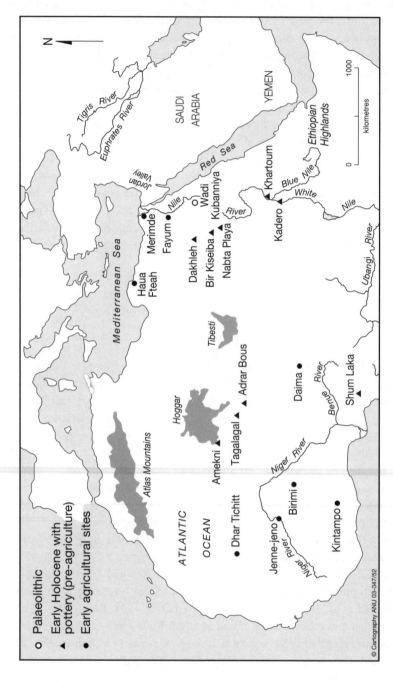

Figure 5.2 Archaeological sites of northern Africa discussed in the text.

○ Palaeolithic
▲ Early Holocene with pottery (pre-agriculture)
● Early agricultural sites

N

Tigris River
Euphrates River
SAUDI ARABIA
YEMEN
Red Sea
Jordan Valley
Ethiopian Highlands
Nile
Mediterranean Sea
Haua Fteah
Merimde
Fayum
Dakhleh
Bir Kiseiba
Nabta Playa
Wadi Kubanniya
Khartoum
Blue Nile
White Nile
Kadero
River
Tibesti
Hoggar
Adrar Bous
Tagalagal
Amekni
Atlas Mountains
Daima
Shum Laka
Benue River
ATLANTIC OCEAN
Dhar Tichitt
Jenne-jeno
Birimi
Kintampo
Niger River
Ubangi River

0   1000
kilometres

© Cartography ANU 03-047/52

When the Wadi Kubanniya campsites were occupied, the alluvium-filled late glacial Nile valley had both low water levels and low evaporation. The floodplain retained seasonal channels and pools of water – a landscape fairly attractive for mobile hunters and gatherers. As the climate became warmer and wetter at the end of the Pleistocene, the increasing Nile flood-power scoured out the alluvium toward the low sea level, producing an incised valley within which there are very few signs of human settlement. With the eventual rise and stabilization of sea level close to its current height during the early Holocene, the Nile Delta was able to recommence growth, and the valley began to refill with the rich alluvial soil which much later was to support the citizens of Pharaonic Egypt.

According to Stanley and Warne (1993), this stabilization and alluviation commenced between 6500 and 5500 BC, although Hassan (1997a) favors an earlier date, starting about 10,000 BC. Whichever is correct, the striking fact remains that the Nile Valley cannot be demonstrated to have been settled by agriculturalists until about 5500–5000 BC, at which time a full agropastoral economy with pottery was introduced from Southwest Asia. Unless an aceramic Neolithic has been totally submerged beneath the Nile alluvium (Midant-Reynes 2000:106), the Nile Valley received its agriculture even later than Greece and Italy, a circumstance which, from the perspective offered in chapter 2, surely reflects the forbidding presence of the Sinai desert barrier between Palestine and the Nile Delta. Like the Californian Indians, early Holocene Egyptians did not need agriculture and did not seek it, until the tables turned and agriculture sought them as a result of dispersal events originating in the southern Levant.

When agriculturalists first entered the Nile Valley at about 5500 BC, other people who made pottery, collected wild sorghum, and, according to some authorities, herded cattle, had already been living at Nabta Playa and Bir Kiseiba in Egypt's Western Desert for possibly 3,000 years, during periodic and brief phases of wetter climate (Wendorf et al. 2001; Dahlberg and Wasylikowa 1996; Wasylikowa and Dahlberg 1999; Close 1996). There is no clear evidence that such populations were living in the Nile Valley itself at this time, but the possibility must be considered. Mid-Holocene dessication of the Sahara with retraction of the summer monsoon finally led to virtual abandonment of Nabta Playa and other oasis settlements by about 4000 BC, and this might have led to a kind of refuge movement into the Nile Valley, where Saharan people would have met and mixed with the descendants of the Southwest Asian Neolithic population responsible for the introduction of the Southwest Asian agricultural tradition into the Nile Valley about 1,500 years earlier. The resulting amalgam was later to develop into one of the most remarkable civilizations of the ancient world, a true synthesis of the Oriental and the African.

Within the Egyptian Neolithic lifestyle are found a number of specific cultural items of presumed Palestinian origin, even though no precise source can be pinpointed. Such items include side-notched and tanged bifacially flaked arrowheads (Helwan points – Figure 3.5/1 – occurring in the PPNA and PPNB in the Levant as well as in the Nile Valley), pear-shaped maceheads, polished stone axes, footed pottery different from the incised and impressed wares of the Sudan and Saharan early Holocene sites, together with emmer wheat, barley, flax and linen, pigs, cattle, sheep, and goats (Arkell 1975; Hassan 1988; Koslowski and Ginter 1989; Smith 1989; Midant-Reynes 2000). These items appear suddenly in the archaeological record, suggesting introduction, except for the cattle which could, according to recent genetic research, have been domesticated from native stock in North Africa (Bradley et al. 1996; Bradley and Loftus 2000; Hanotte et al. 2002).

The western and southern regions of Arabia were also wetter than now in the early and middle Holocene, so a possibility of cultural transmission across the Red Sea or Bab al Mandab must be borne in mind. However, the archaeological record of Arabia so far reveals no clear evidence for Neolithic agriculture (Edens and Wilkinson 1998), despite a presence in southern Arabia of what appear to be early Holocene check dams for trapping soil (McCorriston and Oches 2001). Phillipson (1998:41) notes the presence of villages during the third millennium BC in the Yemen highlands, with domesticated cattle, sheep, goats, and pigs.

In the Neolithic sites of the Fayum depression, the new agricultural economy is represented by deep storage pits lined with basketry and straw matting that could hold up to 200–300 kilograms of grain. The Fayum lithics, with sickle blades, flake axes, and hollow-based projectile points, show no signs of continuity from the preceding microlithic industries of the region. Like the early pottery of the Levant, that of the Fayum sites is chaff-tempered. These sites have not yielded any architectural evidence, but a site at Merimde near the western edge of the Nile delta, approximately contemporary with the Fayum sites, has yielded remains of post and matting shelters and mud-walled oval houses with semi-subterranean floors, arranged along paths. Merimde appears to have covered about 2.4 hectares and has similar pottery and a similar economy to that of the Fayum.

Indeed, the basal level of Merimde also has Helwan points, clay figurines, and herringbone-incised pottery, the latter paralleled in the Yarmukian ceramic Neolithic of the Jordan Valley (Kantor 1992), a period of small village agriculture with associated goat pastoralism established at about 6000 BC, following the PPNC agricultural decline. This decline in itself also offers a strong hint as to why movement into the Nile Valley might have occurred (Hassan 2002, 2003). Sling stones and spindle whorls also suggest Palestinian connections, but architecturally, of course, these Egyptian villages of wattle and daub huts would have appeared very different from the contemporary mud brick villages typical of the Fertile Crescent.

All of this suggests that the Egyptian Predynastic of the millennium prior to Unification was an amalgam of a Southwest Asian economy and technology with cultural traditions of native Nile and Saharan origin, the latter in evidence in the Badarian Neolithic of Upper (southern) Egypt with its black-topped pottery (Hassan 1997b; Midant-Reynes 2000). Which tradition(s) ultimately dominated, in terms of language and population source, is a matter to be discussed later with respect to the ancestry of the Afroasiatic language family.

As far as the rest of Mediterranean North Africa is concerned, details are few, but the Southwest Asian Neolithic economy with sheep, goats, and cattle can certainly be traced during the sixth millennium BC at the cave of Haua Fteah in Cyrenaica, presumably heading west. A spread of pastoral peoples along the North African coastline is of course likely; pottery and evidence for sheep/goat herding occur along the Moroccan and Algerian coastlines dating from about 5500 BC. But the arrival time of cereal agriculture here is less clear, with current estimates not extending back much before 2000 BC (Holl 1998; David Lubell pers. comm.).

So far, therefore, the spread of the Southwest Asian economy into Egypt and its amalgamation with a Saharan tradition of pottery usage and cattle exploitation seems well documented. South of Egypt, the Fertile Crescent cereals soon met a barrier in the monsoonal summer-rainfall climate of Sudan, and their spread into the more suitable climatic conditions of the Ethiopian Highlands seems to have occurred only within the past 3,000 years (Barnett 1999; D'Andrea et al. 1999; Bard et al. 2000). But what of the rest of the African continent? Here we enter an arena of truly gigantic geographical scale.

The Origins of the Native African Domesticates

Two initial questions arise:

1. Which African crops and animals were domesticated, and where?
2. Were these domestications due to independent actions by native Saharan and sub-Saharan hunter-gatherer communities, to stimuli from the spread of Southwest Asian agriculture and animal herding, or to a combination of both factors? Many archaeologists hold the view that increasing dessication of the Sahara after 2000 BC caused herders to move south, wherever their ultimate origins, perhaps to trigger plant domesticatory processes in the Sahel and savanna regions (Wetterstrom 1998; Neumann 1999; Casey 2000; Hassan 2002; Haour 2003).

First of all, let us see what seems to be generally agreed with respect to plant domestication. Figure 5.1 shows the homelands for a number of African crops according to the botanist Jack Harlan, based on *modern* plant distributions (these homelands were certainly more extensive in the early Holocene). Of these, the most significant include the cereals sorghum (*Sorghum bicolor*) and pearl millet (*Pennisetum glaucum*), both domesticated in the dry Sahel and Savanna zone. Then we have African rice (*Oryza glaberrima*) and Guinea yam (*Dioscorea rotundata*), these being crops of the forest–savanna boundary in West Africa. To these we can add oil palm, cowpea, and groundnut in West Africa, and a number of Ethiopian crops such as finger millet (*Eleusine coracana*), the cereal *tef* (*Eragrostis tef*), ground into flour for making flat bread, and the banana-like plant called *ensete* (*Musa ensete*) that provides an edible pulp from the base of its leaves.

All of the domesticated cereals in the above list are annuals, as they are in Southwest Asia and China. But the African cereals have high tendencies toward cross- rather than self-pollination, and so any selection, unconscious or not, by humans for domesticated phenotypes would only work well if the stocks were planted beyond the ranges of wild stands (Willcox 1989:282; Haaland 1995, 1999; Wetterstrom 1998). This is fairly significant since it is possible that the African cereals might not have been so easy to domesticate as those in Southwest Asia. It may have required a greater degree of focused human intention to complete the process.

This being the case, it might come as no surprise to find that the hard evidence for native African plant domestication is very recent in time, commencing about 2000–1500 BC for pearl millet at Dhar Tichitt in Mauretania and Birimi in northern Ghana, and only during the first millennium BC for sorghum and African rice.[1] These dates are bolstered by the evidence that sorghum and pearl millet were taken to north-western South Asia and possibly the Arabian Peninsula during Late Harappan times (ca. 2000–1500 BC; see chapter 4). Prior to 2000 BC, these millets were apparently exploited in Africa as wild plants, regardless of whether or not they were actually *cultivated*.

Indeed, wild millet grains from a number of species, and impressions in pottery, occur in many sites right across the Sahara dating from about 8500 BC onward (Figure 5.2).[2] People were harvesting morphologically wild sorghum and pearl millet during the early Holocene in northern Africa, although evidence for actual cultivation remains elusive. Nevertheless, Randi Haaland (1999) suggests that cultivation *was* occurring in sites in Sudan by about 5000 BC, and makes the important observation that none of the Sudan Mesolithic sites have stone sickles, hence the potential "forcing" of the domestication process suspected for the sickle-using Levant PPN cultures would not have occurred. Domesticated sorghum is not present in north-eastern Africa until Roman times (Rowley-Conwy et al. 1997).

Given the uncertainty over plant domestication, we may ask what can be ascertained about exploitation patterns of the cattle, sheep, and goats whose bones also occur in many of these early pottery-bearing sites? North Africa had native cattle at the end of the Pleistocene, and it is entirely possible that they were domesticated separately from those in Eurasia. But the evidence for an *independent* domestication process for cattle is uncertain. Cattle bones are first found during the El Adam wet phase, dating to about 8000 BC, at Nabta Playa and Bir Kiseiba in western Egypt (Figure 5.2 and 5.3). Many point out that cattle could not have survived in the wild in such marginal regions, even in the Early Holocene (Marshall 1998; Wendorf and Schild 1998; Wendorf et al. 2001; Hassan 1997b, 2000). Fiona Marshall and Elisabeth Hildebrand (2002) have recently proposed a scenario for early cattle domestication in the eastern Sahara, the main prompting agent being a desire for "predictable access to resources." In other words, groups living in environments wet enough from time to time to support cattle, but not wet enough to support them all of the time, turned to herding them instead, and thus moving to good resource areas as the environment dictated. This scenario is most intriguing, since it tends to reverse the order of events that we witness in the Near East. In Saharan Africa, it seems that cattle herding and pottery-making preceded plant domestication, and animal domestication in its early phases went hand-in-hand with mobility, not sedentism.

At present, these suggestions are still under debate. Many archaeologists are rather skeptical, favoring an appearance of domesticated cattle at only about 6000–5000 BC,

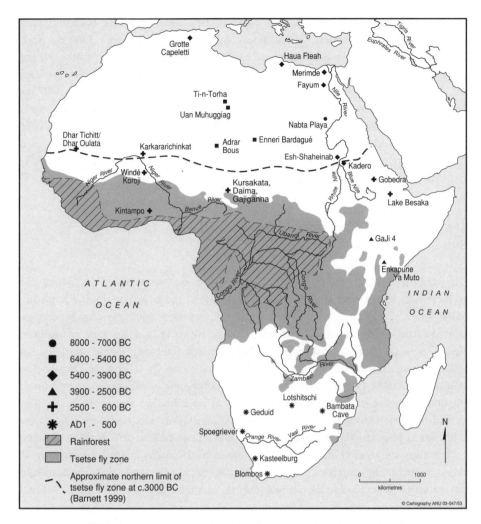

Figure 5.3 Dated sites with evidence for early domesticated cattle in Africa, with the approximate northern boundaries of the tsetse belt shown at 3000 BC and today. Data from Bower 1991; Barnett 1999; Marshall and Hildebrand 2002.

by which time sheep and goat are agreed to have been introduced to Egypt and the Sudan from a Southwest Asian source (MacDonald 2000; Gifford-Gonzalez 2000). At Kadero in Sudan, for instance, domesticated cattle, sheep, and goat all appear together at around 5000 BC. Furthermore, at Dakhleh Oasis in the Egyptian Western Desert, about 400 kilometers northwest of Nabta Playa, neither cattle nor pottery are present in a long and well-dated sequence until about 5000 BC (MacDonald 1998). As Andrew Sherratt (1995:11) points out:

> Although it is still maintained, for instance, that cattle domestication began, quite independently of contemporary Levantine developments, in the Sahara in the seventh millennium BC, what a coincidence it would be if that were really the case!

Africa: An Independent Focus of Agricultural Development? 105

We can conclude at this point that communities with caprovine husbandry are *certainly* attested in northern Africa, particularly in Sudan, at about 5000 BC. Such communities might have been involved earlier in the management of cattle and the cultivation of morphologically wild cereals in the eastern Sahara, the millets perhaps for animal fodder in the first instance (Wetterstrom 1998). Indeed, as we will see later, linguistic reconstructions for the Nilo-Saharan language family make early Holocene cattle keeping or management of some kind in the Sahara a very viable possibility. In addition, Graeme Barker (2003) suggests that Barbary sheep might also have been managed in the early Holocene in the central Sahara. This is rapidly becoming a debate of great interest.

The Development and Spread of Agriculture in Sub-Saharan Africa

The idea that Saharan and Sudanic herders pressed southward out of the Sahara due to increasing dessication after 3000 BC is widespread in the archaeological literature (McIntosh and McIntosh 1988; McIntosh 1994; Casey 1998; 2000). By 2500 BC, domesticated cattle, sheep, and goats had spread as far south as Lake Turkana in northern Kenya, perhaps from a Sudan origin and presumably following a southward retreat, under drying climatic conditions, of the zone of tsetse fly infestation (Figure 5.3) (Gifford-Gonzalez 1998, 2000). These people combined animal herding with hunting and gathering, made pottery, but appear to have had no grain cultivation. The spread of cattle through the belt of tsetse fly infestation occurred very much later with Bantu populations, making an initial appearance below 10°S early in the first millennium AD. Diane Gifford-Gonzalez points to the many central African bovine diseases, including rinderpest, trypanosomiasis (carried by tsetse flies), and malignant catarrhal fever derived from wildebeest, as major reasons for this slowdown in spread.

In the western Sahara, the evidence for cattle exploitation is younger than that in the Nile Valley and Sudan, generally after 3000 BC (Figure 5.3). By 2000 BC, populations belonging to the Kintampo cultural complex of Ivory Coast and Ghana had begun to herd sheep, goats, and possibly cattle. The Kintampo represents a fairly sharp change from preceding Late Stone Age cultures, being associated with wattle and daub house construction in village-sized concentrations, pottery (including figurines of animals and humans), ground stone tools (axes, points, arm rings) and evidence for widespread exchange networks (Anquandah 1993; Stahl 1994:76; Casey 2000; D'Andrea and Casey 2002). Ann Stahl (1993:268) notes that Kintampo pottery is quite homogeneous across a large area, particularly with respect to the popularity of comb-stamped motifs, common also at this time in northern Niger (Roset 1987; Barich 1997).

Evidence from Birimi in northern Ghana shows that Kintampo people grew domesticated pearl millet during the early second millennium BC, as at contemporary sites further north such as Dhar Tichitt in Mauretania (D'Andrea et al. 2001; Neumann 1999; Klee and Zach 1999). In the Kintampo sites they also exploited oil palm and canarium nuts, as did contemporary pottery-using populations living in the Shum Laka rockshelter further east in Cameroon (De Maret 1996; Lavachery 2001). The Kintampo and contemporary sites thus suggest that domesticated pearl millet cultivation was quite widespread in the savanna zones north of the rain forest by 1500 BC, together with caprovine herding.

The Appearance of Agriculture in Central and Southern Africa

In 1500 BC, the whole southern half of the African continent, including the rain forest and probably all regions below the Equator, still remained the terrain of hunters and gatherers. That is, until the unleashing of one of the most striking and far-flung episodes of agricultural spread in world prehistory. This is the spread associated with the expansion of the Bantu languages from their presumed homeland in Cameroon, around and partly through the rain forest and down the whole eastern side of sub-Saharan Africa, until they reached their limits against the Kalahari Desert and the Cape zone of Mediterranean winter rainfall.

By the 17th century, agriculture had spread south to the Great Fish River in South Africa, an area at that time occupied by speakers of the Xhosa language of the Bantu family. The major part of this expansion, from Lake Victoria southward to Natal, took place over 3,500 kilometers in under a millennium. It must rank as one of the most rapid spreads of an agricultural complex, in this case with an Iron Age cultural affiliation, on record (Ehret 1998). We return to the Bantu languages and their dispersal later, but must here plot the archaeological record for the progression of pottery- and iron-using farmers eastward and southward.

Luckily, there seems to be general agreement on the overall dates and cultural contexts for this phenomenon, particularly in the eastern regions of Africa, despite obvious disagreement about the internal structure, the number of "streams," their sources, and so forth (Vansina 1995). In the west, the beginning of agriculture in the rain forest is still rather poorly understood; the appearance here of ceramic and putatively agricultural assemblages seems to be later in time than Kintampo, perhaps commencing with the Imbonga horizon of the Congo Basin about 500 BC (Eggert 1993, 1996; Mercader et al. 2000). But for eastern Africa we can focus on a much clearer overall picture, commencing with David Phillipson's (1993) incorporation of all the early pottery styles in eastern Africa into what he terms the "Chifumbaze complex," commencing west of Lake Victoria in the middle or late first millennium BC (Figure 5.4).

Chifumbaze-style pottery, distinguished by its horizontal zones of incised and stamped patterns, has several local substyles. Urewe around Lake Victoria seems to be the oldest (ca. 500–200 BC), followed rapidly by Kwale of Kenya, Nkope of Malawi and Zambia, Matola of Mozambique (first century AD), and then related Early Iron Age ceramics of the mid-first millennium AD in South Africa. The main burst of expansion probably occurred more quickly than the 1,000-year time span just indicated,

Figure 5.4 Sites of the Chifumbaze complex in eastern and southern Africa. After Phillipson 1993.

being focused in just a few centuries according to David Phillipson (1993:190, 2003; Maggs 1996).

The economy behind this spread, at least in its established phases, contained all the major domesticated animals and cereals of eastern Africa – cattle, sheep, goats, chicken, sorghum, pearl and finger millet. Whether or not these were all present in the earliest Urewe phase is less clear, but Phillipson (1993:188, 2003) believes that they probably were. Evidence for iron working is widespread, and of great importance since iron tools would have allowed very rapid forest clearance for agriculture. Furthermore, by the mid-first millennium AD, the Kenyan coast was coming within the range of trading networks across the Indian Ocean to Southwest Asia and India (Chami and Msemwa 1997), a circumstance which might have played no small role in the arrival in Africa of Southeast Asian crops such as bananas, taro, and the greater yam. The general lifestyle of these agricultural communities was clearly village-based, especially in coastal areas, but greater mobility with a stronger pastoral base developed in the drier inland regions in the south. In general, the whole Chifumbaze complex gives the appearance of being an agro-pastoral "package" with a high degree of cultural homogeneity, notwithstanding strong suggestions of incorporation of native Stone Age cultural traditions in inland regions (e.g., within the Nkope tradition in Zambia).

In terms of directionality, there is perhaps rather less agreement. David Phillipson favors expansion mainly down the eastern side of Africa, with separate Western and Eastern "facies" of the Chifumbaze complex. Christopher Ehret's (1998) reconstruction, based mainly on linguistic evidence, is similar to that of Phillipson. On the other hand, Thomas Huffman, while agreeing generally with Phillipson's concept of a Chifumbaze complex, gives more significance to a secondary spread of the Kalundu Tradition from the lower Congo basin and Angola after AD 100 (Huffman 1989a, 1989b; Herbert and Huffman 1993; Huffman and Herbert 1996). A similar emphasis on this western tradition, but using the term "Western Stream" rather than Kalundu, is favored by James Denbow (1990). According to these scholars, this western stream met and mixed in southeastern Africa with the Kwale and Nkope variants of the Chifumbaze complex which had spread down through eastern Africa from Tanzania.

How such a hypothesis of two separate origins for southern African Bantu-speaking agriculturalists, derived from either side of the African continent, can be equated with the current distribution of the speakers of Western and Eastern Bantu languages is not clear (chapter 10). Currently, Western Bantu languages do not occur in southeastern Africa, as the Huffman and Denbow hypotheses might predict, so we must assume that they have been replaced by the present Eastern Bantu languages. This is an area of great uncertainty.[3]

By AD 500, the dispersal of agricultural village societies through eastern Africa had reached the limits of the summer rainfall belt in Natal. This limit still held when van Riebeeck planted the Dutch flag at Capetown in 1652. However, to the south and west, the fringes of the Kalahari and coastal southwestern Africa had witnessed an introduction of pottery by 2,000 years ago, and sheep herding by 1,600 years ago, but here with no associated agriculture. The introduction of pottery clearly occurred some centuries before any village agriculturalists reached this latitude, and there seems little doubt that the spread reflected the initiative of the native Khoi populations of southern Africa, presumably through connections with herders in Angola or southern Zambia (Sadr 1998; Bousman 1998). The pottery, which is generally pointed-based, shows no affinity to the Chifumbaze complex (Smith 1990; Maggs and Whitelaw 1991; Sealy and Yates 1994). The significance of this is that an indigenous Khoisan hunter-gatherer population of southwestern Africa adopted pottery-making and sheep herding, thereafter remaining in control of their territories until colonial times, owing to the fortunate occurrence of a well-marked southern boundary to the summer rainfall belt upon which the farmers depended. Had southern Africa been entirely monsoonal in rainfall distribution the ultimate result would doubtless have been very different.

Let us now review the germs of an agricultural prehistory for the African continent:

1. With improving climatic conditions, a tradition of wild cereal harvesting (and cultivation?), together with the use of pottery, was spreading through many regions of Saharan and Nilotic Africa by 8000 BC. Some form of cattle management was under development in the eastern Sahara at the same time.
2. Around 5500 BC, the Fertile Crescent agropastoral economy was introduced into Egypt, leading presumably to an amalgamation of both African cattle herders and immigrant Levantine populations. At the same time, sheep and goats (and some West Asian cattle?) were introduced into other regions of northern Africa, such as the Red Sea Hills, via Egypt and possibly also via Arabia/Yemen and the Horn of Africa.
3. Herders moved south with the drying of the Sahara, triggering by 2000 BC the domestication of pearl millet in the Sahel and savanna zones. Herders also moved from Sudan into equatorial east Africa at about 2500 BC. Fertile Crescent crops reached the highlands of Ethiopia at an unknown date, but presumably before 500 BC.
4. After 1000 BC, Bantu-speaking agricultural populations began to spread, in part with a knowledge of iron, from the vicinity of Lake Victoria through eastern and ultimately much of southern Africa. Other Bantu populations spread south through the rain forest into Angola. These spreads triggered an adoption of sheep herding by indigenous Khoisan populations in southern Africa about 2,000 years ago.

All of this is, of course, based essentially on archaeological evidence. Linguistic evidence provides more detail for the recent movements, much in reasonable concordance with the general sequence of events summarized above. As far as the archaeology is concerned, I will close by emphasizing how separate was the course toward farming in sub-Saharan Africa from that in Egypt and the Levant. The Sahara, even allowing for a warmer and wetter early Holocene climate, was clearly a barrier of immense proportions through which neither farmers nor their crops or animals were ever able to spread with ease. Again, the linguistic evidence, with an essential separation of Africans into speakers of Niger-Congo languages in the south and Afroasiatic languages in the north, separated roughly along the southern fringes of the Sahara by Nilo-Saharan languages (the early herders?), reinforces this conclusion very strongly.

Chapter 6
The Beginnings of Agriculture in East Asia

In East Asia, the foci of interest as far as agricultural origins are concerned lie in the middle and lower basins of the Yellow (Huanghe) and Yangzi rivers, and the several smaller river basins, especially the Huai, that lie between them. Like central Africa and India, this is an area of monsoon rainfall that produced a range of domesticated summer cereals, of which rice has evolved into one of the most important foods in the world today (Figure 6.1). In general, this central riverine region of today's China has higher rainfall than Southwest Asia, with a strong and reliable monsoon, although temperature ranges through the year (hot summers, cool to cold winters) are close to those of Southwest Asia by virtue of the similar latitude.

In an overall sense, the agricultural history of central China has been blessed with greater fertility and less environmental degradation than that of Southwest Asia, hence the current massive population density of the region and the absence (so far) of any clear signs of Neolithic environmental damage. However, there are regions of water deficit and long dry season, especially north of the Yangzi and along the southeastern (Fujian) coastline, in the lee of the mountainous island of Taiwan (Figure 6.2). Interestingly, Fujian and neighboring Guangdong are known to have been significant sources of population dispersal not only from Neolithic times onward, but especially during the recent centuries of the "Southern Chinese Diaspora" to Southeast Asia and further regions. The similarly dry region north of the Yangzi was the homeland of Chinese civilization and always a prolific source of both migrating populations and military aggrandizement since at least the Han Dynasty, 2,000 years ago (La Polla 2001).

Early agriculture in China appears to have been as revolutionary as that in Southwest Asia and its development followed a similar early Holocene chronology. Most early Neolithic sites in the middle Yellow valley are on alluvial terraces of fertile wind-blown loess, perfect for rain-fed millet cultivation, derived from Pleistocene

---

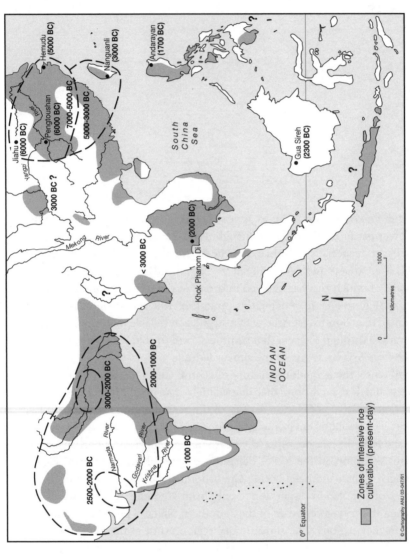

Figure 6.1   The major rice-growing areas (mostly in irrigated fields) of South, East, and Southeast Asia today. Note that intensive rice cultivation tends to correlate with wetter climates (Figure 6.2) on the mainland of Asia, but this is not the case in Island Southeast Asia, where equatorial perhumid conditions are not conducive. Major dated Neolithic sites with rice remains are shown, together with current chronology for domesticated rice dispersal. Modern rice distribution data from Huke 1982b.

Figure 6.3 The locations of major archaeological sites discussed in the text, with the distributions of millet and rice remains.

small numbers in some early Neolithic sites in central China, in both the Yellow and Yangzi basins. Along the Yellow River they are sufficiently common in some regions to suggest a continuity in technological terms from Late Paleolithic into Neolithic, although they cease to occur in some of the major millet-cultivating early villages. If they were indeed reaping knives, their functions were taken over in many of the Neolithic villages by knives of polished stone, shell, pottery, or bone. South of the

Yangzi Basin, microblades are much less common and tend to be outnumbered by the products of pebble-based industries. Occurrences of microblades far to the south at Xiqiaoshan in Guangdong Province and Bukit Tengkorak in Sabah are later in date and it is simply uncertain at this stage if these can be linked to any of the more northerly occurrences.

There is no evidence for primary agricultural development in any other regions of China outside the middle portions of the Yellow, Huai, and Yangzi basins, even though southern China was believed for many years to have been the homeland for rice domestication (T. T. Chang 1976). This remained so until modern archaeological and paleoclimatic data became available to highlight the deep significance of the Yangzi Basin (Glover and Higham 1996; Lu et al. 2002). Claims for very early Holocene agriculture associated with pebble tools in southern Chinese limestone caves have not been convincing to date, and current evidence suggests that rice farming spread into Guangxi about 4500 BC (Tracey Lu, Chinese University of Hong Kong, pers. comm.).

New research, however, hints that significant material south of the Yangzi might be eluding discovery. The caves of Xianrendong and Diaotonghuan, about 150 km south of the Yangzi in northeastern Jiangxi Province, have an appearance of wild rice phytoliths in their deposits at about 11,000 BC. This Terminal Pleistocene appearance was followed by an absence of rice during the ensuing cold phase of the Younger Dryas, then by a return of rice phytoliths, now claimed to be partly from a domestic-ated population, at about 8000–9000 BC (Figure 6.4) (Zhao 1998; Lu et al. 2002). The absence of rice phytoliths during the Younger Dryas reinforces the important observation that we are here right on the northern edge of the range of wild rice distribution, a circumstance that in itself could have been crucial in the shift to domesticated rice, particularly if the transition reflected rapid fluctuations in supply

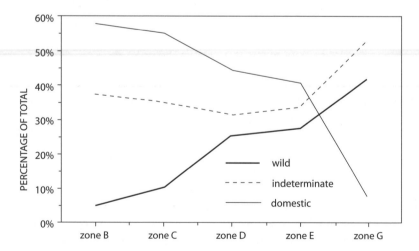

Figure 6.4 Trends in rice exploitation in Diaotonghuan cave, northern Jiangxi, based on analysis of *Oryza* phytoliths by Zhao Zhiyun. Zone G is dated to ca. 11,000 BC, Zone E to ca. 8000–9000 BC, Zone D to ca. 7000 BC, and Zone C to ca. 6000 BC. From Zhao 1998.

owing to climatic oscillations (Yan 1992, 2002; Bettinger et al. 1994; Bellwood 1996b; Cohen 1998).

The inhabitants of these two Jiangxi caves also used round-based and cord-marked pottery, without tripods or ring feet, perhaps as early as 9000 BC.[2] Pig and chicken bones are present, most likely from wild populations in the lower layers of Diaotonghuan, but probably domesticated later. Ground stone axes and arrowheads appear at about 7000 BC. Yuchanyan Cave in Hunan Province, to the southwest of Xianrendong, has also produced rice remains and pottery dating prior to 8000 BC (Chen 1999). But apart from these cave discoveries, information on the actual transition phase into agriculture in China is still sparse.

Far away on the northern side of the Yangzi and Yellow basins lie the fertile agricultural landscapes of Manchuria (especially Liaoning and Jilin), homeland of China's Qing rulers (1644 to 1911) and an important player in the debate to be reviewed in chapter 10 about the origins of the Altaic languages. The paleobotanical record for early agriculture here is sparse, but Gideon Shelach (2000) is a strong advocate for an independent development of plant cultivation in Manchuria. My own view is that a contemporary and linked development of millet cultivation occurred in both the Yellow Basin and Manchuria prior to 6000 BC, while allowing that the early Neolithic of Manchuria (Xinglongwa culture, ca. 6200–5400 BC) is rather different in style from its central Chinese contemporaries. Possibly, native hunter-gatherers here adopted agriculture on the far northern edge of its range, as in Europe and northern Japan (Nelson 1995; Hudson 1999). This region was also the source for the first farmers of the Korean Peninsula, who arrived there with millets by the commencement of the Chulmun pottery phase, prior to 3500 BC. Rice arrived later in Korea, perhaps being transmitted by sea from eastern China (Bale 2001; Crawford and Lee 2003).

Environmental Factors and the Domestication Process in China

The oldest full Neolithic *villages* in China with undisputed evidence of agriculture, in both the Yellow and the Yangzi basins, date to about 7000/6500 BC. By this time, climates were similar to those of the present and postglacial sea level had reached about 10 meters below the present one. Between 6000 and 2000 BC, the sea level peaked above the present level and then began to drop again. Average annual temperatures in the Yellow and Yangzi basins rose to slightly above those of the present and summer monsoon rainfall increased, as revealed by animal distributions and pollen studies (Zhang and Wang 1998; Lu 1998a).

The oldest sites with evidence for agriculture occur in the zone of mid-Holocene overlap between the geographical distributions of wild rice and foxtail millet, from the Yangzi northward through the Huai Valley toward the Yellow River (Figure 6.3). Wild rice *Oryza rufipogon*, progenitor of the domesticated *Oryza sativa*, grew during the mid-Holocene climatic optimum to as far north as the Huai. The Yellow Basin, however, had winters too cold and dry for rice to flourish. Here, on the loess soils drained by the Yellow River and its tributaries, the two most significant wild cereals were the progenitors of the domesticated millets, *Setaria italica* (foxtail millet) and the less important but more drought-resistant *Panicum miliaceum* (broomcorn millet). Both foxtail and broomcorn millet are reported widely in the Neolithic cultures of eastern Europe and the western Eurasian steppes, but how this relates to their contemporary presence in China is unknown. It would appear that northern China still has the oldest dates for their cultivation, from about 6500 BC onward.

Exactly how these crops came to be domesticated and planted in an annual agricultural round is unclear, but a likely scenario reads as follows. As in Southwest Asia, the practice of replanting to maintain or increase supplies of cereals must have developed either during or soon after the Younger Dryas, particularly in "edge-of-range" areas subject to sharp fluctuations in supply. If planting of seed stocks occurred in new territories away from the zones of wild distribution, as hypothesized for Southwest Asia, then each year the relative proportion of naturally non-shattering grain in the crop could have increased, especially if a few panicles were partly ripe at the time of harvest and if the harvesting was by cutting with a knife/sickle or by uprooting. Such a trend would have been assisted by the tendency of wild foxtail millet (*Setaria viridis*) to ripen over a very drawn-out period of up to four months, such that many stands when harvested might be expected to have contained some grain already ripe, amongst which there would be some which had the genotype for non-shattering (Lu 1998b; 2002). Under such circumstances it is not hard to imagine strong selective pressures coming into effect.

Once planting and seed selection began the whole system would have become locked into a snowball of no return, with a rapid domination of non-shattering seed stock, reduction of glume toughness due to winter storage, and a trend toward synchronous ripening, exactly as in the Levant. Indeed, we have no evidence to suggest that the overall sequence of events leading to cereal domestication in China need have been different from that in the Levant. Even the Younger Dryas could have played a similar role in inducing a commitment to planting. But demonstration and proof are elusive indeed.

One problem with the above scenario is that, as noted in chapter 3, quick selection for non-shattering seeds requires use of a sickle or knife, or uprooting. In the rice zone centered on the Yangzi, we lack any pre-agricultural examples of potential harvesting knives, unless some of the rare microblade discoveries can be placed in this category. Such tools are also rare in the oldest rice-zone Neolithic villages (Pengtoushan, Hemudu layer 4), so here the processes of change are harder to visualize. Quite possibly the rice plants were simply uprooted, and a layer up to one meter thick at Hemudu, containing enormous quantities of rice stalks and leaves, suggests that this might have occurred. Whatever the answer, rice appears to have been first domesticated right on the northern edge of its distributional range, in the middle Yangzi and Huai valleys, suggesting, as noted above, that environmentally induced fluctuations in supply were perhaps more important than they were for the hardier millets. Indeed, it seems possible that the domestication process actually *began* with rice and spread later to the millets, but this cannot yet be demonstrated with certainty. My own feeling is that rice domestication is likely to have preceded that of the millets, and indeed might have stimulated the latter as farming populations tried moved north (Bellwood 1995, in press).

Another area of uncertainty concerns the issue of variation within *Oryza sativa*. Were the oldest cultivated rices along the Yangzi ancestral to both the *japonica* (short-grained) and *indica* (long-grained) varieties of modern rice, as suggested by Zhang Wenxu (2002)? Were they ancestral just to *japonica* and was *indica* domesticated separately somewhere to the south, in northeastern India or Thailand perhaps, as suggested by Yo-Ichiro Sato (1999)? Or was *japonica* rice domesticated along the Huai and *indica* along the Yangzi, as suggested by Zhang and Wang (1998)? Many possibilities are being suggested,[3] and the issue is important because it can reflect on the possibility that domesticated Asian rice has more than one homeland. The archaeological likelihood that native *indica* rices were domesticated in northeast India should not be taken lightly, but this need not mean that the domestication process was entirely independent of that for the *japonica* rices in China. A totally independent domestication of rice in India or Mainland Southeast Asia, given current chronologies, seems unlikely, but this need not imply that other wild races, apart from those native to the Yangzi, were never domesticated.

The Archaeology of Early Agriculture in China

Were rice and the millets domesticated within one cultural system, or separately? Rice is present in large quantities by soon after 7000 BC in the Peiligang culture site of Jiahu in the Huai valley, Henan Province, this being a site with a material culture that falls within the Yellow River millet-based tradition (Zhang and Wang 1998; Lu 1998a; Chen 1999). Thus, there is clear overlap in the distributions of the two sets of cereals. Two completely separate origins of agriculture in China are counter-indicated by this pattern. A single center, albeit large and diffuse, seems far more likely (Cohen 2003).

Turning now to the early Neolithic archaeological record, non-readers of Chinese luckily have the masterly 1986 summary of the situation by the late K. C. Chang (Chang Kwang-chih), now a little out of date but still very thorough in its presentation. In the first two editions of this book (1963 and 1968), Chang presented his view that the southern and eastern Chinese Neolithic developed as a result of "Lungshanoid" diffusion from a Yangshao/Longshan agricultural and Neolithic heartland in the North China plain (the Zhongyuan), located around the junctions of the Yellow, Wei, and Fen rivers, where the oldest millet-bearing sites occur. At that time, before the early Yangzi rice-bearing sites were discovered, a Zhongyuan cultural origin was postulated for the whole Chinese Neolithic, and the Lungshanoid was perceived in terms of a secondary dispersal of populations with rice cultivation, stone adzes, and reaping knives, and a set of specific pottery forms (including tripod vessels) to as far south as Guangdong.

By the time of Chang's third edition (1977), archaeology was entering an anti-diffusionist and anti-historical phase. Chang was now beginning to regard the Lungshanoid more as a result of interaction than of diffusion or population dispersal from a heartland region. The most recent fourth edition (1986) maintains this view, wherein the Lungshanoid is seen purely as a convergence phenomenon between an array of later Neolithic cultures located across southern and eastern China during the fourth millennium BC. Interestingly, however, there are hints in a 1996 paper that Chang might have been returning to almost his original views just prior to his death in 2001, owing to the new Yangzi early rice discoveries, since he was suggesting that the Neolithic cultures of southern China and Taiwan could have had a Yangzi origin linked to an actual population dispersal (Chang and Goodenough 1996). By this time, the concept of central China as a large region of early agriculture involving both rice and millets, rather than merely a Yellow River (Yangshao) source with millets only in the first instance, was rapidly becoming more widely accepted.

I have to state at the outset that I believe Chang was generally correct in his early interpretations in the 1960s, even if some of the Yangzi early rice details were still unimagined at that time. I suspect also that we were both in accord in our views during the late 1990s, since I had many occasions to talk with him during visits to Taipei in connection with my research on Austronesian origins. The reason why Late Neolithic China became such a cozy club of cultural interaction at about 3500 BC is because the cultures concerned were already culturally and historically closely related, and probably shared an ultimate common regional origin at the beginning of the Neolithic, at 6500 BC or before. This does not mean that the Chinese Neolithic evolved from one small ancestral society, but it does mean that it evolved within a region characterized by a high degree of communication and interaction, perhaps focused on a chain of quite closely related ethnolinguistic populations.

The Archaeological Record of the Early Neolithic in the Yellow and Yangzi Basins

The archaeological record of the Yellow River points toward an oldest appearance of the Neolithic at about 6500 BC, amongst a group of sites located along the eastern foothills of the highlands that form the western edge of the North China Plain. Other sites were perhaps also located around the edge of the Shandong highlands, at that time either an island or linked to the mainland by swamps and marshes. Annual temperatures at this time were 2–4°C above the present and summer growing-season rainfall might have been a little higher than now. The loess soils of the Yellow valley were capable of supporting permanent agriculture when sufficient moisture was present; loess also has a self-fertilizing propensity, bringing up mineral nutrients by capillary action. Under such conditions, according to Ho (1975), millet agriculture could have supported at least 400 people per square kilometer on a fairly permanent basis.

The oldest Yellow River Neolithic sites formed a continuum with four internal clusters, two centered respectively around the major sites of Cishan and Peiligang

(Figure 6.3), with two smaller groups in the Wei and upper Han valleys. Related but slightly later sites occurred as far west as eastern Gansu (Dadiwan culture), and as far east as Shandong (Houli and Beixin cultures). All the sites of the core region centered around Cishan and Peiligang date between 6500 and 5000 BC. They usually cover between one and two hectares, and they often occur at high densities (e.g., 54 Peiligang-type sites, all under 6 hectares, in an area of 17 by 20 kilometers in central Henan, according to Li Liu 1996:267). Houses were round or square with sunken floors, interspersed with storage pits. Over 300 such pits occurred at Cishan, 80 with millet remains, with a total millet storage capacity estimated for the site of about 100,000 kilograms of grain (Yan 1992). Polished stone axes and serrated stone or shell reaping knives, plus pestles and mortars with four short legs, all attest to an agricultural economy, combined with the keeping of pigs, dogs, and chickens and the collection of considerable quantities of nuts (walnuts, hazelnuts, and *Celtis* seeds). Some sites have cemeteries of extended burials, reinforcing the obvious hints of large and densely concentrated populations.

The pottery of these northern cultures is remarkably alike, and includes simple forms of cord-marked, combed, fingertip-impressed, or incised vessels (even some painted), often on tripods or pedestals. While there are minor cultural differences over the large area represented by these sites, given the overall homogeneity of pattern it is not too hard to visualize a common ancestral form of culture, located quite close in time, from which all these descendant cultures of the Yellow River Basin originated.

Southerly sites of this group, for instance Lijiacun in the upper Han Valley, often contain small quantities of rice as well as millet (Wu 1996). Jiahu in Henan, a Huai basin site with a material culture very close to that of the Peiligang culture, is especially important, as already noted, because it actually appears to have had a rice-based economy. Dated to between 7000 and 5800 BC, Jiahu possibly covered 5.5 hectares, with sunken floored houses in Peiligang style, a cemetery, pottery kilns, and a Peiligang polished stone industry including axes, reaping knives, and typical Peiligang stone mortars on four low legs. The site also has evidence for domesticated pig, dog, and (claimed) cattle; for rice-tempered, cord-marked, and sometimes red-slipped pottery (with some possible sign precursors for later Chinese writing); and quantities of rice husks, grains, and phytoliths (Zhang and Wang 1998; Li et al. 2003). Some of the pottery resembles that from Pengtoushan, a rice-based site in the middle Yangzi Basin, to which we turn below. This is of course extremely significant – Jiahu has two faces, one facing north, one south. It renders untenable the idea that the millets and rice were domesticated by separate communities living in splendid isolation.

It is, of course, the recent discoveries located in the lakelands to the immediate south of the middle Yangzi Valley that have revolutionized our understanding of Neolithic China. The one-hectare site of Pengtoushan near the shoreline of Lake Dongting was founded around 7000 BC, perhaps slightly earlier than any of the millet-based sites of the Yellow River, although the available chronologies still lack the refinement to make this certain (Hunan 1990; Yan 1991). Its layers, 3 to 4 meters thick, contain traces of sand-floored houses, cord-marked and red-slipped pottery with rice-husk tempers, and fairly simple flaked lithics. Reaping knives and mortars of the Peiligang type are absent, the latter perhaps because rice was normally boiled in pots and eaten as a whole-grain food rather than ground into flour (Fujimoto 1983).

Another rice-bearing site at Bashidang, located about 25 kilometers north of Pengtoushan, covered 3 hectares and contained a mixture of houses with sunken floors, ground-level floors, and even pile constructions, together with a starfish-shaped earthen ceremonial platform and a defensive ditch (Hunan 1996; Chen 1999; Yasuda 2000). Bashidang also belongs to the Pengtoushan culture (7000 to 5500 BC), and is stated to contain wooden spade blades and unspecified tools of bone, wood, and bamboo. Chen Xingcan (1999) notes the presence of pottery features found also in the Peiligang culture and in Jiahu. Bashidang has yielded bones of possibly domesticated pigs, dogs, chicken, and cattle, and prolific rice remains (over 15,000 grains).

Presumably, the rice eaten in these early Neolithic sites in the middle Yangzi was grown in wet swampy fields of some kind, close to lakes and river banks. Water caltrop and lotus roots were also grown, like rice both water-loving plants. Although no fields have survived from early Neolithic times, new discoveries at Chengtoushan and Caoxieshan, near Pengtoushan, have yielded remains of small bunded rice fields dating from about 4500–3000 BC, these being so far the oldest actual rice field remains discovered in China (He 1999).

According to Yan Wenming (1992), the majority of the earliest rice-yielding sites known in China are located in the middle and lower Yangzi Basin. Here, we un-doubtedly have at least one origin region for rice cultivation, perhaps the only one. The "heartland" of East Asian agriculture, extending from the Yangzi to the Yellow rivers and incorporating the Pengtoushan and Peiligang/Jiahu foci for both rice and the millets, has given rise to the dispersal of the ancestors of almost half of the world's modern population.

Later Developments (post-5000 BC) in the Chinese Neolithic

By 5000 BC, the Yellow and Yangzi basins were well populated with Neolithic settlements (as this book goes to press, Chinese archaeologists are preparing publications on new sites in the lower Yangzi, with rice cultivation and pile dellings prior to 6000 BC). What kind of cultural relationships can we see now? Are traces of a common regional origin for Chinese Neolithic cultures still evident?

The distributions of the major Chinese Neolithic traditions between 5000 and 3000 BC are shown in Figure 6.5. In the north, the best-known tradition of this period, the Yangshao, was a direct descendant of the Peiligang culture. Also, with little doubt, it was a major (if not the major) direct ancestor of the Han Chinese cultural and linguistic tradition with its 4,000-year dynastic history. Yangshao sites occupy a large area of the middle Yellow River and its tributaries, stretching from Hebei westward to Gansu. Sites are large, with major excavated villages such as Banpocun, Jiangzhai, and Beishouling covering between 5 and 6 hectares, considerably larger than the

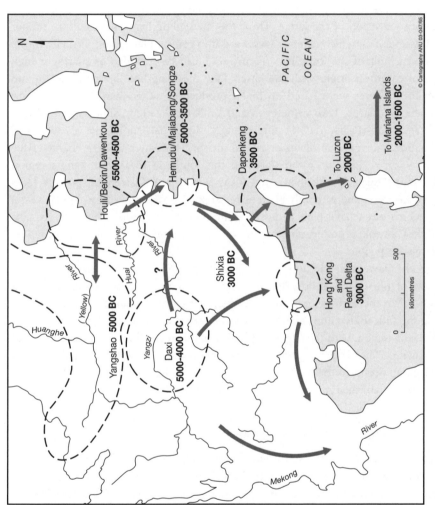

Figure 6.5 The distributions of archaeological cultures in China between 5000 and 3000 BC, showing likely early axes of communication and population spread. Based in part on Chang 1986.

average for the preceding Peiligang culture. The fine details of Yangshao assemblages are not of direct concern here, but village plans, cemeteries, and pottery kilns all attest complex, possibly even ranked, societies with developed technology. Yangshao people also had a system of notation, often scratched on pot rims, which might have been in part ancestral to the Old Chinese script of the Shang dynasty (ca. 1300 BC).

East of the Yangshao we enter the zone of the Dawenkou tradition of Shandong. The first phases of this tradition, termed Houli and Beixin (ca. 6000–4500 BC), were very closely related to the Peiligang culture in pottery forms and may be regarded as an eastern extension of the latter. Thus, the succeeding Dawenkou culture proper (ca. 4500–2500 BC), which extends westward into central Henan and virtually meets the eastern limit of the Yangshao (Figure 6.5), can be regarded as sharing a high degree of common origin with the latter. Like the Yangshao, both the Beixin and Dawenkou cultures were based on millet production rather than rice. Dawenkou settlements are large, with cemeteries and similar indications of social complexity to the Yangshao (Pearson 1981). Interestingly, the burials sometimes show cranial deformation and removal of upper lateral incisors, the latter being a characteristic of several early Neolithic assemblages to the south, in the lower Yangzi region (Majiabang), Fujian (Tanshishan), and Taiwan (Beinan). Dawenkou pottery lacks paddle impression and is mainly plain or red-slipped, characterized by angular vessel forms which often have high pedestals with cut-out decoration. Symbols are also found on Dawenkou pottery that might be related to the notational system used by the Yangshao people.

Thus, the Dawenkou tradition may be seen as a potential link between the Yangshao tradition of the inland Yellow River and the Neolithic panoply of cultures that extends down the eastern coastline of China, to as far as Guangdong and Taiwan. During the fifth millennium BC these coastal cultures included the Majiabang of the Yangzi delta region, with the slightly older Hemudu culture immediately to its south in Zhejiang. The Daxi culture and its predecessors (Zaoshi/Chengbeixi and Tangjiagang) occupied the middle Yangzi, and, by perhaps 3500 BC, the Dapenkeng culture was established in Taiwan and coastal Fujian (Figure 6.5).

South of the Yangzi – Hemudu and Majiabang

The Hemudu culture, to the south of Hangzhou Bay, was one of the most dramatic discoveries by Chinese archaeologists during the 1970s. Prior to the discovery of Pengtoushan, Hemudu was the oldest rice-bearing site in China, dated at its base to 5000 BC. The oldest Hemudu pottery (from the basal layer 4) is fairly unusual in the Chinese context since it lacks ring feet and tripods. It is possible that it represents the incorporation into the rice-growing Neolithic landscape of a group not immediately derivable from the other cultural regions along the middle Yangzi, further upstream. Interestingly, portable pottery stoves occur in this culture, similar to a more recent tradition of pottery stoves still used on boats by "sea nomads" in the islands of Southeast Asia (especially in the southern Philippines and northern Borneo). Hemudu people therefore had links with coastal maritime cousins. Sites of Hemudu type occur on offshore islands in northern Zhejiang, attesting development of a raft or canoe technology (wooden paddles have been found in Hemudu itself).

Hemudu is of extreme importance because of the sheer quantity of material culture recovered, some with remarkable parallels in later cultures across the Pacific, a circumstance perhaps not totally coincidental. The site was located in a marshy zone close to the sea, and waterlogging has led to excellent preservation of organic remains. The most striking items include stepped and shouldered stone adzes with knee-shaped wooden handles, bone spades, pottery spindle whorls, bamboo matting, foundations for long timber houses raised on piles with mortise and tenon joinery (identical to joinery found in Majiabang sites, below),[4] and pieces of bone carved with zoned geometric and curvilinear patterns. Pig, dog, and perhaps water buffalo were domesticated and their droppings have been found in the site. In one 400-square-meter area a layer of rice husks and plant debris up to one meter thick was found, evidently the remains of an ancient threshing floor. According to Yan Wenming (1991, 1992), the site yielded rice remains equivalent to 120,000 kilograms of fresh grain.

Above the basal layer 4 at Hemudu comes layer 3, with pottery like that from Majiabang, a site a little further to the north near Shanghai. The Majiabang culture lies immediately south of the Dawenkou and was culturally quite close to it, as was its Songze cultural successor, both dating overall to 5000–3000 BC. Majiabang pottery has tripods and pedestals, is sometimes red-slipped but rarely cord-marked. It resembles Beixin and Dawenkou pottery fairly closely but is less obviously related to that from Peiligang and Yangshao, as one would expect from the greater degree of geographical separation. Majiabang sites have alluvial or lake-edge locations, suitable for the rice-growing economy of this culture (rice husks were also commonly used to temper pottery).

The Hemudu–Majiabang sequence thus incorporated the results of contacts from at least two directions. The rice-growing economy was presumably brought down the Yangzi or Huai, whereas some of the pottery features of rice-growing Majiabang reflect contacts with millet-growing Shandong to the north. Such linkages suggest that by 5000 BC, if not before, all of the rice and millet-growing cultures of central China, from the middle Yangzi to the environs of Beijing, were interrelated by contacts visible through their farming economies and pottery styles, just as they were a thousand years earlier through the intermediacy of Jiahu. The significance of a cultural ancestry founded in an original Peiligang–Jiahu–Pengtoushan Neolithic heartland of the seventh millennium BC will later become evident.

The spread of agriculture south of Zhejiang

Turning now to the Neolithic archaeological record south of Zhejiang, it is necessary first to recap on a few observations made above. The Neolithic cultures examined so far, in the Yangzi and Yellow Valleys, as well on the coasts of Shandong, Jiangsu, and Zhejiang, show a great deal of intertwining in economy and style, with the most "idiosyncratic" perhaps being that represented in the basal layer 4 at Hemudu, a factor which could in part be due to the superb level of preservation and sheer quantity of material in this site. By 5000 BC, other indications of regionalism in artifact style were undoubtedly starting to appear, and we may expect that by this time there was a separation forming into a Sinitic tradition to the north of the Yangzi (Yangshao and Dawenkou cultures) and a non-Sinitic tradition to the south, ancestral to many of the cultural minority populations of present-day southern China (Hemudu, Majiabang, Zaoshi, and Daxi cultures).

The expansion of Neolithic cultures through southern China seems to have reflected two axes (Figure 6.5). One extended from the Zaoshi, Tangjiagang, and Daxi cultural spheres (ca. 5000 to 3000 BC) of the Middle Yangzi lake district, running southward along river valleys to Guangdong (including Hong Kong) and Hainan. The other extended down the coastline with its myriad offshore islands formed as a result of the postglacial sea-level rise, from Zhejiang to Fujian, Guangdong, and Taiwan. The latter spread appears to have been roughly contemporary with the westerly Zaoshi/Daxi-influenced spread and was probably fueled in part by the succession of rice-growing cultures in the Shanghai/Hangzhou Bay region. Taiwan, with its Austronesian heritage, belongs in my view to this latter tradition, while the inland axis represents that which spread the oldest Neolithic assemblages into Hong Kong, Vietnam, and Thailand.

As far as the eastern stream of Neolithic spread southward is concerned, the Majiabang culture of the Shanghai region had developed into the Songze culture by 4000 BC. Songze pottery is characterized by a continuing presence of tripods and high pedestals, many of the latter with decorative cut-outs.[5] There is a continuation of red-slipping, incised decoration, and cord-marking, as there is in the poorly dated Tanshishan culture to the south in Fujian, which may be derived from the Songze. In northern Guangdong, the site of Shixia reveals the oldest dated presence of rice so far in southeastern mainland China, in plentiful quantities, at about 3000 BC. The Shixia pottery resembles that of both Songze and the following jade-rich Liangzhu culture in the lower Yangzi delta region (ca. 3300–2300 BC; Huang 1992), and Shixia has also produced jade bracelets, rings, and earrings of Liangzhu type. All of this suggests to Charles Higham (1996a, 2003) that the spread of rice cultivation down the Chinese coast through Fujian into Taiwan, and into northern Guangdong, had occurred by 3000 BC.

Currently, the earliest Neolithic sites in Guangdong and Hong Kong appear to lack evidence for rice and to have a fabric tradition emphasizing the use of barkcloth, beaten with distinctive grooved beaters, rather than of textile fibers spun with spindle whorls and woven on a loom. Charles Higham (1996a:79) regards these assemblages as the handiwork of hunters and gatherers ("affluent foragers"). I am not so sure of this, since these earlier sites are numerous, prolific in material culture, often located near good rice-growing soils, and certainly not suggestive of any continuity from the preceding Hoabinhian pebble tool complex. There are strong hints amongst them of a level of population density that we would associate with farming, commencing by perhaps 4000 BC. Given recent findings of plentiful rice and millet remains in sites of this period in southern Taiwan (chapter 7), further research is required, especially in the examination of soil samples for phytoliths of rice and other crops.

The oldest Neolithic sites in Hong Kong and the Pearl Delta (for instance, Xiantouling, Dahuangsha, Hac Sa Wan, Sham Wan, and Chung Hom Wan) date between 4200 and 3000 BC, and comprise numerous coastal midden-like deposits on sandy soils, up to about 1.5 hectares in size (Meacham 1978, 1984–85, 1994; Chau 1993; Chen 1996; Yang 1999). Their painted and incised pottery styles resemble the contemporary Tangjiagang and Daxi pottery complexes of the Middle Yangzi, as well as the Shixia assemblage further north in Guangdong. They are generally associated with stepped and shouldered stone adzes, and they also contain large numbers of barkcloth beaters. Bill Meacham (1995:450) thinks these populations all grew rice and I tend to agree with him, but the evidence is currently very fugitive. The economy of the earliest Neolithic in far southern China still remains something of a mystery, and we will probably have to settle, in the final resort, for a mosaic pattern of regional crop dominances, from rice through to tubers (particularly taro) and tree products.

In general, the pre-Neolithic assemblages of southern China and Mainland Southeast Asia belong to a pebble-tool tradition known as the Hoabinhian, a complex of assemblages found very widely in caves and shell middens that extends back into the Pleistocene and which is clearly indigenous to the region. Although many archaeologists have attempted in the past to show that the Hoabinhian underwent an *in situ* transformation to agriculture, no convincing demonstration of this interesting possibility has ever been presented. Occasional occurrences of sherds of cord-marked pottery in the upper layers of caves probably reflect disturbance, and although the Hoabinhians were clearly plant users and perhaps even plant managers, we have no indication that they ever developed systematic field agriculture (Bellwood 1997b; Higham 1996a; Higham and Thosarat 1998a). Southern China, together with the mainland and island regions of Southeast Asia, belongs to a zone of strong and clear-cut Neolithic spread. Only when we move as far east as New Guinea, as we do in the next chapter, does the fundamental picture change.

Chapter 7
The Spread of Agriculture into Southeast Asia and Oceania

I must confess to having some degree of vested interest in the contents of this chapter since my research career has been spent in the region of concern. Hence I make no apology for presenting a basic summary of views which I have published elsewhere,[1] together with acknowledgments of counter-views where such seem necessary. In terms of environment, history, language, and biology, over the long term, we have essentially three regions of concern, all of course overlapping greatly in environmental and historical context but nevertheless being coherently identifiable. These regions are *Mainland Southeast Asia* (Burma across to Vietnam and West Malaysia), *Island Southeast Asia* (Taiwan, Philippines, Indonesia, East Malaysia, Brunei), and *Oceania* – the islands of the Pacific Ocean from New Guinea eastward (Figure 7.1). The latter are normally divided into the regions termed Melanesia, Micronesia, and Polynesia, although in recent years a tradition, started by Roger Green (1991), has developed of using the term *Near Oceania* for the islands to as far east as the Solomons, and *Remote Oceania* for those beyond. Pleistocene hunter-gatherers reached the islands of Near Oceania over 30,000 years ago, but only Austronesian agriculturalists were able to reach the islands of Remote Oceania, and only within the past 3,500 years.

Within this vast region, only the New Guinea Highlands have yielded data suggestive of independent agricultural origins. The other regions of Southeast Asia and Near Oceania, excluding the New Guinea Highlands, reflect varying degrees of agricultural spread through landscapes previously settled by hunter-gatherers, in extremely complex trajectories. Descendants of some of the earlier populations still survive as hunter-gatherers today, particularly amongst lowland sago gatherers in New Guinea (Roscoe 2002), and as the Negritos (Semang and Agta) of the Malay Peninsula and Luzon (Figure 2.5). Even where they no longer survive as discrete hunter-gatherer populations, the genes of some of these former inhabitants are still present in many regions.

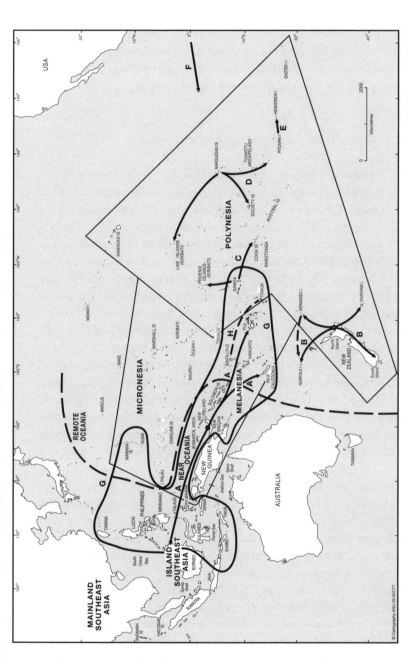

Figure 7.1 Major archaeological regions of Southeast Asia and Oceania. This map also shows some Neolithic instances of long-distance seaborne movement of lithic resources. A) obsidian from New Britain to Borneo and Fiji, over a total of 6500 kilometers at 1000 BC; B) obsidian from Mayor Island after AD 1200; C, D, and E) movements of adze-making basalts in Eastern Polynesia after AD 800 (Weisler 1998; Di Piazza and Pearthree 2001); F) movement of sweet potato from Central or South America into Eastern Polynesia, ca. AD 1200(?). The enclosed area marks the currently known distribution of the red-slipped and stamped pottery styles thought to be associated with the early phases of Austronesian dispersal (information is lacking from much of western Indonesia).

This is significant because, as in Europe, questions arise for Southeast Asia as to the contribution of indigenous hunter-gatherer populations to the eventual agricultural mosaic. Such contributions, especially in a purely genetic sense, are still visible and important today in the Malay Peninsula, parts of the Philippines and eastern Indonesia, and in Island Melanesia. In terms of material culture and language, however, it is my impression that continuity from the pre-agricultural past has not been particularly strong, except in Near Oceania and amongst *some* of the groups who continued a hunting and gathering lifestyle into the recent past (see chapter 2).

The Background to Agricultural Dispersal in Southeast Asia

To understand the creation of a human cultural kaleidoscope on the scale of Southeast Asia, we need first an awareness of some of the major environmental factors. The whole region is tropical, but there is decreasing dry season length as one moves into the equatorial zone between 5° degrees north and south, within which rain falls during much of the year (Figure 6.2). Equatorial populations tend to be small, and in eastern Indonesia often dependent for subsistence on tubers and tree crops such as yams, taro, sago, and bananas. The equatorial zone with its ever-wet rain forest is not especially suitable for rice agriculture (Figure 6.1), and in prehistoric times it would appear that rice and foxtail millet were gradually dropped from the roster of cultivated plants as agricultural populations moved through this zone and eastward into Oceania. According to Robert Dewar (2003), unreliable rainfall regimes in southern Taiwan and the northern Philippines could also have filtered out annual cereals in favor of crops with less seasonal rainfall requirements, such as taro and other tubers (see also Paz 2003). Today, and presumably also in the agricultural past, the greatest population densities occur in the monsoon regions where rainfall distribution is reliable and where rice can flourish, especially in alluvial landscapes in southern China, northern Mainland Southeast Asia, parts of the Philippines, Java, Bali, and the Lesser Sundas.

Nowhere in Southeast Asia is there currently any good evidence for a presence of any form of food production before 3500 BC. This is significant, given that rice was well domesticated by at least 6500 BC along the Yangzi. As with the movement of agriculture from Southwestern Asia into India, so in Mainland Asia we also see an apparent slowing down, in this case apparently caused by cross-latitudinal movement and perhaps hunter-gatherer resistance, rather than by any crossing into a completely different rainfall regime (both China and Southeast Asia are part of the same monsoonal summer rainfall belt). Once on the move, however, Neolithic complexes with pottery, polished stone adzes, shell ornaments, spindle whorls, backcloth beaters, and presumed-domesticated bovids, pigs, and dogs replaced the older hunter-gatherer archaeological complexes of the early and mid-Holocene with orderly precision, generally moving down a north–south axis from southern China through Mainland Southeast Asia toward the Malay Peninsula, and through Taiwan and the Philippines toward Indonesia.[2] Within the Indonesian equatorial zone, the spread of agricultural populations was converted to a latitudinal axis out of the Borneo–Sulawesi–Moluccas region, on the one hand westward into western Indonesia, the Malay Peninsula, and Madagascar, and on the other hand eastward into Oceania.[3] The presence of an independent focus of early food production in New Guinea complicates the Oceanic story, and we return to this later.

Early Farmers in Mainland Southeast Asia

The mainland of Southeast Asia consists of upland terrain separated by a number of very long river valleys, most rising in the eastern fringes of the Himalayas and following generally north–south directions (Figure 6.3). These rivers include the Irrawaddy, the Salween, the Chao Phraya, the Mekong, and the Red (Hong), and all must have served as major conduits of human population movement in the past. Thus, it is not surprising that the Neolithic archaeology of this region shows much stronger connections with China than it does with India, an axis of relationship to be dramatically overturned at about the time of Christ with the spread of the Indic cultural influences which came to dominate the Hindu–Buddhist (pre-Islamic) civilizations of Southeast Asia. Prior to 500 BC we see very few connections between India and Southeast Asia, except for the presumed spreads westward of Austroasiatic (Munda) languages, a topic to which we return in chapter 10.

Unfortunately, the recent rather troubled history of much of Mainland Southeast Asia means that we have few data from countries such as Burma, Laos, and Cambodia. Matters are improving, but for present purposes we must rely on the richer records from Vietnam, Thailand, and Malaysia. In northern Vietnam, the earliest Neolithic is a little obscure with respect to origin and economic basis, as it is along the Guangdong coast. The oldest pottery in Vietnam is cord-marked, vine- or basket-impressed. Because it often occurs in apparent overlap situations with Hoabinhian stone tools in caves, there has been a long-standing assumption that indigenous Hoabinhian hunter-gatherers might have played some role in the beginnings of agriculture in this region. This is still not well demonstrated, but there are coastal Neolithic sites such as the estuarine shell-midden at Da But and the small open site of Cai Beo which probably date to about 4500 BC, and are thus contemporary with the oldest Guangdong Neolithic sites. Da But in particular has oval-sectioned untanged stone adzes that could be derived from Hoabinhian/Bacsonian prototypes. Charles Higham (1996a:78) notes that these sites have no certain traces of agriculture and may thus have been essentially hunter-gatherer and fishing settlements.

Apart from these early and somewhat puzzling sites, Vietnam became part of a widespread Mainland Southeast Asian Neolithic expression between 2500 and 1500 BC, an expression characterized by a distinctive style of pottery decoration comprising incised zones filled with stamped punctations, often made with a dentate or shell-edge tool. Sites of this complex in the Red River Valley are attributed to the Phung Nguyen cultural complex and overlap with the development of bronze metallurgy. It is in this phase that a number of artifact types with strong southern Chinese parallels

---

make a solid appearance. These include shouldered stone adzes, polished stone projectile points, stone bracelets and penannular earrings, and baked clay spindle whorls. More importantly, site sizes during this period became greatly increased, reaching 3 hectares in the cases of Phung Nguyen and Dong Dau. Many sites of this period (including some in southern Vietnam) have good evidence for rice cultivation from about 2000 BC onward, an economy which would have flourished on the fertile alluvial plains of the Red River (Nguyen 1998). Cattle, buffalo, and pigs might have been domesticated during the late Neolithic, but precise data are not available.

Firm data for a spread of rice agriculture by at least 2300 BC are more clearly attested for Thailand (Glover and Higham 1996). As in northern Vietnam, the oldest pottery on the Khorat Plateau of northeastern Thailand and in the lower Chao Phraya Basin has zoned incision infilled with punctation, together with less flamboyant forms of paddle impression, including cord-marking. The former type of decoration is widespread between 2300 and 1500 BC at sites such as Nong Nor, Khok Phanom Di, Non Pa Wai, Tha Kae, and Ban Chiang,[4] and we will meet it again far to the south in Malaysia. The economic record for the Thai Neolithic is especially rich, and most sites have evidence for rice cultivation from the beginning, especially in the form of husk temper in pottery. Nong Nor in central Thailand has no trace of rice at 2500 BC, but nearby and closely related Khok Phanom Di has plentiful evidence from 2000 BC onward, even though the excavators regard the rice as imported in the basal layers (Higham 2004). In northeastern Thailand, Ban Chiang has rice remains which may predate 2000 BC, but in the drier southern part of the Khorat Plateau the first agricultural sites seem to postdate 1500 BC (e.g., Ban Lum Khao in the upper Mun Valley, a west-bank tributary of the Mekong). Domestic animals include pig and dog, but neither seem to be present (except for wild pig) at Nong Nor. At Khok Phanom Di, only the dog is likely to have been domesticated, together possibly with a species of jungle fowl. Domesticated cattle (probably of gaur or banteng ancestry) were present by at least 1500 BC in northeastern Thailand, at Non Nok Tha, Ban Lum Khao, and Ban Chiang. Domesticated water buffalo in Thailand only occur in the Iron Age, after 500 BC.

The wide distribution of the distinctive incised and zone-impressed pottery across parts of far southern China, northern Vietnam, and Thailand after about 2500 BC suggests that this region might express a similar phenomenon to that recognized in other regions of agricultural spread, namely an early homogeneity followed by a later regionalization of cultural style. Because of gaps in the record it is difficult to be certain about this, but this impression has also been remarked upon by Charles Higham (1996c). We certainly find a similar situation in the oldest Neolithic in much of Island Southeast Asia and the western Pacific, and it also becomes very apparent when we examine the oldest Neolithic complexes south of Bangkok, in Peninsular Thailand and Malaysia.

The peninsula from southwestern Thailand to Singapore is about 1,600 kilometers long and a maximum of about 300 kilometers across. It is entirely tropical, with a monsoonal summer wet season in the north, and an equatorial climate with no marked dry season in the south. The interior is mountainous, especially in Malaysia, and contains many areas of limestone with caves and rockshelters. The majority of archaeological assemblages come from cave locations, a circumstance which doubtless biases the record, but from Hoabinhian into Neolithic times there was certainly a very marked shift in cave usage from habitation to burial functions. This may reflect the arrival of agriculture, promoting a sedentary lifestyle in villages as opposed to a mobile lifestyle using temporary camps in caves.

Peninsular Neolithic pottery has cord-marked decoration, with rare incision or red-slipping, often with tripod feet or pedestals. Distinctive vessel tripods with perforations to allow hot air to escape during firing have been found in about twenty sites down almost the whole length of the peninsula, from Ban Kao in western Thailand to Jenderam Hilir in Selangor (Leong 1991; Bellwood 1993). These represent a very consistent tradition of pottery manufacture, although whether exchange or colonization, or both, can explain the widespread homogeneity is not so clear. Stephen Chia (1998) has shown that much of the Malaysian Neolithic pottery was locally made, an argument which would support a hypothesis of colonization rather than exchange. Gua Cha in Kelantan also has fine incised pottery with zoned punctation dating to about 1000 BC, like that discussed above from Vietnam and Thailand (Adi Taha 1985). Cemeteries of extended burials also contain (as grave goods) stone adzes with quadrangular cross-sections, some shouldered or "beaked," stone bark-cloth beaters and bracelets, bone harpoons and fishhooks, and shell beads and bracelets. Many of these artifacts are closely paralleled in the related site of Khok Phanom Di, and especially in the site of Ban Kao, in west-central Thailand, so much so that the term "Ban Kao culture" has been used to designate this peninsular complex by the excavator of Ban Kao, Per Sørensen (1967).

Sørensen had no doubt after his 1965–66 excavations at Ban Kao that the tripod pottery had an origin in "Lungshanoid China," referring at that time to the first edition (1963) of K. C. Chang's book on Chinese archaeology. Since that time, no archaeology has come to light in support of a *direct* derivation of the Ban Kao culture from a Neolithic assemblage in southern China, but the fact remains that the Mainland Southeast Asian Neolithic *as a whole* shows very marked signs of an ultimate southern Chinese inspiration. Sørensen was clearly on the right track. The Ban Kao culture represents a clear movement of Neolithic assemblages down the Malay Peninsula at about 2000–1500 BC, although south of Khok Phanom Di there is no direct archaeological evidence for rice, so the nature of the driving economy remains something of a mystery.

Summarizing the Neolithic record for the Southeast Asian Mainland, we have indications of the spread of a well-defined incised and stamped pottery style associated with rice cultivation in far southern China, Vietnam, and Thailand, between 2500 and 1500 BC. A contemporary but slightly different style of tripod pottery spread down the Malay Peninsula after 2000 BC. These spreads appear to have been rapid, extensive, and with little sign of continuity from local Hoabinhian forebears. The question remains, if there was a movement of farmers out of southern China at this time, did it occur down the major rivers, around the Vietnam coastline, or by both routes? Only future research is going to answer this question.

We must also note, finally, that some recent palynological and phytolith research hints that plant management activities combined with forest clearance might have been present well before 2500 BC on the Southeast Asian mainland (Kealhofer 1996; Penny 1999). Forest clearance does not, of course, necessarily imply agriculture. But the possibility of a Hoabinhian focus on plant management activities long prior to the spread of formal field agriculture, probably with a strong tuber and arboricultural content, must not be overlooked. This might help to explain some of the mysteries of the oldest Neolithic in northern Vietnam referred to above, although we must remember, as we will see more clearly in Island Southeast Asia, that it is unreasonable to expect all sites with a Neolithic material culture to produce evidence for rice agriculture. The absence of rice in some Neolithic sites in Thailand, such as Nong Nor and Non Pa Wai, need not mean that the inhabitants were hunter-gatherers of Hoabinhian ancestry. Their material culture negates this entirely, and it is more likely that the "Neolithic economy" was not monolithic but flexible in differing situations.

Early Farmers in Taiwan and Island Southeast Asia

We now move southeast to the island chains which festoon the coastline of Southeast Asia. In the Taiwan archaeological record we witness the same phenomenon as in the early mainland Neolithic, namely a basal homogeneity followed by increasing regionalization. The oldest Neolithic culture in Taiwan, the Dapenkeng,[5] spread all round the coastline of Taiwan after 3500 BC, with a cord-marked and incised pottery style so similar everywhere that spread with a new population from Fujian replacing or assimilating the earlier Changbinian (a facies of the Hoabinhian) seems assured. Close relationships occur with slightly older Fujian pottery assemblages dating to ca. 4500 BC from sites such as Keqiutou and Fuguodun, the latter on Jinmen (Quemoy) Island.[6]

The Dapenkeng culture is known to have had rice and foxtail millet production, pearl shell reaping knives, spindle whorls, and barkcloth beaters, as a result of recent excavations in the twin sites of Nanguanli East and West that lie buried under 7 meters of alluvial plain near Tainan (Tsang Cheng-hwa in press). Rice is also present as impressions in sherds in a late Dapenkeng context, ca. 2500 BC, in the site of Suogang in the Penghu Islands (Tsang 1992). Furthermore, a pollen diagram from Sun-Moon Lake in the mountainous center of Taiwan indicates a marked increase in large grass pollen, second growth shrubs, and charcoal particles soon after 3000 BC (Tsukada 1967).

Following the period of the Dapenkeng culture there seems to have been internal continuity in Taiwan into the succeeding but more varied cultures of the second millennium BC. These later cultures include, amongst others, the Yuanshan in the Taipei Basin, the Niuchouzi in the southwest, and the Zhangguang and Beinan on the southeastern coast. With the passage of time, so the cultural landscape became more diversified into regional patterns. Yet, at the same time, there was also continuing contact with the Chinese mainland, as may be seen in pottery and stone tool relationships between Taiwan and contemporary mainland cultures such as the Tanshishan of northern Fujian, dating to the third and second millennia BC. Basalt from Penghu was also widely used for adze-making in Taiwan from at least 2500 BC onward (Rolett et al. 2000).

The main point to emphasize is that the Taiwan prehistoric sequence shows no sign of an island-wide *replacement* of population or cultural tradition following the establishment of the Dapenkeng culture at about 3500/3000 BC. There was a relatively continuous history of cultural development into the recent ethnographic past, indicating that Austronesian-speaking populations occupied the whole island until major Chinese settlement began in the 17th century AD. It was at some point in this development, about 2500–2000 BC according to the archaeological record, after the Dapenkeng pottery style had evolved into various regional cord-marked or red-slipped expressions, that the first Neolithic farmers moved south into the Philippines and eventually Indonesia.

Taiwan does provide one other interesting perspective on early farmers and their environmental impact. The Penghu (Pescadores) Archipelago consists of low, sandy, and fairly barren islands that lie in the Taiwan Strait, about 50 kilometers from Taiwan and 100 kilometers from the Fujian mainland. This is a dry rain-shadow area. Today, the Penghu Islands support a small population dependent on fishing and peanut cultivation, there being no good rice soils and little surface water. Field surveys and excavations here by Tsang Cheng-hwa (1992) uncovered 40 prehistoric sites, all of which dated to approximately the third millennium BC, when people grew rice (as noted above, rice impressions occur in pottery from the site of Suogang). The remaining sites belonged mainly to the period with Chinese trade ceramics during and after the Song Dynasty, starting about a millennium ago. The intervening 2,500 years would appear to be associated with no archaeological record at all.

Can we perhaps see in Penghu the results of an early collapse of an agricultural economy under conditions of high population and fairly aggressive rice cropping in a fragile environment? Such a collapse would have been localized, since no such gap is reported from anywhere on Taiwan itself, a much more fertile island. But, if this suggestion is correct there must have been repercussions for increasing agricultural investment, as in the Levantine PPNC or the late pueblo cultures of the American Southwest. It is impossible to *prove* that a collapse of this kind led to the movements of farming pioneers south into the Philippines, but the time and place are right in a general sense.

In the Philippines, northern Borneo, and many regions of eastern Indonesia the oldest Neolithic pottery is characterized by simple forms with plain or red-slipped surfaces, sometimes with incision or stamped decoration and sometimes with perforated ring feet. This phase has no very clear internal divisions at present and it seems to date overall to between 2000 and about 500 BC, when it transforms into a series of more elaborately decorated Early Metal Phase ceramics. In the light of recent research in the Batanes Islands and the Cagayan Valley of northern Luzon, the origins of this red-slipped pottery can be traced to eastern Taiwan assemblages of about 2000 BC, still only hazily reported but presumably the immediate ancestors of the later second

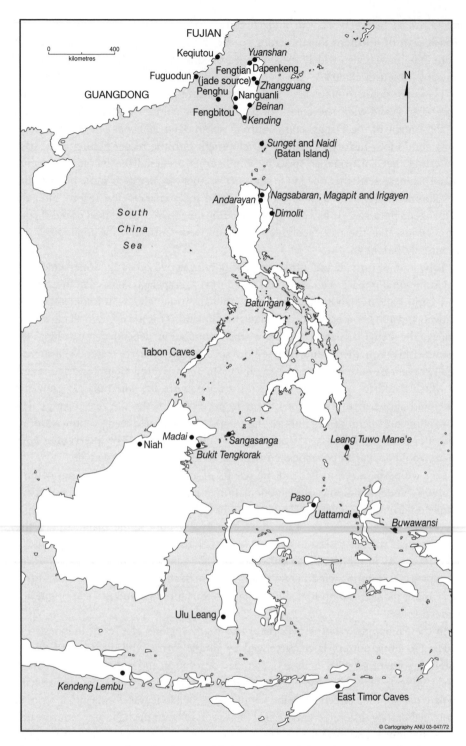

Figure 7.2 Sites (in italics) that have yielded Neolithic red-slipped pottery in Island Southeast Asia.

millennium Beinan and Zhangguang cultures of the east coast and the Yuanshan of northern Taiwan (Figure 7.2). The Fengtian nephrite source in Eastern Taiwan was also a source of Neolithic jade (Lien 2002), used not only in Taiwan but also exported to the Philippines, where bracelets and earrings of Taiwan jade have been found in Neolithic and Early Metal Age sites (dating overall to 1500 BC to early AD) at Anaro on Itbayat Island in the Batanes, at Nagsabaran in the Cagayan Valley, and in Uyaw Cave on Palawan Island.[7]

In the Philippines, this type of red-slipped pottery occurs with dentate-stamped and incised motifs in the Magapit and Nagsabaran shell midden sites in the lower Cagayan Valley of northern Luzon. Dates are from 2000 BC onward at the site of Pamittan, and some of the pottery is remarkably similar to contemporary dentate-stamped pottery from the Lapita cultural complex in Melanesia and western Poly-nesia (Figure 7.3). Open sites at Andarayan in the Cagayan Valley and Dimolit in northeastern Luzon have yielded rice husks in sherds, dated to about 1600 BC at Andarayan (Snow et al. 1986; Michael Graves pers. comm.). Similar pottery, but circle- rather than dentate-stamped, comes from the site of Sunget on Batan Island (Batanes), where it dates from about 1200 BC (Bellwood et al. 2003).

Pottery of similar red-slipped type and second millennium BC date to that from Luzon also comes from Bukit Tengkorak in Sabah (Bellwood and Koon 1989), here with an agate microblade industry of long drills used for shell-working, and imported obsidian carried 3500 kilometers from a source on New Britain in the Bismarck Archipelago (Figure 7.1). Bukit Tengkorak has some rather limited evidence for rice husks in pottery (Doherty et al. 2000:152), and also large quantities of fishbone and fragments of pottery stoves of a type used recently by Bajau "sea nomads" on their boats. The implication here is for a maritime economy, mobile, trade focused, with only a passing interest in field agriculture. Other assemblages with similar red-slipped pottery, but without the agate microblades and New Britain obsidian, and so far also without rice, come from northern Sulawesi, the northern Moluccas, and eastern Java (Figure 7.2). In the rockshelters of Uattamdi and Leang Tuwo Mane'e such assemblages were probably established by 1300 BC or before. Here they also occur with polished stone adzes, shell beads and bracelets, and bones of pig and dog, none present in any older assemblages in this region (Bellwood 1997a).

The implication of all this archaeological material is that a marked cultural break with the Preceramic lithic industries of the Indonesian region occurred across a very large area, possibly commencing by 2000 BC in the Philippines and appearing close to New Guinea, after the loss of rice cultivation, by about 1400 BC. Some of these societies had strong maritime leanings and it was probably from one or more of them that the first settlers reached the Mariana Islands in western Micronesia by 1500 BC or before, situated across a phenomenal 2000 kilometers of open sea to the east of their likely homeland in the Philippines. By 1400 BC, culturally related colonists were also moving into Melanesia to spread the Lapita culture over 5500 kilometers east-ward from the Admiralty Islands to Samoa. The Lapita movement took only 500 years or less to reach its limits in the central Pacific, one of the fastest movements of a prehistoric colonizing population on record.

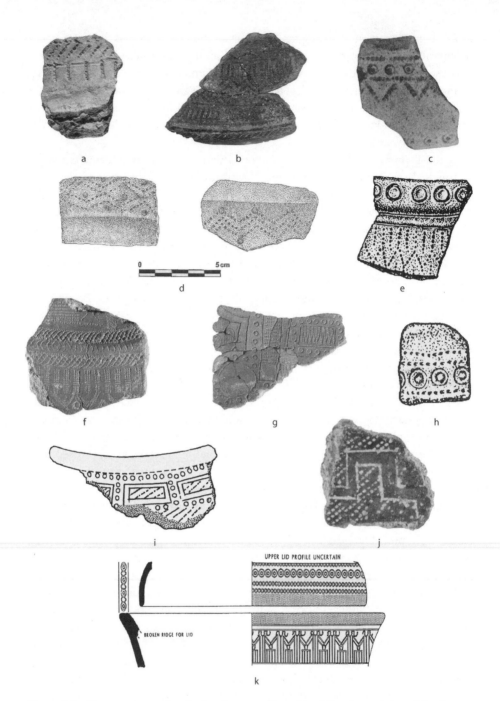

Figure 7.3 Dentate-stamped and related pottery from Island Southeast Asia and Lapita sites in Melanesia (all apart from a) are red-slipped and have lime or white clay infill in the decoration): a) Xiantouling, Guangdong coast, China (pre-3000 BC?); b) Magapit, Cagayan Valley, Luzon (1000 BC); c) Yuanshan, Taipei, Taiwan (1000 BC); d) Nagsabaran, Cagayan Valley (1500 BC); e and h) Batungan Cave, Masbate, central Philippines (800 BC); f) Kamgot, Anir Islands, Bismarck Archipelago (Lapita – 1300 BC); g) Lapita (Site 13), New Caledonia (1000 BC); i and j) Achugao, Saipan, Mariana Islands (1500 BC); k) Bukit Tengkorak, Sabah, 1300 BC.

All of this leads to the fairly astonishing observation that, between 2000 and 800 BC, assemblages with related forms of red-slipped and stamped or incised pottery, shell artifacts, stone adzes, and keeping of pigs and dogs (neither of these animals being native in most of the regions concerned) spread over an area extending almost 10,000 kilometers from the Philippines through Indonesia to the western islands of Polynesia in the central Pacific. The economy driving this expansion was strongly maritime in orientation, but these people were also farmers with domesticated animals. We have no evidence that any of them grew rice in the islands beyond the Philippines and Borneo. It seems that this subtropical cereal faded from the economic repertoire as populations moved toward eastern Indonesia. In the western Pacific, however, there is good archaeological evidence from Lapita sites for production of a range of tubers and fruits, out of a roster of native plants that includes yams, aroids (especially taro), coconut, breadfruit, bananas, pandanus (a starchy fruit), canarium nuts, and many others, all originally domesticated in the tropical regions from Malaysia through to Melanesia (Kirch 1989; Lebot 1998). Neolithic populations either domesticated them, or acquired them from native populations, as they moved southward and eastward through the islands.

Meanwhile, it should be noted that the red-slipped pottery horizon does not appear in western Indonesia, although the Neolithic archaeological record here is currently only poorly understood. Most early pottery assemblages in western Borneo and Java tend to have cord-marked or paddle-impressed surface decoration without red slip. In Borneo, recent research in Kimanis Cave in East Kalimantan by Karina Arifin (pers. comm.) indicates that some sherds of this kind of pottery contain rice impressions. Similar rice impressions occur in pottery in the Niah Caves in Sarawak and in the cave of Gua Sireh near Kuching, the latter with an actual rice grain embedded in a sherd dated to about 2300 BC by AMS radiocarbon (Ipoi and Bellwood 1991; Bellwood et al. 1992; Beavitt et al. 1996; Doherty et al. 2000). My impression from these data, still admittedly faint and unconfirmed by any coherent information from Java or Sumatra, is that a paddle-impressed style of pottery with widespread evidence of rice spread from the Philippines, where similar impressed pottery occurs in Palawan, through Borneo and presumably into western Indonesia, after 2500 BC. This spread was apparently independent of that which carried red-slipped pottery and a non-cereal economy into the Pacific. Its source remains essentially unknown. However, the Malay Peninsula, as noted above, has a Neolithic series of assemblages derived from southern Thailand rather than from Indonesia.[8]

Exactly how this Sundaland series of paddle impressed assemblages relates to the red-slipped pottery tradition to the east is unknown, but a homeland for both amongst populations located in Taiwan and the Philippines at about 2500/2000 BC seems likely. We seem to be looking at a geographical and economic bifurcation, the western branch emphasizing farming and open field cereal cultivation, the eastern branch trending toward a tuber and fruit (arboricultural) focus with a stronger maritime component. Pacific peoples such as the Polynesians are clearly very suitable candidates for descent from the latter tradition. But, as we will see, there is more to early agriculture in the Pacific than simple expansion from Southeast Asia.

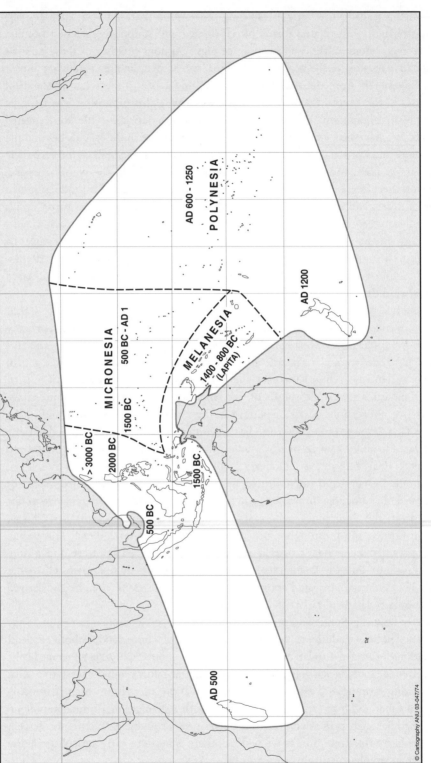

Figure 7.4 The distribution of Austronesian languages, from Madagascar to Easter Island, together with archaeological dates for the spread of Neolithic cultures. These dates also track the initial human settlement of Remote Oceania (as delineated in Figure 7.1).

© Cartography ANU 03-047/74

Early farmers in the Pacific

As far as the human settlement of the islands of Remote Oceania is concerned, we have essentially three "bouts" of colonizing activity. The first, that described as Lapita by archaeologists, led to the settlement of the islands of central and eastern Melanesia, plus western Polynesia to as far east as Samoa, by makers of red-slipped and stamped pottery (Figure 7.4). This occurred very rapidly between about 1350 and 800 BC. Following 800 BC there was an apparent standstill in the central Pacific (Fiji, Tonga, Samoa). The so-called "Nuclear" Micronesian islands, excluding the Mariana and Palau groups in the west, appear to have been settled about 2,500–2,000 years ago, possibly from Melanesia. The final push involved the archipelagos of eastern Polynesia (including New Zealand), settled by aceramic populations between AD 600 and 1250 (pottery-making was abandoned in western Polynesia soon after 2,000 years ago).

This chronology of colonization with its apparent standstills probably owes little in any direct sense to factors of agricultural causation (Bellwood 2001e). The standstills themselves reflect factors of distance, of sea-level fluctuation – many atolls were submerged by higher sea levels 3,000 years ago – and of maritime technology. Large and efficient canoes were not invented instantly, and sea craft underwent technological improvement as the wave of human expansion spread eastward (Anderson 2000). The movement also reflected desires to exploit naïve bird faunas, as well as social factors that encouraged fissioning, and doubtless many other motives, including an interest in finding new sources of exotic exchange items. However, agriculture *was* a crucial factor in the overall equation. Without it, the Pacific would never have been colonized at all on any long-term basis, at least not the smaller islands in Micronesia and Polynesia. Early colonists faced not only sea gaps of increasing width moving eastward into the Pacific Ocean, but also islands of decreasing size and diminishing native subsistence resources. The latter meant that the agricultural economy as a *portable* subsistence lifeline came into its own, together with an expectable focus on marine resources. With the development of substantial ocean-going sea craft, the whole Pacific beyond the Solomons was opened for human settlement.[9]

Thus, we see a vast sweep of agricultural populations moving into new terrain from southern China, through Southeast Asia and into the Pacific Islands, over a time span of about 5,000 years, commencing at about 3500 BC in Taiwan and culminating in the Maori colonization of New Zealand around AD 1250. Within this span of island colonization there are some intriguing instances of long-distance exchange, especially of lithic raw materials (Figure 7.1), that bring home to us the real extent of voyaging ability. Yet, there are two very significant regions that did not form part of this huge voyaging network. One was Australia, a continent of consistent and continuing hunter-gatherer population until European contact. The other was the interior of the massive island of New Guinea, lying just south of the Equator to the east of Indonesia, but so very different from the major Indonesian islands in terms of agricultural, linguistic, and biological history. New Guinea, and particularly the New Guinea Highlands, forms a unique cultural world with a seemingly independent trajectory into some form of food production.

The New Guinea Agricultural Trajectory and its Role in Pacific Colonization

Between 1972 and 1977, excavations led by Jack Golson revealed a series of intercutting drainage ditches belonging to six separate phases of activity, all dug into a swamp on the Kuk tea plantation in the Wahgi Valley, Papua New Guinea Highlands.[10] Radiocarbon dating and a series of dated ash showers established that the sequence might have commenced as early as 8000 BC, although the first phase with really substantial ditches, up to 3 meters deep and traceable over a length of at least 500 meters, was dated at that time to about 5000 BC. The six phases were separated by phases of non-usage of the swamp and succeeded each other through prehistory into recent times, the most recent being characterized by a grid of drainage ditches like those used ethnographically in the New Guinea Highlands for growing the introduced American sweet potato. The assumption made was that the main crops grown at this altitude (1,550 meters above sea level) in the early Holocene would have been taro (*Colocasia esculenta*), pandanus, Australimusa bananas (a native New Guinea section of bananas with vertical fruit stalks), yams, and sugar cane. Today, yams grow in the highlands up to about 1,700–2,000 meters, bananas to about 2,000 meters, and taro to about 2,700 meters (Bayliss-Smith 1988). Presumably, in the last glacial period, these plants would not have grown at all in the broad fertile highland valleys that lie above 1,300 meters, and would have been restricted to lowland areas and to the steeply sloping terrain that surrounds the highlands in most directions. As postglacial temperatures rose, people perhaps moved with the rising upper limits for these plants into the highlands, then as now a region on the "edge of the range" for agricultural activity and thus subject to stress factors that might have stimulated a focus on planting rather than simple collecting.

Since the Kuk findings were published there has been considerable discussion as to just how "agricultural" were the early Holocene Kuk ditches (Spriggs 1996). Some of these questions have now been answered by new research by Tim Denham and his colleagues (2003). Through an analysis of pollen, phytoliths, and starch grains from the Kuk soil profiles, including the fills of prehistoric ditches, they believe that the Kuk landscape was partially cleared for banana cultivation by 4500 BC, and that some of the bananas at this time were being deliberately grown in mounds close to the edge of the swamp. Slightly uncertain evidence for shifting cultivation extends back as far as 8000 BC, but this team dates the first drainage ditch networks to only 2000 BC, younger than the original date favored by Golson. Starch grains indicate cultivation of taro, and phytoliths indicate cultivation of bananas of the Eumusa section to which most modern commercial bananas belong, rather than bananas of the previously suspected but less significant Australimusa section. If this research is upheld, it will make an important case for origin of many cultivated bananas and some taros in New Guinea, rather than in the islands of Southeast Asia, thus marking an important contribution of Papuan horticulture to Austronesian crop rosters as Austronesian settlers moved into the Melanesian region from Indonesia about 1400 BC.

This research reinforces very strongly the idea that some form of gardening economy with planting of tubers and fruit-bearing small trees, utilizing fertile swamp soils wherever they were available, was present in the New Guinea Highlands in the early Holocene. This qualifies to be considered as true and primary agriculture, albeit not a highly expansive system in the absence of cereals and domesticated animals. No evidence is available to indicate that tropical regions further west in Indonesia witnessed such developments prior to the arrival of Austronesian farmers, so perhaps we can ask why agriculture developed specifically in the New Guinea Highlands, and what were its repercussions in terms of population growth and dispersal.

Firstly, New Guinea is unique in having a continuous highland spine almost 2,000 kilometers long, as opposed to the smaller discontinuous areas of highland characteristic of other large tropical islands such as Borneo and Java. The New Guinea highlands, with their large valleys and dense populations, lie mostly between 1,300 and 2,300 meters above sea level (ground frosts start at 2,600 meters). They thus form a large island of non-tropical climate, at least in terms of temperature, within the vast terrain of equatorial lowland which extends right through Island Southeast Asia and into the western Pacific. Such a special kind of region might, perhaps, be expected to have had a special kind of prehistory.

Secondly, by 8500 BC the New Guinea Highland late glacial climate had ameliorated to present conditions and the tree-line had risen almost 2,000 meters in a remarkably short period, perhaps only one millennium, to reach its present altitude at ca. 4,000 meters above sea level (Swadling and Hope 1992; Haberle et al. 1991). A warm climatic situation with a relatively non-seasonal rainfall distribution pattern was thus established, suitable for the development of traditional New Guinea agricultural systems focused on tubers and tree products.

Thirdly, technology seems to have changed very little before, during, or after the advent of agriculture in New Guinea. We see no rapid spreads of new art styles, pottery (never manufactured in the main highlands), or new forms of flaked lithics. Neither are there any recognizable harvesting tools in the oldest agricultural contexts. Except for the appearance of ground stone axes at an uncertain date in the early Holocene, the archaeological face of early agriculture shows no real change at all from the hunter-gatherer background assemblages of the Late Pleistocene. This suggests a fundamental continuity of cultural tradition across the transition, even though the tempo of technological change seems to have been much less marked than in regions such as Southwest Asia, China, or Mesoamerica.

Could New Guinea agriculture have developed first in the lowlands and then spread into the highlands? I rather doubt it, as does Paul Gorecki (1986). The altitudinal locations of early sites in New Guinea have been plotted by Simon Haberle (1994), and a virtual absence of sites of all periods between 500 and 1,300 meters above sea level is very apparent. Coastal sites are also few, and show no signs of early agriculture. Finds of plant remains dated to ca. 4000 BC at Dongan in the lowland Sepik basin (candlenut, canarium, coconut, pandanus, possibly sago) are of great interest here, but all could have been exploited from self-propagated rather than planted trees (Swadling et al. 1991). In the New Guinea lowlands there is no hard evidence for actual plant cultivation, as opposed to possible management, prior to the arrival of Austronesian-speaking populations within the past 3,000 years. The highlands also fit best with the "edge-of-the-range" theory for agricultural origins, as it has been applied to Southwest Asia and China (Bellwood 1996b).

Given the rather special environment of the New Guinea Highlands within the Southeast Asian context, it may be suggested that any early Holocene stress factor, such as a long episode of locally unprecedented drought (Brookfield 1989), would have encouraged a switch to swamp-edge planting of wild tubers and fruits at key altitudes in favorable locations. The unstable climatic conditions at the end of the last glaciation could thus have led to fluctuations in food supplies, and in the case of Kuk Swamp the transition to agriculture occurred within the zone where many cultivated plants, such as taro, banana, and sugar cane, were approaching the altitudinal limits of their growth ranges. Once swamp-edge planting commenced, probably in combination with some degree of swiddening on adjacent terrain (Bayliss-Smith 1988; Denham et al. 2003), it is not hard to visualize communities being propelled toward increasing investment in new forms of production, such as the grassland tillage and tree-fallowing described for the later phases at Kuk by Jack Golson and Don Gardner (1990).

As for agricultural dispersal, it can only be stated that New Guinea does not show the expansive trends so typical of other regions such as the Middle East, Mesoamerica, and China. The archaeological and linguistic records do not indicate any major colonizations from the highlands out into the islands of Melanesia, and the total absence of any agricultural spread into Australia is very striking, despite the fact that it was probably still joined to New Guinea by dry land when the agricultural developments began. Although the Oceanic peoples living beyond New Guinea grew similar crops to the gardeners of the New Guinea Highlands, and might even have acquired some crop varieties from New Guinea sources, the terms they used for them were derived from Austronesian sources in the Philippines and Indonesia rather than from Papuan sources in New Guinea. Perhaps this non-expansive situation reflects in part the isolation of the highlands by inhospitable terrain, and the scourge of malaria afflicting any situations of increasing population density in the surrounding lowlands. However, an eventual spread of farmers from the highlands into the lowlands of New Guinea itself is attested quite well by the linguistic record, to which we return later.

The evidence to hand suggests that the New Guinea transition into some form of food production was perhaps as old a transition as anywhere else in the world, and it was clearly pristine. It might also have had similar causes, if we can take seriously the many current claims for risk management as a major factor in the beginnings of agriculture. From the viewpoint of overall productivity, in its early days the New Guinea agricultural scene was without any domestic animals, until the pig was introduced from Indonesia after 1000 BC, with dog and chicken perhaps later. The fact remains, however, that even *without* any major expansion of New Guinea agriculturalists and their languages into regions further away than Timor, Halmahera, and the Solomon Islands, their biological impact on the phenotype of the western Pacific has been immense. Although the languages and agricultural systems of the Austronesian-speaking populations of Island Southeast Asia and the Pacific Islands for the most part reveal undoubted Southeast Asian, even southern Chinese origins, the same is not true of biological genotypes, at least not in those islands which stretch from New Guinea to Fiji. New Guinea has been a powerhouse in the prehistory of the western Pacific, a circumstance underlined by the fact that its present populations, at least in the Highlands, are with little doubt the direct descendants of populations living on the island during the late Pleistocene. New Guinea, unlike its neighbors, was never seriously colonized by *incoming* agriculturalists. Neither, of course, was Australia, but that seems to reflect isolation and environmental factors rather than any New Guinea-like ability to provide the wherewithal for an independent origin of agriculture.

Chapter 8
Early Agriculture in the Americas

The transitions through time and in space between hunting-gathering and farming are rarely as sharp in the New World as in the Old. One reason for this is that few major meat-producing herd animals were ever domesticated in the Americas, so ancient farmers continued mostly to derive meat from wild resources. The main exception to this generalization, albeit one of fairly restricted regional impact, concerns the domestication of llamas, alpacas, and guinea pigs in the high Andes of Peru and Bolivia. Turkeys were domesticated in Middle America and dogs were also widely eaten, especially in the Maya region, but none of these served as widespread meat staples.

The Americas also lacked the broad base of highly productive cereals available in the Old World, with only maize fulfilling such a role on a large geographical scale, and only after about 2000 BC. The earliest domesticates in the Americas were mainly condiments, fruits, or industrial plants (e.g., chili pepper, gourd, avocado, cotton, and possibly even maize in the first instance) rather than productive staples. In the opinion of Hugh Iltis (2000:37):

> As of now, it may well be said that the reason agriculture came to the New World much later than in the Old was a reflection of both the absence of any large-grained Hordeae [the grass tribe that includes wheat, barley and rye] in the Americas, and of the difficulty mankind had in taming teosinte, its only large-seeded annual grass, and even then one with dubious agricultural potential.

The problems of teosinte (the wild relative of maize) are discussed later, but North America north of Mexico was not a source of any domesticated staples equal in productive capacity to Mesoamerican maize, or to the major tropical American tubers such as manioc and sweet potato. Although some native seed-bearing plants were domesticated in the Mississippi and Ohio basins, these had sunk to only a minor resource compared to maize by AD 1500. Very large areas of North America were also beyond the range of agriculture because of their cold and/or dry mountain and prairie environments, with the northern limit of the 120-day frost-free zone running approximately along the US–Canadian border and just to the north of the Great Lakes. At European contact, about half (probably more) of the land area of the Americas was still occupied by hunters and gatherers (Figure 8.1), and many regions potentially suitable for agriculture in western North America, from California northward, simply had not been reached by farming communities.

Figure 8.1   The major early agricultural zones of the Americas – Andes, Mesoamerica, southwestern USA, Eastern Woodlands – together with probable source regions for early domesticated plants. The dates in bold refer to the approximate dispersal chronology for maize.

The American agricultural economies, still essentially Neolithic in technological terms despite a widespread use of copper (but not iron) for ornaments at European contact, and without draft animals, ploughs, or wheeled transport, were thus not generally as productive as the economies that underpinned the expansive demographic trajectories of the Old World Neolithic and Bronze/Iron Ages. The expansion of agricultural economies in the Americas cannot be expected to be as clear-cut in the archaeological record as in some parts of the Old World, where fully agropastoral food production systems spread extensively through territories of former hunter-gatherers, as for instance in Neolithic Europe, and Iron Age central and southern Africa.

There is another major difference between the Old World and the New, and this is the relative lack of "centricity" in the New World early agricultural record. In the Old World, the Fertile Crescent and central China can be posited as geographically focused regions of early agricultural genesis in terms of their archaeological records and associated botanical and zoological information. In the Americas, it has long been assumed that agriculture evolved first in Mesoamerica and Peru because of their rich archaeological records, albeit with occasional but not widely accepted protestations to the contrary (Lathrap 1977). But it is now becoming apparent that these regions of later high civilization need not have been the *only* loci for initial agriculture, whatever importance they may ultimately have had in the rise of large-scale agricultural societies.

The focus is instead moving, at least in part, toward the lesser-understood (in an archaeological sense) and geographically diffuse tropical lowlands and mid-altitude regions of Middle America and northwestern South America, areas of seasonal forest and broad rivers where the floristic diversity underpinning the central suite of agricultural plants in the Americas (especially maize, beans, and squashes) appears to have been located (Figure 8.1). The picture is made more complicated by the recent verification that the middle Mississippi drainage basin and its tributary valleys contained an independent development of plant domestication. However, as in many regions of the Old World, we need to distinguish conceptually between regions of origin of agriculture as a system of food production, and regions of origin and domestication of individual crop species. The latter were probably far more widespread than the former. While the Americas were quite non-centralized as far as domesticated plant origins are concerned, this need not mean that food production was developed independently in every region where there happened to exist a wild plant species brought into domestication.

Some Necessary Background

The documented settlement of the Americas, from Siberia, occurred about 11,500 BC (Lynch 1999; Fiedel 1999). Until about 3000 BC, all Americans were essentially hunter-gatherers, with a possible but disputed earlier investment in horticultural activity claimed for some tropical regions. Dated macroscopic plant remains for domesticated *staple food plants*, as opposed to snack foods, containers, and condiments, occur only after 4000 BC, and for the most part a great deal later than this (Smith 1995, 2001; Benz 2001; Piperno and Flannery 2001). In fact, with the exception of a small region of unusual precocity in southern Ecuador and northern Peru, virtually the whole tropical American sequence of development from the oldest sedentary agricultural settlements to Late Preclassic Period urbanism occurred between 2000 and 300 BC. This is indeed compaction, more so than the 5,000 years from Pre-Pottery Neolithic Jericho to Protoliterate Uruk, or from Peiligang to the Shang Dynasty. The American cultural sequence in the tropical regions of high population density has a slightly frenetic air – a little late, always in a hurry, ferociously competitive, and remarkably creative.

So far, for the Americas, no one has yet prepared an environmental case to explain the development of early agriculture as complex and detailed as that for the Southwest Asian transition, which currently revolves around environmental change from the Pleistocene into the Holocene and the impact, albeit disputed, of the brief Younger Dryas return to glacial conditions. Yet the Pleistocene–Holocene boundary in the Americas was a period doubtless as well supplied with rapid climatic perturbation as it was in the Old World (Buckler et al. 1998). Because of this, Dolores Piperno and Deborah Pearsall (1998) favor a stress-based model for agricultural origins, focusing both on the Younger Dryas and on declining hunting returns in an increasingly forested early Holocene landscape. However, direct archaeological evidence for such environmental correlations with early agriculture is still elusive. Indeed, if agricultural dependence was a lifestyle that *postdated* 6,000 or even 5,000 years ago in the Americas, any attempt to link it directly in causal fashion with Late Pleistocene–Early Holocene environmental change will be hard to sustain. It has recently been claimed that the establishment of sedentary settlements and agriculture in Peru can be correlated *not* with Early Holocene events, but with higher rainfall along the Pacific coast due to an increasing frequency of El Niño episodes after 5,800 years ago (Sandweiss et al. 1999). The debate continues.

Essentially, we still do not know why agriculture began in the various regions, presumably three, of independent agricultural origin in the New World. Kent Flannery (1986:16) poses some general possibilities which still seem to be as good as any others:

In our model, the end-Pleistocene climatic changes . . . and the growth of world population . . . combined between 10,000 and 5000 BC to bring about a density-dependent shift in human cultural behavior over much of the world. Emigration and high mobility declined in importance, and strategies for dealing with predictable (seasonal) and unpredictable (annual) variation on a local basis began to emerge . . . In Mexico, agriculture may have begun as one of many strategies aimed at reducing the differences between wet and dry years.

In this model, increasing packing of population ("circumscription" in the terms of Robert Carneiro 1970) in the late hunter-gatherer world, plus desires to level out uncertainty and risk, would have been fundamental. The Americas in this sense fit well into the currently most popular worldwide model for the origins of agriculture, this being that it was essentially due to processes of risk minimization in the face of early or middle Holocene fluctuations in environmental circumstances. Such models have already been discussed in previous chapters for the Levant, the eastern Sahara, and the New Guinea Highlands. The major problem for the Americas is that the precise chronologies and geographical/environmental circumstances that lay behind the various cases of agricultural inducement remain rather obscure. Agriculture certainly appears to be younger in the New World than in much of the Old, so we may presumably look for many of the stimuli in the period postdating the Younger Dryas and running down to as recently as 2000 BC. But this is a large haystack in which to look for a small number of needles.

One other general point is worthy of comment. After sedentary life began across the American zones of early agriculture, mainly after 2000 BC, we soon witness some remarkable and unprecedented regional homogeneities in cultural style. The Early and Middle Formative periods of Mesoamerica and the Andes (including the Olmec and Chavin horizons) encompass a great deal of the American early agricultural action. Across many regions there is a degree of uniformity of style in pottery shape and surface decoration, clay figurines, art motifs and designs, even ceremonial center architecture and planning, which requires explanation. Some of these similarities also extend, at approximately the same time, into contemporary North American cultural complexes in the Eastern Woodlands of the USA. Do they reflect independent lines of common ancestry derived entirely from the Palaeoindian hunters of the Clovis horizon and its contemporaries? Or, far more likely in my view, are they due to contemporary Formative-period diffusion and/or population movement, as long ago argued in different ways by James Ford (1969), Gordon Willey (1962), Donald Lathrap (1973, 1977), and many others? Certainly, after 10,000 years of prior occupation of the Americas, we are not witnessing the actions of a single ethnolinguistic population working to invent a unique tradition of agriculture that thereafter spread to all regions. But the similarities most certainly reflect more than mere historical coincidence.

The Geography of Early Agriculture, and General Cultural Trajectories

The regions of early agriculture under examination are four in number. In the south lies the Andean region of southern coastal Ecuador, Peru, Bolivia, and northern Chile. This is a region of Pacific coast deserts, Andean valleys, and intermontane basins, ultimately sloping down eastward toward the rain forests of Amazonia. To the north lies Middle America – northern Colombia/Panama to central Mexico – again a region of great environmental variation from rain forests to semi-deserts and high mountains. The more specific title "Mesoamerica" is usually reserved for the cultural region extending from central Mexico to Honduras and El Salvador, this being the zone occupied by the Classic and Postclassic civilizations. To the north of Mesoamerica, through semi-arid northern Mexico, lies the US Southwest – Arizona,

New Mexico, and parts of Colorado and Utah. Finally, we jump eastward, across the marginally agricultural Great Plains and southern Texas, into the fertile Eastern Woodlands of the USA. These comprise the vast drainage basins of the Mississippi and its major tributaries (Arkansas, Missouri, Tennessee, Ohio), with northward extensions to the Great Lakes and New England. With the exception of the rather nebulous possibility of early manioc agriculture in the Amazon Basin, we have no clear signs of any role for other regions, apart from those listed, in *primary* agricultural origins.

In terms of overall archaeological trajectory, the essential frameworks for the four regions (Figures 8.2, 8.3) are as follows:

1. In the Andes, the oldest pottery commences in the Valdivia I period in Ecuador between 3500 and 3000 BC, with agriculture (apparently without maize at this early date) claimed in association. However, in nearby northern Peru the contemporary early archaeological record of agriculture, prior to 2000 BC, has no pottery (and again no maize), despite the presence of some impressive monumental constructions dating to the Late Preceramic Period, from 3000 BC onward. Pottery and maize both appear, at least in quantity, in Peru's Initial Period (1800–900 BC), during which time the Kotosh religious tradition with its distinctive ceremonial constructions spread over large parts of the northern and central highlands. In the Early Horizon (900 to 200 BC), dramatic evidence for interpolity warfare made an appearance, followed by the remarkable spread of the tightly knit Chavin network of interaction (500 to 200 BC).
2. In Middle America, the first pottery is also generally quite young, being dated in Chiapas, Oaxaca, Valley of Mexico, Puebla, and Costa Rica to about 2000 BC, although claims exist for older pottery in Panama and northern Colombia. From about 4000 BC onward, an early stage of maize domestication is attested in Guila Naquitz cave in Oaxaca, in the Tehuacan Valley in Puebla, and in the Maya lowlands, in all three cases long before the local appearance of pottery. In Mesoamerica proper, however, large ceremonial centers do not appear to be older than pottery usage, in contradistinction to the northern Peruvian situation. By 1000 BC, many regions were coming within the orbit of the Olmec network of interaction, a phenomenon similar to Chavin in Peru.
3. In the Southwestern USA, maize agriculture, pit storage, and large settlements appeared in southern Arizona by 2000 BC (with canal irrigation by 1500 BC). Pottery appeared at about the same time (Jonathan Mabry, pers. comm. 2003). Here, however, the early agriculture was not indigenous, but introduced from Mesoamerica.
4. In the Eastern Woodlands, an independent focus of native seed plant domestication was under way by 2000, perhaps 3000 BC (Bruce Smith, pers. comm. 2003), centered on the Ohio and Tennessee Valleys and adjacent portions of the Mississippi. Maize appeared in this region after 2,000 years ago, ultimately allowing agriculture to spread to its northern limits around the 120-day frost-free line, just north of the latitude of the Great Lakes.

Cal. AD/BC	Peru Coast	Peru/Bolivia Highlands	Colombia/Ecuador Coast	Amazonia	Panama & Southeast Mesoamerica	Maya Region	Western & Central Mesoamerica	Southwestern USA	Eastern Woodlands
AD 1500									Maize dominance
AD 1000								Pueblos	
AD 1	*CHAVIN* Early Horizon (camelids)	*CHAVIN* Early Horizon	San Agustin						Oldest maize Hopewell Adena
1000 BC	Cerro Sechin Sechin Alto Initial Period	maize Initial Period	maize		Early Formative	Early Formative	La Venta *OLMEC* San Lorenzo San José Mogote Ajalpan El Arbolillo *Early Formative*	*BASKETMAKER II* Santa Cruz Bend Las Capas	Poverty Point Early cultivation
2000 BC	El Paraiso Caral Late Preceramic	Kotosh (camelids) La Galgada Late Preceramic	Loma Alto Real Alto	Tutishcainyo				maize	Fibre-tempered Pottery in SE
3000 BC			Valdivia I Puerto Hormiga		Monagrillo				
4000 BC						Earliest Maize Cultivation?	Guila Naquitz maize	Archaic Foragers	
5000 BC			San Jacinto I		maize? manioc?				
6000 BC				Taperinha Pottery	Early Horticulture?				

Figure 8.2 Cultural chronologies for the regions of early agricultural development in the Americas. Dotted lines indicate approximate dates for the regional appearances of pottery.

Incised and stamped pottery
1200 - 800 BC

Las Capas
2000 BC Poverty Point ●
1800 BC

Savannah River
2500 BC

ATLANTIC

OCEAN

20°N

Tehuacan Valley
(Purron)
2500 BC

Caribbean Sea

Puerto Hormiga
3500 BC

●San Jacinto
5000 BC

Monagrillo
3000 BC

0° Equator

Valdivia
3500 BC

2000 BC Taperinha
Huaca Prieta La Galgada **6000 BC**
AMAZONIA
Las Haldas Chavin de Huantar
Aspero Kotosh
El Paraiso

PACIFIC

OCEAN

Lake Titicaca

20°S

ANDES

N

0   500
kilometres
Parallel scale at 0°

© Cartography ANU 03-047/83

Figure 8.3   Archaeological sites that have early pottery in the Americas, with
approximate dates.

Current Opinion on Agricultural Origins in the Americas

According to Dolores Piperno and Deborah Pearsall (1998), the first American
agriculture began very diffusely in the lowland seasonal deciduous forests of Middle
America and northern South America. They suggest that it began in a very small
way, early in the Holocene by about 8000 BC, with no domestic animals, as an
adjunct to a hunting and gathering economy based on a limited investment in house
gardens and shifting agriculture. Piperno and Pearsall are here echoing, but modify-
ing, earlier views on the significance of the lowland tropics by Carl Sauer (1952) and
Donald Lathrap (1970).

At the same time, they are posing a scenario rather different in geographical terms from that favored by Richard MacNeish, as a result of his research in the much drier Tamaulipas and Tehuacan regions of Mexico (Byers 1967; MacNeish 1972, 1992). MacNeish, like Piperno and Pearsall, favored a gradual adoption of agriculture and settling down, but in this case in the semi-arid highland regions of Mesoamerica rather than in the wetter lowlands. Even though MacNeish maintained his views until his death in 2000 (MacNeish and Eubanks 2000), phytolith evidence now suggests that teosinte, widely considered the likely ancestor of maize, was absent in the Mesoamerican highlands until its appearance as a primitive domesticate about 6,000 years ago (Piperno and Flannery 2001; Pohl et al. 1996; Buckler et al. 1998). This absence supports, at face value, a lowland origin for maize.

One can, however, read this absence the other way, as does Hugh Iltis when he makes the intriguing suggestion that teosinte became domesticated into maize *not* in its lowland biological homeland, which probably lay in or close to the Balsas basin of western Mexico, but possibly in a highland region such as Tehuacan, to which ancestral forms must have been taken by humans. To make the situation even more complex, botanist Mary Eubanks favors a derivation of maize not from annual Balsas teosinte at all, but from cross-pollination between a perennial form of teosinte and another grass species *Tripsacum dactyloides*, a cross that probably occurred in highland Mesoamerica (MacNeish and Eubanks 2000). Matsuoka et al. (2002) also favor a highland origin for maize domestication based on genetic analysis.

All of this is, of course, a little confusing for the non-botanist. Highland or lowland? Agricultural origins in the Americas are certainly not transparent and obvious. As Iltis (2000:37) notes, discussing the homeland of maize domestication: "Clearly, we don't know, and much more aggressive archaeology is needed in Mexico." Indeed it is.

The Domesticated Crops

Two general points about American plant domestication require emphasis. Firstly, some of the plants that were domesticated are non-staples in a food sense, for instance chilis, avocados, gourds, tobacco, and cotton. We can expect hunter-gatherers to have favored the growth of such useful plants and to have selected and planted seeds in some instances, as indeed they appear to have done with a species of squash (*Cucurbita pepo*) as early as 8000 BC in Oaxaca (Smith 1997b). The earliest use of teosinte / early maize might also have been for its sugary stalk, like sugar cane (Iltis 2000), and it is possible that primitive maize spread widely during the early Holocene as a source of sugar for alcoholic beverages, to be domesticated as a grain plant later and possibly in more than one location (Smalley and Blake 2003). Such initial movement as a snack food need have little directly to do with the origins of systematic agriculture, being more a case of occasional seed selection for replanting, in other words a variety of hunter-gatherer resource management.

Other plants, however, clearly served as staple foods, for instance maize in its eventual domesticated form in which the cob became the main exploited part, other seed-bearing plants such as chenopods (goosefoot in the Eastern Woodlands, quinoa in the Andes), various species of beans, and tubers such as potato, sweet potato, and manioc. Evidence for domestication of these staples generally falls much later in time than for the condiments and snack foods.

The second point is that a number of these plant species could have been domesticated in more than one region (Figure 8.1). Such possibilities have been raised for cotton, chilis, common and lima beans, some of the squashes, manioc, and even for maize.[1] Multiple domestications are quite possible for plants that have very widespread natural ranges, and we do not need to inflate the number of regions of independent agricultural genesis just because of this. But the situation as a whole does impart an air of diffuseness to the whole agricultural transition in the Americas. If there ever was an American "Fertile Crescent," tightly focused in space and time, it certainly hides from us very successfully.

Maize

Maize was the subsistence foundation for most late prehistoric and ethnographic American farming cultures, except for many groups living on poorer soils in Amazonia who depended mainly upon manioc and other tubers such as sweet potato (and bananas since European contact). Most botanists agree that maize was domesticated from one or more annual varieties of teosinte, the most important apparently being *Zea mays* var. *parviglumis* (Galinat 1985, 1995), which grows today in the Balsas river basin of Michoacan and Guerrero in western Mexico, with a closely related variety living slightly west in Jalisco, one of the possible homelands also for the common bean *Phaseolus vulgaris*. But the exact homeland of *domesticated* maize, as noted above, is a contentious issue.[2] The search goes on, as discussed earlier, and no firm conclusion can be offered here.

Throughout its history, maize has become perhaps the most widespread major food crop in the Americas, extending from 47°N to 43°S and up to about 4,000 meters in altitude. Its early spread into North America beyond the Southwest was not very rapid, perhaps because it is a short-day plant which had to adapt to the increasingly longer days and shorter duration of the summer growing season as it moved northward. Its entry into the southwestern USA occurred about 2000 BC, perhaps only a few centuries after large and productive varieties were first domesticated in Mexico (Matson 2003), but it did not spread into the eastern USA until about the time of Christ, only becoming a dietary mainstay there after AD 500. Maize clearly needed to evolve biologically, via human selection, as it spread.

In the early centuries of maize domestication it is possible that size increase was a slow process, owing to its wind-pollinated habit (as with the African millets), thus requiring conscious human planting in regions away from wild stands in order for improvements to become fixed (Iltis 2000). By 2000 BC, as noted by Kent Flannery (1972), maize had reached a size and level of productivity (cob length about 6 centimeters, yields perhaps 200/250 kilograms/hectare) that could have underpinned intensive production and the resulting Formative efflorescences of population in

Mesoamerica, the Andes, and the southwestern USA (Wilson 1985; Marcus and Flannery 1996:71).

Once in full production, maize clearly revolutionized American Indian life in many regions, certainly in Mesoamerica and the Southwest, even though it was preceded by other crops in the Andes and the eastern USA. Maize matures quickly, can be easily stored (an essential advantage), and has evolved many high-yielding varieties. One drawback is that it is lacking in available niacin, a problem remedied by cooking it in lime water in Mesoamerica and the Southwest, and pounding the kernels with wood ash in the eastern USA (Heiser 1990; niacin deficiency can cause pellagra).

When was maize domesticated? In Mexico, the oldest cobs of domesticated maize, as opposed to teosinte, come from ephemeral occupations in Guila Naquitz cave where the cobs themselves are dated by AMS radiocarbon to about 4250 BC (Piperno and Flannery 2001). Maize cobs from the Coxcatlan Phase layers in San Marcos Cave, in the Tehuacan Valley in Puebla, are AMS dated to about 3600 BC (Long et al. 1989; Benz and Iltis 1990). Carbon isotope analyses of human bone from a Coxcatlan phase burial in the Tehuacan Valley suggest increasing reliance on cereals by about 3500 BC, although this technique does not automatically identify the cereals as being domesticated (Farnsworth et al. 1985). However, Benz and Long (2000) note that maize cobs underwent rapid morphological development between 3500 and 3000 BC in the Tehuacan Valley sequence. Directly dated domesticated maize appears in northeastern Mexico and the Gulf lowlands of Tabasco by 2500 BC, and *Zea* pollen occurs with evidence for agricultural deforestation in the Maya lowlands at about the same time (Smith 1997a; Pope et al. 2001; Pohl et al. 1996).

There is a groundswell of opinion in favor of older dates for maize (see the discussion on stalk sugar above), especially for Middle and South America, where several locations in Panama and Ecuador have maize phytoliths or pollen in deposits dated by association to the early Holocene, back to at least 6000 BC (Piperno and Pearsall 1998; Pearsall 1999; Piperno et al. 2000). To the contrary, Bruce Smith (1995:159) accepts no dates for maize in South America until its clear presence in cob form after 2000 BC at Valdivia in Ecuador, thus rejecting all older dates based on the finding of phytoliths in uncertain archaeological contexts. The debate on this continues, sometimes quite energetically. For instance, at the late Valdivia culture site of La Emerenciana, recent analyses of stable isotopes in human bone and phytoliths from dental calculus and food residues in sherds indicate an increasing presence of maize, perhaps consumed in the form of *chicha* maize "beer," in the coastal Ecuadorian diet by 2200 BC. But maize cannot convincingly be demonstrated to have been present *as a significant staple* in South America before this date. Indeed, and rather ominously for the early dates scenario, maize is completely absent in several large agricultural sites of Late Preceramic date (ca. 2500–2000 BC) in northern Peru.[3]

The extent of the chronological problem for early maize, in this case in Panama, is highlighted by John Hoopes (1996:18):

> Available models for both the introduction and the intensification of maize agriculture in western Panama . . . are based on ambiguous evidence. Given various interpretations

of both microbotanical and macrobotanical data, maize may have been introduced to the region anywhere between the sixth millennium B.C. and the early half of the first millennium A.D. Maize may have been: (1) modified indigenously from an ancient, primitive ancestor; (2) introduced to the region from Costa Rica to the west; (3) brought from central Panama and Colombia to the east; or (4) introduced by some combination of these modes. Pollen and phytolith data indicate the presence of maize at inland rock-shelters in central Panama ca. 5100 B.C . . . However, the earliest *macrobotanical* remains from central Panama, in the form of maize kernels and cob fragments, date no earlier than 300 B.C. Hopefully, rigorous application of the principles of chronometric hygiene will soon help to sort out fundamental problems of this kind.

The other crops

No other American crop can claim such a stature in prehistory as maize and only some of the more important ones can be listed here, together with the small suite of domestic animals. Squashes, of which there were six domesticated species in the Americas, were clearly domesticated several times, presumably independently, in a number of regions, including the Eastern Woodlands, Mesoamerica, and South America (Figure 8.1) (Whitaker 1983; King 1985; Sanjur et al. 2002). The ca. 10,000-year-old AMS-dated seed of *Cucurbita pepo* in the cave of Guila Naquitz in Oaxaca raises the possibility that squashes, and the gourds also found in Guila Naquitz, could have been manipulated by humans from a very early period indeed (Flannery 1986; Smith 1997b). The gourds most probably served as containers rather than food. The seeds of these plants could very easily have been selected and replanted to promote desired characteristics, and also passed from group to group over very large distances, long before the beginnings of any systematic cultivation.

Beans also come in several useful species and had multiple loci of early domestication. Direct dates for these tend to be much younger than for squashes or maize, and the oldest occurrences would appear to be in Late Preceramic sites postdating 2500 BC in Peru and Ecuador (as also for cotton), and only 1000 BC in the Early Formative of Mexico (Smith 1995:163, 2001).[4] Beans appear to be younger than maize in the southwestern USA, and none reached the northeastern USA until about AD 1300 (Hart et al. 2002).

Of other crops, manioc (cassava) pollen is claimed with maize pollen from the Belize lowlands at about 3000 BC, and perhaps 5000 BC in the Gulf lowlands of Tabasco (Pohl et al. 1996; Pope et al. 2001). A charred manioc tuber from the site of Cuello in Belize has been AMS radiocarbon dated to about 600 BC (Hather and Hammond 1994). Piperno and Pearsall (1998) indicate the presence of manioc in Amazonia, its presumed homeland, by at least 2000 BC, and Donald Lathrap earlier made impassioned pleas for manioc to be regarded as the foundation crop for the whole cultural sequence of the agricultural Americas. Olsen and Schaal (1999) have recently sourced domesticated manioc using genetic markers to the southwestern Amazon in Brazil, close to the eastern borders of Peru and Bolivia (Figure 8.1).

Presumed homelands for some other food crops are also shown in Figure 8.1, a map that highlights the diffuseness of agricultural crop origins in the Americas. Yet there are two regions that could well have served as quite focused centers for the domestication of a range of localized crops and domestic animals. One is the highland Andes from central Peru down into Bolivia, between Lakes Junin and Titicaca (Roosevelt 1999b; Shimada 1999). For this region, Bruce Smith (1995) draws together a convincing case for a combined domestication, perhaps commencing around 2000 BC, of the white potato, the chenopod grain crop quinoa (*Chenopodium quinoa*), the meat- and wool-producing and pack-carrying llamas and alpacas, and the humble guinea pig. Duccio Bonavia (1999) believes that camelids and guinea pigs could even have been under some form of domesticatory selection in highland Peru as early as 3500 BC. Remains of quinoa occur together with squash and peanut in occupations in the Nanchoc Valley in northern Peru, apparently predating 4500 BC, but they are of uncertain domesticatory status at this time (Dillehay et al. 1997).

The other region of food-crop origin is the Woodlands of the central-eastern USA, focused on the basins of the Missouri, Ohio, and Middle Mississippi rivers, where a number of grain and oil crops were domesticated after 2000 BC. These crops include such delicacies as goosefoot, knotweed, maygrass, and marsh elder, to which were added the more widespread gourd, squash, and sunflower. The discovery of this independent complex of early agriculture has been one of the major recent achievements of US archaeological research and we return to it in more detail below. Indeed, it serves as a reminder that major developments in prehistory can sometimes be hidden from science for a very long time, a salutory observation for those endeavoring to recognize global patterns from the archaeological record.

Early Pottery in the Americas (Figure 8.3)

The oldest claimed pottery in the Americas, sand-tempered and with incised decoration, made its appearance in what appear to have been hunter-gatherer contexts in the lower Amazon by 6000 BC, for instance at Taperinha (Roosevelt et al. 1991). In northern Colombia, a very different kind of pottery with an organic fiber temper occurs in several sites, the earliest apparently being the inland site of San Jacinto I where an ornately decorated grass-tempered ware is dated to as early as 5000 BC, in association with many large stone-filled cooking pits and food grinding implements (manos and metates). San Jacinto is believed by the excavator (Oyuela-Cayceda 1994, 1996) to have had a wild seed-exploiting economy, with no definite evidence for agriculture, although perhaps in some kind of transition toward it. Other sites with fiber-tempered pottery occur as large doughnut-shaped shell middens on the northern Colombian coast (e.g., Puerto Hormiga; Hoopes 1994).

Elsewhere, similar fiber-tempered pottery and shell middens occur in parts of the southeastern USA (South Carolina, Georgia, northern Florida) by about 2500 BC. A different kind of pottery, Monagrillo sand-tempered, appears in shell middens and rockshelters in Panama by soon after 3500 BC. Suggestions that these early pottery occurrences are, or are not, related to each other are legion, but as John Hoopes (1994) points out, these oldest pottery occurrences in the Americas – currently in the lower Amazon, Colombia, Ecuador, Panama, and the southeastern USA – could well have occurred independently of each other. Being honest, we just do not know.

Were any of these early pottery-using groups associated with any form of agricultural subsistence? The evidence is not clear, although Dolores Piperno and Deborah Pearsall clearly favor an affirmative answer, perhaps for both maize and manioc in the general region of northern South America (Panama, Colombia, Ecuador) by possibly 5000 BC. As discussed above, it is possible that hunter-gatherers were beginning to manipulate these species by this time, particularly if maize was used for its sugary stalk. But if they did, the archaeological sites concerned provide no hard evidence.

Early Farmers in the Americas

Between 2500 and 1000 BC, the archaeological record in the Americas underwent remarkable transformations. Societies capable of constructing sedentary residential complexes with ceremonial monuments, in many cases with positively identified agriculture, appeared across vast regions of the northern Andes, Middle America, the US Southwest and the Eastern Woodlands. In their remarkable sharings, these late Archaic and early Formative cultures testify to the creation of what archaeologists would term a series of "interaction spheres" on a vast scale. It is the explanations for the existences of these interaction spheres, or *horizons* in archaeological classification, that offer some of the most interesting research questions in Americanist archaeology. What roles were played by population movement and the sharing of fairly proximate cultural and linguistic ancestries?

The Andes (Figure 8.4)

The Formative sequence in South America is often stated to begin with the Valdivia cultural complex of the semi-arid southern coastline of Ecuador at about 4000 BC, although the early stages of the sequence are a little unclear and there seems to be only very insecure evidence for sedentary settlements, pottery, and agriculture prior to about 3000 BC (Staller 2001). Four sites have yielded the most important evidence – Valdivia itself, and the riverine sites of Real Alto, Loma Alta, and La Emerenciana. The settlement debris in Real Alto and Loma Alta was arranged in U-shaped mounded plans, open across one end, covering more than one hectare in extent in the case of Real Alto, with sufficient pole and thatch elliptical houses for estimated populations of 150 to 200 people (Damp 1984:582). Although maize phytoliths are claimed to occur in Early Valdivia layers (as discussed above – see Pearsall 2002), actual macrofossils do not include maize until the second millennium BC. Instead, the Early Valdivia domesticated plant repertoire included squash, canavalia beans, the tuber *achira*, and cotton for textiles and fishing gear. Interestingly, the Valdivia people were

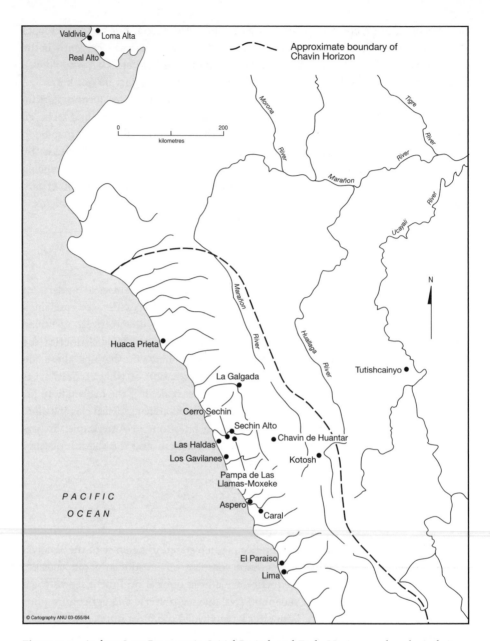

Figure 8.4 Andean Late Preceramic, Initial Period, and Early Horizon archaeological sites and complexes discussed in the text.

capable of making sea crossings, as shown by the existence of a Valdivia shrine on Isla de la Plata, 23 kilometers offshore in the Pacific Ocean (Brunhes 1994:82).

Northern Peru now takes center stage, owing to a remarkable degree of labor investment in some massive residential and ceremonial complexes during the Late Preceramic Period (3000 to 2000 BC), the Initial Period (2000 to 900 BC), and the Early

Horizon (900 to 200 BC). These sites occur along the Pacific desert coast with its permanent rivers, in the lower valleys of some of these rivers, and in the northern and central highlands. Mark Cohen (1977b:164) has suggested, on the basis of site surveys in the Ancon–Chillon valleys of central coastal Peru, that populations might have increased between 15 and 30 times during the Late Preceramic Period, fueled by a combination of agriculture and the rich maritime resources of the cold Humboldt Current. Such phenomenal population growth is attested in the remains of some remarkable Late Preceramic sites in the short coastal river valleys of northern and central Peru – sites such as Huaca Prieta, Aspero, Caral, Las Haldas, Huaynuna, Los Gavilanes, and El Paraiso, the latter with occupation debris extending over 58 hectares. Recent research at Caral in the Supe Valley has revealed six large platform mounds up to 18 meters high around a rectangular open space (Figure 8.5A), together with two sunken circular plazas, and residential complexes, the whole extending over 65 hectares (Shady Solis et al. 2001).

One of the most interesting sites of this phase is La Galgada in the Tablachaca Valley of inland northern Peru (Grieder et al. 1988). Today, La Galgada is in a rather forbidding semi-arid area, 1,100 meters above sea level, that looks very marginal for agriculture. But during the Late Preceramic a ten-kilometer stretch of the valley bottom supported at least 11 agricultural sites. La Galgada, like El Paraiso on the coast, apparently produced cotton in large quantities utilizing a riverine field system fed by irrigation canals. The base of the deposits was not reached during the excavations in the 1980s, but the lowest layers reached date to about 2700 BC and have an architectural style focused on small rooms with "ventilated hearths," four being set atop an oval stone-faced stepped pyramid 15 meters high (Figure 8.5B). Similar rooms have also been excavated at Kotosh, about 300 kilometers southeast of La Galgada, one termed the "Temple of the Crossed Hands" because of the survival of two such adobe reliefs beneath wall niches (Izumi and Terada 1972).

Artifacts found within the dry deposits at La Galgada include twined cotton textiles, netting, barkcloth, turquoise, marine shells, and Amazonian bird feathers, some of these items attesting to wide trade contacts. We witness during this period a remarkable agreement of architectural and artistic style through the northern and central Peruvian highlands, and also in sites on the coast. The significance of this wide horizon-like distribution in the Late Preceramic at about 2000 BC, particularly of ritual paraphernalia, is commented upon by Thomas Pozorski (1996:350):

> Closer similarities early in the sequence suggest that this was the time of greatest communication or influence, apparently in the area of religion or ritual. Subsequent divergence of form . . . reveals that interaction, at least in this sphere, may have waned.

During the Late Preceramic Period in northern and central Peru, apart from significant quantities of maritime resources in coastal regions, subsistence depended on irrigation cultivation of squash (including Mexican *Cucurbita moschata*), beans, sweet potato, potato, *achira*, chili peppers, and avocados (of Mexican origin). Cotton was widely grown, but there are no signs of maize. Michael Moseley (1975) also lists

Figure 8.5   A) The ceremonial area of Caral during the Late Preceramic, about 2500 BC. Large platform mounds and associated residential complexes surround a quandrangular plaza about 600 meters long. From Shady Solis et al. 2001. B) Reconstruction of the ceremonial area at La Galgada during the Late Preceramic Period, ca. 2500 BC. From Grieder et al. 1988.

manioc and the highland tubers *oca* and *ullucu* for Preceramic coastal sites in the Ancon region, near Lima. This suggests that the highlands and lowlands of the northern Andes were in contact at this time, an unsurprising conclusion which is reinforced by some very precise parallels in textile designs and ceremonial architecture, for instance in the above-mentioned rooms with central hearths ventilated by under-floor passages found in the highland sites of La Galgada and Kotosh, and in the lowland Casma Valley sites of Huaynuna and Pampa de las Llamas-Moxeke (Pozorski and Pozorski 1992; Pozorski 1996).

After 2000 BC, during the Initial Period in northern and central Peru, pottery and weaving made their first appearances, as did maize. U-shaped ceremonial centers following Late Preceramic prototypes occur in about twenty coastal sites (Williams 1985). As in the Late Preceramic, there was a continuing widespread degree of ritual and stylistic homogeneity, suggesting powerful linkages between regional populations. Very large polities appear to have been present in the Casma valley, focused on the sites of Sechin Alto and Pampa de las Llamas-Moxeke, the latter covering 220 hectares. Sechin Alto, one of the largest sites in the New World at this time, comprised a U-shaped complex 1.5 kilometers long with a central end platform 44 meters high. The modeled adobe friezes which adorn several of these sites are forebears of the famous Chavin art style which dominated the greater part of the northern Andes during the following Early Horizon.

Thus, by 2000 BC, the northern Andes had developed large agricultural polities with populations of over 1,000 people (Burger 1992:71–72). Many chambers at La Galgada were now converted into tombs, and the well-preserved burials indicate that about half of the population lived to over 40, and only 17.5 percent died younger than 4 years old – not a bad record for a society at this stage of cultural development. Initial Period sites extend down into the Marañon Basin in the east, giving access to the Amazonian rain forests. But it is interesting that we now witness an appearance of inter-polity warfare, graphically represented by the figures of warriors and mutilated captives carved on the blocks facing a stone platform at the coastal site of Cerro Sechin. Demographic pressures were surely building.

During the Early Horizon (900 to 200 BC), maize production increased rapidly in Peru; Ricardo Sevilla (1994) indicates that average cob lengths almost doubled between 500 BC and AD 1. Richard Burger and Nikolaas van der Merwe (1990) note, from stable carbon isotope analysis on human bone, that maize was still not a food staple comparable to native domesticates such as potato and quinoa, and perhaps served mainly as the source for corn beer, *chicha*. Even so, the early part of the Early Horizon was clearly a time of considerable social stress. Michael Moseley (1994) comments on widespread site abandonment along the Peruvian coast at around 800 BC, and raises the possibility of a cause connected with environmental degradation. Shelia and Thomas Pozorski (1987) also point to the possibility of invasion around the end of the Initial Period in parts of northern Peru, leading to some degree of population replacement via warfare. This is not the place to enter into detail about these developments, but their aftermath was the Early Horizon spread of the Chavin artistic and cult horizon over a vast area of northern and central Peru.

The site of Chavin itself perpetuated the U-shaped form of earlier periods in its Old Temple plan, but it also was clearly involved in some way in the formation of a new and remarkably complex art style which spread around 500 BC so quickly, over an area almost 1,000 kilometers long (Figure 8.4), that Peru became virtually a "religious archipelago" in Richard Burger's terms (1992:203). Communities became locked together by a powerful cult with a very standardized iconography, involving both human and feline symbolism. Chavin, of course, long postdates the origins of agriculture in the Andes, but it forms part of a long cycle of fluctuation in Peru from periods of widespread cultural homogeneity, through periods of increasing regionalism, and then back again (Burger 1992:228).

If we stand back and examine the major developments in the early agricultural sequence in the Andes, we see the following trends:

1. Once agriculture was present, developments were rapid in terms of population growth and expansion of the repertoire of domesticated products. A widespread sharing of style and iconography becomes apparent, especially in northern Peru. Varied populations doubtless took part in these developments, but within a network of communication that involved some degree of stylistic and perhaps also linguistic commonality right from the start.
2. The semi-arid environments concerned were always fragile and easily subjected to overexploitation. By 1000 BC, after a millennium of population growth during the Initial Period, warfare and site abandonment suggest that some degree of social and environmental collapse might have occurred, especially along the Pacific coast.
3. Following this, there appears to have been a reformulation of the whole system in terms of a region-wide Chavin horizon of cult, art, and exchange.

The whole Peruvian sequence so far perhaps replicates something of the sequence we see in the Levant, from early farming, through the late PPNB/PPNC decline, into the expansive early ceramic cultures of southeastern Europe and northern Mesopotamia. If my observations are not misplaced, then we need to ask just how coherently related were these Chavin populations, and indeed their immediate predecessors extending back into the Late Preceramic, in terms of language and shared aspects of cultural origin. The overall regional coherence of material culture suggests that levels of relationship in this regard would have been fairly high, more so perhaps than 2,000 years later, during the period of the Inca Empire, when we know that Peru contained some quite deep ethnolinguistic diversity. This increasing diversity over time, following on from the period of early agriculture, is beginning to follow a familiar trend, and we return to these issues from a linguistic perspective in chapter 10.

Amazonia

The Amazonian archaeological record is less detailed than that for the Andes. The expansion of agriculture through Amazonia and the Orinoco basin could have involved an indigenous domestication of manioc, but this is not certain and the oldest pottery from Taperinha in Brazil (Figure 8.3) appears to be associated with a hunter-gatherer population. According to Betty Meggers (1987; Meggers and Evans 1983), three main styles of pottery spread through Amazonia from the northwest, starting at about 2000 BC. She refers to these as, first, the "zoned hachure tradition," with oldest occurrences in Valdivia in Ecuador, Puerto Hormiga in Colombia, Initial Period Peru, and the site of Tutishcainyo in the upper Ucayali Valley of eastern Peru (Figure 8.4); second, the "polychrome tradition," which spread along the *varzea* alluvial bottomlands after 1,800 years ago, possibly from northwest Venezuela; and third, the relatively recent "incised and punctate tradition," which spread from the Orinoco Basin after 1,200 years ago.

The preference of Meggers is clearly for a downstream movement of agriculturalists and pottery traditions through Amazonia, commencing from homelands in the northwestern part of the continent, especially Colombia and the northern Andes. A related view was also favored by Julian Steward (1947), but with a greater emphasis on the Caribbean coastal regions of Venezuela and the Guianas. To the contrary, Donald Lathrap favored the central Amazon Basin itself as the source region for all Mesoamerican and South American early agricultural societies. No strong position is taken on this issue here, but the possibility that agricultural populations entered Amazonia via the upper courses of tributary rivers from the west and northwest carries conviction when examined from the viewpoint of some of the linguistic evidence (Figure 10.10), as well as the likely homeland of manioc (Olsen and Schaal 1999). The Initial Period of Peru, at least with respect to the zoned hachure pottery tradition of sites such as Kotosh (Waira-jirca phase) and Tutishcainyo, must surely be considered a potential origin for some of the early lowland pottery-using societies.

Concerning early Amazonian agricultural subsistence, Anna Roosevelt (1980) has documented a presence of maize in the Middle Orinoco valley by about 800 BC, preceded perhaps by manioc cultivation. But maize agriculture in general appears to have been rather non-intensive in Amazonia until about AD 1000 (Roosevelt 1999b). The expansions of agriculture and pottery into the West Indies appear to have taken place only during the later first millennium BC (Rouse 1992; Keegan 1994; Callaghan 2001). Evidence for early agriculture in Amazonia, if real, remains elusive.

Middle America (with Mesoamerica)

The Middle American sequence of early settlements and agriculture differs a little from that in the Andes, in that there is no clear-cut Preceramic phase of *both* sedentary agricultural settlements *and* monument construction, comparable for instance to sites such as El Paraiso and La Galgada. The specifically Mesoamerican Early Formative sequence nowhere dates convincingly before 2000 BC, and the first large monuments equivalent to those of the Late Preceramic and Initial Periods in Peru were under construction in the Gulf Lowlands of Mexico only by 1000 BC. By this time an area of about 11,000 square kilometers, extending right across Mesoamerica from western Mexico to Honduras, was coming within the orbit of the Olmec interaction network

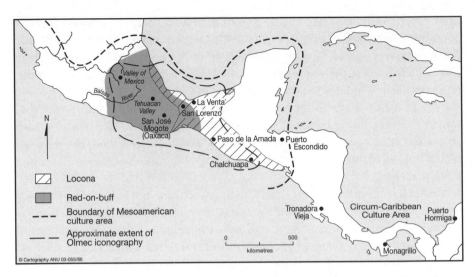

Figure 8.6 Mesoamerican archaeological sites discussed in the text. The map shows the extent of the Olmec Horizon, and the distributions of the Early Formative red-on-buff and Locona pottery traditions, ca. 1600–1000 BC, after Clark 1991.

(Middle Formative), a near-contemporary and very similar phenomenon in a structural sense to the Chavin horizon in Peru.

Examples of Early Formative communities in Mesoamerica dating from about 1800/ 1600 BC and onward are widespread (Figure 8.6). El Arbolillo, Tlatilco, and Coapexco are located in the Valley of Mexico, the latter with a population of possibly 1,000 people (Santley and Pool 1993; Tolstoy 1989; Grove 2000). In the Valley of Oaxaca, settlements between one and three hectares in size with rectangular pole and thatch houses, bell-shaped storage pits, pottery, and human figurines made their appearance during the Espiridion Phase, at about 1700 BC. The Barra, Locona, and Ocos phases of the Soconusco region of Chiapas, between 1800 and 1200 BC, record similar developments. During Locona times, a ceremonial center consisting of oval earthen platforms up to 2.5 meters high was constructed at Paso de la Amada (Lesure 1997).

Further east, pottery appears by 1500 BC in the Chalchuapa region of El Salvador, and at this time there is also a possibility of ceramic relationships between Pacific coastal Mesoamerica and contemporary cultures in Ecuador. Closely related Barahona phase pottery at Puerto Escondido, near the Caribbean coast of Honduras, dates from 1600–1400 BC, and pottery with rocker-stamped decoration and maize agriculture is attested at Tronadora Vieja in inland Costa Rica by soon after 2000 BC, again with possible cultural linkages with Chiapas (Joyce and Henderson 2001; Sharer 1978; Sheets 1984, 2000; Hoopes 1991, 1993).

All of this implies a very solid development of agricultural life with very similar painted, incised, and stamped pottery styles in most parts of Mesoamerica by at least 1500 BC, associated with rapid population growth and an increasing interest in the construction of ceremonial centers with their implications for the rise of power, authority, and increasing warfare (Flannery and Marcus 2003). A settlement study of

Early Formative sites over an area of about 600 square kilometers in the Valley of Guatemala postulates a doubling of population density every 250–300 years at this time, all underpinned by maize agriculture. The authors of this study (Sanders and Murdy 1982:58) refer to "rapid population growth, fissioning of settlement, and lateral expansion of population that is characteristic of a pioneer-farming population with . . . an extensive approach to land use." Joyce Marcus and Kent Flannery (1996:84) estimate a fivefold or tenfold increase in Early Formative population in the Valley of Oaxaca, where by 1200 BC the large settlement of San Jose Mogote covered about 20 hectares, with outlying hamlets spreading over an area of about 70 hectares. Skeletal analyses also indicate continuing levels of good health amongst these early Oaxacan cultivators (Flannery ed. 1976; Whalen 1981; Hodges 1989; Flannery and Marcus 1983, 2000; Christensen 1998).

In terms of regional style zones, John Clark (1991) proposes the existence of two separate interaction spheres in Mesoamerica during the Early Formative, ca. 1500 BC. One incorporates a large region of central Mexico, from the Gulf of Mexico across to the Pacific coast, and has characteristic red-on-buff pottery. The other, termed the Locona style zone, with fluted, incised, and bichrome *tecomates*, incorporates the Isthmus of Tehuantepec and the southern portions of Chiapas and Guatemala (Figure 8.6). Kent Flannery and Joyce Marcus (2000) have recently commented that the boundary between these two zones equates quite closely with the distributions of the Otomanguean language family to the west and the Mixe-Zoque and Mayan families to the east, a topic to be discussed further in chapter 10. The first zone has uncertain western boundaries, but the second extends as far as the eastern boundary of Mesoamerica, located at 1000 BC in Honduras and El Salvador (Sheets 2000:418) and correlating well with the eastern boundary of the Mayan languages.

The culmination of these widening horizons of agricultural spread and interaction in Mesoamerica was the remarkable Middle Formative interaction sphere known as the Olmec horizon (ca. 1200 to 500 BC) (Clark and Pye 2000). Opinions concerning the topic of "Olmec origins" have been very varied, with some favoring the Gulf Coast region, others Chiapas and Guatemala (Bernal 1969; Coe 1989; Lowe 1989; Graham 1989). To my mind, it is quite possible that the Olmec complex, as also Chavin, had no specific origin locus at all (Flannery and Marcus 2000). Instead of being a result of conquest or proselytization, perhaps like Chavin it represented a reemphasis of existing lines of shared ancestry and identity amongst populations already ethnolinguistically related.

Artifacts and rock carvings classified as Olmec occur throughout a very large area of Mesoamerica; Gulf Coast, Valley of Mexico, Guerrero, Puebla, Morelos, Oaxaca, Chiapas, Guatemala, and onward into El Salvador and Honduras. But rather interestingly, from an ethnolinguistic perspective, the Olmec distribution excludes the Maya lowlands (Hammond 2000). David Grove (1989) notes that most Olmec artifacts were produced locally rather than traded, and, as with Chavin in Peru, they occur through all social levels, rather than just in association with an elite (Pye and Demarest 1991). Typical features of Olmec pottery include a dish on a perforated ring stand, gourd-shaped bottles, neckless globular vessels (*tecomates*, like contemporary forms in Peru), flat-based plates, and surface decoration emphasizing infilled incision ("zoned hachure") and grooving. The ceremonial centers of the Gulf lowlands, such as La Venta, now depended upon maize for their subsistence, probably grown on riverine levees (Rust and Leyden 1994; Pope et al. 2001). Obsidian was traded widely from sources in central Mexico, Puebla, and Guatemala.

Most authors today regard the Olmec phenomenon as something imposed through increased interaction between far-flung communities. Perhaps it was, but it is suggested here that such interaction, as with Chavin in Peru, brought together peoples who were already related in much deeper ethnolinguistic senses by virtue of earlier population radiations, following on from the establishment of systematic agriculture. As far as Mesoamerica is concerned, this suggestion is not really new.

In 1969, James A. Ford's massive work on the American Formative was published posthumously. It is a book which today usually rates only a brief dismissal, partly because Ford was under the assumption that all the American early pottery industries spread from a source close to Valdivia in Ecuador. Today, this assumption can probably be rejected (Hoopes 1994). But there was much more to Ford 1969 than this, because for the first time an enormous effort was made to plot some very specific material cultural similarities across the Formative Americas, from Peru to the Eastern Woodlands, focusing on specific categories such as mound construction, blade technologies, barkcloth beaters, grooved axes, manos and metates, stone beads, ear spools and plugs, anthropomorphic pottery figurines, cylinder and button seals, tobacco pipes, and a large array of pottery vessel and decoration types (e.g., *tecomates*, carinated pots, ring feet and tripods, stirrup spouts, red slip and zoned red slip, zoned hachuring, and excising). Close relationships across a vast area between about 1500 and 500 BC were displayed in 22 magnificent charts.

Ford asked one very significant question as the subtitle to his book. Did the resemblances point toward "diffusion or the psychic unity of man?" Ford chose diffusion, following such earlier scholars as Spinden and Kroeber. We are here only concerned with those traits that spread "subsequent to the Colonial Formative" in Ford's terms (Ford 1969:148), dating in terms of current chronology between 2500 and 1000 BC. For these he stressed a pattern of early homogeneity, followed by increasing heterogeneity through time as cultures differentiated. We know today that this period, essentially the Early Formative in Mesoamerican terms, Late Preceramic and Initial Periods in Peruvian terms, was a period of remarkable, indeed unique, cultural and linguistic expansion in the Americas, paralleled only by the initial Paleoindian colonization of the two continents ten thousand years before, and by the expansion of European cultures three thousand years afterward.

The Southwest

The southwestern USA, comprising the states of Nevada, Utah, Arizona, western Colorado, and western New Mexico, was not a locus of independent agricultural development. But it was one of the most important areas in North America for the

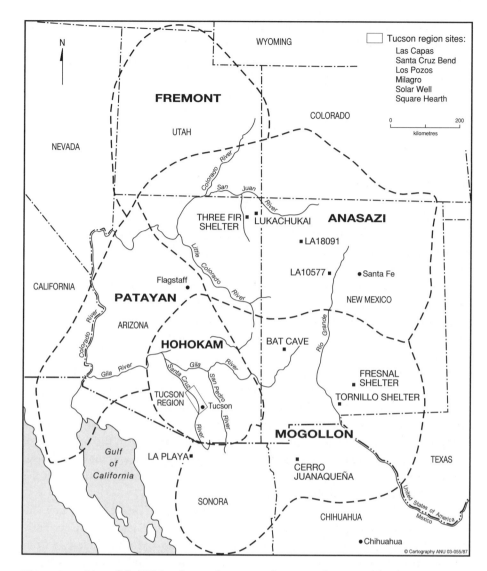

Figure 8.7 Map of the US Southwest showing early sites with maize older than 1000 BC (filled squares), and the approximate boundaries of the subsequent Hohokam, Mogollon, Anasazi, Patayan, and Fremont cultural regions. Data from Coe et al. 1989; Mabry 1998; *Archaeology Southwest* 13, No. 1, pp. 8–9, 1999.

development of agricultural societies, the record of these being most clearly enshrined in the great Anasazi, Mogollon, and Hohokam pueblo ruins of the early second millennium AD (Figure 8.7). Living descendants of these ancient agriculturalists include the extant pueblo-dwelling Hopi, Zuñi, and Rio Grande peoples of parts of northern Arizona and New Mexico.

The Southwest, however, has served not only as an environmental backdrop for the development of pueblo societies with stone or adobe architecture. For instance, the ethnographic Tarahumara of Sonora and Chihuahua in northwestern Mexico did not build pueblos, and were fairly mobile in settlement terms (Hard and Merrill 1992; Graham 1994). The Great Basin of Nevada and Utah and the northern regions of the Colorado Plateau housed mobile hunter-gatherer populations. So did much of the former Anasazi region of the southern Colorado Plateau, as a result of the southward migration of the Athabaskan-speaking Navajo and Apache. This hunter-gatherer migration occurred after AD 1400 (Matson 2003), doubtless assisted by the abandonment of most of the former pueblo settlements by that time.

The southwestern USA, in terms of its agricultural prehistory since about 2000 BC, can be seen as a northerly continuation of Mesoamerica. Indeed, Paul Kirchhoff (1954) used the concept of the "Greater Southwest" to include Mexico north of the Tropic of Cancer. It is a region of semi-desert, steppe, and high altitude forest, interspersed with bands of fertile riverine alluvium. Irrigation was essential in most regions apart from those at very high altitude, and agriculture was limited to the summer months by winter frosts and snow in many upland regions. The major crops in late prehistory were of Mesoamerican origin – especially maize, squash, beans, and cotton – and reached their greatest geographical extent a little before AD 1300, extending to as far north as the Fremont culture of Utah. Also of Mesoamerican origin was the practice of soaking maize in lime water before cooking, and the making of maize flour tortillas.

Since AD 1300, Amerindian agriculture in the Southwest has contracted drastically, some say due to drought and climate change, others to that frequent combination of too many people, overly intensive agriculture, and too fragile an environment. My sympathies are toward the latter explanation, perhaps a combination of both, but this is not a topic to delay us here since we are more concerned with the beginning of agriculture than the end (except insofar as the Fremont culture and the Great Basin are concerned, to both of which we will return in chapter 10 in connection with the origins of the Numic-speaking peoples).

The Southwest has an immensely detailed archaeological record, albeit one still with major gaps in the early agricultural period prior to 400 BC. These gaps are currently being filled, but the lack of evidence until recently for an agricultural lifestyle from the early period between 2000 and 400 BC, beyond sporadic finds of maize, is surely one reason why southwestern archaeologists, with rare exceptions, have in the past held almost universally to the idea that resident late Archaic foragers everywhere adopted maize cultivation to increase economic security and obviate risk (Ford 1985; Wills 1988; Jennings 1989; Minnis 1992; Upham 1994; papers in Roth ed. 1996; Plog 1997; Cordell 1997). This offers essentially a no-moves explanation favoring cultural continuity within the Southwest, from the Archaic to the period of Pueblo decline. Late Archaic hunter-gatherer populations are claimed to have remained essentially mobile with only subsidiary cultivation throughout the final millennium BC, until they began to settle down in settlements of "Basketmaker II" pit houses with irrigation farming after about 400 BC.

However, the idea that the agricultural transition in the Southwest was no more than a long episode of hunter-gatherer adoption *in situ* has always had some detractors, some more strongly opinionated than others. For instance, according to Spencer and Jennings (1977:253): "we can only agree that the first Hohokam were no doubt a group of transplanted Mexican Indians establishing a northern outpost with a technology appropriate for subduing the desert wastes of the Gila and Salt Valleys, where Phoenix, Arizona, now stands." It is perhaps only fair to state that Jesse Jennings (1989) later changed his mind, returning to the prevailing scenario of non-movement. But another founder-figure in Southwestern archaeology, Emil Haury (1986), favored an introduction of maize and pottery into southern Arizona by population movement from Mexico at about 300 BC. Haury, however, like most other southwestern archaeologists, always believed that agriculture was spread by hunter-gatherer adoption into the higher altitude Mogollon and Anasazi regions, and it must be stated here that current research still supports such an explanation (Matson 2003).

One researcher to realize the significance of the period of farming introduction prior to Basketmaker II was Michael Berry (1985:304):

> the introduction of maize farming was accomplished through sociocultural intrusion rather than through diffusion of agriculture to hunter-gatherer populations . . . there is no reason to expect that a successfully adapted hunting and gathering culture would voluntarily adopt a practice that imposes so many constraints on mobility and whose seasonal maintenance and harvest requirements conflict with the seasonality of so many productive wild resources . . . The gradualist model . . . errs in failing to acknowledge the all-or-nothing nature of maize agriculture. It is impossible to sustain a plant that is not self-propagating for any length of time without a total commitment to its planting, maintenance and harvesting on a year to year basis . . . everything seems to point to colonization by small groups of farmers whose cultural ties are ultimately (though probably not directly) traceable to Mesoamerica.

In perhaps the most wide-ranging review of early southwestern agriculture published to date, R. G. Matson (1991) was obliged to take an "on the fence" position on the immigration versus indigenous-adoption issue, perhaps rightly so at that time. He was able to note, however, without taking sides, that maize dependency, pit house settlements, and a new type of side-notched projectile point called the San Pedro Point had appeared in southern Arizona and on the Colorado Plateau by 1000 BC. New discoveries in southern Arizona relate directly to this phase and have completely revolutionized earlier views.

Thank the Lord for the freeway (and the pipeline)

Without rescue archaeology, a major period of North American archaeology would still be shrouded in semi-darkness, as would the beginnings of agriculture in Taiwan (see chapter 7). For many years it has been apparent that maize was eaten widely in the Southwest prior to 1000 BC (Figure 8.7), being particularly well represented in the form of cobs placed in caches inside caves. Some of these sites have a definite Archaic hunter-gatherer "feel," hence the long uncertainty about what all this cave-focused early maize really signified (Simmons 1986; Matson 1991).

During the 1990s, rescue excavations in alluvial and river terrace locations along tributaries of the Gila River in southern Arizona changed everything. At Milagro in the Tucson Basin, excavations on the route of a sewer pipeline in 1993 produced a settlement of oval pithouses, bell-shaped underground storage pits, fired-clay figurines, projectile points, and maize cobs, the latter directly radiocarbon dated to 1200–1000 BC. Some of the pits were calculated to be big enough to hold enough corn to support a family of four, eating only maize, for four months. Pottery in this site only appeared in upper levels, dating to about AD 100 (Huckell et al. 1995). The Milagro findings were a major factor in switching opinion away from a favored highland spread of maize from Mexico into the Southwest, toward a lowland riverine spread.

Already, many other pithouse finds had indicated a major role for maize back to at least 800 BC in the Tucson region. The growing idea that the spread of maize was rapid and large-scale was given support by the discovery of a four-hectare settlement at Cerro Juanaqueña in northern Chihuahua, where maize was again AMS dated to between 1500 and 1000 BC, possibly grown on about 8 km of linear stone-faced terraces associated with the site (although the terraces themselves were also, perhaps primarily, intended for housing and defense against atlatl warfare).[5] Robert Hard and John Roney (1998, 1999) note that maize was not necessarily a staple here; the inhabitants also grew chenopods and amaranth grasses and continued hunting and gathering. However, at the contemporary site of La Playa in Sonora, excavators note that maize was "ubiquitous" and enjoyed by a population in "relatively good health" (Carpenter et al. 1999).

Perhaps the most important discoveries have been made during freeway construction in the basin of the Santa Cruz River, a tributary of the Gila, to the north of Tucson. At a site called Santa Cruz Bend, a large area of 1.2 hectares was stripped of overburden, revealing 730 features, mostly house floors (total of 183) and storage pits, dating to the San Pedro (1200–800 BC), Cienega (800 BC–AD 150), and Agua Caliente phases (AD 150–550) (Mabry 1998). It is possible that only 15 percent of whole site was uncovered, giving some idea of the sheer size of this early farmer village (7–8 hectares). The house floors are all circular with post walls, one being a massive 8.5 meters in diameter and probably a communal structure of some kind. Remains of maize, squash, tobacco, and cotton indicate the agricultural nature of the economy; there was also a decrease of large hunted animals over time, suggesting increasing pressure on the environment owing to population growth. Pottery of crude form appeared in the Santa Cruz Bend site during the Cienega phase, later developing in the Agua Caliente phase into the polished form of *tecomate* which also characterized contemporary pottery all over northern Mexico. Interestingly, the oldest pottery at Santa Cruz Bend does not appear to have been used for cooking, and might have been used for storage.

The most recent and most dramatic results come from Las Capas, another freeway rescue site in the Santa Cruz valley, excavated also by Jonathan Mabry (Muro 1998–9; Mabry 1999). This site has a fully fledged settlement of the San Pedro phase dating from at least 1200 BC (Figure 8.8), associated with circular house floors, irrigation

Figure 8.8 A reconstruction of the Las Capas site through time, showing houses, irrigation canals, and bell-shaped pits for maize storage. Credit: Michael A. Hampshire (reproduced with permission from the artist).

canals, and the usual bell-shaped storage pits (also fairly universal in the Mesoamerican Early Formative at about the same time). In Las Capas, pottery made its appearance at about 900 BC. Also characteristic are the side-notched San Pedro points, perhaps used to tip atlatl darts, which seem to represent a break from earlier local Archaic types. The oldest Las Capas maize is dated to 1500 BC, and to 1700 BC at another site called Los Pozos (Stevens 1999).

Immigrant Mesoamerican farmers in the Southwest?

One important observation made during the research at Santa Cruz Bend was that the rate of alluvial deposition in the vicinity of the site underwent a marked increase at about 1700 BC. Bruce Huckell (1998:64) attributes this increase to climatic factors and notes that roughly synchronous changes occurred in other valleys in the general region. But one must ask here, given the known aggradational effects of human vegetation clearance for early agricultural purposes in other parts of the world, if the first farmers were not also responsible to some degree. If so, an arrival of maize agriculture in the Southwest by soon after 2000 BC seems likely, and indeed is strongly suggested by recent radiocarbon dates.

In a recent conference paper, John Carpenter, Jonathan Mabry, and Sanchez de Carpenter (2002) point to a spread of maize from Mesoamerica into the Tucson Basin by at least 2000 BC, in association with Cortaro and Gypsum projectile points. These are forms that also occur in Mesoamerica, for instance in Coxcatlan Cave in the

Tehuacan Valley and Tlatilco in the Valley of Mexico. They may thus be good evidence for a population movement behind the initial spread of maize farming into Arizona. However, just as I finished writing this chapter I received an e-mail from Jonathan Mabry telling me that maize and pottery have also been found in the Tucson region with a point type called Armijo, which seems to be indigenous to Arizona. This suggests that maize cultivation could have spread very early amongst Archaic hunter-gatherers as well.

My own assumption here is that agricultural introduction occurred with population movement from Mexico, an assumption supported by new interpretations of the history of the Uto-Aztecan language family, to which we return in chapter 10. But we need to ask if this explanation applies to the whole of the Southwest, or if some former hunters might not also have adopted agriculture from the farmers. Many sites with maize, but with hints of the kind of mobility characteristic of hunter-gatherers, occur widely throughout the region, especially in relatively marginal areas away from the major alluvial zones (Whalen 1994; Roth 1996; Gilman 1997). The most recent statement on this issue, by R. G. Matson (2003), accepts a core spread of maize cultivation into Arizona as a result of a movement of agriculturalists from northern Mexico. He raises the possibility that the movement was very rapid, requiring perhaps only 500 years for maize to travel from the Balsas Basin of Guerrero in western Mexico to Arizona.

But Matson also considers other evidence from Basketmaker II sites in the higher altitude eastern (Mogollon) regions of the Colorado Plateau, these being techniques of basketry and sandal manufacture (such items are often found in dry caves), paleoanthropological data, and modern pueblo languages (some being non-Uto-Aztecan). From this evidence he suggests that there was indigenous adoption of agriculture by Archaic hunter-gatherers in this region. A similar viewpoint is taken by Steven LeBlanc (2003). The overall conclusion for the Southwest from the archaeological evidence is therefore that maize agriculture was introduced from Mexico, by 2000 BC and most probably by lowland population movement, albeit with varying degrees of adoption by indigenous hunter-gatherer populations, living at higher altitudes.

Independent Agricultural Origins in the Eastern Woodlands

As in the Southwest, the archaeology of early agriculture in the eastern part of the USA has recently undergone a paradigm shift as a result of the demonstration that a local domestication of annual seed-bearing plants was under way in the Ohio, Cumberland, Tennessee, and middle Mississippi river basins by 2000 BC or before. Although this observation was presaged as early as 1936, most American archaeologists until recently still considered the mound-building Early and Middle Woodland cultures of this region (1000 BC to AD 500) to be essentially hunter-gatherer, prior to the widespread adoption of maize agriculture in the mid- to late first millennium AD. Actual maize remains in the eastern USA so far date back only to about 200 BC, at the Holding site in Illinois, after being introduced possibly across the Caribbean (Riley et al. 1991; Riley et al. 1994). Maize apparently did not reach New England until about AD 650 (Hart et al. 2003).

Yet even with the new knowledge there are still some puzzling aspects. For one thing, the pre-maize native domesticates were apparently absent in large regions of the southern and eastern coastal regions of the USA, being concentrated in the central interior of the Eastern Woodlands, north of about 34 degrees latitude (see the circled area in Figure 10.13). Paradoxically, some of the large mounded ceremonial sites which lie outside the early domestication zone, such as Poverty Point in Louisiana, show few signs of agricultural production, even though their sizes would suggest on comparative grounds that some form of food production was present. Furthermore, agriculture shows few signs of being very significant anywhere before about 500 BC, suggesting that in the Woodlands, as perhaps in northern South America, hunters and gatherers initially toyed with domesticated plants on the edges of fairly rich non-farming economies, as hedges against periods of scarcity. Overall, the Woodlands trajectory toward agriculture has a gentle and gradual feel which perhaps aligns it with that of other forested regions such as the New Guinea Highlands and Amazonia, contrary to the more frenetic pattern of change which we have witnessed in the Middle East, China, Mesoamerica/Southwest, and the Andes.

Let us look first of all at the crops themselves.[6] As in Mesoamerica, it is highly likely that non-food indigenous plants were domesticated first, in this case squash (*Cucurbita pepo*) and gourds, the latter used for containers. Their eventual domestication was due, no doubt, to continuous human selection and planting of seeds around camps. Annual food plants were domesticated as well, including starchy-seeded *Chenopodium berlandieri* (goosefoot, so called because of its leaf shape), and the oily-seeded species *Helianthus annuus* (sunflower) and *Iva annua* (sumpweed or marsh elder). These plants are recognizable as domesticated because of their increasing seed sizes and/or thinner seed coats (Figure 8.9). All are native to the Woodlands, except possibly for the sunflower, which could be of Mexican or Southwestern origin. Some other starchy-seeded annuals such as maygrass, little barley, and knotweed also occur in large quantities in some sites, but do not in themselves reveal clear domesticated characteristics. Apart from squashes and sunflower, none of the above food plants continue in cultivation today.

Of these crops, the chenopods appears to have been the most important; Gayle Fritz (1993) mentions a cache of nine million goosefoot seeds buried in a pit during the early first millennium AD in the floor of Ash Cave in Ohio. Knotweed and little barley apparently did not become common until about 2,000 years ago, by which time maize was also making its initial appearance. The common bean *Phaseolis vulgaris*, like maize of Mesoamerican origin, did not spread into the Eastern Woodlands until about AD 1000.

One of the main proponents of the view that these domesticated plants supported a truly agricultural economy, rather than just being an adjunct to hunting and gathering, has been Bruce Smith (1987, 1992a, 1992b, 1995). He suggests that a "floodplain weed" domestication process occurred in anthropogenically disturbed alluvial terrain

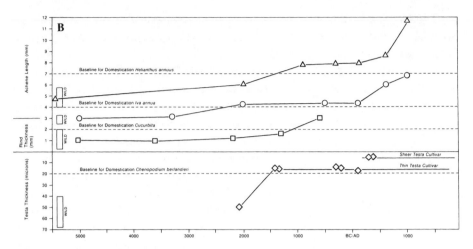

Figure 8.9   Trajectories for the domestication of sunflower, sumpweed, squash, and goosefoot in the Eastern Woodlands. From Smith 1992b. In a recent personal communication (2003), Bruce Smith has informed me that current commencement dates for domestication, in terms of the baselines shown here, fall close to 3000 BC for squash and 2000 BC for sunflower.

along the major rivers, in circumstances of increased mid-Holocene alluvial deposition. Such increased deposition often attracts a climatic explanation but, in view of comments made above about the Tucson Basin, one could perhaps also justify an in-part anthropogenic origin through vegetation clearance. In other words, the increased alluvial deposition could perhaps have been promoted by the transition to field planting on cleared land.

How important in the diet were these native Woodland domesticates? The plants concerned are described by Smith (1992b:208) as having "impressive nutritional profiles and substantial potential harvest yield values." Richard A. Yarnell (1993:17, 1994) estimates, from a number of cave flotation and paleofeces samples, that a possible dietary intake from plants during the period 650–250 BC in Kentucky could have consisted of 40 percent oily seeds (such as sunflower, sumpweed, and squash), 36 percent starchy seeds (chenopods, maygrass, amaranth), 20 percent nuts, and rare greens and fruits. This listing suggests that at least 75 percent of plant food dietary intake came from domesticated garden products. Obviously, regional variation would have spread such percentages for individual crops widely, as shown by Bruce Smith, who indicates chenopods dominating in eastern Tennessee but apparently playing only a minor role in west-central Illinois. Smith (1992b: 200) also suggests that a field 70 by 70 meters, planted with marsh elder and goosefoot, could have provided half the caloric requirements for a ten-person household for six months.

Thus, by the second millennium BC, communities in the central part of the Eastern Woodlands were depending increasingly on plant domestication. By AD 1, early in the Hopewell phase of the Middle Woodland Period, pre-maize systems of agriculture were present through Illinois, Tennessee, Kentucky, and Ohio, extending across the Mississippi into Missouri and Kansas (Adair 1988; O'Brien and Wood 1998). By this time there is ample archaeological evidence for a pattern of small settlements of circular huts, mostly under 2 hectares in size, located along the edges of floodplains and interspersed with burial mounds and "ceremonial centers" (Smith 1992b).

Unlike Mexico, Peru, the Middle East, or China, there is here no ebullient trend toward settlement concentration, at least not until a millennium later during the maize-based Mississippian complex after AD 1000. But some of the Early and Middle Woodland mound complexes are of course of great size; Adena burial mounds of the first millennium BC in Ohio can be up to 20 meters high, constructed over circular posthole structures and supplied with central log-lined burial pits. Such mounds are sometimes associated with complex embanked enclosures enclosing up to 10 hectares (Brose et al. 1985; Webb and Snow 1988; Mainfort and Sullivan 1998). Even more impressive mound and bank constructions, including animal-shaped mounds, together with widespread trading networks enmeshing much of the eastern USA, are characteristic of the following Hopewell phase of the first millennium AD (Figure 10.13) (Brown 1994).

The Early and Middle Woodland periods were also a time of population increase in terms of skeletal data and fertility estimates, an increase continuing onward into the Late Woodland and Mississippian periods (Buikstra et al. 1986). Numerous questions arise, however, with respect to this early agricultural complex. How does pottery technology relate to the Woodland picture? What was the economic status of the people in those very extensive regions around the edges of the confirmed agricultural zone, some also builders of impressive mounds, for whom there appears to be no evidence for farming activity? How did the people who created the Woodland agricultural sites relate to their Archaic predecessors? Was there any population reassortment or replacement across the transition? In many ways, the record in this region is much harder to read coherently than those in central Mesoamerica or northern Peru. This may reflect factors of preservation, but it may also reflect the possibility that the Eastern Woodlands were always much more a region of balance between farming and foraging than were the regions of burgeoning complex civilization. The farming picture seems to be diffuse and muted right down to the period of maize dominance after AD 900.

As far as pottery is concerned, the early fiber-tempered pottery of the southeastern USA, with its possible South American parallels (discussed above), has not yet been found in agricultural contexts. This pottery dates back to perhaps 2500 BC in Georgia and northern Florida and seems everywhere to precede any significant agricultural presence (Peterson 1980; Adair 1988; Walthall 1990; Milanich 1996). Between 1200 and 600 BC, varieties of paddle-impressed, stamped, and incised pottery, mostly with non-fiber tempers, appeared widely to the east of the Mississippi, extending right up to New York State (Jenkins et al. 1986). Whether or not this Early Woodland pottery was derived indigenously from the earlier fiber-tempered wares, or whether there was some input of technique and style from Mesoamerica, as claimed by Ford (1969) and Webb and Snow (1988), is an intriguing question. It is not possible linguistically to have a major migration from Mesoamerica as recent in time as 1000 BC covering most of the eastern USA and replacing earlier languages – on these grounds alone, the Early Woodland peoples must surely be mainly the descendants of Archaic forebears.

But there are some very important "big-picture" aspects to all of this that tend to be overlooked in discussions of regional prehistory. The Early Woodland pottery becomes very widespread at about the same time as the evidence for early agriculture and the beginnings of mound and earthwork construction. This is the case even if the pottery, agriculture, and mounds do not overlap in distribution with absolute precision. Thus, some correlation between pottery and agriculture can be suggested. Furthermore, on the Mesoamerican contact issue, some of the southern sites, for instance Poverty Point in Louisiana, have *tecomate* pottery forms resembling contemporary Mesoamerican pottery. Some southern pottery traditions of the period before 600 BC also have incised and stamped forms of surface decoration which again parallel similar and contemporary styles in Mesoamerica (Ford 1969; Jenkins et al. 1986).

So what does the Early Woodland picture in the eastern USA really tell us? I think we have a non-coincidental association of earthwork monuments, pottery manufacture, and a developing agricultural economy, at least in the central Mississippi basin and its major tributaries, during the Early Woodland Period, from the third millennium BC onward. The evidence suggests that this is a locally generated transition into farming, with some strong evidence for a degree of stylistic contact with Mesoamerica, but not in the first instance for a successful agricultural transfer from Mesoamerica, given that maize clearly took some centuries to adapt to the northerly latitudes.

But what about developments much further to the south, seemingly beyond the range of the Woodland agricultural zone? The impressive 60-hectare site of Poverty Point in Louisiana, for instance, has six massive semi-circular concentric earthworks, a bird-shaped mound with possibly Olmec parallels, figurines, pottery, a possible supporting population of 5,000 people living in 600 houses, all set in a landscape with at least 80 contemporary and culturally related sites. The whole complex dates to the second millennium BC, with dates of 1750 to 1350 BC currently being suggested for Poverty Point itself, and in this region there are stated to be much older mounds dating back to almost 4000 BC (Gibson 1998). Yet Poverty Point has yielded absolutely no evidence of domesticated plants or agriculture at all (Webb 1977; Byrd 1991; Gibson 1996, 1998). Is this due to fugitive evidence? Was some form of pre-domestication cultivation being practiced? Or were the inhabitants of Poverty Point still purely Archaic hunters and gatherers? Were foodstuffs obtained from subject populations? We do not know, but it is somehow hard to imagine that such a massive site could have existed for so long merely supported by collected and hunted food from the local environment.

To the later phases of Woodland prehistory, those connected with the gradual expansion of maize cultivation after 2,000 years ago, we return in chapter 10. For we still have to tease out the ethnolinguistic prehistory of this region in terms of the movement of populations such as the Siouans, Caddoans, and Iroquoians. While the indigenous plant domestication process must have laid the ethnolinguistic foundations in part for these language families, it is clear that major changes and population reassortments also occurred during the first and early second millennia AD. The most intensive episode of expansion of agricultural communities across the Mississippi on to the Great Plains was essentially a phenomenon of this later period of developing maize cultivation, as was the expansion of maize farmers northward to Ontario.

Chapter 9

What Do Language Families Mean for Human Prehistory?

all these dialects preserve several words of a more antient language, which was more universal, and was gradually divided into many languages, now remarkably different. (Johann Reinhold Forster 1778[1])

The central job of comparative-historical linguistics is the identification of groups of genetically related languages, the reconstruction of their ancestors, and the tracing of the historical development of each of the member languages. (Kaufman 1990a:15)

The first eight chapters of this book have detailed the early history of agricultural dispersal from a number of homelands in Asia, Africa, and the Americas. Crops, domestic animals, and new forms of technology spread over vast areas. Burgeoning human populations moved from seasonally mobile camps into sedentary villages and towns. Ancestors, communal tombs, monuments to the gods, and ranked lineages impinged on human affairs with an ever-increasing intensity. The essential social and productive foundations were put in place beneath the long haul to the first literate civilizations.

What did all this mean in real human terms? Who were these early farmers and how do they relate as possible ancestors, in cultural, linguistic, and biological senses, to modern populations? At this point, we must be very strict in keeping apart the implications of the records derived from different disciplines. The archaeological record deals with the *material* aspects of ancient life, not with language or biology. The comparative and historical linguistic record suggests how *languages* might have developed and spread, and is not tied in any absolute way to the history of agricultural systems or human genotypes.

In this chapter and the next, our interest is not with named individual ethnic groups (such as Celts or Chinese), but rather with whole families of languages – for instance, with the Indo-European language family, the Sino-Tibetan family, and so forth. On this whole-family scale, major patterns of expansion in the deep past can be perceived that can, with considerable profit, be compared with the records of agricultural expansion derived from archaeology.

Language families are remarkable phenomena. The largest ones, situated mostly in the Old World, tie together hundreds, sometimes thousands, of languages and communities spread right across continents and oceans. They extend far beyond individual community awareness – how many speakers of English (excluding linguists!) would be aware that their language shares a common origin with Bengali, or have the faintest idea why? They also extend far beyond the reaches of history – related languages ancestral to both English and Bengali were spoken in northwestern Europe and northern India respectively by at least 1500 BC and perhaps earlier; long before the existence of any western European or Indian historical records or great empires.

If we dissect a language family, for example the Austronesian family of Southeast Asia and Oceania, we find a sharing of related forms in lexicon, grammar, and phonology so widespread (Table 9.1) that only a concept of *common ancestry*, of descent from a homeland ancestral linguistic entity, can explain them. Phonological considerations make it clear that the vast majority of these forms did not spread secondarily as borrowings – they descend directly from the source linguistic complex and have undergone the same sound changes over time as the rest of the vocabulary in the languages concerned.

Common ancestry, or phylogenetic relationship to use the terminology of science, is a very powerful concept. This is because language families, like animal species,

Table 9.1 Some widespread Austronesian cognates (blank entries indicate absence of a cognate form). PAN = Proto-Austronesian, Rukai is a Taiwan language, Tagalog is the national language of the Philippines, Rapanui is Easter Island. Courtesy: Malcolm Ross.

	PAN	Rukai	Tagalog	Javanese	Fijian	Samoan	Rapanui
two	*DuSa	dosa	dalawa	lo-ro	rua	lua	rua
four	*Sepat	sepate	āpat	pat	vā	fā	hā
five	*limaH	lima	lima	limo	lima	lima	rima
six	*ʔenem	eneme	ānim	enem	ono	ono	ono
bird	*manuk		manok	manuʔ	manumanu	manu	manu
head louse	*kuCuH	koco	kūto	kutu	kutu	ʔutu	kutu
eye	maCa	maca	mata	moto	mata	mata	mata
ear	*Caliŋa	caliŋa	tēŋa		daliŋa	taliŋa	tariŋa
liver	*qaCey	aθay	atay	ati	yate	ate	ʔate
road	*Zalan	ka-dalan-ane	daan	dalan	sala	ala	ara
pandanus	*paŋuDaN	paŋodale	pandan	pandan	vadra	fala	
coconut	*niuR		niyog	nior	niu	niu	
sugarcane	*tebuS	cubusu	tubo	tebu	dovu	tolo	toa
rain	*quZaN	odale	ulan	udan	uca	ua	ʔua
sky	*laŋiC		lāŋit	laŋit	laŋi	laŋi	raŋi
canoe	*awaŋ	avaŋe	baŋka		waga	vaʔa	vaka
eat	*kaʔen	kane	kāʔin	ma-ŋan	kan-ia	ʔai	kai

cannot form because of the convergence of taxa originally unrelated, such as Germanic and Sinitic languages, or horses and rhinos, to form a single genetic taxon within which all units share a common ancestry. Admittedly, some closely related animal species can interbreed and produce offspring, mostly infertile, and languages that already share close genetic relationship and have previously differentiated only slightly can undergo some degree of "advergence" toward reunification (Renfrew 2001a). Furthermore, speakers of unrelated languages can sometimes be forced together under socially unusual circumstances (e.g., slavery, migrant labor) and obliged to create pidgin languages. But examples of such pidgin developments in language history are quite rare and hardly convincing as explanations for the genesis of whole families of related languages spread over enormous distributions of territory. As noted by Gerrit Dimmendaal (1995:358): "notions of non-genetic or multi-genetic development in historical linguistics are not felicitous." It is quite possible for a language family to *descend* from a pidginized proto-language, but pidginization cannot be a sufficient cause for all later subgroup differentiation within a family. Once taxa begin to separate they usually continue to do so, and convergence by language mixing is not convincing as a major player in language family origins.

Since convergence cannot explain a language family, what can? The answer is expansion from a homeland region, such that a foundation layer of "language" (probably in the form of related dialects), that has spread in some way from a source region, gives rise over time to differentiating daughter languages. The spread factor is of course essential – without it there can be no linguistic foundation for a language family, no matter what circumstances gave rise to the eventual daughter-language differentiation.

Once a linguistic spread has occurred, the circumstances of subsequent differentiation can be quite varied. Communities can stay in contact or split irrevocably as the expansion takes place; they can also be split apart through invasion by other unrelated linguistic groups. They can form borrowing relationships with unrelated linguistic groups, or hide in virtual isolation. Some groups can abandon their original languages and adopt others (*language shift*), just to make the task of historical reconstruction often very difficult. But the fundamental observation that the ancestral languages in a family have *somehow spread outward* from a source region and then diversified is one of the most significant that can be made in any quest for human cultural origins. Language families are manifestly phenomena of divergence, not convergence.[2]

The next question is perhaps obvious. How *do* languages spread over large distances? Do they spread because people who already speak them move into new territories? If this is so, we must explain the reason for their expansionary success, and also explain what has driven/induced them out of their homeland or attracted them to their new utopia. On the other hand, do languages spread because people adopt them, by language shift, with only a minor presence of a native-speaking source population? If this is so, then we must explain why people should abandon their native languages, and often many attached cultural norms.

Many archaeologists and not a few linguists are very blasé about language shift, dismissing it as trivial and everyday. Not so the linguist Marianne Mithun (1999:2), writing of the demise of native American languages:

Speakers of these languages and their descendants are acutely aware of what it can mean to lose a language. When a language disappears, the most intimate aspects of culture can disappear as well: fundamental ways of organizing experience into concepts, of relating ideas to each other, of interacting with other people. The more conscious genres of verbal art are usually lost as well: traditional ritual, oratory, myth, legends, and even humor. Speakers commonly remark that when they speak a different language, they say different things and even think different thoughts. The loss of a language represents a definitive separation of a people from its heritage.

Admittedly, this quote refers to abrupt language death in traumatic circumstances. But even in more gentle circumstances of interaction it is hard to imagine that language loss via shift, even over a period of several generations, would always have been an eagerly embraced outcome of social contact, certainly not on the scale of many of the major language families to be discussed in the next chapter. Multilingualism for many modern societies is a far more attractive alternative to a one-way total shift with language loss.

Other social mechanisms that might explain language spread, all overlapping with population movement and language shift and often involving one or both of them, include trade and a need for lingua francas, "elite dominance" (when an incoming elite tries to impose its language on a larger native population), slavery and forced translocation of population, and population replacement due to disease or war (for discussion see Renfrew 1989, 1992a, 1992b; Nettle 1998, 1999). In my view, these mechanisms taken individually can explain certain situations, but they are not of even validity throughout all circumstances and none of them can explain the entire distributions of major language families.

Immediate questions that are of especial relevance for prehistory include the following:

- Is it possible to determine the homeland region for a major language family?
- Can comparative linguistic reconstructions of the shapes of "family trees" throw light on how proto-languages once spread from homeland regions?
- Is it possible to reconstruct the culture(s) and lifeway(s) attached to the "proto-language" or ancestral language network?
- Is it possible to *date* the proto-language for a major language family, and also the many subsequent regional proto-languages?
- Is it then possible to equate reconstructed linguistic cultures and archaeological cultures in time and space?

Issues of Phylogeny and Reticulation

Linguists, plus those historians, archaeologists, and anthropologists who take an interest in historical comparative linguistics, have tended to view the past of language families as reflecting two processes – phylogenetic mother-language to daughter-language descent (the "family tree" model), and a co-evolutionary model which stresses contemporary interaction between neighboring languages (the "linguistic area" model). According to linguist Bob Dixon (1997), language families exist because of punctuated and relatively short-lived periods of expansion. They also share areal linguistic features as a result of much longer, non-punctuated processes of interaction and borrowing. As he states: "Each language has two possible kinds of similarities to other languages – genetic similarities, which are shared inheritances from a common proto-language; and areal similarities, which are due to borrowing from geographical neighbours" (Dixon 1997:15). There is a third kind of similarity – coincidental resemblance – but this is not of great significance at the level of linguistic classification under discussion here.

In major language families like Indo-European and Austronesian, the results of both processes are always evident. Far-flung languages, often thousands (even tens of thousands) of kilometers apart, share transparent phylogenetic relationships (e.g., English and Bengali, Malay and Tahitian, Navajo and the Athabaskan languages of Canada). On the other hand, languages within different families can share areal features within specific regions. Such "linguistic areas," widely discussed by linguists, include the Indian subcontinent, Mesoamerica, the Balkans, and the Amazon Basin. Yet – and this proviso requires stress – *the languages within these areas always retain their phylogenetic relationships in spite of interaction*. In other words, we do not find the Indian subcontinent to be full of phylogenetically unclassifiable languages that have all blended equal aspects of Indo-European, Dravidian, Tibeto-Burman, and Austroasiatic structure and vocabulary. Neither is this the case in the well-studied Vaupes region of Amazonia, where some groups even practice linguistic exogamy (a person should marry someone from another language group), yet language families such as Arawak and Tucanoan remain essentially coherent despite structural convergence and universal multilingualism (Sorensen 1982; Aikhenvald 1996, 2001).

Another basic and important concept here is that the initial formation of new language families, in Dixon's view, occurs *relatively quickly*. Languages change constantly for both internal (genetic) and external (areal) reasons, as can be verified quite simply by comparing Anglo-Saxon with the English of Chaucer and then E. M. Forster, or by comparing modern Romance languages with Latin, their common ancestor. Because of this, it stands to reason that widespread language families such as Indo-European and Austronesian must have spread to their geographical limits sufficiently recently in time for evidence of common origin to remain in all their component subgroups. Some linguists calculate that a maximum time span for such traces to remain would fall somewhere between 7,000 and 10,000 years ago, beyond which time percentages of shared cognates in basic (culturally universal) vocabulary would drop below about 5–10 percent. Thus, if early Indo-European had taken more than 10,000 years to spread from its homeland to the far reaches of Iceland and Bangladesh, then the Indo-European family would probably not exist at all in the way so clearly identifiable by linguists today. This may seem like an obscure technicality, but it does imply that the major language families of agriculturalist populations that exist today are Holocene, not Pleistocene, phenomena. Their life histories fall well within the time span of agricultural food production.

In the following sections I wish to examine some practical matters of language family phylogeny, making reference for illustrative purposes mainly to the Austronesian languages of Southeast Asia and Oceania, with forays here and there into other families such as Indo-European. The Austronesian family comprises about 1,000 languages spread more than halfway round the world from Madagascar to Easter Island (Figure 7.4) (Bellwood 1991, 1997a; Blust 1995a; Pawley and Ross 1993; Pawley 2003). There are perhaps 350 million Austronesian speakers, mostly in Southeast Asia, especially in Indonesia and the Philippines. Individual languages may have a few hundred indigenous speakers (like many in western Oceania) to upward of 60 million (Javanese). The Austronesians themselves mostly have Asian biological phenotypes, but many Melanesian populations in the western Pacific also speak Austronesian languages, as do Negritos in the Philippines. Cultures varied enormously in the pre-colonial past, from Hindu and Islamic states to forest hunting and gathering bands. Yet, by the logic described above, the Austronesian entity is not merely a result of random patterning in time and space. There is a solid core of shared phylogenetic history, both linguistic and cultural, despite vast geographic spread and the adoption of Austronesian languages by members of other, unrelated ethnic communities, especially in western Melanesia.

Moving now to some definitions, a language *family* is a grouping of languages that shares a unique set of identifying linguistic features, mainly as *retentions* from an earlier stage of linguistic history. Some of these identifying features might indeed be uniquely shared *innovations* generated at the point of origin (the proto-language stage), but without external witnesses in other language families it is impossible to be sure, and this issue takes us into the much-disputed level of *macrofamilies*, a concept to which we will return. Language families consist of *subgroups* of closely related languages, defined by uniquely shared innovations (rather than retentions) similar to derived or autapomorphic characters in biological cladistics. A good example here would be the uniquely shared innovations reconstructed by Robert Blust for the Proto-Malayo-Polynesian subgroup of Austronesian, which includes all Austronesian languages apart from the Formosan languages of Taiwan. These include the use of the enclitic form *-mu* for the second person singular pronoun, the loss of preconsonantal and final *s*, and the verbal prefixes *ma-* and *pa-*. These forms are not found in Formosan languages, and for phonological reasons Blust (1995b:620–621) interprets the situation as reflecting Proto-Malayo-Polynesian innovation, rather than Formosan loss. Such innovations will clearly have occurred during the time period prior to the break-up of the proto-language ancestral to the subgroup, going back as far as the previous ancestral phylogenetic division in the family tree. If they occurred before this last ancestral division they would not, presumably, be unique to one subgroup.

Admittedly, there can be complications in the recognition of cognates that can, in theory, skew the accuracy of historical interpretation. For instance, borrowings, if adopted by all the languages of a subgroup soon after they differentiated, can often mimic cognates. In this case, however, such early borrowings can offer the same historical implications of close geographical relationship as truly cognate (commonly inherited) forms. In addition, shared retentions from a proto-language can often masquerade as shared innovations if they are by chance preserved only by the members of a subgroup and none of their immediate neighbors, such that genuine cognates located more distantly are overlooked or not recorded. The sample density of studied languages clearly matters greatly in such cases; one must know that neighborhood absences are real and not just reflections of an absence of recording.

When family trees are constructed they reveal certain features. All have a reconstructible ancestral formulation – a *proto-language* (or in reality a hierarchy of multiple proto-languages) – that can be presented as a set of reconstructed features. The most important such features for prehistorians trying to reconstruct ancient cultures are ancestral lexical items with their most likely original meanings.[3] The reconstruction of meanings can sometimes be an ambiguous exercise if a reconstructed item has a wide and overlapping range of modern meanings, but in general such proto-lexicons can be a very powerful source of cultural data. For instance, proto-language reconstruction makes it certain that many of the major language families to be discussed later had their roots amongst agricultural peoples, not hunter-gatherers. Linguistic analysis can also sometimes show whether a given cultural trait was present continuously since the existence of the proto-language, or whether it was introduced later. Thus, many material cultural items connected with agriculture, seafaring, fishing, and pottery-making can be shown to go back continuously in the western Pacific to the Proto-Oceanic stage, the ancestral stage (ca. 3500 BP) for all the Austronesian languages of Oceania (Pawley 1981). Likewise, according to Robert Blust (2000a), the rice vocabulary in the Chamorro language of the Mariana Islands in Micronesia was inherited directly from Proto-Malayo-Polynesian about 4,000 years ago, rather than introduced to these islands by borrowing at a later date.

One must ask, however, what was the geographical extent of any specific reconstructed proto-language. Was it a single language spoken in one village, or was it a much broader regional spread of related dialects? Long ago, Gordon Childe (1926:12) suggested for Proto-Indo-European: "The Aryan [Proto-Indo-European] cradle must have had a geographic unity; the linguistic data alone presuppose a block of allied dialects constituting a linguistic continuum within a specific area and under more or less uniform geographical conditions." A similar view is held by Lehmann (1993:15): "Yet is clear that some social group, of whatever size or coherence, at one time spoke the relatively unified language labelled Proto-Indo-European and that this group maintained a specific culture." This need not mean an origin from a single ancestral community such as one village. As Dixon (1997:98) notes, any given language family "may have emanated not from a single language, but from a small areal group of distinct languages, with similar structures and forms." However, the concept of an original linguistic unity cannot be broken down too far in the direction of multiple unrelated languages.

Another aspect of language family trees is that they may be *strong* or *weak*, or indeed both at different times in their courses of development. Strong trees are like

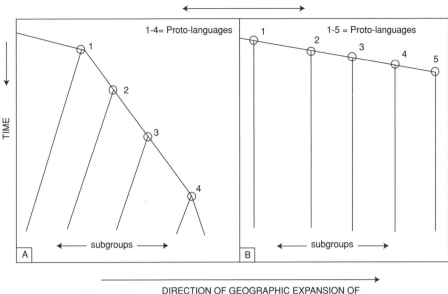

SPACE

TIME

1-4= Proto-languages

1-5 = Proto-languages

subgroups

subgroups

A

B

DIRECTION OF GEOGRAPHIC EXPANSION OF
FOUNDER COMMUNITIES

Figure 9.1 Strong and weak family trees. In A, the nodes are innovation-defined (strong) and well distinguished, by virtue of both geographical and chronological separation. In B, all nodes are innovation-linked (weak) and derived from rapid rake-like dispersal, thus relatively undifferentiated from each other.

"real" trees in shape, with an identifiable root and subsequent sequential branches (Figure 9.1A). As an example, the Polynesian languages developed a strong tree-like structure in their earlier period of differentiation, with a very well-defined proto-language (Proto-Polynesian) that contained, according to Andrew Pawley (1996), a remarkable number of innovations, including up to 1,392 lexical items (although some of these could have undetected cognates outside Polynesia), 14 morphological and 8 grammatical features. These were all created in a unified and well-bounded homeland region situated between about 1000 BC and AD 500 in Western Polynesia, in particular the Tongan and Samoan Islands (Kirch and Green 2001). This implies a long period of standstill, known in this case from archaeological correlations to have lasted more than 1,000 years, during which time populations remained in contact and shared large numbers of widespread linguistic changes that never spread to other neighboring areas such as Fiji or Vanuatu. Polynesian is thus an excellent example of an *innovation-defined* subgroup.[4]

Language families with *weak* phylogenies have rake-like structures with lots of coordinate and independent subgroup branches, and no coherent root (Figure 9.1B). The proto-language vocabularies of the Malayo-Polynesian subgroups of Austronesian in the Philippines, eastern Indonesia, and western Oceania, as reconstructed by Robert Blust (Figure 10.9 inset), share quite a uniform basic vocabulary (Blust 1993;

Pawley 1999). They are essentially *innovation-linked* subgroups in the terminology of Andrew Pawley and Malcolm Ross (1993, 1995). This suggests that subgroup differentiation occurred from a very widely spread dialect chain with no significant build-up of innovations in any region. In this case, the foundation dialect spread was rapid, perhaps under 500 years (very rapid for such a vast area), and there were no major foci of linguistic isolation within which *uniquely* shared innovations could be accumulated (Pawley 1999). As it happens, archaeology supports these historical linguistic reconstructions of rapid primary spread within the Austronesian family very accurately (Bellwood 2000c). English in North America and Australia would no doubt yield similarly rake-like subgroups were tribal societies of Neolithic (and non-literate) type to come back and dominate the world for the next 2,000 years. This is because the spreads of English in both continents were so rapid and so undifferentiated that no points of initial arrival in the respective land masses, and no directions of subsequent spread, would ever be recognizable in the pattern of subsequent phylogenetic differentiation.

The concept of the linguistic family tree can imply that languages split irrevocably once their speakers moved apart. But, in reality, ancient colonists would rarely have passed into such utter isolation that their languages separated with absolute finality. Such might have happened in remote places such as Easter Island, owing to the sheer difficulty of getting there, but in general we would expect communication between spreading daughter dialects to continue for as long as was physically possible. As Pawley and Ross (1995:20) point out, descendants of the Austronesian colonists of the large land masses of New Zealand and Madagascar "were generally mobile enough to maintain fairly cohesive dialect networks over large islands and island groups for up to 1000 years or so." Such broad networks remind one of the broad networks of relative homogeneity characteristic of the earliest Neolithic assemblages in many parts of the world. Thus, dispersal need not lead to immediate isolation, although the rate of diversification will be compounded if groups come into intensive contact with people speaking completely unrelated languages. Such happened with the Austronesian speakers who settled the Papuan-speaking regions of western Melanesia after 3,500 years ago. Their rate of lexical differentiation increased greatly, thus leading in the 1960s to an erroneous opinion, derived from lexicostatisical calculations, that Melanesia was actually the Austronesian homeland (Dyen 1965; Murdock 1968).

As far as language family homelands are concerned it is generally assumed, as in paleontology, that the most likely homelands are those where the deepest (i.e., oldest) subgroup separations, or bifurcations in the family tree, occur. Remember from the above, however, that one needs a strong family tree in order to be able to determine this. Rake-like formations, if they form the whole of a language family, make it essentially impossible to locate a homeland with precision. Luckily, many language families contain both rake-like and tree-like subgrouping structures. For instance, most subgroups of Indo-European have rake-like relationships, but the ancient Anatolian languages have sufficient unique features to make it possible that the Indo-European homeland was located somewhere in Turkey (Drews 2001). Likewise, the Malayo-Polynesian subgroups are also rake-like, as noted above, but the Formosan languages, which do not belong to Malayo-Polynesian and form several separate first-order subgroups within Austronesian, suggest very strongly a Taiwan homeland. Another point to note is that a language family need not always have originated in the center of its current distribution. Such reasoning manifestly does not work for families such as Austronesian, or Benue-Congo (including Bantu), where spreads out of homelands were essentially unidirectional in the early periods.

Introducing the Players

The indigenous language map of the world, as we know it after stripping away the European colonial languages, does not reveal a picture of even gradation in which all languages prior to AD 1500 were equally different from all neighboring languages, without sharp boundaries. If it did, human prehistory would require little explanation; all societies would presumably have evolved *in situ*, hand-in-hand with their neighbors and with only localized reassortments since linguistically competent human societies first spread across the earth.

In fact, the language map of the world shows some very clear-cut patterns of differentiation, not only in clines of diversity, but also in sharp boundaries between language families, most of which are sufficiently bounded and defined in linguistic terms that they stand apart from each other as discrete and unarguable entities. Although there are "problem" languages in this regard, especially the creoles, pidgins, and other linguistic entities which resist genetic classification, the major families of the world are very well founded in terms of comparative linguistic data. They are not merely deceptive crystallizations out of an even mesh of language diversity. As Aikhenvald and Dixon (2001:6) point out, "It is often easier to prove that a set of languages form a genetic unit (a language family) than it is to establish subsidiary genetic units (subgroups) within a family."

Because the component languages within the well-defined families share a common genetic ancestry, and because many of these families had reached (in ancestral form) their current geographical limits well back in prehistoric times, we are forced to assume that they owe their existences to processes which took place long before the rise of conquest states, literacy, world religions, and centralized systems of education and language domination. In other words, they are solidly "prehistoric," pre-literate, and pre-state. Families which certainly spread over vast distances in prehistoric times include Indo-European, Dravidian, "Altaic" (a controversial macrofamily that might include Turkic, Mongolian, and perhaps even Japanese), Uralic, Afroasiatic, Benue-Congo (including Bantu), Austroasiatic, Austronesian, Sino-Tibetan, and many of the major families of the Americas such as Uto-Aztecan, Algonquian, and Arawak (Figures 1.1 and 1.2). Of course, subgroups of many of these families – Germanic, Sinitic, and Malayic, for instance – have undergone considerable expansion in historical times, but this does not negate the observation that the origins of all these families and either much or all of their foundation geographical expansion occurred long before written history began.

On the other hand, some other language families, such as Khoisan and Nilo-Saharan of Africa, probably most of the families of northern Australia, parts of New Guinea and northwestern North America, together with the several small language isolates dotted here and there across the world (e.g., Basque), might have remained relatively static for enormous time spans without significant movement at all, except for contraction due to language competition. Colin Renfrew (1992a, 1992b), for instance, regards such language groups as established very early in the history of modern human global colonization.

If all the major language families of the world imply human population expansions, as suggested here, then we have a situation of immense significance, especially in the Old World where a small number of language families have expanded to enormous extents in quite recent prehistoric time. In order to understand this significance, especially in relation to the archaeological and genetic histories of human populations, we need to understand how languages and language families have evolved in time and space in the minds and mouths of actual *speakers*. We cannot decide this solely from the comparative reconstruction of proto-languages and subgroup relationships since these tell us most directly about the languages themselves, rather than their speakers, just as the archaeological record tells us essentially about material culture and only secondarily about its makers. We need a worldwide comparative viewpoint that must be derived from available historical and ethnographic records of language spread and replacement history, as recorded from the ancient world onward, and from the data of sociolinguistics – the study of language in relation to social factors.

Such comparative data allow us to think seriously about a number of questions important for interpreting ancient language history, even though we are working with gradations of likelihood, not proof. How do languages spread, how fast do they change through time, how do languages compete with and replace each other, what happens when the speakers of different languages interact, and how do the answers to these questions vary according to the socio-economic situation? Isolated pre-literate Neolithic tribes and huge centralized empires with literacy and high levels of ethnic diversity are most unlikely to have undergone identical linguistic histories.

How Do Languages and Language Families Spread?

The only plausible explanation of the currency of [Indo-European] languages so similar over so large an area at the beginnings of historical periods is that they derive from dialects of a fairly homogeneous prehistoric language which had been disseminated by migrations out of a smaller region. (Friedrich 1966)

Language spread without a significant movement of people is seemingly a rare phenomenon in North America. (Foster 1996:67)

Linguists often make the assumption that a true language family, one which can be shown by the comparative study of shared innovations to be internally structured genetically, with an array of reconstructed proto-languages, must owe its existence to some kind of population expansionary process. From a comparative perspective this is the only explanation that makes sense. Historical data indicate that language shift alone, without population movement or some degree of dispersal by the population carrying the target language, has never created anything remotely equaling those vast inter-continental genetic groupings of languages with which we are here concerned. One has only to examine the varying linguistic histories of many the great conquest empires of the past – Assyrian, Achaemenid, Hellenistic, Roman, Mongol, Aztec, even Spanish and British – to realize this. Imperial conquest by itself, without large-scale and permanent settlement by members of the conquering population, generally imposes little apart from loan words in the long term.

Trade also is generally of little significance as a factor behind large-scale language spread. Consider the situation in trader-conscious Papua New Guinea, where the linguistic diversity reached record levels (New Guinea had about 760 languages) in ethnographic times and is only now being leveled by Tok Pisin and English, awesomely backed by the modern muscle of statehood, literacy, television, and the circumvention of group endogamy owing to massive social change (Kulick 1992). Yet even with all this inducement, on a scale totally inapplicable to situations in remote prehistory, the dominance of Tok Pisin remains only a local phenomenon on a whole-Pacific scale. Conquest, trade, and cultural diffusion can spread languages, but never on a trans-continental language family scale unless assisted by another factor, this being *actual movement* of existing speakers of the languages concerned.

Rather than examining at great length here the historical documentation necessary to support these views, I will focus on the example of the seventh century AD Arab conquests out of Arabia, in support of the idea that successful language spread required in the first instance a spread of native speakers. We look first at the spread of the Arabic language itself (Khoury and Kostiner 1990; Goldschmidt 1996; Levtzion 1979; Pentz 1992; Petry 1998). In parts of Jordan and Syria there were already widespread and numerous Arabic-speaking populations who had migrated northward out of Arabia long before the seventh century, so the Muslim conquest here did not require extensive language replacement. The introduction of Arabic into Iraq and Egypt required conquest, and occurred via garrison cities of settled Arab soldiers (about 40,000 in the case of Fustat near Cairo) and their families. So a spread of Arabic, in the first instance, in the mouths of settlers and soldiers is not in doubt, regardless of how many people (in North Africa, for instance) might later have adopted that language.

However, the Arab conquests did not extend into South or Southeast Asia, or even directly into Iran and Pakistan. Thus, the vast majority (perhaps 80 percent) of Muslims in the world today, more in Indonesia than in any other country, do not speak Arabic (apart from loan words) unless they are reciting the Koran, in which case they use seventh-century rather than modern Arabic. As Mansfield (1985:40) notes: "although Arabic language and culture retain a special and predominant place in the world of Islam, only about one fifth of the one sixth of mankind who are Muslims are Arabic speaking." This gives us a major negative example – no population movement, no language spread, regardless of what might have happened with the religion.

The Indonesian experience with the spread of Islam recapitulated that which occurred there a millennium earlier with the spreads of Hinduism and Buddhism from India. In this case there was also no major population movement into Southeast Asia, apart perhaps from a trickle of traders and religious functionaries, despite the profound socio-cultural impact of the Indic religions, modes of kingship, and literally hundreds of Sanskrit, Prakrit, and Tamil loan words in the Malay and Javanese languages (Gonda 1973). Yet Indonesians never converted to the use of Indic languages in any but learned circumstances, and Indonesian and Indian languages do not even share any noticeable typological features as a result of the contact. As Colin Masica (1976:184) points out, religious and political domination alone is not sufficient to promote such convergence; one needs "more intimate, less structured, intercourse."

The moral of all this is that Arabic spread essentially, in the first place, in the mouths of Arabic-speaking settlers in the conquered areas of the Middle East and North Africa only, and in the early years it seems there was very little shift to the language by other non-Arab populations. The whole process was no doubt assisted by the association of Arabic with the Koran, but even this was clearly not a driving factor behind significant language spread. In later centuries, of course, many Middle Eastern and North African populations not of Arab origin must have adopted the Arabic language, but this is a little beside the point. Our interest here is in the original spread and its causation, and this was manifestly not a spread caused by language shift, but by native speaker movement.

If a cosmopolitan language such as Arabic had such difficulty in spreading into regions not settled by Arabs, even aided by a document as linguistically persuasive as the Koran, likewise Sanskrit with the Mahabharata, what hope can we have that Neolithic languages could have spread over the vast distances required to found language families by such means? We see a picture similar to that for Arabic with Latin, which at the end of the Roman Empire only became a lasting vernacular, as the mother tongue of the Romance languages, in those regions close to the heart of the empire favored for intensive settlement by Latin speakers (Iberia, southern France, Romania – rather brutally conquered by Trajan, and Italy itself; Krantz 1988; Brosnahan 1963). Greek died beyond Greece and Asia Minor with the decline of the Hellenistic kingdoms, even though in this case there was some colonization by the followers of Alexander the Great and his successors, albeit in small numbers compared to the surrounding native populations.

Conversely, the English language spread into the Americas and Australasia through massive levels of population movement, backed up by continuous outflow from the source region. However, in other regions dominated by British conquest and control, such as South Asia, much of Africa, and Malaysia, the existing dense populations together with tropical diseases kept the colonization process at bay, as described so lucidly by Alfred Crosby (1986). English in Africa, India, and Malaysia today is mainly spoken by elites and shows no sign of replacing dominant native languages such as Hindi, Tamil, or Malay. According to Breton (1997), there were only 202,000 native

English speakers in India in the 1981 census year, mostly Anglo-Indian, although 11 million people used English as a secondary language (out of a total population of 1,100 million). Dutch today is essentially an extinct language in Indonesia, despite 300 years of colonial government, but with no population movement from the Netherlands into Indonesia on any scale.

Basically, and right at the heart of the matter in terms of the theme of this book, is the observation that a major language family, if it is identified by the comparative method as a genetic unit with a history of differentiation from a common ancestral language (or a series of related dialects), can only have been spread by processes of movement by native speakers, not by language shift alone. The relevance of this observation for recent human prehistory as a whole (given that clear-cut evidence for linguistic relationship of the kind being examined here does not survive for much more than 10,000 years) is quite colossal. Since much of the world is divided amongst quite a small number of major language families, recent human prehistory is perhaps to be written very much in terms of a small number of equivalent massive continent-wide dispersals of population.

But, and this I think is a most important proviso, it should not be assumed that such spreading populations of native speakers were always derived entirely from the localized population amongst whom the language family originated in the first place. The world has far too many situations where biology and language do not agree in precise unison, and such situations demand explanation. As examples we have clear biological differences between western Europeans and South Asians who speak Indo-European languages, and between Melanesians and Filipinos who speak Austronesian languages. Language shift and contact-induced language change obviously matter today and have mattered throughout history, but we must beware of giving them a relevance beyond their due. We consider them in more detail below.

How Do Languages Change Through Time?

It is now necessary to ask if linguistic analysis can provide chronological data independent of those derived from the archaeological record. The answer is a little ambiguous. Linguists reconstructing the history of a language family can generally only go back in time as far as the proto-language at the base of the phylogeny. The dispersal of this proto-language will represent a punctuation, an erasure of any previous linguistic pattern, although traces of previous patterns can sometimes survive in enclaves or so-called "linguistic isolates." Going beyond the family proto-language level takes us into the level of macrofamilies, with lots of attendant controversy owing to the eroded nature of the record and its inherent ambiguity.

Linguistic analysis, in fact, does not yield time depth easily, as will be seen from a perusal of a recent compilation of papers on this topic (Renfrew et al. 2000). Ancient written languages on a world scale are too rare (and too recent) to be of very much assistance in throwing light on the periods under investigation in this book. Some can give rule of thumb ideas about rates of change, derivable for instance by comparing

Coptic with Ancient Egyptian, Romance languages with late classical Latin, or Mandarin with Old Chinese. We can also use the archaeological record quite precisely in island situations where we can be fairly sure that only one population, and that ancestral to the present population, has been in occupation. On these grounds, the Vanuatu languages, for instance, can only have been developing for about 3,000 years, since Vanuatu was first settled then. Maori has closer to 800 years since its arrival in New Zealand. Yet these year counts by themselves do not get us very far in a comparative sense, unless we assume that there is a constant rate, like a mutation rate, by which languages change their vocabularies through time.

Claims for such a regular rate of language change, especially in core vocabulary (common and universal words in all languages, not culturally specific words), have been made by a number of linguists. The most famous is the glottochronological formula developed in the 1950s by Morris Swadesh, which assumes random core-vocabulary replacement in any language of 19.5 percent per 1,000 years (this figure being derived from a 200-word list applied to Romance languages). It is not necessary to examine the mathematical foundations of glottochronology here, but most linguists, at least those who do not reject it altogether, regard it as most useful for the past 500–2,500 years. Like radiocarbon dating, the more one goes back in time the less the quantity of datable material that remains. Linguists who use glottochronology and regard it as relatively accurate include Ehret (1998, 2000, 2003) for African language families, Kaufman (1990a) for American families, and Nichols (1998b), who states that it can be used successfully for language history in general after 6000 BP. As Kaufman (1990a: 27–28) states:

> The fact remains that when applied as it should be applied, glottochronology seems to agree remarkably well with linguistic inferences arrived at by other means, such as branching models based on shared non-trivial innovations or absolute chronology derived from dated monuments.

Not all linguists agree with this rather enthusiastic perspective. Observations that languages seem to have changed at different rates, some being conservative, some innovative, were made almost from the start. Some linguists pointed to a common and intriguing habit in many tribal societies known as word tabooing, which dictates that a sound that occurs both in an everyday word and in the name of a dead person must no longer be uttered. The everyday word thus has to be changed and so the lexicon as a whole can change quite quickly, at least in theory (e.g., Kahler 1978; Chowning 1985). On another tack, Malcolm Ross (1991; also Blust 1991) suggests that, in a dispersal situation, the stay-at-home languages will tend to be more conservative than the migrating ones owing to social dislocation and founder effects; small migrant groups tend to lose and modify linguistic resources more rapidly than the larger and more stable populations back in the homeland.

Perhaps the strongest critic of glottochronology as applied to Austronesian languages has been Robert Blust (2000b), who compared a number of modern Malayo-Polynesian languages within the Austronesian family with their reconstructed common ancestor,

Proto-Malayo-Polynesian (PMP). Logically, if all languages change their basic vocabularies at a uniform rate, then all daughter-languages derived from a common ancestor should be equally different from that ancestor, given that they have each been descending from it for the same length of time. Blust used a 200-word list and was able to show that some Malayo-Polynesian languages, especially certain Polynesian languages and Malay, retain a large number of PMP cognates and have thus had conservative histories. Other languages, mostly in western Melanesia, retain very few PMP cognates and are thus innovative. If one applies glottochronology to these innovative languages one comes up with the erroneous conclusion that the entire Austronesian language family originated in Melanesia, a conclusion completely at odds with the mainstream comparative tradition of linguistics that makes a homeland in Taiwan almost certain.

The main reasons for this puzzling situation seem to be that Austronesian-speaking societies in western Melanesia formed small social groups in which language differences were emphasized as social markers, and many were in intensive contact with speakers of completely unrelated Papuan languages and borrowed frequently from them (Capell 1969; Dutton 1994, 1995; Dutton and Tryon 1994; Ross 2001). The Polynesian and Malay languages existed in linguistically less diverse environments and were spoken by larger and more cohesive groups. The implications of all this are that lexicostatistics documents variation in retention rate, not true phylogeny.

So where does this leave glottochronology? Obviously, languages that have had histories similar to those of the Romance languages might have had similar rates of change, and this seems to be true of Polynesian languages and Malay. Melanesian languages have not had such histories, and once one domino falls it tends to wobble the rest. For deeply prehistoric societies we cannot easily know what the precise linguistic environment might have been, so we can never really know if a given glottochronological date is right or wrong. Nevertheless, in the next chapter I will refer to glottochronological dates in some instances since, en masse, they do seem to show some overall correlation with archaeologial dates for the beginnings of agriculture, at least as far as the major language families with agriculturalist proto-languages are concerned (Bellwood 2000c). There may not be precision here in all circumstances but there is a trend, in the sense that Afroasiatic, Sino-Tibetan, and Uto-Aztecan, to give three examples from many, have glottochronological time depths which tend to agree quite well with the time depths for agriculture in the likely homeland areas. We return to the details later.

Macrofamilies, and more on the time factor

Although language families are recognized as genetic groups by linguists, it is very difficult to reconstruct much deeper genetic groups comprising several families, even though comparative linguistic principles remain the same regardless of whether one is working within or beyond the individual family (Hegedüs 1989; Michalove et al. 1998). This very characteristic of language families, that they cohere within but not convincingly without, supports the view of rapid punctuational origins during which earlier linguistic landscapes were erased by dispersal (Dixon 1997; Aikhenvald and Dixon 2001:9). In addition, language families are not only discrete, but they also appear to have fairly limited time depths, as discussed above. According to Johanna Nichols (1998b), they can only retain genetic identity for about 6,000 to 10,000 years. But I would ask if this is a real statistical limit, or an epiphenomenon of the fact that virtually all major language families have for some reason radiated fairly explosively within precisely this time period, prior to which time such radiations tended hardly to occur. The mere fact that reconstruction at the macrofamily level leads to so much acrimonious and inconclusive debate, when logically it should not do so if language family evolution has always been even and regular, supports the idea of relatively recent starburst-like episodes of language family dispersal from homeland regions. In such cases, any foundation relationships that might exist between different families will be rake-like and always ambiguous.

The answers to the confrontations that divide linguists at this deep level of reconstruction are unlikely to come from within linguistics itself. Multidisciplinary observations, especially from the archaeological record, can perhaps provide some essential help. For instance, Colin Renfrew and I were suggesting over a decade ago that many language families originated in and spread from a small number of specific regions where agriculture began early in the Holocene (Bellwood 1989; Renfrew 1991). This is because farming is a more efficient driver of language family dispersal in previously inhabited landscapes than hunting and gathering (allowing, of course, that hunters can spread far and rapidly if there is virtual prior depopulation). These agriculturalist language families, on geographical grounds, might share homeland relationships of a macrofamily nature, even if clear demonstration of such will always be highly elusive.

Thus, language inter-family relationships, even if only reflecting early borrowing and propinquity of homeland rather than true common ancestry, could have firm foundations in historical events. Before trying to reconstruct such events, however, it is necessary to consider in more detail how languages replace and influence each other through time and space.

Languages in Competition – Language Shift

The essential factor in long-distance language spread and continuing long-term survival in vernacular form at the whole population level, especially in pre-state circumstances, is a sufficiency of population movement at the base of the dispersal. Ephemeral languages of trade or government that fade away as soon as the organizational structure beneath them is removed are of little historical interest for the issues discussed here. The significance of population movement can be established by analyzing any major historical situation.

But languages rarely spread through uninhabited voids, except in cases of initial human colonization of new lands. Native populations will sometimes adopt languages brought in by outsiders who represent larger (in demographic terms), more powerful, and more prestigious cultures, although this need not happen in all cases. Indeed, if colonists/conquerors do not have a demographic advantage over the long term, for instance the Normans in England, the British in Malaysia, the Dutch in Indonesia, and even the Hellenistic Greeks in central Asia, then their languages will rarely be adopted as the vernacular by large, healthy, and culturally viable native populations. Nevertheless, language shift is important and must be an essential ingredient in explaining the many cases in large-scale human patterning where linguistic and biological distributions show discordance.

Spreading languages also have a natural attraction for speakers of other more local languages in areas of high linguistic diversity – they allow access to widespread contacts and resources otherwise only available through laborious processes of multilingualism. Thus, they can become lingua francas – success breeds more success, at least for a time. As Cooper notes (1982:17): "nothing stops the spread of a lingua franca more surely than the existence of a rival lingua franca." But in the early days of agricultural dispersal the other lingua francas were surely few and far between. It is likely that the early spread of Austronesian languages into Melanesia was lubricated because Proto-Oceanic (the reconstructed proto-language of the period of Austronesian colonization beyond the Bismarck Archipelago) represented a useful degree of uniformity, perhaps as a lingua franca, throughout a network of highly diversified coastal Papuan languages.

If we are to understand the past through the lens of comparative linguistics we need to understand a little about why language shift can occur. Some linguists take the view that languages spread automatically by shift, with no movement of native speakers of the target languages (the ones being shifted to) at all (Nichols 1997b). I am not aware of any historical, anthropological, or linguistic data that render such a view very convincing, at least not on the large-scale language family canvas under consideration here. Language shift is not a simple matter, as anyone who has tried to learn a second language will know (the "foreign accent" problem). The very important factor termed "language loyalty" (Haugen 1988) generally means that a population will not give up its native language unless it is already bilingual in both this and the target language to which the shift will eventually occur. Even then, multilingualism can be stable and long lasting. Eventual shift will require deep influence from the culture that "owns" the target language, influence that will normally require a pre-existing substantial presence of native speakers amongst the linguistically different native population (Nettle 1998, 1999).

There must also be a reason for the shift to occur. In the case of the Agta Negrito hunter-gatherers of the Philippines, all of whom adopted Austronesian languages long ago, the shifts were probably due to a wish to trade and to provide field labor in return for agricultural produce, plus a generally increasing encapsulation of the Agta by Austronesian farmers. The original shift seems to have operated as a process of creolization, according to Lawrence Reid (1994a, 1994b), followed later by a "decreolization" process as encapsulation and the intensity of Austronesian influence became stronger.

There can also be active forces working against language shift in situations where one might expect it to occur. Heath and Laprade (1982:137) describe 16th-century

Indian reluctance to learn Spanish in the Andes, preferring instead to adopt the important Indian languages Quechua and Aymara, which were also used widely in Spanish missions for translation of the Bible:

> Castilian did not spread into workaday technical uses for a majority of the Indians. It became the sometime language of administrative and judicial affairs, and the tongue of those who were able to gain access to the creole class. Its use was primarily restricted to urban areas, . . . in the countryside it remained limited to uses in churches and governmental units. For the majority of rural Indians, it was grafted onto religious rituals, sacred texts, and polite associations with their oppressors. In some cases, the high-prestige language was adopted by the Indians in low-prestige functions, and the language was debunked even by those who learned it (e.g., in its use by Indian males when they were drunk). From the colonial policy perspective, there was a great disparity between the potential and actual spread of Castilian.

Interestingly, of course, many millions of American Indians still speak their native languages today – not all have simply converted to Spanish or Portuguese. As another example, Joseph Errington (1998) describes Indonesian resistance to adopting Javanese as a national language and lingua franca, despite the fact that it is the native language of the ruling Javanese elite. Instead, the leaders of independent Indonesia in 1947 chose Malay, a trader language used across Indonesia since Islamic times and thus a neutral language not tied to ethnicity or control. In Errington's terms, the spread of Malay, as Bahasa Indonesia, has been miraculous and unique, as any traveler to the remotest corners of Indonesia will have observed. But even so, Bahasa Indonesia is not replacing Javanese in Java itself, where instead we have the formation of a stable diglossia in which both languages mutually influence each other.

The moral of all this is that language shift is not an automatic result of contact between speakers of different languages, even if one is more "prestigious" than the other. Neither is it an inevitable final state amongst bi- or multilingual populations. It is an important process, but one that is completely unconvincing as an explainer of language family spreads over vast distances by Neolithic or Formative farmers.

Languages in competition – contact-induced change

As noted, when speakers of two different languages are brought together by the in-migration of one of the groups, it is not a foregone conclusion that one language will automatically scoop the pool and replace the other. Stable situations can evolve in which many languages coexist because the majority of the population is either bi- or multilingual. In such situations the small local languages can often undergo "one-way leaning" toward the models provided by the more widely spoken community languages, by means of a process termed metatypy by the linguist Malcolm Ross (1997, 2001). Metatypy is one aspect of a large field of contact-induced language change, a field that runs from limited borrowing of a few vocabulary items, through metatypy, to "interference through shift," a process whereby a population that adopts a new language will also modify that language by carrying over aspects of their previous language. Such modifications can often involve far more than just a "foreign accent" factor and can sometimes lead to considerable structural change in the successful language, as in the many regional versions of modern English spoken by aboriginal populations across the world.[5] Many of these contact-induced processes of change, however, stop short of actual language replacement.

Contact-induced change on a deep level, beyond superficial borrowing, will normally only operate if the speakers of two or more languages in contact are bi- or multilingual. As Marianne Mithun (1999:314) points out: "Cultural traits are of course more easily diffused than linguistic ones, which require intensive contact and in many cases bilingualism." As noted above, such bilingualism will not in itself encourage language shift, and amongst healthy and demographically viable populations the result is likely to be long-term situations of contact-induced change. This process has already been referred to as reticulation, the operation of areal diffusion for long periods between much shorter dispersive punctuations. In extreme cases, if the reticulation is allowed to run unchecked for several millennia, the result can be a breakdown of subgrouping structure altogether. Dixon (1997) claims this for many Australian languages, and George Grace (1990) suggests it to be the case for the Austronesian languages of New Caledonia, where languages lose forms and then borrow them back from widespread neighboring languages with such intensity that discrete languages no longer exist.

As Grace also notes, however, this situation is rather extreme. The great majority of Austronesian languages elsewhere are far more amenable to application of the comparative method. It seems that such extreme cases of areal diffusion exist mainly amongst small-scale egalitarian societies with limited systems of political integration, especially in those that lack formal descent groups (Foley 1986).[6] Societies with corporate land-holding descent groups, and especially chiefdoms and states, usually contain more homogeneous and widespread languages owing to their much larger networks of communication and control (e.g., Dahlin et al. 1987 for the Maya lowlands). Situations of extreme areal interaction have little relevance for language spread, or for the episodes of agricultural population dispersal in which we are most interested.

We have now reviewed most of the features of the linguistic record that need to be taken into account in the reconstruction of linguistic prehistory. These comparative observations are most useful for guidance, and, as noted, can never make any given interpretation an absolute certainty. But having them in the background can make the inferences to be presented on language family dispersal a great deal more convincing. As far as language spread at the family level is concerned, population movement would appear to be far more convincing as a long-distance mover than other more reticulative forms of inter-population contact.

Chapter 10

The Spread of Farming: Comparing the Archaeology and the Linguistics

This chapter examines the patterns of origin and dispersal for the major agriculturalist language families, as visible from the viewpoint of comparative linguistics. The question at this point is whether the foundation "layers" of language families/subgroups, and Neolithic/Formative farming economies and material cultures, could have spread together.

First of all, Figure 1.3 encapsulates current understanding of the archaeological record pertaining to the origins and spreads of the major agricultural systems and the cultures associated with them, as dealt with in chapters 3 to 8. It is not necessary to justify these conclusions further at this point, although I would not be so unwise as to claim that they are fixed and immutable. New data might impose changes, yet my feeling is that we have enough of a world archaeological record to make it unlikely that any complete upheaval will occur.

The distributions of the major agriculturalist languages at AD 1500 are delineated in Figures 1.1 and 1.2, together with those of the major hunter-gatherer families. If the homelands and directions of spread of agricultural systems and technologies, as modeled in Figure 1.3, were indeed concurrent with the homelands and directions of spread of the major agriculturalist language families, then we should expect a number of correlations. Relevant language families should have their putative homelands located within or close to agricultural homelands; they should overlap or intersect geographically within or close to agricultural homelands; and they should have dispersal histories that commence chronologically within agricultural homeland areas and then become progressively younger with distance away from such homelands.

To see if there are such correlations, we turn to the history of the major agriculturalist language families themselves, those that cover large extents of terrain in agricultural latitudes and that have reconstructed agricultural terminology, including names for crops and domesticated animals, in their proto-languages. As far as these target language families are concerned, there are three essential arenas of linguistic reconstruction that are of immediate interest, these being the identification of homelands, the identification of early cultural vocabularies (especially those pertaining to agriculture), and the histories of expansion and dispersal of their major subgroups. Questions of macrofamily affiliation for individual language families also arise.

Western and Central Eurasia, and Northern Africa

The major language families to be considered in this region are Indo-European, Afroasiatic, and (Elamo-)Dravidian. The Indo-European and Afroasiatic families today occupy much of the area covered in prehistory by the Southwest Asian agropastoral combination of crops and animals, and it is possible that Dravidian originated also within this region. Indo-European and Afroasiatic are flanked to the south and east respectively by the African and East Asian monsoonal zones, with their quite different rainfall regimes and domesticated plant species, and to the north by regions beyond the range of Neolithic farmers. There are disputed linguistic claims that these three families belong in one macrofamily, termed Nostratic, and we return to this concept later.

Indo-European

We begin with Indo-European (IE – Figure 10.1), since this is by far the most studied language family in the world, and also the one that has driven much of the debate over how one determines deep language history. No discussion of Indo-European can begin without a reference to Sir William Jones, who in 1786 commented on similarities between Sanskrit, Greek, Latin, Gothic, Celtic, and Persian, and added the famous phrase that they must have been "sprung from some common source, which, perhaps, no longer exists" (Pachori 1993:175; Johann Reinhold Forster anticipated Jones by about a decade with his comments on Austronesian!). In 1890, von Bradtke divided the IE languages into two groups in terms of a sound change in the word for "one hundred," thus defining Greek, Italic, Germanic, and Celtic (and later, Tocharian and Anatolian) as a *centum* group, and Baltic, Slavic, Albanian, Armenian, and Indo-Iranian as a *satem* group. At first sight, the geography of all this looks rather odd, but explanations are offered below.

Indo-European from the Pontic steppes?

The first, and long dominant, "world view" of IE origins developed through the middle and later years of the 20th century, with contributions from both archaeologists and linguists. This is the Pontic steppes theory, with a homeland located in Ukraine and southern Russia, north of the Black and Caspian Seas, and a dispersal associated with conquests by late Neolithic and Chalcolithic/Early Bronze Age

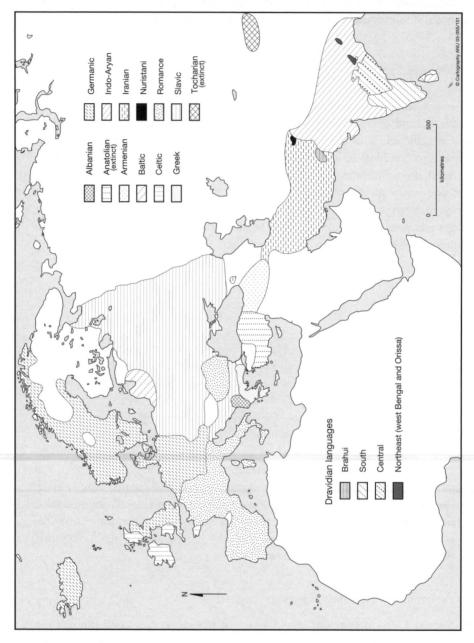

Figure 10.1 The distributions of the major subgroups of the Indo-European and Dravidian language families, after Ruhlen 1987.

pastoralists who had knowledge of horse-riding and use of the wheel for transport. No proposed family trees for IE actually demand a Pontic homeland, and we return to subgrouping matters below. The Pontic steppes theory has basically been driven by a congregation of assumptions, unrelated to linguistic subgrouping *per se*, that can be listed as follows:

1. Linguistic reconstructions of terms for wheeled vehicles to a relatively early stage of IE support a homeland in the Pontic steppes, where carts are known to date back to about 3000 BC in the archaeological record (Anthony 1995; Bakker et al. 1999).
2. Certain aspects of reconstructed Proto-IE society could be taken to imply patrilineality and pastoralism, the latter again pointing to the rather dry Pontic steppe region, albeit not in any specific way.
3. Some linguists have an intuition, backed by glottochronology, that the IE languages cannot be more than 5,000 or 6,000 years old, and thus late Neolithic or Early Bronze Age, but not early Neolithic or Mesolithic, in archaeological terms.
4. The Anatolian languages (discussed further below) are stated by many historians and linguists to be non-native to Anatolia, and thus of no relevance for IE homeland questions.

Within the archaeological literature, for this is where it has been most strongly propounded, the Pontic steppes hypothesis was clearly stated by Gordon Childe in 1926, and then taken up in many publications by Marija Gimbutas (e.g., 1985, 1991). In Gimbutas' formulations, the early IE populations spread by migration of patriarchal horse-riding pastoralists from the Pontic steppes between 4500 and 2500 BC, in up to four successive waves. These people constructed burial mounds (*kurgans*), and formed an elite who imposed their IE languages upon a matriarchal (and non-IE) Neolithic population with goddess-centered rather than patrilineal ideologies. As Gimbutas (1985:185) once stated of Neolithic Anatolia: "the great neolithic civilization of this region is the antithesis of all the characteristics understood as Proto-Indo-European."

The Pontic steppes origin has been supported (with variations on some of the Gimbutas details) by scholars too numerous to discuss individually. Currently, one of its strongest proponents is archaeologist David Anthony (1991, 1995; Anthony and Brown 2000), who has examined both the archaeological and the linguistic records for evidence of early horse riding and wheeled vehicles on the Eurasian steppes. In Anthony's most recent formulations, horse riding could have been practiced north of the Black Sea as early as 3500 BC, and the Proto-Indo-Europeans might thus have spread together with horses, wheeled vehicles, and a full agropastoral economy from the steppes, entering Europe by about 3000 BC.

All these reconstructions, of course, require processes of "elite dominance" for the Proto-Indo-European (PIE) populations to impose their languages on the much larger Neolithic populations already spread across Europe, processes in my view based more in guesswork than sociolinguistic reality. Indeed, all four assumptions listed above as being at the base of the hypothesis are now under attack from many sides.

For instance, Jim Mallory (1997), one of the staunchest supporters of a Pontic homeland, is clearly no longer convinced that domesticated horses and wheeled vehicles *must* be reconstructed to PIE (although wild horses could be another matter). Neither are linguists James Clackson (2000), Robert Coleman (1988:450), Calvert Watkins (1985), and historian Igor Diakonov (1985). The reconstructed PIE vocabulary[1] was not exclusively pastoralist, and neither is the archaeological record entirely pastoralist from the relevant period on the steppes (Mallory 1997; Anthony and Brown 2000). Recent research on horse domestication by archaeologist Marsha Levine (et al. 1999) suggests much later dates for horse riding, only late second millennium BC and thus irrelevant for PIE dispersal. Many linguists are now willing to entertain suggestions that PIE could be older than 5,000 years (see below), and the idea that the Anatolian languages were not native to Anatolia (and thus not relevant for IE homeland questions) has no strong factual basis. But the fundamental nail in the coffin of the Pontic steppes hypothesis was hammered by Colin Renfrew (1987), when he asked how a *kurgan*-based expansion of late Neolithic and Bronze Age conquering pastoralists across most of Europe could have left absolutely no corresponding continent-wide horizon in the archaeological record.

Where did PIE really originate and what can we know about it?

In order to determine the true homeland of PIE, we must understand the phylogeny of the IE major subgroups. However, many linguists have pointed out that there is no well-stratified family tree for IE with consecutive bifurcations and a clear root. With the possible exception of Anatolian, all the IE families form a rake-like pattern of descent, running in parallel from a very widespread basal linguistic forebear. The fact that some subgroups, such as Romance, Slavic, Germanic, and Indo-Iranian, spread very extensively long after PIE times does not affect this basic rake formation, but merely adds "bushes" on the ends of the tines. The existing subgroups of IE separated from one another very early in the history of IE diversification, and no obvious homeland therefore springs forth from the shape of the tree itself.

This rake-like phylogeny of IE suggests a very wide dispersal of early IE languages, followed by maintenance of contacts in different directions (as indicated by overlapping isoglosses) for perhaps a millennium, according to Johanna Nichols (1998a, 1998b) and Calvert Watkins (1998), prior to the development of mutual unintelligibility and the separation of distinct subgroups. However, there is one subgroup, discovered with the translation early last century of second-millennium BC Hittite and the discovery of several other ancient Anatolian languages (Lydian, Lycian, Palaic, and Luwian), that renders a *completely* rake-like foundation for IE increasingly untenable.

Today, increasing numbers of linguists regard the Anatolian languages as a single branch of IE, coordinate with a second branch containing all the other subgroups. If this view is correct, then the Anatolian languages *must* be relevant for the IE homeland question. In addition, several Russian linguists claim that PIE shares loan words with Proto-Semitic, presumably located in the northern Levant, and also with Proto-Kartvelian, one of the three language families in the Caucasus (Gamkrelidze and

Ivanov 1985, 1995; Gamkrelidze 1989; Dolgopolsky 1987; Klimov 1991). The geography of these borrowings has led some of these scholars to place the IE homeland in Anatolia, particularly in its eastern portion. These observations are not yet accepted by all linguists – Johanna Nichols (1997a) uses the Kartvelian loans to place the IE homeland close to the Ural Mountains, although this viewpoint seems not to have attracted any further supporters.

Gamkrelidze and Ivanov (1995) strongly favor an eastern Anatolian homeland for PIE, but still accept the viewpoint of the Pontic school, that wheeled vehicles, and also a non-specific knowledge of metal, are reliable PIE reconstructions. This forces them to favor a Chalcolithic or Bronze Age date for PIE dispersal, with movements out of Anatolia west into Greece and the Balkans, and northeast via the Caucasus and then westward into Europe around the north of the Black Sea. In their major 1995 work they suggest the Chalcolithic Halafian culture of northern Mesopotamia and southeastern Turkey (ca. 5500–5000 BC), characterized by highly competent production of kiln-fired painted pottery, as a possible identification for PIE. But archaeological support for this view is so far unconvincing.

Anatolia is therefore coming into focus as the most likely homeland region for PIE, at least according to a sound but not absolute consensus amongst modern linguists. There is increasing agreement that languages ancestral to subgroups including Greek, Tocharian of the Tarim Basin, Italic, and Celtic began to spread first (or stay at home in the case of Anatolian), these all forming a major segment of the *centum* group referred to above, which also includes Germanic (Ringe et al. 1998; Drews ed. 2001; Gray and Atkinson 2003). Suggestions are also being made that certain poorly understood languages of ancient Europe, such as Minoan and Etruscan, once considered non-IE in the absence of any detailed understanding, could be witnesses for subgroups that moved extremely early from the IE (or Indo-Hittite) homeland (Renfrew 1998, 1999).

The reconstructed PIE vocabulary certainly does not rule out an Anatolian homeland, and indeed supports it to a degree, especially if we accept the claim of Gamkrelidze and Ivanov that there was a term for "mountain," which in turn tends to rule out the flat Pontic steppes. Other items of a more cultural nature that can be reconstructed back to PIE include the Southwest Asian domesticated animals and horses, the latter perhaps wild, an unspecified term for grain (perhaps wheat and/or barley), the plough (the simple ard rather than the mold-board plough that actually turns a sod), and weaving and the use of wool. This listing is sufficient to demonstrate the possibility that PIE could have been an early farming society – it evidently was not a hunter-gatherer one. However, the nature of the PIE vocabulary will always be a little uncertain if the phylogeny of the language family is not fully agreed upon. For instance, if the Anatolian subgroup really does link to all the others at the base of the IE family tree, then *only* items that have Anatolian witnesses can truly be reconstructed within the PIE vocabulary.

As for the date of PIE, most linguists have recently opted for dates sometime between 3500 and 7000 BC. Russell Gray and Quentin Atkinson (2003) have used computational methods derived from evolutionary biology in order to find the tree with the smallest number of evolutionary changes required to generate recorded IE vocabularies. Using chronological calibrations derived from changes in historically recorded languages, they offer a date for PIE close to 7000 BC, followed by initial divergence of Anatolian, Tocharian, and Greek/Armenian (in that order), with the other subgroups differentiating later and being more rake-like in their relationships. In a similar analysis, Peter Forster and Alfred Toth (2003) use phylogenetic network methods derived from evolutionary biology to offer a similar time depth for PIE of 8100±1900 BC for PIE. These are important contributions, which give very strong support to an Anatolian homeland and a Neolithic initial dispersal.

Colin Renfrew's contribution to the Indo-European debate

In 1987, a book entitled *Archaeology and Language* pushed the debate over the Indo-European homeland and date of dispersal to a new level of intensity. In it, British archaeologist Colin Renfrew set out in detail his hypothesis that PIE had spread from Anatolia into Europe with the first Neolithic farmers. The publication was followed by considerable discussion, some percipient, as in the case of Andrew and Susan Sherratt's 1988 suggestion that other language families could have followed a similar trajectory to Indo-European, thus leading to radial outflows of language from agri-cultural heartland areas. Sixteen years after the publication of *Archaeology and Language*, Renfrew (2003) still maintains his basic stance on the correlations between farming dispersal and the spread of language families. His most recent expositions on IE favor a homeland in south-central Anatolia during the period when farmers first spread into Greece, at about 7000–6500 BC (Renfrew 1999, 2001a). This initial spread continued into Europe to give rise to the Italic and Celtic subgroups, with Tocharian splitting off quite early (5000 BC?) to the north of the Black Sea to move across the steppes into central Asia. This early movement seems generally to have given rise to the *centum* languages, whereas the *satem* subgroups in eastern Europe (Baltic, Slavic, and Albanian) maintained a situation of "advergence" characterized by shared innova-tions in a Balkan *sprachbunde*, this latter reflecting many of the social characteristics that Marija Gimbutas originally associated with the basal layer of IE. Interestingly, the Indo-Iranian languages also relate most closely to eastern European *satem* languages, thus giving hints for the ultimate origins of the IE languages of the Indian subcontinent.

Renfrew's basic reconstruction clearly favors a "stratified" phylogeny for IE, a little different from the rake-like pattern normally favored by linguists, but one recently promulgated by a variety of mathematical approaches (Warnow 1997; Ringe et al. 1998; Gray and Atkinson 2003). The reconstruction of the earliest period of IE dispersal into Europe favored by Renfrew is shown in Figure 10.2. Archaeologically, the over-all spread occurred between about 7000 BC (Greece) and 4000 BC (Britain). During this 3,000-year period there was undoubtedly very great genetic interchange between incoming farmers and Mesolithic natives, especially in northern Europe, although there is little evidence for anything approaching "creolization" in the linguistic record. There are claims for substrata involving plant names, river names, and other geo-graphical terms, perhaps of non-IE origin (Markey 1989; Polomé 1990; Schmidt 1990;

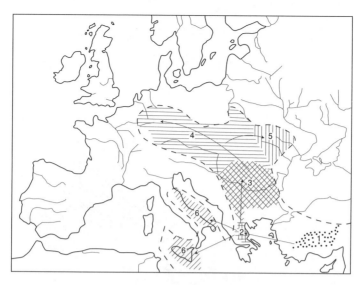

Figure 10.2 Colin Renfrew's reconstruction of the Indo-European homeland in central Anatolia and the first expansions of Indo-European languages into Europe. From Renfrew 1999.

Vennemann 1994; Kitson 1996; Dolgopolsky 1993). Norbert Strade (1998) also suggests that the Germanic languages spread over a Uralic substratum by a process involving considerable language shift. Besides Uralic, the coastal fringes of Europe certainly harbored a number of other languages in Roman times that might have been non-IE, with Basque of the Pyrenees being perhaps the best-known (Zvelebil and Zvelebil 1988; Sverdrup and Guardans 1999 term these languages "Paleoeuropean"). But many of the ancient languages are only poorly understood, if understood at all, and opinions on IE versus non-IE status for them seem to swing widely, especially in cases like Pictish and Etruscan. We can only note that the spread of IE through most of Europe south of the Baltic does not seem to have been associated with massive levels of contact-induced language change, of the type we see, for instance, amongst some of the Austronesian languages of Melanesia. This suggests that the IE spread occurred through coherent processes of population expansion.[2]

Afroasiatic

The Afroasiatic (AA) language family (Figure 10.3) contains six subgroups, of which Ancient Egyptian (or Coptic in historical times), Semitic, and Berber are agreed by most linguists to form a single node (*Boreafrasian* of Christopher Ehret 1995, with several phonological innovations). Chadic and Cushitic form separate subgroups, as does a poorly known and small language subgroup in southwestern Ethiopia, termed Omotic.[3] The present-day widespread distribution of Semitic languages in North Africa does not reflect *in situ* descent directly from the earliest history of this

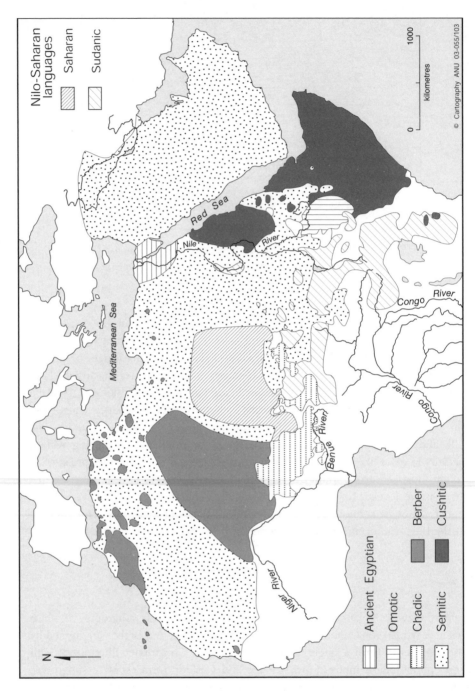

Figure 10.3 The distributions of the major subgroups of the Afroasiatic and Nilo-Saharan language families, after Ruhlen 1987.

family, since Arabic spread very widely after the seventh-century Arab conquests, and the ancestors of the more diverse Ethiopic languages (including Amharic), also in the Semitic subgroup, spread from Arabia during the second millennium BC (Ehret 2000).

There are two quite separate bodies of opinion concerning AA prehistory. One school, for which linguists Christopher Ehret (1979, 1995, 2003), Lionel Bender (1982), and Roger Blench (1993, 1999) are perhaps the main proponents, favors a homeland in northeastern Africa on the grounds that five of the six AA subgroups (excluding Semitic) occur only in Africa, including those perceived to be the most ancient in phylogenetic terms. The precise location of the homeland varies a little according to author, oscillating through Ethiopia and Sudan toward the Red Sea coast, where live the Beja, apparently representing a very early linguistic split within the Cushitic subgroup. These linguists tend to regard early AA expansion as pre-agricultural, although not pre-herding in Ehret's view, thus perhaps to be equated with population spread into the eastern Sahara consequent upon the postglacial wetter climatic conditions after about 10,000 years ago. Ehret (2003), for instance, states that Cushitic, Chadic, Berber, and Semitic all have independently derived agricultural proto-vocabularies, but that Proto-Cushitic already had some cattle vocabulary at the time of its break-up, and thus may have had an incipient herding economy.

The other major school, composed mainly of Russian linguists, strongly favors a Southwest Asian and specifically Levant homeland. This opinion is based entirely on vocabulary reconstruction rather than the "center-of-gravity" assumptions of the Northeast Africa school. Apart from one rather isolated claim for an AA expansion out of the Levant during the Aurignacian over 30,000 years ago (McCall 1998), the core case for the Levant school is based on the following observations:

1. Glottochronological considerations, calibrated against data on ancient Egyptian and Semitic languages (Greenberg 1990:12), suggest that PAA is perhaps a little older than PIE (between 10,000 and 7000 BC).
2. The reconstructed vocabulary of PAA does not contain any specifically agricultural cognates, but it does include names for a number of plants and animals that are of Asian, not North African origin (sheep, goat, barley, chickpea, for instance: Blazek 1999; Militarev 2000, 2003). Militarev favors early agricultural correlations.
3. Proto-Semitic is of undoubted Levant origin and has a full agropastoral vocabulary (Dolgopolsky 1993; Diakonoff 1998).

These observations do not form conclusive proof of a Levant origin for the whole AA family, and we seem to be sitting on a slightly unyielding fence. My suspicions, with Colin Renfrew (1991), are that PAA does indeed have a Levant rather than a Northeast African origin, but I have to admit that this view is based more on an understanding of the record of early Holocene population movement than of any absolute markers of linguistic phylogeny. The spread of Neolithic cultures from the Levant into Egypt at about 5500 BC, or perhaps before, combined with the possibility of a PPNB movement of caprovine herders down the western side of the Arabian Peninsula in the wetter conditions of the early Holocene, are suggestive of a bifurcatory movement of early farmers and pastoralists, with sheep, goats, wheat, and barley, into Africa by two routes:

1. Southern Levant into Egypt, leading eventually to further movement of early Berber languages and goat herding into the northern Sahara.
2. A separate movement, mainly pastoralist with sheep and goat herding rather than agriculture, through western Arabia and across to East Africa, leading to Cushitic, Chadic, and presumably Omotic.

Taking linguistic and archaeological evidence into consideration, it is also possible that the movement through Arabia occurred first, perhaps a millennium or more before that into Egypt. Linguistically, this would explain why Cushitic, Omotic, and Chadic are believed by many linguists to be deeper in a phylogenetic sense than the other families (unless there has been a great deal of contact-induced change, as in the case of the western Melanesian languages within Austronesian). It would also explain why the Egyptian Neolithic as known at present started *after* the PPNB, during the Pottery Neolithic.

This view of a Levant origin takes into account details of the archaeological record, of proto-vocabulary reconstruction, and of existing evidence for population movement during the early Holocene. The opposing view of an African origin is based on linguistic subgrouping data and has no archaeology in support, unless one guess-links AA dispersal to the warmer and wetter climate of the Sahara in the early Holocene. But this, of course, cannot explain Semitic, which reveals no direct traces at all of an African origin, and it also runs up against the view, widely held, that the early Nilo-Saharan languages would be better candidates for a linkage with the early Holocene Saharan cattle herders. A Levant origin for AA fits the general picture better, as it is currently understood, than does an African origin. The testing of this hypothesis lies in the future – for instance in the archaeology of Ethiopia and the linguistics of the little-known Omotic subgroup.

Elamite and Dravidian, and the Indo-Aryans

South Asia contains languages that belong to four quite separate families – Indo-European (Indo-Aryan subgroup, in turn a subgroup of Indo-Iranian), Dravidian, Munda (part of the larger Austroasiatic family of Southeast Asia), and Tibeto-Burman (Figures 10.1, 10.4, 10.7, 10.8A). Today, Indo-Aryan (IA) languages are dominant in the north, and it is often assumed that they have achieved this dominance at the expense of the other language families. As I will explain below, this may not be quite so transparent as it might appear. That IA languages have replaced others in northern India and Pakistan is clear, but that these others were necessarily all Dravidian or Munda is not so clear at all.

One of the historical documents that is often brought forward as a witness for IA invasion from the northwest is the compilation of hymns and supplicatory chants known as the Rigveda, an oral creation of the middle or late second millennium BC, committed to writing in the late first millennium BC. Parts of the Rigveda describe battles and attacks on cities in the region of Punjab, and many earlier authorities regarded this compilation as a record of the conquest, by incoming Indo-Aryan-speaking pastoralists, of a Dravidian-speaking Harappan civilization already in decline. The discovery of apparent massacres at Mohenjo-Daro once appeared to support the idea, but current radiocarbon dates indicate that the Mature Indus Phase had ended by 1900 BC, long before the events described in the Rigveda took place. Instead, modern scholars regard the Rigveda as recording events in a Punjab that was already Indo-Aryan and had long been so (Erdosy 1989, 1995; Witzel 1995). We can no longer blame the followers of Indra for the Mature Harappan decline.

In order to put South Asia in a "Post-Rigveda" linguistic perspective we need first to review what modern linguists state about language history, in the first instance of Dravidian. In 1974, linguist David McAlpin (1974, 1981) proposed the existence of a language macrofamily that he termed "Elamo-Dravidian," based on a comparison between the Dravidian languages of South Asia and Elamite texts found in the Achaemenid palaces at Persepolis in southwestern Iran (late sixth to fifth centuries BC) (see also Blazek 1999). The ancient Elamite language was used from the late third millennium BC into Achaemenid times, and its early history is best documented from cuneiform documents found in the huge city mound of Susa in Khusistan (Potts 1999). Even older pictographic and numerical texts, dating from about 2800 BC and known as "Proto-Elamite," have been found in several sites from Susa across the Iranian Plateau to Shahr-i-Sokhta in eastern Iran, but these tablets remain undeciphered and no definite link with the true Elamite language of a millennium later can yet be demonstrated. Elamite civilization was urban, closely related to that of the Sumerians and Akkadians, and occupied large areas of Iran prior to the dominance of the Indo-European Medes and Persians in the first millennium BC.

The Dravidian languages themselves, except for the outlier of Brahui in the Indus valley, are today confined to central and southern India (Figure 10.1). Internal reconstruction of proto-vocabularies and subgrouping structure has proceeded quite far in terms of the Indian members of the family, such that we can guess at a northerly South Asian homeland in a general sense. But McAlpin's Elamo-Dravidian lies too far back in time to be amenable to linguistic proof, even though many Dravidianists, including Kamil Zvelebil (1985), have commented on it favorably. The issue is also confused by the massive overlay of IA languages in the northwest, erasing the linguistic footprints of deeper time levels. Brahui could be a remnant of a once more widespread layer of Dravidian that existed in the Indus Valley, but in reality it seems to be a very poorly recorded language, of uncertain historical significance (Coningham 2002:86 quotes Elfenbein's view that it could even represent a Medieval migration from the south).

At present, most linguists seem to agree that the Dravidian languages of southern and central India (with Brahui remaining uncertain) shared a common ancestor around

2500 BC, with a reconstructed agricultural vocabulary that contained terms at least for cattle, date, and plough (Southworth 1975, 1990, 1992, 1995; Gardner 1980). Dorian Fuller (2003) suggests that terms for some native South Indian crops such as mung bean and horsegram reconstruct back to very early stages within Dravidian, and he also regards the whole family as being of southern Indian pre-agricultural origin. If he is correct, then McAlpin's claims for links with Elamite become less credible. Unfortunately, the linguistic data do not seem to be firm enough to clinch the matter. If McAlpin is correct, and if the Dravidian glottochronological estimates are worth anything (they fit well with the dated archaeological record for the spread of agriculture in South India), then any genetic linkages between Elamite and Dravidian must have predated 2500 BC by a long period.

Before moving further into the Elamo-Dravidian conundrum, it is necessary to return to the Indo-Aryan languages. The separation of the Indo-Iranian languages from the remainder of Indo-European was a relatively late process in the totality of IE history, according to majority linguistic opinion. Many scholars place the Indo-Iranian homeland in the steppe lands to the north of the Black Sea, running eastward toward the Caspian, favoring a movement toward Iran and India at about 2000 BC or soon afterward (Anthony 1991; Parpola 1988, 1999; Mallory 1989; Masica 1991; Kuzmina 2001). The Indo-Iranian languages belong to the *satem* group, so in this regard their closest subgroup relatives are Armenian, Slavic, Albanian, and Baltic. The Bronze Age Andronovo steppe culture with its emphasis on herding was distributed from north of the Caspian toward the Hindu Kush during the second millennium BC, and this is believed by many to be the most likely source for the migrating Indo-Aryans, who split into their Iranian and Indic branches as they moved through what are now Turkmenistan and Uzbekistan. From this viewpoint, the IA arrival in the Indus region occurred at about the time of Mature Harappan decline, or later. Needless to say, this reconstruction depends in part upon a view of the early Indo-Aryans as essentially a pastoralist people, a view that has no clear archaeological justification within the South Asian subcontinent itself, or within the Rigveda, or within the family tree of the Indo-European languages.[4]

Against this mainstream reconstruction we have a number of statements of disagreement. Colin Renfrew (1987:208) tentatively raised the possibility that the Indo-Iranian languages could have originated from the Mehrgarh Neolithic, representing a spread from the Indo-European homeland in Anatolia. However, the linguistic position within IE of the Indo-Aryan languages would seem not to support an antiquity as far back as 6000 BC, even allowing for a fair degree of linguistic diversity in the form of the Nuristani (Kafiri or Dardic) languages of the Hindu Kush region of Afghanistan. Another argument against an equation of the early Indo-Iranians with the Andronovo culture, or with its contemporary in the Amu Darya and Syr Darya basins (the mellifluously tagged Bactrian Margiana Archaeological Complex), has recently been put forward by C. C. Lamberg-Karlovsky (2002). This is that one cannot equate archaeological cultures with languages at all. Such a statement represents a great challenge.

A multidisciplinary scenario for South Asian prehistory

I would first like to point to an important observation that I do not believe has been made before. The distribution of the Indo-Aryan languages, even today (but excluding Sri Lanka), corresponds remarkably with that of the Chalcolithic cultures of the northwestern Deccan and the Ganges–Yamuna Basin. These are all characterized by a use of copper and painted pottery, usually in black on a red background, and include the Ahar, Malwa, and Jorwe cultures of Rajasthan and Maharashtra, and the Ochre Coloured Pottery and Black and Red Ware cultures of the Ganges Basin. They also, of course, include the Mature and post-Harappan. In the Ganges Basin, as discussed in chapter 4, a strong argument can be made for cultural continuity in archaeological terms from perhaps 3000 BC into historical (Buddhist and Hindu) times (Liversage 1992). Because of this, a hypothesis of Indo-Aryan continuity through the same time-span should be taken seriously.

The Dravidian languages as spoken today cover the region of the Southern Neolithic, with its villages of circular houses and cattle pastoralism, and domestication of a number of south Indian cereals and legumes. These southern sites have a distinct character, despite some obvious signs of connection with the northwestern Deccan. Again, continuity in southern India seems likely from Neolithic through to Early Historical times, with the marked exception of the Early Historical spread of an Indo-Aryan language in the form of Sinhalese to Sri Lanka.

Taking into account the above details, and bearing in mind the many points of view currently in circulation, I would offer the following scenario for South Asia as a whole (Figure 10.4).

1. During the Neolithic of Iran and Baluchistan, from 7000 BC onward into Early Harappan times, an Elamo-Dravidian linguistic continuum (following McAlpin) was spread from Khusistan to the Indus and perhaps beyond. Early Indo-Iranian speakers moved into Iran from the steppe lands to the north during Neolithic times, exactly when being uncertain.

2. The Harappan civilization itself, like that of Mesopotamia, was surely polyglot. My hunch here is that the language of the pictographic Harappan script was a relative of Elamite, rather than a close relative of the Dravidian languages currently spoken in southern India. The common people of the civilization would have spoken both ancestral Indo-Aryan and Elamo-Dravidian languages, just as their Mesopotamian contemporaries spoke Sumerian, Akkadian, Elamite, and even Eblaite if one traveled up the Euphrates far enough. But since we cannot decipher the Indus script we will never know the finer details.

3. During the time span of the Early Harappan, starting perhaps 3500 BC, farming settlements spread into Gujarat and Rajasthan. By 3000 BC they were spreading into the Ganges Basin. Even earlier, perhaps as early as 5000 BC, hunter-gatherers in camps such as Bagor in Rajasthan were acquiring cattle and caprovines from Indus-region farming villages, and commencing a pastoralist/herding specialization (Lukacs 2002). Following the distributional argument adumbrated above, did the

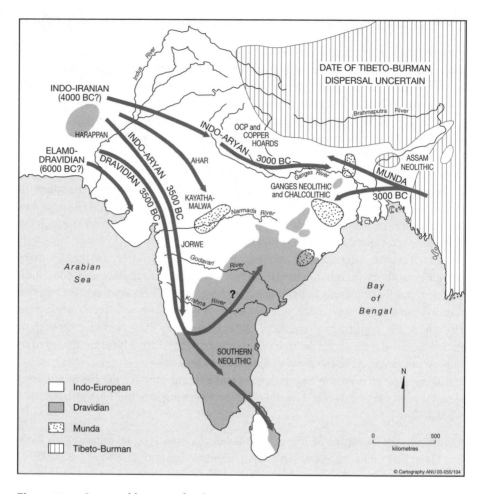

Figure 10.4 Suggested language family movements in South Asia.

village settlements mainly house Indo-Aryan-speaking agricultural populations, and were the herders of cattle and caprovines Dravidian speakers of native South Asian origin, both populations existing in a mutualistic relationship on the borderlands of the burgeoning Indus city-scape?

4. A number of sites in the northwestern region of India are noted as having unusual basal features, for instance the circular houses at Navdatoli and Balathal, and even perhaps the cow dung fill of the stone-walled enclosure (ca. 2800 BC) at the latter site. Could these represent an early Dravidian presence? We will never know, but my suspicion is that a linked farming and herding population, with both Indo-Aryan and Dravidian components, continued to move southward through Maharashtra toward Karnataka after 3000 BC. Specializations continued toward village farming on the one hand, and cattle herding on the other, but with much overlap between the two economic modes. If the village farmers were indeed Indo-Aryans, they seemingly limited themselves to Maharashtra

and northward, where their Southwest Asian winter cereals would still grow well, albeit with irrigation when necessary. In this scenario, the pastoralist Dravidians pushed onward into the Deccan, Karnataka, and southern India, there to develop their own style of millet agriculture and cattle corralling.

5. It is likely that no Dravidians moved into the Ganges Valley, and that the Chalcolithic farmers of the OCP phase, presumably Indo-Aryans, were the first agriculturalists here (at least until they met the ancestral Mundas, but more on these later).

This reconstruction has the Indo-Aryans and Dravidians together undertaking the agricultural and pastoralist colonization of a formerly hunter-gatherer India, with the latter adopting a more mobile herding lifestyle and continuing southward into Karnataka and the southern Deccan, but not the Ganges plains. Modern Hindi, spoken widely on the latter, has derived about 30 percent of its agricultural terms from linguistic sources that were neither IA, nor Dravidian, nor Munda (Masica 1979). Walter Fairservis and Franklin Southworth (1989) refer to this source as "language X." The Gangetic location of Hindi thus counter-indicates a Dravidian substratum in this region. Did "language X" belong to some pre-IA farming population of the Ganges Basin? I find this hard to accept in the absence of any clear linguistic survivals, but further speculation seems unwarranted.

The IA languages Gujerati and Marathi of northwestern India do carry a number of Dravidian loans, so a former presence of Dravidian speech here is not in question. Were the early Dravidians confined mainly to the southern part of the Indus realm, extending into Gujarat, Maharashtra, and perhaps Rajasthan? Were the early Indo-Aryans initially confined to the northern part of the Indus realm, later moving south (and east) to mingle with and eventually replace Dravidian languages in Gujarat and Masharashtra, but not Karnataka or southern India (Figure 10.4)? The basal structures at Navdatoli and Balathal offer some faint support for this view.

There remains one other group that interacted eventually with both IAs and Dravidians in the northeastern peninsular regions of India. These are the Mundas, an Austroasiatic-speaking population whose ultimate linguistic origin was in Mainland Southeast Asia (Figure 10.7). Reconstructions of Proto-Munda indicate cognates for rice, millets, and legumes, so there is little doubt that this population introduced rice cultivation into northeastern India, perhaps at about 3000 BC (Zide and Zide 1976; Southworth 1988; Higham 2003). Interestingly, according to the linguistic analyses of F. B. J. Kuiper (1948), Dravidian and Munda languages were in contact *prior* to any IA presence in eastern India, presumably somewhere in the current overlap zone between these two families in Andhra Pradesh, Orissa, and southern Bihar. This suggests that the Dravidian settlement of the Deccan was a fairly rapid affair after it got under way at about 3000 BC. However, it is not clear how far Munda languages originally spread up the Ganges river system, and Franklin Southworth (1988) has suggested that their greatest extent was never very much larger than now, perhaps due to competition from IA and Dravidian. This suggests that the three language families concerned all spread into the subcontinent at roughly the same time – a considerable historical coincidence, the results of which are still visible in the Indian ethnolinguistic landscape today.

Indo-European, Afroasiatic, Elamo-Dravidian, and the Issue of Nostratic

We have already raised the question of whether or not language families can be subgrouped into macrofamilies. Some linguists reject the idea without question, on the grounds of imperfections in methodology and the possibility that observed similarities can be due to chance (Dixon 1997). I do not wish to become embroiled in a debate about research methodology amongst linguists, but for a decade or more I have been intrigued, as has Colin Renfrew (1991), by the possibility that some macrofamily hypotheses could be reflecting important developments in archaeological prehistory, especially in terms of the linked origins and radial dispersals of agricultural peoples out of homeland regions.[5]

One of the most significant language macrofamilies, promoted especially by Russian comparative linguists since the 1960s, is Nostratic. In its basic form, Nostratic is stated to include Indo-European, Afroasiatic, Kartvelian of the southern Caucasus, Uralic, Altaic, and Dravidian, all of which are claimed to share either some degree of common origin, or at least to have shared early histories with a fair degree of inter-family contact.[6] More recently, Joseph Greenberg (2000) has put forward a competing hypothesis, involving a Eurasiatic macrofamily that includes Indo-European, Uralic, Yukaghir of Siberia, Altaic (including Korean and Japanese), Ainu of Hokkaido, Gilyak, Chukotian, and Eskimo-Aleut.

With lists of language families as long as these, it is perhaps not surprising that some linguists express exasperation. Archaeologists also find them a little hard to handle. Obviously, in the case of Greenberg's Eurasiatic, all these diverse populations cannot be connected with any agricultural radiation and the concept, if real, presumably reflects the initial colonizations of northern latitudes by modern humans, who after all did not reach the Americas until after 15,000 years ago. The survival of some degree of archaic linguistic residue is perhaps not surprising.

But Nostratic could be a different matter, since many of its constituent language families were potentially very deeply involved in agricultural radiations out of the Middle East into Europe, North Africa, and Asia. This is so for Indo-European, Afroasiatic, and Elamo-Dravidian. Kartvelian, as a stay-at-home family in the mountainous and remote Caucasus, also fits this model geographically, although the Caucasus does have two other language families that are not part of the Nostratic grouping. One of the latter (Nakh-Dagestanian) apparently had an agriculturalist proto-language with a glotto-chronological age of about 6,000 years according to Johanna Nichols (in Wuethrich 2000), but little appears to be known about the history of Kartvelian in this regard.

The other two members of the Nostratic macrofamily, Uralic and Altaic, pose different problems. The Uralic language family includes the Finnish and Hungarian, both of course languages of farming peoples today. But the basic consensus appears to be that Uralic derived originally from a hunter-gatherer spread across postglacial northern Europe and Asia. Kalevi Wiik (2000) has recently published a reconstruction of Uralic linguistic history which has many of the speakers descending from the original hunter-gatherer populations of postglacial northern Europe, later to be influenced by incoming Indo-European-speaking agriculturalists. Other linguists note that Proto-Uralic reveals close connections with Indo-European languages, especially Iranian, but there is no consensus as to whether these links reflect shared ancestry or more recent borrowing during the period of Iranian linguistic domination of the steppes, prior to the spread of Turkic languages after about 500 BC. I cannot claim to know the answers for Uralic, but it is clear that the language family cannot be regarded as connected with any agricultural population radiation out of Southwest Asia.

Altaic poses a different problem, this being that the most likely homelands for its chief subgroups (Turkic, Mongolian, and Tungusic) are agreed by almost all linguists to be in Mongolia and Manchuria, far to the east of any close connection with the other members of Nostratic. We return to Altaic matters later, allowing that a southwestern origin for the family close to Southwest Asia is most unlikely.

We are thus left with the three language families with which we began – Indo-European, Afroasiatic, and Elamo-Dravidian – as representing agriculturalist dispersal out of Southwestern Asia. One might argue that, unless one accepts the Nostratic idea in its entirely, one should not adopt it at all, and such a conclusion would doubtless please a number of linguists. I am not sure what I would reply to such a doubtful linguist in this regard, but to an archaeologist I would state that the reconstructed history of agriculturalist dispersal from Southwest Asia makes an associated and radial dispersal model for these three language families very appealing. Proto-Nostratic need not be such a wild idea after all.

Indeed, some linguists have tried to identify the cultural vocabulary, location, and possible date for Proto-Nostratic. Alan Bomhard (1996) locates a homeland loosely south of the Caucasus at the end of the Pleistocene. Aharon Dolgopolsky (1998) suggests that Proto-Nostratic had no clear agricultural reconstructions, but did have terms for barley, bovids, sheep, and goat, again favoring a pre-agricultural homeland within Southwest Asia (although Dolgopolsky does not attempt to locate one). Perhaps the Natufian and its contemporaries occupied a position quite centrally within the Nostratic equation, although it is clear that precise cultural affiliations for Proto-Nostratic will always remain elusive.

Saharan and Sub-Saharan Africa: Nilo-Saharan and Niger-Congo

Nilo-Saharan

We now move south toward sub-Saharan Africa to examine, in the case of the Nilo-Saharan family, one of the likely predecessors to the remarkable domination of Northern Africa by Afroasiatic and especially Semitic languages in the past few millennia. The Nilo-Saharan language family is very diverse, so much so that some linguists refuse to accord it true family status. It has a rather spotty and stretched-out distribution that seems to show clear evidence of overlay by the recent spreads of Semitic and Niger-Congo languages (Figure 10.3).

In a paper written over two decades ago, Nicholas David (1982) equated the spread of the Sudanic branches of Nilo-Saharan with the development of sorghum cultivation and cattle and goat herding. Modern archaeology would deny a truly domesticated status to sorghum at such an early date, but cultivation of wild forms is not at all unlikely. The most detailed scheme for Nilo-Saharan unfolding has since been developed by Christopher Ehret (1993, 1997, 2000, 2003). This favors an ultimate origin for Proto-Nilo-Saharan during the terminal Pleistocene along the Middle Nile, amongst hunter-gatherer populations who possibly began their first phase of expansion with the improving postglacial climate. According to Ehret, the Northern Sudanic branch of Nilo-Saharan then acquired cattle herding by about 9000 BC, together with pottery-making. Plant cultivation and sheep/goat herding appeared slightly later, by about 7000 BC, when cultivation was first adopted by the Central Sudanic populations. After 5000 BC this Saharan agropastoral complex, associated by this time with both Nilo-Saharan and Cushitic (Afroasiatic) populations, began to spread south with increasing Saharan desiccation, eventually to reach Lake Turkana in Kenya by about 3000 BC. Further expansion within East Africa by Nilotic speakers within the Nilo-Saharan family, fueled in Ehret's view by a successful warlike ideology, has continued into recent centuries (Ehret 2003:171).

Ehret's chronologies correlate with the archaeological record (see chapter 5) for early Holocene cattle management and pottery-making in the Sahara, even if there are no archaeological indications that any of the early Holocene sorghums or millets were actually domesticated. The most interesting question concerns the ancient extent of Nilo-Saharan, prior to the incursions of Afroasiatic and Niger-Congo languages. Did Nilo-Saharan languages once cover the whole Sahara? Or just the eastern portions where they are found today? And if the latter, what languages were once spoken in the western Sahara? Niger-Congo? We do not have answers to these questions. But it is important to reflect on the suggestion that Nilo-Saharan, or at least its Sudanic subgroup, could in the first instance have been another, albeit very shadowy, example of a farming (or herding)/language dispersal.

Niger-Congo, with Bantu

The Niger-Congo language family is largest in the world in terms of number of languages – 1,436 according to one source, with possibly 300 million speakers (Williamson and Blench 2000). The whole family, and especially its Bantu subgroup, covers a vast area of sub-Saharan Africa with almost no survivals of substratum languages and isolates, except for the Khoisan languages in the far southwest of the continent, and the Hadza, Sandawe, and South Cushitic languages in Tanzania. The

Figure 10.5   The major subgroups of the Niger-Congo family. Courtesy Roger Blench.

Bantu languages in particular can be clearly subgrouped owing to the recency and phenomenal extent of their spread.

The area of greatest subgroup diversity of the Niger-Congo languages is in West Africa (Figure 10.5), and this is clearly where the whole family first developed. In this section we will be mainly concerned with the Bantu subgroup owing to the enormous extent of its spread – the remaining subgroups to the west are greater in time depth. Roger Blench (1993, 1999) suggests that the original Proto-Niger-Congo vocabulary was probably pre-agricultural, thus the initial existence of the family might have been somewhere amongst a *sprachbunde* of early Holocene hunting and gathering populations spread quite widely throughout West Africa. In terms of rough estimates from glottochronology, this phase should predate 5000 BC, long before any signs of agriculture appear in the archaeological record. Niger-Congo at base, therefore, is not an agriculturalist language family, even though its enormous expansion east of the Niger River was without doubt agriculturally driven.

The major spreads of the agriculturalist Niger-Congo subgroups, according to the majority of linguists, have occurred within the past 5,000 years. The most significant involved the Bantu-related subgroups. Proto-Benue-Congo, for instance, has a reconstructed agricultural vocabulary. The slightly younger Proto-Bantu, with a time-depth close to 3,000–4,000 years in terms of the archaeological record, had terms for oil palm, yams, beans, groundnuts, dog, goat, pottery, and pigs (or perhaps wild warthogs according to Vansina 1990). At this stage there were no iron tools, cattle, cereals, or Southeast Asian crops such as bananas and taro in the Bantu homeland region. But it is clear that the eventual Bantu expansion was later to be assisted greatly by these highly significant technological and economic introductions, all of which became available in eastern Africa just before the most rapid phase of Eastern Bantu expansion during the first millennium AD.

The Bantu speakers originated in Cameroon, perhaps initially in grassland areas north of the rain forest (see page 107 for pertinent archaeological data). There appears to have been an early separation into Western and Eastern subgroups, prior to 1000 BC, and this is visible in Clare Holden's (2002) family tree for the Bantoid and Bantu languages shown in Figure 10.6. The Eastern Bantu groups began to spread eastward along the northern fringes of the rainforest, to reach Lake Victoria by about 1000 BC. The Western Bantu, with pottery, oil palms, and yams, were perhaps moving southward into the West African rain forest at about the same time, eventually emerging into the savannas of Angola. The arrival of Asian bananas during the first millennium BC probably stimulated this movement, such that the rain-forest region was quite densely settled by Western Bantu farmers by AD 500–1000. Jan Vansina (1990:257) offers a mechanism for the Western Bantu spread close to my own model of "founder rank enhancement" for Austronesians (Bellwood 1996d), suggesting that "emigration became preferable to a continued life as a perpetual junior in an over-crowded homeland."

Christopher Ehret (1997, 1998, 2000) has recently offered a very detailed linguistically based appraisal of Eastern Bantu dispersal. The Eastern Bantu who entered the Great Rift Valley of East Africa about 3,000 years ago came into contact with cattle herders and millet cultivators speaking Cushitic and Nilo-Saharan languages, and also with Khoisan-speaking hunters and gatherers whose Hadza and Sandawe descendants still occupy small areas southeast of Lake Victoria. From the former groups they adopted sorghum and pearl millet to add to their predominantly tuberous domesticated plant roster. They also acquired iron metallurgy, and a little later, by the beginning of the first millennium AD, they added cattle, sheep, and donkeys, together with Southeast Asian crops and domesticated Asian chickens. The result was to be one of the most rapid episodes of farming spread in world history.

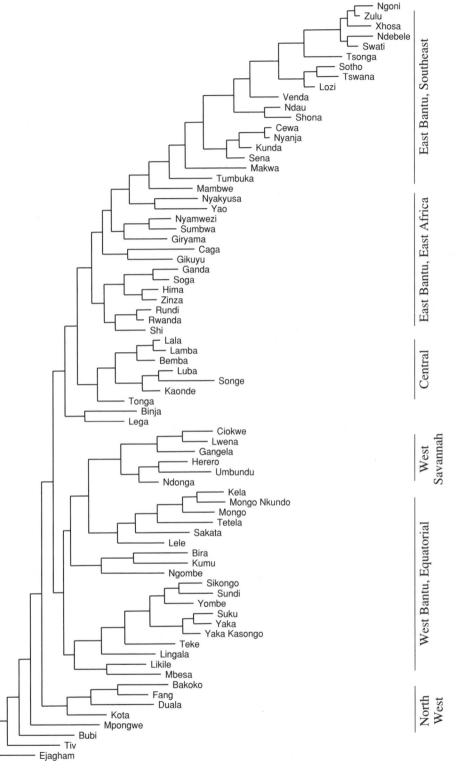

Figure 10.6 Clare Holden's (2002) maximum-parsimony tree of 75 Bantoid and Bantu languages, showing clearly the separate Western and Eastern subgroups, and the long "tail" of Eastern Bantu languages extending into the southeastern corner of the African continent. Bantu language data are from Bastin et al. 1999.

Questions arise as to how many separate directional "streams" of population movement occurred within the Bantu dispersal as a whole, and this issue was raised from the archaeological perspective in chapter 5. Of the linguists, Christopher Ehret favors two separate dialect continua spreading side by side in the southern expansion of Eastern Bantu, down the Great Rift Valley and through East Africa. He calls these the Kaskazi and Kusi dialect continua, and plots their spreads southward toward the Zambesi between 700 and 200 BC. Eventually, speakers of these dialects and their descendants traveled over 3,000 kilometers in under a millennium, from Kenya into Mozambique. Jan Vansina (1995) appears to favor a more complex pattern of spread, more like a continuously expanding backward-and-forward mesh of related communities, rather than a stream-like process.

This debate may reflect little more than differences of scale. Vansina's reconstruction is acceptable on the local village scale, since over a decade or so any distances moved might not have been very great. But an early computer demographic simulation by Collett (1982), based on the huge distances of spread and the relatively short time depths available, suggested that quite large groups might on occasion have moved or leapfrogged over large distances. Clare Holden's (2002) maximum parsimony (tree building) computational study, using 95 basic vocabulary items from 75 Bantoid and Bantu languages, indicates that the Eastern Bantu languages have a unique common ancestor (Western Bantu ones apparently do not), and that this common ancestor spread consistently through adjacent geographical regions with little borrowing between languages once they were in place. In other words, the Eastern Bantu family tree represents differentiation *in situ* since initial settlement, with little subsequent interference through areal processes.

Overall, the Bantu dispersal was one of the most dramatic examples of language/ farming dispersal in world history, and there is quite remarkable agreement between the archaeological and linguistic records on its reality.

East and Southeast Asia, and the Pacific

The Chinese and Mainland Southeast Asian language families

The earliest Neolithic cultures of the Yellow and Yangzi basins enshrine the ancestry of not just the Sinitic peoples. Neolithic China contains the common roots of many other populations in East and Southeast Asia, plus Oceania. Thus, while the Yangshao culture could conceivably be ancestral to the Han Chinese, so likewise the contemporary Neolithic cultures of Fujian and Taiwan could be ancestral to the Austronesians, and those of southern China to the Austroasiatic- and Tai-speaking peoples. However, these oldest Neolithic cultures long predate the precipitation of any sharply defined modern ethnolinguistic identities. This is sometimes a very hard concept to get across to modern lecture audiences, who react with puzzlement when told that many Southeast Asian cultures appear to have ultimate origins in southern China at about 7,000 years ago. People find it hard to think of "China" as ever having been anything other than just like modern China – full of people speaking Chinese languages, looking like Chinese, and presumably identifying in some way as "Han."

This concept of an unchanging ethnic landscape is utterly wrong. A voluminous historical record tells us that Han Chinese populations have spread within the past 2,500 years, following the Eastern Zhou and Qin military conquests, over much of what is now China south of the Yangzi. This type of situation, whereby the languages of dominant populations have erased earlier linguistic landscapes, even within the same family, is of course very common across the world and can render the true course of ethnolinguistic history sometimes hard to discern (Diamond and Bellwood 2003). The replacement of the Anatolian languages by first Greek and later Turkish creates similar problems for reconstructing the Indo-European homeland, just as the replacement of many indigenous languages by English and Spanish creates similar problems in the Western Hemisphere.

Within China and Southeast Asia there are three language families which appear to represent primary dispersals of agricultural populations through landscapes that were mostly occupied previously by hunting and gathering groups. These are the Sino-Tibetan, Austroasiatic, and Austronesian families. In addition, Japanese evidently spread to Japan around 300 BC with Yayoi rice farmers from Korea, replacing the languages of Jomon "hunter-gatherers" (Hudson 1999, 2003). A similar case for Neolithic spread could perhaps be made for the remote antecedents of Korean itself, and we return to Japanese and Korean later in connection with the "Altaic" language family. The present-day distributions of Austroasiatic and Sino-Tibetan are shown in Figures 10.7 and 10.8 (for Austronesian see Figure 7.4).

The Austroasiatic language family, the most widespread and also the most geographically fragmented language family in Mainland Southeast Asia and eastern India, includes approximately 150 languages in two major subgroups; Mon-Khmer of Southeast Asia, and Munda of northeastern India. The Mon-Khmer subgroup is the largest and contains Mon, Khmer, and Vietnamese, as well as Khasi in Assam, the Aslian languages of Peninsular Malaysia, and Nicobarese (Parkin 1991). We have already met the Munda languages of Bihar, Orissa, and West Bengal in the discussion of South Asia. The very disjointed distribution of the Austroasiastic family today suggests that it represents the oldest major language dispersal recognizable in Southeast Asia, one overlain by many expansive languages of later civilizations such as Burmese and Karen (both Tibeto-Burman), Thai, Malay, Khmer, and Vietnamese (the last two being Austroasiatic).

One observation of great interest is that the reconstructed vocabulary of Proto-Austroasiatic contained terms for rice cultivation (Pejros and Schnirelman 1998; Mahdi 1998; Higham 2003). The possibility that Austroasiatic languages were once spoken very widely in southern China, with place-name traces even as far north as the Yangzi River, is also worthy of note (Norman and Mei 1976). The homeland of Austroasiatic is not clear owing to massive overlying expansion of other language families, but most linguists suggest southern China or northern mainland Southeast Asia. Pejros and Schnirelman (1998) suggest a homeland near the middle Yangzi.

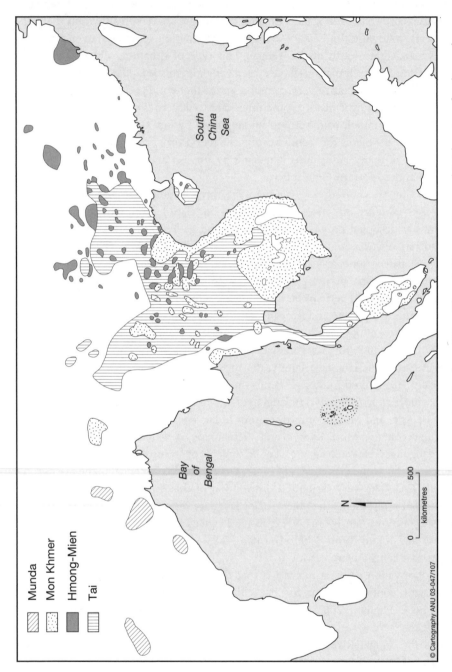

Figure 10.7 The distributions of the Austroasiatic (Munda and Mon-Khmer), Hmong-Mien, and Tai language families and their major subgroups, after Ruhlen 1987.

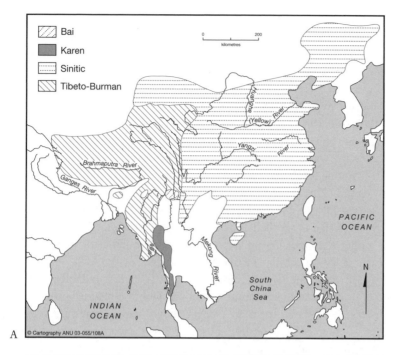

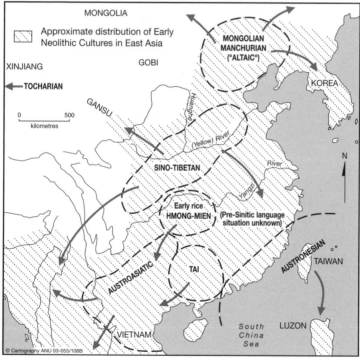

Figure 10.8 A) The distributions of the major subgroups of the Sino-Tibetan language family, after Ruhlen 1987. B) Suggested homelands for the major language families of China and Southeast Asia.

We turn now to the great modern population juggernaut represented by Sino-Tibetan (Figure 10.8). In recent years, linguists have given some remarkably divergent opinions on the homeland for this family. Ilya Peiros (1998) suggests northern South Asia, George van Driem (1999, 2003) favors Sichuan, James Matisoff (1991, 2000) points to the Himalayan Plateau. Juha Janhunen (1996:222) presents in my view the most likely homeland hypothesis by associating the early Sino-Tibetan languages with the Yellow River Neolithic (Yangshao culture), but this is partly based on archaeological reasoning. Jerry Norman (1988:17) merely states that the homeland is unknown, but notes that, on the way to the Yellow River, the early Sino-Tibetan languages borrowed from early Hmong-Mien and early Austroasiatic languages, thus implying a slightly southerly origin. This is quite likely, given that Proto-Sino-Tibetan also has strong reconstructions for rice cultivation (Pejros and Schnirelman 1998; Sagart 2003).

Clearly, the range of views here is extremely varied. Sino-Tibetan subgrouping is rake-like rather than tree-like in structure, a possible indicator of a fast and wide-spread early radiation, similar to that reconstructed for the Malayo-Polynesian languages within Austronesian. As already noted, such fast radiations do not lend themselves to homeland identification, and van Driem (2003) uses the metaphor of "fallen leaves" to describe the Sino-Tibetan subgrouping situation. Given this, and the erasure of much early patterning caused by Sinitic expansion, my own preference would be to move straight into the reasoning behind the farming/language dispersal hypothesis. This would place the homeland of Sino-Tibetan in the agricultural heartland area of central China, as preferred by Janhunen, and to a lesser extent by van Driem (Sichuan is a little west of the core region of Neolithic development, but it does border on the middle Yangzi). Such reasoning might be deemed unacceptably dependent upon the archaeology, but central China has unbroken and impressive cultural continuity from Neolithic into Chinese historical times. No other region within the Sino-Tibetan distribution can compete in this regard.

Of the other Mainland Southeast Asian language families, Hmong-Mien is most likely to have originated closest to the central Yangzi early rice zone, although the actual dispersal of this group as hill tribes into Southeast Asia has been relatively recent and due in part to pressure from the Chinese state. Peiros (1998:160) suggests that a combined Austroasiatic/Hmong-Mien grouping could have a glottochronological age of about 8,000 years, but whether Austroasiatic and Hmong-Mien languages are indeed related genetically is a matter for linguists to decide – the prospect is at least interesting since such genetic relationship would automatically imply propinquity of homeland. The Hmong-Mien family may also have provided a substratum for the Sinitic language of the kingdom of Chu in the middle Yangzi basin, during the later first millennium BC (Ballard 1985).

The Tai languages are, as a group, not of great antiquity, with a diversification history dating within the past 4,000 years according to Peiros (1998; see also Ostapirat in press). Their homeland probably lay in the southern Chinese provinces of Guizhou, Guangxi, and Guangdong, the latter occupied today by Sinitic languages. The ultimate spread of the Tai family into Thailand and Laos probably reflected Chinese demographic and military pressure, and has occurred mainly within the past 1,000 years.

According to Laurent Sagart (in press), the initial break-up of the Tai languages occurred during a period of contact with Malayo-Polynesian languages within the Austronesian family. This is an interesting observation, and one which probably places the initial genesis of Tai within Neolithic times in coastal southern China and Northern Vietnam.

As far as these four language families are concerned, we can perhaps hypothesize on linguistic grounds that, around 6000 BC, ancestral Hmong-Mien languages were located to the immediate south of the middle Yangzi, with early Austroasiatic languages further to the southwest and early Tai languages to the southeast (Figure 10.8B). In the first instance, only the Austroasiatic and Sino-Tibetan groups underwent expansion, with Hmong-Mien and Tai presumably remaining relatively circumscribed by these expansions until later.

Austronesian

The Austronesian family is the most widespread in the world, representing one of the most phenomenal records of colonization and dispersal in the history of mankind (Blust 1995a; Bellwood 1991, 1997a; Pawley 2003). Austronesian languages are now spoken in Madagascar, Taiwan, parts of southern Vietnam, Malaysia, the Philippines, and all of Indonesia except for the Papuan-speaking regions in and around New Guinea (Figure 7.4). They are also spoken right across the Pacific, to as far east as Easter Island, encompassing about 210 degrees of longitude, or more than halfway around the earth's circumference at the equator. Because of the wealth of comparative research carried out on the Austronesian languages it is possible to draw some very sound conclusions, using purely linguistic evidence, concerning the region of origin of the family, the directions of its subsequent spread, and also the vocabularies of important early proto-languages, particularly Proto-Austronesian and its most significant daughter, Proto-Malayo-Polynesian. The Malayo-Polynesian languages do not include those of Taiwan, but incorporate the vast remaining distribution of the family from Madagascar to Easter Island.

The reconstruction of overall Austronesian linguistic prehistory which is most acceptable today, and which fits best with all independent sources of evidence, is that favored by the linguist Robert Blust (1995a, 1999). Reduced to its essentials, this reconstruction favors a geographical expansion beginning in Taiwan, the location of Proto-Austronesian and of the majority of the primary subgroups of Austronesian (at least nine out of ten, according to Blust). Subsequent Malayo-Polynesian dispersal then encompassed the Philippines, Borneo, and Sulawesi, finally spreading in two branches, one west to Java, Sumatra, and the Malay Peninsula (the Western Malayo-Polynesian languages), the other east into Oceania (Figure 10.9 inset).

The Proto-Austronesian vocabulary, sourced to Taiwan, indicates an economy well suited to marginal tropical latitudes with cultivated rice, millet, and sugarcane, domesticated dogs, pigs, and possibly water buffalo, weaving, and the use of canoes (sails are less certain at this stage). The vocabulary of Proto-Malayo-Polynesian, perhaps of northern Philippine genesis, adds a number of tropical economic indicators

---

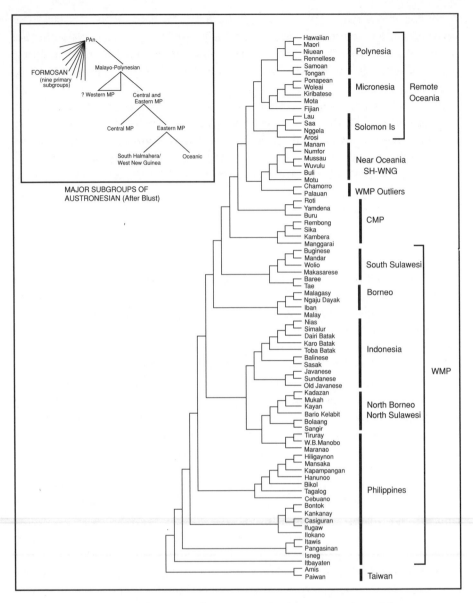

Figure 10.9 This phylogenetic tree of 77 Austronesian languages is derived from a parsimony analysis by Russell Gray and Fiona Jordan (2000). The tree shows considerable agreement with the linguistic subgroups of Robert Blust (inset) and reflects historical relationships, not just geographical ones (e.g., Malagasy and Ngaju Dayak are subgrouped, in accord with the comparative linguistic evidence for their very close relationship, even through they are located 8,000 kilometers apart). WMP = Western Malayo-Polynesian, SH-WNG = South Halmahera–West New Guinea.

which are not well attested in the earlier Proto-Austronesian stage, since Taiwan lies partly outside the tropics. These include taro, breadfruit, banana, yam, sago, and coconut, and their presences reflect the shift away from rice toward a greater dependence on tubers and fruits in equatorial latitudes (Zorc 1994; Pawley and Pawley 1994; Dewar 2003).

As indicated by Blust (1993) and Pawley (1999, 2003), the early Malayo-Polynesian languages spread very far very quickly, before linguistic differentiation was able to develop. As an example, the oldest Malayo-Polynesian language in western Oceania (Proto-Oceanic, probably located in the Bismarck Archipelago) shared almost 90 percent of its basic vocabulary with Proto-Malayo-Polynesian, located perhaps in the northern Philippines almost 5,000 kilometers away. Such rake-like relationships between subgroups are a very strong indicator of a rapid foundation spread, at least from the northern Philippines to the central Pacific. A fairly rapid "express train" model of Austronesian linguistic expansion from Taiwan is also supported by a maximum parsimony analysis of Austronesian vocabularies by Russell Gray and Fiona Jordan (2000). Their tree of subgrouping relationships is shown in Figure 10.9.

Of course, much Austronesian dispersal occurred long after the Neolithic – to southern Vietnam and Madagascar, for instance, both probably Iron Age movements. But the foundation spread into Remote Oceania was fundamentally based on agricultural subsistence and Neolithic voyaging technology. Other factors such as presences of naïve faunas and desires for founder status were certainly significant too, but these are a little peripheral for the broad scale of this discussion. Essentially, in the hierarchy of "causes" of Austronesian dispersal, the development of agriculture in Neolithic China and Taiwan played the most significant foundation role.

Piecing it together for East Asia

The data reviewed so far for eastern Asia suggest the following inferences based on the comparative linguistic and archaeological data sets:

1. Linguistically, a series of language families founded with agricultural and domestic animal vocabularies evolved in central and southern China, with extensions into the northern fringes of Southeast Asia and Taiwan (Figure 10.8B). Three of these language families – Austroasiatic, Sino-Tibetan, and Austronesian – underwent major expansions long before history began, in the latter case with very firm phylogenetic reconstructions indicating spread southward from Taiwan into Indonesia and Oceania. Linguistic dating estimates for the foundation proto-languages in these families, albeit rather impressionistic, indicate ages generally between 7,000 and 4,000 years ago – post-hunter-gatherer and pre-Iron Age in cultural terms.

    Numerous linguistic hypotheses suggest that these families share basal relationships, implying their derivations from regions quite close together in space.[7] However, I would not be so unwise as to claim that all relationships are ones of common descent; arguments for early borrowing also are numerous. The suggestion here is that early forms of the major families – Sino-Tibetan, Austroasiatic,

Hmong-Mien, Austronesian, and Tai – were at one time located sufficiently close together for some degree of sharing of common heritage. Laurent Sagart's claims for links between Austronesian and Sino-Tibetan, via the intermediacy of the Dawenkou culture of the Shandong Neolithic (ca. 4000 BC), are of particular interest here, in the light of recent discoveries of foxtail millet and the ritual extraction of upper lateral incisor teeth in both Neolithic Shandong and Taiwan.[8]

2. Archaeologically, rice and millet cultivation in central China precede any evidence for agriculture in Southeast Asia by about 3,000 years. After 3000 BC there was a spread of Neolithic cultures through the mainland and islands of Southeast Asia, in radiocarbon terms decreasing in age southward toward Malaysia and into Island Southeast Asia and the Pacific. The northerly cultures grew rice, whereas those along the equator in Island Southeast Asia depended on fruits and tubers. Related pottery and other artifact forms suggest ultimate origins for these complexes in the southern China–Taiwan region, with accretions of other native crops in Indonesia and the western Pacific. As far as Austronesian is concerned, a standstill of about 1,000 years in Taiwan, before Neolithic cultures spread further into the Philippines, is documented by both the archaeological and the linguistic records.

At this point, it would take a very determined skeptic indeed to suggest that these patterns are totally unrelated and coincidental. The suggestion that early agricultural economies, and foundation layers of language families, spread hand in hand is a very powerful one in the Asia-Pacific situations discussed (Bellwood 1991, 1996b, 2001a, 2001b, 2003).

"Altaic," and some difficult issues

Outside the East Asian Neolithic heartland, with its extensions into Southeast Asia and Oceania, we have two regions with quite different cultural and linguistic trajectories, in both cases a little difficult to interpret. The first comprises Mongolia and Manchuria. The main language family of northeast Asia is termed Altaic, which has three major subgroups – Turkic, Mongolian (including Mongol, the language of the Great Khans – rulers of Yuan dynasty China), and Tungusic (including Manchu, the language of the Qing dynasty rulers of China from 1644 to 1911). Some linguists also regard Korean, Japanese (both now single languages), and the Ainu language of Hokkaido as being affiliated with Altaic (Ruhlen 1987:127).

Altaic poses two immediate problems. One is the belief of some linguists that it belongs in the Nostratic macrofamily. But in terms of the internal structure of the family, with the deepest subgroups in Mongolia and Manchuria, a Southwest Asian homeland would seem to be impossible. Another problem is that some linguists dispute the veracity of Altaic as a true family, regarding it as several separate families and isolates linked by areal and borrowing factors.[9] Furthermore, Altaic dispersal cannot at present be equated with the Neolithic. But it can be related, especially in the cases of Japanese and Turkic, to more recent expansions of agricultural and pastoralist populations.

Juha Janhunen (1996) regards the Altaic languages as developing initially in Manchuria and Inner Mongolia, with clear separation into the Turkic, Mongolic, Tungusic, and Japonic subgroups by 2,500 years ago. Prior to this time, linguistic relationships are hard to reconstruct, but the ultimate roots of the whole family probably are to be found amongst the rich Neolithic cultures of Manchuria. Millet farmers with pottery and large villages, different in cultural tradition from the early farmers of the Yellow River, were well established on the fertile southern Manchurian plains by 6000 BC. Early agricultural dispersal for these pioneers, except into Korea, was probably circumscribed by decreasing rainfall in the west (Mongolia), decreasing temperature to the north (Siberia), and other farmers to the south (the early Sino-Tibetans). During the first millennium BC, however, the Turkic languages began to spread westward with horse riding and pastoralism from Mongolia toward central Asia, replacing Indo-Iranian languages on the Asian steppes and ultimately arriving in Turkey with the Seljuk invasions of the 11th century AD (Parpola 1999; Nichols 2000:643).

For Japanese, both Janhunen and Hudson (1999, 2003) favor linguistic origins in Early Bronze Age Korea, the language being taken by Yayoi rice farmers across to northern Kyushu during the later part of the first millennium BC. The Yayoi immigrants mixed with the Final Jomon, partly hunter-gatherer inhabitants of the Japanese islands, to form the roots of the Japanese people and language of today. Modern Japanese is not so transparently related to modern Korean that such a history is clear and obvious – Hudson suggests with linguistic backing that Japanese descends from the former Koguryo language of Korea, eclipsed in historical times by the Silla language that forms the basis of modern Korean. Seen from this perspective, however, the spread of the Japanese language with Yayoi rice farmers into Japan about 2,500 years ago can be regarded as an instance of agriculturalist movement into a former hunter-gatherer territory, albeit not of course a Neolithic movement (Yayoi had bronze and iron). In this regard, the Yayoi dispersal to Japan equates best with the iron-using dispersal of the Bantu speakers in Africa.

The Trans New Guinea Phylum

New Guinea is often reputed to contain some of the highest linguistic diversity in the world, and this may be true in terms of the overall time depth of internal development, without major language replacement from external sources. Apart from coastal pockets of Austronesian speakers whose ancestors arrived after 3,000 years ago, the New Guinea languages belong in several Papuan "phyla," to use the lexicostatistical term applied to them by linguists in the 1970s. In that decade, linguists realized that many of the Highlands languages were remotely related, especially in terms of pronoun sets, and grouped them into a Trans New Guinea Phylum (TNGP).

In his culture-historical surveys, linguist Stephen Wurm (1982, 1983) reconstructed a hypothetical spread of the TNGP languages, firstly from west to east through Highland New Guinea more than 6,000 years ago, then back in an east to west direction from the vicinity of the Markham Valley, this later movement occurring for the most part within the past 3,500 years. Wurm chose this second date owing to the presence of numerous Austronesian loans, especially terms for pigs and dogs, in eastern TNGP languages. Eventually, TNGP languages came to occupy most of the New Guinea mainland, with the marked exception of the Sepik (north center) and Bird's Head (western tip) regions. Five hundred of the 740 Papuan languages recognized by Wurm were stated to belong to TNGP, which also extends to parts of interior Timor, and to the small islands of Alor and Pantar in eastern Nusa Tenggara.

After the early 1980s, the TNGP concept languished almost forgotten for many years. William Foley (1986) did not recognize its existence in his major survey of Papuan languages, noting in general that they had undergone too much borrowing for a family tree model to be applied successfully. Recently, however, linguists Andrew Pawley (in press) and Malcolm Ross have noted that the TNGP is well defined on pronoun sets, but it is very hard to subgroup internally, with about 50 small groups each having only short time depths, suggesting much recent population movement. The phylum seems to be of New Guinea Highlands origin, perhaps eastern rather than western, and it is likely to be deeper in time depth than Austronesian. Pawley also raises, but does not elaborate, the possibility that the early spread of the TNGP could have been connected with an early spread of agriculture in the Highlands, a spread that commenced archaeologically by at least 6,000 years ago (pages 142–5). It is surely not coincidental that Highland New Guinea witnessed both a very early internal development of agriculture, plus maintenance of a set of indigenous language phyla that successfully resisted encroachment by Austronesian languages. One cannot state the same for the major islands of Indonesia, where Austronesian languages are universal. For TNGP, early Holocene dispersal with swamp and swidden farming techniques seems an option well worthy of consideration.

The Americas – South and Central

In the Americas, agriculturalist expansion was subject to much more geographical circumscription than in the Old World, especially in the apparent absence of ocean-going sailing vessels. Mesoamerica is a relatively narrow isthmus, and the Americas as a whole are oriented north–south (Diamond 1994). Because of the great extent of land at high latitudes and altitudes, very large areas of North America and southern South America never saw prehistoric agriculture at all. American agriculturalist language families, on average, covered quite small areas compared to their Old World counterparts. Many had very fragmented geographical distributions owing to the spread of European languages in the past few centuries, erasing indigenous languages in many areas with almost no traces. However, this is no cause to give up – American early farmers have many fascinating archaeolinguistic secrets to reveal.

The language families of the Americas that are recognized by the majority of linguists are shown in Figure 1.2. Linguistic estimates of time depth place most of the agriculturalist ones between 6,000 and 3,500 years old. Thus, they have clearly not occupied their present ranges since the Americas were first colonized, but have all spread roughly within the time range for the development of agriculturalist societies. Recently, I surveyed some of the time-depth estimates by linguists for the larger of these American families, and came up with the following *average* age for each one (Bellwood 2000c):[10]

Otomanguean	4000 BC
Je	3400 BC
Uto-Aztecan	3300 BC
Chibchan	3000 BC
Tupian	2750 BC
Panoan	2600 BC
Quechua and Aymara	2500 BC
Arawak	2375 BC
Mayan	2200 BC
Iroquoian	2000 BC
Mixe-Zoquean	1500 BC
Algonquian	1200 BC
Caddoan	AD 1

As in the Old World, the New World language families have been grouped together into macrofamilies in a bewildering variety of ways. The most celebrated classification is that by Joseph Greenberg (1987), who regarded all American families as belonging to one Amerind macrofamily, apart from the Na-Dene (including Athabaskan) and Eskimo-Aleut languages brought in by Holocene hunter-gatherer immigrants from Siberia. The linguistic literature still waxes hot over Amerind, and in my view it simply reflects widely shared linguistic residues from the initial settlement of the Americas at about 11,500 BC.

South America

In 1915, Herbert Spinden (1915:275) suggested that "The lines of agricultural migration over the greater part of South America may be indicated in the grouping of the various language stocks." This would be a very useful observation, if only we could know how the groupings had come about. Unfortunately, many linguists and ethnographers are clearly of the opinion that present-day language distributions, especially in Amazonia, reflect colonial period disruptions rather than any "pristine" pre-contact situation (Wüst 1998; Dixon and Aikhenvald 1999). Terence Kaufman estimates that 50 percent of the South American languages existing at Spanish contact in the 16th century are now extinct, hindering any attempts to identify homelands and dispersal histories from the present extremely fragmented and scattered language family distributions.

Amazonian ethnography and ethnohistory indicate clearly how extensive has been much recent population movement. Napoleon Chagnon (1992), writing of the

Yanomama in the Orinoco headwaters of Amazonia, describes an agricultural population living in large villages that fission very frequently owing to a range of social disputes and occasions for violence. Until recently the Yanomama were able to expand freely into virgin lowland rainforest, and Chagnon explicitly compares this situation with that which might have occurred in the early centuries of the spread of agriculture. Social reasons for Yanomama movement include problems with wife-exchange in situations of male polygyny, and also rapid population growth. Yanomama villages have between 40 and 250 inhabitants and are relocated every 3–5 years, with women who survive to age 50 averaging 8.2 births (Merriwether et al. 2000). Gardens tend to be used for only three years before reverting to long-term fallow, a factor which obviously leads to a continual demand for new land, especially amongst peripheral groups. Yanomama population is now growing fast, despite high infant and adult male mortality (the latter due to warfare), perhaps a reflection in part of the acquisition of steel axes and Asian bananas since Spanish contact.

It is unknown how far the Yanomama pattern of expansion can be read back into prehistory, when their ancestors presumably were either hunter-gatherers or depended on some form of cultivation. What is most interesting here, however, is the situation of continuous "bursting out" into new lands under conditions of very powerful social circumscription. Ernest Migliazza (1985) notes that Yanomama expansion could have been assisted by a retreat of Arawak and Carib-speaking populations, who occupied much of the Yanomama region until about 1800.[11] Exactly how this retreat was encouraged is not clear, but warfare and headhunting could have played major roles.

The broader significance of the high Yanomama rates of fissioning and migration becomes clear when one examines an ethnolinguistic map of the whole of northern South America, east of the Andes. Such a map was prepared by Curt Nimuendajú in 1944, and the version reissued by Brazilian authorities in 1980 (too large and complex to reproduce here) reveals the full nature of the incredible mosaic in and around Amazonia (Mapa 1980). For instance, Tupian languages have moved right around the southeastern highlands of Brazil, to encapsulate the formerly hunter-gatherer Je language family. The Amazon basin incorporates widespread patches of Arawak, Carib, Tupian, Panoan, and Tucanoan languages. Isolates and very small language groupings abound. According to linguist Alexandra Aikhenvald (2002:2), referring to the Amazonian families:

> All the major language families are highly discontinuous. For instance, Arawak languages are spoken in over ten locations north of the Amazon, and in over ten south of the Amazon. The language map of Amazonia thus resembles a patchwork quilt where over a dozen colours appear to be interspersed at random. Frequent migrations and language contact bring about extensive borrowing and grammatical change . . . This produces a linguistic situation unlike those found in most other parts of the world, creating difficulties for distinguishing between similarities due to genetic retention and those due to areal diffusion.

Obviously, this is not fertile linguistic territory for the farming/language dispersal hypothesis, not because of historical impossibility but because of the enormous difficulties of tracking the past. How one is to interpret the history behind these Amazonian language distributions is not clear, but there are, scattered through the linguistic literature, observations that allow us at least to make a try.

The first observation is that a number of major language families have agricultural terms in their proto-vocabularies, especially for maize, and often manioc. According to Esther Matteson and colleagues (1972), such families include Chibchan, Tucanoan, and Arawakan. They reconstruct a widely shared term for corn, derived from a form like *iSi-ki/'im, for Proto-Arawak, Proto-Mayan, Proto-Otomanguean, and Proto-Panoan. Payne (1991) also presents widespread Arawak cognates for maize, sweet potato, manioc, and pottery. These observations, if verified (and they have been challenged on methodological grounds), suggest that some of the major Amazonian families could have spread after an acquisition of agriculture.

In terms of actual homelands, the situation is rather diffuse. We have no reason to suspect that the perhaps related early Quechua and Aymara languages were ever spoken anywhere but in the Andes, so presumably we can equate early versions of these with some of the first farmers in Peru and Bolivia almost 5,000 years ago. However, the expansion of Quechua in Inca and Spanish times doubtless erased many minority languages, and it is also unclear what linguistic affiliations existed in the pre-Inca civilizations such as Chavin, Mochica, Nazca, Huari, Tiahuanaco (Tiwanaku), and Chimu. One rather interesting reconstruction sources the early Quechua languages to the central Peruvian highlands, roughly from Ayacucho northward to the region south of Cajamarca, and the Aymara languages to southern Peru and Bolivia (Bird et al. 1983–84). The authors suggested that Quechua languages were carried southward with specific varieties of maize to the Cuzco region during the Huari (Wari) Period, dating to about AD 600, where they replaced Aymara languages. The result of this spread in southern Peru was a series of Aymara-influenced Quechua dialects, later to be spread much more widely through Andean South America by the Incas. The Tiahuanaco (Tiwanaku) people in Bolivia (ca. AD 800) spoke either Aymara or Puquina (now extinct) languages (Kolata 1993:34), whereas the northern coastal Chimu kingdom of the pre-Inca period perhaps used now extinct languages unrelated to Quechua.

For Amazonia, Dixon and Aikhenvald (1999:17) observe that Arawak, Carib, and Tupian are demonstrably related genetically, and this circumstance alone should be sufficient to suggest a common homeland. Aikhenvald (1999:75) places the Arawak homeland in Upper Amazonia, between the Rio Negro and the Orinoco. Rodriguez (1999:108) places the Tupian homeland in Rondonia, near the eastern boundary of Bolivia. Both these locations are close to the Andes. Another linguist, Ernest Migliazza (1982), proposed a series of homelands based on lexicostatistical calculations for the Tupian, Carib, Arawak, and Pano-Tacanan (Panoan plus Tacanan) language families. His proposals are shown in Figure 10.10, in which it can be seen that the suggested homelands for Panoan, Tupian, and Arawak are all very close to the eastern edge of

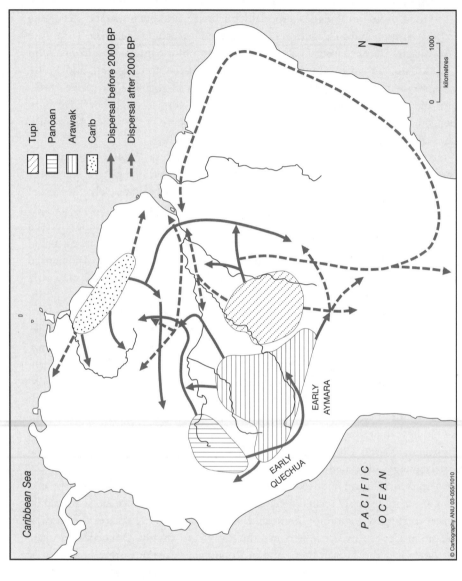

Figure 10.10 Postulated centers of dispersal for the Tupian, Panoan, Arawak, and Carib language families, according to Ernest Migliazza (1982). Based on Prance 1982. Used by permission of Columbia University Press.

the Andes, running along the eastern lowlands of Peru and into northern Bolivia. Migliazza's conclusions for the Proto-Arawak homeland were also reached by Noble (1965).

All the above authors seem to agree upon upstream rather than downstream Amazonian homelands, except for Carib, although Aikhenvald and Migliazza disagree on the precise location for early Arawak. Carib dispersal could relate to a development of manioc cultivation, but this is of course pure guesswork with our present level of knowledge. Carib appears to have spread later than the upper Amazonian families, and it did not spread at all into the Caribbean islands until historic times, owing to the prior presence there of the Arawak languages from which ethnographic Taino culture descended (Villalon 1991). Irving Rouse (1992) suggests a date in the late first millennium BC for the movement of Arawak languages into the West Indies.

It is very difficult to summarize the situation for South America, but the possibility that the very extensive Arawak, Panoan, and Tupian families all commenced their spreads downriver, with the inception of agriculture along the eastern marches of the Andes, prior to 2000 BC, seems to me to be a strong working hypothesis. Gordon Lathrap in 1970 argued differently, deriving most populations from the Middle Amazon, with colonizing movements upriver rather than downriver. The past 30 years of archaeological and linguistic research have not supported this opinion. Beyond this, apart from recognizing Quechua and Aymara as the stay-at-home languages of populations in the Andean farming homeland, we can make little further progress as far as South America is concerned.

Middle America, Mesoamerica, and the Southwest

Middle America is a little easier to handle than South America, owing in part to smallness of scale and to the unequivocally agricultural nature of the relevant proto-languages. Only four language families need concern us – these being Otomanguean (a large grouping that includes Zapotec and Mixtec of Oaxaca); Mayan of Chiapas, Guatemala, and the Yucatan Peninsula; Mixe-Zoquean of the Isthmus of Tehuantepec; and the remarkable Uto-Aztecan, which records one of the clearest cases of agricultural expansion in the Americas. One could perhaps add Chibchan of eastern Middle America; Lyle Campbell (1997) notes that Proto-Chibchan had terms for maize and manioc, and suggests a homeland in Costa Rica or Panama at about 3000 BC.

Commencing with Otomanguean, a reconstruction of Proto-Otomanguean lexical items by Rensch (1976) gave terms for maize and tortilla, chili, squash/gourd, sweet potato, cotton, tobacco, turkey, pottery, and weaving. Terence Kaufman (1990b) offered similar semantic reconstructions to Rensch (albeit with some differences in the actual proto-forms), and placed the Otomanguean homeland at about 4000 BC between the Valley of Mexico and Oaxaca. Kent Flannery and Joyce Marcus (1983) suggested that the separation of the Zapotec and Mixtec branches of the family occurred after the Coxcatlan phase (ca. 3500 BC) in the Tehuacan Valley of Puebla, with its early domesticated maize. A specific claim for a Tehuacan homeland was also presented by Josserand et al. (1984).

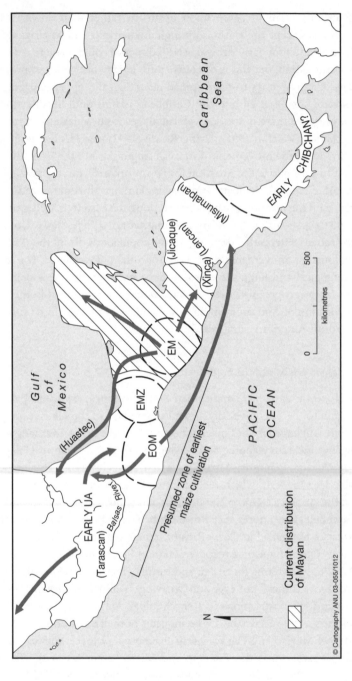

Figure 10.11 Reconstructed language family homelands for Mesoamerica. Languages in brackets are isolates that do not belong to any of the major Mesoamerican language families (Misumalpan may be related to Chibchan). This map suggests how early Uto-Aztecan (UA) dispersal could have brought speakers of UA languages into contact with speakers of early Mixe-Zoque (MZ) languages. EOM = Early Otomanguean, EMZ = Early Mixe-Zoque, EM = Early Mayan. (See also Figure 8.6.)

Whatever the exact homeland, the viewpoint that the early Otomanguean languages spread in central Mexico with the inception of maize agriculture seems hard to refute. However, the Otomangueans were not alone in this process. Circumscription, in the form of adjacent but linguistically different early farming populations, also commencing their own expansions, rapidly hemmed them in. Immediately to the east, even more circumscribed in the long run, were the Mixe-Zoquean speakers, a group who appear to have been intimately associated with the genesis of the Olmec horizon of Middle Formative Mesoamerica. Campbell and Kaufman (1976) suggested a glottochronological date of 1500 BC for the break-up of Proto-Mixe-Zoquean, considerably later than that offered for Proto-Otomanguean. This perhaps reflects a maintenance of linguistic unity for a relatively long period in a constrained area, since we clearly have no good reason from the archaeological record to assume that the Mixe-Zoqueans adopted farming any later than the Otomangueans. Soeren Wichmann (1998) reconstructs a large agricultural vocabulary for Proto-Mixe-Zoquean, with terms for manioc, squash, sweet potato, and bean.

It is interesting to reflect also on the observation by Wichmann that Mixe-Zoquean and Uto-Aztecan could be genetically related. If this is not a reflection of shared inheritance from Palaeoindian or Archaic linguistic substrata, it could indicate that the early forms of these two language families were once adjacent, presumably somewhere in central Mexico. The glimmerings of a scenario for this are presented in Figure 10.11.

The Mayan language family, according to Kaufman (1976) and Campbell (1997), originated in the Highlands of Chiapas or Guatemala at about 2000 BC, again with a large agricultural vocabulary including terms for maize, manioc, sweet potato, bean, chili, and squash. Did it relate genetically or via borrowing to any of the other families? The Mesoamerican linguistic literature has been peppered for many years with debates about deeper-level relationships, for instance between Mixe-Zoquean and Mayan, or Mixe-Zoquean and Uto-Aztecan. There seems little reason to become deeply involved in these debates, but I would suggest, as with all the confusing and cross-cutting claims for macrofamily affiliations in East Asia, that we might be witnessing a situation where all the major proto-languages were to some degree *in contact*, or at least at one time located within a zone characterized by a fair amount of areal diffusion. Such a possibility was raised in 1978 by Witkowski and Brown, who placed Mayan, Otomanguean, Mixe-Zoquean, and others in a Proto-Mesoamerican macrofamily, adding the comment (1978:942):

> Plausibly, plant domestication, which was beginning about the time Proto-Mesoamerican was spoken, triggered a vast population increase leading to the linguistic diversity that presently characterizes these languages.

This suggestion was attacked strongly by Campbell and Kaufman on the grounds that the claimed relationships could be due to chance vocabulary resemblances,[12] and the situation seems to have languished unresolved since. But I remain highly intrigued by the possibilities.

Figure 10.12 The distribution of the Uto-Aztecan language family. From Miller 1983.

Uto-Aztecan

We now turn to the most widespread Mesoamerican family of all, Uto-Aztecan, so-called because of its very extensive distribution in 1519, ranging from the urbanized Nahua-speaking Aztecs of Tenochtitlan (Mexico City) to the nomadic Paiute and Shoshone hunter-gatherers of the Great Basin, over 3,000 kilometers away to the north (Figure 10.12). As noted by Spencer and Jennings (1977:xvi):

> One is struck by the military and governmental development of the pre-Columbian Aztec state in Mexico and yet at the same time must consider that the Indians of the Great Basin . . . who by any standard possessed the simplest brand of culture, spoke a related tongue.

Uto-Aztecan was one language family that escaped the circumscription of Mesoamerica since it was on the northwestern edge of the early Mesoamerican agricultural zone.

Eventually, the early Uto-Aztecans emerged in the US Southwest as the ultimate inspirers of the Hohokam, Mogollon, and Anasazi pueblo traditions (Figure 8.7).

The Uto-Aztecan-speaking agriculturalist populations evidence some very deep-seated and widespread cultural links, especially between the Hopi of northern Arizona, now isolated from their linguistic cousins by Navajo expansion, and many Mexican populations such as the Cora and Huichol of Nayarit, and the Nahua-speaking (Aztec) populations of central Mexico (Hedrick et al. 1974; Kelley 1974; Kelley and Kelley 1975; Bohrer 1994). These links are mainly of a ritual nature and include the "volador" ritual, the concept of a four-cornered world and the village as a navel, rain gods at the four corners, corn planting in counterclockwise spirals, water serpent myths, a fire god, a corn mother, snake cults, circular kiva-like temples, curing and funerary observances, prayer sticks, corn ear fetishes, smoking to the directions, sand painting, landownership patterns, and use of the true loom (only found in the Southwest in North America). As Ellis (1968:85) noted: "The parallels between the Huicholes and the Pueblos in religious traits are so marked that one can hardly see how they could exist without direct contact between the two peoples . . . Once upon a time, the Utaztecans probably were one people."

The Uto-Aztecan languages today form a number of subgroups. On lexicostatistical grounds, linguist Wick Miller in 1984 recognized a Southern Uto-Aztecan, which included the languages of central and northern Mexico (Sonoran and Aztecan groups, including Cora, Huichol, and Nahuatl), then three coordinate subgroups in the US Southwest – 1) Hopi of northern Arizona, 2) Takic of southeastern California, and 3) Tubatulabal of southeastern California, plus the Numic languages (including Paiute and Shoshone) of the Great Basin (Figure 10.12). The latter two subgroups incorporate traditional hunter-gatherer populations, whereas the Southern Uto-Aztecans and Hopi are maize farmers. Miller noted that these four subgroups are all coordinate, thus drawing attention to an observation made by other linguists, to the effect that the Uto-Aztecan family tree is distinctly rake-like, with no clear root (Lamb 1958; Fowler 1994; Foster 1996:91; Hill 2001). Such a situation makes a homeland rather hard to discern, and the problem has been exacerbated by the incursions of Athabaskan and Yuman speakers into former Uto-Aztecan territories, pushing a geographical discontinuity through much of Arizona and leaving the Hopi isolated far to the north of the other, Southern Uto-Aztecan, maize farmers. Much of the original distribution of Uto-Aztecan languages has thus been lost or masked.

Until recently, the majority of linguists, with archaeologists in close support, regarded the early Uto-Aztecans as foragers who lived somewhere in eastern California or the Great Basin, that is in the USA rather than Mexico (Hopkins 1965; Nichols 1983–84; Lathrap and Troike 1983–84; Miller 1984; Foster 1996). The Nahuatl-speaking Aztecs were believed to have spread into the Valley of Mexico after AD 500, according to ethnohistorical accounts and linguistic data (Fowler 1989; Kaufman 2001; Beekman and Christensen 2003). Miller placed the Uto-Aztecan homeland on lexicostatistical grounds in eastern California, where the Takic sub-group exists today. Groups who moved south into Mesoamerica then adopted maize farming, which according to Miller later spread back into the US Southwest, but not back as far as the Hopi of northern Arizona owing to the intervening expansion of the Yuman languages. Hence, in Miller's view, the Hopi adopted their maize agriculture independently of the Mexican members of the Uto-Aztecan language family.

This forager-focused view of Uto-Aztecan origins has not always held sway without opposition. As early as 1957, Kimball Romney suggested that the early Uto-Aztecans dispersed with maize agriculture from the northern Sierra Madre of Mexico. Some moved southward into Mesoamerica, others northward toward the Great Basin, where the Numic populations eventually converted from farming back to hunting and gathering. In hindsight, Romney's view was remarkably perceptive. A number of other linguists and archaeologists have proposed homelands in the same general region as Romney, particularly in Sonora (Goss 1968; Hale and Harris 1979; Fowler 1983). But almost nobody, apart from Romney, visualized until recently an agricultural as opposed to a forager origin.

In the past few years, the whole picture for Uto-Aztecan origins has been revolutionized. For me, it began during a sabbatical semester in the Anthropology Department at the University of California in Berkeley in 1992. Here, I was given a golden opportunity to read into the American literature and to see if my developing ideas of farming and language dispersal in the Old World could be applied in the New. Uto-Aztecan intrigued me as a most promising language family in this regard, partly because of its great extent within Mesoamerica (Bellwood 1997c). In 1999, I received an opportunity to visit the University of Arizona in Tucson, where I was taken by Bill Longacre and Jonathan Mabry to visit the Las Capas archaeological site, with its early maize remains and irrigation channels (Figure 8.8). I also gave a seminar at the University of Arizona entitled "Austronesian prehistory and Uto-Aztecan prehistory: similar trajectories?" Sitting in the audience was University of Arizona linguist Jane Hill, who was clearly quite interested in what I had to say.

Exactly what I did say is no longer in the forefront of my memory, but I stressed that, like Austronesian, Uto-Aztecan appeared to have all the makings of a language family that spread from Mexico with maize farming. Using new lexical data recorded for Hopi in northern Arizona, Jane Hill went on to publish a major paper in 2001, in which she offered seven crucial observations about early Uto-Aztecan:

1. Proto-Uto-Aztecan lexical reconstructions do not rule out a Mesoamerican homeland.
2. Uto-Aztecan has a rake-like primary division into five subgroups – Northern Uto-Aztecan (Hopi, Numic, Tubatulabal, and Takic), Tepiman, Taracahitan, Tubar, and Corachol-Aztecan (Figure 10.12). These subgroups, based on shared innovations, differ from those recognized by Miller using lexicostatistical criteria.
3. A substantial maize-related vocabulary reconstructs to Proto-Uto-Aztecan, with six probable and three possible terms including corn cob, popcorn, tortilla, and griddle. Terms for beans do not reconstruct back as far as Proto-Uto-Aztecan.
4. The Proto-Uto-Aztecan cultivation vocabulary was not borrowed from another language family such as Mixe-Zoquean, but represents original innovation.

5. The Proto-Uto-Aztecan homeland was in Mesoamerica, probably between 2500 and 1500 BC, perhaps not far from the great Classic Mesoamerican city complex at Teotihuacan in the valley of Mexico (ca. AD 1600), where new epigraphic research suggests that a Uto-Aztecan language might have been in use (Dakin and Wichmann 2000).[13] If the Uto-Aztecan homeland really was near here, it could have been quite close to the contemporary homelands of the Otomanguean and Mixe-Zoquean families, the latter evidently a major source of loans into early Nahuatl (Kaufman 2001).
6. The archaeological record for the Southwest indicates a spread of maize cultivation from Mesoamerica at about 4,000 years ago, with beans and squash slightly later (chapter 8).
7. Given this reconstruction, it is very likely that the Northern Uto-Aztecan groups recorded as hunter-gatherers in ethnographic times had all converted from farming to foraging at some time in the prehistoric past.

In a subsequent paper, Hill (2003) has expanded discussion of the Northern Uto-Aztecan "devolution" by pointing out that some of the foraging populations in the Owens Valley of eastern California and the Great Basin practiced cultivation-type activities with wild plants, as already pointed out in chapter 2. She suggests that these Numic populations might have evolved out of a part of the former Fremont complex of maize cultivators and interstitial foragers located in the better-watered parts of the eastern Great Basin and Colorado Plateau (Figure 8.8), after a 12th–13th-century drought (or was it human overexploitation?) caused the decline of pueblo communities over much of the Southwest. Perhaps the ancestral Numic speakers were the foragers in the Fremont equation, who simply stayed at home while some of the farmer groups moved away.[14] Following this transformation, Numic speakers then radiated with their successful foraging adaptation into those drier parts of the Great Basin that previously were not Uto-Atecan speaking, ultimately into Idaho and Wyoming.

Hill (2002) also suggests that some of the other minor language families of the Southwest, especially Yuman and Kiowa-Tanoan, could have spread with the adoption of maize cultivation, in these cases secondarily by borrowing from Uto-Aztecan populations. Other maize farmers such as the Zuñi and Keres of the New Mexico pueblos clearly did not expand very far since their languages are isolates – perhaps they experienced circumscription through being surrounded by other maize farming populations quite early on. The Apache and Navajo are, of course, Athabaskan speakers whose ancestors moved as hunters into the region after the decline of the pueblos, and thus they had no connection with early maize farming at all.

On the issue of the Numic languages within Northern Uto-Aztecan, Jane Hill's account of conversion from farming to foraging *in situ* as a result of environmental decline in the southeastern Great Basin is at odds with the mainstream view of archaeologists, who have mostly regarded the Numic speakers as eternal foragers located in the Great Basin or somewhere close to it, for instance in southeastern California, since the Archaic. The most celebrated version of such a view is that by

Bettinger and Baumhoff (1982; Young and Bettinger 1992), who proposed that Numic speakers migrated into the Great Basin from southeastern California between 1,000 and 650 years ago, as a result of a competitive and successful economic adaptation involving seed processing.

In my view, however, Hill's suggestion of a Numic "devolution" *in situ* out of a prior Uto-Aztecan population of maize farmers, followed by spread throughout the Great Basin, accords best with the multidisciplinary evidence for the origins of these ethnographic hunter-gatherers. A possible historical trajectory for them is as follows:

1. Uto-Aztecan maize farmers spread into Utah from the south between 2,500 and 2,000 years ago, during a relatively supportive climatic phase,[15] to create the Fremont culture, based on a combination of maize cultivation with hunting and collection.
2. By 650 years ago, Fremont maize agriculture had declined and the Great Basin henceforth could only support foragers. The Numic speakers, as suggested by Hill, were derived from former Fremont and northern Anasazi farmer/foragers who simply stayed in place instead of moving to better-watered terrain. Eventually they spread out as successful mobile foragers and plant managers, to reach the limits shown in Figure 10.12.

Eastern North America

The remaining agricultural region of the prehistoric Americas comprises the eastern tall grass plains of the US midwest, and the Eastern Woodlands. This is a roughly quadrangular block of territory, divided down the middle by the Mississippi Basin, with its Missouri, Ohio, Arkansas, and Tennessee tributary systems. The northern limits of the region run to the latitude of the Great Lakes. Outside this quadrangle, the Great Plains proper and most of Canada were either too dry or too cold to support prehistoric farming, and farming never reached the west coast of North America in prehistory.

The Eastern Woodlands in particular have suffered much linguistic extinction as a result of European settlement, but there are five language families that are possible candidates for an initial generation through some form of farming dispersal. These are Caddoan, Siouan, and Iroquoian (reputedly sharing distant genetic links according to some linguists), together with Algonquian and Muskogean (likewise, according to some linguists, distantly related) (Figure 1.2). All of these families appear to have expanded within the past 4,000 years, according to glottochronological estimates, with Siouan and Iroquoian being marginally the most diverse.

Because of the high rates of language loss, the precise homelands and expansion histories of these five language families are not easy to reconstruct. But it is still evident that Iroquoian, Siouan, and Algonquian tend to converge geographically within the zone marked in Figure 10.13 as the homeland of post-2000 BC interior riverine seed crop cultivation. Admittedly, Iroquoian lies a little to the east of this zone, but this family now has a broken distribution, with Cherokee (Southern

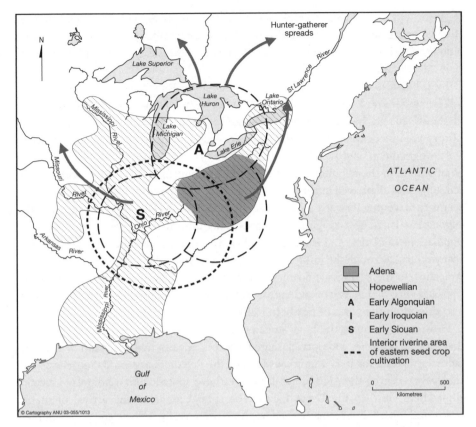

Figure 10.13 Reconstructed language family homelands for the Eastern Woodlands. The map shows the interior riverine area of early seed crop cultivation (after Scarry 1993; Cordell and Smith 1996), and the distributions of the Adena and Hopewellian burial mound and ceremonial complexes (after Coe et al. 1989). The language family homelands shown are fairly hypothetical, as discussed in the text.

Iroquoian) being geographically separated from the main block of Northern Iroquoian languages. Likewise, Siouan proper has become separated by a geographical gap from Catawba in South Carolina. Nevertheless, it is likely that all three did once intersect within the circle in Figure 10.13, and have individually radiated out of it. This, at least, sounds convincing in principle, although it is no doubt impossible at this late date to prove from linguistic resources alone.

Algonquian and Muskogean

Unfortunately, these two language families contain little information that can positively support or negate the applicability of the early farming dispersal hypothesis in eastern North America. According to Mary Haas (1969:62), both could have shared a common ancestor about 5,000 years ago, although this is not agreed upon by all linguists, and even if true it would seem to relate to pre-agricultural circumstances. Both language families are relatively non-diverse internally, with Algonquian having a divergence history of perhaps 3,500 to 3,000 years, Muskogean much less, perhaps only 2,000 years.

Most linguists who have ventured a homeland for Algonquian focus on the Great Lakes region. Frank Siebert (1967) placed it between Lake Ontario and Lake Huron at about 1200 BC, based on a reconstruction of about 50 Proto-Algonquian natural history reconstructions. Terms for maize, beans, and squash do not reconstruct to Proto-Algonquian, and Ives Goddard (1979) and Michael Foster (1996:99) have both commented on the rake-like structure of the Algonquian family "tree," with nine or ten subgroups all derived independently from Proto-Algonquian. No linguist, however, seems to have put forward a historical hypothesis to explain the vast spread of the Algonquian languages, ranging ethnographically from the extensive hunter-gatherer populations of central and eastern Canada (Cree, Ojibwa, Montagnais-Naskapi, plus many others), through the hunters of the northern Great Plains (Blackfoot, Cheyenne, Arapaho), to the small-scale farming and foraging populations of the Middle Mississippi and Ohio basins. Wiyot and Yurok, two languages distantly related to Algonquian, also existed on the coast of northern California.

How can we explain the huge spread of Algonquian? Its limited degree of genetic diversity, at least in widespread shared lexicon, means that we cannot claim an eternal existence for it as a *sprachbunde* since the Paleoindian period. Somehow, and relatively recently, the Algonquian languages have spread from a homeland located somewhere close to the Great Lakes. The spread predated the arrival of maize, beans, and squash, but certainly need not have been totally Archaic and purely hunter-gatherer. The great problem here is that words for the native seed crops cultivated in the Eastern Woodlands are not recorded in the languages that have survived to the present, and we meet this problem later in connection with Siouan and Iroquoian. So, if the early Algonquians did maintain fields of cultivated goosefoot and sumpweed, we are never likely to find any witnesses in the linguistics.

But all is perhaps not lost. Archaeologist Stuart Fiedel (1987, 1990, 1991) has reconstructed an early Algonquian homeland amongst pottery-using Early or Middle Woodland cultures of the northeast. The options, centered on the period between 600 and 200 BC, include the Point Peninsula culture of Ontario and the Adena culture of the Ohio valley. Fiedel allows for some cultivation of gourd and squash, but not maize, which is not yet present in the archaeological record. By 200 BC, according to Fiedel's glottochronological dating, Algonquians had reached New England, but many of the Eastern Algonquian languages only spread during the first millennium AD, just prior to the arrival of the Northern Iroquoians (after AD 700).

My own suggestion, offered purely as a working hypothesis, would be that the central and eastern Algonquians (excluding the genetically distant Plains languages and those in northern California) could have undergone some degree of expansion during the late Archaic and Early Woodland periods following the acquisition of indigenous seed crop cultivation in the Mississippi and Ohio valleys. The eventual acquisition of maize agriculture could have stimulated expansion further, perhaps on a much larger geographical scale, but by this time there was growing territorial competition from other groups such as the Iroquoians and Siouans.

The Canadian Algonquian hunters such as the Cree and Ojibwa represent from this perspective another specialization that probably reflected the location of Proto-Algonquian somewhere close to the northern edge of the zone of agricultural viability. Whether these hunters replaced other populations in Canada I cannot be sure,[16] but my inclination is to regard them as akin to the Punan of Borneo, able to spread just as their farmer cousins, but for reasons that could have involved demands from more settled societies for furs and other wild resources.

The essential conclusion, therefore, is that Algonquian expansion may have reflected agricultural dispersal in part, but certainly not in totality. However, when we move to examine Muskogean, the picture (perhaps deceptively) seems to be simpler. Muskogean occupies an area of the southeastern USA east of the lower Mississippi, and is thus more limited in extent than Algonquian. It is not a diverse language family internally, and Proto-Muskogean seems to have existed only about 2,000 years ago according to lexical comparisons. To the west of it existed a number of isolated and now extinct languages such as Natchez, Tunica, Chitimacha, Tonkawa, and Atakapa, suggesting that the spread of Muskogean itself was somewhat constrained to within the modern states of Mississippi, Alabama, and Georgia. Foster (1996) suggests a connection for Muskogean languages with the Mississippian culture (AD 1000–1500) and a possibly aggressive spread southeastward at that time, although some earlier movement following on from the spread of maize cultivation and ridged field construction into the southeastern USA after AD 200 (Riley 1987) can be considered likely. Muskogean seems to be too young for any early connection with the region of indigenous seed crop domestication in the Eastern Woodlands, and it is perhaps significant that its distribution falls mostly outside that region. So, for Muskogean, are we looking at late, maize-related, expansion during the Late Woodland and Mississippian periods? I suspect so.

Iroquoian, Siouan, and Caddoan

Iroquoian and Siouan, in particular, have clear histories of spread that could very likely have commenced within the Early Woodland cultures of the Eastern region of seed crop agriculture. Neither had maize terms in their proto-languages, although the less diverse and younger Caddoan most probably did (Rankin n.d.; Mithun 1984).

Ethnographically, and in late prehistoric archaeology, the Iroquoians of the northeastern states of the USA (parts of New York, southern Ontario, Quebec, Pennsylvania, and Ohio) were intensive farmers of maize, beans, and squash, living in palisaded villages of long timber houses. They had a complex political structure with tribal councils, multi-tribal confederations, and matrilineal inheritance of ranked chiefly titles (Snow 1994). The assumption of most archaeologists and linguists is that the Iroquoians conquered a territorial wedge through the eastern Algonquians, commencing around AD 700 according to Fiedel (1991), although Foster (1996:99–101) prefers the reverse scenario of an Algonquian movement around an Iroquoian wedge already in place.

As with the other Eastern Woodlands families, linguistic reconstruction rules out an early economy of maize cultivation for the Iroquoians. Marianne Mithun (1984) dated Proto-Iroquoian to about 2000 BC, and regarded the separation of Cherokee in the southern Appalachians as the first identifiable phylogenetic division. Between Cherokee and the Northern Iroquoian languages there is a substantial geographical gap with no coherent linguistic information – whether the Iroquoian languages once occupied a single large territory is uncertain. Mithun states that the Proto-Iroquoians did not have agriculture, but this brings up the problem mentioned above, that words for the native seed crops do not survive in modern Iroquoian and Siouan languages and so we could never expect to find linguistic witnesses for them anyway. Terms for maize, field, to plant, and pottery reconstruct back as far as Proto-Northern Iroquoian only, a subgroup that Mithun regarded as expanding after 2,000 years ago.

A number of archaeologists have attempted to trace back into prehistory the Northern Iroquoian cultural markers of maize and longhouses. This is a fairly simple matter going back into the large palisaded longhouse settlements of the Owasco phase, dating from about AD 1300 in New York and Pennsylvania. Beyond this it becomes more difficult, and opinions tend to be based on assumptions of cultural continuity through time. Some researchers, for instance Willey (1958) and Snow (1984), were willing to consider Northern Iroquoian origins in New York and Pennsylvania amongst Early Woodland assemblages of the first millennium BC. But in his recent papers, Dean Snow (1994, 1995, 1996) favors fairly late Northern Iroquoian expansion, deriving about AD 600 from the Clemson's Island culture of central Pennsylvania, only entering New York State about AD 1150 with the Owasco culture and its immediate antecedents. Here, it replaced an earlier Point Peninsula tradition claimed to be associated with Algonquian speakers.

In Ontario, Gary Warrick (2000) favors a similar appearance of archaeologically recognizable Iroquoians during the Princess Point Phase, after AD 500. The Princess Point Iroquoians grew maize, and their Uren Phase descendants at about 1300 underwent very rapid demographic growth, leading to a late pre-European population density stated by Warrick to be akin to that postulated for the contemporary Valley of Mexico. Fifty late prehistoric Iroquoian villages have been excavated in Ontario alone in the past 20 years (Warrick 2000:420). By 1534, the Iroquoian population in the northeastern USA is estimated to have been 100,000 people.

Dean Snow's view of a relatively late northward migration of Iroquoians with maize agriculture obviously fits well with a farming dispersal hypothesis, even though many archaeologists still regard the Iroquoians as a non-migratory population whose ancestors have been indigenously in place since Early Woodland or even Archaic times (Wright 1984; Clermont 1996; Warrick 2000; Hart and Brumbach 2003). The record suggests some initial expansion with seed crop cultivation after 2000 BC, leading to a separation of the Southern and Northern subgroups, followed much later by expansion of the Northern Iroquoians consequent upon the acquisition of maize.

Turning now to Siouan, we find a situation that resembles that for Iroquoian quite closely. This family also has a disjunct distribution, with most Siouan languages occurring west of the Mississippi, apart from isolated Catawba in Carolina, and Tutelo,

Ofo, and Biloxi (all extinct) in the Ohio Valley. Linguistically, the origin of the Siouan family is agreed to lie within the eastern part of its current range, perhaps between the two main areas of distribution that survive today (Rankin n.d.; Foster 1996). Both Rankin and Foster agree on a date around 2000 BC for the break-up of Proto-Siouan, and Rankin suggests that the four major subgroups (Missouri River, Mandan, Mississippi valley, and Ohio valley) were all linguistically separate by 500 BC.[17] He also notes that no agricultural terms can be reconstructed for Proto-Siouan. Maize terms, certainly, arrived in the Siouan vocabulary well after the Proto-Siouan stage.

In terms of the archaeological record, it looks as if the early Siouan languages, like early Iroquoian and Algonquian, arose within the general area of native Eastern Woodlands seed crop domestication. By 500 BC, some Siouan languages had already been carried across the Mississippi River into the Missouri Basin, where reported occurrences of the native Eastern Woodlands crops (chenopod, amaranth, squash, and sumpweed) date to as early as 2,000 years ago in Nebraska and Kansas (Kansas City Hopewell, Middle Woodland Phase; Adair 1988, 1994; Snow 1996:166). Maize occurs in this region as early as AD 200 in the Trowbridge site near Kansas City, together with squash and sumpweed (*Iva annua*), but it did not become common until the late first millennium AD. Indeed, numerous sources agree that the intensive spread of maize farming and large villages on to the eastern plains occurred only between AD 700 and 1000.

Archaeologically, it is of course impossible to decide just when Siouan populations moved west of the Mississippi – whether in 500 BC or AD 1000. Wedel (1983) favored the later date as far as the eastern plains were concerned, but this does not rule out a much earlier presence along the Mississippi River itself. O'Brien and Wood (1998:345) suggest a date of about AD 900 for Siouan movement into Missouri, during the Oneota Phase. Such late chronologies would be supported by the ethnographic focus on maize cultivation recorded for most Siouan speakers, apart from the Crow on the western short grass plains who switched in the 19th century to bison hunting on horseback. The Mandan of Dakota in particular constructed very large palisaded villages in late prehistory, supported by farming of maize, beans, squash, sunflower, and tobacco.

But such a late chronology is not supported by the linguistic observation that the major subgroups of Siouan were already separating by 500 BC. Admittedly, linguistic dates are very imprecise, but my inclination is to suggest that the initial phases of Siouan expansion occurred during the Woodland Period with its focus on native seed crops (see pages 176–7), and that considerable later expansion, especially in a westerly direction, might have occurred consequent upon the adoption of maize farming by AD 1000. The first stage of Siouan expansion could thus be represented somewhere within the widespread shared iconography of the Adena and Hopewell Phases, whereas the later maize-related spread could be reflected in the "sameness and uniformity" of material culture noted by Linda Cordell and Bruce Smith (1996:259) in the Late Woodland Phase between AD 400 and 800.

Our final language family, Caddoan, appears to be only about 2,000 years old (like Muskogean; Campbell 1997), although Foster (1996) dates Proto-Caddoan much earlier, to 1500–1300 BC. The Caddoans (who include the Arikara, Pawnee, and Wichita) are all agriculturalists, and Perttula (1996) dates the appearance of a distinctive Caddoan archaeological tradition to about AD 800, with earthen ceremonial mounds and maize cultivation. In the absence of any very informative debate on Caddoan linguistic prehistory I can only suggest that it might represent a fairly late prehistoric maize-related spread, like Muskogean.

Having run the gamut of the Eastern Woodlands language families, we can now take stock (Figure 10.13). This region does not have the clarity of evidence in support of farming dispersal that occurs in some other parts of the world, in part because of fragmentary language survival, and in part because the vocabulary relevant for the native seed crops has not been preserved. The Algonquian, Iroquoian, and Siouan families present some shadowy evidence for an initial generation and dispersal history set within the phases of population growth represented by the Adena and Hopewell Traditions of the first millennium BC, dispersals assisted perhaps by increasing reliance on indigenous forms of plant cultivation. In distributional terms, Siouan might fit such an Adena-Hopewell origin more strongly than Algonquian or Iroquoian, but this can only be surmise given the disjointed distributions of these language families. The arrival of maize agriculture then set off further expansion, especially of the Northern Iroquoians and the western Siouans, and perhaps also gave rise to the eventual expansions of the Muskogeans and Caddoans. Perhaps this is as far as we can go in establishing the merits of a farming dispersal hypothesis for the Eastern Woodlands. But I would add that the overall pattern of overlap between language family homelands and agricultural homelands does seem to work almost as well in the Eastern Woodlands as it does in Mesoamerica, the Middle East, China, or West Africa. Whether my readership will agree is for the future to decide.

Did the First Farmers Spread Their Languages?

This chapter has brought together what might appear to be a rather bewildering quantity of information, often rather vague and contested, on the history of the major agriculturalist language families. Does this information support the three correlations between farming and linguistic homelands suggested at the start of this chapter? These three correlations were as follows: language families should have their putative homelands located within or close to agricultural homelands, they should intersect geographically within or close to agricultural homelands, and they should have dispersal histories that commence chronologically within agricultural homeland areas and then become progressively younger with distance away from such homelands.

My feeling at this point is that radially patterned dispersals of language families and early farming systems from agricultural homeland areas can be traced to a degree much greater than we could expect from chance alone. Indo-European, Afroasiatic, and Elamo-Dravidian radiate from around the Southwest Asian region of early farming. Likewise, Sino-Tibetan, Austroasiatic, and Austronesian, not to mention Tai, Hmong-Mien, and Altaic, all emanated from the Chinese region, albeit not all during the Neolithic. New Guinea has its Trans New Guinea Phylum, while West Africa spawned the Niger-Congo languages. In the Americas, we have just reviewed some rather hazy evidence that Quechua, Aymara, Arawak, and Panoan (with Tupian being less specific) developed in or fairly close to the Andes of Peru. Mayan, Chibchan, Mixe-Zoque, Otomanguean, and Uto-Aztecan developed within Mesoamerica. Algonquian, Iroquoian, and Siouan perhaps had some connection with the early development of seed cropping in the Eastern Woodlands.

These radial patterns of genesis and spread of agriculturalist language families and early forms of farming do not occur at random all over the world. There is no evidence for them, for instance, in Europe, central Asia, southern Africa, the lower Amazon or the lower Mississippi. No one, to my knowledge, has ever claimed that Proto-Indo-European was spoken in the United Kingdom, that rice cultivation began in Sulawesi, or that maize cultivation began in New York (or if they have, I haven't read their works). I am unable to prove that the suggested correlations can only be explained in the manner suggested, but there is clearly sufficient correlation within the spatial and chronological patterns to make the farming/language dispersal hypothesis worthy of a great deal more attention than it has received so far.

Chapter 11

Genetics, Skeletal Anthropology, and the People Factor

Critics of the early farming dispersal hypothesis usually raise the crunch-time question: never mind the languages and archaeology, what about the people? Did languages and farming lifestyles spread through unmoving populations of hunter-gatherers simply by *cultural diffusion* (i.e., adoption, borrowing, acculturation), or did they spread because of the demographic expansion (via *demic diffusion*) of populations whose ancestors already possessed the relevant languages and farming lifestyles? For some regions of the world, biological data are too few to inform usefully and directly on such questions. For other regions, such as western Eurasia and Southeast Asia/Oceania, the debates are quite heated and schools of opinion can be discerned emerging from the steam. This is because both kinds of movement are, of course, logically possible, and can be eloquently argued for, even though the biological data do not clinch the matter with the finality that some protagonists might hope for.

The phenomenon of actual population spread is referred to in this chapter as demic diffusion, following the terminology used in their classic study of Neolithic Europe by archaeologist Albert Ammerman and geneticist Luca Cavalli-Sforza (1984:6). Demic diffusion in prehistoric contexts would have occurred, at least in optimal continental circumstances, via a *wave of advance*, in which continuous demographic growth in non-circumscribed frontier situations would have prompted a population boundary to expand outward by gradual or saltational means. The inward (or backward) direction would have been demographically "full," settled by populations that had reached optimal size after the wave of advance had moved on beyond them. Ammerman and Cavalli-Sforza calculated, using archaeological C14 dates, that a Neolithic wave of advance spread from southeast to northwest through Mesolithic Europe at an *average* rate of around 1 kilometer per year (see also Fort and Mendez 1999; and Fort 2003 for comparable calculations for the Pacific). They noted also that actual rates of spread on the ground would have varied greatly because of environmental barriers and differing carrying capacities.

Ammerman and Cavalli-Sforza most emphatically did *not* suggest that the Neolithic farmers simply drove all the Mesolithic foragers in Europe into extinction – critics of the wave of advance model sometimes jump unfairly to this conclusion without good reason. Instead, they advocated continuing genetic admixture between the two groups as the wave of advance progressed (1984:128–130), such that the ultimate cultural and linguistic descendants of a "Middle Eastern" population commencing with 100 percent "farmer" genes, upon reaching the Atlantic limits, *could* have found themselves (had they noticed!) with almost 100 percent "native forager" genes, at least in theory (Krantz 1988:93; Cavalli-Sforza 2003). Such a process would have established what geneticists term a *demic cline* – a geographical gradient away from an origin in the occurrence of one or more genes. The essence here is a continuous watering-down of an expanding genetic configuration, away from its original state, by inexorable local input from an ever-unfolding native genetic landscape (Renfrew 2001c, 2003). It need hardly be stressed that Neolithic farmers could not have spread in the way 19th-century European colonists migrated to North America and Australasia, with constant back-up from source in the form of flotillas of ships carrying thousands of people. Neolithic expansion was more of an insistent creep, with occasional jumps, than a sudden and overwhelming sonic boom.

We return to genes and clines later, first making the point that this is not a chapter on the technicalities of population genetics, biochemistry, and mathematical computation. Interest here is in the *historical* observations that paleoanthropologists and geneticists can make about ancient human populations, rather than in the analyses and computations of the genetic data themselves. Archaeologists in search of population history should at least attempt to understand the historical reasoning processes of linguists and biologists, just as reverse accommodations should also take place.

Are There Correlations between Human Biology and Language Families?

In 1774, on Cook's Second Voyage to discover the Great Southern Continent, Johann Reinhold Forster mused "What occasions the inhabitants of O-Taheitee to be so much distinguished from the Mallicolese?" (Thomas et al. 1996:175). He had noted that the Tahitians of Polynesia and the Malekulans of Vanuatu (Melanesia) spoke languages (now known as Austronesian) with many words in common, yet the people were so different in physical appearance. Austronesians are physically very varied, just as are speakers of Afroasiatic (e.g., Arabs and Ethiopians), Indo-European (e.g., Bengalis and Norwegians), and Altaic languages (e.g., Turks and Mongolians), to name just a few of the more obvious cases. The speakers within these language families seem unlikely to have descended *entirely* from single founder biological populations in the few millennia since the linguistic dispersals occurred, at least not in terms of our current understanding of rates of biological change in humans. But do these patterns reflect language movements through unmoving but already highly differentiated populations, or do they reflect population movements leading to a kaleidoscope of admixture between incoming and indigenous groups?

We might begin by asking if there are any demonstrable geographical correlations today between patterns of linguistic and biological variation on a worldwide canvas. If there are, then it stands to reason that such correlations could result from past episodes of demic diffusion, when population expansions occurred that carried *both* genes and languages. In 1988 and 1994, Luca Cavalli-Sforza and his colleagues addressed this question from a worldwide perspective, utilizing genetic distance analyses of 42 modern populations in terms of their frequencies of 120 different classical genetic markers. They claimed that the resulting genetic tree of populations resembled closely a tree of populations classified by language family membership, a claim recently restated (with qualifications) by Daniel Nettle and Louise Harriss (2003), using the same gene frequency data. Basically, genetic distances and languages correlate quite closely in Europe, East and Central Asia, but rather less well in West Africa, Southwest and Southeast Asia. Nettle and Harriss rightly point out that strong cases of correlation could result from situations of past demic diffusion, whereas weaker situations allow for more population mixing. Furthermore, by controlling for the influence of purely geographical factors in their analysis, they are able to refute the complaint that such correlations simply reflect geographical proximity, rather than factors of correlated genetic and linguistic origin.[1]

Do genes record history?

Luca Cavalli-Sforza has asked, "can the history of humankind be reconstructed on the basis of today's genetic situation?" (Cavalli-Sforza and Cavalli-Sforza 1995:106). Well might we ask, given that identification of ancient DNA from bone is a technique still in its infancy, having so far yielded few data significant for the questions addressed in this book (Pääbo 1999). The question of whether genetic data drawn from the blood, hair, or saliva of modern sample populations can be used as direct witnesses for the histories of whole populations who lived many millennia ago is a very fundamental one. A mind-modeling of what might have happened in a Neolithic situation involving population growth will quickly show why.

If we begin with a Neolithic source population, dependent upon farming and with a healthy rate of demographic growth, then during every generation a few members of the group will wish to seek new land, with their families, sometimes close to the source region, sometimes further afield, depending on the varied realities of geography and environment, social competition, and desire for founder status. If allowed, as for instance in situations where early farmers were surrounded by hunter-gatherers rather than other equally territorial farmers, the wave of advance will spread out gradually, yet continually, in theory involving interbreeding with surrounding hunter-gatherer populations, perhaps mainly via forager female/farmer male parenthood if the ethnographic record is any guide. There will be a continuous watering-down of the original farmer genetic profile as the frontier spreads away from the source region.

But now impose upon the foundation genetic edifice that has resulted from such a farming dispersal several *subsequent* millennia of continuing mutation, natural selection, and genetic drift. Impose also cultural and natural events such as invasions, massacres, epidemics, and natural disasters, and we might wonder how the source genetic configuration could ever possibly survive at all to be still traceable into the present. That such tracing can occur at all is quite remarkable, and in part due to the careful attention paid by geneticists to both the clinal geography of multiple genetic markers studied in combination (e.g., Ammerman and Cavalli-Sforza 1984), and to the phylogenetic analysis of non-recombining mitochondrial DNA and Y-chromosome lineages as they spread through space and mutate through time.[2]

Currently, geneticists engage in considerable debate about the historical significances of their data, especially of the trans-continental clines that are often visible in both the nuclear and non-recombining genetic systems. To understand the genesis of these clines, it is necessary also to be aware of the roles of natural selection (especially through climate and disease), and the factors of chance in reproductive strategies that can have a major effect on the survival of lineages.

For instance, Ronan Loftus and Patrick Cunningham (2000) note, actually in this instance discussing the mtDNA of African cattle:

> in a population where females leave on average one surviving daughter per generation, any single mother has only a two percent chance of contributing her mtDNA to a population one hundred generations later.

Thus, some of the mitochondrial lineages that characterized a population at source can disappear through genetic drift as the generations pass by, ultimately to be replaced by other lineages that have either mutated or have become incorporated through intermarriage. Such lineages need have no bearing on the ultimate origin of the core population. These stochastic processes will be enhanced in small populations that tend to undergo periodic isolation, as for instance in small islands or rugged terrain.

In fact, mtDNA lineage distributions and mutation ages have to be handled with extreme care when the history of a whole human population is at stake, rather than just that of the lineage itself. Molecular clock forms of dating, whereby mtDNA and Y-chromosome lineages are given mutation ages according to assumed rates of nucleotide sequence mutation through time, can be particularly contentious. This issue is far too complex for further discussion here, but many geneticists have misgivings about the accuracy of such dating methods (e.g., Bradley and Loftus 2000:248; Cavalli-Sforza 2003:85). Perhaps it is not surprising that Erika Hagelberg (2000:5–6) has recently stated that genetic data "cannot provide clear-cut evidence of historical events . . . We cannot simply look at DNA of so-called native peoples and expect to reconstruct the past."

Nevertheless, geneticists are currently making many grand claims for the histories of populations, including those populations attached to language families, so we turn now to relevant early farming situations where genetic or skeletal data can reflect usefully upon issues of demic versus cultural diffusion. The focus is quite heavily on

Neolithic Europe and Austronesia, because of the high intensities of debate and publication in these regions.

Southwest Asia and Europe

This is the classic area for debate over cultural versus demic diffusion models for the spread of farming. The original demic diffusion model of Ammerman and Cavalli-Sforza required active population growth along an expanding frontier, moving across Europe from southeast to northwest at an average rate of one kilometer per annum and incorporating indigenous hunter-gatherer populations along the way. Principal components analysis of the genetic data suggested that this particular movement, the major one of three identified in the data, accounted for about 30 percent of the genetic variation in modern European populations (Figure 11.1 upper left).

This model has spawned enormous debate over the past 20 years, most fairly inconclusive until the eruption of mtDNA analysis during the mid-1990s. Alan Fix (1999) has recently suggested that the major southeast-to-northwest cline identified by Cavalli-Sforza and his colleagues, especially in terms of HLA genes, could reflect the effects of selection caused by the farming economy itself, for instance through the associated spread of diseases originating from domesticated animals (zoonotic diseases), or the spread of malaria amongst relatively large and densely settled Neolithic populations, even in temperate latitudes. He does not rule out demic diffusion as a significant process in the genetic foundations of Neolithic Europe, but feels instead that genetic data cannot really illuminate its significance. Cavalli-Sforza himself, supported strongly by Italian geneticist Guido Barbujani and other colleagues, feels conversely that the observed cline is so complex that it must result to a degree from population movement rather than natural selection alone (Cavalli-Sforza and Cavalli-Sforza 1995:149; Barbujani et al. 1998). Other critics, however, point out that the cline is not *in itself* dateable to any particular period in time, and could just as well be Paleolithic as Neolithic in origin.

The debate has become more lively in recent years with the increasing emphasis on the analysis of haploid markers in mitochondrial DNA and on the Y-chromosome. Interpretations of the data have become complex and varied in the extreme, but two schools of historical interpretation appear to be consolidating. One, basing its historical reconstructions on the *phylogenetic* analysis of mtDNA and Y-chromosome lineages, regards most modern Europeans as having essentially local Paleolithic ancestries, with input of Southwest Asian genes during the Neolithic accounting for very little of the modern patterning. This school favors cultural rather than demic diffusion, and its views have most recently been summarized by Martin Richards (2003). The strongest opposed viewpoint favoring demic diffusion derives from modeling the consequences of admixture between postulated Paleolithic European and Neolithic Southwest Asian gene pools, using both the non-recombining systems as well as nuclear DNA.

In order to put this debate into perspective I will review some of the most significant recent opinions in chronological order, subsequent to the classic 1984 study by

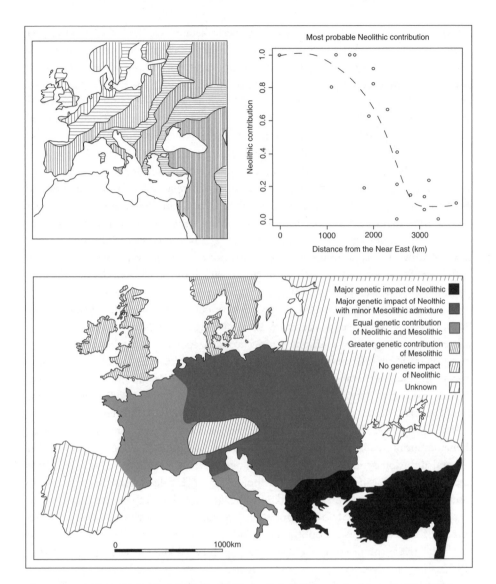

Figure 11.1   Upper left: The clinal distribution of markers in 91 nuclear genetic systems from southwest to northwest across Europe, identified by principal components analysis. This is the first principal component within the data and it accounts for about 30% of the total variation. After Cavalli-Sforza and Minch 1997. Upper right: A plot of the most probable Neolithic contribution to the modern Y chromosome genotype, as assessed by Chihki et al. 2002 for European genetic samples against their geographic distance from the Levant. After Bentley et al. 2003. Lower: A model for Mesolithic–Neolithic genetic admixture in Europe based on demographic assumptions and the archaeological record. After Lahr et al. 2000.

Ammerman and Cavalli-Sforza. In 1991, a genetic distance analysis of 26 polymorphic genetic systems by Sokal, Oden, and Wilson resulted in the statement: "We conclude that the spread of agriculture through Europe was not simply a case of cultural diffusion, but involved significant differential reproduction of the new farmers whose origins can be traced to the Near East." Full support was given to theories of linked Neolithic and Indo-European spreads across Europe, and allowance was made for "diffusive gene flow between the neolithic farmers and mesolithic groups."

Although Sokal and his team qualified their conclusions in the following year (Sokal et al. 1992), the demic diffusion model for Neolithic and Indo-European spread was soon given further support from a spatial autocorrelation analysis of genetic and linguistic similarities among Eurasian populations by Guido Barbujani and colleagues (1994). Alberto Piazza and colleagues (1995) then used synthetic genetic maps to claim, in agreement with Luca Cavalli-Sforza, that a Neolithic spread through Europe from Southwest Asia accounted for 26 percent of modern genetic variation.

In 1995, Sokal teamed up with Barbujani to return to the issue of demic diffusion, concluding from a computer simulation of five models of microevolution in European populations that: "The genetic structure of current populations speaking Indo-European languages seems therefore to largely reflect a Neolithic expansion . . . Allele-frequency gradients among Indo-European speakers may be due either to incomplete admixture between dispersing farmers, who presumably spoke Indo-European, and pre-existing hunters and gatherers (as in the traditional demic diffusion hypothesis), or to founder effects during the farmers' dispersal" (Barbujani et al. 1995:109). The demic diffusion model was becoming well established.

Indeed, by 1996, an unbiased observer might have drawn the conclusion that demic diffusion had won the day, at least for Neolithic Europe. However, the cultural diffusion school was clearly not going to give in quietly. Martin Richards and colleagues, basing their views on molecular clock calculations and patterns of internal phylogenetic diversity in mtDNA lineages, concluded that "the major extant [mtDNA] lineages throughout Europe predate the Neolithic expansion and . . . the spread of agriculture was a substantially indigenous development accompanied by only a relatively minor component of contemporary Middle Eastern agriculturalists" (Richards et al. 1996:185).

Debate naturally ensued over this paper, and battle lines started to emerge (Cavalli-Sforza and Minch 1997; Richards et al. 1997; Barbujani et al. 1998). The Richards team restated the value of a phylogeographic approach focused on molecular ages for MtDNA lineages, whereas the Barbujani team countered (1998:489): "We do not think that the age of a group of [mtDNA] haplotypes can be mechanically equated to the age of the population from which they came, especially if these haplotypes are also found elsewhere . . . inferences from population history must be based on measures of genetic diversity between populations, not between molecules."

In 1998, Antonio Torroni and colleagues entered the debate on the side of the cultural diffusionists, by suggesting that most European mtDNA lineages spread with ancestral populations emerging from late glacial refugia, particularly from Iberia. They claimed also that Southwest Asian mtDNA haplogroup H accounted for between

40 and 60 percent of mtDNA lineages in western Europe, but removed this from Neolithic consideration by giving it an age of more than 25,000 years.

Cultural (non-demic) diffusion received another boost when Bryan Sykes (1999a) restated that the Southwest Asian contribution to the European mtDNA pool was only between 20 and 30 percent, and further claimed that 70 percent of the European mtDNA gene pool originated in the post-glacial re-peopling of Europe, between 11,000 and 14,000 years ago. Martin Richards and colleagues (2000) then restated the case for a Paleolithic inheritance using what they termed "founder analysis," reemphasizing that most European mtDNA lineages expanded after the last glaciation and that under 25 percent of the modern mtDNA pool in Europe was brought in during the Neolithic. However, they remained open to debate on these issues, concurring that: "it is important to bear in mind that these values indicate the likely contribution of each prehistoric expansion to the composition of the *present-day* mtDNA pool. Extrapolating from this information to details of the demography at the time of the migration, although of course highly desirable for the reconstruction of archaeological processes, is unlikely to be straightforward" (Richards et al. 2000:1272).

In 2000, Ornella Semino and colleagues brought Y-chromosome data into the fray, suggesting that about 78 percent of European Y-chromosome variation related to Paleolithic expansions from glacial refugia in Iberia and Ukraine. They attributed about 22 percent of the modern variation to four haplotypes that spread during the Neolithic from the Levant, thus supporting the claims by Richards and Sykes for only a low Neolithic contribution based on mtDNA.

Between 1996 and 2000, therefore, cultural diffusion was making a strong comeback, even though the percentages actually offered by each school for the Neolithic contribution to the overall European gene pool overlapped considerably, generally between 20 and 30 percent. However, the demic diffusion school was not slow to reply. Lounès Chikhi and colleagues (1998a, 1998b) identified a cline across Europe in molecular DNA markers that paralleled closely the original cline in classical protein markers proposed by Cavalli-Sforza and Piazza. Their own molecular clock calculations placed the population expansion that led to this cline squarely in the Neolithic, and they argued for younger dates for the so-called Paleolithic mtDNA lineages.

Zoë Rosser and colleagues (2000) then indicated clines in two Y-chromosome haplogroups that today account for 45 percent of European variation. These clines were stated, slightly cautiously since they are also strongly influenced by geography, to be good evidence for significant demic diffusion of Neolithic farmers from Southwest Asia. The authors suggested that much of the genetic patterning in Europe may have developed with the spread of Indo-European languages (see also Simoni et al. 2000).

By 2001, Y-chromosome data were sufficiently detailed for Peter Underhill and colleagues (2001a; Underhill 2003) to summarize worldwide patterns, showing that European and west/central Asian populations are closely related in terms of Y haplogroups, particularly when compared to sub-Saharan African and East Asian populations. Two of the Y haplogroups concerned, III and part of VI, could have spread into Europe by Neolithic expansion, and it was acknowledged that the Y-chromosome data support the model of demic diffusion with population admixture, from south-east to northwest across Neolithic Europe.

In 2002, Lounès Chikhi and colleagues analyzed 22 binary markers on the Y-chromosome in order to model situations of admixture, followed by genetic drift, between two "ideal" populations, one using modern Near Eastern samples to represent a "Neolithic" mode, the other using Basque and Sardinian samples to represent a "Paleolithic" mode. An essential assumption here is that the real genetic patterning present in the Near East and western Europe 10,000 years ago is unknowable, so only a modeling process of this type will lead to realistic conclusions. The authors concluded that the Neolithic contribution to modern European Y-chromosomes must have been about 50 percent on average, far higher than either the original estimate by Cavalli-Sforza or that from the mtDNA phylogeographic approach of Martin Richards (both under 30 percent). There is geographical variation, however, with a Near Eastern component of 85–100 percent in southeastern Europe, but only 15–30 percent in France (Figure 11.1 upper right).

By 2002, the supporters of both cultural and demic diffusion had fired many salvos, and the debate is far from over. In 2003, as I finalize this chapter, a compilation of genetics papers on Europe has just been published by the McDonald Institute, as part of a worldwide review of the farming/language dispersal hypothesis (Bellwood and Renfrew 2003). Guido Barbujani and Isabelle Dupanloup, together with Luca Cavalli-Sforza, and Lounès Chikhi, restate the case for significant demic diffusion of a South-west Asian Neolithic population into Europe. Barbujani and Dupanloup note how the results of admixture between farmers and foragers will vary in terms of just *when* in the historical sequence the interbreeding became significant; in other words, for-agers would have had far greater genetic impact if they interbred early on with small groups of expanding farmers, much greater than if they went into an early isolation-ist mode and only emerged much later on to face a farmer population increased by several generations of rapid internal population growth. They conclude "At present, we think there are good reasons to take sides with the earlier (Ammerman and Cavalli-Sforza 1984) rather than with the later (Semino et al. 2000) studies by Cavalli-Sforza's group, and to maintain that a large fraction of the European gene pool is derived from the genes of ancestors who did not live in Europe, but in the Levant, until the Neolithic" (Barbujani and Dupanloup 2003:430).

From the cultural diffusion perspective, Martin Richards and colleagues in the same volume restate the case for only a low proportion of Near Eastern genes across Europe, in fact only about 20 percent, but they also suggest that when the small numbers of Near Eastern farmers did move, they moved far and rapidly. They (2003:464) conclude that "Farming dispersal models may yet have a rôle to play in explaining language expansions. But grand syntheses based on demic diffusion and the wave of advance, in which farming, languages and genes all expand together, should become a thing of the past." I could not agree more, and sense from this statement a desire for a middle ground.

The middle ground will perhaps be found after more careful consideration of the obvious fact that Europe cannot be considered a single "place" for purposes of

Mesolithic to Neolithic transition models. Whatever overall percentage of genes the Neolithic farmers brought into Europe, the actual results of farmer–forager interbreeding must have varied across the continent, with the Southwest Asian component necessarily being largest in the south and east, and smallest in the west and north. This has come more into focus with a paper by Roy King and Peter Underhill (2002), in which it is claimed that there are very significant correlations between the distributions of painted pottery and anthropomorphic figurines in Neolithic archaeological contexts in the Levant, Anatolia, and southeastern Europe, and the distribution of a particular Y-chromosome haplogroup termed Eu9. This correlation supports a hypothesis of demic diffusion, at least of males, out of Southwest Asia to as far west as southern France. In addition, analysis of ancient bone from LBK contexts in France and Germany has indicated the presence of mtDNA lineages of Southwest Asian origin – direct evidence for the movement of at least some females during the Neolithic (Jones 2001:161).

As in the earlier *Archaeogenetics* volume produced by the McDonald Institute (Renfrew and Boyle 2000), the debate over demic vs. cultural diffusion for Neolithic Europe still remains very lively. The dust has not settled yet and there is no obvious neat and tidy genetic reconstruction for the whole of Europe that can be presented in a nutshell. This being the case, can we extract any useful data, independently of the genetics, from the results of skeletal analysis and observations of visible biological characters?

The most obvious example of the latter is the cline in hair and eye pigmentation that runs from relatively dark in the Levant and along the Mediterranean, to light (fair hair, blue eyes) around the North and Baltic Seas and in Scandinavia (Sidrys 1996). At first sight, this could indicate a relative isolation of northern Europeans from any Levantine or Mediterranean influence, but the situation is not really so simple. Natural selection for pale pigmentation via Vitamin D synthesis over a period of 6,000 years, in cold climate circumstances where humans covered themselves with clothing, together with assortative mating, could in theory also have produced the observed cline.

Paleodemographic data also have a contribution to make. An age-at-death analysis of skeletons in European Neolithic cemeteries has recently allowed Jean-Pierre Bocquet-Appel (2002) to suggest a rapid increase in birth rate immediately following the adoption or spread of agriculture in Europe, followed much later by a rising mortality rate. The earliest farmers were clearly fertile, and Bocquet-Appel draws the conclusion: "With the data currently available, this [pan-European Mesolithic to Neolithic] transition is characterized by a clear rupture with the previous stationary regime of foragers over a period of some 500 years." However, farmer fecundity need not automatically mean demic diffusion of pre-existing farmers, since foragers can also adopt farming and lessen their birth intervals. Bocquet-Appel's results only underpin the reality of rapid early farmer demographic growth.

Another source of skeletal data involves metric and morphological analysis of crania from ancient cemeteries and other archaeological contexts in order to determine population affinities. Slovimil Vencl (1986) analyzed skeletal evidence from central

Europe to suggest a tenfold increase in population numbers from the Mesolithic into the Neolithic, and a complete population replacement across the transition, with hunter-gatherers holding out only in areas sub-optimal for farming. A more recent multivariate analysis of cranial data from Turkey and the Levant, plus southeastern and Mediterranean Europe, suggests three conclusions (Pinhasi and Pluciennik in press):

1. PPNB populations in the Levant and Anatolia were very varied.
2. Southeastern European Neolithic peoples were probably drawn from a central Anatolian Neolithic population represented by the burials from Çatalhöyük.
3. Mediterranean populations originated from a greater degree of Mesolithic-Neolithic admixture than those in southeastern Europe.

As the authors point out, these conclusions are more precise geographically than those drawn from genetic analyses, the latter being "of insufficient resolution for regional assessment." Their conclusions are rather similar to those drawn by Marta Lahr and colleagues (2000), based on demographic modeling and the archaeological record. These are shown in Figure 11.1 (lower), and indicate something a little similar to the first principal component of Cavalli-Sforza, in that there is an obvious cline from Anatolia, through Greece and the Balkans, into central and then Mediterranean and western Europe. A recent strontium isotope analysis of female skeletons from LBK contexts in the Rhineland perhaps tells us how such a cline might have originated, in this case via the in-marrying or capture of non-local (Mesolithic?) females who grew up in, and thus acquired chemical signatures in their bones from, upland areas away from the riverine landscape favored for LBK farming (Bentley et al. 2003).

I have deliberately gone into the European situation in depth because of the vast quantity of data available for that region. Clearly, and despite obvious disagreements, the indications point consistently to a "common sense" scenario that requires a Neolithic population to spread in from the southeast and to gradually "disappear" in a genetic sense as the wave of advance spread toward the northwest. The disagreements relate to the strength of this wave of advance, not to its very existence. The perspective I am offering in this book leads me to believe, with geneticists such as Lounès Chikhi and Guido Barbujani, that the strength of this advance was considerable, and that Mesolithic populations, while contributing genes in a markedly clinal fashion, did not contribute very much to the resulting patterns of archaeology and language in Europe, except in situations where they survived temporarily in relative isolation. For other regions of the world we do not have anywhere near such a density of data, but we also have interesting debates.

South Asia

The debate for this region is really only just starting, compared to Europe. In 1996, Giuseppe Passarino and colleagues published evidence for a "dilution" of an ancient mtDNA marker in northern India by Caucasoid populations coming in from western Asia, thus supporting a demic spread of Indo-Europeans into India. In 2001, Lluis

Quintana-Murci and colleagues carried this perspective further with an analysis of Y-chromosomes, suggesting two episodes of demic diffusion from the northwest. The first, represented by Y-chromosome haplogroup 9, accounts for 30 to 60 percent of Southwest Asian lineages and ~20 percent of those in Pakistan and northern India. This haplogroup is stated to relate to Elamo-Dravidian movement from Iran. The second, represented by Y-chromosome haplogroup 3, is common in central Asia and northern India, and is stated to record the movement of Indo-European speakers. The spread of haplogroup 9 occurred between 4,000 and 6,000 years ago, haplogroup 3 between 3,500 and 4,500. The authors conclude "The geographical distributions, observed clines, and estimated ages of Hg-9 and Hg-3 chromosomes in southwestern Asia all support a model of demic diffusion of early farmers from southwestern Iran – and nomads from western and central Asia – into India, bringing the spread of genes and cultures (including language)" (Quintana-Murci et al. 2001:541).

Support for cultural diffusion models is not lacking in this region, however. Toomas Kivisild and colleagues (2003) claim that the northern Indian Y-chromosome lineages could be more ancient than Quintana-Murci and colleagues suggest, indeed much older than the Neolithic. They allow an estimate of only ~8 percent of "Neolithic" lineages in South Asia, thus arguing for only a very small amount of population movement from the west associated with early farmers and Indo-Aryans.

This rather brief review indicates that the conclusions for Asia are no firmer than those for Europe. Can we add more from skeletal anthropology? Brian Hemphill and colleagues (1991) have summarized a great deal of data on Harappan and related skeletal populations, noting a progressive decline in dental health since the early Neolithic, and the possibility of a population change in terms of non-metric dental characters between 6000 and 4500 BC. They also note that the population resident at Mohenjo-Daro during the Harappan was morphologically different from other Harappan populations. The Harappans as a whole resembled Iranian populations in cranial terms, whereas the older Neolithic population at Mehrgarh resembled that from Chalcolithic Inamgaon in Maharashtra. It is not clear if such observations can be related usefully to questions of Indo-Aryan and Elamo-Dravidian origins, but they certainly do not support any total isolation of the subcontinent since the Paleolithic.

Africa

In 1987, Laurent Excoffier and colleagues noted close relationships between African major linguistic populations and the genetic geography of the Rhesus blood group system, protein systems, and DNA molecules. Bantu-speakers were stated to be fairly homogeneous genetically, and distinct from Afroasiatic-speakers. Southern Bantu populations revealed evidence for past admixture with Khoisan populations. In 1996, Himla Soodyall and colleagues suggested that a distinctive mtDNA 9-base-pair deletion, different in origin from a similar deletion found in many East Asian populations, spread widely during Bantu expansion, also being found through admixture in Pygmy populations. The deletion, however, does not occur in other Niger-Congo speakers in West Africa, and so probably originated after Bantu expansion had commenced.

Genetic support for demic diffusion as part of the Bantu spread is thus quite firm. In 1996, Elizabeth Watson and colleagues analyzed African mtDNA sequences to indicate much greater nucleotide sequence variability amongst hunter-gatherer populations than amongst farmers and pastoralists. The results were interpreted to suggest that the farmers and pastoralists (including Bantu-speakers) have increased their population sizes relatively recently, whereas the hunter-gatherers have had stable population sizes. In 1997, Estella Poloni and colleagues showed that Y-chromosome lineage variation is well correlated with language family distributions in Africa and Eurasia. Their Y-chromosome molecular clock calculations suggested that speakers of Niger-Congo languages began to spread around 4,000 years ago, Afroasiatic speakers around 8,900 years ago, and Indo-European speakers around 7,400 years ago.

Poloni et al. also showed that Afroasiatic-speakers in Ethiopia share Y-chromosome haplotypes with people in Southwest Asia, but have essentially local mtDNA lineages. Some Khoisan populations in the south have admixtures of Niger-Congo Y-chromosome lineages with Khoisan mtDNA. Both these situations suggest a tendency for males to disperse further than females, and consequently to have a wider genetic impact. This view was given further support in 2001, when Peter Underhill and colleagues (2001a) indicated that Bantu migration is strongly marked by the distribution of Y-chromosome haplogroup III, but Bantu mtDNA haplogroups are more localized.

The African genetic data thus seem to agree closely on the significance of Bantu population expansion. For other populations, including Afroasiatic-speakers, the data are not so clear (Barbujani et al. 1994), and research still has rather a long way to go.

East Asia

The most recent worldwide population tree published by Luca Cavalli-Sforza and Marcus Feldman (2003), based on analysis of polymorphisms in 120 protein systems in 1915 human populations, groups Southeast Asians with Pacific Islanders (excluding New Guinea), and then at a higher level with New Guineans and Australian Aborigines. A completely separate extra-African group, comprising the rest of out-of-Africa mankind, includes Northeast Asians, American Indians, and Europeans. Such high-level groupings do not inform greatly about the issues under debate here and probably reflect mainly Pleistocene movements of modern humans, in two spread processes into northern and southern East Asia respectively. Subsequent expansions of farming populations have been essentially confined to within each of these two zones rather than across both, the only exception in prehistoric times perhaps being the expansion of Tibeto-Burman speakers into Southeast Asia. Much, of course, depends on where one places the boundary between northern and southern East Asia – presumably in terms of this analysis it falls somewhere in central China, north of the regions whence the dispersals of Austroasiatic, Tai, Hmong-Mien, and Austronesian peoples are claimed to have begun (Figure 10.8B). Tatiana Karafet and colleagues (2001) also underline distinctions between Northeast and Southeast Asian populations in Y-chromosome haplogroups, linking central Asian Turkic populations and Tibeto-Burman speakers to Northeast Asians.[3]

In contrast to the above, Peter Underhill and colleagues (2001a) imply closer north–south Asian relationships in terms of the spread of group VII Y-chromosome lineages, stating that that they probably originated in northern China and spread with millet and rice agriculture on a large scale, analogous to the spread of group III lineages by Bantu-speakers. Group VII lineages dominate all of the East Asian mainland, from northern China to Thailand.

This observation of close relationships right through East Asia is supported very strongly by analyses of ancient crania. Johan Kamminga and Richard Wright (1988) have observed that Late Paleolithic crania from China, particularly from the Upper Cave at Zhoukoudian, were not morphologically ancestral to the modern East Asian population, raising the possibility that the latter spread from an unknown homeland in Neolithic times. These Paleolithic people instead resembled the pre-Japanese Jomon population of Japan between about 12,000 and 2,000 years ago, prior to the arrival there of Yayoi rice farmers. In China, fully Mongoloid cranial features first appear in the early Neolithic, for instance at the site of Jiahu in the Huai valley (Chen and Zhang 1998). Peter Brown (1998, 1999) extends these observations to the whole of China, contending that Paleolithic skulls such as those from Liujiang and Minatogawa, as well as Upper Cave, are not Mongoloid at all, whereas Neolithic samples from sites such as Dawenkou, Jiangzhai (Yangshao culture), and Jiahu most certainly are.

Considerable population replacement during the Chinese Neolithic is therefore indicated from the skeletal perspective, as likewise during the expansion of Yayoi rice agriculturalists from Korea into Japan at about 300 BC (Hudson 1999, 2003). The genetic perspective seems to differ, and debate will doubtless continue.

Southeast Asia and Oceania (mainly Austronesians)

A great deal of the genetic and skeletal research in this region has been driven by a scholarly obsession with the origins of the Polynesians. I have already summarized elsewhere the results of much of this research (Bellwood 1978a, 1993, 1997a), concluding that pre-Neolithic populations in Island Southeast Asia, especially Indonesia, formed a westerly extension of the Australomelanesian population that had been established in the western Pacific (including Australia) since at least 40,000 years ago. Neolithic population movements, especially of Austronesian speakers into the islands and of Austroasiatic speakers on the Southeast Asian mainland, then brought in Asian (Southern Mongoloid) genotypes that mixed with those of the preceding populations, being even absorbed by them in Island Melanesia and to a lesser extent in the Malay Peninsula and eastern Indonesia. The result is that today one can see a cline from Asian into Australomelanesian characteristics running from north to south and from west to east, from Island Southeast Asia into Island Melanesia, and southward down the Malay Peninsula. The cline from Melanesia into Polynesia trends in the opposite direction, with Asian characters coming back in high proportion as one moves into eastern Polynesia and eastern Micronesia.

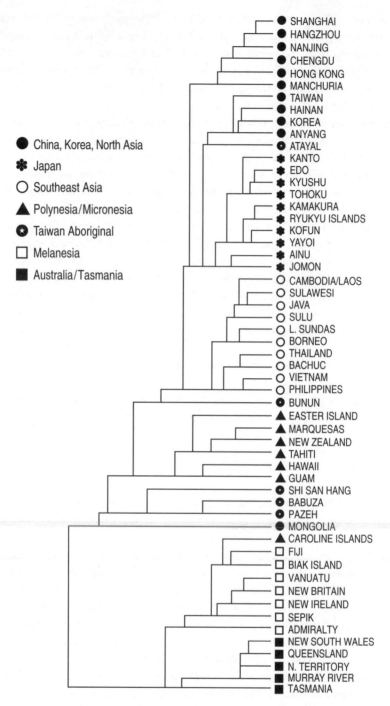

Figure 11.2 Diagram of relationships between Asian and Oceanic populations based on a cluster analysis of 29 cranial measurements recorded on 53 male samples. The samples are of various dates from possibly Neolithic and Bronze Age to relatively recent. From Pietrusewsky and Chang 2003.

The peoples of New Guinea, despite developing very early and independent agriculture, cannot really be shown to have expanded very far in a geographical sense, except in terms of genetic contribution to many present-day Austronesian speakers in eastern Indonesia (especially Moluccas and eastern Lesser Sundas) and Island Melanesia, eastward to Fiji. Recent mtDNA research does, however, indicate a lack of lineage diversity in the New Guinea Highlands that could relate to agriculturally driven population dispersal (Hagelberg et al. 1999:149).

The most complete analysis of East Asian and Oceanic cranial data is that by Michael Pietrusewsky (1999), whose cluster analysis (shown in Figure 11.2) expresses not just geographical but also phylogenetic relationships. In East Asia, this tree clearly separates Jomon and Ainu populations from Japanese. It also indicates the fairly high degree of diversity present in "Chinese" samples, and links all Southeast Asians with these in a large Asian branch at the top of the diagram. Close to this Asian branch come Polynesians and Micronesians, with Melanesians and Australians having very different cranial characteristics and belonging in a separate branch of their own. Perhaps most interestingly, in view of the discussion to follow, is Pietrusewsky's recent conclusion (Pietrusewsky and Chang 2003:293) that "Connections between Taiwan aboriginal groups and cranial series from Polynesia suggest that Taiwan's aboriginal inhabitants may have been the ancestral source of these inhabitants of remote Oceania." It is also worth noting that the deep divisions between East and Southeast Asians favored by some geneticists (above) are not visible in these cranial data.

We now move to the genetics, beginning with the broad question of Austronesian origins and dispersals and picking up the thread in 1995 when Alan Redd, Terry Melton, and colleagues published their analyses of the distribution of a feature within mtDNA known as the 9-base-pair deletion (Redd et al. 1995; Melton et al. 1995). This deletion contains a number of lineages defined by specific nucleotide substitutions. One, involving a substitution at position 16247, has become known as the "Polynesian motif" because it dominates in most modern Polynesian populations. Redd and colleagues suggested that this lineage spread from eastern Indonesia into Oceania at about 5,500 years ago. The ultimate source of the Austronesians as a whole, and of the substitution at position 16261 that occurred prior to 16247, was stated to be Taiwan, a view reached independently at the same time by Bryan Sykes and colleagues (1995), also using mtDNA data. Terry Melton and colleagues (1998) reemphasized that the ancestral mtDNA substitutions (excluding 16247) within the 9-base-pair deletion haplogroup had spread into Southeast Asia and Oceania through a Taiwan bottleneck (see also Hagelberg et al. 1999; Hagelberg 2000).

These conclusions are in accord with those of several other biochemists and geneticists. Koji Lum and Rebecca Cann (1998) have noted that Polynesian mtDNA very clearly links these people with Southeast Asians rather than Melanesians, a conclusion also drawn by Andrew Merriwether and colleagues (1999), who stress very firmly that Polynesian maternal ancestry cannot be derived to any major degree from Melanesia. All authorities agree that the Polynesian mtDNA motif (with the 16247 substitution) originated in eastern Indonesia rather than in Taiwan, where only the antecedent mutations are present, a situation suggesting that the mutation might have occurred during the dispersal process itself.

By 1998, Koji Lum and colleagues (1998, 2002) were already noting that about 30 percent of Polynesian nuclear genes are probably Melanesian, and this they related to extensive male gene flow from Papuan into Austronesian communities as the Austronesian dispersal progressed eastward. In a sense, the mtDNA story was beginning to look like an "express train" from Southeast Asia into the Pacific, to use the metaphor of Jared Diamond (1988), whereas the nuclear DNA and (later on) the Y-chromosome stories would be seen to relate more to Darwin's "entangled bank" metaphor as used by John Terrell (1988). Women traveled early and far with the initial migrants, but their female descendants stayed essentially in place, whereas males have always had a propensity to roam (Hage and Marck 2003 discuss these observations from an anthropological perspective).

The concept of considerable male-mediated gene flow from Papuan into Austronesian populations in Oceania was soon given further stimulus by Y-chromosome research. Manfred Kayser and colleagues (2000) claimed that three Polynesian Y-chromosome haplotypes found in a small sample of Cook Islanders could have originated in Melanesia, even though they also occur in Island Southeast Asia. Their conclusions differed from those presented in another study by Bing Su and colleagues (2000), who regarded all Polynesian Y-chromosomes as being derived from Southeast Asia, with none at all from Melanesia. Such difficulties reflect in part an analysis of different markers by the different research teams, and Kayser states that the results of both analyses could be compatible.

One such compatible conclusion was announced in 2001, when Cristian Capelli and colleagues (2001) provided an overall Y-chromosome view of Pacific, Southeast Asian, and southern Chinese relationships. Austronesian dispersal from southern China and Taiwan into Island Southeast appears to be well recorded by their Y haplogroups H and L (now more commonly termed O3: Cox 2004), the latter having an apparent origin during the early Holocene and occurring widely and frequently in South China, southern Taiwan, Island Southeast Asia, and Polynesia. Eastern Indonesians and Melanesians have haplogroups that are mainly indigenous to the western Pacific region (Cox 2004). Polynesians reveal great variation as a result of genetic drift, but basically they combine both the Melanesian and the "Austronesian" haplogroups in proportions that differ from one island group to another.

All the Y-chromosome information on Austronesians presented so far fits quite well with what we can read from the archaeology and linguistics. An expanding population with Y-chromosome haplogroups that probably originated in southern China/Taiwan mixed increasingly with indigenous populations as it moved southward and eastward, virtually disappearing eventually in a genetic sense in Island Melanesia, but continuing eastward again through a series of founder bottlenecks into Polynesia. Using a different set of Y-chromosome data, Peter Underhill and colleagues (2001b) state: "The Y-chromosome results support a pattern of complex interrelationships between Southeast Asia, Melanesia, and Polynesia, in contrast to mtDNA and linguistic data, which uphold a rapid and homogeneous Austronesian expansion. The Y-chromosome data highlight a distinctive gender-modulated pattern of differential gene flow in the history of Polynesia." Matthew Hurles and colleagues, working with satellite markers within the Y-chromosome, provide the additional conclusion: "[our] study, while not strongly supporting the hypothesis of a rapid Austronesian expansion from Taiwan, is not necessarily incompatible with it. Biological and cultural origins can become uncoupled to varying degrees" (Hurles et al. 2002:301; Hurles 2003).

So, can we relax now with a conclusion from genetics that Austronesian prehistory witnessed initial fairly clear-cut dispersal from southern China and Taiwan, via Island Southeast Asia, into Oceania, accompanied by considerable intermixing with indigenous populations, and eventually with a considerable quantity of male-focused gene flow out of Melanesia? I certainly believe that we can, but a team of mtDNA researchers comprising Martin Richards, Stephen Oppenheimer, and Bryan Sykes have recently stated otherwise (Richards et al. 1998; Oppenheimer and Richards 2001a, 2001b, 2003). They claim that Polynesians are of separate biological origin from other Austronesians, since the "Polynesian motif" can in their opinion be clocked to a mutation in eastern Indonesia that occurred between 5,500 and 34,500 years ago. Because this motif does not appear to occur in its "final" form with the mutation at position 16247 in Taiwan, the Philippines, or much of Indonesia, and because their calculated age range precedes any archaeological or linguistic evidence for Austronesian dispersal, they claim that Polynesians are derived from Pleistocene populations located in eastern Indonesia, perhaps somewhere east of the Wallace Line (Sulawesi, Moluccas, or Lesser Sundas). They also suggest that the whole of the Austronesian dispersal in the linguistic sense might have originated in eastern Indonesia, a hypothesis also foreshadowed in Y chromosome research by Bing Su and colleagues (2000; but see contrary arguments by Reid 2001).

Linguistically and archaeologically, deriving all Austronesian-speaking populations from Pleistocene forebears in eastern Indonesia is not a credible proposition. To claim a biological dispersal of Austronesian-speaking peoples from eastern Indonesia to Taiwan would involve movement in a direction completely opposed to that of the archaeology and the languages. This is no doubt possible, but extremely unlikely given any balanced worldwide comparative view of multidisciplinary human history. But what of the Polynesians and the Polynesian mtDNA motif? There are problems here, since firstly, this motif also occurs in Madagascar in high frequency, a situation that recently led Bryan Sykes (1999b:109) to claim that Madagascar was settled by Polynesians sailing south of Australia. However, not only do the Malagasy languages derive in the main from southern Borneo, but Madagascar prehistory since settlement occurred about AD 500 is fully ceramic, whereas Polynesians lost pottery making about 2,000 years ago. There is absolutely nothing in the archaeological or linguistic records that could possibly bring Malagasy settlers, with their Malay-mediated Sanskrit loans (Adelaar 1995), from Polynesia.

Instead, we seem to have three possibilities to explain the situation recognized by Oppenheimer and Richards with the Polynesian motif:

1. If populations with a Polynesian-like and Asian-derived morphology had spread into eastern Indonesia long before the period of Austronesian dispersal, then the haplotype could have been acquired from them much later by the Austronesian populations ancestral to Polynesians. This is possible in theory, and would allow for a greater level of accommodation between the two opposing reconstructions. The main problem is that there is no skeletal evidence to indicate the presence of such a Polynesian-like population in eastern Indonesia prior to the Holocene, although this may simply reflect lack of data.

2. The molecular clock calculation for the origin of the Polynesian motif may be wrong, given that there is now a voluminous literature of debate and disagreement about this kind of chronological calculation. If wrong, then perhaps the mutation could have occurred during Austronesian dispersal after 4,000 years ago in eastern Indonesia. In other words, is the place of origin of the Polynesian motif correct, but the calculated date of its mutation wrong?[4]

3. Could early Austronesians have picked up the Polynesian motif from an indigenous source in eastern Indonesia, initially through only one or two female individuals, whose descendants soon thereafter, as a result of considerable fecundity in bottleneck situations, raised the frequency of its occurrence in the ancestral Polynesian (Lapita) population? This option seems possible, but is only necessary if a Pleistocene date for the origin of the Polynesian motif is supported by future calculations.

Oppenheimer and Richards also suggest that the alpha-globin genes of Polynesians (which code for part of the hemoglobin molecule) most likely originated east of the Wallace Line. This may be correct, but since abnormal hemoglobins are involved throughout the tropical Old World in defenses against malaria it seems likely that natural selection lies behind the situation, rather than population origin factors themselves. Eastern Indonesia and Melanesia, even today, still have very virulent forms of malaria, and early Austronesians were probably initially without any genetic variants that confer resistance (Serjeantson and Gao 1995; Fix 2002).

This review of Austronesian genetic ancestry has gone into detail since this region, like Europe, has one of the densest debates between archaeologists, linguists, and biologists currently under way anywhere in the world. As it happens, just after this chapter was drafted, I was asked to read a PhD thesis by Murray Cox (2003), a biochemist from the University of Otago in New Zealand and now based in the Leverhulme Centre for Human Evolutionary Studies in Cambridge. Cox has reviewed the Y and mtDNA data for Austronesians in detail, and points out that, perhaps as expected, modern Austronesians only reveal (so far) about 20 percent of the genes likely to have been carried by their Neolithic Austronesian ancestors, an average situation perhaps similar to that for Europe. But Cox also recalculates the age of the Polynesian motif, bringing it much closer to overlap with the period of Austronesian migration, and of similar Holocene age to Asian Y-chromosome haplogroup O3, as discussed above. Cox clearly favors what he terms a "Modified Out of Taiwan Model" for Austronesian dispersal, which is basically the model that I favor.

Finally, one other region overlapping with Austronesia where there has recently been debate over population history is the Malay Peninsula, with its marked population variations running from southern Thailand toward Singapore. My own view is that three major population movements into the Peninsula are represented in present patterns of diversity (Bellwood 1993, 1997a). The Semang Negritos are descendants of early Hoabinhian foragers who spread widely through the Peninsula, probably moving inland as postglacial sea levels rose in the early Holocene. According to David Bulbeck (2003), they ultimately acquired shorter stature within the past few millennia in the interior rain-forest environment. They were followed by ancestral Senoi farmers who moved down from southern Thailand about 4,000 years ago, bringing Neolithic artifacts and Austroasiatic ("Aslian") languages into the Peninsula, the latter being eventually adopted by the Semang foragers, just as Negritos in the Philippines have adopted Austronesian languages. The ancestors of the third major group, the Austronesian-speaking Malays, arrived during the Iron Age, about 500 BC or later, from western Borneo and/or Sumatra.

This relatively simple series of cultural and biological successions, which in my view still explains the situation best, has also been examined by anthropologist Geoffrey Benjamin (1985). He favors the view that the two Aslian populations are of indigenous Peninsula origin and have basically differentiated their lifestyles, languages, and phenotypes *in situ* as a result of social and economic factors (e.g., mobile hunting vs. sedentary farming, group exogamy vs. endogamy, differential involvement in trade). Benjamin's view has recently been upheld by David Bulbeck (2004) from a skeletal perspective. Geneticist Alan Fix (1999, 2000, 2002) also favors Benjamin's hypothesis of internal cultural and biological genesis, but concludes that modern genetic data cannot really prove or disprove the occurrence of ancient migrations, noting on several occasions that history may not be read simply from gene trees.

For what it is worth, genetic research (Saha et al. 1995) suggests that the Semai Senoi of Malaysia and the Khmers of Cambodia are fairly closely related in their blood genetic markers (proteins and enzymes), and if this is an indication of shared ancestry then it is much easier to locate it in prehistoric, perhaps Neolithic times, than in historical times. The Khmer empire of Angkor certainly never stretched as far as the jungled interior of Peninsular Malaysia, and we have no evidence that any significant gene flow into the southern Malay Peninsula occurred as recently as this (ca. 12th century AD). I can only conclude that the Malay Peninsula is still an enigmatic region and simple answers to population history will not come easily.

The Americas

The Americas do not offer very rich data on specific questions of farming population and language family ancestry, and I must also confess to a lack of access to many of the relevant sources. But a few observations are of great interest. For instance, Sloan Williams and colleagues (2002) note that modern Yanomama village populations in Venezuela and Brazil, with high levels of within-village endogamy, can be clearly differentiated from each other in terms of nuclear genetic markers. The genetic distances between these village populations also correlate well with their recorded histories of fission. In addition, Nelson Fagundes and colleagues (2002) have found that mtDNA relationships follow linguistic relationships very clearly amongst Tupian-speakers in Brazil. This is very hopeful news for those interested in tracking the populations associated with language families back through time.

But when Williams et al. used mtDNA sequences as opposed to nuclear genetic data for differentiating Yanomama village populations, they were found not to work so well, apparently owing to sex-specific migration and sampling issues. In this re-gard, therefore, it is interesting that Ripan Malhi and colleagues (2003) suggest that mtDNA haplotypes in Mexico and the US Southwest relate more to geography than to language groupings. They state that early Uto-Aztecan languages were spread by male rather than female migrations, the former perhaps being identifiable through the wide distribution of a nuclear marker called Albumin*Mexico. The prospect of females staying close to home and males migrating makes a degree of sense, but one wonders how the claimed results reflect sampling and other factors.

In addition, the Americas were settled so recently in time that the major degree of biological differentiation that we see between populations of Old World origin has never had time to develop. Most population movements in the past, especially incre-mental rather than long-distance ones, would probably have mingled people already quite closely related in terms of genetic descent. If the Americas are to provide genetic data useful for questions of farming dispersal, much more research will be needed.

Did Early Farmers Spread through Processes of Demic Diffusion?

There is no single answer to this question, since local situations clearly differ. Demic diffusion alone can never have been the source of any language family or agricultural complex. But demic diffusion, with constant processes of population mixing, sex-specific differential migration, and successive bottlenecks, presents a much more likely conclusion. Allowing for such a combination of processes means we are not forced into having the Neolithic Britons genetically identical to the Neolithic Anatolians, or the modern Solomon Islanders genetically identical to the modern Formosans.

As the lengthy biological debates continue, for instance about the origins of the Europeans or the Austronesians, such middle-of-the-road conclusions become in-creasingly self-evident. But this does not mean that the human past is just a formless pattern of drift, with no foci of innovation or dispersal ever present. We cannot regard the human archaeological, linguistic, and biological records as merely the products of mutation and drift "in place" since humans in some sentient form first spread across the earth. To give all ancient societies an equal role in the creation of a formless and creolized past is just as unfair to those long dead and forgotten as is the opposite polarization, represented by total domination and replacement of earlier populations. We need a balance, so perhaps it is time to move toward a conclusion.

Chapter 12

The Nature of Early Agricultural Expansion

The spreads of early agricultural populations, through regions formerly occupied by hunter-gatherers, created many basic patterns in the distributions of languages, cultures, and genotypes that still survive today across large parts of the temperate and tropical regions of the earth. However, dispersal did not occur out of all regions of agricultural origin. Neither did languages, cultures, and genotypes always spread in perfect unison. The totality of the human past has been very complex indeed.

Are there any cross-cultural generalizations that can be made about how and why the various agricultural "unfoldings" differed in spatial and temporal expression? Can early farming spreads be classified in terms of observable and sometimes quantifiable variables, such as rate of frontier movement, overall chronology, and degree of isomorphism in linguistic, cultural, and biological patterns?

In order to approach these questions we consider first of all two polar situations. At one extreme, the replacement of population and culture is total, or close to it. At the other extreme, languages and cultural configurations are adopted by indigenous populations, with no expansion of externally derived population at all. As previous chapters should have indicated, both these extremes are highly unlikely ever to have occurred in reality, at least not in previously occupied landscapes. But we can, for heuristic purposes, still list ideal expectations for them.

In the first situation, of complete ethnolinguistic and population replacement, there will be no significant substratum survival (and none at all in landscapes previously unoccupied). Barring subsequent population expansions, which of course start the process all over again, the linguistic pattern will reveal no isolates, no traces of pidginization or interference through language shift, and there should be fairly even rates of lexical change across subgroups. The archaeological pattern will be widespread and stylistically homogeneous to begin with, breaking down gradually into regional expressions with the passage of time. Stylistic patterns should lose homogeneity fairly evenly, reflecting time and geography rather than hybridization. Genetic and skeletal evidence should indicate population replacement.

In the second situation, of cultural and linguistic dispersal through adoption/shift only, with no population movement, substratum survival will be complete. The linguistic pattern will probably reveal lots of isolates where shift did not occur, strong evidence for interference through language shift, and great variation in rates of lexical change according to the varying structures of the indigenous adopting societies. The archaeological pattern will show stylistic diversity continuing from prior time periods, but with addition of the new technological and economic elements driving the cultural dispersal (e.g., agriculture, ground stone, pottery). Genetic and skeletal evidence should indicate population continuity.

Possible situations which fall between these two extremes are of course almost infinite in variation. They will be revealed most clearly by any disequilibrium between the archaeological, linguistic, and biological sources of data. For instance, language can often show evidence of "strong" spread, with no interstitial isolates and few substratum traces, while patterning in human biology can be more diverse. This is the case in eastern Indonesia and Island Melanesia, where it can perhaps be explained by a hypothesis of powerful Austronesian linguistic dispersal through both native-speaker movement and language shift, but with a relatively much greater degree of mixing between Asian and Melanesian biological populations. Material culture falls somewhere in-between – the components are not so locked together as are the structural elements of a language, but not so free to recombine attributes as are chromosomes.

Homeland, Spread, and Friction Zones, plus Overshoot

In a recent review of the many issues surrounding early farming dispersal (Bellwood 2001b), I found it useful to visualize four different zonal concepts as involved in processes of agricultural origin and spread.

1. Homeland or starburst zones reveal upwelling patterns with radial spread, high suitability for agriculture, and of course considerable hunter-to-farmer continuity across the agricultural transitions. Examples include the major regions of agricultural and language family origin discussed in previous chapters.
2. Spread zones (following earlier usage of this term, with a slightly different meaning, by linguist Johanna Nichols) fall close to the replacement extreme described above, with widespread levels of homogeneity and strong indications of temporal discontinuity in cultural trajectory. Rates of spread tend to be high, until environmental or demographic limitations intervene. Some examples of Neolithic or Formative spread zones are illustrated in Figure 1.3.
3. Friction zones are characterized by genetic admixture and cultural reticulation between hunters and farmers. Some friction zones lie at the end of the road for agriculture, for instance in northern and western Europe, where climatic factors

or high hunter-gatherer densities backed by coastlines imposed barriers to further spread. In these cases, rates of farming spread slowed down markedly. But in other cases, for instance lowland New Guinea with respect to Austronesian spread, the friction zone was not at the end of the line, but rather a salient in its middle. In the case of the Lapita settlement of western Oceania, the rate of spread was extremely rapid because rich resources continued beyond western Melanesia, in previously uninhabited Oceanic islands. On the other hand, Austronesian dispersal was very slow to penetrate New Guinea itself from relatively nearby Lapita sources (Table 12.1). Thus, the friction zone concept refers essentially to a relatively high degree of reticulation, but not necessarily to a fast or slow rate of foundation spread.

4. Finally, we have those zones of overshoot where farmers found themselves, for varying reasons, in adverse environments and so modified their economies accordingly. The southern Maoris, the Punan of Borneo, and the Numic speakers of the Great Basin would appear to be excellent examples of this.

Looking at a sample of spread and friction zones on a worldwide basis, combined with issues of tempo, one comes up with some interesting observations (Table 12.1). Jared Diamond (1994) is quite correct to point out that early farmers tended to move more rapidly along latitudes than across them, mainly because environments remain similar along latitudes, and the crucial factor of day length that triggers germination in cereals and legumes changes little. But we do have cases of rapid cross-latitudinal spread – Iron Age farmers in eastern and southern Africa, for instance. We also have converse cases of very slow spread along latitudes, for instance from the Indus into India. The reason for this was essentially the latitudinal switch in this region from a winter to a summer rainfall regime. Fundamental shifts in rainfall seasonality stopped agriculturalists (as opposed to pastoralists) from spreading into southwestern Africa, also California, they slowed down the spread into northern India, and rendered the spread of the southwest Asian farming system that entered Egypt a very difficult matter in terms of the rest of Africa. Although wheat and other winter crops eventually made their way to the Ethiopian Highlands, they never spread further.

So one conclusion I would draw from Table 12.1 is that changes in rainfall seasonality formed much greater barriers to early farmers than changes in temperature (except when the growing season shrank below length requirements for the available crops). But there are exceptions, and one of these is southern China. The longitudinal spread through southern China into Southeast Asia was much slower than that into southern Africa, at least until Austronesian maritime technology lifted the lid and allowed the rapid sea-borne colonization of Island Southeast Asia and Oceania. The climates of southern China and southeastern Africa were not sufficiently different from the relevant homeland climates, in my view, to be the sole causes of the differences in dispersal rate. Instead, technological development was often as important as environmental suitability in the lubrication or hindrance of agricultural spread. In southern China the technology was purely Neolithic at the time of farming dispersal, and here the population densities of preexisting hunter-gatherer

Table 12.1 Rates of spread of farming as determined from the archaeological record, compared against latitude, environmental variables, and the prior presences of hunter-gatherer populations. The rates are subject to chronological uncertainties, but trends rather than absolute precision are the goal. See also Bellwood 2001b:186–187, wherein some earlier calculations, now somewhat amended, were presented.

Situation of Neolithic/Formative spread	Time required for spread (approx.)	Distance in km (approx.)	Rate (km per century)	Latitudinal difference between origin and endpoint	Degree of environmental change
		SPREAD ZONES			
Italy to Portugal (Cardial Neolithic)	200 years (Zilhao 2001)	c.2000 if moving coastally	10 (maritime)	Nil	Very little
Hungary to France (LBK)	400 years (Gronenborn 1999)	1000	2.5	<5 degrees	Very little
Zagros to Baluchistan PPN (Mehrgarh)	500 years (LeBlanc 2003)	1600	3.2	5 degrees	Very little
Philippines to Samoa (Redslip/Lapita)	1000 years (Bellwood 2001)	8500	8.5 (maritime) (cf. Fort 2003)	Nil in terms of degrees from equator	Very little
Central Mexico to Arizona	500 years (LeBlanc 2003; Matson 2003)	1850	3.7	12 degrees	Little, but desert barriers
Lake Victoria to Natal (Chifumbaze)	700 years (Phillipson 1993)	3000	4.3 (Iron Age)	30 degrees	Major in terms of winter temperature, but no change in rainfall seasonality
		FRICTION ZONES			
Neolithic, from LBK to Britain	1300 years (Price 2000)	500	0.4	Nil	Very little (hunter-gatherer resistance?)
Neolithic, Yangzi to Hong Kong	2500 years	1000	0.4	8 degrees	Very little (hunter-gatherer resistance?)
Chalcolithic, Baluchistan to Haryana and eastern Rajasthan	3000 years	1000	0.33	Nil	Major: Mediterranean to summer monsoonal
New Britain (Lapita) to southern Papua	1300 years (Kirch 2000:119)	1000	0.8 (maritime)	5 degrees	Very little

populations, especially in rugged or coastal terrain, were evidently significant. In Africa, spreading Bantu farmers had access to iron tools, a major technological advantage.

The carrying capacities of agricultural landscapes, and the negative impacts wrought upon them by climate change and human overexploitation, are also of course extremely relevant as determinants of rates of spread of pioneer farmers. So too are the production levels of the agricultural and pastoral systems themselves. David Harris (2003), for instance, regards cereal systems as more expansive than tuber systems, an opinion amply substantiated by the archaeological record.

Some of the above might seem rather obvious when it is spelt out in this way. Yet there is an immense amount of detail and understanding to be squeezed out of comparative data such as this. Table 12.1, for instance, shows some of the variations in rates of spread that we can expect under spread zone and friction zone conditions. It will be noted how maritime and Iron Age spreads can be very fast indeed. My suspicion is that the rate of spread of farming increased *very rapidly* as the degree of environmental difficulty declined and as technological capacity increased. Without a need for any adjustment to differing environmental circumstances, cereal-based cultures in spread mode could generate sufficient demographic impetus to snowball along very far and very fast indeed.

The Stages within a Process of Agricultural Genesis and Dispersal

The above discussion has been concerned mainly with patterns of dispersal. Let us now turn to patterns of development through time. It can be hypothesized that agricultural systems have developed fundamentally through the following very generalized stages.

1. *Pre-farming.* During terminal phases of hunting and gathering we can expect deep cultural heterogeneity if populations had already been in place for many millennia. This would be so even in cases of high latitude or arid zone repopulation consequent upon terminal Pleistocene environmental change, since most agricultural dispersals took place many millennia after the final amelioration that occurred, prior to the onset of the Younger Dryas, even in the Middle East.
2. *Transition to farming.* With trends toward agricultural production during the Holocene we can expect increasing sedentism, population density, and social complexity to have developed. With the establishment of farming, larger communities allowed village-endogamous mating networks to operate, even though the archaeological record reveals widening spheres of interaction for the movement of raw materials, concepts, and aspects of style. In such circumstances, certain languages could have been used for communication across wide areas, perhaps normally through stable bilingualism rather than language replacement. Specific loan words for cultural items could have spread over very large distances within such networks. In Neolithic/Formative circumstances such languages were

most probably natural languages, with genetic relatives, rather than pidgins of the types formed during the process of European colonial expansion and population relocation. Did such languages form the roots for subsequent language families?

3. *Ensuing dependence upon farming, and dispersal.* With increasing population growth, environmental impact, inter-group conflict, and demand for increased agricultural production, expansion from homeland/starburst regions began, centrifugal in pattern and derived mainly from peripheries rather than inner core regions. Expanding populations on peripheries would have shared many features of language and style due to previous interaction. Such sharing need not always indicate genetic relationship, although it may well do so in cases where two groups spread in different directions from a common homeland region. The resulting outward dispersals would thus contain many aspects of both genetic and prior borrowing relationship, in practice ambiguously intertwined. Meanwhile, the core regions, being circumscribed, would have had opportunities to intensify production in the direction of "civilization," even though in reality only a small number of regions were ever able to take this course. Others simply stabilized, some declined.

In general, we may expect the greatest degrees of correlation between patterns of material culture, language, and biology to occur in this third phase, at the cusp of an expansion as it progresses or hops through new territory. Such episodes will sometimes produce more homogeneous cultural patterns than existed in the agricultural homeland itself, since they will have predominantly phylogenetic (dispersal-based) rather than interactive foundations, consequent upon population and language spread, not upwelling. With settling-in comes reticulation, mixing with native populations, and assimilation. The intensity of reticulation will depend on local circumstances, including the relative demographic balance between newcomers and natives, the chronology and tempo of the mixing, technological differences, assortative mating patterns, and so forth. Newcomers can also bring in disease and warfare, but in pre-state early farmer circumstances we should expect native hunter-gatherer populations to survive genetically, even if not through language or material lifestyle in the long term.

The overall shape of the past is here regarded as one of dispersal-based pulsation at intervals, with reticulation in the periods (often extremely long periods) between. We cannot expect that the results of all past dispersals will be unambiguously obvious in present-day linguistic and biological patterns. But the major ones should be.

Perhaps the final conclusion should be that language families and early agricultural economies spread through hunter-gatherer landscapes in prehistory essentially through population growth and dispersal, but with admixture. Hunter-gatherer adoption was not the sole or main mechanism of spread, although it was of increasing importance as the prime conditions for demic diffusion of farmers became attenuated. Being indigenous is always a matter of degree.

For me, the excitement of research into the early farming dispersal hypothesis comes from its immense significance for the world as we know it today, or at least in its pre-colonial form prior to AD 1500. Our language families, our agricultural systems, even our races (whatever animosities one might harbor toward this concept) reflect the impacts of early agricultural dispersal very visibly indeed, even millennia after the events of concern passed from memory. Archaeology is of little value unless we can relate it to the here and now, and this is one arena in which it can broadcast its significance very lucidly indeed.

Another aspect of excitement for me is the fact that all populations in the world have somehow been involved in these early farming dispersals in some way or another, whether as initiators or receivers. Our world needs a story to bring peoples together, not to isolate their ancestors as archaeologically impressive but parochial one-off experiments. The human ability to migrate and successfully populate new environments was one of the greatest assets of the ancestors of all peoples in the world, at all levels from hunters through ancient farmers to early states. I hope that the future world order will harness this energy, which to me shows no signs of dissipation, in a humane and civilized way.

Notes

1. The literature on issues of phylogeny and reticulation in prehistory is rather large, but for differing perspectives see Bellwood 1996c, 2001a, 2001b, 2001c, 2001d; Kirch and Green 2001; Moore 1994; Prentiss and Chatters 2003; Shennan 2002; Terrell ed. 2001.

Chapter 2

1. Chen Chi-lu 1987 discusses Taiwan; Terrell 1986:191 discusses Pitcairn; Borrie 1994 discusses Australia. See also Birdsell 1957 for Tristan da Cunha and the Bass Strait Islands.
2. For instance, the need to carry children while gathering food over a very wide area, periodically low levels of fat intake, and longer periods of breast-feeding necessitated by a dearth of soft weaning foods. For discussion of these points see Blurton Jones 1986; Cohen 1980; Kelly 1995; Lee 1979, 1980.
3. On these health issues see, e.g., Handwerker 1983; Roosevelt 1984; Meiklejohn and Zvelebil 1991; Fox 1996; Jackes et al. 1997a, 1997b. For Thailand, skeletal anthropologists Domett 2001, and Pietrusewsky and Douglas 2001, do not find that health declined continuously with the development of agriculture. Pechenkina et al. 2002 state un-equivocally that health decline began late rather than early in the Chinese Neolithic. Early Near Eastern farmers seem to have been essentially healthy without signs of malnutrition (e.g., Moore et al. 2000).
4. Higham and Thosarat 1994; Tayles 1999. Khok Phanom Di is not technically an *earliest* agricultural site – it dates to only 2000 BC (as opposed to rice-growing cultures at 7000 BC in the Yangzi Basin) and probably represents a movement of rice agriculturalists from a homeland region further north into a swampy coastal environment where malaria rapidly became endemic. Malaria is known to cause spontaneous abortion, hence its devastating effect on infant mortality here. Although the possession of abnormal haemoglobin alleles

---

can give some protection for heterozygotes, homozygotes will succumb either to malaria or to anemia.

5. Bender 1978; Hayden 1990, 1992, 1995; Runnels and van Andel 1988; Dickson 1989. See also Chang 1981, 1986; Thorpe 1996 and Price and Gebauer 1995 for recent statements in favor of affluence models, in which agriculture commenced as a supplement to other food sources in relatively rich environments. Farrington and Urry (1985) favour an initial domestication of "culturally valued foodstuffs" rather than staples.

6. For example, Kennedy 1969 for northern New Zealand; Graham 1994 for northern Mexico.

7. Levant – Lieberman 1998; Moore et al. 2000; Turkey – Rosenberg et al. 1998; Sudan – Haaland 1997; Mexico – Niederberger 1979.

8. Pennington 1996; Gomes 1990; Kelly 1995; Rosenberg 1998.

9. While checking proofs I discovered Bruce Smith's (2003) suggestion that "low-level food production" of between 30 and 50 percent of total dietary intake, combined with continuing foraging, was a stable adaptation for many societies in prehistory. This is contrary to what is being suggested in this chapter, even though Smith's two main prehistoric examples – eastern USA pre-maize agriculture and the Jomon of Japan – appear to be well chosen. But the ethnographic examples of low-level food production that he identifies, namely the Austronesian-speaking Nuaulu of equatorial Seram Island in eastern Indonesia, and the Numic (Uto-Aztecan) speaking Paiute and Shoshone populations of the Owens Valley of eastern California and the Great Basin, all in my view descend from ancestral agricultural societies (see pp. 243–4 for the Numic speakers). In other words, the ancestors of these modern groups adopted a partial or entirely hunting and gathering lifestyle after moving into environments inimical to successful agriculture, as described in more detail later in this chapter. So, while low-level food production can exist in theory, my feeling is that it has always been a child of marginal environments, where farmers necessarily retracted into food collection or where foragers were able to invest in minor cultivation without too much competition from other farmers. Such societies represent the ends, rather than the sources, of historical trajectories of agricultural expansion.

10. Gellner 1988; Eder 1987; A.B. Smith 1990, 1998; Ingold 1991; Bird-David 1990, 1992.

11. Examples include Mbuti-Bantu interaction in central Africa (Bahuchet et al. 1991); Semang-farmer exchange in Malaysia (Dunn 1975; Endicott and Bellwood 1991; Gregg 1979–80; Endicott 1997); and Agta-Filipino exchange in the Philippines (Headland and Reid 1989; Peterson 1978; Headland 1986).

12. Wilmsen and Denbow (1990) favor a continuous moving in and out of pastoralism for the San since about AD 600, as does Schrire (1980). The neighboring linguistically and biologically related Khoikhoi (or Khoekhoe) adopted pastoralism as much as 1,500–2,000 years ago (Barnard 1992; A.B. Smith 1993). But other scholars regard many of the San, especially the remoter groups, as always having been "genuine" hunter-gatherers (Solway and Lee 1990, Lee and Guenther 1990; Yellen 1990; also Lee 1979 on !Kung history). Archaeology gives strong support to the view that San and Khoi have been relatively separate since 1500 BP, and that the San have an independent hunter-gatherer prehistory (Smith 1993). See also Bird-David 1992; Kent 1992; Jolly 1996; Sadr 1997.

13. Peterson 1976; Chase 1989. Jones and Meehan (1989), and Yen (1995), also note that Arnhem Land Aboriginal groups exploited many wild plants which were cultivated elsewhere outside Australia – yams, taro, pandanus, and rice. No attempts to domesticate these plants in Australia have ever been recorded. Aboriginal populations at European

contact showed no signs whatever of being in transition to agriculture, despite occasional contacts with Papuan gardeners in the Torres Strait Islands.

14. Binford (1980) presented a classification of hunter-gatherer societies, which clearly resembles that of Woodburn, in which he distinguished *forager* and *collector* variants. Foragers are very mobile and move frequently from one resource zone to another in relatively non-seasonal environments. Collectors inhabit more seasonal environments which induce them to store food and generally to be more sedentary in their settlement patterns. Collectors come closer to the delayed return societies of Woodburn. Binford relates his two variants to environmental (non-seasonal versus seasonal) factors rather than to social factors such as presence or absence of circumscription. In reality, it seems likely that both pairs of factors have a role to play in inducing cultural variation. See Keeley 1988 for a similar division of hunter-gatherers into simple and complex types.

15. Schwartz 1963. See also Sather 1995 for the view that such specializations of economy within a single ethnic group, from hunter-gatherer to farmer, characterized Austronesian societies in general from very early times (e.g., from the Proto-Malayo-Polynesian linguistic phase, ca. 2500 BC).

16. See Headland 1993; Berreman 1999; and also Bellwood 1997a; Blust 1989; Hoffman 1986; Sandbukt 1991 and Headland 1993 for general discussion of these issues. Brosius 1991 and Sellato 1994 are against this view of an agricultural origin for the Punan of Borneo – Sellato (1994:7) terms them "an autonomous original culture of nomadic hunter-gatherers."

17. References for these cases: Nurse et al. 1985 (Africa); Guddemi 1992 (Sepik); Gardner 1993; Zide and Zide 1976 (India). For debate on the Okiek see Blackburn 1982; Chang 1982; Newman 1995:173–174.

18. Lathrap 1969; Stearmann 1991; Kent 1992. The issue of whether the Amazonian hunters and gatherers descend from cultivating or hunting founder societies is interesting but rather insoluble (Rival 1999; Roosevelt 1999a). A continuous hunter-gatherer ancestry seems likely for many Je speaking groups in Southeast Amazonia, but perhaps not for other groups who speak languages also spoken by farming populations. This is an area of much uncertainty.

19. See Zvelebil and Rowley-Conwy 1986; Rowley-Conwy 2001; Gregg 1988 for such possibilities in Neolithic Europe.

20. Ancient peoples often maintained contacts over quite large distances, so in some ways it is counter-productive to argue over whether or not these regions witnessed *absolutely pristine* developments towards agriculture in isolation. The most significant observation for each of them is that they present very strong hints that agriculture was essentially an internal development.

Chapter 3

1. Childe 1936; Bar-Yosef and Belfer-Cohen 1992; Bellwood 1989, 1996b; Sherratt 1997b.

2. On these environmental changes see Byrne 1987; Bottema 1995; Butzer 1995; Bar-Yosef 1996; Hillman 1996; Sanlaville 1996; Simmons 1997; Hillman et al. 2001; van Andel 2000; Chappell 2001; Cappers and Bottema 2002.

3. General accounts may be found in Heiser 1990; Evans 1993; Smith 1995; Harlan 1995; Willcox 1999; Zohary and Hopf 2000.

4. In hulled wheats and barley (all wild cereals are hulled) the grains are enclosed by tough cases termed glumes, which protect them from predators and the elements during dormancy. In many domesticated cereals (e.g., bread wheat) the grains are only held loosely within much-reduced glumes. These are much easier to thresh and are sometimes referred to as naked-grained cereals. Hulled cereals continued to be grown throughout prehistory in many regions because they were more disease- and drought-resistant than the naked varieties. For the distributions of wild and domesticated cereals and legumes in archaeological sites in the Levant, see Garrard (1999) and Colledge (2001).

5. For example, wild barley occurs in Natufian contexts at Wadi Hammeh 27 (Edwards 1991) and Hayonim Cave (Capdevila 1992); in PPNA contexts at Netiv Hagdud and Gilgal, both in the Jordan Valley (Bar-Yosef 1991; Kislev 1997); and also in PPNA contexts at Jerf el Ahmar and Dja'de on the Middle Euphrates in northern Syria (Willcox 1996).

6. Sites of the earliest agricultural phases in Southwest Asia and the Yellow River Valley of northern China normally produce large numbers of stone mortars and grinders. As Wright (1994) points out, these would also have been needed in Southwest Asia to grind flour, assuming that ancient people ate their cereals, as they do now, in various baked bread or cake preparations (Molleson 1994).

7. Goring-Morris and Belfer-Cohen 1998. For overall reviews of the Natufian see Bar-Yosef and Belfer-Cohen 1989a; Gilead 1991; Byrd 1989; Henry 1989; Belfer-Cohen 1991; Bar-Yosef and Valla eds. 1991; Olszewski 1991; Anderson ed. 1992; Bar-Yosef 1998b; Belfer-Cohen and Bar-Yosef 2000; Bar-Yosef 2003.

8. Henry 1989, 1991; Moore and Hillman 1992; Hillman 1996; Hillman et al. 2001; Bar-Yosef 1996, 1998a, 1998b, 2002; Harris 2002.

9. On commensals, compare Belfer-Cohen and Bar-Yosef 2000; Edwards 1989; Lieberman 1991, 1993, 1998. On social differentiation see Olszewski 1991; Byrd and Monahan 1995; Kuijt 2000b.

10. Although as Ofer Bar-Yosef (pers. comm.) has pointed out to me, there is no proof that the early pottery was used for cooking.

11. Some botanists favor at least a small presence of domesticated cereals in the PPNA, for instance at Jericho (Hopf 1983) and Tell Aswad near Damascus (Miller 1992), but dates for these sites are uncertain (see Stordeur 2003 for doubts over the presence of the PPNA at Tell Aswad). Kislev (1992, 1997) believes that domesticated cereal remains do not occur until the PPNB, after 8500 BC (see also Willcox 1996 for the northern Levant), and also points out that the occasional cereal fragments with domesticated morphology from PPNA sites could just represent rare non-shattering individuals in wild populations. The precise chronology for the appearance of morphologically domesticated cereals thus remains a little obscure. For further discussion see Harris 1998a; Garrard 1999; Edwards and Higham 2001; papers in Cappers and Bottema 2002; and Colledge et al. 2004.

12. In favor of a southern Levant origin see McCorriston and Hole 1991; Bar-Yosef 1994:53; Bar-Yosef and Meadow 1995. For a central Levant origin see Bar-Yosef 2003. For northern Levant see Gopher 1994; Hillman 1996; Cauvin 2000; Lev-Yadun et al. 2000. Opinions change rapidly!

13. On these sites see Aurenche 1989; Betts 1994; Hillman et al. 2001; Mottram 1997; Nadel et al. 1991; Stordeur et al. 1997; Stordeur 2000; Watkins et al. 1989; Watkins 1992; Willcox 1996.

14. Rosenberg 1994, 1999; Rosenberg and Redding 1998; Özdogan and Balkan-Atli 1994; Pringle 1998; Rosenberg et al. 1998. Rowley-Conwy (2001) doubts that the pigs were actually domesticated at Hallan Çemi, as opposed to hunted intensively.

15. In addition to Hallan Çemi, see also Henry et al. 1999 on a possible shift from hunting and gathering directly into goat herding in an arid region of the southern Levant. Domestication of goats is claimed for the Younger Dryas in the Lebanon Mountains by Wasse (2001), although there would appear to be no archaeological evidence directly in support of such an early date.

16. Note here the suggestion by Roberts 2002 that forest clearance was already under way in Anatolia and the Levant immediately after the end of the Younger Dryas.

17. For instance, Cauvin 1988, 1993, 2000; Aurenche 1989; Rollefson 1989; Goring-Morris and Belfer-Cohen 1998; Bar-Yosef 2003.

18. Perhaps the doorways were high in the walls to discourage the entry of vermin; note the doors about 60 centimeters above the ground in the Jordanian site of Basta, and the peculiar "port-holes" in the Iranian site of Ganj Dareh. At any rate, doorways are rarely found in the foundation structures which have survived for archaeological examination, and in sites such as Çatalhöyük (now shown to be of PPN foundation date – Cessford 2001) and Ba'ja there are suggestions for entry via roof trap-doors. Many cubicle structures could have served as foundations for 2-storey constructions, as at Basta and Ba'ja (Gebel and Hermansen 1999). Interestingly, but entirely coincidentally, anyone familiar with later PPNB cellular architecture will probably feel at home amongst the pueblo constructions of the ancient and modern Southwest of the USA. Twelfth-century Pueblo Bonito, Chetro Ketl, and Aztec Ruin, and the modern multi-story apartment buildings in Taos Pueblo, come to mind especially.

19. On the ritual buildings and constructions discussed in these paragraphs, see Stordeur 2000 (Jerf el Ahmar); Hauptmann 1999 (Göbekli Tepe and Nevali Çori); Rollefson 1998 (Ain Ghazal); Verhoeven 1997 (Sabi Abyad); Schirmer 1990 (Çayönü); Goring-Morris 2000 and Keys 2003 (Kfar HaHoresh); Gebel and Hermansen 1999 (Ba'ja); Schmidt 2003 and many articles in the journal *Neo-Lithics* (Göbekli Tepe). See also general discussions in Kuijt 2000b.

20. For instance, Aurenche and Calley 1988; Cauvin 1988, 2000; Aurenche 1989; Bar-Yosef and Belfer-Cohen 1989b, 1991; Gopher and Gophra 1994; Miller 1991; Garfinkel 1994; Banning 1998:215.

21. It is often extremely hard to know whether an episode of environmental degradation in the presence of a large human population was caused by the activity of that population alone, or whether independent adverse environmental changes (e.g., a drying climate) acted as a prime mover. Both can cause degradation, but a natural change could presumably only be established as the primary cause from multiple pollen cores, including some from regions where human activity is not in evidence. The Middle East does not have such a wonderful pollen record for the time period in question. Many scholars tend to blame humans for "catastrophes" of this type, particularly when they occur in the Holocene amongst societies at a high level of population density and social complexity.

Chapter 4

1. Simmons 1998, 1999. It is not absolutely clear that Neolithic farmers exterminated these animals; a different population of hunters could possibly have arrived a little before them.

2. Demoule and Perlès 1993; Demoule 1993; Halstead 1996; van Andel and Runnels 1995; Runnels and Murray 2001.

3. Bailey et al. 2002 discuss the transition from tells in the southern Balkans to more short-lived settlements in the northern Balkans.

4. The debate is between Fox (1996: in favor of Neolithic population immigration, supported by Zilhão 2000, 2001) and Jackes et al. (1997a, 1997b: against Neolithic immigration, supported by Ribé et al. 1997). Whatever the answer, analyses of stable isotopes in human bone certainly indicate a major dietary change from Mesolithic into Neolithic in Portugal (Zilhão 2000:162).

5. Gronenborn (1999:143) also discusses evidence from pottery decoration that Neolithic traditions of both Danubian and Mediterranean origin met and mixed in northern France. See also Sherratt 1997a:fig. 13.1. The Hoguette pottery tradition of the Rhineland might indeed reflect Mesolithic adoption of pottery from a southern Cardial source, rather than from the LBK (Street et al. 2001).

6. This section on the LBK is compiled from many sources, useful ones being Keeley and Cahen 1989; Keeley 1992; Kooijmans 1993; Bogucki 1987, 1988, 1996a, 1996b; Bogucki and Grygiel 1993; Staüble 1995; Sherratt 1997a; Gronenborn 1999; Kruk and Milisauskas 1999; Bradley 2001; Collard and Shennan 2000; Shennan 2002:247–251.

7. Note that Raemakers (2003) favors a much more rapid switch from Mesolithic to Neolithic in the lower Rhine than most other authors, suggesting that the apparent long overlap might just be an epiphenomenon of site preservation factors. Otherwise, this section on Ertebølle and TRB is compiled from Arias 1999; Price 1987, 1996; Price and Gebauer 1992; Rowley-Conwy 1984, 1995, 1999; Solberg 1989; Midgley 1992; Zvelevil 1996a, 1996b; Street et al. 2001; Nowak 2001.

8. For instance, Midgley (1992), Bogucki (1996b), Price (1996), Thomas (1996), Nowak (2001) and Zvelebil (1996a, 1996b, 1998, 2000) all believe in some degree of Mesolithic input into the post-Ertebølle TRB culture, some more strongly than others.

9. Schild (1998) attributes many of the pottery finds to stratigraphic mixing, so some caution is required in accepting this concept of a Jomon-like non-agricultural "Neolithic" for the eastern Baltic region.

10. For instance, the Balbridie Neolithic timbered hall in Scotland, dated to 4000 BC (Fairweather and Ralston 1993), and some early Neolithic houses in Ireland (Grogan 2002)). Other recent northwest European and British Neolithic evidence suggestive of sharp dietary and cultural change from Mesolithic into Neolithic is offered by Rowley-Conwy 2000; Kimball 2000; Schulting 2000; Dark and Gent 2001. Recent stable isotope studies on ancient bones also suggest a marked shift from riverine or coastal to "terrestrial" (i.e., plant-based) diets across the Mesolithic–Neolithic boundary in various regions of Europe (e.g., Bonsall et al. 1997 for the Danube Basin; Richards and Hedges 1999 for northern Europe and Iberia; Zilhão 2000 for Iberia; Schulting and Richards 2002 for Wales; Richards et al. 2003 for Denmark). This counteracts the view that the Mesolithic economy simply went on regardless into the Early Neolithic (but see Milner et al. 2004 for cautions).

11. Note here that only in southern New Zealand, beyond the range of agriculture, did these people actually become permanent hunter-gatherers. The tropical Polynesians and North Island Maoris reverted to their ancestral agricultural economy as the natural resources became scarcer due to overexploitation.

12. General accounts of Mehrgarh can be found in Lechevallier and Quivron 1979; Jarrige and Meadow 1980, 1992; Jarrige 1993; Costantini 1981; Meadow 1989, 1993, 1998.

13. Claims for a very early appearance of agriculture in Sri Lanka exist but are unsupported by firm archaeological evidence (Deraniyagala 2001).

14. On African millets and legumes in South Asia see Possehl 1986; Kajale 1991; Reddy 1997; Weber 1991, 1998, 1999; Blench 2003. But see Rowley-Conwy et al. 1997 and Fuller 2001 for doubts concerning some sites, also Wigboldus 1996 who believes that all the African millets in India are of medieval date or later, a view not well supported by an increasing number of archaeological finds.

15. References on Pre-Harappan archaeology are voluminous, but pertinent ones for this section include R.P. Singh 1990; Kajale 1991 (both general paleobotanical reviews); Dhavalikhar and Possehl 1992 (Gujarat); Shudai 1996–97; Sonawane 2000 (Gujarat); Chakrabarti 1999; Misra 2001; Possehl 2002.

16. See IAR 1981–82: 19–20 (Gufkral); Buth and Kaw 1985 (Burzahom); Dikshit 2000.

17. By the end of the third millennium BC the African millets had reached the eastern fringes of the Harappan region, as had rice (Fujiwara 1993). Various crop combinations involving millets and rice are reported from sites of the early second millennium BC in Gujarat, such as Rojdi (Weber 1991, 1993, 1999, 1998) and Rangpur (Rao 1962–63). See also Possehl 1986; Fuller 2002, 2003.

18. Sources on these cultures are many, but see Chakrabarti 1999; Clason 1977; Dhavalikar 1988, 1994, 1997; Dhavalikar et al. 1988; Kajale 1996a; Misra 1997; Misra et al. 1995, Shinde 1991, 1994, 2000; Thomas 2000.

19. See V. D. Misra 2002 for cord-marking on Ochre Coloured pottery. Cord-marked pottery was made with a paddle and anvil, the paddle (normally a wooden beater) being wrapped with some form of cordage or basketry and used to beat the outer surface of the pot prior to firing. It is very common in Chinese and Mainland Southeast Asian Neolithic contexts, as well as in the Japanese Jomon.

20. Chirand lacks cord-marked pottery but otherwise has pottery similar to that from Neolithic Koldihwa; Misra 1977:116. Narhan I, dated from about 1300 BC (Singh 1994), has rice, hexaploid wheats, pearl millet, barley, *zebu* cattle, BRW and cord-marked pottery, and small items of copper.

21. References for these sites include Liversage 1992; Dhavalikar 1997; R. P. Singh 1990; A. K. Singh 1998; P. Singh 1994, 1998; Sathe and Badam 1996.

22. Liversage 1992; Allchin and Allchin 1982 are in favor of continuity; Lal 1984 against.

Chapter 5

1. On sub-Saharan domestication records for specific crops, see MacDonald 1998; Rowley-Conwy et al. 1997; Wetterstrom 1998; D'Andrea and Casey 2002; and papers in van der Veen 1999.

2. On the various occurrences of early pottery in northern Africa see Mohammad-Ali 1987; Roset 1987; Krzyzaniak 1991; Muzzolini 1993; Haaland 1993, 1999; Close 1995, 1996; Barich 1997; Wasylikowa et al. 1997; Wetterstrom 1998; Hassan 1998; Midant-Reynes 2000; Cremaschi and di Lernia 2001; Wendorf et al. 2001.

3. David Phillipson (pers. comm.) agrees that there was some dispersal of early farming communities in West Africa along or close to the Atlantic coast southward to northern Angola, but feels that there is little evidence in support of a Western Bantu spread southeastward across the continent.

Chapter 6

1. The possibility that arboriculture and field agriculture were present in Jomon Japan must not be overlooked – rice was present in some regions of Japan from Middle Jomon times onward, and millets were fairly universal. For Jomon agricultural activity in general see Imamura 1996; Crawford and Chen 1998; D'Andrea 1999; and several papers in Yasuda 2002.
2. MacNeish and Libby 1995; MacNeish et al. 1998; MacNeish 1999; Zhao 1998; Pringle 1998; Zhang 1999; Chen 1999. The dates offered for cultural developments for Xianrendong and Diaotonghuan vary somewhat according to author.
3. See, for instance, the variety of opinions given in the various papers in *Antiquity* 72, 1998, Special Section on Rice Domestication, and in Yasuda 2002. Many translations of Chinese articles on rice origins are available in the Ancient Chinese Rice Archaeological Project web site www.carleton.ca/~bgordon/Rice/. The DNA evidence for a separate origin of *indica* and *japonica*, however, does appear to be very strong (Bautista et al. 2001).
4. And, for what it is worth, very similar to joinery in prehistoric New Zealand! Hemudu carpentry, adze handles, and wooden tops closely resemble those of late prehistoric Maoris (e.g., Bellwood 1978b for the Lake Mangakaware excavations). This does not mean that Maori ancestry should be traced directly to Hemudu, but it does mean that many aspects of Austronesian material culture and technology in the Pacific can be traced back to coastal Neolithic China.
5. Such perforations were perhaps made in the first instance to allow hot gases to escape from inside the pedestal during firing. Pottery of this shape occurs from Neolithic China right through Island Southeast Asia into the Lapita cultural complex in western Melanesia.

Chapter 7

1. Recent surveys include Bellwood 1992, 1996a, 1996b, 1997a, 1998a, 1998b, 2000a, 2000b, 2001f, Bellwood and Hiscock in press. See also Higham 1996a, 1996b, 2002, 2004; Higham and Thosarat 1998a; Spriggs 1989, 1999, 2003; and many chapters in Glover and Bellwood eds. 2004. Other, more Pacific-focused surveys include Kirch 1997, 2000; Spriggs 1997a; Bellwood 2001e.
2. Items such as spindle whorls and bovid bones do not generally occur in the Neolithic of Island Southeast Asia, at least not south of northern Luzon in the Philippines. This statement merely generalizes about a trend.
3. Madagascar was settled in the mid-first millennium AD by Indonesian agriculturalists, probably in the main from southern Borneo, with linguistic influences from Malay and Javanese (Adelaar 1996; Vérin and Wright 2000). At present there is no clear evidence for any older population on the island (but see MacPhee and Burney 1991). This chapter does not deal further with Madagascar, which geographically is, of course, part of Africa. But this island might have played a role in the spread of Southeast Asian crops such as bananas, taro, and the greater yam into tropical Africa.
4. Recent reports which deal specifically with these sites include Higham and Bannanurag 1990 and onward; Higham and Thosarat 1994; Higham and Thosarat 1998b; White 1982, 1997; Pigott and Natapintu 1996–97.
5. In this chapter I use pinyin spellings for Taiwan place names.

6. On these assemblages see Chang 1995; Bellwood 1997b, 2000b; Yang 1995; Tsang 1992, 1995. Tsang Cheng-hwa of the National Museum of Prehistory in Taiwan (2004) also sees close relationships between early Taiwan pottery and that of the Guangdong coastal Neolithic sites. Tianlong Jiao of the Bishop Museum in Honolulu is currently preparing new data on coastal Fujian sites for publication.

7. This information comes from current research by Hung Hsiao-chun (ANU, Canberra), Yoshi Iizuka (Academia Sinica, Taipei), Eusebio Dizon (National Museum, Manila) and the author. The Batanes Islands have produced a 3,500-year sequence with very close ties to Taiwan maintained for at least the first 2,000 years of this time span. For preliminary results see Bellwood et al. 2003.

8. In Bellwood 1997a:237–238) I raised the possibility of a Neolithic movement to Borneo from the Malay Peninsula. It was made in the light of linguistic parallels between Aslian and Sarawak Austronesian languages suggested by Adelaar (1995), but discussions with Sander Adelaar since then have convinced me that the linguistic explanation is somewhat different. The details are not essential for present purposes.

9. Hunter-gatherers would not have found sufficient food for long-term survival on small and isolated Oceanic islands. Although small islands were often colonized in Indonesia by as much as 35,000 years ago, they were always close to larger ones such that the population could be peripatetic when necessary (Bellwood et al. 1998). In terms of boat technology, hunter-gatherer populations were able to reach the islands of Indonesia, New Guinea, and Australia before 35,000 years ago, but in order to do this they normally only had to cross narrow sea gaps with land visible on the other side. They probably paddled bamboo rafts in monsoon-determined periods of quiet ocean surface. Maximum distances up to 200 kilometers, from New Guinea to the Admiralty Islands or from mainland Asia/Japan to Okinawa, were also crossed, but rarely. The more recent Austronesian agriculturalist populations were able to cross distances of 2000 kilometers or more, from 1500 BC onward (e.g., Philippines to Guam), using sailing canoes with outriggers (Anderson 2000).

10. On the Kuk research and its implications, see Golson 1977; Golson and Gardner 1990; Swadling and Hope 1992; Bayliss-Smith and Golson 1992; Haberle and Chepstow-Lusty 2000; Denham et al. 2003; Denham 2003; Haberle 2003.

Chapter 8

1. For suggestions of multiple origin see Pickersgill 1989; Hastorf 1999; Jones and Brown 2000. Bonavia and Grobman 1989 suggest it for maize, clearly very likely if maize spread initially as a source of sugar and was later domesticated for its cob (Smalley and Blake 2003).

2. Note also that Mangelsdorf et al. 1964 regarded early wild maize as an independent species distinct from teosinte.

3. For current debate see Tykot and Staller 2002; Staller and Thompson 2002. Pearsall 2002 still favors older dates, suggesting that maize was common at Valdivia in Ecuador by 3500 BC, according to a presence of maize phytoliths in the deposits. Previous discussions of maize dating in South America include Bird 1990; Wilson 1985; Hastorf and Johannessen 1994; Piperno 1998; Hastorf 1999; Lynch 1999. Large Pre-ceramic sites older than 2000 BC without maize in northern Peru include La Galgada (Grieder et al. 1988), Huaynuna

(Pozorski and Pozorski 1990), Aspero (Feldman 1985) and El Paraiso (Quilter et al. 1991). There is still much uncertainty.

4. Hastorf (1999:45) claims domesticated common beans (*Phaseolis vulgaris*) from about 8000 BC in Peru, but Smith (2001:1325) indicates AMS dates for this species in Mexico back to only 300 BC.

5. For an aerial photograph of Cerro Juanaqueña, see LeBlanc 2003.

6. References on the domestication history of the crops of the Eastern Woodlands are very numerous. Some of the most thorough include Ford 1985 (many papers); Keegan 1987 (many papers); Adair 1988; Jennings 1989; Fritz 1990; Smith 1992a, 1992b, 1995; Scarry 1993 (many papers); Green 1994 (many papers); Johannessen and Hastorf 1994 (many papers); Hart 1999.

Chapter 9

1. After his return from Cook's Second Voyage, discussing the languages that today are termed Austronesian (Thomas et al. 1996:190).

2. For instance, according to Hines (1998:284): "I can see no reason to resist the notion that in the vast periods of prehistory, and over the vast geographical ranges of the world's major language phyla, dispersal, isolation (in my view the critical factor) and divergence were dominant trends." See also Ross 1997 for an excellent discussion of this point. Coleman 1988, Nichols 1997a, Dolgopolsky 1993, and Hayward 2000 all reject convergence between unrelated languages as a source of language families, and reject in particular the theory of Trubetzkoy (1939) that Indo-European has no homeland at all, and is purely a result of convergence.

3. For an excellent example of the use of a reconstructed proto-language together with the archaeological record, in this case to build up a record of the culture and lifestyle of the Proto-Polynesians, see Patrick Kirch and Roger Green 2001. But Soeren Wichmann (2003) notes, following the recent successful decipherment of many Mayan inscriptions, that reconstructed proto-languages can often be quite imperfect in detail.

4. Innovation-defined (tree-like) subgroups and innovation-linked (rake-like) subgroups are discussed in more technical detail by Andrew Pawley and Malcolm Ross 1993, 1995; Ross 1997. These issues are also discussed by Nichols (1997a), who associates rake-like subgroup relationships with what she terms "spread zones." Nichols (1998b:136) also suggests that all the major branches of Indo-European had already diverged within 1,000 years of the existence of Proto-Indo-European, thus forming a rake-like distribution owing to rapid dispersal.

5. Ross (1994) gives a good example of interference through shift in New Ireland, where the Kuot people, former speakers of a Papuan language, have adopted an Austronesian language and in the process have modified the latter with an input of Papuan phonology.

6. This might not have been true of pre-contact New Caledonia, but there is not space here to go further into this matter.

Chapter 10

1. The PIE vocabulary is discussed in many sources. See Watkins 1985; Mallory 1996; Mallory and Adams 1997; Anthony 1995; Lehmann 1993; Gamkrelidze and Ivanov 1995. Comrie 2003 suggests that a reconstruction for "plough" demands a post-Neolithic date

for PIE, but use of the ard surely goes back to the beginnings of agriculture and animal domestication in Europe, and possibly southwestern Asia too.

2. In 1988, American biological anthropologist Grover Krantz (1988) published, seemingly quite independently of Colin Renfrew, a similar hypothesis of Neolithic spread out of Anatolia for the early IE languages. Krantz set out a number of rather compelling principles that still carry much conviction today – for instance, populations and languages do not normally spread far unless there is a compelling reason, and some technological or numerical superiority would normally be required on the part of those doing the moving into previously inhabited regions. Krantz' precise reconstructions for European, and Indo-European, prehistory need not be detailed here – suffice it to say that he regarded Neolithic Europe as an arena for both IE and Afro-Asiatic expansion, noting that the *kurgan* (Pontic steppes) hypothesis was untenable.

3. Some linguists dispute the existence of AA, for instance Campbell 1999, who doubts the membership of Omotic and Chadic.

4. According to Kumar (1988), the Rigvedic texts have many references to agriculture. A term for barley also reconstructs to proto-Indo-Aryan according to Masica (1979), although many crop words were borrowed, as we would expect from an understanding of the archaeological prehistory of India.

5. Renfrew 1989, 1991, 1992a, 1992b; Bellwood 1989; and see also similar ideas in Sherratt and Sherratt 1988, who were perhaps the first to propose such a radial model. A number of archaeologists were clearly coming independently to such conclusions in the late 1980s. In more recent papers (e.g., 2001b), Renfrew has become more cautious about the reality of macrofamilies.

6. Basic references on Nostratic (in English) include Kaiser and Shevoroshkin 1988; Shevoroshkin and Manaster Ramer 1991; Shevoroshkin 1992; Bomhard and Kerns 1994; Bomhard 1996; Dolgopolsky 1998; and see a wide range of discussion from many viewpoints in Renfrew and Nettle 1999. Nostratic is based on a number of lexical cognates, especially pronouns. Claims for 600 or more widespread cognates now exist in the literature (Michalove et al. 1998).

7. Frequent suggestions are for Austronesian–Austroasiatic relationships (e.g., Reid 1988, 1996); Austronesian–Tai relationships (e.g., Benedict 1975), and also Austronesian–Sino–Tibetan relationships (Sagart 1994, 2002, 2003). See Egerod 1991; Blust 1996 and Sagart et al. in press for current debate.

8. Sagart 1994, 2002; see Chang 1986:162 for Dawenkou tooth extraction.

9. Some of the great variation in opinion can be gauged by examining Unger 1990; Bomhard 1990; Miller 1991; Janhunen 1996.

10. These dates are merely averages of estimates by several linguists. For data see Migliazza 1982; Kaufman 1990a; and other sources listed in Bellwood 2000c:129–130.

11. The Yanomama speak a language related to Panoan.

12. See discussion in *American Anthropologist* 82:850–857 (1980), 83:905–911 (1981) and 85:362–372 (1983).

13. But see also the arguments against a Nahuatl affiliation for Teotihuacan given by Kaufman 2001; Beekman and Christensen 2003.

14. Jane Hill has suggested to me (pers. comm.) that the Fremont population could have been multi-linguistic, involving possibly some Tanoan speakers as well.

15. Kelly 1997:22 suggests that summer rainfall from the southwest might have been greater then than now. See also Madsen and Simms 1998.

16. Figure 3.4 in Snow 1996 suggests that Canada north of the Great Lakes and the St Lawrence was relatively free of human population during the Archaic.

17. Rankin does not include Catawba as a Siouan language, although Foster includes it within a Siouan-Catawba grouping.

Chapter 11

1. As argued, for instance, by Bateman et al. (1990). In agreement with Cavalli-Sforza and colleagues, Barbujani and Sokal (1990) claim that language affiliations of European populations have played a major role in maintaining genetic differences, whereas adaptations to different environments do not appear to have been significant in this regard.

2. Mitochondrial DNA is transmitted through females, and produces enzymes that power cells and convert food into energy. The Y-chromosome is transmitted through males and is the one that determines biological maleness in the offspring. The most important observation about these genetic systems is that they do not recombine at meiosis in each generation, and so they pass through time as true lineages that only change through occasional mutations. Such mutations are amenable to molecular clock calculations of their ages if there are calibration scales available, but dating of this type can be highly problematic.

3. See also Kivisild et al. 2002 for similar observations that mtDNA lineages differentiate Northeast from Southeast Asian populations, but also underlining the significance of Yayoi immigration into Japan from Korea. On the other hand, Tajima et al. (2002) suggest a close grouping of Han Chinese with many Southeast Asian populations. The debate is too new for much consensus to have emerged.

4. The week before final proof reading I attended a conference on Human Migrations in Continental East Asia and Taiwan, held in the University of Geneva (June 2004). Jean Trejaut from the Mackay Memorial Hospital in Taipei here offered a new coalescence age of only 6,900 years for the Polynesian motif, together with an age for the ancestral form of only 10,000 years in Taiwan or China. These ages are calibrated against ages for the human–chimp lineage split, and represent more than a halving of the Oppenheimer and Richards estimate. I do not know which age is correct for the mutation of the Polynesian motif, but the true answer, if it can ever be found, will no doubt be interesting.

References

Adair, M. 1988 *Prehistoric Agriculture in the Central Plains*. Lawrence: University of Kansas Department of Anthropology.

Adair, M. 1994 Corn and culture history in the central Plains. In S. Johannessen and C. Hastorf eds., *Corn and Culture in the Prehistoric New World*, pp. 315–34. Boulder: Westview.

Adelaar, K.A. 1995 Borneo as a cross-roads for comparative Austronesian linguistics. In P. Bellwood, J.J. Fox and D. Tryon eds., *The Austronesians: Comparative and Historical Perspectives*, pp. 75–95. Canberra: Dept Anthropology, Research School of Pacific and Asian Studies, Australian National University.

Adelaar, K.A. 1996 Malagasy culture history: some linguistic evidence. In J. Reade ed., *The Indian Ocean in Antiquity*, pp. 487–500. London: Kegan Paul International.

Adi Haji Taha 1985 The re-excavation of the rockshelter of Gua Cha, Ulu Kelantan, West Malaysia. *Federation Museums Journal* 30.

Agrawala, R.C. and Kumar, V. 1993 Ganeshwar-Jodhpura culture: new traits in Indian archaeology. In G. Possehl ed. *Harappan Civilization: A Recent Perspective*, pp. 79–84. New Delhi: Oxford & IBH.

Aikhenvald, A. 1996 Areal diffusion in northwest Amazonia – the case of Tariana. *Anthropological Linguistics* 38:73–116.

Aikhenvald, A. 1999 The Arawak language family. In R. Dixon and A. Aikhenvald eds., *Amazonian Languages*, pp. 65–106. Cambridge: Cambridge University Press.

Aikhenvald, A. 2001 Areal diffusion, genetic inheritance, and problems of subgrouping: a North Arawak case study. In A. Aikhenvald and R. Dixon eds., *Areal Diffusion and Genetic Inheritance*, pp. 167–94. Oxford: Oxford University Press.

Aikhenvald, A. 2002 *Language Contact in Amazonia*. Oxford: Oxford University Press.

Aikhenvald, A. and Dixon, R. 2001 Introduction. In A. Aikhenvald and R. Dixon eds., *Areal Diffusion and Genetic Inheritance: Problems in Comparative Linguistics*, pp. 1–26. Oxford: Oxford University Press.

Akkermans, P. 1993 *Villages in the Steppe*. Ann Arbor: International Monographs in Prehistory.

Alexander, J. 1978 Frontier studies and the earliest farmers in Europe. In D. Green, C. Haselgrove and M. Spriggs eds., *Social Organisation and Settlement*, pp. 13–30. Oxford: BAR International Series (Supplementary) 47(i).

Allchin, B. and Allchin, R. 1982 *The Rise of Civilization in India and Pakistan*. Cambridge: Cambridge University Press.

Allchin, R. 1963 *Neolithic Cattle Keepers of South India*. Cambridge: Cambridge University Press.

Allen, H. 1974 The Bagundji of the Darling Basin. *World Archaeology* 5:309–22.

Ammerman, A.J. and Cavalli-Sforza, L.L. 1984 *The Neolithic Transition and the Genetics of Populations in Europe*. Princeton: Princeton University Press.

Andel, T. van 2000 Where received wisdom fails: the mid-Palaeolithic and early Neolithic climates. In C. Renfrew and K. Boyle eds., *Archaeogenetics*, pp. 31–40. Cambridge: McDonald Institute for Archaeological Research.

Andel, T. van and Runnels, C. 1995 The earliest farmers in Europe. *Antiquity* 69:481–500.

Andel, T. van, Zangger, E. and Demitrack, A. 1990 Land use and soil erosion in prehistoric and historic Greece. *Journal of Field Archaeology* 17:379–96.

Anderson, A. 1989 *Prodigious Birds*. Cambridge: Cambridge University Press.

Anderson, A. 2000 Slow boats from China. In S. O'Connor and P. Veth eds., *East of Wallace's Line*, pp. 13–50. Rotterdam: Balkema.

Anderson, P. 1994 Reflections on the significance of two PPN typological classes. In H.G. Gebel and S.F. Kozlowski eds., *Neolithic Chipped Stone Industries of the Levant*, pp. 61–82. Berlin: Ex Oriente.

Anderson, P. ed. 1992 *Préhistoire de l'Agriculture*. Paris: CNRS (Monographie du CRA 6).

Anquandah, J. 1993 The Kintampo complex. In T. Shaw, P. Sinclair, B. Andah and A. Okpoko eds., *The Archaeology of Africa*, pp. 255–60. London: Routledge.

Anthony, D. 1991 The archaeology of Indo-European origins. *Journal of Indo-European Studies* 19:193–222.

Anthony, D. 1995 Horse, wagon and chariot: Indo-European languages and Archaeology. *Antiquity* 69:554–64.

Anthony, D. and Brown, D. 2000 Eneolithic horse exploitation in the Eurasian steppes. *Antiquity* 74:75–86.

Araus, J.L. et al. 1999 Crop water availability in early agriculture. *Global Change Biology* 5:201–12.

Arias, P. 1999 The origins of the Neolithic along the Atlantic coast of Continental Europe. *Journal of World Prehistory* 13:403–64.

Arkell, A.J. 1975 *The Prehistory of the Nile Valley*. Leiden: Brill.

Armit, I. and Finlayson, B. 1992 Hunter-gatherers transformed: the transition to agriculture in northern and western Europe. *Antiquity* 66:664–76.

Aurenche, O. and Calley, S. 1988 L'architecture de l'Anatolie du Sud-Est au Néolithique acéramique. *Anatolica* 15:1–24.

Aurenche, O. 1989 La néolithisation au Levant et sa première diffusion. In O. Aurenche and J. Cauvin eds., *Néolithisations*, pp. 3–36. Oxford: International Series 516.

Bader, N.O. 1993 Tell Maghzaliyah. In N. Yoffee and J.J. Clark eds., *Early Stages in the Evolution of Mesopotamian Civilization*, pp. 7–40. Tucson: University of Arizona Press.

Bahuchet, S., McKey, D. and de Garine, I. 1991 Wild yams revisited. *Human Ecology* 19:213–44.

Bailey, D., Andreescu, R. et al. 2002 Alluvial landscapes in the temperate Balkans Neolithic; transitions to tells. *Antiquity* 76:349–55.

Bakker, J., Kruk, J. et al. 1999 The earliest evidence of wheeled vehicles in Europe and the Near East. *Antiquity* 73:778–90.

Bale, M. 2001 The archaeology of early agriculture in the Korean Peninsula. *Bulletin of the Indo-Pacific Prehistory Association* 21:77–84.

Ballard, W.L. 1985 The linguistic history of South China: Miao-Yao and southern dialects. In G. Thurgood et al. eds., *Linguistics of the Sino-Tibetan Area: The State of the Art*, pp. 58–89. Canberra: Pacific Linguistics C-87.

Banning, E.B. 1998 The Neolithic Period. *Near Eastern Archaeology* 61/4:188–237.

Barbujani, G, Bertorelle, G. and Chikhi, L. 1998 Evidence for Palaeolithic and Neolithic gene flow in Europe. *American Journal of Human Genetics* 62:488–91.

Barbujani, G. and Dupanloup, I. 2003 DNA variation in Europe: estimating the demographic impact of Neolithic dispersals. In P. Bellwood and C. Renfrew eds., *Examining the Farming/Language Dispersal Hypothesis*, pp. 421–34. Cambridge: McDonald Institute for Archaeological Research.

Barbujani, G., Pilastro, A. et al. 1994 Genetic variation in North Africa and Eurasia: Neolithic demic diffusion vs. Palaeolithic colonization. *American Journal of Physical Anthropology* 95:137–54.

Barbujani, G. and Sokal, R. 1990 Zones of sharp genetic change in Europe are also linguistic boundaries. *Proceedings of the National Academy of Sciences* 87:1816–9.

Barbujani, G., Sokal, R. and Oden, N. 1995 Indo-European origins: a computer-simulation test of five hypotheses. *American Journal of Physical Anthropology* 96:109–32.

Bard, K., Coltorti, M. et al. 2000 The environmental history of Tigray (northern Ethiopia) in the Middle and Late Holocene. *African Archaeological Review* 17:65–86.

Barich, B. 1997 Saharan Neolithic. In J. Vogel ed., *Encyclopaedia of Precolonial Africa*, pp. 389–94. Walnut Creek: Sage.

Barker, G. 2003 Transitions to farming and pastoralism in North Africa. In P. Bellwood and C. Renfrew eds., *Examining the Farming/Language Dispersal Hypothesis*, pp. 151–62. Cambridge: McDonald Institute for Archaeological Research.

Barnard, A. 1992 *Hunters and Herders of Southern Africa*. Cambridge: Cambridge University Press.

Barnett, T. 1999 *The Emergence of Food Production in Ethiopia*. Oxford: BAR International Series 763.

Barnett, W.K. 1995 Putting the pot before the horse. In W.K. Barnett and J. Hoopes eds., *The Emergence of Pottery*, pp. 79–88. Washington: Smithsonian.

Bar-Yosef, O. 1991 The Early Neolithic of the Levant. *Review of Archaeology* 12/2:1–18.

Bar-Yosef, O. 1994 The contributions of Southwest Asia. In M.H. Nitecki and D.V. Nitecki eds., *Origins of Anatomically Modern Humans*, pp. 23–66. New York: Plenum.

Bar-Yosef, O. 1996 The impact of Late Pleistocene–Early Holocene climatic changes on humans in Southwest Asia. In L.G. Strauss et al. eds., *Humans at the End of the Ice Age*, pp. 61–78. New York: Plenum.

Bar-Yosef, O. 1998a On the nature of transitions. *Cambridge Archaeological Journal* 8:141–63.

Bar-Yosef, O. 1998b The Natufian culture in the Levant. *Evolutionary Anthropology* 6:159–77.

Bar-Yosef, O. 2002 The role of the Younger Dryas in the origin of agriculture in West Asia. In Y. Yasuda ed., *The Origins of Pottery and Agriculture*, pp. 39–54. New Delhi: Roli.

Bar-Yosef, O. 2003 The Natufian Culture and the Early Neolithic: social and economic trends in Southwestern Asia. In P. Bellwood and C. Renfrew eds., *Examining the Language/Farming Dispersal Hypothesis*, pp. 113–26. Cambridge: McDonald Institute for Archaeological Research.

Bar-Yosef, O. and Belfer-Cohen, A. 1989a The origins of sedentism and farming communities in the Levant. *Journal of World Prehistory* 3:447–498.

Bar-Yosef, O. and Belfer-Cohen, A. 1989b The Levantine PPNB interaction sphere. In Herschkovitz, I. *People and Culture in Change*, pp. 59–72. Oxford: BAR International Series 508.

Bar-Yosef, O. and Belfer-Cohen, A. 1991 From sedentary hunter-gatherers to territorial farmers in the Levant. In S.A. Gregg ed., *Between Bands and States*, pp. 181–202. Center for Archaeological Investigations, Occasional Paper 9, Southern Illinois University.

Bar-Yosef, O. and Belfer-Cohen, A. 1992 From foraging to farming in the Mediterranean Levant. In A.B. Gebauer and T.D. Price eds., *Transitions to Agriculture in Prehistory*, pp. 21–48. Madison: Prehistory Press.

Bar-Yosef, O. and Meadow, R. 1995 The origins of agriculture in the Near East. In T.D. Price and A.B. Gebauer eds., *Last Hunters First Farmers*, pp. 39–94. Santa Fe: School of American Research.

Bar-Yosef, O. and Valla, F.R. eds. 1991 *The Natufian Culture in the Levant*. Ann Arbor: International Monographs in Prehistory.

Bastin, Y., Coupez, A. and Mann, M. 1999 Continuity and divergence in the Bantu languages: perspectives from a lexicostatic study. Tervuren, Belgium: Musée Royale d'Afrique Centrale, *Annales, Sciences Humaines*, vol. 162.

Bateman, R., Goddard, I. et al. 1990 Speaking of forked tongues. *Current Anthropology* 31:1–24.

Bautista, N.A., Solis, R. et al. 2001 RAPD, RFLP and SSLP analyses of phylogenetic relationships between cultivated and wild species of rice. *Genes and Genetic Systems* 76(2):71–9.

Bayliss-Smith, T. 1988 Prehistoric agriculture in the New Guinea Highlands: problems in defining the altitudinal limits. In J. Bintliff et al. eds., *Conceptual Issues in Environmental Archaeology*, pp. 153–60. Edinburgh University Press.

Bayliss-Smith, T. and Golson, J. 1992 Wetland agriculture in New Guinea Highland prehistory. In B. Coles ed., *The Wetland Revolution in Prehistory*, pp. 15–28. Exeter: Prehistoric Society and WARP.

Beaglehole, J.C. 1968 *The Journals of Captain James Cook. I: The Voyage of the Endeavour 1768–1771*. Cambridge: Hakluyt Society.

Bean, L.J. and Lawton, H. 1976 Some explanations for the rise of cultural complexity in California with comments on proto-agriculture and agriculture. In L.J. Bean and T.C. Blackburn eds., *Native Californians*, pp. 19–40. Socorro: Ballena Press.

Beavitt, P., Kurui, E. and Thompson, G. 1996 Confirmation of an early date for the presence of rice in Borneo. *Borneo Research Bulletin* 27:29–37.

Beekman, C. and Christensen, A. 2003 Controlling for doubt and uncertainty through multiple lines of evidence: a new look at the Mesoamerican Nahua migrations. *Journal of Archaeological Method and Theory* 10:111–164.

Belfer-Cohen, A. 1991 The Natufian in the Levant. *Journal of World Prehistory* 20:167–86.

Belfer-Cohen, A. and Bar-Yosef, O. 2000 Early sedentism in the Near East. In I. Kuijt ed., *Life in Neolithic Farming Communities*, pp. 19–37. New York: Kluwer.

Belfer-Cohen, A. and Hovers, E. 1992 In the eye of the beholder: Mousterian and Natufian burials in the Levant. *CA33*:463–72.

Bellwood, P. 1978a *Man's Conquest of the Pacific*. Auckland: Collins.

Bellwood, P. 1978b *Archaeological Research at Lake Mangakaware, Waikato*. Dunedin: Otago Studies in Prehistoric Anthropology 12.

Bellwood, P. 1983 The great Pacific Migration. *Encyclopaedia Britannica Yearbook of Science and the Future for 1984*, pp. 80–93.

Bellwood, P. 1988 A hypothesis for Austronesian origins. *Asian Perspectives* 26:107–17.

Bellwood, P. 1989 Foraging towards farming. *Review of Archaeology* 11/2:14–24.

Bellwood, P. 1991 The Austronesian dispersal and the origins of languages. *Scientific American* 265/1:88–93.

Bellwood, P. 1992 Southeast Asia before history. In N. Tarling ed., *The Cambridge History of Southeast Asia*, vol. I, pp. 55–136. Cambridge: Cambridge University Press.

Bellwood, P. 1993 Cultural and biological differentiation in Peninsular Malaysia: the last 10 000 years. *Asian Perspectives* 32:37–60.

Bellwood, P. 1995 Early agriculture, language history and the archaeological record in China and Southeast Asia. In C-t. Yeung and Brenda Li eds., *Conference Papers on Archaeology in Southeast Asia*, pp. 11–22. University of Hong Kong Museum and Art Gallery.

Bellwood, P. 1996a Early agriculture and the dispersal of the Southern Mongoloids. In T. Akazawa and E. Szathmary eds., *Prehistoric Mongoloid Dispersals*, pp. 287–302. Tokyo: Oxford University Press.

Bellwood, P. 1996b The origins and spread of agriculture in the Indo-Pacific region. In D. Harris ed., *The Origins and Spread of Agriculture and Pastoralism in Eurasia*, pp. 465–98. London: University College Press.

Bellwood, P. 1996c Phylogeny and Reticulation in prehistory. *Antiquity* 70:881–90.

Bellwood, P. 1996d Hierarchy, founder ideology and Austronesian expansion. In J. Fox and C. Sather eds., *Origin, Ancestry and Alliance*, pp. 18–40. Canberra: Department of Anthropology, Comparative Austronesian Project, ANU.

Bellwood, P. 1997a *Prehistory of the Indo-Malaysian Archipelago*. Revised edition. Honolulu: University of Hawaii Press.

Bellwood, P. 1997b Taiwan and the prehistory of the Austronesian-speaking peoples. *Review of Archaeology* 18/2:39–48.

Bellwood, P. 1997c Prehistoric cultural explanations for the existence of widespread language families. In P. McConvell and N. Evans eds., *Archaeology and Linguistics: Aboriginal Australia in Global Perspective*, pp. 123–34. Melbourne: Oxford University Press.

Bellwood, P. 1998a Human dispersals and colonizations in prehistory – the Southeast Asian data and their implications. In K. Omoto and P.V. Tobias eds., *The Origins and Past of Modern Humans – Towards Reconciliation*, pp. 188–205. Singapore: World Scientific.

Bellwood, P. 1998b From Bird's Head to bird's eye view: long term structures and trends in Indo-Pacific Prehistory. In J. Miedema, C. Odé and R. Dam eds., *Perspectives on the Bird's Head of Irian Jaya, Indonesia*, pp. 951–75. Amsterdam: Rodopi.

Bellwood, P. 2000a Some thoughts on understanding the human colonization of the Pacific. *People and Culture in Oceania* 16:5–17.

Bellwood, P. 2000b Formosan prehistory and Austronesian dispersal. In D. Blundell ed., *Austronesian Taiwan*, pp. 337–65. Taipei: SMC Publishing.

Bellwood, P. 2000c The time depth of major language families: an archaeologist's perspective. In C. Renfrew, A. McMahon and L. Trask eds., *Time Depth in Historical Linguistics*, pp. 109–40. Cambridge: McDonald Institute for Archaeological Research.

Bellwood, P. 2001a Archaeology and the historical determinants of punctuation in language family origins. In A. Aikhenvald and R. Dixon, eds., *Areal Diffusion and Genetic Inheritance: Problems in Comparative Linguistics*, pp. 27–43. Oxford: Oxford University Press.

Bellwood, P. 2001b Early agriculturalist population diasporas? Farming, languages and genes. *Annual Review of Anthropology* 30:181–207.

Bellwood, P. 2001c Archaeology and the history of languages. *International Encyclopaedia of the Social and Behavioral Sciences*, Vol. 1, pp. 617–22. Amsterdam: Pergamon.

Bellwood, P. 2001d Cultural evolution: phylogeny versus reticulation. *International Encyclopaedia of the Social and Behavioral Sciences*, Vol. 5, pp. 3052–7. Amsterdam: Pergamon.

Bellwood, P. 2001e Polynesian prehistory and the rest of mankind. In C. Stevenson, G. Lee and F. Morin eds., *Pacific 2000*, pp. 11–25. Los Osos CA: Easter Island Foundation.

Bellwood, P. 2001f Southeast Asia Neolithic and Early Bronze. In P. Peregrine and M. Ember eds., *Encyclopaedia of Prehistory, Vol. 3: East Asia and Oceania*, pp. 287–306.

Bellwood, P. 2003 Farmers, foragers, languages, genes: the genesis of agricultural societies. In P. Bellwood and C. Renfrew eds., *Examining the Farming/Language Dispersal Hypothesis*, pp. 17–28. Cambridge: McDonald Institute for Archaeological Research.

Bellwood, P. in press. Examining the farming/language dispersal hypothesis in the East Asian context. In L. Sagart, R. Blench and A. Sanchez-Mazas eds., *The Peopling of East Asia: Putting Together Archaeology, Linguistics and Genetics*. London: RoutledgeCurzon.

Bellwood, P., Gillespie, R., Thompson, G.B., Vogel, J., Ardika, I.W. and Datan, I. 1992 New dates for prehistoric Asian rice. *Asian Perspectives* 31:161–70.

Bellwood, P. and Hiscock, P. in press. Hunters, farmers and long distance colonizers – Australia, Island Southeast Asia and Oceania during the Holocene. In C. Scarre ed., *The Human Past*. London: Thames and Hudson.

Bellwood, P. and Koon, P. 1989 Lapita colonists leave boats unburned. *Antiquity* 63: 613–22.

Bellwood, P., Nitihaminoto, G. et al. 1998 35,000 years of prehistory in the northern Moluccas. In G. Bartstra ed., *Bird's Head Approaches*, pp. 233–74. Rotterdam: Balkema.

Bellwood, P. and Renfrew, C. eds. 2003 *Examining the Farming/Language Dispersal Hypothesis*. Cambridge: McDonald Institute for Archaeological Research.

Bender, B. 1978 Gatherer-hunter to farmer: a social perspective. *World Archaeology* 10: 204–22.

Bellwood, P., Stevenson, J. et al. 2003 Archaeological and palaeoenvironmental research in Batanes and Ilocos Norte Provinces, Northern Philippines. *Bulletin of the Indo-Pacific Prehistory Association* 23:141–62.

Bender, L. 1982 Livestock and linguistics in north and east African ethnohistory. *Current Anthropology* 23:316–7.

Bendremer, J. and Dewar, R. 1994 The advent of prehistoric maize in New England. In S. Johannessen and C. Hastorf eds., *Corn and Culture in the Prehistoric New World*, pp. 369–94. Boulder: Westview.

Benedict, P. 1975 *Austro-Thai Language and Culture*. New Haven: HRAF Press.

Benjamin, G. 1985 In the long term: three themes in Malayan cultural ecology. In K.L. Hutterer, T. Rambo and G. Lovelace eds., *Cultural Values and Human Ecology in Southeast Asia*, pp. 219–78. Ann Arbor: University of Michigan, Center for S and SE Asian Studies.

Bentley, R., Chikhi, L. and Price, D. 2003 The Neolithic transition in Europe: comparing broad scale genetic and local scale isotopic evidence. *Antiquity* 77:63–6.

Benz, B. 2001 Archaeological evidence of teosinte domestication from Guila Naquitz, Oaxaca. *Proceedings of the National Academy of Sciences* 98:2104–6.

Benz, B. and Iltis, H. 1990 Studies in archaeological maize I. *American Antiquity* 55:500–11.

Benz, B. and Long, A. 2000 Prehistoric maize evolution in the Tehuacan Valley. *Current Anthropology* 41:459–65.

Bernal, I. 1969 *The Olmec World*. Berkeley: University of California Press.

Berreman, G.D. 1999 The Tasaday controversy. In R.B. Lee and R. Daly eds., *The Cambridge Encyclopaedia of Hunters and Gatherers*, pp. 457–64. Cambridge: Cambridge University Press.

Berry, M.S. 1985 The age of maize in the Greater Southwest. In R. Ford ed., *Prehistoric Food Production in North America*, pp. 279–308. University of Michigan, Museum of Anthropology, Anthropological papers 75.

Bettinger, R., Madsen, D. and Elston, R.G. 1994 Prehistoric settlement categories and settlement systems in the Alashan Desert of Inner Mongolia. *Journal of Anthropological Archaeology* 13:74–101.

Bettinger, R.L. and Baumhoff, M.A. 1982 The Numic spread. *American Antiquity* 47:485–503.

Betts, A. 1994 Qermez Dere: the chipped stone assemblage. In H.G. Gebel and S.F. Kozlowski eds., *Neolithic Chipped Stone Industries of the Levant*, pp. 189–204. Berlin: Ex Oriente.

Binford, L. 1968 Post-Pleistocene adaptations. In S.R. and L.R. Binford eds., *New Perspectives in Archaeology*, pp. 313–41. Chicago: Aldine.

Binford, L. 1980 Willow smoke and dogs tails. *American Antiquity* 45:4–20.

Bird, R., Browman, D. and Durbin, M. 1983–4 Quechua and maize: mirrors of central Andean culture history. *Journal of the Steward Anthropological Society* 15(1 and 2): 187–240.

Bird, R.M. 1990 What are the chances of finding maize in Peru dating before 1000 BC? *American Antiquity* 55:828–40.

Bird-David, N. 1990 The giving environment. *Current Anthropology* 31:189–96.

Bird-David, N. 1992 Beyond "the original affluent society": a culturalist reformulation. *Current Anthropology* 33: 25–48.

Birdsell, J.B. 1957 Some population problems involving Pleistocene man. *Cold Spring Harbour Symposia on Quantitative Biology* 22: 47–69.

Blackburn, R. 1982 In the land of milk and honey: Okiek adaptations to their forests and neighbours. In E. Leacock and R.B. Lee eds., *Politics and History in Band Societies*, pp. 283–305. Cambridge: Cambridge University Press.

Blazek, V. 1999 Elam: a bridge between Ancient Near East and Dravidian India? In R. Blench and M. Spriggs eds., *Archaeology and Language IV*, pp. 48–78. London: Routledge.

Blench, R. 1993 Recent developments in African language classification and their implications for prehistory. In T. Shaw et al. eds., *The Archaeology of Africa*, pp. 126–38. London: Routledge.

Blench, R. 1999 The languages of Africa. In R. Blench and M. Spriggs eds., *Archaeology and Language IV*, pp. 29–47. London: Routledge.

Blench, R. 2003 The movement of cultivated plants between Africa and India in prehistory. In K. Neumann, A. Butler and S. Kahlheber eds., *Food, Fuel and Fields: Progress in African Archaeobotany*, pp. 273–99. Köln: Heinrich-Barth-Institute.

Blumler, M. 1998 Introgression of durum into wild emmer and the agricultural origin question. In A. Damania, J. Valkoun, G. Willcox and C. Qualset eds., *The Origins of Agriculture and Crop Domestication*, pp. 252–68. Aleppo: ICARDA.

Blurton-Jones, N. 1986 Bushman birth spacing: a test for optimal interbirth intervals. *Ecology and Sociobiology* 7:91–105.

Blust, R. 1989 Comment (on Headland and Reid 1989). *Current Anthropology* 30: 53–4.

Blust, R. 1991 Sound change and migrational distance. In R. Blust ed., *Current Trends in Pacific Linguistics*, pp. 27–42. Canberra: Pacific Linguistics C-117.

Blust, R. 1993 Central and Central-Eastern Malayo-Polynesian. *Oceanic Linguistics* 32: 241–93.

Blust, R. 1995a The prehistory of the Austronesian-speaking peoples: a view from language. *Journal of World Prehistory* 9: 453–510.

Blust, R. 1995b The position of the Formosan languages. In P.J-K. Li, D-A. Ho, Y-K. Huang, C-W. Tsang and C-Y. Tseng eds., *Austronesian Studies Relating to Taiwan*, pp. 585–650. Taipei: Academia Sinica, Institute of History and Philology, Symposium Series 3.

Blust, R. 1996 Beyond the Austronesian homeland: the Austric hypothesis and its implication for archaeology. In W. Goodenough ed., *Prehistoric Settlement of the Pacific*, pp. 117–40. Philadelphia: American Philosophical Society.

Blust, R. 1999 Subgrouping, circularity and extinction. In E. Zeitoun and P. J-K. Li eds., *Selected papers from the Eighth International Conference on Austronesian Linguistics*, pp. 31–94. Taipei: Academia Sinica, Institute of Linguistics.

Blust, R. 2000a Chamorro historical phonology. *Oceanic Linguistics* 39/1: 83–122.

Blust, R. 2000b Why lexicostatistics doesn't work. In C. Renfrew, A. McMahon and L. Trask eds., *Time Depth in Historical Linguistics*, pp. 311–32. Cambridge: McDonald Institute for Archaeological Research.

Bocquet-Appel, J-P. 2002 Palaeoanthropological traces of a Neolithic demographic transition. *Current Anthropology* 43:637–50.

Bogucki, P. 1987 The establishment of agrarian communities on the North European Plain. *Current Anthropology* 28:1–24.

Bogucki, P. 1988 *Forest Farmers and Stockherders*. Cambridge: Cambridge University Press.

Bogucki, P. 1996a Sustainable and unsustainable adaptations by early farming communities of central Poland. *Journal of Anthropological Archaeology* 15:289–311.

Bogucki, P. 1996b The spread of early farming in Europe. *American Scientist* 84:242–53.

Bogucki, P. and Grygiel, R. 1993 The first farmers of central Europe. *Journal of Field Archaeology* 20:399–426.

Bohrer, V.L. 1994 Maize in Middle American and Southwestern United States agricultural traditions. In S. Johannesen and C. Hastorf eds., *Corn and Culture in the Prehistoric New World*, pp. 469–512. Boulder: Westview.

Bomhard, A. 1990 A survey of the comparative phonology of the so-called "Nostratic" languages. In P. Baldi ed., *Linguistic Change and Reconstruction Methodology*, pp. 331–58. Berlin: Mouton de Gruyter.

Bomhard, A. 1996 *Indo-European and the Nostratic Hypothesis*. Charleston: Signum.

Bomhard, A. and Kerns, J. 1994 *The Nostratic Macrofamily*. Berlin: Mouton de Gruyter.

Bonavia, D. 1999 The domestication of Andean camelids. In G. Politis and B. Alberti eds., *Archaeology in Latin America*, pp. 130–47. London: Routledge.

Bonavia, D. and Grobman, A. 1989 Andean maize: its origins and domestication. In D. Harris and G. Hillman eds., *Foraging and Farming*, pp. 456–70. London: Unwin Hyman.

Bonsall, C. et al. 1997 Mesolithic and Neolithic in the Iron Gates: a palaeodietary perspective. *Journal of European Archaeology* 5:50–92.

Borrie, W.D. 1994 *The European Peopling of Australasia*. Canberra: Demographic Program RSSS, Australian National University.

Boserup, E. 1965 *The Conditions of Agricultural Growth*. Chicago: Aldine.

Bottema, S. 1995 The Younger Dryas in the Eastern Mediterranean. *Quaternary Science Reviews* 14:883–91.

Bousman, C.B. 1998 The chronological evidence for the introduction of domesticated stock into southern Africa. *African Archaeological Review* 15:133–50.

Bower, J. 1991 The Pastoral Neolithic of East Africa. *Journal of World Prehistory* 5:49–82.

Bradley, D. and Loftus, R. 2000 Two eves for *Taurus*? Bovine mitochondrial DNA and African cattle domestication. In R. Blench and K. MacDonald eds., *The Origins and Development of African Livestock*, pp. 244–50. London: UCL Press.

Bradley, D.G., MacHugh, D., Cunningham, P. and Loftus, R. 1996 Mitochondrial diversity and the origins of African and European cattle. *Proceedings of the National Academy of Sciences* 93:5131–5.

Bradley, R. 2001 Orientations and origins: a symbolic dimension to the long house in Neolithic Europe. *Antiquity* 75:50–5.

Braidwood, R. 1960. The agricultural revolution. *Scientific American* 203:130–48.

Breton, R. 1997 *Atlas of the Languages and Ethnic Communities of South Asia*. Walnut Creek: Altamira.

Broodbank, C. 1999 Colonization and configuration in the insular neolithic of the Aegean. In P. Halstead ed., *Neolithic Society in Greece*, pp. 15–41. Sheffield: Sheffield Academic Press.

Broodbank, C. and Strasser, T.F. 1991 Migrant farmers and the Neolithic colonization of Crete. *Antiquity* 65:233–45.

Brookfield, H. 1989 Frost and drought through time and space. *Mountain Research and Development* 9: 306–21.

Brose, D.S., Brown, J.A. and Penney, D.W. 1985 *Ancient Art of the American Woodland Indians*. New York: Abrams.

Brosius, P. 1990 *After Duwagan*. Ann Arbor: University of Michigan, Center for S and SE Asian Studies.

Brosius, P. 1991 Foraging in tropical rain forests: the case of the Penan of Sarawak. *Human Ecology* 19:123–50.

Brosnahan, L. 1963 Some historical cases of language imposition. In J. Spencer ed., *Language in Africa*, pp. 7–24. Cambridge: Cambridge University Press.

Brown, I.W. 1994 Recent trends in the archaeology of the Southeastern USA. *Journal of Archaeological Research* 2:45–112.

Brown, P. 1998 The first Mongoloids? *Acta Anthropologica Sinica* 17:260–75.

Brown, P. 1999 The first modern East Asians? In K. Omoto ed., *Interdisciplinary Perspectives on the Origins of the Japanese*, pp. 105–26. Kyoto: International Research Center for Japanese Studies.

Brunhes, K. 1994 *Ancient South America*. Cambridge: Cambridge University Press.

Buckler, E., Pearsall, D. and Holtsford, T. 1998 Climate, plant ecology, and Central American Archaic plant subsistence. *Current Anthropology* 39:152–64.

Buikstra, J.E., Konigsberg, L. and Bullington, J. 1986 Fertility and the development of agriculture in the prehistoric Midwest. *American Antiquity* 51:528–46.

Bulbeck, D. 2003 Hunter-gatherer occupation of the Malay Peninsula from the Ice Age to the Iron Age. In J. Mercader ed., *Under the Canopy*, pp. 119–60. New Brunswick: Rutgers University Press.

Bulbeck, D. 2004 Indigenous traditions and exogenous influences in the early history of Peninsular Malaysia. In I. Glover and P. Bellwood eds., *Southeast Asia: From Prehistory to History*, pp. 314–36. London: RoutledgeCurzon.

Burger, R. 1992 *Chavin and the Origins of Andean Civilization*. London: Thames and Hudson.

Burger, R. and van der Merwe, N. 1990 Maize and the origin of highland Chavin civilization. *American Anthropologist* 92:85–95.

Buth, G. and Kaw, R. 1985 Plant husbandry in Neolithic Burzahom, Kashmir. *Current Trends in Geology* VI, pp. 109–13. New Delhi: Today and Tomorrow's Printers and Publishers.

Butler, V. 2000 Resource depression on the Northwest Coast of North America. *Antiquity* 74:649–61.

Butzer, K. 1995 Environmental change in the Near East and human impact on the land. In J. Sasson ed., *Civilizations of the Ancient Near East*, vol. 1, pp. 123–51. New York: Scribner's Sons.

Byers, D.S. ed. 1967 *The Prehistory of the Tehuacan Valley, Vol. 1: Environment and Subsistence*. Austin: University of Texas Press.

Byrd, B. 1989 Natufian settlement variability and economic adaptations. *Journal of World Prehistory* 3:159–98.

Byrd, B. and Monahan, C. 1995 Death, mortuary ritual, and Natufian social structure. *Journal of Anthropological Archaeology* 14:251–87.

Byrd, K.M. ed. 1991 *The Poverty Point Culture*. Geoscience and Man Vol. 29. Baton Rouge: Louisiana State University.

Byrne, R. 1987 Climate Change and the Origins of Agriculture. In L. Manzanilla ed., *Studies in the Neolithic and Urban Revolutions*, pp. 21–34. Oxford: BAR. International Series 349.

Callaghan, R.A. 2001 Ceramic age seafaring and interaction potential in the Amtilles: a computer simulation. *Current Anthropology* 42:308–13.

Campbell, L. 1997 *American Indian Languages*. New York: Oxford University Press.

Campbell, L. 1999 Nostratic and linguistic palaeontology in methodological perspective. In C. Renfrew and D. Nettle eds., *Nostratic: Examining a Language Macrofamily*, pp. 179–230. Cambridge: McDonald Institute for Archaeological Research.

Campbell, L. and Kaufman, T. 1976 A linguistic look at the Olmecs. *American Antiquity* 41:80–9.

Cane, S. 1989 Australian Aboriginal seed grinding and its archaeological record. In D. Harris and G. Hillman eds., *Foraging and Farming*, pp. 99–119. London: Unwin Hyman.

Capdevila, R.B. 1992 Quelques aspects des restes paléobotaniques prélevés sur la terrasse de Hayonim. In P.C. Anderson ed., *Préhistoire de l'Agriculture*, pp. 225–30. Paris: CNRS (Monographie du CRA 6).

Capell, A. 1969 *A Survey of New Guinea Languages*. Sydney: Sydney University Press.

Capelli, C., Wilson, J.F. et al. 2001 A predominantly indigenous paternal heritage for the Austronesian-speaking peoples of Insular Southeast Asia and Oceania. *American Journal of Human Genetics* 68:432–43.

Carneiro, R. 1970 A theory of the origin of the state. *Science* 169:733–8.

Cappers, R. and Bottema, S. eds. 2002 *The Dawn of Farming in the Near East*. Berlin: Ex Oriente.

Carpenter, J., Mabry, J. and Sanchez de Carpenter, G. 2002 O'Odham origins: reconstructing Uto-Aztecan prehistory. Paper presented at Annual Meeting of the Society for American Archaeology, Denver.

Carpenter, J., Sanchez de Carpenter, G. and Villalpando, E. 1999 Preliminary investigations at La Playa, Sonora, Mexico. *Archaeology Southwest* 13(1):6.

Casey, J. 1998 The ecology of food production in West Africa. In G. Connah ed., *Transformations in Africa*, pp. 46–70. London: Leicester University Press.

Casey, J. 2000 *The Kintampo Complex*. Oxford: BAR International Series 906.

Cauvin, J. 1988 La néolithisation de la Turquie du Sud-Est dans sa contexte proche-oriental. *Anatolica* 15:69–80.

Cauvin, J. 1993 La séquence néolithique PPNB au Levant Nord. *Paléorient* 19(1):23–28.

Cauvin, J. 2000 *The Birth of the Gods and the Origins of Agriculture*. Cambridge: Cambridge University Press.

Cauvin, J., Hodder, I., Rollefson, G., Bar-Yosef, O. and Watkins, T. 2001 The birth of the gods and the origins of agriculture. *Cambridge Archaeological Journal* 11:105–22.

Cavalli-Sforza, L.L. 2003 Demic diffusion as the basic process of human expansions. In P. Bellwood and C. Renfrew eds., *Examining the Farming/Language Dispersal Hypothesis*, pp. 79–88. Cambridge: McDonald Institute for Archaeological Research.

Cavalli-Sforza, L.L. and Cavalli-Sforza, F.C. 1995 *The Great Human Diasporas*. Reading, MA: Addison-Wesley.

Cavalli-Sforza, L. and Feldman, M. 2003 The application of molecular genetic approaches to the study of human evolution. *Nature Genetics Supplement* 33:266–75.

Cavalli-Sforza, L.L., Menozzi, P. and Piazza, A. 1994 *The History and Geography of Human Genes*. Princeton: Princeton University Press.

Cavalli-Sforza, L. and Minch, E. 1997 Palaeolithic and Neolithic lineages in the European mitochondrial gene pool. *American Journal of Human Genetics* 61:247–51.

Cavalli-Sforza, L., Piazza, A. et al. 1988 Reconstruction of human evolution: bringing together genetic, archaeological and linguistic data. *Proceedings of the National Academy of Sciences* 85:6002–6.

Cessford, C. 2001 A new dating sequence for Çatalhöyük. *Antiquity* 75:717–25.

Chagnon, A. 1992 *Yanomamö*. Fort Worth: Harcourt Brace Jovanovich.

Chakrabarti, D. 1999 *India: An Archaeological History*. New Delhi: Oxford University Press.

Chami, F. and Msemwa, P. 1997 A new look at culture and trade on the Azanian coast. *Current Anthropology* 38:673–7.

Chang, C. 1982 Nomads without cattle: East African foragers in historical perspective. In E. Leacock and R.B. Lee eds., *Politics and History in Band Societies*, pp. 269–82. Cambridge: Cambridge University Press.

Chang, C. and Tourtelotte, P. 1998 The role of agro-pastoralism in the evolution of steppe culture in the Semirechye area of southern Kazakhstan. In V. Mair ed., *The Bronze Age and Early Iron Age Peoples of Eastern Central Asia*, pp. 238–63. Washington: Institute for the Study of Man.

Chang, K.C. 1981 The affluent foragers in the coastal areas of China. *Senri Ethnological Studies* 9:177–86.

Chang, K.C. 1986 *The Archaeology of Ancient China*. 4th edn. New Haven: Yale University Press (Previous editions 1963, 1968, 1977).

Chang, K.C. 1995 Taiwan Strait archaeology and the Protoaustronesians. In P.J-K. Li, D-A. Ho, Y-K. Huang, C-W. Tsang and C-Y. Tseng eds., *Austronesian Studies Relating to Taiwan* pp. 161–84. Taipei: Academia Sinica, Institute of History and Philology, Symposium Series 3.

Chang, K.C. and Goodenough, W. 1996 Archaeology of southern China and its bearing on the Austronesian homeland. In W. Goodenough ed., *Prehistoric Settlement of the Pacific*, pp. 36–56. Philadelphia: American Philosophical Society.

Chang, T-T. 1976 The rice cultures. *Philosophical Transactions of the Royal Society of London: Series B* 275:143–55.

Chappell, J. 2001 Climate before agriculture. In A. Anderson, I. Lilley and S. O'Connor eds., *Histories of Old Ages*, pp. 171–84. Canberra: Pandanus.

Chase, A. 1989 Domestication and domiculture in northern Australia: a social perspective. In D. Harris and G. Hillman eds., *Foraging and Farming*, pp. 42–54. London: Unwin Hyman.

Chau Hing-wah ed. 1993 *Collected Essays on the Culture of the Ancient Yue People in South China*. Hong Kong: Urban Council.

Chen Chi-lu 1987 *People and Culture*. Taipei: Southern Materials Center.

Chen Dezhen and Zhang Juzhong 1998 The physical characteristics of the Early Neolithic human in Jiahu site. *Acta Anthropologica Sinica* 17:205–11.

Chen Xingcan 1996 Xiantouling Dune Site. *Bulletin of the Indo-Pacific Prehistory Association* 15:207–10.

Chen Xingcan 1999 On the earliest evidence for rice cultivation in China. *Bulletin of the Indo-Pacific Prehistory Association* 18:81–94.

Chia, S. 1998 Prehistoric Pottery Sources and Technology in Peninsular Malaysia. *Federation Museums Journal* 33.

Chikhi, L., Destro-Bisol, G. et al. 1998a Clinal variation in the nuclear DNA of Europeans. *Human Biology* 70: 643–57.

Chikhi, L., Destro-Bisol, G. et al. 1998b Clines of nuclear DNA markers suggest a largely Neolithic ancestry of the European gene pool. *Proceedings of the National Academy of Sciences* 95:9053–8.

Chikhi, L., Nichols, R. et al. 2002 Y genetic data support the Neolithic demic diffusion model. *Proceedings of the National Academy of Sciences* 99:11008–13.

Childe, V. 1926 *The Aryans: A Study of Indo-European Origins*. London: Paul, Trench, Trubner.

Childe, V.G. 1928 *The Most Ancient East*. London: Kegan Paul, Trench, Trubner.

Childe, V.G. 1936/1956 *Man Makes Himself*. London: Watts.

Chowning, A. 1985 Rapid lexical change and aberrant Melanesian languages. In A. Pawley and L. Carrington eds., *Austronesian Linguistics at the 15th Pacific Science Congress*, pp. 169–98. Canberra: Pacific Linguistics C-88.

Christensen, A.F. 1998 Colonization and microevolution in Formative Oaxaca, Mexico. *World Archaeology* 30:262–85.

Clackson, J. 2000 Time depth in Indo-European. In C. Renfrew, A. McMahon and L. Trask eds., *Time Depth in Historical Linguistics*, pp. 441–54. Cambridge: McDonald Institute for Archaeological Research.

Clark, J.D. and Khanna, G.S. 1989 The site of Kunjhun II. M. Kenoyer ed., *Old Problems and New Perspectives in the Archaeology of South Asia*, pp. 29–46. Madison: Dept Anthropology, University of Wisconsin.

Clark, J.E. 1991 The beginnings of Mesoamerica. In W.R. Fowler ed., *The Formation of Complex Society in Southeastern Mesoamerica*, pp. 13–26. Boca Raton: CRC Press.

Clark, J.E. and Pye, M. eds. 2000 *Olmec Art and Archaeology in Mesoamerica*. Washington DC: National Gallery of Art.

Clason, A.T. 1977 *Wild and Domestic Animals in Prehistoric and Early Historic India*. Lucknow: The Eastern Anthropologist Vol. 30, No. 3.

Clermont, N. 1996 The origin of the Iroquoians. *The Review of Archaeology* 17/1:59–64.

Close, A. 1995 Few and far between: early ceramics in North Africa. In W.K. Barnett and J.W. Hoopes eds., *The Emergence of Pottery*, pp. 23–37. Washington: Smithsonian.

Close, A. 1996 *Plus ça change*: the Pleistocene–Holocene transition in northeast Africa. In L.G. Strauss, B.V. Eriksen, J.M. Erlandsen and D. Yesner eds., *Humans at the End of the Ice Age*, pp. 43–60. New York: Plenum.

Coe, M. 1989 The Olmec Heartland: evolution of ideology. In R.J. Sharer and D.C. Grove eds., *Regional Perspectives on the Olmec*, pp. 68–84. Cambridge: Cambridge University Press.

Coe, M., Snow, D. and Benson, E. 1989 *Atlas of Ancient America*. New York: Facts on File.

Cohen, D. 1998 The origins of domesticated cereals and the Pleistocene–Holocene transition in China. *Review of Archaeology* 19/2:22–9.

Cohen, D.J. 2003 Microblades, pottery, and the nature and chronology of the Palaeolithic-Neolithic transition in China. *Review of Archaeology* 24/2:21–36.

Cohen, M.N. 1977a *The Food Crisis in Prehistory*. New Haven: Yale University Press.

Cohen, M.N. 1977b Population pressure and the origins of agriculture: an archaeological example from the coast of Peru. In C.A. Reed ed., *Origins of Agriculture*, pp. 135–78. The Hague: Mouton.

Cohen, M.N. 1980 Speculations on the evolution of density measurement and regulation in *Homo sapiens*. In M.N. Cohen, R.S. Malpass and H.G. Klein eds., *Biosocial Mechanisms of Population Regulation*, pp. 275–304. New Haven: Yale University Press.

Coleman, R. 1988 Comment. *Current Anthropology* 29:449–53.

Collard, M. and Shennan, S. 2000 Processes of culture change in prehistory: a case study from the European Neolithic. In C. Renfrew and K. Boyle eds., *Archaeogenetics*, pp. 89–97. Cambridge: McDonald Institute for Archaeological Research.

Colledge, S. 2001 *Plant Exploitation on Epipalaeolithic and Early Neolithic Sites in the Levant.* Oxford: BAR International Series 986.

Colledge, S., Conolly, J. and Shennan, S. 2004 Archaeobotanical evidence for the spread of farming in the Eastern Mediterranean. *Current Anthropology* 45.

Collett, D.P. 1982 Models of the spread of the Early Iron Age. In C. Ehret and M. Posnansky eds., *The Archaeological and Linguistic Reconstruction of African History*, pp. 182–98. Berkeley: University of California Press.

Comrie, B. 2003 Farming dispersal in Europe and the spread of the Indo-European language family. In P. Bellwood and C. Renfrew eds., *Examining the Language/Farming Dispersal Hypothesis*, pp. 409–20. Cambridge: McDonald Institute for Archaeological Research.

Coningham, R. 2002 Deciphering the Indus script. In S. Settar and R. Korisettar eds., *Indian Archaeology in Retrospect*, vol. 2, pp. 81–103. New Delhi: Manohar.

Cooper, R. 1982 A framework for the study of language spread. In R. Cooper ed., *Language Spread*, pp. 5–36. Bloomington: Indiana University Press.

Cooper, Z. 1996 Archaeological evidence of maritime contacts: the Andaman Islands. In H.P. Ray and J-F. Salles eds., *Tradition and Archaeology*, pp. 239–46. New Delhi: Manohar.

Cordell, L. 1997 *Archaeology of the Southwest.* 2nd edn. San Diego: Academic.

Cordell, L. and Smith, B. 1996 Indigenous farmers. In B.G. Trigger and W.E. Washburn eds., *The Cambridge History of the Native Peoples of the Americas, Vol. 1, North America, Part 1*, pp. 201–66. Cambridge: Cambridge University Press.

Costantini, L. 1981 The beginning of agriculture in the Kachi Plain: the evidence of Mehrgarh. In B. Allchin ed., *South Asian Archaeology 1981*, pp. 29–33. Cambridge: Cambridge University Press.

Cowgill, G.L. 1975 On causes of ancient and modern population changes. *American Anthropologist* 77: 505–25.

Cox, M. 2003 *Genetic Patterning at Austronesian Contact Zones.* Unpublished PhD thesis, University of Otago, Dunedin, New Zealand.

Cox, M. 2004 Biogeographical boundaries? Re-establishing "Melanesia" in biological history. *Manuscript.*

Crawford, G. and Chen Shen 1998 The origins of rice agriculture: recent progress in East Asia. *Antiquity* 72:858–66.

Crawford, G. and Lee, G. 2003 Agricultural origins in the Korean Peninsula. *Antiquity* 77:87–95.

Cremaschi, M. and di Lernia, S. 2001 Environment and settlements in the mid-Holocene palaeo-oasis of Wadi Tanezzuft (Libyan Sahara). *Antiquity* 75:815–24.

Crosby, A.W. 1986 *Ecological Imperialism.* Cambridge: Cambridge University Press.

D'Andrea, C. 1999 The dispersal of domesticated plants into north-eastern Japan. In C. Gosden and J. Hather eds., *The Prehistory of Food*, pp. 166–83. London: Routledge.

D'Andrea, C. and Casey, J. 2002 Pearl millet and Kintampo subsistence. *African Archaeological Review* 19:147–74.

D'Andrea, C., Klee, M. and Casey, J. 2001 Archaeobotanical evidence for pearl millet (*Pennisetum glaucum*) in sub-Saharan West Africa. *Antiquity* 75:341–8.

D'Andrea, C., Lyons, D. et al. 1999 Ethnoarchaeological approaches to the study of prehistoric agriculture in the Highlands of Ethiopia. In M. van der Veen ed., *The Exploitation of Plant Resources in Ancient Africa*, pp. 101–22. New York: Kluwer Academic.

Dahlberg, J.A. and Wasylikowa, K. 1996 Image and statistical analyses of early sorghum remains (8000 BP) from the Nabta Playa archaeological site. *Vegetation History and Archaeobotany* 5:293–9.

Dahlin, B., Quizar, R. and Dahlin, A. 1987 Linguistic divergence and the collapse of preclassic civilization in southern Mesoamerica. *American Antiquity* 52:367–82.

Dakin, K. and Wichmann, S. 2000 Cacao and chocolate: a Uto-Aztecan perspective. *Ancient Mesoamerica* 11:55–75.

Damp, J.E. 1984 Architecture of the Early Valdivia village. *American Antiquity* 49:573–85.

Dark, P. and Gent, H. 2001 Pests and diseases of prehistoric crops: a yield 'honeymoon' for early grain crops in Europe? *Oxford Journal of Archaeology* 20:59–78.

David, N. 1982 Prehistoric and historical linguistics in central Africa: points of contact. In C. Ehret and M. Posnansky eds., *The Archaeological and Linguistic Reconstruction of African History*, pp. 78–95. Berkeley: University of California Press.

Deavaraj, D. et al. 1995 The Watgal excavations: an interim report. *Man and Environment* XX(2):57–74.

Demoule, J-P. 1993 Anatolie et Balkans: la logique évolutive du Néolithique égéen. *Anatolica* 19:1–18.

Demoule, J-P. and Perlès, C. 1993 The Greek Neolithic: a new review. *Journal of World Prehistory* 7:355–416.

Denbow, J. 1990 Congo to Kalahari. *African Archaeological Review* 8:139–76.

Denham, T. 2003 Archaeological evidence for mid-Holocene agriculture in the interior of Papua New Guinea: a critical review. *Archaeology in Oceania* 38:159–76.

Denham, T., Haberle, S. et al. 2003 Origins of agriculture at Kuk Swamp in the Highlands of New Guinea. *Science* 301:189–93.

Dennell, R. 1992 The origins of crop agriculture in Europe. In C.W. Cowan and P.J. Watson eds., *The Origins of Agriculture*, pp. 71–100. Washington: Smithsonian.

Dentan, R.K., Endicott, K., Gomes, A.G. and Hooker M.B. 1997 *Malaysia and the Original People*. Boston: Allyn and Bacon.

Deraniyagala, S.U. 2001 Man before Vijaya in Sri Lanka. In L. Prematilleke ed., *Men and Monuments*, pp. 54–62. Sri Lanka: Central Cultural Fund.

Dergachev, V. 1989 Neolithic and Bronze Age cultural communities of the steppe zone of the USSR. *Antiquity* 63:793–802.

Dewar, R. 2003 Rainfall variability and subsistence systems in Southeast Asia and the western Pacific. *Current Anthropology* 44:369–88.

Dhavalikar, M. 1988 *The First Farmers of the Deccan*. Pune: Ravish.

Dhavalikar, M. 1994 Early farming communities of central India. *Man and Environment* XIX:159–68.

Dhavalikar, M. 1997 *Indian Protohistory*. New Delhi: Books & Books.

Dhavalikar, M., Sankalia, H.D. and Ansari, Z. 1988 *Excavations at Inamgaon*. 2 vols. Pune: Deccan College.

Dhavalikhar, M.K. and Possehl, G. 1992 The Pre-Harappan Phase at Prabhas Patan. *Man and Environment* XVII/1:71–8.

Di Piazza, A. and Pearthree, E. 2001 Voyaging and basalt exchange in the Phoenix and Line Archipelagoes. *Archaeology in Oceania* 36:146–52.

Diakonoff, I. 1998 The earliest Semitic society. *Journal of Semitic Studies* 43/2:209–19.

Diakonov, I. 1985 On the original home of the speakers of Indo-European. *Journal of Indo-European Studies* 13:92–174.

Diamond, J. 1988 Express train to Polynesia. *Nature* 336:307–8.

Diamond, J. 1994 Spacious skies and tilted axes. *Natural History* 1994, part 5:16–22.

Diamond, J. 1997 *Guns, Germs and Steel*. London: Jonathan Cape.

Diamond, J. 2002 Evolution, consequences and future of plant and animal domestication. *Nature* 418:34–41.

Diamond, J. and Bellwood, P. 2003 Farmers and their languages: the first expansions. *Science* 300:597–603.

Dickson, D.B. 1989 Out of Utopia. *Journal of Mediterranean Archaeology* 2:297–302.

Dikshit, K.N. 2000 A review of Palaeolithic culture in India with special reference to the Neolithic culture of Kashmir. *Man and Environment* XXV/2:1–6.

Dillehay, T.D., Rossen, J. and Netherly, P. 1997 The Nanchoc Tradition: the beginnings of Andean civilization. *American Scientist* 85:46–55.

Dimmendaal, G. 1995 Do some languages have a multi-genetic or non-genetic origin? In R. Nicolai and F. Rottland eds., *Cinquième Colloque de Linguistique Nilo-Saharienne*, pp. 358–92. Köln: Köppe.

Dixon, R. 1997 *The Rise and Fall of Languages*. Cambridge: Cambridge University Press.

Dixon, R. and Aikhenvald, A. 1999 Introduction. In R. Dixon and A. Aikhenvald eds., *Amazonian Languages*, pp. 1–22. Cambridge: Cambridge University Press.

Doherty, C., Beavitt, P. and Kurui, E. 2000 Recent observations of rice temper in pottery from Niah and other sites in Sarawak. *Bulletin of the Indo-Pacific Prehistory Association* 20: 147–52.

Dolgopolsky, A. 1987 The Indo-European homeland and lexical contacts of Proto-Indo-European with other languages. *Mediterranean Language Review* 3:7–31.

Dolgopolsky, A. 1993 More about the Indo-European homeland problem. *Mediterranean Language Review* 6:230–48.

Dolgopolsky, A. 1998 *The Nostratic macrofamily and Linguistic Palaeontology*. Cambridge: McDonald Institute for Archaeological Research.

Dollfus, G. 1989 Les processus de néolithisation en Iran – bilan des connaissances. In O. Aurenche and J. Cauvin eds., *Néolithisations*, pp. 37–65. Oxford: BAR International Series 516.

Domett, K. 2001 *Health in Late Prehistoric Thailand*. Oxford: BAR International Series 946.

Donahue, R., Burroni, D., Coles, G., Colten, R. and Hunt, C. 1992 Petriolo III South. *Current Anthropology* 33:328–32.

Drews, R. ed. 2001 *Greater Anatolia and the Indo-Hittite Language Family*. Washington DC: Institute for the Study of Man.

Driem, G. van 1999 A new theory on the origin of Chinese. *Bulletin of the Indo-Pacific Prehistory Association* 18:43–58.

Driem, G. van 2003 Tibeto-Burman phylogeny and prehistory: languages, material culture and genes. In P. Bellwood and C. Renfrew eds., *Examining the Language/Farming Dispersal Hypothesis*, pp. 233–50. Cambridge: McDonald Institute for Archaeological Research.

DuFresne, A. et al. 1998 A preliminary analysis of microblades, blade cores and lunates from Watgal. *Man and Environment* XXIII/2:17–44.

Dunn, F.L. 1975 *Rain-Forest Collectors and Traders*. Monographs of the Malaysian Branch of the Royal Asiatic Society No. 5.

Dutton, T. 1994 Motu-Koiari contact in Papua New Guinea. In T. Dutton and D. Tryon eds., *Language Contact and Change in the Austroneaian World*, pp. 181–232. Berlin: Mouton de Gruyter.

Dutton, T. 1995 Language contact and change in Melanesia. In P. Bellwood, J. Fox and D. Tryon eds., *The Austronesians*, pp. 192–213. Canberra: Dept Anthropology, Research School of Pacific Studies, Australian National University.

Dutton, T. and Tryon, D. eds. 1994 *Language Contact and Change in the Austronesian World*. Berlin: Mouton de Gruyter.

Dye, T. and Komori, E. 1992 A pre-censal population history of Hawai'i. *New Zealand Journal of Archaeology* 14:113–28.

Dyen, I. 1965 *A Lexicostatistical Classification of the Austronesian Languages*. International Journal of American Linguistics Memoir 19.

Early, J. and Headland, T. 1998 *Population Dynamics of a Philippine Rainforest People*. Gainesville: University of Florida Press.

Edens, C. and Wilkinson, T. 1998 Southwest Arabia during the Holocene. *Journal of World Prehistory* 12:55–119.

Eder, J. 1987 *On the Road to Tribal Extinction*. Berkeley: University of California Press.

Edwards, P. 1989 Problems of recognizing earliest sedentism: the Natufian example. *Journal of Mediterranean Archaeology* 2:5–48.

Edwards, P. 1991 Wadi Hammeh 27. In O. Bar-Yosef and F.R. Valla eds., *The Natufian Culture in the Levant*, pp. 123–48. Ann Arbor: International Monographs in Prehistory.

Edwards, P. and Higham, C. 2001 Zahrat adh-Dhra' 2 and the Dead Sea Plain at the dawn of the Holocene. In A. Walmsley ed., *Australians Uncovering Ancient Jordan*, pp. 139–52. Sydney: Research Institute for Humanities and Social Sciences, University of Sydney.

Egerod, S. 1991 Far Eastern languages. In S. Lamb and E. Mitchell eds., *Sprung from Some Common Source*, pp. 205–31. Stanford: Stanford University Press.

Eggert, M. 1993 Central Africa and the archaeology of the equatorial rainforest. In T. Shaw, P. Sinclair, B. Andah and A. Okpoko eds., *The Archaeology of Africa*, pp. 289–329. London: Routledge.

Eggert, M. 1996 Pots, farming and analogy: early ceramics in the equatorial rainforest. *Azania* Special Volume XXIX–XXX:332–8.

Ehret, C. 1979 On the antiquity of agriculture in Ethiopia. *Journal of African History* 20:161–77.

Ehret, C. 1993 Nilo-Saharans and the Saharo-Sudanese Neolithic. In T. Shaw, P. Sinclair, B. Andah and A. Okpoko eds., *The Archaeology of Africa*, pp. 104–25. London: Routledge.

Ehret, C. 1995 *Reconstructing Proto-Afroasiatic*. Berkeley: University of California Press.

Ehret, C. 1997 African languages: a historical survey. In J. Vogel ed., *Encyclopaedia of Precolonial Africa*, pp. 159–66. Walnut Creek: Sage.

Ehret, C. 1998 *An African Classical Age*. Charlottesville: University Press of Virginia.

Ehret, C. 2000 Testing the expectations of glottochronology against the correlations of language and archaeology in Africa. In C. Renfrew, A. McMahon and L. Trask eds., *Time Depth in Historical Linguistics*, pp. 373–400. Cambridge: McDonald Institute for Archaeological Research.

Ehret, C. 2003 language family expansions: broadening our understandings of cause from an African perspective. In P. Bellwood and C. Renfrew eds., *Examining the Farming/Language Dispersal Hypothesis*, pp. 163–76. Cambridge: McDonald Institute for Archaeological Research.

Ehret, C. and Posnansky, M. eds. 1982 *The Archaeological and Linguistic Reconstruction of African History*. Berkeley: University of California Press.

Ellis, F.H. 1968 What Utaztecan ethnography suggests of Utaztecan prehistory. In E.H. Swanson ed., *Utaztecan Prehistory*, pp. 53–105. Pocatello: Museum of Idaho University, Occasional Papers 22.

Endicott, K. 1997 Batek history, interethnic relations, and subgroup dynamics. In R.L. Winzeler ed., *Indigenous Peoples and the State*, pp. 30–50. New Haven: Yale University Southeast Asia Studies Monograph 46.

Endicott, K. and Bellwood, P. 1991 The possibility of independent foraging in the rain forest of Peninsular Malaysia. *Human Ecology* 19:151–87.

Erdosy, G. 1989 Ethnicity and the Rigveda. *South Asian Studies* 5:35–47.

Erdosy, G. 1995 Language, material culture and ethnicity. In G. Erdosy ed., *The Indo-Aryans of Ancient South Asia*, pp. 1–31. Berlin: Walter de Gruyter.

Errington, J. 1998 Shifting Languages. Cambridge: Cambridge University Press.

Evans, L. 1993 *Crop Evolution, Adaptation and Yield*. Cambridge: Cambridge University Press.

Excoffier, L., Pellegrini, B. et al. 1987 Genetics and history of Sub-Saharan Africa. *Yearbook of Physical Anthropology* 30:151–94.

Fagundes N., Bonatto, S. et al. 2002 Genetic, geographic, and linguistic variation among South American Indians: possible sex influence. *American Journal of Physical Anthropology* 117:68–78.

Fairservis, W. and Southworth, F. 1989 Linguistic archaeology and the Indus Valley culture. In J. Kenoyer ed., *Old Problems and New Perspectives in the Archaeology of South Asia*, Madison: Dept. of Anthropology, University of Wisconsin, pp. 183–92.

Fairweather, A.D. and Ralston, I. 1993 The Neolithic timber hall at Balbridie. *Antiquity* 67:313–23.

Farnsworth, P., Brady, J., DeNiro, M. and MacNeish, R. 1985 A re-evaluation of the isotopic and archaeological reconstructions of diet in the Tehuacan valley. *American Antiquity* 50:102–16.

Farrington, I. and Urry, J. 1985 Food and the early history of cultivation. *Journal of Ethnobiology* 5:143–57.

Feldman, R.A. 1985 Preceramic corporate architecture. In C.B. Donnan ed., *Early Ceremonial Architecture in the Andes*, pp. 71–92. Washington, DC: Dumbarton Oaks Research Library and Collection.

Fellner, R. 1995 *Cultural Change and the Epipalaeolithic of Palestine*. Oxford: BAR International Series 599.

Fentress, M. 1985 Water resources and double cropping in Harappan food production. In V.N. Misra and P. Bellwood eds., *Recent Advances in Indo-Pacific Prehistory*, pp. 359–68. New Delhi: Oxford & IBH.

Fiedel, S. 1987 Algonquian origins. *Archaeology of Eastern North America* 15:1–11.

Fiedel, S. 1990 Middle Woodland and Algonquian expansion: a refined model. *North American Archaeologist* 11:209–30.

Fiedel, S. 1991 Correlating archaeology and linguistics: the Algonquian case. *Man in the Northeast* 41:9–32.

Fiedel, S. 1999 Older than we thought: implications of corrected dates for Paleoindians. *American Antiquity* 64:95–115.

Fix, A. 1999 *Migration and Colonization in Human Evolution*. Cambridge: Cambridge University Press.

Fix, A. 2000 Genes, languages and ethnic groups: reconstructing Orang Asli prehistory. *Bulletin of the Indo-Pacific Prehistory Association* 19:11–16.

Fix, A. 2002 Foragers, farmers and traders in the Malayan Peninsula: origins of cultural and biological diversity. In K. Morrison and L. Junker eds., *Forager-traders in South and Southeast Asia*, pp. 185–202. Cambridge: Cambridge University Press.

Flam L. 1999 The prehistoric Indus river system and the Indus Civilization in Sindh. *Man and Environment* XXIV/1:35–70.

Flannery, K. 1969 Origins and ecological effects of early domestication in Iran and the Near East. In P. Ucko and G.W. Dimbleby eds., *The Domestication and Exploitation of Plants and Animals*, pp. 73–100. London: Duckworth.

Flannery, K. 1972 The origins of the village as a settlement type in Mesoamerica and the Near East. In P. Ucko, R. Tringham and G. Dimbleby eds., *Man, Settlement and Urbanism*, pp. 23–53. London: Duckworth.

Flannery, K. ed. 1976 *The Early Mesoamerican Village*. Orlando: Academic.

Flannery, K. 1986 The problem and the model. In K.V. Flannery ed., *Guila Naquitz*, pp. 1–18. Orlando: Academic.

Flannery, K. ed. 1986 *Guila Naquitz*. Orlando: Academic.

Flannery, K. and Marcus, J. eds. 1983 *The Cloud People*. Orlando: Academic.

Flannery, K. and Marcus, J. 2000 Formative Mexican chiefdoms and the myth of the "Mother Culture". *Journal of Anthropological Archaeology* 19:1–37.

Flannery, K. and Marcus, J. 2003 The origin of war: new ^{14}C dates from ancient Mexico. *Proc. National Academy of Sciences (USA)* 100:11801–5.

Foley, W. 1986 *The Papuan Languages of New Guinea*. Cambridge: Cambridge University Press.

Ford, J.A. 1969 *A Comparison of Formative Cultures in the Americas*. Washington DC: Smithsonian.

Ford, R. ed. 1985 *Prehistoric Food Production in North America*. University of Michigan, Museum of Anthropology, Anthropological Papers 75.

Forster, P. and Toth, A. 2003 Toward a phylogenetic chronology of ancient Gaulish, Celtic, and Indo-European. *Proc. National Academy of Sciences (USA)* 100: 9079–84.

Fort, J. 2003 Population expansion in the western Pacific (Austronesia): a wave of advance model. *Antiquity* 77: 520–30.

Fort, J. and Mendez, V. 1999 Time delayed theory of the Neolithic transition in Europe. *Physical Review Letters* 82:867–71.

Foster, M. 1996 Language and the culture history of North America. In I. Goddard ed., *Handbook of North American Indians*, vol. 17, pp. 64–110. Washington DC: Smithsonian.

Fowler, C. 1983 Lexical clues to Uto-Aztecan prehistory. *International Journal of American Linguistics* 49:224–57.

Fowler, C. 1994 Corn, beans and squash: some linguistic perspectives from Uto-Aztecan. In S. Johannessen and C. Hastorf eds., *Corn and Culture in the Prehistoric New World*, pp. 445–68. Boulder: Westview.

Fowler, W. 1989 *The Cultural Evolution of Ancient Nahua Civilizations*. Norman: University of Oklahoma Press.

Fox, C.L. 1996 Physical anthropological aspects of the Mesolithic–Neolithic transition in the Iberian Peninsula. *Current Anthropology* 37:689–94.

Fox, R.B. 1953 The Pinatubo Negritos. *Philippine Journal of Science* 81:173–414.

Friedrich, P. 1966 Proto-Indo-European kinship. *Ethnology* 5:1–36.

Fritz, G.J. 1990 Multiple pathways to farming in precontact eastern North America. *Journal of World Prehistory* 4:387–436.

Fritz, G.J. 1993 Early and Middle Woodland Period paleoethnobotany. In C.M. Scarry ed., *Foraging and Farming in the Eastern Woodlands*, pp. 39–56. Gainesville: University Press of Florida.

Fujimoto, T. 1983 Grinding-slabs, hand-stones, mortars, pestles, and saddle querns 1. *Bulletin of the Department of Archaeology, Faculty of Letters, University of Tokyo* 2:73–5.

Fujiwara, H. 1993 Research into the history of rice cultivation using phytolith analysis. In D.M. Pearsall and D. Piperno eds., *Current Research in Phytolith Analysis*, pp. 157. Philadelphia: MASCA Research Papers in Science and Archaeology 10.

Fuller, D. 2001 Harappan seeds and agriculture: some considerations. *Antiquity* 75:410–4.

Fuller, D. 2002 Fifty years of archaeobotanical studies in India: laying a solid foundation. In S. Settar and R. Korisettar eds., *Indian Archaeology in Retrospect*, vol. 3, pp. 247–363. New Delhi: Manohar.

Fuller, D. 2003 An agricultural perspective on Dravidian historical linguistics. In P. Bellwood and C. Renfrew eds., *Examining the Farming/Language Dispersal Hypothesis*, pp. 191–215. Cambridge: McDonald Institute for Archaeological Research.

Fuller, D. and Madella, M. 2002 Issues in Harappan archaeology: retrospect and prospect. In S. Settar and R. Korisettar eds., *Indian Archaeology in Retrospect*, Vol. 2, pp. 317–90. New Delhi: Manohar.

Galinat, W.C. 1985 Domestication and diffusion of maize. In R. Ford ed., *Prehistoric Food Production in North America*, pp. 245–278. University of Michigan, Museum of Anthropology, Anthropological Papers 75.

Galinat, W. 1995 The origin of maize: grain of humanity. *Economic Botany* 49:3–12.

Gamkrelidze, T. 1989 Proto-Indo-Europeans in Anatolia. *Journal of Indo-European Studies* 17:341–50.

Gamkrelidze, T. and Ivanov, V. 1985 The Ancient Near East and the Indo-European question. *Journal of Indo-European Studies* 13:3–48.

Gamkrelidze, T. and Ivanov, V. 1995 *Indo-European and the Indo-Europeans*. Berlin: Mouton de Gruyter.

Garasanin, M. and Radovanovic, I. 2001 A pot in house 54 at Lepenski Vir 1. *Antiquity* 75:118–25.

Gardner, P. 1980 Lexicostatistics and Dravidian differentiation *in situ*. *Indian Linguistics* 41:170–80.

Gardner, P.M. 1993 Dimensions of subsistence foraging in South India. *Ethnology* 32:109–44.

Garfinkel, J. 1994 Ritual burial of cultic objects: the earliest evidence. *Cambridge Archaeological Journal* 4/2:159–88.

Garfinkel, Y. 1987 Yiftahel. *Journal of Field Archaeology* 14:199–212.

Garrard, A. 1999 Charting the emergence of cereal and pulse domestication in South-west Asia. *Environmental Archaeology* 4:67–86.

Gaur, R.C. 1983 *Excavations at Atranjikhera*. Delhi: Motilal Banarsidass.

Gebel, H.G. and Bienert, H-D. 1997 Ba'ja hidden in the Petra Mountains. In H. Gebel. Z. Kafafi and G. Rollefson eds., *The Prehistory of Jordan, II. Perspectives from 1997*, pp. 221–62. Berlin: Ex Oriente.

Gebel, H.G. and Hermansen, B. 1999 Ba'ja Neolithic Project 1999. *Neo-Lithics* 3(99):18–21.

Geertz, C. 1963 *Agricultural Involution*. Berkeley: University of California Press.

Gellner, E. 1988 *Plough, Sword and Book*. London: Collins Harvill.

Gibson, J.L. 1996 Poverty Point and Greater Southeastern prehistory. In K. Sassaman and D. Anderson eds., *Archaeology of the Mid-Holocene Southeast*, pp. 288–305. Gainesville: University of Florida Press.

Gibson, J.L. 1998 Broken circles, owl monsters, and black earth midden. In R. Mainfort and L. Sullivan eds., *Ancient Earthen Enclosures*, pp. 17–30. Gainesville: University of Florida Press.

Gifford-Gonzalez, D. 1998 Early pastoralists in East Africa: ecological and social dimensions. *Journal of Anthropological Archaeology* 17:166–200.

Gifford-Gonzalez, D. 2000 Animal disease challenges to the emergence of pastoralism in sub-Saharan Africa. *African Archaeological Review* 17:95–139.

Gilead, I. 1991 The Upper Palaeolithic period in the Levant. *Journal of World Prehistory* 5:105–50.

Gilman, P.A. 1997 *Wandering Villagers*. Arizona State University Anthropological Papers 49.

Gimbutas, M. 1985 Primary and secondary homelands of the Indo-Europeans. *Journal of Indo-European Studies* 13:185–202.

Gimbutas, M. 1991 Deities and symbols of Old Europe. In S. Lamb and E. Mitchell eds., *Sprung from Some Common Source*, pp. 89–121. Stanford: Stanford University Press.

Gkiasta, M., Russell, T. et al. 2003 Neolithic transition in Europe: the radiocarbon record revisited. *Antiquity* 77:45–62.

Glover, I. and Bellwood, P. eds. 2004 *Southeast Asia: From Prehistory to History*. London: RoutledgeCurzon.

Glover, I.C. and Higham, C.F. 1996 New evidence for early rice cultivation. In D. Harris ed., *The Origins and Spread of Agriculture and Pastoralism in Eurasia*, pp. 412–41. London: UCL Press.

Goddard, I. 1979 Comparative Algonquian. In L. Campbell and M. Mithun eds., *The Languages of Native America*, pp. 70–132. Austin: University of Texas Press.

Goldschmidt, A., 1996 *A Concise History of the Middle East*. Boulder: Westview.

Golson, J. 1977 No room at the top. In J. Allen, J. Golson and R. Jones eds., *Sunda and Sahul*, pp. 601–38. London: Academic.

Golson, J. and D. Gardner 1990 Agriculture and sociopolitical organisation in New Guinea Highlands prehistory. *Annual Review of Anthropology* 19:395–417.

Gomes, A.G. 1990 Demographic implications of villagisation among the Semang of Malaysia. In B. Meehan and N. White eds., *Hunter-Gatherer Demography: Past and Present*, pp.126–38. Sydney: Oceania Monograph 39.

Gonda, J. 1973 *Sanskrit in Indonesia*. 2nd edn. New Delhi: International Academy of Indian Culture.

Gopher, A. 1994 Southern-Central Levant PPN cultural sequences. In H.G. Gebel and S.F. Kozlowski eds., *Neolithic Chipped Stone Industries of the Levant*, pp. 387–92. Berlin: Ex Oriente.

Gopher, A., Abbo, S. and Lev-Yadun, S. 2001 The "when", the "where" and the "why" of the Neolithic revolution in the Levant. In M. Budje ed., *Documenta Praehistorica* XXVIII, pp. 49–62. Ljubljana (ISSN 1408–967X).

Gopher, A. and Gophra, R. 1994 Cultures of the eighth and seventh millennia BP in the southern Levant. *Journal of World Prehistory* 7:297–353.

Gorecki, P. 1986 Human occupation and agricultural development in the Papua New Guinea Highlands. *Mountain Research and development* 6:159–66.

Goring-Morris, A.N. 2000 The quick and the dead. In I. Kuijt ed., *Life in Neolithic Farming Communities*, pp. 103–36. New York: Kluwer.

Goring-Morris, A.N. and Belfer-Cohen, A. 1998 The articulation of cultural processes and Late Quaternary environmental changes in Cisjordan. *Paléorient* 23/2:71–93.

Gosden, C. and Hather, J. eds. 1999 *The Prehistory of Food*. London: Routledge.

Goss, J. 1968 Culture-historical inference from Utaztecan linguistic evidence. In E. Swanson ed., *Utaztecan Prehistory*, pp. 1–42. Pocatello: Occasional Papers of the Museum of Idaho University, No. 22.

Grace, G. 1990 The "aberrant" (vs. "exemplary") Melanesian languages. In P. Baldi ed., *Linguistic Change and Reconstruction Methodology*, pp. 156–73. Berlin: Mouton de Gruyter.

Graham, J. 1989 Olmec diffusion: a sculptural view from Pacific Guatemala. In R.J. Sharer and D.C. Grove eds., *Regional Perspectives on the Olmec*, pp. 227–46. Cambridge: Cambridge University Press.

Graham, M. 1994 *Mobile Farmers*. Ann Arbor: International Monographs in Prehistory, Ethno-archaeological Monograph 3.

Gray, R. and Atkinson, Q. 2003 Language tree divergence times support the Anatolian theory of Indo-European origin. *Nature*, 426: 435–9.

Gray, R. and Jordan, F. 2000 Language trees support the express-train sequence of Austronesian expansion. *Nature* 405:1052–5.

Green, R. 1991 Near and Remote Oceania – disestablishing "Melanesia" in culture history. In A. Pawley ed., *Man and a Half*, pp. 491–502. Auckland: Polynesian Society.

Green, W. ed. 1994 *Agricultural Origins and Development in the Mid-Continent*. Iowa City: University of Iowa Press.

Greenberg, J. 1987 *Language in the Americas*. Stanford: Stanford University Press.

Greenberg, J. 1990 Commentary. *Review of Archaeology* 11/2:5–14.

Greenberg, J. 2000 *Indo-European and its Closest Relatives: the Eurasiatic Language Family. Vol. 1: Grammar*. Stanford: Stanford University Press.

Gregg, S. 1979–80 A material perspective of tropical rainforest hunter-gatherers: the Semang of Malaysia. *Michigan Discussions in Anthropology* 15/1–2:117–35.

Gregg, S.A. 1988 *Foragers and Farmers*. Chicago: University of Chicago Press.

Grieder, T., Mendoza, A.B., Smith, C.E. and Malina, R.M. 1988 *La Galgada, Peru*. Austin: University of Texas Press.

Grogan, E. 2002 Neolithic houses in Ireland: a broader perspective. *Antiquity* 76:517–25.

Gronenborn, D. 1999 A variation on a basic theme: the transition to farming in southern central Europe. *Journal of World Prehistory* 13:123–212.

Groube, L. 1970 The origin and development of earthwork fortification n the Pacific. In R. Green and M. Kelly eds., *Studies in Oceanic Culture History*, vol. 1, pp. 133–64. Honolulu, Bishop Museum: Pacific Anthropological Records 11.

Grove, D. 1989 Olmec: what's in a name? In R.J. Sharer and D.C. Grove eds., *Regional Perspectives on the Olmec*, pp. 8–16. Cambridge: CUP.

Grove, D. 2000 The Preclassic societies of the Central Highlands of Mesoamerica. In R. Adams and M. MacLeod eds., *The Cambridge History of the Native Peoples of the Americas II, Mesoamerica, Part 1*, pp. 122–55. Cambridge: Cambridge University Press.

Guddemi, P. 1992 When horticulturalists are like hunter-gatherers: the Sawiyano of Papua New Guinea. *Ethnology* 31:303–14.

Haaland, R. 1993 Aqualithic sites of the Middle Nile. *Azania* 28:47–86.

Haaland, R. 1995 Sedentism, cultivation and plant domestication in the Holocene Middle Nile region. *Journal of Field Archaeology* 22:157–74.

Haaland, R. 1997 The emergence of sedentism. *Antiquity* 71:374–85.

Haaland, R. 1999 The puzzle of the late mergence of domesticated sorghum in the Nile valley. In C. Gosden and J. Hather eds., *The Prehistory of Food*, pp. 397–418. London: Routledge.

Haas, M. 1969 *The Prehistory of Languages*. The Hague: Mouton.

Haberle, S. 2003 The emergence of an agricultural landscape in the highlands of New Guinea. *Archaeology in Oceania* 38:149–58.

Haberle, S.G. 1994 Anthropogenic indicators in pollen diagrams: problems and prospects for Late Quaternary palynology in New Guinea. In J. Hather ed., *Tropical Archaeobotany: Applications and New Developments*, pp. 172–201. London: Routledge.

Haberle, S.G. and Chepstow-Lusty, A.G. 2000 Can climate influence cultural development? A view through time. *Environment and History* 6:349–69.

Haberle, S.G., Hope, G.S. and DeFretes, Y. 1991 Environmental change in the Baliem Valley, montane Irian Jaya, Republic of Indonesia. *Journal of Biogeography* 18:25–40.

Hage, P. and Marck, J. 2003 Matrilineality and the Melanesian origin of Polynesian Y chromosomes. *Current Anthropology* 44, Supplement:121–7.

Hagelberg, E. 2000 Genetics *in the Study of Human History: Problems and Opportunities*. University of Amsterdam, Kroon Lecture Series no. 20.

Hagelberg, E., Kayser, M. et al. 1999 Molecular genetic evidence for the human settlement of the Pacific. *Philosophical Transactions of the Royal Society of London, Biological Sciences* 354:141–52.

Hale, K. and Harris, D. 1979 Historical linguistics and archaeology. In A. Ortiz ed., *Handbook of North American Indians, Vol. 9, Southwest*, pp. 170–7. Washington: Smithsonian.

Halstead, P. 1996 The development of agriculture and pastoralism in Greece. In D. Harris ed., *The Origins and Spread of Agriculture and Pastoralism in Eurasia*, pp. 296–309. London: UCL Press.

Hammond, N. 2000 The Maya Lowlands: pioneer farmers to merchant princes. In R. Adams and M. MacLeod eds., *The Cambridge History of the Native Peoples of the Americas II, Mesoamerica, Part 1*, pp. 197–249. Cambridge: Cambridge University Press.

Handwerker, W.P. 1983 The first demographic transition. *American Anthropologist* 85:5–27.

Hanotte, O., Bradley, D. et al. 2002 African pastoralism: genetic imprints of origins and migrations. *Science* 296:336–9.

Hansen, J. 1991 *The Paleoethnobotany of Franchthi Cave*. Bloomington: Indiana University Press.

Hansen, J. 1992 Franchthi Cave and the beginnings of agriculture in Greece and the Aegean. In P.C. Anderson ed., *Préhistoire de l'Agriculture*, pp. 231–48. Paris: CNRS.

Haour, A. 2003 One hundred years of archaeology in Niger. *Journal of World Prehistory* 17:181–234.

Hard, R.J. and Merrill, W.C. 1992 Mobile agriculturalists and the emergence of sedentism: perspectives from northern Mexico. *American Anthropologist* 94:601–20.

Hard, R.J. and Roney, J.R. 1998 A massive terraced village complex in Chihuahua, Mexico, 3000 years before present. *Science* 279:1661–4.

Hard, R.J. and Roney, J.R. 1999 Cerro Juangqueña. *Archaeology Southwest* 13/1:4–5.

Harlan, J. 1992 Indigenous African agriculture. In C.W. Cowan and P.J. Watson eds., *The Origins of Agriculture*, pp. 59–70. Washington DC: Smithsonian.

Harlan, J. 1995 *The Living Fields*. Cambridge: CUP.

Harris, D. 1977a Alternative pathways toward agriculture. In C.A. Reed ed., *Origins of Agriculture*, pp. 179–243. The Hague: Mouton.

Harris, D. 1977b Subsistence strategies across Torres Strait. In J. Allen, J. Golson and R. Jones eds., *Sunda and Sahul*, pp. 421–64. London: Academic Press.

Harris, D. 1998a The origins of agriculture in Southwest Asia. *Review of Archaeology* 19/2:5–11.

Harris, D. 1998b The spread of Neolithic agriculture from the Levant to western central Asia. In A. Damania, J. Valkoun, G. Willcox and C. Qualset eds., *The Origins of Agriculture and Crop Domestication*, pp. 65–82. Aleppo: ICARDA.

Harris, D. 2002 Development of the agro-pastoral economy in the Fertile Crescent during the Pre-Pottery Neolithic period. In S. Bottema and R. Cappers eds., *The Transition from Foraging to Farming in Southwest Asia*, pp. 67–84. Berlin: Ex Oriente.

Harris, D. 2003 The expansion capacity of early agricultural systems: a comparative perspective on the spread of agriculture. In P. Bellwood and C. Renfrew eds., *Examining the Farming/Language Dispersal Hypothesis*, pp. 31–40. Cambridge: McDonald Institute for Archaeological Research.

Harris, D., Gosden, C. and Charles, M. 1996 Jeitun: recent excavations at an Early Neolithic site in southern Turkmenistan. *PPS* 62:423–42.

Hart, J. 1999 Maize agriculture evolution in the Eastern Woodlands of North America. *Journal of Archaeological Method and Theory* 6:137–80.

Hart, J., Asch, D. et al. 2002 The age of the common bean (*Phaseolus vulgaris*) in the northern Eastern Woodlands of North America. *Antiquity* 76:377–85.

Hart, J. and Brumbach, H. 2003 The death of Owasco. *American Antiquity* 68:737–52.

Hart, J., Thompson, R. and Brumbach, H. 2003 Phytolith evidence for early maize (*Zea mays*) in the northern Finger Lakes region of New York. *American Antiquity* 68:619–40.

Hassan, F. 1981 *Demographic Archaeology*. New York: Academic.

Hassan, F. 1988 The predynastic of Egypt. *Journal of World Prehistory* 2:135–86.

Hassan, F. 1997a Holocene palaeoclimates of Africa. *African Archaeological Review* 14:213–30.

Hassan, F. 1997b Egypt: beginnings of agriculture. In Vogel, J. ed., *Encyclopaedia of Precolonial Africa*, pp. 405–9. Walnut Creek: Sage.

Hassan, F. 1998 The archaeology of North Africa at Kiekrz 1997. *African Archaeological Review* 15:85–93.

Hassan, F. 2000 Climate and cattle in North Africa: a first approximation. In Blench, R. and MacDonald, K. eds., *The Origins and Development of African Livestock*, pp. 61–86. London: UCL Press.

Hassan, F. 2002 Palaeoclimate, food and culture change in Africa: an overview. In Hassan, F. ed., *Droughts, Food and Culture*, pp. 11–26. New York: Kluwer.

Hassan, F. 2003 Archaeology and linguistic diversity in North Africa. In P. Bellwood and C. Renfrew eds., *Examining the Farming/Language Dispersal Hypothesis*, pp. 127–34. Cambridge: McDonald Institute for Archaeological Research.

Hastorf, C. 1999 Cultural implications of crop introductions in Andean prehistory. In C. Gosden and J. Hather eds., *The Prehistory of Food*, pp. 35–58. London: Routledge.

Hastorf, C. and Johannessen, S. 1994 Becoming corn-eaters in prehistoric America. In S. Johannessen and C. Hastorf eds., *Corn and Culture in the Prehistoric New World*, pp. 427–44. Boulder: Westview.

Hather, J. and Hammond, N. 1994 Ancient Maya subsistence diversity. *Antiquity* 68:330–5.

Haugen, E. 1988 Language and ethnicity. In A. Jazayery and W. Winter eds., *Languages and Cultures*, pp. 235–44. Berlin: Mouton de Gruyter.

Hauptmann, H. 1999 The Urfa region. In M. Özdoğan and N. Başgelen eds., *Neolithic in Turkey*, pp. 65–86. Istanbul: Arkeoloji ve Sanat Yayinlari.

Haury, E.H. 1986 Thoughts after sixty years as a Southwestern archaeologist. In J.J. Reid and D.E. Doyel eds., *Emil W. Haury's Prehistory of the American Southwest*, pp. 435–64. Tucson: University of Arizona Press.

Hayden, B. 1990 Nimrods, piscators, pluckers and planters. *Journal of Anthropological Archaeology* 9:31–69.

Hayden, B. 1992 Models of domestication. In A.B. Gebauer and T.D. Price eds., *Transitions to Agriculture in Prehistory*, pp. 11–19. Madison: Prehistory Press.

Hayden, B. 1995 An new overview of domestication. In T.D. Price and A.B. Gebauer eds., *Last Hunters First Farmers*, pp. 273–300. Santa Fe: School of American Research.

Hayward, R. 2000 Is there a metric for convergence? In C. Renfrew, A. McMahon and L. Trask eds., *Time Depth in Historical Linguistics*, pp. 621–42. Cambridge: McDonald Institute for Archaeological Research.

He Jiejun 1999 Excavations in Chengtoushan in Li County, Hunan Province, China. *Bulletin of the Indo-Pacific Prehistory Association* 18:101–4.

Headland, T. ed. 1993 *The Tasaday Controversy*. Washington: American Anthropological Association.

Headland, T. 1986 *Why Foragers do not Become Farmers*. Ann Arbor: University Microfilms International.

Headland, T. 1997 Limitation of human rights – Agta Negritos. *Human Organisation* 56:79–90.

Headland, T. and Reid, L. 1989 Hunter-gatherers and their neighbours from prehistory to the present. *Current Anthropology* 30:43–66.

Heath, S. and Laprade, R. 1982 Castilian colonization and indigenous languages: the cases of Quechua and Aymara. In R. Cooper ed., *Language Spread: Studies in Diffusion and Social Change*, pp. 118–47. Bloomington: Indiana University Press.

Hedrick, B.C., Kelley, J.C. and Riley, C.R. eds. 1974 *The Mesoamerican Southwest*. Carbondale: Southern Illinois University Press.

Hegedüs, I. 1989 The applicability of exact methods in Nostratic research. In V. Shevoroshkin ed., *Explorations in Language Macrofamilies*, pp. 30–9. Bochum: Brockmeyer.

Heiser, C. 1988 Aspects of unconscious selection and the evolution of domesticated plants. *Euphytica* 37:77–81.

Heiser, C. 1990 *Seed to Civilization*. Cambridge, MA: Harvard University Press.

Hemphill, B. et al. 1991 Biological adaptations and affinities of Bronze Age Harappans. In R.H. Meadow ed., *Harappa Excavations 1986–1990*, pp. 137–82. Madison: Prehistory Press.

Henry, D.O. 1989 *From Foraging to Agriculture*. Philadelphia: University of Pennsylvania Press.

Henry, D.O. 1991 Foraging, sedentism and adaptive vigour in the Natufian. In G.A. Clark ed., *Perspectives on the Past*, pp. 353–70. Philadelphia: University of Pennsylvania Press.

Henry, D.O. et al. 1999 Investigation of the Early Neolithic site of Ain Abu Nekheileh. *Neo-Lithics* 3/99:3–5.

Herbert R.K. and Huffman, T.N. 1993 A new perspective on Bantu expansion and classification. *African Studies* 52:53–76.

Herschkovitz, I. Speirs, M, Frayer, D., Nadel, D., Wish-Baratz, S. and Arensburg, B. 1995 Ohalo II H2: a 19,000 year old skeleton from a water-logged site at the Sea of Galilee, Israel. *American Journal of Physical Anthropology* 96:215–34.

Hester, J.J. 1962 *Early Navajo Migrations and Acculturation in the Southwest*. Santa Fe: Museum of New Mexico, Papers in Anthropology No. 6.

Heun, M. Schafer-Pregl, R. et al. 1997 Site of einkorn wheat domestication identified by DNA fingerprinting. *Science* 278:1312–4.

Higgs, E.S. and Jarman, M. 1972 The origins of animal and plant husbandry. In E.S. Higgs ed., *Papers in Economic Prehistory*, pp. 3–14. Cambridge: Cambridge University Press.

Higham, C. 1996a *The Bronze Age of Southeast Asia*. Cambridge: Cambridge University Press.

Higham, C. 1996b A review of archaeology in Mainland Southeast Asia. *Journal of Archaeological Research* 4:3–50.

Higham, C. 1996c Archaeology and linguistics in Southeast Asia: implications of the Austric hypothesis. *Bulletin of the Indo-Pacific Prehistory Association* 14:110–118.

Higham, C. 2002 *Early Cultures of Mainland Southeast Asia*. London: Thames and Hudson.

Higham, C. 2003 Languages and farming dispersals: Austroasiatic languages and rice cultivation. In P. Bellwood and C. Renfrew eds., *Examining the Language/Farming Dispersal Hypothesis*, pp. 223–32. Cambridge: McDonald Institute for Archaeological Research.

Higham, C. 2004 Mainland Southeast Asia from the Neolithic to the Iron Age. In I. Glover and P. Bellwood eds., *Southeast Asia: From Prehistory to History*, pp. 41–67. London: RoutledgeCurzon.

Higham, C. and Bannanurag (Thosarat), R. eds. 1990 and onwards *The Excavation of Khok Phanom Di*. London: Society of Antiquaries. 5 vols.

Higham, C. and Thosarat, R. 1994 *Khok Phanom Di*. Fort Worth: Harcourt, Brace, Jovanovich.

Higham, C. and Thosarat, R. 1998a *Prehistoric Thailand*. Bangkok: River Books.

Higham, C. and Thosarat, R. eds. 1998b *The Excavation of Nong Nor: a prehistoric site in central Thailand*. Oxford: Oxbow Books.

Hill, J. 2001 Proto-Uto-Aztecan: a community of cultivators in central Mexico? *American Anthropologist* 103:913–34.

Hill, J. 2002 Toward a linguistic prehistory of the Southwest: "Aztec-Tanoan" and the arrival of maize cultivation. *Journal of Anthropological Research* 58:457–76.

Hill, J. 2003 Proto-Uto-Aztecan cultivation and the Northern Devolution. In P. Bellwood and C. Renfrew eds., *Examining the Farming/Language Dispersal Hypothesis*, pp. 331–40. Cambridge: McDonald Institute for Archaeological Research.

Hillman, G. 1989 Late Palaeolithic plant foods from Wadi Kubanniya in Upper Egypt. In D. Harris and G. Hillman eds., *The Origins and Spread of Agriculture and Pastoralism in Eurasia*, pp. 207–39. London: UCL Press.

Hillman, G. 1996 Late Pleistocene changes in wild plant-foods available to hunter-gatherers of the northern Fertile Crescent; possible preludes to cereal cultivation. In D. Harris ed., *The Origins and Spread of Agriculture and Pastoralism in Eurasia*, pp. 159–203. London: UCL Press.

Hillman, G. 2000 The plant food economy of Abu Hureyra 1. In A. Moore, G. Hillman and A. Legge *Village on the Euphrates: From Foraging to Farming at Abu Hureyra*, pp. 327–99. New York: Oxford University Press.

Hillman, G. and Davies, M. 1990 Measured domestication rates in wild wheat and barley. *Journal of World Prehistory* 4:157–222.

Hillman, G., Hedges, R., Moore, A., Colledge, S. and Pettitt, P. 2001 New evidence of late glacial cereal cultivation at Abu Hureyra on the Euphrates. *The Holocene* 11:383–93.

Hines, J. 1998 Archaeology and language in a historical context: the creation of English. In R. Blench and M. Spriggs eds., *Archaeology and Language III*, pp. 283–94. London: Routledge.

Hitchcock, R. 1982 Patterns of sedentism among the Basarwa of eastern Botswana. In E. Leacock and R.B. Lee eds., *Politics and History in Band Societies*, pp. 223–68. Cambridge: Cambridge University Press.

Ho, Ping-ti 1975 *The Cradle of the East*. Chicago: University of Chicago Press.

Hodges, D.C. 1989 *Agricultural Intensification and Prehistoric Health in the Valley of Oaxaca, Mexico*. Ann Arbor, Museum of Anthropology, University of Michigan, Memoir 22.

Hoffman, C.L. 1986 *The Punan: Hunters and Gatherers of Borneo*. Ann Arbor: UMI Research Press.

Holden, C. 2002 Bantu language trees reflect the spread of farming across sub-Saharan Africa: a maximum parsimony analysis. *Proceedings of the Royal Society of London B* 269:793–9.

Hole, F. 1998 The spread of agriculture to the eastern arc of the Fertile Crescent. In A. Damania, J. Valkoun, G. Willcox and C. Qualset eds., *The Origins of Agriculture and Crop Domestication*, pp. 83–92. Aleppo: ICARDA.

Hole, F. 2000 New radiocarbon dates for Ali Kosh, Iran. *Neo-Lithics* 1/2000:13.

Holl, A. 1998 The dawn of African pastoralisms. *Journal of Anthropological Archaeology* 17:81–96.

Hoopes, J. 1991 The Isthmian alternative. In W.R. Fowler ed., *The Formation of Complex Society in Southeastern Mesoamerica*, pp. 171–92. Boca Raton: CRC Press.

Hoopes, J. 1993 A view from the south: prehistoric exchange in Lower Central America. In J.E. Ericson and T.G. Baugh eds., *The American Southwest and Mesoamerica*, pp. 247–82. New York: Plenum.

Hoopes, J. 1994 Ford revisited. *Journal of World Prehistory* 8:1–50.

Hoopes, J. 1996 Settlement, subsistence and the origins of social complexity in Greater Chiriqui. In F.W. Lange ed., *Paths to Central American Prehistory*, pp. 15–48. Niwot: University of Colorado Press.

Hopf, M. 1983 Jericho plant remains. In K.M. Kenyon and T.A. Holland eds., *Excavations at Jericho, Vol. 5*, pp. 576–621. London: British School of Archaeology in Jerusalem.

Hopkins, N. 1965 Great Basin prehistory and Uto-Aztecan. *American Antiquity* 31:48–60.

Hours, F. et al. 1994 *Atlas des Sites du Proche Orient*. 2 vols. Lyon: Maison de l'Orient méditerranean.

Huang Tsui-mei 1992 Liangzhu – a late neolithic jade-yielding culture in southeastern coastal China. *Antiquity* 66:75–83.

Huckell, B. 1998 Alluvial stratigraphy of the Santa Cruz Bend Reach. In J. Mabry ed., *Archaeological Investigations of Early Village Sites in the Middle Santa Cruz Valley. Analysis and Synthesis*, vol. 1, pp. 31–56. Tucson: Center for Desert Archaeology, Archaeological Papers 19.

Huckell, B., Huckell, L.W. and Fish, S.K. 1995 *Investigations at Milagro*. Tucson: Center for Desert Archaeology, Technical Report No. 94–5.

Hudson, M. 1999 *Ruins of Identity*. Honolulu: University of Hawaii Press.

Hudson, M. 2003 Agriculture and language change in the Japanese Islands. In P. Bellwood and C. Renfrew eds., *Examining the Farming/Language Dispersal Hypothesis*, pp. 311–8. Cambridge: McDonald Institute for Archaeological Research.

Huffman, T.N. 1989a *Iron Age Migrations*. Johannesburg: Witwaterstrand University Press.

Huffman, T.N. 1989b Ceramics, settlements and Late Iron Age migrations. *African Archaeological Review* 7:155–82.

Huffman, T.N. and Herbert, R.K. 1996 A new perspective on Eastern Bantu. *Azania* Special Volume XXIX–XXX:27–36.

Huke, R. 1982a *Agroclimatic and Dry-Season Maps of South, Southeast and East Asia*. Los Baños, Philippines: International Rice Research Institute.

Huke, R. 1982b *Rice Area by Type of Culture: South, Southeast and East Asia*. Los Baños, Philippines: International Rice Research Institute.

Hunan Institute of Archaeology 1990 Preliminary report on excavations at the Early Neolithic site of Pengtoushan. *Wenwu* 1990/8:17–29 (in Chinese).

Hunan Institute of Archaeology 1996 Excavation of an Early Neolithic site at Bashidang. *Wenwu* 1996/12:26–39 (in Chinese).

Hunn, E.S. and Williams, N.M. 1982 Introduction. In N.M. Williams and E.S. Hunn eds., *Resource Managers: North American and Australian Hunter-Gatherers*, pp. 1–16. Boulder: Westview.

Hurles, M. 2003 Can the hypothesis of language/agriculture co-dispersal be *tested* with archaeogenetics? In P. Bellwood and C. Renfrew eds., *Examining the Farming/Language Dispersal Hypothesis*, pp. 299–310. Cambridge: McDonald Institute for Archaeological Research.

Hurles, M., Nicholson, J. et al. 2002 Y chromosomal evidence for the origins of Oceanic-speaking peoples. *Genetics* 160:289–303.

IAR 1982 *Indian Archaeology – A Review*. New Delhi: Archaeological Survey of India.

Iltis, H. 2000 Homoerotic sexual translocations and the origin of maize. *Economic Botany* 54:7–42.

Imamura, K. 1996 *Prehistoric Japan*. Honolulu: University of Hawaii Press.

Ingold, T. 1991 Comments. *Current Anthropology* 32:263–5.

Inizan, M-L. and Lechevallier, M. 1994 L'adoption du débitage laminaire par pression au Proche-Orient. In H.G. Gebel and S.F. Kozlowski eds., *Neolithic Chipped Stone Industries of the Levant*, pp. 23–32. Berlin: Ex Oriente.

Ipoi, D. and Bellwood, P.S. 1991 Recent research at Gua Sireh (Serian) and Lubang Angin (Gunung Mulu National Park), Sarawak. *Bulletin of the Indo-Pacific Prehistory Association* 11:386–405.

Izumi, S. and Terada, K. 1972 *Excavations at Kotosh, Peru*. Tokyo: University of Tokyo Press.

Jackes, M., Lubell, D. and Meiklejohn, C. 1997a On physical anthropological aspects of the Mesolithic–Neolithic transition in the Iberian Peninsula. *Current Anthropology* 38:839–46.

Jackes, M., Lubell, D. and Meiklejohn, C. 1997b Healthy but mortal: human biology and the first farmers of Western Europe. *Antiquity* 71:639–58.

Janhunen, J. 1996 *Manchuria: an Ethnic History*. Helsinki: Suomalais-Ugrilainen Seura.

Jarrige, J-F. and Meadow R.H. 1980 The antecedents of civilization in the Indus Valley. *Scientific American* 243/2:102–11.

Jarrige, J-F. and Meadow R.H. 1992 Melanges Fairservis. In G.L. Possehl ed. *South Asian Archaeology Studies*, pp. 163–78. New Delhi: Oxford & IBH.

Jarrige, J-F. 1993 Excavations at Mehrgarh. In G. Possehl ed., *Harappan Civilization: A Recent Perspective*, pp. 79–84. 2nd edition. New Delhi: Oxford & IBH.

Jenkins, N.J., Dye, D.H. and Walthall, J.A. 1986 Developments in the Gulf Coastal Plain. In K. Farnsworth and T. Emerson eds., *Early Woodland Archaeology*, pp. 546–63. Kampsville, IL: Center for American Archaeology, Kampsville Seminars in Archaeology, vol. 2.

Jennings, J.D. 1989 *Prehistory of North America*. 3rd edition. Mountain View: Mayfield.

Jensen, H., Schild, R., Wendorf, F. and Close, A. 1991 Understanding the Late Palaeolithic tools with lustrous edges from the Nile Valley. *Antiquity* 65:122–8.

Jing, Y. and Flad, R. 2002 Pig domestication in ancient China. *Antiquity* 76:724–32.

Jolly, P. 1996 Symbiotic interaction between black farmers and south-eastern San. *Current Anthropology* 37:277–306.

Jones, M. 2001 *The Molecule Hunt*. London: Allen Lane.

Jones, M. and Brown, T. 2000 Agricultural origins: the evidence of modern and ancient DNA. *The Holocene* 10:769–76.

Jones, R. and Meehan, B. 1989 Plant foods of the Gidjingali. In D. Harris and G. Hillman eds., *Foraging and Farming*, pp. 120–35. London: Unwin Hyman.

Josserand, K., Winter, M. and Hopkins, N. eds. 1984 *Essays in Otomanguean Culture History*. Nashville: Vanderbilt University Publications in Archaeology 31.

Joyce, R. and Henderson, J. 2001 Beginnings of village life in eastern Mesoamerica. *Latin American Antiquity* 12:5–24.

Kahler, H. 1978 Austronesian comparative linguistics and reconstruction of earlier forms of the language. In S. Wurm and L. Carrington eds., *Proceedings of the Second International Conference on Comparative Austronesian Linguistics*, Fascicle 1, pp. 3–18. Canberra: Pacific Linguistics Series C-61.

Kaiser, M. and Shevoroshkin, V. 1988 Nostratic. *Annual Review of Anthropology* 17:309–29.

Kajale, M.D. 1991 Current status of Indian palaeoethnobotany. In J. Renfrew ed., *New Light on Early Farming*, pp. 155–89.

Kajale, M. 1996a Palaeobotanical investigations at Balathal. *Man and Environment* XXI/1:98–102.

Kajale, M.D. 1996b Neolithic plant economy in parts of Lower Deccan and South India. In I. Abstracts – The Sections of the XIII International Congress of Prehistoric and Protohistoric Sciences, Forli, Sept. 1996, pp. 67–70.

Kamminga, J. and Wright, R. 1988 The Upper Cave at Zhoukoudian and the origins of the Mongoloids. *Journal of Human Evolution* 17:739–67.

Kantor, H. 1992 Egypt. In R.W. Ehrich ed., *Chronologies in Old World Archaeology*, vol. 1, pp. 3–21. Chicago: University of Chicago Press.

Karafet, T., Xu, L. et al. 2001 Paternal population history of East Asia. *American Journal of Human Genetics* 69:615–28.

Kaufman, T. 1976 Archaeological and linguistic correlations in Mayaland and associated areas of Meso-America. *World Archaeology* 8:101–18.

Kaufman, T. 1990a Language history in South America. In D. Payne ed., *Amazonian Linguistics*, pp. 13–73. Austin: University of Texas Press.

Kaufman, T. 1990b Early Otomanguean homelands and cultures: some premature hypotheses. *University of Pittsburgh Working Papers in Linguistics*, vol. I, pp. 91–136.

Kaufman, T. 2001 The history of the Nawa language group from earliest times to the sixteenth century. http://www.albany.edu/anthro/maldp/Nawa.pdf.

Kayser, M., Brauer, S. et al. 2000 Melanesian origin of Polynesian Y chromosomes. *Current Biology* 10:1237–46.

Kealhofer, L. 1996 The human environment during the terminal Pleistocene and Holocene in northeastern Thailand. *Asian Perspectives* 35:229–54.

Keally, C., Taniguchi, Y. and Kuzmin, Y. 2003 Understanding the beginnings of pottery technology in Japan and neighboring East Asia. *Review of Archaeology* 24/2:3–14.

Keegan, W. 1987 Diffusion of maize from South America. In W.F. Keegan ed., *Emergent Horticultural Economies of the Eastern Woodlands*, pp. 329–44. Center for Archaeological Investigations, Southern Illinois University at Carbondale.

Keegan, W. ed. 1987 *Emergent Horticultural Economies of the Eastern Woodlands*. Carbondale, Southern Illinois University, Center for Archaeological Investigations, Occasional Paper 7.

Keegan, W. 1994 West Indian Archaeology I. Overview and foragers. *Journal of Archaeological Research* 2:255–84.

Keeley, L.H. 1988 Hunter-gatherer economic complexity and "population pressure": a cross-cultural analysis. *Journal of Anthropological Archaeology* 7:373–411.

Keeley, L.H. 1992 The introduction of agriculture to the western North European Plain. In A.B. Gebauer and T.D. Price eds., *Transitions to Agriculture in Prehistory*, pp. 81–96. Madison: Prehistory Press.

Keeley, L.H. 1995 Protoagricultural practices amongst hunter-gatherers. In T.D. Price and A.B. Gebauer eds., *Last Hunters First Farmers*, pp. 243–272. Santa Fe: School of American Research.

Keeley, L. 1996 *War before Civilization*. New York: Oxford University Press.

Keeley, L.H. 1997 Frontier warfare in the early Neolithic. In D.L. Martin and D.W. Frayer eds., *Troubled Times*, pp. 303–19. Amsterdam: Gordon and Breach.

Keeley, L.H. and Cahen, D. 1989 Early Neolithic Forts and Villages in NE Belgium: A Preliminary Report. *Journal of Field Archaeology* 16: 157–76.

Kelley, J.C. 1974 Speculations on the culture history of Northwestern Mesoamerica. In B. Bell ed., *The Archaeology of West Mexico*, pp. 19–39. Jalisco: West Mexican Society for Advanced Study.

Kelley, J.C. and Kelley, E.A. 1975 An alternative hypothesis for the explanation of Anasazi culture history. In T.R. Frisbie ed., *Collected Papers in Honour of Florence Hawley Ellis*, pp. 178–223. Norman: Hooper.

Kelly, R. 1997 Late Holocene Great Basin prehistory. *Journal of World Prehistory* 11:1–50.

Kelly, R.L. 1995 *The Foraging Spectrum*. Washington: Smithsonian.

Kennedy, J. 1969 *Settlement in the Bay of Islands 1772*. Dunedin: Otago University Studies in Prehistoric Anthropology 3.

Kent, S. 1992 The current forager controversy. *Man* 27:45–70.

Kent, S. 1996 Cultural diversity among African foragers: causes and implications. In S. Kent ed., *Cultural Diversity among Twentieth-Century Foragers*, pp. 1–18. Cambridge: Cambridge University Press.

Kent, S. ed. 1989 *Farmers as Hunters*. Cambridge: Cambridge University Press.

Kertesz, R. and Makkay, J. eds. 2001 *From the Mesolithic to the Neolithic*. Budapest: Archaeolingua.

Keys, D. 2003 Pre-Christian rituals at Nazareth. *Archaeology* 56/6:10.

Khoury, P. and Kostiner, J. 1990 Introduction. In P. Khoury and J. Kostiner eds., *Tribes and State Formation in the Middle East*, pp. 1–22. Berkeley: University of California Press.

Kimball, M. 2000 *Human Ecology and Neolithic Transition in Eastern County Donegal, Ireland*. Oxford: BAR British Series 300.

King, F.B. 1985 Early cultivated cucurbits in eastern North America. In R. Ford ed., *Prehistoric Food Production in North America*, pp. 73–98. University of Michigan, Museum of Anthropology, Anthropological Papers 75.

King, R. and Underhill, P. 2002 Congruent distribution of Neolithic painted pottery and ceramic figurines with Y-chromosome lineages. *Antiquity* 76:707–14.

Kirch, P.V. 1989 Second millennium BP arboriculture in Melanesia. *Economic Botany* 43: 225–40.

Kirch, P.V. 1997 *The Lapita Peoples*. Oxford: Blackwell.

Kirch, P.V. 2000 *On the Road of the Winds*. Berkeley: University of California Press.

Kirch, P.V. and Green, R.C. 2001 *Hawaiki: Ancestral Polynesia*. Cambridge: Cambridge University Press.

Kirchhoff, P. 1954 Gatherers and farmers in the Greater Southwest: a problem in classification. *American Anthropologist* 56:529–60.

Kislev, M.E. 1992 Agriculture in the Near East in the VIIth millennium BC. In P.C. Anderson 1992, *Préhistoire de l'Agriculture*, pp. 87–94. Paris: CNRS (Monographie du CRA 6).

Kislev, M.E. 1997 Early agriculture and paleoecology of Netiv Hagdud. In O. Bar-Yosef and A. Gopher eds., *An Early Neolithic Village in the Jordan Valley. Part I: The Archaeology of Netiv Hagdud*, pp. 209–36. Cambridge, MA: Peabody Museum of Archaeology and Ethnology.

Kitson, P. 1996 British and European river names. *Trans. Philological Society* 94:73–118.

Kivisild, T., Rootsi, S. et al. 2003 The genetics of language and farming spread in India. In P. Bellwood and C. Renfrew eds., *Examining the Farming/Language Dispersal Hypothesis*, pp. 215–22. Cambridge: McDonald Institute for Archaeological Research.

Kivisild, T., Tolk, H. et al. 2002 The emerging limbs and twigs of the East Asian mtDNA tree. *Molecular Biology and Evolution* 19:1737–51.

Klee, M. and Zach, B. 1999 The exploitation of wild and domesticated food plants at settlement mounds in north-east Nigeria. In M. van der Veen ed., *The Exploitation of Plant Resources in Ancient Africa*, pp. 81–8. New York: Kluwer Academic.

Klimov, G. 1991 Some thoughts on Indo-European-Kartvelian relations. *Journal of Indo-European Studies* 19:193–222.

Knapp, B. and Meskell, L. 1997 Bodies of evidence on prehistoric Cyprus. *Cambridge Archaeological Journal* 7:183–204.

Kohler-Rollefson, I. 1988 The aftermath of the Levantine Neolithic Revolution. *Paléorient* 14/1:87–94.

Kolata, A. 1993 *The Tiwanaku*. Oxford: Blackwell.

Kooijmans, L. 1993 The Mesolithic/Neolithic transformation in the Lower Rhine Basin. In P. Bogucki ed., *Case Studies in European Prehistory*, pp. 95–146. Boca Raton: CRC.

Korisettar, R., Venkatasubbaiah, P. and Fuller, D. 2002 Brahmagiri and beyond: the archaeology of the southern Neolithic. In S. Settar and R. Korisettar eds., *Indian Archaeology in Retrospect*, Vol. 1, pp. 151–237. New Delhi: Manohar.

Koslowski, S. and Ginter, B. 1989 The Fayum Neolithic in the light of new discoveries. In L. Krzyzaniak and M. Kobusiewicz eds., *Late Prehistory of the Nile Basin and the Sahara*, pp. 157–80. Poznan: Poznan Anthropological Museum.

Kozlowski, S. 1992 *Nemrik 9. Vol. 2: House No 1/1A/1B*. Warsaw: Warsaw University Press.

Kozlowski, S.K. 1994 Chipped Neolithic industries at the Eastern Wing of the Fertile Crescent. In H.G. Gebel and S.F. Kozlowski eds., *Neolithic Chipped Stone Industries of the Levant*, pp. 143–72. Berlin: Ex Oriente.

Kozlowski, S.K. 1999 *The Eastern Wing of the Fertile Crescent*. Oxford: BAR International Series 760.

Krantz, G. 1988 *Geographical Development of European Languages*. New York: Lang.

Kruk, J. and Milisauskas, S. 1999 *The Rise and Fall of Neolithic Societies*. Krakow: Polskiej Akademii Nauk.

Krzyzaniak, L. 1991 Early farming in the Middle Nile Basin. *Antiquity* 65:515–32.

Kuchikura, Y. 1988 Food use and nutrition in a hunting and gathering community in transition, Peninsular Malaysia. *Man and Culture in Oceania* 4:1–30.

Kuijt, I. 1994 Pre-Pottery Neolithic A settlement variability. *Journal of Mediterranean Archaeology* 7:165–92.

Kuijt, I. 1996 Negotiating equality through ritual. *Journal of Anthropological Archaeology* 15:313–36.

Kuijt, I. 2000a People and space in early agricultural villages. *Journal of Anthropological Archaeology* 19:75–102.

Kuijt, I. ed. 2000b *Life in Neolithic Farming Communities*. New York: Kluwer.

Kuiper, F. 1948 *Proto-Munda Words in Sanskrit*. Amsterdam: Verhandelingen der Koninklijke Nederlandsche Akademie van Wetenschappen, Afdeling Letterkunde 51, Part 3.

Kulick, D. 1992 *Language Shift and Cultural Reproduction*. Cambridge: Cambridge University Press.

Kumar T. 1988 *History of Rice in India*. Delhi: Gian.

Kushnareva, O. 1997 *The southern Caucasus in Prehistory*. Philadelphia: University of Pennsylvania.

Kuzmina, E. 2001 The first migration wave of Indo-Aryans to the south. *Journal of Indo-European Studies* 29, parts 1 and 2:29–40.

Ladizinsky, G. 1999 Identification of the lentil's wild genetic stock. *Genetic Resources and Crop Evolution* 46:115–8.

Lahr, M., Foley, R. and Pinhasi, R. 2000 Expected regional patterns of Mesolithic–Neolithic human population admixture in Europe based on archaeological evidence. In C. Renfrew and K. Boyle eds., *Archaeogenetics*, pp. 81–88. Cambridge: McDonald Institute for Archaeological Research.

Lal, M. 1984 *Settlement History and Rise of Civilization in Ganga-Yamuna Doab*. Delhi: B.R.

Lamb, S. 1958 Linguistic prehistory in the Great Basin. *International Journal of American Linguistics* 24:95–100.

Lamberg-Karlovsky, C.C. 2002 Archaeology and language: the Indo-Iranians. *Current Anthropology* 43:63–88.

LaPolla, R. 2001 The role of migration and language contact in the development of the Sino-Tibetan language family. In A. Aikhenvald and R. Dixon, eds., *Areal Diffusion and Genetic Inheritance: Problems in Comparative Linguistics*, pp. 225–54. Oxford: Oxford University Press.

Lathrap, D. 1969 The "hunting" economies of the tropical forest zone of South America. In R. Lee and I. De Vore eds., *Man the Hunter*, pp. 23–29. Chicago: Aldine.

Lathrap, D. 1970 *The Upper Amazon*. London: Thames and Hudson.

Lathrap, D. 1973 The antiquity and importance of long distance trade. *World Archaeology* 5:170–86.

Lathrap, D. 1977 Our father the cayman, our mother the gourd. In C. Reed ed., *Origins of Agriculture*, pp. 713–52. The Hague: Mouton.

Lathrap, D. and Troike, R. 1983–4 Californian historical linguistics and archaeology. *J. Steward Anthropological Society* 15: 99–157.

Lavachery, P. 2001 The Holocene archaeological sequence of Shum Laka rock shelter. *African Archaeological Review* 18:213–47.

Layton, R. et al. 1991 The transition between hunting and gathering and the specialised husbandry of resources. *Current Anthropology* 32:255–74.

Le Brun, A. 1989 *Fouilles récentes à Khirokitia*. Paris: Editions Recherche sue les Civilizations.

LeBlanc, S. 2003a *Constant Battles*. New York: St Martin's.

LeBlanc, S. 2003b Conflict and language dispersal – issues and a New World example. In P. Bellwood and C. Renfrew eds., *Examining the Farming/Language Dispersal Hypothesis*, pp. 357–65. Cambridge: McDonald Institute for Archaeological Research.

Lebot, V. 1998 Biomolecular evidence for plant domestication in Sahul. *Genetic Resources and Crop Evolution* 46: 619–28.

Lechevallier, M. and Quivron, G. 1979 The Neolithic in Baluchistan: new evidences from Mehrgarh. In H. Härtel ed., *South Asian Archaeology 1979*, pp. 71–92. Berlin: Dietrich Reimer.

Lee, R.B. 1979 *The !Kung San*. Cambridge: Cambridge University Press.

Lee, R.B. 1980 Lactation, ovulation, infanticide, and women's work: a study of hunter-gatherer population regulation. In M.N. Cohen, R.S. Malpass and H.G. Klein eds., *Biosocial Mechanisms of Population Regulation*, pp. 321–48. New Haven: Yale University Press.

Lee, R.B. and Daly, R. eds. 1999 *The Cambridge Encyclopaedia of Hunters and Gatherers*. Cambridge: Cambridge University Press.

Lee, R.B. and Guenther, M. 1990 Oxen or onions? The search for trade (and truth) in the Kalahari. *Current Anthropology* 32:592–602.

Legge, A.J. and Rowley-Conwy, P. 1987 Gazelle killing in Stone Age Syria. *Scientific American* 257(8):88–95.

Legge, A.J. and Rowley-Conwy, P. 2000 The exploitation of animals. In A. Moore, G. Hillman and A. Legge, *Village on the Euphrates: From Foraging to Farming at Abu Hureyra*, pp. 424–71. New York: Oxford University Press.

Lehmann, W. 1993 *Theoretical Bases of Indo-European Linguistics*. London: Routledge.

Leong Sau Heng 1991 Jenderam Hilir and the mid-Holocene prehistory of the west coast plain of Peninsular Malaysia. *Bulletin of the Indo-Pacific Prehistory Association* 10:150–60.

Lesure, R.G. 1997 Early Formative platforms at Paso de la Amada, Chiapas, Mexico. *Latin American Antiquity* 8:217–35.

Levine, M., Rassamakin, Y., Kislenko, A. and Tatarintseva, N. 1999 *Late Prehistoric Exploitation of the Eurasian Steppes*. Cambridge: McDonald Institute for Archaeological Research.

Levtzion, N., 1979 Toward a comparative study of Islamization? In N. Levtzion ed., *Conversion to Islam*, pp. 1–23. New York: Holmes and Meier.

Lev-Yadun, S., Gopher, A. and Abbo, S. 2000 The cradle of agriculture. *Science* 288:1602–3.

Li Xueqin, Harbottle, G. et al. 2003 The earliest writing? *Antiquity* 77:31–44.

Lieberman, D.E. 1991 Seasonality and gazelle hunting at Hayonim Cave. *Paléorient* 17:47–57.

Lieberman, D.E. 1993 The rise and fall of seasonal mobility amongst hunter-gatherers. *Current Anthropology* 34:599–632.

Lieberman, D.E. 1998 Natufian "sedentism" and the importance of biological data for estimating reduced mobility. In T. Rocek and O. Bar-Yosef eds., *Seasonality and Sedentism*, pp. 75–92. Cambridge, Mass.: Peabody Museum, Harvard University.

Lien Chao-mei 2002 The jade industry of Neolithic Taiwan. *Bulletin of the Indo-Pacific Prehistory Association* 22:55–62.

Liu, L. 1996 Settlement patterns, chiefdom variability, and the development of early states in north China. *Journal of Anthropological Archaeology* 15:237–88.

Liversage, D. 1992 On the origins of the Ganges civilization. In P. Bellwood ed., *Man and His Culture: A Resurgence*, pp. 245–66. New Delhi: Books and Books.

Loftus, R. and Cunningham, P. 2000 Molecular genetic analysis of African zeboid populations. In Blench, R. and MacDonald, K. eds., *The Origins and Development of African Livestock*, pp. 251–8. London: UCL Press.

Long, A., Benz, B., Donahue, D., Jull, A. and Toolin, L. 1989 First direct AMS dates on early maize from Tehacan, Mexico. *Radiocarbon* 31:1030–35.

Lourandos, H. 1991 Palaeopolitics: resource intensification in Aboriginal Australia and Papua New Guinea. In T. Ingold, D. Riches and J. Woodburn eds., *Hunters and Gatherers. Vol. 1: History, Evolution and Social Change*, pp. 148–60. Oxford: Berg.

Lourandos, H. 1997 *Continent of Hunter-Gatherers*. Cambridge: Cambridge University Press.

Lowe, G.W. 1989 The heartland Olmec: evolution of material culture. In R.J. Sharer and D.C. Grove eds., *Regional Perspectives on the Olmec*, pp. 33–67. Cambridge: CUP.

Lu Houyuan, Liu Zhenxia, Wu Naiqin et al. 2002 Rice domestication and climate change: phytolith evidence from East China. *Boreas* 31:378–85.

Lu, T. 1998a *The Transition from Foraging to Farming and the Origin of Agriculture in China*. Oxford: BAR International Series 774.

Lu, T. 1998b Some botanical characteristics of green foxtail (*Setaria viridis*) and harvesting experiments on the grass. *Antiquity* 72:902–7.

Lu, T. 2002 A green foxtail millet (*Setaria viridis*) cultivation experiment in the middle Yellow River Valley. *Asian Perspectives* 41:1–14.

Lukacs, J. 2002 Hunting and gathering strategies in prehistoric India. In K. Morrison and L. Junker eds., *Forager-Traders in South and Southeast Asia*, pp. 41–61. Cambridge: Cambridge University Press.

Lum, K and Cann, R. 1998 mtDNA and language support a common origin of Micronesians and Polynesians in Island Southeast Asia. *American Journal of Physical Anthropology* 105:109–19.

Lum, K., Cann, R. et al. 1998 Mitochondrial and nuclear genetic relationships among Pacific Island and Asian populations. *American Journal of Human Genetics* 63:613–24.

Lum, K., Jorde, L. and Schiefenhovel, W. 2002 Affinities among Melanesian, Micronesians and Polynesians: a neutral, biparental genetic perspective. *Human Biology* 74:413–30.

Lynch, T.F. 1999 The earliest South American lifeways. In F. Salomon and S. Schwartz eds., *The Cambridge History of the Native Peoples of the Americas III, South America, Part 1*, pp. 188–263. Cambridge: Cambridge University Press.

Mabry, J. 1999 Changing concepts of the first period of agriculture in the southern Southwest. *Archaeology Southwest* 13/1:2.

Mabry, J. B. ed. 1998 *Archaeological Investigations of Early Village Sites in the Middle Santa Cruz Valley. Analyses and Synthesis, Parts I and II*. Tucson: Center for Desert Archaeology, Archaeological Papers 19.

MacDonald, K. 1998 Before the Empire of Ghana. In G. Connah ed., *Transformations in Africa*, pp. 71–103. London: Leicester University Press.

MacDonald, K. 2000 The origins of African livestock: indigenous or imported? In R. Blench and K. MacDonald eds., *The Origins and Development of African Livestock*, pp. 2–17. London: UCL Press.

MacHugh, D.E. and Bradley, D.G. 2001 Livestock genetic origins: goats buck the trend. *Proc. National Academy of Sciences* 98:5382–4.

Macknight, C. 1976 *Voyage to Marege*. Carlton: Melbourne University Press.

MacNeish, R. 1972 The evaluation of community patterns in the Tehuacan Valley. In P. Ucko, R. Tringham and G. Dimbleby eds., *Man, Settlement and Urbanism*, pp, 67–93. London: Duckworth.

MacNeish, R. 1992 *The Origins of Agriculture and Settled Life*. Norman: University of Oklahoma Press.

MacNeish, R. 1999 A Palaeolithic–Neolithic sequence from South China, Jiangxi Province PRC. In K. Omoto ed., *Interdisciplinary Perspectives on the Origins of the Japanese*, pp. 233–55. Kyoto: International Research Center for Japanese Studies.

MacNeish, R. and Eubanks, M. 2000 Comparative analysis for the Rio Balsas and Tehuacan models for the origins of maize. *Latin American Antiquity* 11:3–20.

MacNeish, R. and Libby, J. eds. 1995 *Origins of Rice Agriculture. The Preliminary Report of the Sino-American Jiangxi (PRC) Project – SAJOR*. University of Texas at El Paso: El Paso Centennial Museum, Publications in Anthropology 13.

MacNeish, R., Cunnar, G, Zhijun Zhao and Libby, J. 1998 *Re-Revised Second Report of the Sino-American Jiangxi (PRC) Origin of Rice Project*. Andover, MA: Andover Foundation for Archaeological Research.

MacPhee, R. and Burney, D. 1991 Dating of modified femora of extinct dwarf *Hippopotamus* from southern Madagascar. *Journal of Archaeological Science* 18:695–706.

Madsen, D. and Simms, S. 1998 The Fremont complex: a behavioural perspective. *Journal of World Prehistory* 12:255–336.

Madsen, D.B. and Rhode, D. 1994 *Across the West*. Salt Lake City: University of Utah Press.

Maggs, T. 1996 The Early Iron Age in the extreme south: some patterns and problems. *Azania* Special Volume XXIX–XXX:171–8.

Maggs, T. and Whitelaw, G. 1991 A review of recent archaeological research on food-producing communities in southern Africa. *Journal of African History* 32:3–24.

Mahdi, W. 1998 Linguistic data on transmission of Southeast Asian cultigens to India and Sri Lanka. In R. Blench and M. Spriggs eds., *Archaeology and Language* II, pp. 390–415. London: Routledge.

Maier, U. 1996 Morphological studies of free-threshing wheat ears from a Neolithic site in southwest Germany, and the history of naked wheats. *Vegetation History and Archaeobotany* 5:39–55.

Mainfort, R.C. and Sullivan, L.P. 1998 Explaining earthen enclosures. In R. Mainfort and L. Sullivan eds., *Ancient Earthen Enclosures*, pp. 1–16. Gainesville: University of Florida Press.

Malhi, R., Mortensen, H. et al. 2003 Native American mtDNA prehistory in the American Southwest. *American Journal of Physical Anthropology* 120:108–24.

Malone, C. 2003 The Italian Neolithic. *Journal of World Prehistory* 17:235–312.

Mallory, J. 1989 *In Search of the Indo-Europeans*. London: Thames and Hudson.

Mallory, J. 1996 The Indo-European phenomenon: linguistics and archaeology. In A. Dani and J. Mohen eds., *History of Humanity*, vol. II, pp. 80–91. Paris: Unesco.

Mallory, J. 1997 The homelands of the Indo-Europeans. In R. Blench and M. Spriggs eds., *Archaeology and Language I*, pp. 93–121. London: Routledge.

Mallory, J. and Adams, D. eds. 1997 *Encyclopaedia of Indo-European Culture*. London: Fitzroy Dearborn.

Mangelsdorf, P., MacNeish, R. and Galinat, W. 1964 Domestication of corn. *Science* 143: 538–45.

Mansfield, P. 1985 *The Arabs*. 2nd edition. Harmondsworth: Penguin.

Mapa 1980 *Mapa Etno-Historico do Brasil e Regioes Adjacentes*. Fundacao Instituto Brasileiro de Geografia e Estatistica.

Marcus, J. and Flannery. K. 1996 *Zapotec Civilization*. London: Thames and Hudson.

Maret, P. de 1996 Pits, pots and the Far-West streams. *Azania* Special Volume XXIX–XXX: 318–23.

Markey, T. 1989 The spread of agriculture in western Europe. In D. Harris ed., *The Origins and Spread of Agriculture and Pastoralism in Eurasia*, pp.585–606. London: UCL Press.

Marshall, F. 1998 Early food production in Africa. *Review of Archaeology* 19/2: 47–57.

Marshall, F. and Hildebrand, E. 2002 Cattle before crops: the beginnings of food production in Africa. *Journal of World Prehistory* 16:99–144.

Masica, C. 1976 *Defining a Linguistic Area: South Asia*. Chicago: University of Chicago Press.

Masica C. 1979 Aryan and Non-Aryan elements in north Indian agriculture. In M. Deshpande and P. Hook eds., *Aryan and Non-Aryan in India*, pp. 55–152. Ann Arbor: Michigan Papers on South and Southeast Asia 14.

Masica, C. 1991 *The Indo-Aryan Languages*. Cambridge: Cambridge University Press.

Matisoff, J. 1991 Sino-Tibetan linguistics: present state and future prospects. *Annual Review of Anthropology* 20: 469–504.

Matisoff, J. 2000 On the uselessness of glottochronology for subgrouping Tibeto-Burman. In C. Renfrew, A. McMahon and L. Trask eds., *Time Depth in Historical Linguistics*, pp. 333–72. Cambridge: McDonald Institute for Archaeological Research.

Matson, R.G. 1991 *The Origins of Southwestern Agriculture*. Tucson: University of Arizona Press.

Matson, R.G. 2003 The spread of maize agriculture into the US Southwest. In P. Bellwood and C. Renfrew eds., *Examining the Farming/Language Dispersal Hypothesis*, pp. 341–56. Cambridge: McDonald Institute for Archaeological Research.

Matsuoka, Y., Vigouroux, Y, Goodman, M. et al. 2002 A single domestication for maize shown by multilocus microsatellite genotyping. *Proceedings of the National Academy of Sciences* 99: 6080–84.

Matteson, E., Wheeler, A. et al. 1972 *Comparative Studies in Amerindian Languages*. The Hague: Mouton.

McAlpin, D. 1974 Towards Proto-Elamo-Dravidian. *Language* 50:89–101.

McAlpin, D. 1981 Proto-Elamo-Dravidian: the Evidence and its Implications. *Transactions of the American Philosophical Society* 71(3). Philadelphia.

McCall, D. 1998 The Afroasiatic language phylum: African in origin, or Asian? *Current Anthropology* 39:139–44.

McCorriston, J. and Hole, F. 1991 The ecology of seasonal stress and the origins of agriculture in the Near East. *American Anthropologist* 93:46–69.

McCorriston, J. and Oches, E. 2001 Two Early Holocene check dams from southern Arabia. *Antiquity* 75:675–6.

McIntosh, S.K. and McIntosh, R. 1988 From stone to metal: new perspectives on the later prehistory of West Africa. *Journal of World Prehistory* 2:89–133.

McIntosh, S.K. 1994 Changing perceptions of West Africa's past. *Journal of Archaeological Research* 2:165–98.

Meacham, W. 1978 *Sham Wan, Lamma Island*. Hong Kong Archaeological Society, Journal Monograph III.

Meacham, W. 1984–5 Hac Sa Wan, Macau. *Journal of the Hong Kong Archaeological Society* XI:97–105.

Meacham, W. 1994 *Archaeological Investigations on Chek Lap Kok Island*. Hong Kong: Hong Kong Archaeological Society.

Meacham, W. 1995 Middle and Late Neolithic at "Yung Long South". In C. Yeung and B. Li eds., *Archaeology in Southeast Asia*, pp. 445–66. Hong Kong: University of Hong Kong Museum and Art Gallery.

Meadow, R. 1989 Continuity and change in the agriculture of the Greater Indus Valley. In J.M. Kenoyer ed., *Old Problems and New Perspectives in the Archaeology of South Asia*, pp. 61–74. Madison: University of Wisconsin Archaeological Reports 2.

Meadow, R.H. 1993 Animal domestication in the Middle East. In G. Possehl ed., *Harappan Civilization: A Recent Perspective*, pp. 295–322. 2nd edition. New Delhi: Oxford & IBH.

Meadow, R.H. 1998 Pre- and proto-historic agricultural and pastoral transformations in northwestern South Asia. *Review of Archaeology* 23/2: 22–29.

Meggers, B. 1987 The early history of man in Amazonia. In T.C. Whitmore and G.T. Prance eds., *Biogeography and Quaternary History in Tropical America*, pp. 151–74. Oxford: Clarendon Pres.

Meggers, B. and Evans, C. 1983 Lowland South America and the Antilles. In J.D. Jennings ed., *Ancient South Americans*, pp. 287–335. San Francisco: Freeman.

Mehra, K. 1999 Subsistence changes in India and Pakistan. In C. Gosden and J. Hather eds., *The Prehistory of Food*, pp. 139–46. London: Routledge.

Meiklejohn, C. and Zvelebil, M. 1991 Health status of European populations at the agricultural transition. In H. Bush and M. Zvelebil eds., *Health in Past Societies*, pp. 129–45. Oxford: BAR International Series 567.

Meiklejohn, C. et al. 1992 Artificial cranial deformation. *Paléorient* 18/2:83–98.

Melton, T., Clifford, S. et al. 1998 Genetic evidence for the Proto-Austronesian tribes in Asia. *American Journal of Human Genetics* 63:1807–23.

Melton, T., Peterson, R. et al. 1995 Polynesian genetic affinities with Southeast Asian populations as identified by mitochondrial DNA analysis. *American Journal of Human Genetics* 57:403–14.

Mercader, J, Garcia-Heras, M. and Gonzalez-Alvarez, I. 2000 Ceramic tradition in the African forest. *Journal of Archaeological Science* 27:163–82.

Merriwether, A., Friedlaender, J. et al. 1999 Mitochondrial DNA is an indicator of Austronesian influence in Island Melanesia. *American Journal of Physical Anthropology* 110:243–70.

Merriwether, A., Kemp, B. et al. 2000 Gene flow and genetic variation in the Yanomama as revealed by mitochondrial DNA. In C. Renfrew ed., *America Past, America Present*, pp. 89–124. Cambridge: McDonald Institute for Archaeological Research.

Michalove, P., Georg, S. and Manaster Ramer, A. 1998 Current issues in linguistic taxonomy. *Annual Review of Anthropology* 27:451–72.

Midant-Reynes, B. 2000 *The Prehistory of Egypt*. Oxford: Blackwell.

Midgley, M. 1992 *TRB Culture*. Edinburgh: Edinburgh University Press.

Migliazza, E. 1982 Linguistic prehistory and the refuge model. In G. Prance ed., *Biological Diversification in the Tropics*, pp. 497–522. New York: Columbia University Press.

Migliazza, E. 1985 Languages of the Orinoco-Amazon region. In H. Manelis-Klein and L. Stark eds., *South American Indian Languages*, pp. 17–139. Austin: University of Texas Press.

Milanich, J.T. 1996 *The Timucua*. Oxford: Blackwell.

Militarev, A. 2000 Towards the chronology of Afrasian (Afroasiatic) and its daughter families. In C. Renfrew, A. McMahon and L. Trask eds., *Time Depth in Historical Linguistics*, pp. 267–307. Cambridge: McDonald Institute for Archaeological Research.

Militarev, A. 2003 The prehistory of a dispersal: the Proto-Afrasian (Afroasiatic) farming lexicon. In P. Bellwood and C.Renfrew eds., *Examining the Farming/Language Dispersal Hypothesis*, pp. 135–50. Cambridge: McDonald Institute for Archaeological Research.

Miller, N. 1991 The Near East. In W. van Zeist et al. eds., *Progress in Old World Palaeoethnobotany*, pp. 133–60. Rotterdam: Balkema.

Miller, N. 1992 The origins of plant cultivation in the Near East. In C.W. Cowan and P.J. Watson eds., *The Origins of Agriculture*, pp. 39–58. Washington: Smithsonian.

Miller, R. 1991 Genetic connections among the Altaic languages. In S. Lamb and E. Mitchell eds., *Sprung from Some Common Source*, pp. 293–327. Stanford: Stanford University Press.

Miller, W. 1983 Uto-Aztecan Languages. In A. Ortiz ed., *Handbook of North American Indians*, Vol. 10, pp. 113–24. Washington: Smithsonian.

Miller, W. 1984 The classification of the Uto-Aztecan languages based on lexical evidence. *International Journal of American Linguistics* 50:1–24.

Milner, N., Craig, O. et al. 2004 Something fishy in the Neolithic? *Antiquity* 78:9–22.

Mindzie, C., Doutrelepont, H. et al. 2001 First archaeological evidence of banana cultivation in central Africa during the third millennium before present. *Vegetation History and Archaeobotany* 10:1–6.

Minnis, P.E. 1992 Earliest plant cultivation in the desert borderlands of North America. In C.W. Cowan and P.J. Watson eds., *The Origins of Agriculture*, pp. 121–42. Washington DC: Smithsonian.

Misra, V.D. 1977 *Some Aspects of Indian Archaeology*. Allahabad: Prabhat Prakashan.

Misra, V.D. 2002 A review of the Copper Hoards and the OCP culture. In S. Settar and R. Korisettar eds., *Indian Archaeology in Retrospect*, Vol. 1, pp. 277–86. New Delhi: Manohar.

Misra, V.N. 1973 Bagor – a late mesolithic settlement in north-west India. *World Archaeology* 5:92–110.

Misra, V.N. 1997 Balathal: a Chalcolithic settlement in Mewar, Rajasthan. *South Asian Studies* 13:251–73.

Misra, V.N. 2001 Prehistoric human colonization of India. *Journal of Bioscience* 26, No. 4, Supplement, pp. 491–531.

Misra, V.N. 2002 Radiocarbon chronology of Balathal and its implications. Paper presented at 17th IPPA Congress, Taipei, September 2002.

Misra, V.N. et al. 1995 The excavations at Balathal. *Man and Environment* XX/1:57–80.

Mithun, M. 1984 Iroquoian origins: problems in reconstruction. In M. Foster et al. eds., *Extending the Rafters*, pp. 237–81. Albany: State University of New York Press.

Mithun, M. 1999 *The Native Languages of North America*. Cambridge: Cambridge University Press.

Mohammad-Ali, A. 1987 The Neolithic of central Sudan. In A. Close ed., *Prehistory of Arid North Africa*, pp. 123–36. Dallas: Southern Methodist University Press.

Molleson, T. 1994 The eloquent bones of Anu Hureyra. *Scientific American* 271/2:60–65.

Moore, A. and Hillman, G. 1992 The Pleistocene to Holocene transition and human economy in Southwest Asia. *American Antiquity* 57:482–94.

Moore, A., Hillman, G. and Legge, A. 2000 *Village on the Euphrates: From Foraging to Farming at Abu Hureyra*. New York: Oxford University Press.

Moore, J. 1994 Putting anthropology back together again. *American Anthropologist* 96: 925–48.

Moseley, M.E. 1975 *The Maritime Foundations of Andean Civilization*. Menlo Park: Cummings.

Moseley, M.E. 1994 New light on the horizon. *Review of Archaeology* 15/2:26–41.

Mottram, M. 1997 Jerf el-Ahmar: the chipped stone industry of a PPNA site on the Middle Euphrates. *Neo-Lithics* 1/97:14–16.

Moulins, D. de 1997 *Agricultural Changes at Euphrates and Steppe Sites in the Mid-8th to Mid-6th Millennium BC*. Oxford: BAR International Series 683.

Murdock, G.P. 1967 *Ethnographic Atlas*. New Haven: HRAF Press.

Murdock, G.P. 1968 Genetic classification of the Austronesian languages. *Ethnology* 3:117–26.

Muro, M. 1998–9 Not just another roadside attraction. *American Archaeology* 2/4:10–16.

Muzzolini, A. 1993 The emergence of a food-producing economy in the Sahara. In T. Shaw, P. Sinclair, B. Andah and A. Okpoko eds., *The Archaeology of Africa*, pp. 227–39. London: Routledge.

Nadel, D. and Herschkovitz, I. 1991 New subsistence data and human remains from the earliest Levantine Epipalaeolithic. *Current Anthropology* 32:631–5.

Nadel, D. and Werker, E. 1999 The oldest ever brush hut plant remains from Ohalo II, Jordan Valley, Israel (19,000 BP). *Antiquity* 73:755–64.

Nadel, D. et al. 1991 Early Neolithic arrowhead types in the southern Levant. *Paléorient* 17/1:109–19.

Nelson, S. 1995 Introduction. In S, Nelson ed., *The Archaeology of Northeast China*, pp. 1–18. London: Routledge.

Nettle, D. 1998 Explaining global patterns of linguistic diversity. *Journal of Anthropological Archaeology* 17:354–74.

Nettle, D. 1999 *Linguistic Diversity*. Oxford: Oxford University Press.

Nettle, D. and Harriss, L. 2003 Genetic and linguistic affinities between human populations in Eurasia and West Africa. *Human Biology* 75:331–44.

Neumann, K. 1999 Charcoal from West African savanna sites. In M. van der Veen ed., *The Exploitation of Plant Resources in Ancient Africa*, pp. 205–20. New York: Kluwer Academic.

Newman, J.L. 1995 *The Peopling of Africa*. New Haven: Yale University Press.

Nguyen Xuan Hien 1998 Rice remains from various archaeological sites in North and South Vietnam. In M. Klokke and T. de Bruijn eds., *Southeast Asian Archaeology* 1996, pp. 27–40. University of Hull, Centre for Asian Studies.

Nichols, J. 1997a The epicentre of the Indo-European linguistic spread. In R. Blench and M. Spriggs eds., *Archaeology and Language I*, pp. 122–48. London: Routledge.

Nichols, J. 1997b Modeling ancient population structures and movement in linguistics. *Annual Review of Anthropology* 26:359–84.

Nichols, J. 1998a The Eurasian spread zone and the Indo-European dispersal. In R. Blench and M. Spriggs eds., *Archaeology and Language II*, pp. 220–66. London: Routledge.

Nichols, J. 1998b The origins and dispersals of languages. In N. Jablonski and L. Aiello eds., *The Origin and Diversification of Language*, pp. 127–70. San Francisco: Memoirs of the Californian Academy of Science 24.

Nichols, J. 2000 Estimating the dates of early American colonization events. In C. Renfrew, A. McMahon and L. Trask eds., *Time Depth in Historical Linguistics*, pp. 643–64. Cambridge: McDonald Institute for Archaeological Research.

Nichols, M. 1983–4 Old California Uto-Aztecan. *J. Steward Anthropological Society* 15:23–46.

Niederberger, C. 1979 Early sedentary economy in the Basin of Mexico. *Science* 203:131–42.

Nissen, H., Muheisen, M. and Gebel, H.G. 1987 Report on the first two seasons of excavation at Basta. *Annual Report of the Department of Antiquities of Jordan* 31:79–118.

Noble, G. 1965 Proto-Arawakan and its Descendants. *International Journal of American Linguistics* 31/3, part II.

Norman, J. 1988 *Chinese*. Cambridge: Cambridge University Press.

Norman, J. and Tsu-lin Mei 1976 The Austroasiatics in ancient south China: some lexical evidence. *Monumenta Serica* 32: 274–301.

Nowak, M. 2001 The second phase of Neolithization in east-central Europe. *Antiquity* 75: 582–92.

Nurse, G.T., Weiner, J.S. and Jenkins T. 1985 *The Peoples of Southern Africa and their Affinities*. Oxford: Clarendon Press.

O'Brien, M.J. and Wood, W.R. 1998 *The Prehistory of Missouri*. Columbia: University of Missouri Press.

Olsen, K. and Schaal, B. 1999 Evidence on the origin of cassava: phylogeography of *Manihot esculenta*. *Proceedings of the National Academy of Sciences* 96:5586–91.

Olszewski, D. 1991 Social complexity in the Natufian? In G.A. Clark ed., *Perspectives on the Past*, pp. 322–40. Philadelphia: University of Pennsylvania Press.

Oppenheimer, S. and Richards, M. 2001a Fast trains, slow boats, and the ancestry of the Polynesian islanders. *Science Progress* 84:157–81.

Oppenheimer, S. and Richards, M. 2001b Slow boat to Melanesia? *Nature* 410:166–7.

Oppenheimer, S. and Richards, M. 2003 Polynesians: devolved Taiwanese rice farmers or Wallacean maritime traders with fishing, foraging and horticultural skills. In P. Bellwood and C.Renfrew eds., *Examining the Farming/Language Dispersal Hypothesis*, pp. 287–98. Cambridge: McDonald Institute for Archaeological Research.

Ostapirat, W. in press Kra-dai and Austronesians. In L. Sagart, R. Blench and A. Sanchez-Mazas eds., *The Peopling of East Asia: Putting Together Archaeology, Linguistics and Genetics*. London: RoutledgeCurzon.

Oyuela-Cayceda, A. 1994 Rocks versus clay: the evolution of pottery technology in the case of San Jacinto 1, Colombia. In W. Barnett and J. Hoopes eds., *The Emergence of Pottery*, pp. 133–44. Washington DC: Smithsonian.

Oyuela-Cayceda, A. 1996 The study of collector variability in the transition to sedentary food producers in northern Colombia. *Journal of World Prehistory* 10:49–93.

Özdoğan, M. 1997a Anatolia from the last glacial maximum to the Holocene climatic optimum. *P 23/2:25–38*.

Özdoğan, M. 1997b The beginning of Neolithic economies in southeastern Europe: an Anatolian perspective. *J. European Archaeology* 5/2:1–33.

Özdoğan, M. 1998 Anatolia from the last glacial maximum to the Holocene climatic optimum. *Paléorient* 23/2:25–38.

Özdoğan, M. 1999 Çayönü. In M. Özdoğan and B. Başgelen eds., *Neolithic in Turkey* pp. 35–64. Istanbul: Arkeoloji ve Sanat Yayinlari.

Özdoğan, M. and Balkan-Atli, N. 1994 South-East Anatolian chipped stone sequence. In H.G. Gebel and S.F. Kozlowski eds., *Neolithic Chipped Stone Industries of the Levant*, pp. 205–6. Berlin: Ex Oriente.

Özdoğan, M. and Başgelen, N. 1999 *Neolithic in Turkey*. Istanbul: Arkeoloji ve Sanat Yayinlari.

Pääbo, S. 1999 Ancient DNA. In B. Sykes ed., *The Human Inheritance*, pp. 119–34. Oxford: Oxford University Press.

Pachori, S. 1993 *Sir William Jones: a Reader*. Delhi: Oxford University Press.

Paddayya, K. 1993 Ashmound investigations at Budihal. *Man and Environment* XVIII/1:57–88.

Paddayya, K. 1998 Evidence of Neolithic cattle-penning at Budihal. *South Asian Studies* 14: 141–53.

Pardoe, C. 1988 The cemetery as symbol. *Archaeology in Oceania* 23:1–16.

Parkin, R. 1991 *A Guide to Austroasiatic Speakers and their Languages*. Honolulu: University of Hawai'i Press.

Parpola, A. 1988 The coming of the Aryans to Iran and India. *Studia Orientalia* 64: 195–302.

Parpola, A. 1999 The formation of the Aryan branch of Indo-European. In R. Blench and M. Spriggs eds., *Archaeology and Language III*, pp. 180–210. London: Routledge.

Passarino, G. 1996 Pre-Caucasoid and Caucasoid genetic features of the Indian population. *American Journal of Human Genetics* 59:927–34.

Pawley, A. 1981 Melanesian diversity and Polynesian homogeneity: a unified explanation for language. In K. Hollyman and A. Pawley eds., *Studies in Pacific Languages and Cultures*, pp. 269–309. Auckland: Linguistic Society of New Zealand.

Pawley, A. 1996 On the Polynesian subgroup as a problem for Irwin's continuous settlement hypothesis. In J.M. Davidson et al. eds., *Oceanic Culture History*, pp. 387–410. Dunedin: New Zealand Journal of Archaeology Special Publication.

Pawley, A. 1999 Chasing rainbows: implications of the rapid dispersal of Austronesian languages for subgrouping and reconstruction. In E. Zeitoun and P. J-K. Li eds., *Selected papers from the Eighth International Conference on Austronesian linguistics*, pp. 95–138. Taipei: Institute of Linguistics, Academia Sinica.

Pawley, A. 2003 The Austronesian dispersal: languages, technologies and people. In P. Bellwood and C. Renfrew eds., *Examining the Farming/Language Dispersal Hypothesi*, pp. 251–74. Cambridge: McDonald Institute for Archaeological Research.

Pawley, A. in press The chequered career of the Trans New Guinea hypothesis: recent research and its implications. In A. Pawley, R. Attenborough, R. Hide and J. Golson eds., *Papuan Pasts*. Adelaide: Crawford House Australia.

Pawley, A. and Green, R. 1975 Dating the dispersal of the Oceanic languages. *Oceanic Linguistics* 12: 1–67.

Pawley, A. and Pawley, M. 1994 Early Austronesian terms for canoe parts and seafaring. In A. Pawley and M. Ross eds., *Austronesian Terminologies: Continuity and Change*, pp. 329–62. Canberra: Pacific Linguistics Series C-127.

Pawley, A. and Ross, M. 1993 Austronesian historical linguistics and culture history. *Review of Anthropology* 22:425–59.

Pawley, A. and Ross, M. 1995 The prehistory of the Oceanic languages: a current view. In P. Bellwood, J. Fox and D. Tryon eds., *The Austronesians*, pp. 39–74. Canberra: Dept Anthropology, Research School of Pacific Studies, Australian National University.

Payne, D. 1991 A classification of Maipurean (Arawakan) languages based on shared lexical retentions. In D. Derbyshire and G. Pullum eds., *Handbook of Amazonian Languages*, vol. 3, pp. 355–499. New York: Mouton de Gruyter.

Paz, V. 2003 Island Southeast Asia: spread of friction zone? In P. Bellwood and C. Renfrew eds., *Examining the Farming/Language Dispersal Hypothesis*, pp. 275–85. Cambridge: McDonald Institute for Archaeological Research.

Pearsall, D. 1999 The impact of maize on subsistence systems in South America. In C. Gosden and J. Hather eds., *The Prehistory of Food*, pp. 419–37. London: Routledge.

Pearsall, D. 2002 Maize is *still* ancient in prehistoric Ecuador. *Journal of Archaeological Science* 29:51–5.

Pearson, R. 1981 Social complexity in Chinese coastal Neolithic sites. *Science* 213:1078–86.

Pechenkina, E., Benfer, R. and Wang Zhijun 2002 Diet and health changes at the end of the Chinese Neolithic. *American Journal of Physical Anthropology* 117:15–36.

Peiros, I. 1988 Comparative Linguistics in Southeast Asia. Canberra: Pacific Linguistics Series C-142.

Pejros, I. and Schnirelman, V. 1998 Rice in Southeast Asia. In R. Blench and M. Spriggs eds., *Archaeology and Language* II, pp. 379–89. London: Routledge.

Peltenberg, E., Colledge, S. et al. 2000 Agro-pastoral colonization of Cyprus in the 10th millennium BP: initial assessments. *Antiquity* 74:844–53.

Peltenberg, E., Colledge, S., Croft, P. et al. 2001 Neolithic dispersals from the Levantine Corridor: a Mediterranean perspective. *Levant* 33:35–64.

Pennington, R.L. 1996 Causes of early human population growth. *AJPA* 99:259–74.

Penny, D. 1999 Palaeoenvironmental analysis of the Sakhon Nakhon Basin, northeast Thailand. *Bulletin of the Indo-Pacific Prehistory Association* 18:139–50.

Pentz, P., 1992 *The Invisible Conquest*. Copenhagen: National Museum of Denmark.

Perlès, C. 1999 The distribution of *magoules* in eastern Thessaly. In P. Halstead ed., *Neolithic Society in Greece*, pp. 42–56. Sheffield: Sheffield Academic Press.

Perlès, C. 2001 *The Early Neolithic in Greece*. Cambridge: Cambridge University Press.

Perrin, T. 2003 Mesolithic and Neolithic cultures co-existing in the upper Rhone Valley. *Antiquity* 77:732–9.

Perry, W. 1937 (1924) *The Growth of Civilization*. Harmondsworth: Penguin.

Perttula, T. 1996 Caddoan area archaeology since 1990. *Journal of Archaeological Research* 4:295–348.

Peterson, D.A. 1980 The introduction, use and technology of fibre-tempered pottery in the southeastern USA. In D.L. Browman ed., *Early Native Americans*, pp. 363–72. The Hague: Mouton.

Peterson, J. 1978 *The Ecology of Social Boundaries*. Urbana: University of Illinois Press.

Peterson, N. 1976 Ethnoarchaeology in the Australian Iron Age. In G. Sieveking, I. Longworth and K. Wilson eds., *Problems in Economic and Social Archaeology*, pp. 265–76. London: Duckworth.

Peterson, N. 1993 Demand sharing. *American Anthropologist* 95:860–74.

Petry, C. ed., 1998 *The Cambridge History of Egypt*. Cambridge: Cambridge University Press.

Phillipson, D. 1993 *African Archaeology*. 2nd edn. Cambridge: Cambridge University Press.

Phillipson, D. 1998 *Ancient Ethiopia*. London: British Museum Press.

Phillipson, D. 2003 Language and farming dispersals in sub-Saharan Africa, with particular reference to the Bantu-speaking peoples. In P. Bellwood and C. Renfrew eds., *Examining the Farming/Language Dispersal Hypothesis*, pp. 177–87. Cambridge: McDonald Institute for Archaeological Research.

Piazza, A., Rendine, S. et al. 1995 Genetics and the origin of European languages. *Proceedings of the National Academy of Sciences* 92:5836–40.

Pickersgill, B. 1989 Cytological and genetic evidence on the domestication and diffusion of crops within the Americas. In D. Harris and G. Hillman eds., *Foraging and Farming*, pp. 426–39. London: Unwin Hyman.

Pietrusewsky, M. 1999 Multivariate cranial investigations of Japanese, Asian, and Pacific Islanders. In K. Omoto ed., *Interdisciplinary Perspectives on the Origins of the Japanese*, pp. 65–104. Kyoto: International Research Center for Japanese Studies.

Pietrusewsky, M. and Chang, C. 2003 Taiwan Aboriginals and peoples of the Asia-Pacific region: multivariate craniometric comparisons. *Anthropological Science* (Japan) 111:293–332.

Pietrusewsky, M. and Douglas, M. 2001 Intensification of agriculture at Ban Chiang: is there evidence from the skeletons? *Asian Perspectives* 40:157–78.

Pigott, V. and Natapintu, S. 1996–7 Investigating the origins of metal use in prehistoric Thailand. In D. Bulbeck ed., *Ancient Chinese and Southeast Asian Bronze Age Cultures*, vol. II, pp. 787–808. Taipei: SMC Publishing.

Pinhasi, R. and Pluciennik, M. in press A regional biological approach to the spread of agriculture to Europe. *Current Anthropology*.

Piperno, D. 1998 Paleoethnobotany in the tropics from microfossils. *Journal of World Prehistory* 12:393–450.

Piperno, D. and Flannery, K. 2001 The earliest archaeological maize (*Zea mays* L.) from highland Mexico. *Proceedings of the National Academy of Sciences* 98: 2101–3.

Piperno, D. and Pearsall, D. 1998 *The Origins of Agriculture in the Lowland Neotropics*. San Diego: Academic.

Piperno, D.R., Ranere, A., Holst, I. and Hansell, P. 2000 Starch grains reveal early root crop horticulture in the Panamanian tropical forest. *Nature* 407: 894–7.

Plog, S. 1997 *Ancient Peoples of the American Southwest*. New York: Thames and Hudson.

Pohl, M., Pope, K. et al. 1996 Early agriculture in the Maya Lowlands. *Latin American Antiquity* 7:355–72.

Polomé, E. 1990 The Indo-Europeanization of northern Europe: the linguistic evidence. *Journal of Indo-European Studies* 18:331–8.

Poloni, E., Semino. O. et al. 1997 Human genetic affinities for Y-chromosome P49a,f/*Taq*1 haplotypes show strong correspondence with linguistics. *American Journal of Human Genetics* 61:1015–35.

Polunin, I. 1953 The medical natural history of Malayan aborigines. *Medical Journal of Malaya* 8/1: 62–174.

Pope, K., Pohl, M., Jones, J. et al. 2001 Origin and environmental setting of ancient agriculture in the lowlands of Mesoamerica. *Science* 292:1370–3.

Possehl, G. 1986 African millets in South Asian prehistory. In J. Jacobsen ed., *Studies in the Archaeology of India and Pakistan*, pp. 237–56. New Delhi: Oxford & IBH.

Possehl, G. 1997 The transformation of the Indus civilization. *Journal of World Prehistory* 11:425–72.

Possehl, G. 2002 *The Indus Civilization*. Walnut Creek, C : Altamira.

Possehl, G. and Kennedy, K. 1979 Hunter-gatherer/agriculturalist exchange in prehistory: an Indian example. *Current Anthropology* 20:592–3.

Potts, D. 1999 *The Archaeology of Elam*. Cambridge: Cambridge University Press.

Pozorski, S. and Pozorski, T. 1987 *Early Settlement and Subsistence in the Casma Valley, Peru*. Iowa City: University of Iowa Press.

Pozorski, S. and Pozorski, T. 1992 Early civilization in the Casma Valley, Peru. *Antiquity* 66:845–70.

Pozorski, T. 1996 Ventilated hearth structures in the Casma Valley, Peru. *Latin American Antiquity* 7:341–53.

Pozorski, T. and Pozorski, S. 1990 Huaynuna, a late Cotton Preceramic site on the north coast of Peru. *Journal of Field Archaeology* 17:17–26.

Prance, G. ed. 1982 *Biological Diversification in the Tropics*. New York: Columbia University Press.

Prentiss, W. and Chatters, J. 2003 Cultural diversification and decimation in the prehistoric record. *Current Anthropology* 44:33–58.

Price, T.D. and Gebauer, A.B. 1995 New Perspectives on the Transition to Agriculture. In T.D. Price and A.B. Gebauer eds., *Last Hunters First Farmers*, pp. 3–20. Santa Fe: School of American Research.

Price, T.D. ed. 2000 *Europe's First Farmers*. Cambridge: Cambridge University Press.

Price, T.D. 1987 The Mesolithic of Western Europe. *Journal of World Prehistory* 1:225–306.

Price, T.D. 1996 The first farmers of southern Scandinavia. In D. Harris ed. 1996, pp. 346–62.

Price, T.D. and Gebauer, A. 1992 The final frontier: first farmers in northern Europe. In A.B. Gebauer and T.D. Price eds., *Transitions to Agriculture in Prehistory*, pp. 97–116. Madison: Prehistory Press.

Price, T.D., Bentley, R.A. et al. 2001 Prehistoric human migration in the *Linearbandkeramik* of central Europe. *Antiquity* 75:593–603.

Pringle, H. 1998 The slow birth of agriculture. *Science* 282:1446–50.

Pye, M.E. and Demarest, A. 1991 The evolution of complex societies in southeast Mesoamerica. In W.R. Fowler ed. *The Formation of Complex Society in Southeastern Mesoamerica*, pp. 77–100. Boca Raton, FL: CRC Press.

Quilter, J. Ojeda, B. et al. 1991 Subsistence economy of El Paraiso, an early Peruvian site. *Science* 251:277–83.

Quintana-Murci, L., Krausz, C. et al. 2001 Y-chromosome lineages trace diffusion of people and languages in southwestern Asia. *American Journal of Human Genetics* 68:537–42.

Quintero, L. and Wilke, P. 1995 Evolutionary and economic significance of naviform core-and-blade technology in the southern Levant. *Paléorient* 21:17–33.

Quintero, L., Wilke, P. and Waines, G. 1997 Pragmatic studies of Near Eastern Neolithic sickle blades. In H. Gebel, Z. Kafafi and G. Rollefson eds., *The Prehistory of Jordan, II. Perspectives from 1997*, pp. 263–86. Berlin: Ex Oriente.

Raemakers, D. 2003 Cutting a long story short? The process of neolithization in the Dutch delta re-examined. *Antiquity* 77:740–8.

Rai, N. 1990 *Living in a Lean-to*. Ann Arbor: University of Michigan Monograph in Anthropology 80.

Rankin, R. n.d. On Siouan chronology. Unpublished manuscript (via personal communication).

Rao, S.N. 1977 Continuity and survival of Neolithic traditions in northeastern India. *Asian Pespectives* 20: 191–205.

Rao, S.R. 1962–3 Excavations at Rangpur. *Ancient India* 18 & 19:5–207.

Raymond, J.S. 1981 The maritime foundations of Andean civilization: a reconsideration of the evidence. *American Antiquity* 46:806–21.

Redd, A. J., Takezaki, N. et al. 1995 Evolutionary history of the COII/tRNA^{Lys} intergenic 9 b.p. deletion in human mitochondrial DNAs from the Pacific. *Molecular Biology and Evolution* 12:604–15.

Reddy, S.N. 1997 If the threshing floor could talk. *Journal of Anthropological Archaeology* 16: 162–87.

Reid, L. 1988 Benedict's Austro-Tai hypothesis: an evaluation. *Asian Perspectives* 26:19–34.

Reid, L. 1994a Unravelling the linguistic histories of Philippine Negritos. In T. Dutton and D. Tryon eds., *Language Contact and Change in the Austroneaian World*, pp. 443–76. Berlin: Mouton de Gruyter.

Reid, L. 1994b Possible non-Austronesian lexical elements in Philippine Negrito languages. *Oceanic Linguistics* 33:37–72.

Reid, L. 1996 The current state of linguistic research on the relatedness of the language families of East and Southeast Asia. *Bulletin of the Indo-Pacific Prehistory Association* 15: 87–92.

Reid, L. 2001 Comment. *Language and Linguistics* 2:247–52. Academia Sinica, Taipei.

Renfrew, C. 1987 *Archaeology and Language*. London: Jonathan Cape.

Renfrew, C. 1989 Models of change in language and archaeology. *Transactions of the Philological Society* 87:103–65.

Renfrew, C. 1991 Before Babel. *Cambridge Archaeological Journal* 1:3–23.

Renfrew, C. 1992a World languages and human dispersals: a minimalist view. In J. Hall and I. Jarvie eds., *Transition to Modernity*, pp. 11–68. Cambridge: Cambridge University Press.

Renfrew, C. 1992b Archaeology, genetics and linguistic diversity. *Man* 27:445–78.

Renfrew, C. 1998 Word of Minos. *Cambridge Archaeological Journal* 8:239–64.

Renfrew, C. 1999 Time depth, convergence theory, and innovation in Proto-Indo-European. *Journal of Indo-European Studies* 27:257–93.

Renfrew, C. 2000 Archaeogenetics: towards a population prehistory of Europe. In C. Renfrew and K. Boyle eds., *Archaeogenetics*, pp. 3–12. Cambridge: McDonald Institute for Archaeological Research.

Renfrew, C. 2001a The Anatolian origins of Proto-Indo-European and the autochthony of the Hittites. In R. Drews ed., *Greater Anatolia and the Indo-Hittite Language Family*, pp. 36–63. Washington, DC: Institute for the Study of Man.

Renfrew, C. 2001b At the edge of knowability: towards a prehistory of languages. *Cambridge Archaeological Journal* 10: 7–34.

Renfrew, C. 2001c From molecular genetics to archaeogenetics. *Proceedings of the National Academy of Sciences* 98:4830–32.

Renfrew, C. 2003 'The emerging synthesis': the archaeogenetics of language/farming dispersals and other spread zones. In P. Bellwood and C. Renfrew eds., *Examining the Farming/Language Dispersal Hypothesis*, pp. 3–16. Cambridge: McDonald Institute for Archaeological Research.

Renfrew, C. and Boyle, K. eds. 2000 *Archaeogenetics*. Cambridge: McDonald Institute for Archaeological Research.

Renfrew, C., McMahon, A. and Trask, L. eds. 2000 *Time Depth in Historical Linguistics*. 2 vols. Cambridge: McDonald Institute for Archaeological Research.

Renfrew, C. and Nettle, D. 1999 *Nostratic: Examining a Linguistic Macrofamily*. Cambridge: McDonald Institute for Archaeological Research.

Rensch, C. 1976 *Comparative Otomanguean Phonology*. Bloomington: Indiana University Press.

Ribé, G., Cruells, W. and Molist, M. 1997 The Neolithic of the Iberian Peninsula. In M. Diaz-Andrieu and S. Keay eds., *The Archaeology of Iberia*, pp. 65–84. London: Routledge.

Richards, M., Price, T.D. and Koch, E. 2003 Mesolithic and Neolithic subsistence in Denmark: new stable isotope data. *Current Anthropology* 44: 288–94.

Richards, M. 2003 The Neolithic invasion of Europe. *Annual Review of Anthropology* 32:135–62.

Richards, M., Corte-Real, H. et al. 1996 Palaeolithic and Neolithic lineages in the European mitochondrial gene pool. *American Journal of Human Genetics* 59:185–203.

Richards, M., Macaulay, V. and Bandelt, H-J. 2003 Analyzing genetic data in a model-based framework: inferences about European prehistory. In P. Bellwood and C. Renfrew eds., *Examining the Language/Farming Dispersal Hypothesis*, pp. 459–66. Cambridge: McDonald Institute for Archaeological Research.

Richards, M., Macaulay, V. et al. 2000 Tracing European founder lineages in the Near Eastern mtDNA pool. *American Journal of Human genetics* 67:1251–76.

Richards, M., Macaulay, V. et al. 1997 Reply to Cavalli-Sforza and Minch. *American Journal of Human Genetics* 61:251–4.

Richards, M., Oppenheimer, S. and Sykes, B. 1998 mtDNA suggests Polynesian origins in eastern Indonesia. *American Journal of Human Genetics* 63:1234–6.

Richards, M.P. and Hedges, R. 1999 A Neolithic revolution? New evidence of diet in the British Neolithic *Antiquity* 73:891–7.

Richardson, A. 1982 The control of productive resources on the Northwest Coast of North America. In N.M. Williams and E.S. Hunn eds., *Resource Managers: North American and Australian Hunter-Gatherers*, pp. 93–112. Boulder: Westview.

Richerson, P., Boyd, R. and Bettinger, R. 2001 Was agriculture impossible during the Pleistocene but mandatory during the Holocene? *American Antiquity* 66:387–411.

Riley, T. 1987 Ridged-field agriculture and the Mississippian economic pattern. In W.F. Keegan ed., *Emergent Horticultural Economies of the Eastern Woodlands*, pp. 295–304. Center for Archaeological Investigations, Southern Illinois University at Carbondale.

Riley, T., Walz, G. et al. 1994 Accelerator mass spectrometry (AMS) dates confirm early *Zea mays* in the Mississippi River Valley. *American Antiquity* 59:490–8.

Riley, T., Edging, R. and Rossen, J. 1991 Cultigens in prehistoric eastern North America. *Current Anthropology* 31:525–41.

Rimantiené, R. 1992 The Neolithic of the eastern Baltic. *Journal of World Prehistory* 6:97–143.

Rindos, D. 1980 Symbiosis, instability and the origins and spread of agriculture. *Current Anthropology* 21:751–72.

Rindos, D. 1984 *The Origins of Agriculture*. Orlando: Academic.

Rindos, D. 1989 Darwinism and its role in the explanation of domestication. In D. Harris and G. Hillman eds., *Foraging and Farming*, pp. 27–41. London: Unwin Hyman.

Ringe, D., Warnow, T. and Taylor, A. 1998 Computational cladistics and the position of Tocharian. In V.H. Mair ed., *The Bronze Age and Early Iron Age Peoples of Eastern Central Asia*, pp. 391–414. Philadelphia: Institute for the Study of Man.

Rival, L.M. 1999 Introduction: South America. In R.B. Lee and R. Daly eds., *The Cambridge Encyclopaedia of Hunters and Gatherers*, pp. 77–85. Cambridge: Cambridge University Press.

Roberts, N. 2002 Did prehistoric landscape management retard the post-glacial spread of woodland in Southwest Asia? *Antiquity* 76:1002–10.

Rodriguez, A. 1999 Tupi. In R. Dixon and A. Aikhenvald eds., *Amazonian Languages*, pp. 107–24. Cambridge: Cambridge University Press.

Rolett, B., Chen Wei-chun and Sinton, J. 2000 Taiwan, Neolithic seafaring and Austronesian origins. *Antiquity* 74:54–61.

Rollefson, G. 1989 The late aceramic Neolithic of the Levant: a synthesis. *Paléorient* 15/1:168–73.

Rollefson, G. 1998 Ain Ghazal (Jordan): ritual and ceremony III. *Paléorient* 24/1:43–58.

Rollefson, G. and Kohler-Rollefson, I. 1993 PPNC adaptations in the first half of the 6th millennium BC. *Paléorient* 19:33–42.

Romney, A. 1957 The genetic model and Uto-Aztecan time perspective. *Davidson Journal of Anthropology* 3:35–41.

Roodenberg, J. 1999 Ilipinar, an early farming village in the Iznik Lake region. In M. Özdoğan and N. Başgelen eds., *Neolithic in Turkey*, pp. 193–202. Istanbul: Arkeoloji ve Sanat Yayinlari.

Roosevelt, A.C. 1980 *Parmana*. New York: Academic.

Roosevelt, A.C. 1984 Population, health and the evolution of subsistence. In M.N. Cohen and G.J. Armelagos eds., *Palaeopathology at the Origins of Agriculture*, pp. 559–83. New York: Academic.

Roosevelt, A.C. 1999a Archaeology [South America]. In R.B. Lee and R. Daly eds., *The Cambridge Encyclopaedia of Hunters and Gatherers*, pp. 86–91. Cambridge: Cambridge University Press.

Roosevelt, A.C. 1999b The maritime, highland, forest dynamic and the origins of complex culture. In F. Salomon and S. Schwartz eds., *The Cambridge History of the Native Peoples of the Americas III, South America, Part 1*, pp. 264–349. Cambridge: Cambridge University Press.

Roosevelt, A.C., Housley, R.A., da Silviera, M., Maranca, S. and Johnson, R. 1991 Eighth millennium pottery from a prehistoric shell midden in the Brazilian Amazon. *Science* 254:1621–4.

Roscoe, P. 2002 The hunters and gatherers of New Guinea. *Current Anthropology* 43:153–62.

Rosen, A. 2001 Phytolith evidence for agro-pastoral economies in the Scythian period of southern Kazakhstan. In J. Meunier and F. Colin eds., *Phytoliths: Applications in Earth Sciences and Human History*, pp. 183–98. Lisse: Balkema.

Rosenberg, M. 1994 A preliminary description of lithic industry from Hallan Çemi. In H.G. Gebel and S.F. Kozlowski eds., *Neolithic Chipped Stone Industries of the Levant*, pp. 223–38. Berlin: Ex Oriente.

Rosenberg, M. 1998 Cheating at musical chairs. *Current Anthropology* 39:653–82.

Rosenberg, M. 1999 Hallan Çemi. In M. Özdoğan and N. Başgelen eds., *Neolithic in Turkey*, pp. 25–34. Istanbul: Arkeoloji ve Sanat Yayinlari.

Rosenberg, M., Nesbitt, R., Redding, R.W. and Peasnall, B.J. 1998 Hallam Çemi, pig husbandry and post-Pleistocene adaptations along the Taurus-Zagros Arc. *Paléorient* 24/1:25–42.

Rosenberg, M. and Redding, R. 1998 Early pig husbandry in southwestern Asia. In S. Nelson ed., *Ancestors for the Pigs*, pp. 55–64. Philadelphia: MASCA Research Paper 15.

Roset, J-P. 1987 Palaeoclimatic and cultural conditions of Neolithic development in the Early Holocene of northern Niger. In A. Close ed., *Prehistory of Arid North Africa*, pp. 211–34. Dallas: Southern Methodist University Press.

Ross, M. 1991 How conservative are sedentary languages? Evidence from western Melanesia. In R. Blust ed., *Current Trends in Pacific Linguistics*, pp. 433–57. Canberra: Pacific Linguistics C-117.

Ross, M. 1994 Areal phonological features in north central New Ireland. In T. Dutton and D. Tryon eds., *Language Contact and Change in the Austronesian World*, pp. 551–72. Berlin: Mouton de Gruyter.

Ross, M. 1997 Social networks and kinds of speech community event. In R. Blench and M. Spriggs eds., *Archaeology and Language I*, pp. 209–61. London: Routledge.

Ross, M. 2001 Contact-induced change in Oceanic languages in north-west Melanesia. In A. Aikhenvald and R. Dixon, eds., *Areal Diffusion and Genetic Inheritance: Problems in Comparative Linguistics*, pp. 134–66. Oxford: Oxford University Press.

Rosser, Z., Zerjal, T. et al. 2000 Y-chromosomal diversity in Europe is clinal and influenced primarily by geography, rather than by language. *American Journal of Human Genetics* 67: 1526–43.

Roth, B.J. ed. 1996 *Early Formative Adaptations in the southern Southwest*. Madison: Prehistory Press Monograph in World Archaeology 25.

Rouse, I. 1992 *The Tainos*. New Haven: Yale University Press.

Rowley-Conwy, P. 1984 The laziness of the short-distance hunter. *Journal of Anthropological Archaeology* 3:300–24.

Rowley-Conwy, P. 1995 Making first farmers younger: the west European evidence. *Current Anthropology* 36:346–52.

Rowley-Conwy, P. 1999 Economic prehistory in southern Scandinavia. In J. Coles, R. Bewley and P. Mellars eds., *World Prehistory*, pp. 125–59. London: British Academy.

Rowley-Conwy, P. 2000 Through a taphonomic glass, darkly: the importance of cereal cultivation in prehistoric Britain. In J.P. Huntley and S. Stallibrass eds., *Taphonomy and Interpretation*, pp. 43–53. Oxford: Oxbow.

Rowley-Conwy, P. 2001 Time, change and the archaeology of hunter-gatherers. In C. Panter-Brick, R. Layton and P. Rowley-Conwy eds., *Hunter-Gatherers: an Interdisciplinary Perspective*, pp. 39–72. Cambridge: Cambridge University Press.

Rowley-Conwy, P., Deakin, W. and Shaw, C. 1997 Ancient DNA from archaeological sorghum (*Sorghum bicolor*) from Qasr Ibrim, Nubia. *Sahara* 9:23–34.

Ruhlen, M. 1987 *A Guide to the World's Languages*. Vol. 1. Stanford: Stanford University Press.

Runnels, C. and Van Andel, T.H. 1988 Trade and the origins of agriculture in the eastern Mediterranean. *Journal of Mediterranean Archaeology* 1:83–109.

Runnels, C. and Murray, P. 2001 *Greece Before History*. Stanford: Stanford University Press.

Rust, W.R. and Leyden, B.W. 1994 Evidence of maize use at Early and Middle Preclassic La Venta Olmec sites. In S. Johannessen and C. Hastorf eds., *Corn and Culture in the Prehistoric New World*, pp. 181–202. Boulder: Westview.

Sadr, K. 1997 Kalahari archaeology and the Bushman debate. *Current Anthropology* 38: 104–12.

Sadr, K. 1998 The first herders at the Cape of Good Hope. *African Archaeological Review* 15: 101–32.

Sagart, L. 1994 Proto-Austronesian and the Old Chinese evidence for Sino-Austronesian. *Oceanic Linguistics* 33:271–308.

Sagart, L. 2002 Sino-Tibetan-Austronesian: an updated and improved argument. Unpublished paper presented at the 9th International Congress of Austronesian Linguistics, Canberra.

Sagart, L. 2003 The vocabulary of cereal cultivation and the phylogeny of East Asian languages. *Bulletin of the Indo-Pacific Prehistory Association* 23:127–36.

Sagart, L. in press Malayo-Polynesian features in the AN-related vocabulary in Kadai. In L. Sagart, R. Blench and A. Sanchez-Mazas eds., *The Peopling of East Asia: Putting Together Archaeology, Linguistics and Genetics*. London: RoutledgeCurzon.

Saha, N., Mak, J. et al. 1995 Population genetic study among the Orang Asli (Semai Senoi) of Malaysia. *Human Biology* 67:37–57.

Sahi, M. 2001 Ochre Coloured Pottery: its genetic relationship with Harappan ware. *Man and Environment* 26/2:75–88.

Sahlins, M. 1968 Notes on the original affluent society. In R. Lee and I. De Vore eds., *Man the Hunter*, pp. 85–9. Chicago: Aldine.

Sandbukt, Ø. 1991 Tributary tradition and relations of affinity and gender among the Sumatran Kubu. In T. Ingold, D. Riches and J. Woodburn eds., *Hunters and Gatherers. Vol. 1: History, Evolution and Social Change*, pp. 107–116. Oxford: Berg.

Sanders, W.T. and Murdy, C.N. 1982 Cultural evolution and ecological succession in the Valley of Guatemala 1500 BC – AD 1524. In K. Flannery ed. *Maya Subsistence*, pp. 19–63. New York: Academic.

Sandweiss, D., Maasch, K. and Anderson, D. 1999 Transitions in the Mid-Holocene. *Science* 283:499–500.

Sanjur, O., Piperno, D. et al. 2002 Phylogenetic relationships among domesticated and wild species of *Cucurbita*. *Proc. National Academy of Sciences* 99:535–40.

Sanlaville, P. 1996 Changements climatiques dans la région Levantine à la fin du Pleistocene. *Paléorient* 22:7–30.

Santley, R.S. and Pool, C.A. 1993 Prehispanic exchange relationships among Central Mexico, the Valley of Oaxaca, and the Gulf Coast of Mexico. In J.E. Ericson and T.G. Baugh eds., *The American Southwest and Mesoamerica*, pp. 179–211. New York: Plenum.

Sathe, V. and Badam, G. 1996 Animal remains from the Neolithic and Chalcolithic periods at Senuwar. *Man and Environment* XXI:43–8.

Sather, C. 1995 Sea nomads and rainforest hunter-gatherers. In P. Bellwood, J. Fox and D. Tryon eds., *The Austronesians*, pp. 229–68. Canberra: Australian National University, Dept. Anthropology Research School of Pacific and Asian Studies.

Sato, Y-I. 1999 Origin and dissemination of cultivated rice in the eastern Asia. In K. Omoto ed., *Interdisciplinary Perspectives on the Origins of the Japanese*, pp. 143–53. Kyoto: International Research Center for Japanese Studies.

Sauer, C.O. 1952 *Agricultural Origins and Dispersals*. New York: American Geographical Society.

Scarre, C. 1992 The Early Neolithic of western France and megalithic origins in Atlantic Europe. *Oxford Journal of Archaeology* 11:121–54.

Scarry, M. ed. 1993 *Foraging and Farming in the Eastern Woodlands*. Gainesville, FL: University Press of Florida.

Schild, R. 1998 The perils of dating open-air sandy sites of the North European Plain. In M. Zvelebil, L. Domanska and R. Dennell eds., *Harvesting the Sea, Farming the Forest*, pp. 71–6. Sheffield: Sheffield Academic Press.

Schirmer, W. 1990 Some aspects of building at the 'aceramic-neolithic' settlement at Çayönü Tepesi. *World Archaeology* 21:363–87.

Schmidt, K. 1990 The postulated Pre-Indo-European substrates in Insular Celtic and Tocharian. In T. Markey and J. Greppin eds., *When Worlds Collide*, pp. 179–203. Ann Arbor, MI: Karoma.

Schmidt, K. 2002 The 2002 excavations at Göbekli Tepe. *Neo-Lithics* 2/02: 8–13.

Schmidt, K. 2003 The 2003 campaign at Göbekli Tepe. *Neo-Lithics* 2/03:3–8.

Schrire, C. 1980 An enquiry into the evolutionary status and apparent identity of San hunter-gatherers. *Human Ecology* 8: 9–32.

Schrire, C. 1984 Wild surmises on savage thoughts. In C. Schrire ed., *Past and Present in Hunter-Gatherer Studies*, pp. 1–26. Orlando, FL: Academic.

Schulting, R. 2000 New AMS dates from the Lambourn long barrow. *Oxford Journal of Archaeology* 19:25–35.

Schulting, R. and Richards, M. 2002 Finding the coastal Mesolithic in southwest Britain. *Antiquity* 76:1011–25.

Schwartz, D. 1963 Systems of areal integration. *Anthropological Forum* 1:56–97.

Sealy, J. and Yates, R. 1994 The chronology of the introduction of pastoralism to the Cape, South Africa. *Antiquity* 68:58–67.

Sellato, B. 1994 *Nomads of the Borneo Rainforest*. Honolulu: University of Hawaii Press.

Semino, O., Passarino, G. et al. 2000 The genetic legacy of Paleolithic *Homo sapiens sapiens* in extant Europeans: a Y chromosome perspective. *Science* 290:1155–9.

Serjeantcson, S. and Gao, X. 1995 *Homo sapiens* is an evolving species: origins of the Austronesians. In Bellwood, P. Fox, J.J. and Tryon, D. eds., *The Austronesians: Comparative and Historical Perspectives*, pp. 165–80. Canberra: Dept Anthropology, Research School of Pacific and Asian Studies, Australian National University.

Sevilla, R. 1994 Variation in modern Andean maize and its implications for prehistoric patterns. In S. Johannessen and C. Hastorf eds., *Corn and Culture in the Prehistoric New World*, pp. 219–44. Boulder: Westview.

Shady Solis, R., Haas, J. and Creamer, W. 2001 Dating Caral, a Preceramic site in the Supe Valley on the central coast of Peru. *Science* 292:723–6.

Sharer, R. 1978 *The Prehistory of Chalchuapa, El Salvador*. Philadelphia: University of Pennsylvania Press.

Sharma, G.R. et al. 1980 *Beginnings of Agriculture*. Allahabad: Abinash Prakashan.

Sheets, P. 1984 The prehistory of El Salvador: an interpretative summary. In F.W. Lange and D.L. Stone eds., *The Archaeology of Lower Central America*, pp. 85–112. Albuquerque: University of New Mexico Press.

Sheets, P. 2000 The southeastern frontiers of Mesoamerica. In R. Adams and M. MacLeod eds., *The Cambridge History of the Native Peoples of the Americas II, Mesoamerica, Part 1*, pp. 407–448. Cambridge: Cambridge University Press.

Shelach, G. 2000 The earliest Neolithic cultures of northeast China. *Journal of World Prehistory* 14:363–414.

Shennan, S. 2002 *Genes, Memes and Human History*. London: Thames and Hudson.

Sherratt, A. 1980 Water, soil and seasonality in early cereal cultivation. *World Archaeology* 11:313–30.

Sherratt, A. 1995 Reviving the grand narrative. *Journal of European Archaeology* 3/1:1–32.

Sherratt, A. 1997a *Economy and Society in Prehistoric Europe*. Edinburgh: Edinburgh University Press.

Sherratt, A. 1997b Climatic cycles and behavioural revolutions. *Antiquity* 71:271–87.

Sherratt, A. and Sherratt, S. 1988 The archaeology of Indo-European: an alternative view. *Antiquity* 62:584–95.

Shevoroshkin, V. and Manaster Ramer, A. 1991 Some recent work on the remote relations of languages. In S. Lamb and E. Mitchell eds., *Sprung from Some Common Source*, pp. 89–121. Stanford, CA: Stanford University Press.

Shevoroshkin, V. ed. 1992 *Reconstructing Languages and Cultures*. Bochum: Brockmeyer.

Shimada, I. 1999 Evolution of Andean diversity: regional formations. In F. Salomon and S. Schwartz eds., *The Cambridge History of the Native Peoples of the Americas III, South America, Part 1*, pp. 350–517. Cambridge: Cambridge University Press.

Shinde, V. 1991 Craft specialization and social organisation in the Chalcolithic Deccan. *Antiquity* 65:796–807.

Shinde, V. 1994 The Deccan Chalcolithic: a recent perspective. *Man and Environment* XIX: 169–78.

Shinde, V. 2000 The origin and development of the Chalcolithic in central India. *Bulletin of the Indo-Pacific Prehistory Association* 19:125–36.

Shinde, V. 2002 The emergence, development and spread of agricultural communities in South Asia. In Y. Yasuda Y. ed., *The Origins of Pottery and Agriculture*, pp. 89–115. New Delhi: Roli.

Shudai, H. 1996–7 Searching for the Early Harappan Culture. *Indian Archaeological Studies* 18:40–51 (Tokyo).

Sidrys, R. 1996 The light eye and hair cline. In K. Jones-Bley ed., *The Indoeuropeanization of Northern Europe*, pp. 330–49. Washington, DC: Journal of Indo-European Studies Monograph 17.

Siebert, F. 1967 The original home of the Proto-Algonquian people. *National Museum of Canada Bulletin* 214:13–47.

Simmons, A.H. 1986 New evidence for the early use of cultigens in the American Southwest. *American Antiquity* 51:73–89.

Simmons, A.H. 1997 Ecological changes during the late Neolithic in Jordan. In H. Gebel. Z. Kafafi and G. Rollefson eds., *The Prehistory of Jordan, II. Perspectives from 1997*, pp. 309–18. Berlin: Ex Oriente.

Simmons, A.H. 1998 Of tiny hippos, large cows and early colonists in Cyprus. *Journal of Mediterranean Archaeology* 11:232–41.

Simmons, A.H. 1999 *Faunal Extinction in an Island Society*. New York: Kluwer.

Simoni, L., Calafell, F. et al. 2000 Geographic patterns of mtDNA diversity in Europe. *American Journal of Human Genetics* 66:262–768.

Singh, A.K. 1998 Excavations at Imlidih Khurd, District Gorakhpur, India. Paper presented at IPPA Conference, Melaka, July 1998.

Singh, O.K. 1997 *Stone Age Archaeology of Manipur*. Manipur: Amusana Institute of Antiquarian Studies.

Singh, P. 1994 *Excavations at Narhan*. Varanasi: Banaras Hindu University.

Singh, P. 1998 Early farming cultures of the Middle Ganga Valley. Paper presented at IPPA Conference, Melaka, July 1998.

Singh, R.P. 1990 *Agriculture in Protohistoric India*. Delhi: Pratibha Prakashan.

Skak-Nielson, N.V. 2003 How did farming come to southern Scandinavia? *Fornvännen* 98:1–12.

Smalley, J. and Blake, M. 2003 Sweet beginnings: stalk sugar and the domestication of maize. *Current Anthropology* 44:675–704.

Smith, A.B. 1989 The Near Eastern connection. In L. Krzyzaniak and M. Kobusiewicz eds., *Late Prehistory of the Nile Basin and the Sahara*, pp. 69–78. Poznan: Poznan Anthropological Museum.

Smith, A.B. 1990 On becoming herders: Khoikhoi and San ethnicity in southern Africa. *African Studies* 49:51–73.

Smith, A.B. 1993 On subsistence and ethnicity in pre-colonial South Africa. *Current Anthropology* 34:439.

Smith, A.B. 1998 Keeping people on the periphery: the ideology of social hierarchies between hunters and herders. *Journal of Anthropological Archaeology* 17:201–15.

Smith, B.D. 1987 The independent domestication of indigenous seed-bearing plants in eastern North America. In W.F. Keegan ed., *Emergent Horticultural Economies of the Eastern Woodlands*, pp. 3–47. Center for Archaeological Investigations, Southern Illinois University at Carbondale.

Smith, B.D. 1992a Prehistoric plant husbandry in eastern North America. In C.W. Cowan and P.J. Watson eds., *The Origins of Agriculture*, pp. 101–20. Washington DC: Smithsonian.

Smith, B.D. 1992b *Rivers of Change*. Washington, DC: Smithsonian.

Smith, B.D. 1995 *The Emergence of Agriculture*. New York: Scientific American.

Smith, B.D. 1997a Reconsidering the Ocampo Caves. *Latin American Antiquity* 8:342–83.

Smith, B.D. 1997b The initial domestication of *Cucurbita pepo* in the Americas 10,000 years ago. *Science* 276:932–4.

Smith, B.D. 2001 Documenting plant domestication. *Proceedings of the National Academy of Sciences* 98:1324–6.

Smith, B. 2003 Low-level food production. *Journal of Archaeological Research* 9: 1–43.

Smith, P. 1972 *The Consequences of Food Production*. Reading: Addison-Wesley.

Snow, B.E., Shutler, R., Nelson, D., Vogel, J.S. and Southon, J. 1986 Evidence of early rice cultivation in the Philippines. *Philippine Quarterly of Culture and Society* 14:3–11.

Snow, D. 1984 Iroquois prehistory. In M. Foster et al. eds., *Extending the Rafters*, pp. 241–57. Albany: State University of New York Press.

Snow, D. 1991 Upland prehistoric maize agriculture in the eastern Rio Grande and its peripheries. In K.A. Spielmann ed., *Farmers, Hunters and Colonists*, pp. 71–88. Tucson: University of Arizona Press.

Snow, D. 1994 *The Iroquois*. Oxford: Blackwell.

Snow, D. 1995 Migration in prehistory: the Northern Iroquoian case. *American Antiquity* 60:59–79.

Snow, D. 1996 The first Americans and the differentiation of hunter-gatherer cultures. In B.G. Trigger and W.E. Washburn eds., *The Cambridge History of the Native Peoples of the Americas*, Vol. 1, North America, Part 1, pp. 125–99. Cambridge: Cambridge University Press.

Sokal, R., Oden, N. and Thomson, B. 1992 Origins of the Indo-Europeans: genetic evidence. *Proceedings of the National Academy of Sciences* 89:7669–73.

Sokal, R., Oden, N. and Wilson, C. 1991 Genetic evidence for the spread of agriculture in Europe by demic diffusion. *Nature* 351:143–4.

Solberg, B. 1989 The Neolithic transition in southern Scandinavia. *Oxford Journal of Archaeology* 8:261–96.

Solway, J.S. and Lee, R.B. 1990 Foragers, genuine or spurious? Situating the Kalahari San in history. *Current Anthropology* 31: 109–46.

Sonawane, V.H. 2000 Early farming communities of Gujarat, India. *Bulletin of the Indo-Pacific Prehistory Association* 19:137–46.

Soodyall, H., Vigiland, L. et al. 1996 mtDNA control-region sequence variation suggests multiple independent origins of an "Asian-specific" 9-bp deletion in Sub-Saharan Africans. *American Journal of Human Genetics* 58:595–608.

Sorensen, A. 1982 Multilingualism in the northwest Amazon. In J. Pride and J. Holmes eds., *Sociolinguistics*, pp. 78–93. Harmondsworth: Penguin.

Sørensen, P. 1967 The Neolithic cultures of Thailand (and north Malaysia) and their Lungshanoid relationships. In Barnard, N. ed., *Early Chinese Art and its Possible Influence in the Pacific Basin*. Vol. 2, pp. 459–506. New York: Intercultural Arts Press.

Southworth, F. 1975 Cereals in South Asian prehistory. In K. Kennedy and G. Possehl eds., *Ecological Backgrounds of South Asian Prehistory*, pp. 52–75. Ithaca: South Asia Program, Cornell University.

Southworth, F. 1988 Ancient economic plants of South Asia. In M. Jazayery and W. Winter eds., *Language and Culture*, pp. 649–68. Berlin: Mouton de Gruyter.

Southworth, F. 1990 The reconstruction of prehistoric South Asian language contact. In E. Bendix ed., *The Uses of Linguistics*, pp. 207–34. Annals of the New York Academy of Science vol. 583.

Southworth, F. 1992 Linguistics and archaeology. In G. Possehl ed., *South Asian Archaeology Studies*, pp. 81–6. New Delhi: Oxford & IBH.

Southworth, F. 1995 Reconstructing social context from language. In G. Erdosy ed., *The Indo-Aryans of Ancient South Asia*, pp, 258–77. Berlin: Walter de Gruyter.

Spencer, R.F. and Jennings, J.D. eds. 1977 *The Native Americans*. 2nd edition. New York: Harper & Row.

Spielmann, K.A. and Eder, J. 1994 Hunters and farmers: then and now. *Annual Review of Anthropology* 23:303–23.

Spinden, H. 1915 The origin and distribution of agriculture in America. In *Proceedings of the 19th International Congress of Americanists, Washington, 1915*, pp. 269–76. Nendeln: Kraus Reprint (1968).

Spriggs, M. 1989 The dating of the Island Southeast Asian Neolithic. *Antiquity* 63:587–612.

Spriggs, M. 1996 Early agriculture and what went on before in Island Melanesia: continuity or intrusion? In D. Harris ed., *The Origins and Spread of Agriculture and Pastoralism in Eurasia*, pp. 524–37. London: University College Press.

Spriggs, M. 1997a *The Island Melanesians*. Oxford: Basil Blackwell.

Spriggs, M. 1997b Landscape catastrophe and landscape enhancement. In P. Kirch, P. and T. Hunt eds., *Historical Ecology in the Pacific Islands*, pp. 80–104. New Haven: Yale University Press.

Spriggs, M. 1999 Archaeological dates and linguistic subgroups in the settlement of the Island Southeast Asian-Pacific region. *Bulletin of the Indo-Pacific Prehistory Association* 18:17–24.

Spriggs, M. 2003 Chronology of the Neolithic transition in Island Southeast Asia and the western Pacific. *Review of Archaeology* 24/2:57–80.

Stahl, A.B. 1993 Intensification in the west African Late Stone Age: a view from central Ghana. In T. Shaw, P. Sinclair, B. Andah and A. Okpoko eds., *The Archaeology of Africa*, pp. 261–73. London: Routledge.

Stahl, A.B. 1994 Innovation, diffusion and culture contact: the Holocene archaeology of Ghana. *Journal of World Prehistory* 8:51–112.

Staller, J. and Thompson R. 2002 A multidisciplinary approach to understanding the initial introduction of maize into coastal Ecuador. *Journal of Archaeological Science* 29:33–50.

Staller, J.E. 2001 Reassessing the developmental and chronological relationships of the Formative of coastal Ecuador. *Journal of World Prehistory* 15:193–256.

Stanley, D.J. and Warne, A.G. 1993 Sea level and initiation of Predynastic culture in the Nile Delta. *Nature* 363:425–8.

Staüble, H. 1995 Radiocarbon dates of the earliest Neolithic in central Europe. *Radiocarbon* 37:227–37.

Stearmann, A.M. 1991 Making a living in the tropical forest: Yuqui foragers in the Bolivian Amazon. *Human Ecology* 19: 245–60.

Stevens, M. 1999 Spectacular results from modest remains. *Archaeology Southwest* 13/1, pp. 4–5.

Steward, J.H. 1947 American culture history in the light of South America. *Southwestern Journal of Anthropology* 3:85–107.

Stordeur, D. 2000 Les bâtiments communautaires de Jerf el Ahmar et Mureybet horizon PPNA. *Paléorient* 26: 29–44 (see also *Neo-Lithics* 1/2000:1–4).

Stordeur, D. 2003 Tell Aswad: resultats préliminaire des campagnes 2001 et 2002. *Neo-Lithics* 1/03:7–15.

Stordeur, D., Helmer, D. and Willcox, G. 1997 Jerf el Ahmar: un nouveau site de l'horizon PPNA sur le moyen Euphrate Syrien. *Bulletin de la Société Préhistorique française* 94:282–5.

Strade, N. 1998 An interdisciplinary approach to the role of Uralic hunters and gatherers in the ethnohistory of the early Germanic area. In K. Julku and K Wiik eds., *The Roots of Peoples and Languages of Northern Eurasia 1*, pp. 168–79. Turku: Finno-Ugric Historical Society.

Street, M., Baales, M. et al. 2001 Final Palaeolithic and Mesolithic research in reunified Germany. *Journal of World Prehistory* 15:365–453.

Su, B., Jin, L. et al. 2000 Polynesian origins: insights from the Y chromosome. *Proceedings of the National Academy of Sciences* 97:8225–8.

Sumegi, P. and Kertesz, R. 2001 Palaeogeographic characteristics of the Carpathian Basin – an ecological trap during the early Neolithic? In R. Kertesz and J. Makkay eds., *From the Mesolithic to the Neolithic*, pp. 405–16. Budapest: Archaeolingua.

Sverdrup, H. and Guardans, R. 1999 Compiling words from extinct non-Indoeuropean languages in Europe. In V. Shevoroshkin and P. Sidwell eds., *Historical Linguistics and Lexicostatistics*, pp. 201–58. Melbourne: Association for the History of Language.

Swadling, P. and Hope, G. 1992 Environmental change in New Guinea since human settlement. In J. Dodson ed., *The Naive Lands*, pp. 13–42. Melbourne: Longman Cheshire.

Swadling, P., Araho, N. and Ivuyo, B. 1991 Settlements associated with the inland Sepik-Ramu Sea. *Bulletin of the Indo-Pacific Prehistory Association* 11: 92–112.

Sykes, B. 1999a The molecular genetics of European ancestry. *Philosophical Transactions of the Royal Society of London, Biological Sciences* 354:131–40.

Sykes, B. 1999b Using genes to map population structure and origins. In B. Sykes ed., *The Human Inheritance*, pp. 93–118. Oxford: Oxford University Press.

Sykes, B., Leiboff, A. et al. 1995 The origins of the Polynesians: an interpretation from mitochondrial lineage analysis. *American Journal of Human Genetics* 57:1463–1475.

Taavitsainen, J.-P., Simola, H. and Gronlund, E. 1998 Cultivation history beyond the periphery. *Journal of World Prehistory* 12:199–253.

Tajima, A., Pan, I-H. et al. 2002 Three major lineages of Asian Y chromosomes: implications for the peopling of east and southeast Asia. *Human Genetics* 110:80–8.

Taketsugu, I. 1991 *Research on Chinese Neolithic Culture*. Translated by Mark Hudson. Tokyo: Yamakawa Shuppansha.

Tayles, N. 1999 *The Excavation of Khok Phanom Di. Vol. V: The People*. London: Society of Antiquaries.

Tchernov, E. 1997 Are Late Pleistocene environmental factors, faunal changes and cultural transformations culturally connected? *Paléorient* 23/2:209–28.

Telegin, D.J. 1987 Neolithic cultures of the Ukraine and adjacent areas and their chronology. *Journal of World Prehistory* 1:307–31.

Terrell, J. 1986 *Prehistory in the Pacific Islands*. Cambridge: Cambridge University Press.

Terrell, J. 1988 History as a family tree, history as an entangled bank. *Antiquity* 62:642–57.

Terrell, J. ed. 2001 *Archaeology, Language and History*. Westport, CT: Bergin and Garvey.

Testart, A. 1988 Some major problems in the social anthropology of hunter-gatherers. *Current Anthropology* 29: 1–32.

Thomas, J. 1996 The cultural context of the first use of domesticates in continental Central and Northwest Europe. In D. Harris ed., *The Origins and Spread of Agriculture and Pastoralism in Eurasia*, pp. 310–22. London: UCL Press.

Thomas, N., Guest, H. and Dettelbach, M. eds. 1996 *Observations Made During a Voyage Round the World* (by Johann Reinhold Forster). Honolulu: University of Hawai'i Press.

Thomas, P.K. 2000 Subsistence based on animals in the Chalcolithic Culture of Western India. *Bulletin of the Indo-Pacific Prehistory Association* 19:147–51.

Thorpe, I. 1996 *The Origins of Agriculture in Europe*. London: Routledge.

Tolstoy, P. 1989 Coapexco and Tlatilco. In R.J. Sharer and D.C. Grove eds., *Regional Perspectives on the Olmec*, pp. 85–121. Cambridge: Cambridge University Press.

Torroni, A., Bandelt, H-J. et al. 1998 mtDNA analysis reveals a major late Palaeolithic population expansion from southwestern to northeastern Europe. *American Journal of Human Genetics* 62:1137–1152.

Troy, C., MacHugh, D. et al. 2001 Genetic evidence for Near Eastern origins of European cattle. *Nature* 410:1088–91.

Trubetzkoy, N. 1939 Gedanken uber das Indogermanenproblem. *Acta Linguistica* 1:81–9.

Tsang Cheng-hwa 1992 *Archaeology of the P'eng-hu Islands*. Taipei: Institute of History and Philology, Academia Sinica.

Tsang Cheng-hwa 1995 New archaeological data from both sides of the Taiwan Straits. In P. Li, et al. eds., *Austronesian Studies Relating to Taiwan*, pp. 185–226. Taipei: Institute of History and Philology, Academia Sinica.

Tsang Cheng-hwa in press Recent discoveries of the Tapenkeng culture in Taiwan: implications for the problem of Austronesian origins. In L. Sagart, R. Blench and A. Sanchez-Mazas eds., *The Peopling of East Asia: Putting Together Archaeology, Linguistics and Genetics*. London: RoutledgeCurzon.

Tsukada, M. 1967 Vegetation in subtropical Formosa during the Pleistocene glaciations and the Holocene. *Palaeogeography, Palaeoclimatology and Palaeoecology* 3:49–64.

Tykot, R. and Staller, J. 2002 The importance of early maize agriculture in coastal Ecuador. *Current Anthropology* 43:666–77.

Underhill, A.P. 1997 Current issues in Chinese Neolithic archaeology. *Journal of World Prehistory* 11:103–60.

Underhill, P., Passarino, G. et al. 2001a The phylogeography of Y chromosome binary haplotypes and the origins of modern human populations. *Annals of Human Genetics* 65:43–62.

Underhill, P., Passarino, G. et al. 2001b Maori origins, Y-chromosome haplotypes and implications for human history in the Pacific. *Human Mutation* 17:271–80.

Underhill, P. 2003 Inference of Neolithic population histories using Y-chromosome haplotypes. In P. Bellwood and C. Renfrew eds., *Examining the Language/Farming Dispersal Hypothesis*, pp. 65–78. Cambridge: McDonald Institute for Archaeological Research.

Unger, J. 1990 Japanese and what other Altaic languages. In P. Baldi ed., *Linguistic Change and Reconstruction Methodology*, pp. 547–61. Berlin: Mouton de Gruyter.

Unger-Hamilton, R. 1989 The Epi-Palaeolithic southern Levant and the origins of cultivation. *Current Anthropology* 30:88–103.

Unger-Hamilton, R. 1991 Natufian plant husbandry in the southern Levant. In O. Bar-Yosef and F.R. Valla eds. 1991 *The Natufian Culture in the Levant*, pp. 483–520. Ann Arbor, MI: International Monographs in Prehistory.

Upham, S. 1994 Nomads of the Desert West. *Journal of World Prehistory* 8:113–68.

Urry, J. and Walsh, M. 1981 The lost "Macassar language" of northern Australia. *Aboriginal History* 5:91–108.

Vamplew, W. ed. 1987 *Australians: Historical Statistics*. Sydney: Fairfax, Syme and Weldon.

Vansina, J. 1990 *Paths in the Rainforest*. Madison: University of Wisconsin Press.

Vansina, J. 1995 New linguistic evidence and "the Bantu expansion." *Journal of African History* 36:173–95.

Veen, M. van der ed. 1999 *The Exploitation of Plant Resources in Ancient Africa*. New York: Kluwer Academic.

Vencl, S. 1986 The role of hunting-gathering populations in the transition to farming: a central-European perspective. In M. Zvelebil ed., *Hunters in Transition*, pp. 43–51. Cambridge: Cambridge University Press.

Venkatasubbaiah, P.C. and Kajale, M. 1991 Biological remains from Neolithic and Early Historic sites in Cuddapah District. *Man and Environment* XVI/1:85–97.

Vennemann, T. 1994 Linguistic reconstruction in the context of European Prehistory. *Trans. Philological Society* 92:215–84.

Verhoeven, M. 1997 The 1996 excavations at Tell Sabi Abyad II. *Neo-Lithics* 1/97:1–3.

Verhoeven, M. 2002 Ritual and ideology in the Pre-Pottery Neolithic B of the Levant and southeast Anatolia. *Cambridge Archaeological Journal* 12:233–58.

Vérin, P. and Wright, H. 1999 Madagascar and Indonesia: new evidence from archaeology and linguistics. *Bulletin of the Indo-Pacific Prehistory Association* 18:35–42.

Vierich, H. 1982 Adaptive flexibility in a multi-ethnic setting: the Basarwa of the southern Kalahari. In E. Leacock and R.B. Lee eds., *Politics and History in Band Societies*, pp. 213–22. Cambridge: Cambridge University Press.

Villalon, M. 1991 A spatial model of lexical relationships among 14 Cariban varieties. In M. Key ed., *Language Change in South American Indian Languages*, pp. 54–94. Philadelphia: University of Pennsylvania Press.

Vitelli, K.D. 1995 Pots, potters and the shaping of Greek Neolithic society. In W. Barnett and J. Hoopes eds., *The Emergence of Pottery*, pp. Washington: Smithsonian.

Walthall, J.A. 1990 *Prehistoric Indians of the Southeast*. Tuscaloosa: University of Alabama Press.

Warnow, T. 1997 Mathematical approaches to computational linguistics. *Proceedings of the National Academy of Sciences* 94:6585–90.

Warrick, G. 2000 The precontact Iroquoian occupation of southern Ontario. *Journal of World Prehistory* 14:415–66.

Wasse, A. 2001 The wild goats of Lebanon: evidence for early domestication? *Levant* 31:21–34.

Wasylikowa, K. and Dahlberg, J. 1999 Sorghum in the economy of the Early Neolithic nomadic tribes at Nabta Playa, southern Egypt. In M. van der Veen ed., *The Exploitation of Plant Resources in Ancient Africa*, pp. 11–32. New York: Kluwer Academic.

Wasylikowa, K., Mitka, J., Wendorf, F. and Close, A. 1997 Exploitation of wild plants by the early Neolithic hunter-gatherers of the Western Desert, Egypt. *Antiquity* 71:932–41.

Watkins, C. 1985 *The American Heritage Dictionary of Indo-European Roots*. Boston, MA: Houghton Mifflin.

Watkins, C. 1998 An Indo-European linguistic area and its characteristics. In A. Aikhenvald and R. Dixon eds., *Areal Diffusion and Genetic Inheritance*, pp. 44–63. Oxford: Oxford University Press.

Watkins, T. 1992 The beginning of the Neolithic. *Paléorient* 18/1:63–75.

Watkins, T., Baird, D. and Betts, A. 1989 Qermez Dere and the early aceramic Neolithic of northern Iraq. *Paléorient* 15/1:19–24.

Watson, E., Bauer, K. et al. 1996 mtDNA sequence diversity in Africa. *American Journal of Human Genetics* 59:437–44.

Watson, J. and Woodhouse, J. 2001 The Kintampo Archaeological Research Project. *Antiquity* 75:813–4.

Webb, C.H. 1977 *The Poverty Point Culture*. Geoscience and Man Vol. 17. Baton Rouge, LA: Louisiana State University.

Webb, W.S. and Snow, C.E. 1988 *The Adena People* (reprint of 1945 original). Knoxville, TN: University of Tennessee Press.

Weber, S.A. 1991 *Plants and Harappan Subsistence*. New Delhi: Oxford & IBH.

Weber, S.A. 1993 Changes in plant use at Rojdi. In G. Possehl ed., *Harappan Civilization*, 2nd Edition, pp. 287–94. New Delhi: Oxford & IBH.

Weber, S.A. 1998 Out of Africa: the initial impact of millets in South Asia. *Current Anthropology* 39:267–73.

Weber, S.A. 1999 Seeds of urbanism: palaeoethnobotany and the Indus Civilization. *Antiquity* 73:813–26.

Wedel, W. 1983 The prehistoric Plains. In J. Jennings ed., *Ancient North Americans*, pp. 203–41. San Francisco, CA: Freeman.

Weisler, M. 1998 Hard evidence for prehistoric interaction in Polynesia. *Current Anthropology* 39:521–32.

Wells, B., Runnels, C., Zangger, E. 1993 In the shadow of Mycenae. *Archaeology* 46/1: 46–58, 63.

Wendorf, F. and Schild, R. 1998 Nabta Playa and its role in northeast African prehistory. *Journal of Anthropological Archaeology* 17:97–123.

Wendorf, F., Schild, R. et al. 2001 *Holocene Settlement of the Egyptian Sahara. Vol. 1: The Archaeology of Nabta Playa*. New York: Kluwer.

Wendorf, F., Schild, R. and Close, A. eds. 1980 *Loaves and Fishes*. Dallas, TX: Southern Methodist University, Dept. Anthropology.

Wetterstrom, W. 1998 The origins of agriculture in Africa. *Review of Archaeology* 19/2:30–46.

Whalen, M. 1981 *Excavations at Santo Domingo Tomaltepec*. Ann Arbor, MI: Museum of Anthropology, University of Michigan, Memoir 12.

Whalen, M. 1994 Moving out of the Archaic on the edge of the Southwest. *American Antiquity* 59:622–38.

Whitaker, T.W. 1983 Cucurbits in Andean prehistory. *American Antiquity* 48:576–85.

White, J.C. 1982 *Ban Chiang*. Philadelphia: University Museum.

White, J.C. 1997 A brief note on new dates for the Ban Chiang cultural tradition. *Bulletin of the Indo-Pacific Prehistory Association* 17:103–6.

Whitehouse, R. 1987 The first farmers in the Adriatic and their position in the Neolithic of the Mediterranean. In J. Guilaine et al. eds., *Premières Communautés paysannes en Méditerranean Occidentale*, pp. 357–66. Paris: CNRS.

Wichmann, S. 1998 A conservative look at diffusion involving Mixe-Zoquean languages. In R. Blench and M. Spriggs eds., *Archaeology and Language II*, pp. 297–323. London: Routledge.

Wichmann, S. 2003 Contextualizing proto-languages, homelands and siatant genetic relationship. In P. Bellwood and C.Renfrew eds., *Examining the Farming/Language Dispersal Hypothesis*, pp. 321–30. Cambridge: McDonald Institute for Archaeological Research.

Widmer, R.J. 1988 *The Evolution of the Calusa*. Tuscaloosa: University of Alabama Press.

Wigboldus, J. 1996 Early presence of African millets near the Indian Ocean. In J. Reade ed., *The Indian Ocean in Antiquity*, pp. 75–88. London: Kegan Paul.

Wiik, K. 2000 Some ancient and modern linguistic processes in northern Europe. In C. Renfrew, A. McMahon and L. Trask eds., *Time Depth in Historical Linguistics*, pp. 463–80. Cambridge: McDonald Institute for Archaeological Research.

Wilke, P.J. et al. 1972 Harvest selection and domestication in seed plants. *Antiquity* 46:203–9.

Willcox, G. 1989 Some differences between crops of Near Eastern origin and those from the tropics. In C. Jarrige ed., *South Asian Archaeology 1989*, pp. 291–9. Madison: Prehistory Press.

Willcox, G. 1996 Evidence for plant exploitation and vegetation history from three Early Neolithic pre-pottery sites on the Euphrates (Syria). *Vegetation History and Archaeobotany* 5:143–52.

Willcox, G. 1999 Agrarian change and the beginnings of cultivation in the Near East. In Gosden and Hather eds., *The Prehistory of Food*, pp. 478–99. London: Routledge.

Willcox, G. 2002 Geographical variation in major cereal components and evidence for independent domestication events in western Asia. In R. Cappers and S. Bottema eds., *The Dawn of Farming in the Near East*, pp. 133–40. Berlin: Ex Oriente.

Willey, G. 1958 An archaeological perspective on Algonkian–Gulf links. *Southwestern Journal of Anthropology* 14:265–71.

Willey, G. 1962 The early great styles and the rise of pre-Columbian civilizations. *American Anthropologist* 64:1–14.

Williams, C. 1985 A scheme for the early monumental architecture of the central coast of Peru. In C.B. Donnan ed., *Early Ceremonial Architecture in the Andes: A Conference at Dumbarton Oaks, 26 and 27 October 1982*, pp. 227–39. Washington, D.C.: Dumbarton Oaks Research.

Williams, S., Chagnon, N. and Spielman, R. 2002 Nuclear and itochondrial genetic variation in the Yanomamö. *American Journal of Physical Anthropology* 117:246–59.

Williamson, K. and Blench, R. 2000 Niger-Congo. In B. Heine and D. Nurse eds., *African Languages: an Introduction*, pp. 11–42. Cambridge: Cambridge University Press.

Willis, K. and Bennett, K. 1994 The Neolithic transition – fact or fiction? *The Holocene* 4: 326–30.

Wills, W.H. 1988 *Early Prehistoric Agriculture in the American Southwest*. Santa Fe, CA: School of American Research.

Wilmsen, E.N. and Denbow, J.R. 1990 Paradigmatic history of San-speaking peoples. *Current Anthropology* 31: 489–524.

Wilson, D.J. 1985 Of maize and men. *American Anthropologist* 83:93–120.

Winter, J.C. and Hogan, P.F. 1986 Plant husbandry in the Great Basin and adjacent North Colorado Plateau. In C.J. Londie and D.D. Fowler eds., *Anthropology of the Desert West*, pp. 119–44. Salt Lake City, UT: University of Utah Press.

Witkowski, S. and Brown, C. 1978 Mesoamerican: a proposed language phylum. *American Anthropologist* 80:942–4.

Witzel, M. 1995 Early Indian history: linguistic and textual parameters. In G. Erdosy ed., *The Indo-Aryans of Ancient South Asia*, pp, 85–125. Berlin: Walter de Gruyter.

Woodburn, J. 1982 Egalitarian societies. *Man* 17:431–51.

Woodburn, J. 1991 African hunter-gatherer social organisation: is it best understood as a product of encapsulation? In T. Ingold, D. Riches and J. Woodburn eds., *Hunters and Gatherers. Vol. 1: History, Evolution and Social Change*, pp. 31–64. Oxford: Berg.

Wright, J. 1984 The cultural continuity of the Northern Iroquoian-speaking peoples. In M. Foster et al. eds., *Extending the Rafters*, pp. 283–99. Albany: State University of New York Press.

Wright, K. 1994 Ground-stone tools and hunter-gatherer subsistence in Southwest Asia: implications of the transition to farming. *American Antiquity* 59:238–63.

Wu Yaoli 1996 Prehistoric rice agriculture in the Yellow River Valley. *Bulletin of the Indo-Pacific Prehistory Association* 15: 223–4.

Wuethrich, B. 2000 Learning the world's languages – before they vanish. *Science* 288:1156–9.

Wurm, S.A. 1982 *Papuan Languages of Oceania*. Tübingen: Gunter Narr Verlag.

Wurm, S.A. 1983 Linguistic prehistory in the New Guinea area. *Journal of Human Evolution* 12:25–35.

Wüst, I. 1998 Continuities and discontinuities: archaeology and ethnoarchaeology in the heart of the eastern Bororo territory, Mato Grosso, Brazil. *Antiquity* 72:663–75.

Yan Wenming 1991 China's earliest rice agriculture remains. *Bulletin of the Indo-Pacific Prehistory Association* 10: 118–26.

Yan Wenming 1992 Origins of agriculture and animal husbandry in China. In C.M. Aikens and Song Nai Rhee eds., *Pacific Northeast Asia in Prehistory: Hunter-Fisher-Gatherers, Farmers, and Sociopolitical Elites*, pp. 113–24. Pullman: Washington State University Press.

Yan Wenming 2002 The origins of rice agriculture, pottery and cities. In Y. Yasuda Y. ed., *The Origins of Pottery and Agriculture*, pp. 151–6. New Delhi: Roli.

Yang Cong 1995 The prehistoric kiln sites and ceramic industry of Fujian. In C. Yeung and B. Li eds., *Archaeology in Southeast Asia*, pp. 267–84. Hong Kong: University of Hong Kong Museum and Art Gallery.

Yang Yaolin 1999 Preliminary investigations of the Xiantou Ling prehistoric cultural remains. *Bulletin of the Indo-Pacific Prehistory Association* 18:105–16.

Yanushevich, Z.V. 1989 Agricultural evolution north of the Black Sea. In D. Harris and G. Hillman eds., *Foraging and Farming*, pp. 607–19. London: Unwin Hyman.

Yarnell, R.A. 1993 The importance of native crops during the Late Archaic and Woodland Periods. In M. Scarry ed., *Foraging and Farming in the Eastern Woodlands*, pp. 13–26. Gainesville, FL: University Press of Florida.

Yarnell, R.A. 1994 Investigations relevant to the native development of plant husbandry in eastern North America. In W. Green ed., *Agricultural Origins and Development in the Mid-Continent*, pp. 7–24. Iowa City, IA: University of Iowa Press.

Yasuda, Y. 2000 The oldest remains of a Chinese circular walled fortification. *Newsletter of the Grant-in-Aid Program for COE Research Foundation* 3/1:1–4. Kyoto: International Research Center for Japanese Studies.

Yasuda, Y. ed. 2002 *The Origins of Pottery and Agriculture*. New Delhi: Roli.

Yellen, J. 1990 The transformation of the Kalahari !Kung. *Scientific American* 262/4:96–105.

Yen, D.E. 1995 The development of Sahul agriculture with Australia as bystander. *Antiquity* 69 (Special Number 265): 831–47.

Young, D. and Bettinger, R. 1992 The Numic spread: a computer simulation. *American Anthropologist* 57:85–99.

Zarins, J. 1990 Early pastoral nomadism and the settlement of Lower Mesopotamia. *Bulletin of the American Schools of Oriental Research* 280:31–65.

Zeist, W. van 1988 Some aspects of early Neolithic plant husbandry in the Near East. *Anatolica* 15:49–67.

Zeist, W. van and Bottema, S. 1991 *Late Quaternary Vegetation of the Near East*. Wiesbaden: Ludwig Reichert.

Zhang Chi 1999 The excavations at Xianrendong and Diaotonghuan, Jiangxi. *Bulletin of the Indo-Pacific Prehistory Association* 18: 97–100.

Zhang Juzhong and Wang Xiangkun 1998 Note son the recent discovery of ancient cultivated rice at Jiahu, Henan province. *Antiquity* 72:897–901.

Zhang Wenxu 2002 The Bi-Peak-Tubercle of rice. In Y. Yasuda Y. ed., *The Origins of Pottery and Agriculture*, pp. 205–16. New Delhi: Roli.

Zhao Zhiyun 1998 The Middle Yangtze region in China is one place where rice was domesticated. *Antiquity* 72:885–96.

Zide, A. and Zide, N. 1976 Proto-munda cultural vocabulary: evidence for early agriculture. In P.N. Jenner, L.C. Thompson and S. Starosta, *Austroasiatic Studies*, pp. 1295–1334. Honolulu: Oceanic Linguistics Special Publication 13.

Zilhão, J. 1993 The spread of agro-pastoral communities across Mediterranean Europe. *Journal of Mediterranean Archaeology* 6:5–63.

Zilhão, J. 2000 From the Mesolithic to the Neolithic in the Iberian Peninsula. In T.D. Price ed., *Europe's First Farmers*, pp. 144–82. Cambridge: Cambridge University Press.

Zilhão, J. 2001 Radiocarbon evidence for maritime pioneer colonization at the origins of farming in west Mediterranean Europe. *Proceedings of the National Academy of Sciences* 98: 14180–5.

Zohary, D. 1996 The mode of domestication of the founder crops of Southwest Asian agriculture, In D. Harris ed., *The Origins and Spread of Agriculture and Pastoralism in Eurasia*, pp.142–58. London: UCL Press.

Zohary, D. 1999 Monophyletic vs. polyphyletic origin of the crops on which agriculture was founded in the Near East. *Genetic Resources and Crop Evolution* 46:133–42.

Zohary, D. and Hopf, M. 2000 *Domestication of Plants in the Old World*. 3rd edition. Oxford: Clarendon.

Zorc, D. 1994 Austronesian culture history through reconstructed vocabulary. In A. Pawley and M. Ross eds., *Austronesian Terminologies: Continuity and Change*, pp. 541–95. Canberra: Pacific Linguistics Series C-127.

Zvelebil, K. 1985 Dravidian and Elamite – a real break-through? *Journal of the American Oriental Society* 94:384–5.

Zvelebil, M. 1989 On the transition to farming in Europe. *Antiquity* 63:379–83.

Zvelebil, M. 1996a The agricultural frontier and the transition to farming in the circum-Baltic region. In D. Harris ed., *The Origins and Spread of Agriculture and Pastoralism in Eurasia*, pp. 323–45. London: UCL Press.

Zvelebil, M. 1996b Farmers our ancestors and the identity of Europe. In P. Graves-Brown, S. Jones and C. Gamble eds., *Cultural Identity and Archaeology*, pp. 145–66. London: Routledge.

Zvelebil, M. 1998 Agricultural frontiers, Neolithic origins, and the transition to farming in the Baltic region. In M. Zvelebil, L. Domanska and R. Dennell eds., *Harvesting the Sea, Farming the Forest*, pp. 9–27. Sheffield: Sheffield Academic Press.

Zvelebil, M. 2000 The social context of the agricultural transition in Europe. In C. Renfrew and K. Boyle eds., *Archaeogenetics*, pp. 57–79. Cambridge: McDonald Institute for Archaeological Research.

Zvelebil, M. and Rowley-Conwy, P. 1986 Foragers and farmers in Atlantic Europe. In M. Zvelebil ed., *Hunters in Transition*, pp. 67–95. Cambridge: Cambridge University Press.

Zvelebil, M. and Zvelebil, K. 1988 Agricultural transition and Indo-European dispersals. *Antiquity* 62:574–83.

Index

NB: A number of categories are pooled (see bold entries), for instance agriculture, animals, language families, legumes, tree and shrub products, and tubers.

Spinden, H.   233
squashes   147–8, 154–61, 170, 172, 175,
   237–9, 243, 246–9
Sri Lanka   87, 92
Starcevo   73–4
Steward, J.   165
Strade, N.   207
Sudan   23, 103, 106
sugarcane   142–4, 227
Sumer, Sumerian   65–6, 211
sunflower   158, 175–6, 249
Sunget   137
Suogang   134–5
Surkotada   90
Susa   65, 211
Swadesh, M.   194
Sykes, B.   259, 267, 269

Taiwan   14, 111, 124, 134–9, 222, 266–72, 291
   Formosan languages   185, 188–9, 195,
      227–30
Tangjiagang   126–7
Tanshishan   124–6, 135
Taperinha   158, 165
Tarim Basin   86
Tasaday   37
Tavoliere Plain   74–5
Tehuacan Valley   151, 156, 173–4, 237
Tekkalakota   93
Tell Aswad   57
Tell Halula   56, 57, 66
Tell Maghzalia   61
Tell Ramad   63, 73
teosinte, see cereals, maize
Teotihuacan   243
Tepe Guran   64
Terrell, J.   268
Tha Kae   132
Thailand Neolithic   132–3
Thessaly   72
Tibeto–Burman, see language families,
   Sino–Tibetan
Tiwanaku   235
Tlatilco   166, 174
Tocharian   86, 205–6
Torroni, A.   258
Toth, A.   206

TRB culture   79–80
tree and shrub products   42–3, 121, 139
   avocados   146, 154, 161
   bananas   36, 97–8, 103, 109, 130, 139,
      142–4, 155, 229, 234
   betel nut   93
   breadfruit   229
   canarium   107, 139, 143
   candlenut   143
   chili pepper   146, 154–5, 161, 237
   coconut   139, 143, 229
   cotton   146, 154–5, 159–63, 170, 172, 237
   oil palm   106–7, 220
   pandanus   139, 142–3
   sago   38, 130, 143, 229
Tripolye   86
Tronadora Vieja   166
Tsang Cheng–hwa   135
tsetse fly   106
tubers   42–3, 277
   achira   159–61
   manioc   33, 146–7, 151, 155–9, 164–5,
      235–9
   (white) potato   155, 158
   sweet potato   16–17, 33, *7.1*, 142, 146–7,
      155, 161, 235, 237–9
   taro   33, 35, 40, 97, 109, 127, 130, 139,
      142–4, 220, 229
   yams   35, 40, 97–8, 109, 130, 139, 142,
      220, 229
Turkey, see Anatolia
Turkic languages, see language families,
   Altaic
Turkmenistan   85–6
Tutishcainyo   165

Uattamdi   137
Umm Dabaghiyah   63
Underhill, P.   259, 261, 264–5, 268
Utnur   92
Uyaw Cave   137

Valdivia   156, 159–60, 165, 168
Valley of Guatemala   167
Valley of Mexico   166, 237, 241, 248
Vansina, J.   220
Vaupes region   184